HANDBOOK OF THE ECONOMICS OF EDUCATION

VOLUME

INTRODUCTION TO THE SERIES

The aim of the *Handbooks in Economics* series is to produce Handbooks for various branches of economics, each of which is a definitive source, reference, and teaching supplement for use by professional researchers and advanced graduate students. Each Handbook provides self-contained surveys of the current state of a branch of economics in the form of chapters prepared by leading specialists on various aspects of this branch of economics. These surveys summarize not only received results but also newer developments, from recent journal articles and discussion papers. Some original material is also included, but the main goal is to provide comprehensive and accessible surveys.

The Handbooks are intended to provide not only useful reference volumes for professional collections but also possible supplementary readings for advanced courses for graduate students in economics.

KENNETH J. ARROW and **MICHAEL D. INTRILIGATOR**

HANDBOOK OF THE ECONOMICS OF EDUCATION

VOLUME

Edited by

ERIC A. HANUSHEK

STEPHEN MACHIN

LUDGER WOESSMANN

Amsterdam • Boston • Heidelberg • London • New York • Oxford
Paris • San Diego • San Francisco • Singapore • Sydney • Tokyo
North-Holland is an imprint of Elsevier

North-Holland is an imprint of Elsevier
525 B Street, Suite 1900, San Diego, CA 92101-4495, USA
Radarweg 29, 1000 AE Amsterdam, The Netherlands

First edition 2011

Copyright © 2011 Elsevier B.V. All rights reserved

No part of this publication may be reproduced, stored in a retrieval system or transmitted in any form or by any means electronic, mechanical, photocopying, recording or otherwise without the prior written permission of the publisher

Permissions may be sought directly from Elsevier's Science & Technology Rights Department in Oxford, UK: phone (+44) (0) 1865 843830; fax (+44) (0) 1865 853333; email: permissions@elsevier.com. Alternatively you can submit your request online by visiting the Elsevier web site at http://elsevier.com/locate/permissions, and selecting *Obtaining permission to use Elsevier material*

Notice
No responsibility is assumed by the publisher for any injury and/or damage to persons or property as a matter of products liability, negligence or otherwise, or from any use or operation of any methods, products, instructions or ideas contained in the material herein. Because of rapid advances in the medical sciences, in particular, independent verification of diagnoses and drug dosages should be made

Library of Congress Cataloging-in-Publication Data
A catalog record for this book is available from the Library of Congress

British Library Cataloguing in Publication Data
A catalogue record for this book is available from the British Library

ISBN: 978-0-444-53429-3

For information on all North-Holland publications
visit our website at elsevierdirect.com

Printed and bound in the USA
Transferred to Digital Printing, 2011

Working together to grow
libraries in developing countries

www.elsevier.com | www.bookaid.org | www.sabre.org

ELSEVIER   BOOK AID International   Sabre Foundation

CONTENTS

Contributors ix
Introduction xi

1. Econometric Methods for Research in Education   1
Costas Meghir and Steven Rivkin

  1. Introduction   2
  2. Wage Equations and the Returns to Education   6
  3. The Returns to Education and Labor Force Participation   40
  4. Education Policy and the Estimated Returns to Education   46
  5. Estimation of School Input Effects   48
  6. Conclusions   82
  References   83

2. The Economics of International Differences in Educational Achievement   89
Eric A. Hanushek and Ludger Woessmann

  1. Introduction   91
  2. Economic Motivation   96
  3. International Tests of Educational Achievement   98
  4. Determinants of International Educational Achievement   111
  5. Economic Consequences of International Educational Achievement   160
  6. Conclusion and Outlook   191
  References   192

3. Education and Family Background: Mechanisms and Policies   201
Anders Björklund and Kjell G. Salvanes

  1. Background and Motivation   202
  2. How Important Is Family Background for Final Educational Attainment?   204
  3. Theory: A Taxonomy of Effects   211
  4. How the Family Affects the Child   216
  5. What Education Policy Can Do at Different Stages of the Educational Career: Lessons from Research on Reforms   236
  6. Conclusions   241
  7. Acknowledgements   243
  References   243

4. **Peer Effects in Education: How Might They Work, How Big Are They and How Much Do We Know Thus Far?** — 249
   Bruce Sacerdote

   1. Introduction and Overview — 250
   2. Models of Peer Effects — 253
   3. Identification of Peer Effects — 256
   4. Empirical Results on Peer Effects in Primary and Secondary Education — 260
   5. Going Beyond Test Scores — 268
   6. Effects in Post-Secondary Education — 269
   7. Conclusions — 271
   References — 273

5. **Teacher Compensation and Collective Bargaining** — 279
   Michael Podgursky

   1. Introduction — 280
   2. Studies of Relative Teacher Pay — 281
   3. Quantity versus Quality Tradeoffs — 283
   4. Comparing Teacher and Nonteacher Compensation — 286
   5. Teacher Pay and Student Achievement — 289
   6. Structure of Teacher Compensation — 290
   7. Trends in Market-Based Pay — 301
   8. Teacher Collective Bargaining — 305
   9. Conclusion — 309
   10. Acknowledgements — 310
   References — 310

6. **Licensure: Exploring the Value of this Gateway to the Teacher Workforce** — 315
   Dan Goldhaber

   1. Background — 316
   2. Theoretical Arguments for and Against Teacher Licensure — 318
   3. Teacher Licensure Systems in the U.S. and Abroad — 321
   4. Empirical Evidence on the Impact of Teacher Licensure — 325
   5. Concluding Thoughts — 335
   References — 337

7. **The Economics of Tracking in Education** — 341
   Julian R. Betts

   1. Introduction — 342
   2. Theoretical Foundations: Lessons for Various Empirical Approaches — 344

	3. Tracking and School Resources	349
	4. Empirical Approaches to Estimating the Effects of Tracking	351
	5. Conclusion and Outline of a Possible Research Agenda for the Future	375
	6. Acknowledgements	380
	References	380

8. School Accountability   383

David Figlio and Susanna Loeb

1. Introduction — 384
2. The Rationale for School-Based Accountability — 386
3. The Nature of Accountability — 388
4. Accountability Might Not Improve School Performance — 397
5. Evidence on Student Outcomes — 402
6. Accountability and Teacher Labor Markets — 412
7. Directions for Future Research — 416
References — 417

9. The GED   423

James J. Heckman, John Eric Humphries, and Nicholas S. Mader

1. Introduction — 424
2. Institutional Background and Functions of the GED — 426
3. The Effects of GED Certification — 432
4. Changes and Growth in the GED Test Taking Population — 458
5. Adverse Consequences of the GED — 471
6. Conclusion — 478
References — 480

10. Housing Valuations of School Performance   485

Sandra E. Black and Stephen Machin

1. Introduction — 486
2. Using Housing Expenditures to Value School Quality — 486
3. Data Issues Relating to House Prices and School Quality — 489
4. Empirical Methodologies and Review of Evidence — 493
5. Conclusions — 515
6. Acknowledgements — 516
References — 516

11. Apprenticeship **521**
Stefan C. Wolter and Paul Ryan

1. Introduction	522
2. Firm Behavior in Providing and Financing Apprenticeship Training	524
3. Empirical Observations on the Specificity of Human Capital, Net Cost of Apprenticeship Training and the Business Cycle	539
4. Outcomes for Apprentices	550
5. Institutional Foundations of Apprenticeship	553
6. Conclusions	569
References	570

Index 557

CONTRIBUTORS

Julian R. Betts
UC San Diego and NBER

Anders Björklund
Stockholm University and IZA

Sandra E. Black
University of Texas at Austin, IZA, CESifo, and NBER

David Figlio
Northwestern University, CESifo, and NBER

Dan Goldhaber
University of Washington

Eric A. Hanushek
Stanford University, University of Texas at Dallas, NBER, and CESifo

James J. Heckman
University of Chicago, American Bar Foundation, University College Dublin, and Yale University

John Eric Humphries
University of Chicago

Susanna Loeb
Stanford University and NBER

Stephen Machin
University College London, London School of Economics, and CESifo

Nicholas S. Mader
University of Chicago

Costas Meghir
University College London, IFS, IFAU, CESifo, and IZA

Michael Podgursky
University of Missouri – Columbia

Steven Rivkin
Amherst College, University of Texas at Dallas, CESifo, and NBER

Paul Ryan
Cambridge University

Bruce Sacerdote
Dartmouth College and NBER

Kjell G. Salvanes
Norwegian School of Economics and Business Administration, CEE, CESifo and IZA

Ludger Woessmann
University of Munich, Ifo Institute for Economic Research, CESifo, and IZA

Stefan C. Wolter
University of Bern and CESifo

INTRODUCTION

The economics of education has flourished as a research field since the publication of Volumes I and II of this Handbook. There has been a big upsurge in new (predominantly, though not exclusively, empirical) research by economists on education and education policy. This economic research continues to be extremely practical, with an explicit aim to better understand how education is acquired, how it affects economic and social outcomes of interest, and how it can inform public policy. The chapters in this new volume (Volume III), and in the companion Volume IV that is already in preparation, focus upon this new research, and its grounding with past economics of education research.

There are several reasons for the explosion of research in this area. One is the very significant improvement in data availability and quality. There are now more and better data to address core questions in the economics of education. These include international data on test scores, high quality administrative data, and rich register data in the Scandinavian countries. A second, related, reason for the upsurge of work, including publishing in the top journals of the economics profession, is the expansion of research separately accumulating in many countries around the world. The coverage of the new volumes—in terms of choice of topics, authorship, and editorship—is meant to reflect this globalization of research in the economics of education. A third aspect, focused on in detail in a number of the chapters in this volume, is the use of new methodological approaches that overlap with significant developments that have been made in other areas of economics. Finally, there has been a heightened policy relevance attached to economics of education research. Many governments want more evidence-based policy, and this has been particularly true in terms of education.

All of these have resulted in the economics of education being a thriving and burgeoning specialist field within economics. The topics covered by the chapters of the current volume step into some of the most obvious gaps that have become evident with the newly emerging research. While there are antecedents to the work in each of the chapters, recent research has taken the ideas into new and productive areas. The first two chapters cover developments in the econometric methods used and the emerging work with the international test score data. The next two chapters deal with family background and peers as much-researched determinants of educational outcomes beyond the traditional school resource inputs. Next are two chapters addressing specific topics related to the teaching profession: salary setting and licensure. Three chapters address separate institutional features of the school system: educational tracking, school accountability, and the GED as a credential for school dropouts. The final two chapters relate to valuation of school quality on the housing market and to apprenticeship as a specific combination of formal education with work-based training that is widely used in several countries, respectively.

We are grateful to all authors contributing to the new volume, as we appreciate (from own experience) how much of a task it is to produce a handbook chapter that both covers the existing literature and provides ideas that lead into the future. Their expertise, enthusiasm, and hard work are highly appreciated. We also gratefully acknowledge the professional support in the *Handbooks in Economics* series, especially by the general editors Kenneth Arrow and Michael Intriligator and by Scott Bentley, Kathleen Paoni, Stacey Walker, and others at Elsevier. We also thank CESifo, which provided financial support and facilities to hold the inaugural meeting of the CESifo research network's Economics of Education area in Munich in September 2009 where initial drafts of the chapters of Volumes III and IV were presented and discussed.

Education is widely recognized as an important determinant of a wide range of economic and social outcomes. Through use of rich data and study of issues of high contemporary policy relevance, study of the economics of education is one of the primary areas of research attraction across the economics profession, appealing to new Ph.D. students and experienced researchers alike. The significant bodies of research studied in this volume suggest that it is highly likely that Volume IV will not be the last in this series, as study of education acquisition and its economic and social impact will undoubtedly remain a fertile research ground for the foreseeable future.

Eric Hanushek
Stephen Machin
Ludger Woessmann
May 2010

CHAPTER 1

Econometric Methods for Research in Education

Costas Meghir* and Steven Rivkin**

*University College London, IFS, IFAU, CESifo, and IZA
**Amherst College, University of Texas at Dallas, CESifo, and NBER

Contents

1. Introduction	2
2. Wage Equations and the Returns to Education	6
2.1 Pricing of human capital	6
2.2 A model of education choice and wages	8
2.3 Estimation	14
2.3.1 Estimation by simulation	17
2.4 Estimating the wage returns to education in Mincer wage equations	19
2.4.1 Nonparametric models	23
2.4.2 Heterogeneous returns to years of education and nonparametric models	25
2.4.3 Education choice and wages: A simple illustration and discussion	30
2.5 Identification and estimation of the wage returns to education in the dynamic discrete education choice model	32
2.6 Using bounds to estimate the returns to education	34
2.7 A special case: Binary educational choice	38
3. The Returns to Education and Labor Force Participation	40
3.1 Bias to the estimated returns when participation is ignored	40
3.2 Accounting for nonparticipation	41
3.3 Nonparticipation and endogeneity	44
4. Education Policy and the Estimated Returns to Education	46
5. Estimation of School Input Effects	48
5.1 Housing choice	49
5.2 Learning dynamics	50
5.3 Estimation of class size effects	55
5.3.1 Model	55
5.3.2 Discussion of empirical analyses	57

Acknowledgements: This paper has been prepared for the *Handbook of the Economics of Education*. We thank Rick Hanushek, Jim Heckman, and Jeremy Lise for comments and discussions. We also thank Zohar Perla for her excellent research assistance. Costas Meghir thanks the ESRC under the Professorial Fellowship RES-051-27-0204 and the ESRC Centre for Microeconomic Analysis of Public Policy at the Institute for Fiscal Studies for funding this research. Steven Rivkin would like to thank the Smith Richardson Foundation, the Spencer Foundation, the Hewlett Foundation, and the Packard Humanity Institute for supporting his work on the modeling of student achievement and teacher value-added. Responsibility for any errors is ours alone.

5.4 Estimation of teacher value-added	66
5.5 Estimation of the housing market capitalization of school quality	73
5.6 Estimation of the effects of competition, choice, and accountability	77
6. Conclusions	82
References	83

Abstract

This paper reviews some of the econometric methods that have been used in the economics of education. The focus is on understanding how the assumptions made to justify and implement such methods relate to the underlying economic model and the interpretation of the results. We start by considering the estimation of the returns to education both within the context of a dynamic discrete choice model inspired by Willis and Rosen (1979) and in the context of the Mincer model. We discuss the relationship between the econometric assumptions and economic behavior. We then discuss methods that have been used in the context of assessing the impact of education quality, the teacher contribution to pupils' achievement, and the effect of school quality on housing prices. In the process we also provide a summary of some of the main results in this literature.

1. INTRODUCTION

The rising return to schooling and growing evidence in support of education as a primary determinant of economic growth has elevated the importance and visibility of research on human capital formation including both the determinants of enrollment and attainment and the determinants of education quality. Such research must address complications introduced by the myriad and inter-related decision-making processes of families, teachers, administrators, and policy makers. A variety of methods have been used to identify causal relationships, ranging from structural models based on utility maximization to experimental and quasi-experimental approaches, yielding a growing body of often contradictory evidence.

Although the various approaches differ in the degree to which theoretical models of decision-making underlay the empirical specifications, the simple dichotomy between structural approaches on the one hand and experimental or quasi-experimental on the other does not hold up in most applications. As we highlight throughout the chapter, the interpretation, the usefulness, and even the identification of estimates typically relies implicitly if not explicitly on a set of assumptions about underlying behavior. Importantly, the introduction of heterogeneity in treatment effects magnifies the importance of such assumptions.

Rather than dividing this chapter by methods, we divide it into two parts largely in parallel to the division of research on human capital formation into quantity (years of schooling) and quality. The first part Section 2 focuses on the estimation of wage equations and the return to schooling, framed by a Roy model of education decision-making, originally suggested by

Willis and Rosen (1979), that incorporates heterogeneity in returns to schooling across both individuals and three levels of schooling and allows for comparative advantage in the sense that individuals need not be best at both education and the labor market. This model not only provides a flexible description of the process through which human capital is acquired through schooling, but it also provides a framework for discussing the identification issues that arise when estimating education effects on wages with empirical methods not based directly on models that articulate the full structure of the process of human capital acquisition.

We then turn to the various methods used to estimate education effects on wages, highlighting the restrictions that must be fulfilled in order to generate consistent estimates of the return to schooling. The natural starting point is the estimation of the full structural model. We describe its estimation based both on maximum likelihood and on newly developed simulation methods.

Next we describe methods that can be used to estimate Mincer wage equations in which education is taken to be a continuous variable. First, we discuss approaches to identification under the assumption that the return to schooling is constant both with respect to the years of education and across individuals. We then permit the wage return to schooling to vary with the level of education and discuss the use of nonparametric IV estimators when the shape of the relationship between wages and years of education is not known. Next we allow for heterogeneity across individuals and consider general nonseparable models with respect to years of education and unobserved heterogeneity. This takes us to the frontier of research as far as this class of models is concerned. Importantly, it becomes clear that identification and interpretation of results depends on the nature of schooling choice. Indeed the implied restrictions on economic behavior, required for identification, are quite stringent and can be interpreted as restrictions on the information possessed by the individual when making education choices.

Following discussion of the Mincer wage equation we return to the Roy model with potentially unordered schooling choices and discuss approaches to identification of the effects of education on wages. There we discuss conditions that allow identification "at infinity", an argument that depends on the availability of enough continuous instruments such that there are sets of values of these instruments where the, individuals facing such values make a choice of a particular education level with probability one. In such sets there is no selection. If the instruments are independent of the unobservables in the wage equation and under some further conditions, identification is achieved. However, it is unlikely that such an identification strategy has much empirical significance. At this point we either need to acknowledge the need for further parametric assumptions, beyond those implied from theory and beyond the standard IV assumptions, or we need to resort to set identification. In this case we focus on bounding the distribution of wages for each education group, rather than attempting to obtain point estimates. The various assumptions used in the point identification approach, such as instrument exclusion, can be used here; some can even be relaxed to allow for instruments to shift the distribution of wages in one direction (monotonicity).[1] The approach can be very fruitful, because it provides an intermediate position where a number of theoretical restrictions are used, making the estimates interpretable within a broad theoretical framework, while not using auxiliary assumptions that are both controversial and do not follow from theory.

Section 3 discusses the problem introduced by missing wages for labor force nonparticipants. We compare a fully structural approach that in practice will have to rely on assumptions beyond those implied by theory and an approach based on bounds.[2] Allowing for both endogenous education choice and endogenous labor force participation does make identification more stringent. At the same time bounds are also less informative. Of course ignoring these issues poses serious problems with interpretation. Identification will have to rely on exploiting the restrictions from theory as well as further assumptions, such as those specifying the distribution of unobservables. Despite the shortcomings of having to make assumptions that do not relate directly to theory, the approach that ignores these issues leads to results that have limited interpretation. Moreover, although most identification theorems proposed hitherto rely on identification at infinity arguments, it is possible that further progress can be made by exploiting further restrictions from theory; one possibility is to explore the use of restrictions from other related decisions. The potential for this can be seen when comparing the identification of pure discrete choice models with those that combine discrete choice with continuous outcome variables, such as the education and wages model we discuss.[3] Moreover when considering bounds, it is clear that identification can be obtained without an "identification at infinity" argument. Characterizing the underlying behavioral conditions for this would be an important advance.

Section 3.3 justifies the idea of a Roy model of education and wages by suggesting that each education level may correspond to a different input in production, these inputs not being perfectly substitutable for each other. We argued that in an economy with a changing supply of educated workers of differing levels, the relative wages and the returns to education will change over time. We also refer to evidence that demonstrates the importance of such considerations. In view of this, we close this section by discussing the implications for policy of placing education choice and wages within a general equilibrium framework. A number of authors have shown that without such

---

[1] See Manski (1994).
[2] See Blundell, Gosling, Ichimura, and Meghir (2007).
[3] Contrast Magnac, Thierry, and Thesmar (2002) with Heckman and Navarro (2007) for example.

a framework it is very difficult to design and think of policy.[4] This again emphasizes the need for a model not only for the interpretation of the estimates but also for understanding what the estimates imply for policy.

Section 5 turns to empirical methods used in research on school and teacher quality. Although it begins with the presentation of an education production function model and discussion of the multiple levels of choices that determine the matching of students, teachers, and schools, this model does not provide the unifying framework of the Roy model, discussed in the previous sections. Given the range of issues covered in research on education quality, we believe it to be more productive to focus on conceptual frameworks tailored to specific issues. We do, however, begin this section with general discussions of housing choice and the dynamics of the process of knowledge acquisition.

In Section 5 we look at the different research areas that have received substantial attention in recent years, and within each we juxtapose various empirical and estimation methods. Specifically, we focus on a small number of papers on class size, teacher quality, capitalization of school quality into house prices, and competition, choice, and accountability. The proliferation of administrative and survey data in recent years has facilitated research on these and other education topics, and we have selected papers that vary by both type of data and empirical method. The methods include controls for observables, instrumental variables, regression discontinuity as a special case of IV, use of random lotteries as a special case of IV, difference-in-differences, fixed effects with large administrative data sets, and the use of data generated by experiments.

As in earlier sections we highlight the inter-relationship among the structure of underlying choices, treatment effects, identification conditions, and meaning of the estimates. Estimators differ according to the assumptions required for identification and assumptions concerning the distribution of treatment effects along various dimensions, though most of these estimators do not come from behavioral models that predict the structure of treatment effects. Nonetheless, we focus on the inter-dependencies among underlying behavior, identification conditions, and interpretation throughout this discussion.

In the case of research on class size, we first present a model of education production based on Lazear (2001) that highlights potential dimensions over which the benefits of smaller classes might vary and then evaluate a series of different estimators with that framework as a backdrop. In addition to describing the methods and identifying assumptions, this compares estimators according to the degree to which they capture class-size–related general equilibrium effects on the quality of instruction; some estimators capture cross-sectional differences in teacher quality associated with smaller classes, some capture changes over time in state average teacher quality, while others isolate the *ceteris paribus* effect of smaller classes.

---

[4] See Heckman, Lochner, and Taber (1998), Lee (2005), Lee and Wolpin (2006), and Gallipoli, Meghir, and Violante (2008).

The description of research on the semiparametric estimation of the variance in teacher quality begins with a discussion of the behavioral responses of families, teachers, and administrators that complicate estimation. It then describes different approaches to estimating the variance and to accounting for sorting both between and within schools.

The discussion of research on housing market capitalization focuses narrowly on boundary fixed effects estimators (see Chapter 10 for a comprehensive treatment of this issue). Two of the three papers adopt reduced-form approaches, while the third develops a discreet choice framework with which to model housing choice and heterogeneity in the preferences for both school quality and peer characteristics.

The section on choice and accountability examines different types of incentives including competition from public and private schools and state accountability systems. Nonrandom family take-up of choice options complicates estimation of choice effects, while the nonrandom distribution of accountability system adoption date and character complicate efforts to identify accountability system impacts. Each paper takes a different approach to account for unobserved heterogeneity.

The chapter concludes with a synthesis of the key commonalities and differences between work on the return to schooling and on school quality and the ways in which the proliferation of administrative and survey data affect the structure of empirical analyses. It highlights remaining challenges and areas for additional work.

2. WAGE EQUATIONS AND THE RETURNS TO EDUCATION

The aim of this section is to discuss the estimation of the returns to education. We place wages and education choice within a simple competitive general equilibrium framework. In this model forward-looking individuals choose an education level; each level is associated with its own wage process. The allows us to clarify the notion of returns to education and to discuss clearly identification issues. Once we have defined the model of education choice and wages we digress to the simpler world of Mincer wage equations and discuss identification issues within that context. In a simple version of that model, as shown by Mincer (1958, 1974), the returns to education can be estimated directly from the relationship of wages and education, because the only cost to education is the opportunity cost—there are no direct costs such as fees. Moreover in many contexts we may be interested in the impact of education on wages in and of itself. Following the discussion of identification of Mincer type models we return to the identification issues of the dynamic model we originally introduced. One of the main themes of this section will be the extent to which we can interpret estimates on the wage returns to education without saying much about the process of education choice.

2.1 Pricing of human capital

Our starting point is that production involves k types of human capital; the type of human capital that an individual possesses is determined by the level of education they have attained. Here the levels considered will be statutory schooling, high school and college. The wage received by an individual will we the product of the aggregate price of her type of human capital (W_{kt}) with the amount she brings to the market (h_{kit}), say $w_{kit} = W_{kt}h_{kit}$, where k denotes the type of human capital and h_{kit} is the amount in efficiency units that individual i possesses in time period t.[5] The literature on modeling wages concentrates on understanding how to model the constituents of h_{kit}, which will be a function of education, ability, and possibly experience, age and other factors that enhance individual productivity and skills. Thus the returns to education in a competitive economy will depend both on how each education level is priced in the market (i.e., how W_{kt} is determined) and how education contributes to the formation of h_{kit}. The way pricing may change in the future is a source of aggregate uncertainty, while possible future shocks to human capital h_{kit} will be a source of idiosyncratic uncertainty.

Consider first pricing in a competitive market. Suppose there are three levels of education: less than high school (S^L), high school (S^H) and college (S^C). Now suppose we can represent aggregate production by the function

$$Q_t = A_t [\delta_S H_{St}^\rho + \delta_H H_{Ht}^\rho + \delta_C H_{Ct}^\rho]^{\alpha/\rho} K_t^{1-\alpha}$$

where $\delta_i > 0$ ($i = C, H, S$), $\delta_C + \delta_H + \delta_S = 1$, $\rho \leq 1$, $0 \leq \alpha \leq 1$ and where H_{jt} is the sum of total human capital employed of type j in period t. In efficiency units this is $H_{jt} = \sum_{i=1}^N h_{kit}$, where h_{kit} is the human capital of type k supplied by individual i in period t. In a competitive equilibrium prices satisfy

$$\frac{W_{jt}}{W_{St}} = \frac{\delta_j}{\delta_S} \left(\frac{H_{jt}}{H_{St}}\right)^{\rho-1} \qquad j = C, H \qquad (1.1)$$

Thus the relative prices of the two types of human capital will vary depending on the ratio of demands $\frac{H_j}{H_S}$, so long as $\rho < 1$. The source of aggregate uncertainty are changes in the relative value of the δs, such as skill biased technical change. When $\rho = 1$ the inputs are perfectly substitutable and the relative prices are invariant to changes in $\frac{H_j}{H_S}$. The relative pay can change however in response to changes in technology as expressed by changes in $\frac{\delta_j}{\delta_S}$. The resulting wage equation for individual i who has obtained educational level k can then be represented as

$$\ln w_{kit} = \ln W_{kt} + \ln h_{kit} \qquad (1.2)$$

When $\rho = 1$, and with no changes in technology this simplifies to

$$\ln w_{it} = \ln W_t + \ln h_{it} \qquad (1.3)$$

which is now common across education groups. Wage equations based on years of education only, without regard to the type of education received can be interpreted through, and is inspired by, the work of Mincer.

---
[5] See for example Heckman, Jayne-Farrar, and Todd (1996).

One way of estimating the parameters is to use Equation (1.1) and write

$$\log \frac{W_{jt}}{W_{St}} = \log\left(\frac{\delta_j}{\delta_S}\right) + (\rho - 1)\log\left(\frac{H_{jt}}{H_{St}}\right) + \varepsilon_{jS} \quad (1.4)$$

To implement this we need measures of $\frac{W_{jt}}{W_{st}}$ and of $\frac{H_{jt}}{H_{st}}$. These can be obtained as follows. First we estimate wage equations for each level of schooling. The time dummies in the equations for level S is a measure (up to an additive constant) of $\log W_{St}$. An estimate of individual human capital can then be obtained by using the relationship

$$h_{kit} = \exp(\log w_{kit} - \log W_{kt})$$

Aggregating the estimate of this quantity and assuming the sample is representative (or grossing it up with the sample weights) allows us to construct $\log\left(\frac{H_{jt}}{H_{st}}\right)$. If the errors in Equation (1.4) relate to changes in technology, then human capital is endogenous. One strategy is to instrument $\log\left(\frac{H_{jt}}{H_{st}}\right)$ by the total number of people of these two skill levels, whether they are working or not. This uses the medium-term availability of the resource as the instrument. An alternative would be to use dynamics, that is lags in human capital, as instruments.

The empirical evidence suggests that $\rho < 1$ and hence that different levels of human capital are not perfectly substitutable. Katz and Murphy (1992) and Heckman, Lochner, and Taber (1998) both estimate the elasticity of substitution $\left(\frac{1}{1-\rho}\right)$ between unskilled and skilled workers to be about 1.4, although alternative estimates suggest even lower values. Gallipoli, Meghir, and Violante (2008) estimate the elasticity of substitution between statutory schooling, high school, and college for the U.S. using instrumental variables. They find that the same elasticity of substitution can be imposed across all pairwise comparisons; they estimate this to be between 1.5 and 2.[6] It is safe to say that the consensus in the literature is that different types of human capital are not perfectly substitutable for each other.

2.2 A model of education choice and wages

Given the discussion above it follows that we should model education as choosing a specific level; we should then estimate life cycle wage profiles within each sector. This is similar to the Roy (1951) model, and the empirical basis for this has been formulated by Willis and Rosen (1979). Keane and Wolpin (1997) have taken this further, allowing also for occupational choice and modeling the entire career.[7]

Consider an individual who has just completed statutory schooling and will decide on completing high school and then on whether to complete college. We will take

---

[6] They consider less than high school, high school, some college, and college. They could not reject the restriction of one elasticity of substitution.

[7] Variations of this model have been used by Attanasio, Meghir, and Santiago (2009) where only the discrete education choice is modeled and Gallipoli, Meghir, and Violante (2008) who model educational choice, wages, labor supply, and intergenerational transfers. Heckman and Navarro (2007) use a version of this model to analyze identifiability of returns to education and of the dynamic discrete choice models.

these as two sequential decisions, to which the individual needs to commit successively. Once schooling is over the individual works and earns depending on the level of schooling received. The earnings function for each level of education is given by

$$\begin{aligned} \log w_i^S &= m^S(age, X_i) + \tau_i^S + \varepsilon_{it}^S & \text{statutory schooling} \\ \log w_i^H &= m^H(age - e^H, X_i) + \tau_i^H + \varepsilon_{it}^H & \text{high school} \\ \log w_i^C &= m^C(age - e^C, X_i) + \tau_i^C + \varepsilon_{it}^C & \text{college} \end{aligned} \quad (1.5)$$

where e^H and e^C represent the additional years of schooling, over and above the statutory ones needed to obtain a high school and college degree respectively and where X_i are observable characteristics that influence individual earnings. It would be straightforward to include age and other time varying characteristics so long as we made the assumption of perfect foresight. In a later section we show how the model can be generalized to include endogenous experience and nonparticipation. We have abstracted from the aggregate fluctuations in the prices of human capital, but in this simple environment allowing for aggregate shocks is relatively straightforward.

These earnings functions include a number of important features: first, earnings growth with respect to potential experience, in other words, age minus years of education differ depending on the level of education, allowing for the possibility of complementarity between education level and age. Second, each individual has a sector-specific level of ability ($\tau_i^0, \tau_i^H, \tau_i^C$). This implies heterogeneous returns to education, with respect to unobservables (as well as possibly through observables). We will assume here that this heterogeneity is in the individual's information set when making the education choice. This assumption is not innocuous and does affect the way we estimate the model. Third, the stochastic structure of earnings will differ across groups. For example, the variance or persistence of shocks may differ depending on the chosen sector. This is particularly important when considering models that allow for risk aversion. The model has abstracted from other important issues, such as endogenous experience and nonparticipation.

Now consider the flow of utility. We assume that individuals incur observable monetary costs $\kappa^H(Z^H)$ and $\kappa^C(Z^C)$ for high school and college, respectively. These will include fees, cost of books, transport costs, and so on, and may depend on observable characteristics $Z_i = \{Z_i^H, Z_i^C\}$. Individuals will also incur unobservable costs per unit of time spent in education, which we can interpret as effort. These we will assume are heterogeneous and we denote them by F_i. Taking all this into account, the flow utility for high school and for college is respectively

$$\begin{aligned} u_i^H &= \kappa^H(Z_i^H) + F_i + \nu_i^H & \text{high school} \\ u_i^C &= \kappa^C(Z_i^C) + \alpha F_i + \nu_i^C & \text{college} \end{aligned} \quad (1.6)$$

where the coefficient α reflects the fact that effort and time spent in college can be different than in high school and where the ν^H and ν^C represent random shocks to the costs of education. The high school utility ν_i^H shock is revealed when the individual needs to decide to go to high school or start working. Similarly the college shock is revealed after high school when the college decision needs to be made. The assumed timing of such shocks is critical for the model: the fact they are revealed sequentially, implies that the decision to continue to the next level will include an option value to continue further; thus, as we shall see, attending high school has value for the earnings that are expected and because of the option of attending college, whose value will depend on the shock that has not been realized yet. We will simplify the model further by assuming that once the individual has dropped out of the formal education system they can no longer return and they work until a fixed retirement age of say 60. In a more detailed model we would allow for endogenous retirement or at least the recognition that retirement age differs by education group and is probably higher for the more educated. The expected utility from working having achieved education level S, H, or C respectively, as viewed at the time the decision will be made is

$$V_i^{WS} = w_{i0}^S + E\sum_{t=e^S+1}^{60} \beta^t w_{it}^S = \exp(\tau_i^S) A^S(X_i) \quad \text{statutory school earnings}$$

$$V_i^{WH} = w_{ie^H}^H + E\sum_{t=e^H+1}^{60} \beta^t w_{it}^H = \exp(\tau_i^H) A^H(X_i) \quad \text{high school earnings} \quad (1.7)$$

$$V_i^{WC} = w_{ie^C}^C + E\sum_{t=e^C+1}^{60} \beta^t w_{it}^C = \exp(\tau_i^C) A^C(X_i) \quad \text{college earnings}$$

where β is the personal discount and $A^J(X) = \sum_{t=e^J+1}^{40} \beta^t \exp[m^H(t-e^J, X_i)], J = S, H, C$, with e^i being the age at which education level i is completed. The expectation is taken over future wage shocks. Now consider the decision process for someone who just completed statutory schooling. The value of attending high school will be given by the sum of the current costs of schooling (u_i^H) and the option value of either going to college or starting work as a high-school graduate. Thus the value of attending high school is given by

$$V_i^H = \kappa^H(Z_i^H) + F_i + v_{it}^H + \beta E \max\{V_i^C, V_i^{WH}\}$$
$$= \tilde{V}_i^H + v_i^H$$

where the expectation is over all future wage shocks and the shock to the cost of attending college v_i^C. The value of attending college is given by

$$V_i^C = \kappa^C(Z_i^C) + \alpha F_i + v_i^C + \beta E V_i^{WC}$$
$$= \tilde{V}_i^C + v_i^C$$

The first decision is to attend high school or not. The decision rule is

$$\text{attend high school} \Leftrightarrow V_i^H > V_i^S \qquad (1.8)$$

If the individual does not attend high school then they enter the labor market until retirement. If they do attend, in the next period they need to decide whether to continue with college. The decision rule is again

$$\text{attend college} \Leftrightarrow V_i^C > V_i^{WH} \qquad (1.9)$$

At the point of making the education decision the individual is assumed to know the experience profiles of each education sector as well as the permanent heterogeneity components τ_i^C, τ_i^H, and τ_i^S. They also know the costs of education (both direct and effort costs). Interestingly, this model allows for comparative advantage (as in Willis and Rosen (1979)) in the sense that individuals need not be best at both education and the labor market: they may be very good at the medium skill labor market (high τ_i^H) and not so good at education (low F_i) or perhaps a negative αF_i. Thus both the mechanism of selection into different education levels and the resulting relationship between education and unobserved components of wages are complex and not necessarily in an easy-to-predict direction.

To estimate the model or use it for simulations we must first solve it, that is, compute expressions for the value functions that will allow us to implement the decision rules in Equations (1.8) and (1.9). In the context of this particularly simple model this is easy to do, but in more complex models it can be computationally time consuming.

Given a set of parameters and given the distribution of unobserved heterogeneity, the discounted value of further schooling and/or work can be computed by projecting earnings forward based on the wage equation for the relevant education sector. Thus, for example,

$$V_i^{WS} = w_{i0}^S + E \sum_{t=e^S+1}^{60} \beta^t w_{it}^S$$

The next step involves a conditional expectation with respect to the distribution of the shocks. Here we either need to make an explicit distributional assumption about the shocks $v_i^C - v_i^H$ or we need to see if such a distribution can be identified nonparametrically. In a parametric context these could be assumed normal, for example; since the decision is discrete we normalize the variance to be one. The distribution is first needed to write down the expected value function for the next period, which involves the future optimal decision to continue schooling:

$$E \max\{V_i^C, V_i^{WH}\} = E\left(V_i^C | v_i^C - v_i^H > \widetilde{V}_i^{WH} - \widetilde{V}_i^C\right) \Pr\left(v_i^C - v_i^H > \widetilde{V}_i^{WH} - \widetilde{V}_i^C\right)$$
$$+ E\left(V_i^{WH} | v_i^C - v_i^H < \widetilde{V}_i^{WH} - \widetilde{V}_i^C\right) \Pr\left(v_i^C - v_i^H < \widetilde{V}_i^{WH} - \widetilde{V}_i^C\right)$$

The missing components to evaluate this expression are $\widetilde{V}_i^{WH} = E \sum_{t=e^H+1}^{60} \beta^t w_{it}^H$ and $\widetilde{V}_i^C$. Given a wage equation and a discount factor we can easily compute $\widetilde{V}_i^{WH}$, which is the present discounted value of mean earnings.

In a model that is linear in earnings, the value beyond working life can be set to zero, without loss of generality. However, a practical difficulty is that we may be missing wages for older individuals, during working life and this needs to be accounted for. Suppose we observe individuals up to some age (it could differ between individuals), then we either need to assume how earnings will evolve beyond that age or we need to introduce a terminal value function whose parameters will be estimated alongside the remaining parameters of the model. If we have enough data to estimate the age-earnings profile only up to a specific age T, the terminal value function will be a function of the state variables at that age as well as of observed X_i and unobserved characteristics and unobserved heterogeneity. In our simple model the state is just the education level. Thus we can specify

$$V_i^{JT} = \exp(\gamma_0^J(X_i) + \gamma_1^J(X_i)\tau_i^J) \text{ for } J = S, H, C \qquad (1.10)$$

where we have used the exponential to restrict the function to be positive. Then we can compute $\widetilde{V}_i^{WJ}$ as follows

$$\widetilde{V}_i^{WJ} = \sum_{t=s+1}^{T_i} \beta^t \hat{w}_{it}^J + \beta^{T_i+1} V_i^{JT}$$

where $\hat{w}_{it}^J$ is the expected wage conditional on unobserved heterogeneity τ^J. Thus, now for a given set of parameters, we can compute all future values required to construct the probability of attaining a particular level of education, conditional on τ.

The average life cycle returns to college *vis-à-vis* high school from the perspective of someone who has just completed high school is

$$\Delta^{C/H} = E\left[\frac{V^C - V^{WH}}{V^{WH}}\right]$$

where the expectation is taken with respect to the unobservables. This measure includes both the wage gains of going to college over the life cycle as well as accounting for the individual direct and opportunity costs of education. This measure will allow for the effects of education on other dimensions of behavior, such as expected endogenous and exogenous spells out of work, which can be elements of more complex models.[8]

---

[8] See, for example, Adda, Dustmann, Meghir, and Robin (2009).

In this model the returns to education are heterogeneous, depending on the unobserved components of wages and educational costs. The individual wage returns to college, at any specific point in the lifecycle take the form

$$\Delta W_i^{C/H} = m^C(age - e^C) - m^H(age - e^H) + \tau_i^C - \tau_i^H + \varepsilon_{it}^C - \varepsilon_{it}^H$$

Since the wage returns[9] to education are heterogeneous in this model, there are many different concepts of such returns.[10] The average wage return to one level of education L relative to another L' (*average treatment effect, or ATE*) at a specific age is given by

$$\Delta_{ATE}^{L/L'}(age, X_i, L, L') \equiv$$

$$E(\ln w_i^L - \ln w_i^{L'}|X_i) = m^L(age - e^L, X_i) - m^{L'}(age - e^{L'}, X_i)$$

The return relative to L' for those who chose $J = L$ (*average treatment on the treated, or ATT*) is given by

$$\Delta_{ATT}^{L/L'}(age, Z_i, X_i, L, L') \equiv E(\ln w_i^L - \ln w_i^{L'}|X_i, J = L)$$
$$= m^L(age - e^L, X_i) - m^{L'}(age - e^{L'}, X_i) \qquad (1.11)$$
$$+ [E(\tau_i^L|age, Z_i, X_i, J_i = L) - E(\tau_i^{L'}|age, Z_i, X_i, J_i = L)]$$

Note that in Equation (1.11) the last expression is the average labor market ability relating to high-school education for those *who chose to attend college*. In all cases, estimation of the returns of interest (e.g., ATE or ATT or the entire distribution) will require estimating some aspect at least of the distribution of the τ^J. Just to emphasize this point, if we ignore this issue and we just compare wages across sectors, the estimate of the returns we will obtain will have the form

$$D^{L/L'} = \left[m^L(age - e^L, X_i) - m^{L'}(age - e^{L'}, X_i) \right]$$
$$+ \left\{ E(\tau_i^L|age, Z_i, X_i, J_i = L) - E(\tau_i^{L'}|age, Z_i, X_i, J_i = L') \right\}$$

While the first term in square brackets is indeed $\Delta_{ATE}^{L/L'}(age)$ and reflects the gains obtained as a result of attending college over high school, the term in {} brackets represents the differences in composition between the two groups. This differs from the expression in the square brackets in Equation (1.11), which represents the average ability for education level L of those who chose L minus the average ability for level L' *of the same group of individuals*, those who chose L.

---

[9] Henceforth we will refer loosely to the "returns to education" as the effect of education on wages.
[10] See Heckman, LaLonde, and Smith (1999).

2.3 Estimation

The model described above has left a number of objects unspecified. These include the functional forms for the direct costs of schooling $\kappa^J(Z_i^J)$, $J = H, C$, the functional form for the wage equations and the distribution of preferences and wages induced by the random vector $(F_i, \tau_i^0, \tau_i^H, \tau_i^C, \nu_i^H, \nu_i^C, \varepsilon_i^0, \varepsilon_i^H,)$. The identifiability of such a model is an important point of discussion. Indeed Magnac, Thierry, and Thesmar (2002) have shown that the discrete choice model, without any direct link to outcomes such as wages, is underidentified.[11] In their context they prove that we can identify the static utilities (here direct costs of education) if we fix the discount rate, the distribution of preferences, and the utility of a reference choice. The implication is that in a discrete choice model, forward looking dynamics have little empirical content; for example we cannot distinguish nonparametrically between a forward looking model and a static one (discount rate zero) without further restrictions. However, this framework is perhaps asking too much from the data and it is perhaps not too surprising that with just discrete decisions and no other restrictions we cannot identify much. Heckman and Navarro (2007) argue that using the cross equation restrictions between educational choice and wages, as implied by a model where educational choices depend on labor market gains, and putting some (factor) structure on the distribution of unobservables is crucial for identification, although not sufficient. We discuss these identification issues below. Here we address estimation in a fully parametric context. That is, we specify all missing functional forms, including the distribution of unobservables, up to an unknown finite set parameters.

There are numerous ways to implement estimation; for particularly complex models a number of simulation approaches have been developed, including simulated method of moments and indirect inference.[12] Here we describe maximum likelihood because the model we presented is relatively simple. We briefly discuss the implementation of simulation estimators for this type of model below.

The estimation approach suggested by Rust (1987), known as *nested fixed point* (NFP) algorithm involves starting at some initial parameter vector; solving the model to obtain the future value functions V_i^C, V_i^{WH} at all possible values of observables and unobservables; followed by the evaluation of the the likelihood function. Once this is evaluated at the parameter vector, an update of the parameters can be found based on a suitable optimization algorithm, such as Gauss-Newton; when the updated parameter vector has been obtained the process starts again with the solution of the model and so on, until convergence. The model will also have to be solved in intermediate steps so as to be able to compute the derivatives of the likelihood during the Gauss Newton iterative process or other derivative based method. It is thus crucial to solve the model in a computationally efficient way.

Su and Judd (2008) note than in many cases the NFP algorithm can become extremely time consuming and possibly infeasible because of the huge number of times

---

[11] See also Rust (1994).
[12] See McFadden (1989), Pakes and Pollard (1989) and Gourieroux, Monfort, and Renault (1993) amongst others.

it needs to solve the full dynamic programming problem. They propose an alternative approach based on mathematical programming subject to equilibrium constraints that simultaneously solves for the value function and estimates the parameters θ. Effectively, they treat the unknown value functions as parameters to be estimated and define the link between the value functions and the structural parameters as a set of nonlinear constraints on the parameters. Once set up in this way any standard optimization algorithm can be used. They find one obtains both speed and accuracy gain in the Rust type problem.

To see how the model can be solved we start by constructing the probabilities of educational attainment *conditional* on unobserved heterogeneity, as shown below

An individual is observed having just statutory education. They are then observed for T_i periods in the labor market. The probability of this level of schooling is

$$P_i^S = \Pr(\text{statutory schooling}) \\ = \Pr\left(v_i^H < EV_i^{WS} - \kappa^{H\prime} Z_i^H - F_i - \beta E \max\{V_i^C, V_i^{WH}\}\right) \quad (1.12)$$

This probability depends on the costs of high school, on the stream of earnings resulting from work at this level of qualification, as well as on the benefits of continuing education into college, which is expressed as a comparison between the benefits of college and the stream of future incomes from high school. Interestingly, even if the benefits from high school may be low for a particular individual, because say τ_i^H happens to be very low they may still choose to attend high school because their benefits from college may be very high. This illustrates why final educational attainment cannot in general be represented as an ordered discrete choice regression model, which will have implications below for the identification and estimation of the wage returns to education.[13] From an economic point of view this highlights the notion that each education level may represent a different sector and individuals may have a comparative advantage for a more advanced sector, without being particularly good at the intermediate level.

Now consider what is the probability of observing someone completing high school and then going on to work. They prefer to continue after statutory schooling and stop after high school. To write down the probability of this event we will assume that the schooling shocks $v^J, J = S, H, C$ are independent over time and that all the dependence in the sequential decisions comes from F_i. Then the probability of high school completion with no further college is

$$P_i^H \equiv \Pr(\text{high school and not college}) \\ = \left[1 - \Pr\left(v_{it}^H < \beta EV_i^{WS} - \kappa^{H\prime} Z_i^H - F_i - \beta E \max\{V_i^C, V_i^{WH}\}\right)\right] \\ \times \Pr\left(v_{it+1}^C - v_{it+1}^H < \kappa_i^{H\prime} Z_i^H - \kappa_i^{C\prime} Z_i^C + (1-\alpha) F_i + \beta\left[E\max\{V^C, V_i^{WH}\} - EV_i^{WC}\right]\right) \quad (1.13)$$

---

[13] See Cameron and Heckman (1998).

Finally, the probability of completing college can be written as

$$P_i^C \equiv \Pr(\text{college})$$
$$= \left[1 - \Pr\left(v_{it}^H < \beta EV_i^{WS} - \kappa^{H\prime}Z_i^H - F_i - \beta E\max\{V_i^C, V_i^{WH}\}\right)\right]$$
$$\times \left[1 - \Pr\left(v_{it+1}^C - v_{it+1}^H < \kappa_i^{H\prime}Z_i^H - \kappa_i^{C\prime}Z_i^C + (1-\alpha)F_i + \beta\left[E\max\{V^C, V_i^{WH}\} - EV_i^{WC}\right]\right)\right] \quad (1.14)$$

This sequence of probabilities also illustrates the way that the distribution of characteristics (observable and unobservable) evolves as individuals progress through schooling: all else being equal individuals with the lowest values of F are the first to stop school. The selection that happens next very much depends on the relative importance of effort costs F for high school and college. If F is more important for high school than college ($\alpha < 1$) then individuals with the highest values of F will actually drop out and not go to college. If on the other hand effort is more important for college, the persons with highest value of F will complete college and then enter the labor market.

Now suppose we observe earnings for an individual over T_i periods. The key complexity here relates to the stochastic structure of earnings, that is, the way that the error terms ε evolve over time. In this context we will deal with the simplest case where the ε are all independently and identically distributed over time. However, other more realistic assumptions in the literature include cases where the ε are a random walk or have an autoregressive structure.

We suppose that observations on earnings start immediately after full-time education is completed. Thus if $t = 1$ for the first observation of someone who started working following statutory schooling, $t = e_H + 1$ for someone with a high school degree, and $t = e_C + 1$ for someone with college. With i.i.d. errors the density of the sequence of earnings for the ith individual can be written as

$$L_i^J \equiv L(w_{is...}w_{iT_i}|J_i, \tau_i, X_i, \theta) = \prod_{t=e_i}^{T_i} g^J(w_i|t - e_i, X_i, \tau_i^{J_i}, \theta) \quad (1.15)$$

where J_i is the level of education achieved, g^J is the density of wages for those with education J, and θ is the vector of parameters. Putting all the pieces together, the likelihood function for an individual who has followed education stream J and is observed working until age T_i is

$$L_i(w_{is...}w_{iT_i}, J_i|Z_i, \tau_i, \theta) = P_i^J(J_i|Z_i, F_i, \tau_i, \theta) L_i^J(w_{is...}w_{iT_i}|J_i, \tau_i, \theta) \quad (1.16)$$

All probabilities and wages depend on unobserved heterogeneity components. The distribution of unobservables needs to be estimated together with the rest of the parameters. The model includes four unobservables, namely $\tau_i = (\tau_i^S, \tau_i^H, \tau_i^C)$, and F which needs to be integrated out. Integrating out the unobserved heterogeneity implies that we average over all possible values, using as weights the probability of each possible value. The weights, as well as the possible values of unobserved heterogeneity constitute unknown parameters of the model. The individual contribution to the likelihood now becomes

$$E_{F,\tau}[L_i(w_{is...}w_{iT_i}, J_i|Z_i, F, \tau, \theta)] = \int_{F,\tau} P_i^J(J_i|Z_i, F, \tau, \theta) L_i^J(w_{is...}w_{iT_i}|J_i, \tau, \theta) dG(F, \tau)$$

where $G(F, \tau)$ is the four-dimensional distribution of unobserved heterogeneity. Note that we are allowing for correlation between the factors.

A key complication in practice is that such high dimensional integrals can take a long time to compute and while this level of generality is very attractive, in that it allows very general sorting patterns into different education groups, the computational difficulty could make the whole problem prohibitive, particularly in the context of richer and more complex models including other decisions such as labor supply.

We can keep some of the advantages of the original specification and simplify the problem substantially by assuming that there are just two factors, one that enters education as before (F) and one that enters wages (τ). The effect of the unobservable in each of the wages is controlled for by a coefficient α^J ($J = H, C$). The coefficient on the wages for statutory schooling is normalized to one since τ is not observed.

Whatever the specifics of the distribution of unobserved heterogeneity, the sample loglikelihood for N individuals is

$$Log\, L = \sum_{i=1}^{N} \log\left\{\int_{F,\tau} P_i^J(J_i|Z_i, X_i, F, \tau, \theta) L_i^J(w_{is...}w_{iT_i}|J_i, X_i, \tau, \theta) dG(F, \tau)\right\} \quad (1.17)$$

The estimation problem relates to obtaining estimates for the unknown parameters θ and the distribution $G(F, \tau)$ by maximizing $LogL$ in Equation (1.17).

2.3.1 Estimation by simulation

Many structural models are often too complex to estimate based on maximum likelihood. Since the seminal work of Lerman and Manski (1981), McFadden (1989), and Pakes and Pollard (1989) simulation approaches and in particular simulated methods of moments have offered a useful alternative that allow us to approach much more complex models.

The first step in simulated method of moments is to decide on a set of moments that can identify the parameters on the model. In our education choice model the proportions attending each level of education, mean wages, and variance of wages by education, all conditional on the exogenous variables, would be suitable moments. These can be estimated directly from the data. Denote these by $\hat{q}$. Given a value for the parameter vector θ, which includes the distribution of unobservables, we can simulate education choices and life cycle profiles of wages from the model. The same moments that were estimated from the data can now be constructed from the simulated data. Denote these simulated moments by $q^s(\theta)$, where s denotes the number of simulations. An estimate of the covariance matrix of the estimated moments is $\hat{\Omega}$. Then the simulated method of moments minimizes the function

$$Q(D|\theta) = (\hat{q} - q^s(\theta))' \hat{\Omega}^{-1} (\hat{q} - q^s(\theta)) \tag{1.18}$$

with respect to θ, where D is the data used to compute the moments Precision will improve with the number of simulations S used to compute $q^s(\theta)$ as well as with the degree of overidentification, that is, the number of moments over and above those needed to exactly identify the model.

A note of caution is called for: while maximum likelihood uses all the information and restrictions implied by the model, given the available data, method of moments do not. In linear models it is easy to see what moments identify the model; however in highly nonlinear models choosing the set of moments that can identify the model may be difficult in practice. Moreover it is complicated if not intractable to check formally that the chosen moments identify the model: this would involve checking that the 2nd derivative matrix of the criterion function is negative definite around the optimum. Thus the cost of moving away from maximum likelihood is the lack of clear rules for choosing the right moments to match.

Returning to the estimation problem, if the criterion function 18 is smooth then a derivative based method, such as Gauss Newton, is appropriate. This may not be always the case. Recently Chernozhukov and Hong (2003) have offered an estimation approach that borrows from Bayesian estimation methods and is particularly suitable for complex problems and nonsmooth criteria functions. Borrowing from the Bayesian literature they define the "quasi posterior" distribution of the parameters as

$$g_N(\theta|D) \propto \exp(-NQ(D|\theta))\pi(\theta) \tag{1.19}$$

where $\pi(\theta)$ is a suitable prior. Asymptotically the prior will not matter, but in any fixed sample the choice will affect the parameter estimates. The key result by Chernozhukov and Hong (2003) is that if we draw a sample of parameters $\theta^{(k)}$ from $g_N(\theta|D)$, where k denotes one random draw, then the sample mean of the $\{\theta^{(k)}, k = 1, K\}$ converges asymptotically to θ. To draw random vectors from $g_N(\theta|D)$ we can use Markov Chain Monte Carlo methods (Chib, 2001). This works as follows: guess an initial value for θ, say $\theta^{(0)}$, solve and simulate the model and compute the corresponding $\exp(-NQ(D|\theta))\,\pi(\theta)$, which is $g_N(\theta^{(0)}|D)$ up to an unknown constant of integration. Now define an update of θ by

$$\theta^{(k+1)} = \theta^{(k)} + \eta \tag{1.20}$$

where η is a random vector drawn from a distribution such that it respects any constraints on the parameter space. For example, for parameters that cover the entire real line, η could be normal with some variance to be chosen by us and modified as the sampling proceeds until we reach a stationary distribution. Once the stationary distribution has been reached the sampling needs to remain the same.[14] We thus proceed as follows: compute the value of $g_N(\theta^{(k}+1)|D)$. The next element of the sample space that we will keep is

$$\begin{array}{ll} \theta^{(k+1)} & \text{with probability } p = \max\left(1, \dfrac{\exp(-NS(D|\theta^{(k+1)}))\pi(\theta^{(k+1)})}{\exp(-NS(D|\theta^{(k)}))\pi(\theta^{(k)})}\right) \\ \theta^{(k)} & \text{otherwise} \end{array} \qquad (1.21)$$

Note that the constant of integration cancels out from 21 and hence never needs to be computed. This algorithm leads to a sample drawn from $g_N(\theta|D)$. The estimator is then the average of the draws from the stationary distribution, and the confidence intervals can be obtained directly from the quantiles of the sampled parameters. This approach can work well, even if the criterion function $Q(D|\theta)$ is not smooth because no derivatives are required.

Overall simulation methods require programming the solution of the model and our ability to simulate it but do not require the computation of an often intractable likelihood function. Such approaches promise to give a fresh impetus to the use of structural models. This is particularly important because, as we shall see, most methods that look simpler rely implicitly for their interpretation on particularly strong assumptions about individual behavior.

2.4 Estimating the wage returns to education in Mincer wage equations

Most of the work on the returns to education has not followed the approach described above; rather it has used the framework of the Mincer equations where educational attainment is summarized by years of education. Thus we digress to discuss the methods used that are based on years of education. The theoretical foundations for such a model can be found in the work of Mincer (1958, 1974). Heckman, Lochner and Todd (2003) have an excellent analysis of the theoretical foundations of the Mincer wage equation and on its empirical relevance.

The key differences in the underlying choice model that leads to the Mincer equation is the absence of direct costs of education and the absence of any uncertainty when education choice is made. Moreover, education is seen as enhancing human capital but not changing its nature: different education levels are perfectly substitutable for each other. The basic Mincer equation can be written as

---

[14] For implementation details of Markov Chain Monte Carlo methods see Robert and Casella (1999).

$$\ln w_{it} = a_t + bs_i + cx_{it} + dx_{it}^2 + u_{it} \tag{1.22}$$

where s_i represents the years of schooling and x_{it} represents years of actual work experience. This relationship is derived in Mincer (1974) and results from prelabor market investments in schooling and post-school training. In the simplest form of the Mincer model, where there are no direct costs of schooling but only an opportunity cost, and no heterogeneity in discount rates, the coefficient on schooling is the return to education and will be equal to the interest rate. However, in more complex models, where there are direct costs and possibly heterogeneity in discount rates and in costs, this is no longer true. So the first (well-known) point is that in general just using a wage equation does not provide us with enough information to estimate the return to education, but just the educational premium for wages; this is just part of the story. In what follows, we refer to the *wage return* to education as the effect of extra education on wages earned, rather than the full return, which would include a complete accounting of the costs and benefits.[15]

Relaxing a number of assumptions underlying the Mincer model, we can end up with a relationship that is both nonlinear in education and where the returns differ across individuals. Perhaps the easiest way of justifying this equation is via the human capital production function, which can take a variety of functional forms, and then price out human capital by the equilibrium in the labor market.

We can simplify the problem by replacing actual experience (the number of periods worked) and including potential experience ($Age_{it} - s_i$) in a linear fashion to start with. We will also abstract from all other relevant observable characteristics and we will drop the time subscript. However we will allow the baseline wage to be different across individuals by specifying that a depends on individual i (a_i) due to unobserved labor market ability. Thus we get

$$\ln w_i = a + bs_i + cAge_i + [a_i - a]$$

If differences in ability are known at the time the individual makes educational choices and are taken into account by them, the years of education will depend on them and be endogenous.[16] This means that $E[a_i - a|s_i] = q(s_i)$ where $q(s_i)$ is some nontrivial function of schooling s. In this simple framework, suppose we have a variable z_i which satisfies the rank condition $E(s_i|z_i) \neq 0$ (correlated with education) and the exclusion restriction $E(a_i - a|z_i) = 0$. Then the instrumental variable estimator is the sample analog of

$$b = \frac{E((z_i - \bar{z})\ln w_i)}{E(s_i(z_i - \bar{z}))} \tag{1.23}$$

---

[15] The Mincer equation can also be viewed as a restrictive version of the Roy model, where the unobservables are the same across education groups.

[16] See Griliches (1977a,b) for one of the first and comprehensive discussions of the role of ability in wage equations.

which can be implemented by replacing the numerator with the sample covariance of z and log wages and the denominator by the sample covariance between z and years of schooling. The resulting estimator is consistent, that is, it converges to the true value b as the sample tends to infinity, under the stated conditions.

Of course the key difficulty is finding variables that somehow affect schooling and do not affect wages. Because of the linearity of the relationship our task is made easier: even a binary instrumental variable would be sufficient to estimate b. An obvious possibility is to use variables that reflect the cost of schooling when the individual was making these decisions. The key problem of course is that such cost-related variables may also be related to the future productivity of the individual when they enter the labor market. A number of variables have been used in the literature in this respect. For example, Card (1995) discusses the use of distance from school as an instrument, which reflects both time and money costs of schooling. While this is clearly a cost related variable and is correlated with schooling it may also be correlated with individual ability. This is because individuals and schools are unlikely to be randomly allocated.[17] An example is individuals living in a city tend to be higher ability and probably more dynamic and ambitious. At the same time the increased population density will mean that schools are on average closer to individuals.

Other instruments relate to changes in legislation. Prominent examples include the use of changes in compulsory schooling laws by Harmon and Walker (1995). They exploit the fact that compulsory schooling increased twice in the U.K., from 14 to 15 and then from 15 to 16. However, because their estimation involves comparing outcomes across successive cohorts, they are not able to allow for other confounding factors that may influence productivity and the returns to education experience of each of the successive cohorts.

Meghir and Palme (2005) directly evaluate the impact of an educational reform that increases compulsory schooling and abolishes early streaming at 12 years of age. In their case they are able to exploit the fact that the reform was introduced gradually across different municipalities in Sweden, which meant that at the same point in time there were municipalities operating different school systems and whose workers would eventually end up in the same labor market. This implied that they could compare across cohorts living in municipalities that switched education system between the cohorts to those living in municipalities that kept the old system for both cohorts (or indeed who were in the new system for both cohorts). The results showed clear benefits for individuals from lower socioeconomic groups both in terms of educational attainment and wages; for those from higher socioeconomic groups there was no effect of education but an adverse effect on

---

[17] See also Card (2001) on this point.

their earnings over the life cycle. Indeed the nature and scope of the reforms were such that we would expect them to affect wages directly as well as possibly through years of education. Hence in this case the reform does not provide a valid instrument for the returns to education, but can be evaluated as a policy in itself.[18]

This brings up an important point of general interest: it is often the case that reforms are used as instruments for estimating returns to education. However, if the reforms changed other aspects of education, such as its quality, it is no longer an excludable instrument for the quantity of education. The reforms to the number of compulsory years of schooling are a strong case at point: if we increase the number of compulsory years of schooling, we may change both the peer group of those who would have continued anyway and possibly the pupil teacher ratio. And if we do increase the resources, we will change the composition of the secondary teacher population, all of which can have a direct effect on wages. In most plausible cases the reform will not be excludable from the wage equation *a priori*.

Angrist and Krueger (1991) use the quarter of birth of an individual as an instrument for education in a wage equation. Quarter of birth interacts with the laws on compulsory schooling to generate differences among individuals who happen to have been born on different dates: the reason this instrument may explain differences in the amount of schooling received is because a student can drop out of school on their 16th birthday; hence depending on the month of birth, some individuals have effectively fewer months of compulsory schooling than others. Interestingly this instrument acts at the individual level and does not affect aggregate schooling, as do reforms to the schooling laws mentioned above. Angrist and Krueger show that there are differences in total schooling by month of birth. However, the differences are small and this particular study led to the important literature on the effects of using instruments that are only weakly correlated with the variable to be instrumented (here schooling). One of the conclusions of this literature is that when an instrument is weak, the estimated results are biased toward OLS (see Bound, Jaeger and Baker (1995) and Staiger and Stock (1997)). A further issue with quarter of birth is whether it is excludable as an instrument from the wage equation: children born in different quarters start attending school at different ages, which may well have an impact on their performance. The effect may be small, but it has to be compared with the small effect that quarter of birth has on attained schooling.

In a interesting paper Acemoglu and Angrist (1999) combine compulsory schooling reforms as instruments that change both the individual level of education and the aggregate one with quarter of birth; it argues that reforms change only individual decisions but have no aggregate effect. Their purpose is to distinguish between the private and the social returns to education; this brings to the fore the issues we discussed earlier: reforms to compulsory schooling laws affect directly those individuals who would have dropped out anyway.

---

[18] It did however allow inferences to be made on the effects of streaming on groups whose socioeconomic background was such that their educational attainment could not be affected by the change in the compulsory schooling laws.

However, because they increase education for a number of people at the same time, they change the composition and amount of educated individuals in the state. If education has externalities, that is, social returns over and above the private ones, then using reforms as an instrument should pick up these effects; the estimated returns to education will be different from those measured by an instrument that "varied" individual levels of education but not the aggregate. Indeed they will be larger if education has positive external effects. To measure the contribution of the external effects they then use quarter of birth instruments to identify the private returns as in Angrist and Krueger (1991). The difference of the two estimates should be the externality effect of education. However, if the reforms also affect the quality of education and equilibrium returns, the estimates obtained with the reforms will be confounded by General Equilibrium (GE) effects and quality differences. A further issue arises if returns to education are heterogeneous because, even under the monotonicity assumption the instruments may be measuring the returns corresponding to different types of individuals. Moreover, with GE and peer effects monotonicity may no longer be valid. In general it is particularly difficult to find satisfactory instruments for education returns without embedding the problem within the a structural model, which allows us to account for such confounding factors.

2.4.1 Nonparametric models

When the wage returns to education are not constant but depend on education, as would be the case if the effect of schooling on wages were nonlinear, the instrumental variables approach becomes more demanding. Dropping age for notational simplicity, a general way of describing the problem is through the following model

$$\ln w_i = b(s_i) + u_i \qquad (1.24)$$

where now $b(s_i)$ is some *unknown* function, and education may be endogenous. The econometric problem of using instrumental variables in this nonparametric context has been addressed by Newey and Powell (2003) and Darolles, Florens and Renault (2002). The estimator is defined based on the assumption that $E(u|Z) = 0$ as in the usual linear instrumental variables context. This restriction means that the error term u is mean independent of *any* nonlinear function of z. However, this is not sufficient: we also need a suitable rank condition. Thus in this regard Newey and Powell (2003) introduce the critical rank condition that any function of education $\delta(s)$ can be predicted by Z. To restate their proposition 2.1:

[Proposition 2.1, Newey and Powell (2003) page 1567] *If $E(u|Z) = 0$ then $b(s)$ in 24 is identified if and only if for all $\delta(s)$ with finite expectation $E(\delta(s)|Z) = 0$ implies $\delta(s) = 0$.*

The importance of this result lies in its implications (or requirements) for identification. The practical difficulty is finding instruments that can satisfy these conditions: the rank condition is much more demanding than the equivalent one in a linear context because it requires that the instrument can produce predictions of any nonlinear function of education and that all these predictions are full rank. However, the practical importance of this theorem lies in what it tells us about the identifiability of such general nonlinear relationships.

Suppose we do have an instrument satisfying the conditions, we now briefly describe implementing an estimator for the function $b(s_i)$. To understand how the non-parametric estimator works we will start with the simple case where the education variable takes K distinct values (1 year to 22 years say) and we have an instrument Z which takes M distinct values; imagine this as reflecting discrete costs of schooling. The exclusion restriction effectively implies that the values of this instrument have been randomly allocated to individuals.[19] Since s_i takes K discrete values, $g(s_i)$ also takes K discrete values. The exclusion restriction implies that $E(\ln w - b(S)|Z = z^j) = 0$.[20] This implies the following set of equations

$$E(\ln w|Z = z_j) = E(b(S)|Z = z_j) \quad j = 1, \ldots, M \quad (1.25)$$

This represents a system of M equations with K unknowns. For example, the first equation will have the form

$$E(\ln w|Z = z_1) = \Sigma_k b(S = s_k) \Pr(S = s_k|Z = z_1)$$

For this system of equations to have a unique solution for the K unknowns $b(S = s_k)$, $k = 1, \ldots, K$, we need the matrix whose (j, k) element is $\Pr(S = s_k|Z = z_j)$ to have rank K. This means that the instrument has to take at least K values and that the probability of different levels of schooling vary sufficiently with the instrument. This rank condition is the discrete analog of the Newey and Powell condition.

To implement this, define the sample average log w when the instrument takes the value z^j by $\bar{y}^j$ whose value is determined by $\bar{y}^j = \frac{1}{N_j}\sum_{i=1}^{N}(1(Z_i = z^j)\ln w_i)$, where $1(Z_i = z^j)$ is one whenever in the sample the instrument take the value z^j and N_j is the number of such sample points. Denote by $p_{kj} = \Pr(S = s_k|Z = z^j)$ and by $\hat{p}_{kj}$ the sample estimate of this probability. The sample analog of 25 is the set of equations

$$\bar{y}^j = \sum_{k=1}^{K} b_k \hat{p}_{kj} \quad j = 1, \ldots, M \quad (1.26)$$

---

[19] The theory requires the instrument just to be mean independent of the residuals, conditional on other observable characteristics. Hence the assumptions are weaker than complete randomization that indices full independence.

[20] We use a capital to denote a random variable and a lower case to denote a specific realization.

where $b_k = b(S = s^k)$ is the set of k unknown values. Estimating g then involves simply solving the system of equations in (1.26). For the exact identification case ($M = K$) this simply means

$$\hat{g} = \hat{P}^{-1}\bar{y} \qquad (1.27)$$

where $\hat{g}$ is the $K \times 1$ vector of all $\hat{g}_k$s and $\hat{P}$ is the $K \times K$ matrix of probabilities of the $\hat{p}_{kj}$. For the overidentified case ($M > K$ and rank(P) = K) the estimator of g_k would minimize the distance

$$D(g) = (\bar{y} - Pg)'\Omega^{-1}(\bar{y} - Pg)$$

with respect to the vector g. In the above, Ω is a suitable covariance matrix.

Extending this procedure to the continuous education case, involves solving an "illposed inverse" problem, where in general the matrix $\hat{P}$ in Equation (1.27) is not invertible in finite samples. The approach to solving this is called regularization, which involves adding a component to P so that it becomes invertible, for example replacing P by $P^* = P + \lambda_N I$, λ_N being a scalar that declines (at a suitable rate) as the sample size N goes to infinity and I being the identity matrix. Darolles, Florens and Renault (2002) and Newey and Powell (2003) offer solutions to the estimation problem in more general terms than we described here.

The key implication of this discussion is that a wage equation that is linear or nonlinear in years of education can in principle be estimated by instrumental variables, without saying much about the structure of the education choice model, other than the standard conditions on the instruments. The most important restriction that has been imposed in this discussion is that the returns to education are homogeneous, or more precisely that education choice does not depend on heterogeneous returns to education.

2.4.2 Heterogeneous returns to years of education and nonparametric models

If individuals have different learning abilities the wage returns to education may differ across individuals. A simple way of expressing this is to rewrite the Mincer model as

$$\ln w_i = a_i + b_i s_i + cAge_i \qquad (1.28)$$

where a_i and b_i are unobservables. Now rewrite the above in the form

$$\ln w_i = a + bs_i + cAge_i + [a_i - a + (b_i - b)s_i]$$

where the term in square brackets $[a_i - a + (b_i - b)s_i]$ is the residual. If the individual takes account of a_i and b_i in choosing s_i, or indeed if any mechanism allocating schooling to individuals depends on a_i and b_i then OLS will be inconsistent for $b = E(b_i)$. So the question is how can we estimate b or other interesting features of the *distribution* of the wage returns. These may include the impact of education level s for those who choose that level (analogous to the effect of treatment on the treated). When s_i is binary, this is the subject of the extensive treatment effects literature, which has also been extended to continuous treatments.[21] We discuss the binary or multiple discrete case in Section 2.5, when we go back to our theoretical framework of education choice and wages.

To start off we define the reduced form model for education choice. Thus we specify

$$S = P(Z) + V \qquad (1.29)$$

where we define $P(Z) \equiv E(S|Z)$.

The first important lesson from this literature is that Instrumental Variables as defined in Equation (1.23) is not consistent for the average parameter $b = E(b_i)$, that is for the average returns to education, without further restrictions. Heckman and Vytlacil (1998) show that IV is consistent for $E(b_i)$ with the additional assumption that $E((b_i - b)v_i|Z) = 0$, implied by the stronger assumption $(A, B, V) \perp\!\!\!\perp Z$, where the capital letters are the random variables and a_i, b_i and v_i are their specific realizations respectively.

To see that this is a strong assumption suppose that the instrument Z was randomized. In the standard IV framework, this would be sufficient for identification, because randomization guarantees that $E(a_i|Z) = 0$. Now however, we need to take a stance about the actual model generating educational choices. Suppose for instance that the true model generating educational choices took the form $S = D(Z, u)$ where u is unobserved heterogeneity. While $(a_i, b_i, u_i) \perp\!\!\!\perp Z$ is guaranteed by randomization we require the stronger assumption that $(a_i, b_i, v_i) \perp\!\!\!\perp Z$ for $v = S - E[D(Z, u)|Z]$ or at that $E[b_i v_i|Z] = 0$; this does not follow without further assumptions. The implication of this discussion is clear: even if the assumptions underlying IV are valid, the interpretation of IV coefficients is unclear and will depend on the structure of the education model itself. We now go deeper into this issue.

More generally, suppose the education model is nonlinear in education s_i so that we can write (ignoring other variables)

$$\ln w = g(S, e) \qquad (1.30)$$

where e is a vector of unobserved characteristics and where S will in general depend on e. A number of papers have attempted to tackle this important problem in various ways, by making different assumptions and considering identification of different aspects of the model. These include Chesher (2003), Altonji and Matzkin (2005), Imbens and Newey (2009), and Florens, Heckman, Meghir, and Vytlacil (2008).[22] Without getting into too much detail we briefly review some of these here.

---

[21] See Heckman and Robb (1985), Heckman, LaLonde, and Smith (1999), Imbens and Angrist (1994), Florens, Heckman, Meghir, and Vytlacil (2008), Imbens and Newey (2009), and Altonji and Matzkin (2005) among many others.

[22] Blundell and Powell (2004) show identification and estimation for nonseparable models with a binary dependent variable.

Altonji and Matzkin develop two approaches. In the one that is most relevant to our problem they make a conditional independence assumption that the distribution of the error term $f(\cdot)$ is such that $f(e|Z, S) = f(e|Z)$, that is, conditional on Z the distribution of the error term does not depend on schooling. In this case e can be a two-dimensional vector of errors that affects log wages in some arbitrary way. The authors identify the average effect of schooling on wages at each level of schooling s, so $E\left(\frac{\partial g(S,e)}{\partial s}|S=s\right)$, based on their assumption.

Chesher (2003) develops identification results for the impact of the endogenous variable (here schooling) on quantiles of the distribution of the outcome. His identification results rely on weaker-than-usual *local* independence conditions; these require that specific quantiles of the distributions of the unobservables are insensitive to changes in the instrument. He also requires that the outcome of interest, here the wage, is monotonically related to the unobservables. In this his model is more restrictive than that of Florens et al. (2008) and Imbens and Newey. If all quantiles of the unobservables are insensitive to the instrument, then global identification follows.

One issue that is important is that the local independence conditions do not have a clear relationship with an underlying choice model. While we can specify sufficient conditions on behavior for full independence to be satisfied, no such conditions have been specified for local independence, when full independence is not valid.

Imbens and Newey (2009) consider a general case where e in Equation (1.30) is a vector of unobservables, and hence they allow for a completely flexible specification of heterogeneity in Equation (1.30). To prove identification they specify the equation assigning values to the endogenous variable, which in our case is the model of education choice, to take the form

$$S = P(Z, U) \qquad (1.31)$$

where the function P is *strictly monotonic* in U. They define the control variate $V = F_{S|Z}(S, Z)$; in a binary choice context this would be the probability of $S = 1$ given Z.

The core of the identification result in their paper is based on the following three assumptions:
1. The function P in 31 is *strictly monotonic* in U.
2. The errors (U, e) are independent of Z, that is, $(U, e) \perp\!\!\!\perp Z$. This implies that S and e are independent conditional on V.
3. The support of V given S is the same as the support of S.

To understand the meaning of this last assumption, return to the definition of V and suppose Z does not affect V for some $S = s'$; in this case the support of V given $S = s'$ would be degenerate. Thus this assumption requires Z to affect V, which makes it equivalent to a rank condition. However, it also has another important implication because it requires Z to be able to span the entire support of V whatever schooling level we consider. To see why this may be restrictive, suppose U is unobserved ability and Z are the observable costs. The assumption effectively requires that Z varies in such a way as to ensure that all ability levels (U) are represented within each schooling level S.

Under these assumptions the authors prove identification of the "quantile structural function," that is, they can identify the quantiles of $g(S, e)$, defined as $q(\tau, S)$ where τ stands for the quantile of $g(S, e)$. This allows them to identify quantile effects, that is, how changes in education change the τth quantile of wages ($q(\tau, S = s) - q(\tau, S = s')$). They also derive a number of other identification results under weaker assumptions, which are beyond the scope of this chapter.

Florens, Heckman, Meghir, and Vytlacil (2008) consider a more restrictive class of models, but obtain identification under a weaker rank condition, namely that of measurable separability, discussed below. The class of models they consider take the following nonseparable form

$$\ln w = m(S, \varepsilon) \equiv g(S) + \varepsilon_0 + \sum_{k=1}^{K} S^k \varepsilon_k \quad (1.32)$$

where the function $g(\cdot)$ is not known. The model discussed in Newey and Powell (2003) and Newey, Powell, and Vella (1999) is one where $K = 0$. More generally, this function is nonseparable in education S and unobserved heterogeneity. The restrictions vis-á-vis Imbens and Newey (2009) is that $g(S)$ has to be differentiable up to the order K and the maximum value of heterogeneous terms K needs to be known in advance. In the context of Florens et al. (2008), no identification results have been proved for the case where K is unknown and has to be estimated. The object of interest for the Florens et al. (2008) core identification result is the *average treatment effect*, or the average wage return to education at each level of education S. This is defined as

$$\Delta^{ATE}(s) = \frac{\partial g(s)}{\partial s} = E_\varepsilon \left[\frac{\partial m(S, \varepsilon)}{\partial S} \right] \quad (1.33)$$

The econometric problem is to identify $\frac{\partial g(s)}{\partial s}$ or even the function $g(S)$. As stated above, standard instrumental variables will not work. Florens et al. (2008) make the following assumptions (omitting some technical details).

1. The function g is differentiable to the $K th$ order.
2. Control function: $E(\varepsilon_j | Z, S) = r_j(V)$ for $j = 0, \ldots, K$, where $r_j(\cdot)$ is a known or identifiable function and V is defined in Equation (1.29).
3. Rank condition (measurable separability): S and V are measurably separated, that is, any function of S almost surely equal to a function of V must be almost surely equal to a constant.

Theorem [from Florens et al. (2008), Theorem 1, p 1197] *Given assumptions 1, 2 and 3 above the average wage returns to education in Equation (1.33) as well as the wage returns to education for those who chose schooling level, $S = s$ are identified.*

This identification theorem defines conditions under which we can actually identify the wage returns to education even with errors that enter in a nonseparable way and in a very general fashion. It is important of course to understand the limitations implied by the assumptions.

Assumption 1 precludes any kinks or discontinuities in the relationship between education and wages; discontinuities could be induced by sheepskin effects, where wages may jump discontinuously upon graduation for instance.

Assumption 2 is similar (but not identical) to the usual exclusion restriction. It states that all the dependence between the unobservables in the education equation and the educational assignment rule can be expressed through some known or identifiable function of the residual in the educational equation reduced form. This assumption is the same as the one used in Heckman (1979) and many others since;[23] in Heckman (1979) the control function is the Mills ratio. Imbens and Newey (2009) use the same concept of a control variate. This control variate induces conditional independence between schooling and unobserved heterogeneity. The third assumption is a rank condition: it requires sufficient independent variation of V and S; if the instrument Z did not "explain" S this condition would not be satisfied. Note however, that measurable separability does not require the support of V given S to be the same as the support of V. As such it is a weaker assumption than the one used by Imbens and Newey (2009).

These assumptions seem overly technical; we need to explain what they mean in terms of economic behavior. Unfortunately, necessary and sufficient conditions are not available. Florens et al. (2008) provide sufficient conditions on a structural model of education choice for the conditions to be satisfied. In particular they posit a model where the education choice can be written as in Equation (1.31) where U is a continuous scalar random variable and P is an increasing function of U. This is restrictive, because it requires that just one unobservable factor characterizes educational choice and that this variable is monotonically related to education. For example, if the level of education depends on unobservable costs and on labor market ability then S will depend on two unobserved factors that may not be possible to aggregate them into one satisfying the monotonicity assumption. Florens et al. (2008) show that if the instrument Z is independent of all unobservables in the model, that is, $Z \perp\!\!\!\perp (U, \varepsilon_0, \varepsilon_1, \ldots, \varepsilon_K)$, then under the assumption of measurable separability between U and S, assumptions 2 and 3 of the theorem are satisfied and identification of the average wage return to education follows. Hence results obtained under the control function

---

[23] See Heckman and Robb (1985) and Newey, Powell, and Vella (1999).

assumption can be interpreted in the context of any education choice model that can be expressed as $S = S(Z, U)$, which is monotonic in U.

2.4.3 Education choice and wages: A simple illustration and discussion

Florens, Heckman, Meghir, and Vytlacil (2008) present the following example to illustrate the issues. Suppose that the discounted annualized earnings flows for s years of education is $W(s)$

$$W(s) = \varphi_0 + (\varphi_1 + \varepsilon_1)s + \frac{1}{2}\varphi s^2 + \varepsilon_0$$

and the cost function for schooling is

$$C(s, Z) = C_0(Z) + (C_1(Z) + v_1)s + \frac{1}{2}C_2(Z)s^2 + v_0 \quad (1.34)$$

where ε_k and $v_k (k = 0, 1)$ are, respectively, unobserved heterogeneity in the wage level and in the cost of schooling. We impose the normalizations that $E(\varepsilon_k) = 0$, $E(v_k) = 0$, for $k = 0,1$. We implicitly condition on variables such as human capital characteristics that affect both wages and the costs of schooling. The Z are factors that only affect the cost of schooling, such as tuition costs.

Assume that agents choose their level of education to maximize wages minus costs. Let S denote the resulting optimal choice of education. S solves the first-order condition

$$(\varphi_1 - C_1(Z)) + (\varphi_2 - C_2(Z))S + \varepsilon_1 - v_1 = 0$$

Assuming that $\varphi_2 - C_2(Z) < 0$ for all Z, the second-order condition for a maximum will be satisfied. This leads to an education choice equation (assignment to treatment intensity rule)

$$S = \frac{\varphi_1 - C_1(Z) + \varepsilon_1 - v_1}{C_2(Z) - \varphi_2}$$

This choice equation satisfies the monotonicity restriction discussed above and if Z is randomized it will be jointly independent of ε_k and v_k ($k = 0, 1$). This implies the control function assumption and the model is identified without knowledge of or further restrictions on the functional form of the wage and the education choice equations.

However this result is sensitive to changes in both the degree of heterogeneity in wages or directly in the cost function because both can affect the structure of educational choice. Consider the same example as before, except now the second derivative of W_d is also stochastic:

$$W_s = \varphi_0 + (\varphi_1 + \varepsilon_1)s + \frac{1}{2}(\varphi_2 + \varepsilon_2)s^2 + \varepsilon_0$$

In itself this poses no problem, except that in an optimizing model it will change the structure of educational choice; this now becomes

$$S = \frac{\varphi_1 - C_1(Z) + \varepsilon_1 - \nu_1}{C_2(Z) - \varphi_2 - \varepsilon_2}$$

In this case, the structural model makes S a function of $V = (\varepsilon 1 - \nu 1, \varepsilon 2)$, which can satisfy the independence assumption if Z is randomized, that is $Z \perp\!\!\!\perp (V, \varepsilon_0, \varepsilon_1, \varepsilon_2)$ *but* V is not a scalar error. We can still construct an education model depending monotonically on one error term but this new error term will not generally be independent of Z: define a residual $\widetilde{V} = F_{S|Z}(S|Z)$; the "reduced form" education choice equation can then be written as $S = \widetilde{g}(Z, \widetilde{V}) = F_{S|Z}^{-1}(\widetilde{V}|Z)$, which is increasing in $\widetilde{V}$. Thus S is strictly increasing in a scalar error term $\widetilde{V}$ that is independent of Z by construction. However, Z is not independent of $(\widetilde{V}, \varepsilon_0, \varepsilon_1, \varepsilon_2)$ as required by the identification theorem, despite the fact that it is independent of the original errors $(V, \varepsilon_0, \varepsilon_1, \varepsilon_2)$. To see why, note that

$$\Pr(\widetilde{V} \leq v | Z, \varepsilon_0, \varepsilon_1, \varepsilon_2) =$$

$$\Pr\left[\nu_1 : \frac{\varphi_1 - C_1(Z) + \varepsilon_1 - \nu_1}{C_2(Z) - \varphi_2 - \varepsilon_2} \leq F_{S|Z}^{-1}(v) | Z, \varepsilon_0, \varepsilon_1, \varepsilon_2\right] \neq \Pr(\widetilde{V} \leq v | \varepsilon_0, \varepsilon_1, \varepsilon_2)$$

In the above, varying Z changes the set of $\nu 1$ for which the condition is true and hence the distribution of $\widetilde{V}$ depends on Z.

This example illustrates how the specification of the educational choice model has implications for the identifiability of the wage returns to education. As emphasized by Heckman, LaLonde and Smith (1999) and Abbring and Heckman (2007) informational assumptions can play an important role: here if the individual knows and takes into account the complete structure of wages, the educational choice model becomes such that the sufficient assumptions for identification used by most papers in this literature may no longer be valid depending on the degree of heterogeneity in the wage equation. Hence even in a nonparametric framework and with randomized instruments, the interpretation of results will depend crucially on the model driving educational choice: randomization of the instruments is not sufficient in this respect. Thus, what transpires from the above is that identification depends on the nature of education choice, beyond the simple statement that a valid instrument is available.[24] This contrasts to an extent with what is known about models with homogeneous effects.

In the next section we will consider explicitly educational choice as discrete. This framework permits consideration of identification and estimation issues based on richer models of educational choice.

---

[24] Valid in the traditional sense of being uncorrelated to unobservables and correlated with education.

2.5 Identification and estimation of the wage returns to education in the dynamic discrete education choice model

We now return to the dynamic multisector model of education choice described in Section 2.2. This is a more complex model because it recognizes the sequential nature of education choice and allows for uncertainty, which gets revealed gradually between different educational stages. It also allows for the possibility of comparative advantage for a particular educational level.[25] Our aim is to review approaches to identifying and estimating measures of the returns to education, such as the average treatment effect or the local average treatment effect.

There is a vast literature on discrete treatment effects and their identification. Some of the most important results are presented in Heckman and Robb (1985), Heckman, LaLonde, and Smith (1999), Imbens and Angrist (1994), Heckman and Vytlacil (2005), Carneiro, Heckman, and Vytlacil (2010) and many others. Most papers define statistical assumptions that lead to identification. Some make the additional important step of relating these assumptions to the underlying economic behavior, a prime example being Vytlacil (2002).

We focus on two issues that arise when using the model of Section 2.2 as an organizing framework. First, to what extent is the full model nonparametrically identified, and second, if the full model is not identified, under what conditions can we at least identify the marginal distribution of earnings for each education level so as to get to the average returns to education.

Magnac and Thesmar (2002) explicitly analyze the identification in dynamic discrete choice models with uncertainty where the data only include the discrete choices as well as observations on the relevant state variables. In our case these would be the education choices and the variables determining the costs of education respectively (Z). No observations on outcomes motivating such choices, such as income, are observed. They show that even in the absence of persistent unobserved heterogeneity the model is seriously underidentified: to identify the within period utility, without functional form restrictions one needs to know the distribution of the shocks, the discount factor, and the current and future preferences for a reference alternative. Exclusion restrictions between alternatives can improve things but not by much.

However, when we observe outcome variables such as earnings and when we can link the choice of a level of education to the observed outcome, as in the model presented in Section 2.2, the prospects for identification improve. Heckman and Navarro (2007) present a number of identification theorems relating to the dynamic structural model itself and to the distribution of earnings in each education level. Many of the issues can be understood by taking the simpler framework of Heckman, Urzua and Vytlacil (2006a,b) (HUV henceforth).

[25] See, for example, Heckman and Sedlacek (1985).

Consider first a simple framework where education choice can be expressed as a once-and-for-all choice at a point in time. Individuals choose the level of education among a set of possible levels. However the levels are not necessarily ordered. The underlying reason why the choices are not ordered are the dynamics: it is possible that an individual choosing between dropping out of school or attending high school could choose the former, in the absence of any other choice, but that if the choice of college is added, then they could progress to college (via high-school graduation). HUV study identification of models with discrete treatments and unordered choices and provide identification results, which we outline briefly here.

Write the net payoff to education as

$$R^J(Z^J, X) = \vartheta^J(Z^J, X) - V^J, \qquad J = S, H, C \qquad (1.35)$$

where Z^J is the set of variables that affect education choice J; these could be the costs that affect a particular education level, such as fees or transport costs to the closest educational institution. Because of dynamics, all Z^J may be the same (see below). Let $Z = \{Z^S, Z^H, Z^C\}$. The payoff to education is earnings and is given by 5. Now make the following assumptions, as in HUV

1. The unobservables are jointly independent of Z, X, and age: $(\tau^S + \varepsilon_t^J, V^J, J = S, H, C) \perp\!\!\!\perp \{Z, age, X_i\}$
2. The support (supp) of the functions $\vartheta^J(Z^J, X)$ and $m^J(age, X)$ are independent of each other so that

$$supp\{\vartheta^J(Z^J, X), m^J(age, X), J = S, H, C\} =$$
$$\vartheta^S(Z^S, X) \times m^S(age, X) \times \vartheta^H(Z^H, X) \times m^H(age, X) \times \vartheta^C(Z^C, X) \times m^C(age, X)$$

3. The structures of the functions $\vartheta^J(Z^J, X)$ and of the variables Z^J is such that their support is at least as large as the support of V^J:

$$\text{supp}\{\vartheta^J(Z^J, X)\} \supseteq \text{supp}\{V^J\}$$

4. Given age and Z, X has full rank

These assumptions imply that we can find combinations of values of Z such that the probability of any choice J becomes 1. Within that "limit set," as Heckman and Navarro (2007) call them, we can identify the marginal distribution of earnings Y^J conditional on age and X. The latter follows from the independence assumption that ensures that the distribution of earnings is the same for whatever value of Z and by the rank condition that ensures that whatever the value of Z and age there is sufficient variation in X. In addition if all we are interested is average earnings given X and age, then all we need is that the errors in the earnings equation are mean independent of Z, age, and X.

This identification result suggests an estimation strategy for mean earnings. Suppose the only X regressor was age. Then we can estimate mean earnings for education level J at age a as

$$\hat{Y}(a,J) = \frac{\sum_{i=1}^{N} K(\hat{p}(Z_i) - 1) Y_i^J (age_i = a)}{\sum_{i=1}^{N} K(\hat{p}(Z_i) - 1)}$$

where $K(\hat{p}(Z_i) - 1)$ is a kernel giving maximum weight when $\hat{p}(Z_i) = 1$. This is a weighted average of the earnings of (potentially) all individuals with education level J, with the weights being higher the higher the predicted probability of attaining that level. The weights toward individuals with probability equal to one of achieving this level increase as the sample size increases, but at a rate that is slower than the sample size increase. Clearly this estimation procedure is only justified if the limit sets exist in the population and the assumptions detailed above are justified. Below we discuss further the support assumptions and the consequences of them being violated. But before this we turn to the model that is explicitly dynamic.

The question is how different is the dynamic context in terms of the required assumptions for identifying the marginal distributions of earnings corresponding to different education levels. By examining Equations 1.12, 1.13 and 1.14 it is apparent that all probabilities depend on all Zs so long as these are all known when the decisions are made sequentially over time. Second, it is also apparent that the probabilities are nonlinear functions of unobserved heterogeneity and the decision problem is not separable in observables and unobservables as in Equation 1.35. The education choice model has the non-separable form

$$R^J = \vartheta^J(Z, X, e), \qquad J = S, H, C \qquad (1.36)$$

where R^J is the life cycle value of alternative J and where e is a vector of unobservables. Of course there is some structure to this, which will matter both in terms of understanding whether the assumptions are valid or not and for identifying the dynamic discrete choice model. Heckman and Navarro (2007) make assumptions on the primitives of the model so that the support conditions discussed above carry over to this context. As before, we need to be able to argue that the required limit sets exist. Given they exist, the same identification argument applies as before.

2.6 Using bounds to estimate the returns to education

The idea of limit sets is interesting intellectually but in practice it is highly unlikely that we observe suitable variables such that the limit sets exist. The variables we observe are likely to have limited support; for example it is unlikely that we will observe such a range of fees that at one end all attend college (presumably this would require a hefty subsidy) and at the other no one did. Even combining this with other cost type variables like distance from college, we are not likely to find a set where the probabilities of attendance reach the limit or even come close; the condition that the distribution of earnings conditional on other observables is the same within such limit sets, is even less likely to be satisfied. However, such identification strategies help us understand the nature of the problem and can sometimes points to other strategies. One strategy is to use the model we described in section 2.2 or other such suitable specification, imposing distributional and other functional form assumptions. Indeed, even if the model is conceptually identified this may be a way of improving efficiency in practice. A diametrically opposite alternative is to make minimal assumptions and follow the route of partial identification and use bounds as discussed in Manski (1994), Manski and Pepper (2000), and Blundell, Gosling, Ichimura, and Meghir (2007). In the context of this discussion the last of those three is particularly useful: it offers an alternative approach to learning something about the distribution of earnings with minimal assumptions and illustrates clearly the identification problem and how the limit set assumption resolves it.

Suppose we wish to identify the marginal distribution of earnings given a level of education J for individuals with characteristics X, $F(Y^J|X)$. Based on the law of iterated expectations we can write

$$F(Y^{J=j} < y|X) = F(Y^J < y|X, J=j)\Pr(J=j|X) + F(Y^J < y|X, J \neq j)\Pr(J \neq j|X)$$

where $F(Y^J < y|X, J \neq j)$ is the distribution of earnings corresponding to level J for those that did not choose level J. This is not observed and without further assumptions all we can say is that it lies in the closed interval $[0,1]$. Then this implies the "worst case" bounds

$$F(Y^J < y|X, J=j)\Pr(J=j|X)$$
$$\leq F(Y^{J=j} < y|X) \leq$$
$$F(Y^J < y|X, J=j)\Pr(J=j|X) + \Pr(J \neq j|X)$$

Because of the lack of any exclusion restrictions, the lower and upper bounds can never be equal; in other words, without further assumptions the distribution of earnings in each education group are never identified and of course neither is any notion of a wage return to education.

Now suppose we do possess a set of instruments Z as above from which education in level J is independent. The assumption is that $F(Y^{J=j} < y|Z, X) = F(Y^{J=j} < y|X)$. Thus Z is excluded from earnings. However, these affect both the probability of selecting education choice J and through selection they also affect the conditional distributions. Thus for each value of the instruments Z and each education level J we have that

$$F(Y^J < y|Z, X, J = j) \Pr(J = j|Z, X)$$
$$\leq F(Y^{J=j} < y|X) \leq$$
$$F(Y^J < y|Z, X, J = j) \Pr(J = j|Z, X) + \Pr(J \neq j|Z, X)$$

Since the distribution of earnings does not depend on Z we can choose the best bounds across Zs. Thus the tightest bounds are

$$\max_Z \{F(Y^J < y|Z, X, J = j) \Pr(J = j|Z, x)\}$$
$$\leq F(Y^{J=j} < y|X) \leq \qquad (1.37)$$
$$\min_Z \{F(Y^J < y|Z, X, J = j) \Pr(J = j|Z, x) + \Pr(J \neq j|Z, X)\}$$

This links the approach with the earlier discussion: given the exclusion restrictions and assuming the distribution of X is not degenerate given Z, a necessary and sufficient condition for the distribution of earnings to be identified is that the upper and lower bounds in Equation 1.37 are equal. The existence of limit sets as discussed in Heckman and Navarro (2007) would imply such an equality. However this is just a sufficient condition, and it is possible that the bounds are equal without the limit set assumption. The difficulty is understanding how such conditions may relate to an underlying model of choice and whether we can expect them to hold.

If identification is not obtainable, that is if

$$\max_Z \{F(Y^J < y|Z, X, J = j) \Pr(J = j|Z, x)\} < $$
$$\min_Z \{F(Y^J < y|Z, X, J = j) \Pr(J = j|Z, x) + \Pr(J \neq j|Z, X)\} \qquad (1.38)$$

for some or all X, then we can only obtain bounds on the distribution of earnings and thus bounds on its quantiles. Moreover, without bounds on the support of Y^J we cannot obtain bounds on means and variances and other moments, other than the order statistics. In this case we need to either impose restrictions on the support or compare the order statistics as a measure of the wage returns to education. To see how this works suppose we wish to compare quantile q. Define $w^{ql}(J = j, Z, X)$ as the w that solves the equation

$$q = F(w|Z, X, J = j) \Pr(J = j|Z, X) \qquad (1.39)$$

and $w^{qu}(Z, X, J = j)$ as the solution to

$$q = F(w|Z, X, J = j) \Pr(J = j|Z, X) + (1 - \Pr(J = j|Z, X)) \qquad (1.40)$$

Thus the upper bound of the qth quantile for a particular value of Z is equal to the $q/\Pr(J = j|Z, X)$ quantile of the observed distribution of earnings for those with education level j. The lower bound is the $(q - (1 - \Pr(J = j|Z, X)))/\Pr(J = j|Z, X)$ quantile of the same observed distribution. To then use the exclusion restriction, the best bounds can be obtained by

$$\max_Z \{w^{ql}(Z, X, J = j)\} \leq w^q(X, J = j) \leq \max_Z \{w^{qu}(Z, X, J = j)\}$$

Now suppose we define the wage returns to education as the difference in the medians of the two distributions. This measure of gain is bounded by

$$w^{ql}(X, J = C) - w^{qu}(X, J = H) \leq \Delta^{C/H} \leq w^{qu}(X, J = C) - w^{ql}(X, J = H) \quad (1.41)$$

where $q = 0.5$. This is not equivalent to the wage returns usually presented, which corresponds to comparing means. Thus, lack of point identification has led us to compare different aspects of the distribution of earnings across education groups.

To implement the bounds approach we can directly estimate the conditional distribution of earnings given each education group. Blundell, Gosling, Ichimura, and Meghir (2007) (henceforth, BGIM) (in the context of selection into work rather than education—see below) use

$$\hat{F}_N(w|J=j, age=a, Z=z) = \frac{\sum_{i=1}^N \Phi\left(\frac{w-w_i}{h}\right) I(J=j) \kappa_{az}(age_i, z_i)}{\sum_{i=1}^N I(J=j) \kappa_a(age_i, z_i)}$$

In the above, $\hat{F}_N(\cdot)$ denotes the estimated distribution and $\Phi\left(\frac{w-w_i}{h}\right)$ is the standard normal distribution function; it is used instead of the indicator function $1(w_i \leq w)$ to provide some smoothness. As the sample size gets bigger we can reduce h, then this function becomes zero very fast as observations above w are used, and is one for values of w_i even slightly lower than w. For the sample size in the BGIM study h was set at a fifth of the standard deviation of wages. For the function $\kappa_{az}(age_i, z_i)$ BGIM use

$$\kappa_a(age_i, z_i) = \left(\frac{age_i - a}{3} + 1\right)^2 \left(\frac{age_i - a}{3} - 1\right)^2 I(|age_i - a| < 3) \varphi_k(z_i)$$

where

$$\varphi_k(z_i) = \left(\frac{z_i - z_k}{0.2} + 1\right)^2 \left(\frac{z_i - z_k}{0.2} + 1\right)^2 I(|z_i - z_k| \leq 0.2)$$

Once the distributions of wages and the probability of attainment conditional on Z have been estimated, we can then apply 38 to bound the distribution, which can then be used to estimate the bounds to the quantiles. Here an interesting observation can be made: the bounds that depend on the exclusion restrictions Z may cross. This can happen either because the restrictions are wrong or because the sample is small. We can thus devise a test of the null hypothesis that the bounds are equal against the alternative that the lower bound is above the upper bound. Rejecting implies the restrictions are invalid. The test has power against the alternative, but cannot detect invalid restrictions that do not lead to the bounds crossing. BGIM discuss such tests and implement it using the bootstrap. Kitagawa (2010) derives formally a test for independence in a similar context.

2.7 A special case: Binary educational choice

Many problems in the broad area of education and training can be represented as the impact of a binary treatment, whose choice may be endogenous. A prime example is the impact of vocational training. In this case the wage equation would take the form

$$\ln w_i = a + b_i T_i + u_i \tag{1.42}$$

or in counterfactual notation used in the treatment effects literature

$$\begin{aligned} \ln w_i^0 &= a + u_i \\ \ln w_i^1 &= a + b_i + u_i \end{aligned} \tag{1.43}$$

where w_i^0 represents wages in the no training state and w_i^1 represents wages in the training state. Estimation and identification of this model has been widely analyzed with some of the key results to be found in Heckman, LaLonde, and Smith (1999). We do not reproduce these here; however we complete our discussion of instrumental variables by pointing out the interpretation of this estimator in this context.

Suppose we possess a binary instrument Z; for example an indicator as to whether some individuals are facing a different policy environment, such as a training subsidy, and which we take as having been randomly allocated. Suppose the model is the simple Roy model with just a binary education/training choice ($T_i = \{1, 0\}$).

Instrumental variables for this problem have been analyzed by Imbens and Angrist (1994). Define $T(1)$ and $T(0)$ to be indicators of whether an individual would take up training when $Z = 1$ and $Z = 0$ respectively. They assume that the instrument Z is jointly independent from all unobservables, that is, ($\ln w_0$, $\ln w_1$, $T(1)$, $T(0)$ ⊥⊥ Z); they also make a critical monotonicity assumption: no person who would have obtained training when facing environment $Z = 0$ refrains from training when $Z = 1$. In terms of the notation above we have that for all individuals $T(1) \geq T(0)$.[26] Under these assumption they show that using Z as an instrument in the above regression (Equation 1.42) will identify the effect of T on wages for those choosing $T = 1$ when facing $Z = 1$ (e.g., when offered the subsidy) and who would have chosen $T = 0$ if instead they faced $Z = 0$ (no subsidy).[27] The effect is known as the *local average treatment effect* (LATE). LATE is not invariant to the choice of instrument: different policies that act on different margins, that is, induce different types of individuals into training, can lead to different estimates of the effect if it is heterogeneous. However, in each case the effect can be interpreted as causal. What is under question is the external validity/generalizability of the estimate. We are left with a situation where we can

---

[26] Obviously all that matters is that Zi induces either no movement or movement in the same direction for all individuals. So we need to have either that T(1) ≥ T(0) for all individuals or alternatively that T(0) ≥ T(1) for all individuals.
[27] That is, the effect for those for whom T(1) = 1 and T(0) = 0.

estimate the impact of training in some specific context, but we cannot necessarily generalize to other contexts.

Vytlacil (2002) shows that the LATE assumptions are equivalent to those of the traditional selection model. Thus the LATE assumptions are satisfied if and only if the training choice can be represented by a threshold crossing model, such that

$$T = 1 \Leftrightarrow \varsigma > g(Z) \qquad (1.44)$$

where the unobservables in Equations 1.44 and 1.42 satisfy the independence assumption $(\varsigma, b, u) \perp\!\!\!\perp Z$. This means that if we can transform the decision rule implied by an economic model into the form of Equation 1.44 with all unobservables jointly independent of Z, then that economic model is consistent with the assumptions implied by LATE.

Important cases where these conditions may not be satisfied is when there are general equilibrium effects or peer/congestion effects. Suppose that Z represents a subsidy to college education and suppose that many individuals take up college education. This may well discourage individuals with say high lnw_i^0 from attending college, when they may have done so without the subsidy.

Heckman and Vytlacil (2005) provide an elegant way of interpreting LATE and placing it in a broader family of treatment effects.[28] Suppose we represent binary education choice by a threshold crossing model, which satisfies the monotonicity restriction (Vytlacil, 2002)

$$\Pr(T_i = 1|Z) = \Pr(\kappa(Z) < v)$$

An individual is defined as marginal with respect to this training choice if $\kappa(Z) = v$: given Z, the unobservable characteristics are such that the benefits and costs of training exactly outweigh each other. A small increase of the benefits will draw this person in. The marginal treatment effect at some value of Z is the effect of training on individuals who are just indifferent between accepting training and not, such that $b^{MTE}(z) = E(b_i|\kappa(Z = z) = v$. For convenience we can rewrite this relationship by defining $\kappa^u(Z) = F(\kappa(Z))$ so that we can define the marginal individual as $\kappa^u(Z = z) = p$ where $p \in [0, 1]$. Now consider a policy that increases Z from a to b. Then the LATE parameter is the average effect for all those individuals in the range $[\kappa^u(Z = a), \kappa^u(Z = b)]$. If on the other hand the policy increases the value of Z by some fixed value, and assuming the LATE assumptions are valid at all Z, then LATE will be an average across different LATE values corresponding to the different starting points for Z. More generally, with Z being continuous, one can imagine estimating an MTE parameter at all levels of Z. Heckman and Vytlacil (2005) show that the average MTE is the average treatment effect. Moreover, all treatment effect parameters, such as the average effect

---

[28] See also Carneiro, Heckman, and Vytlacil (2010).

of treatment on the treated, can be expressed as weighted averages of the MTE over different relevant ranges. From a policy perspective, the MTE offers us a way of estimating the marginal benefit in terms of our outcome variable (such as wages) of a small increase in say the incentive to obtain training.

Heckman and Vytlacil (2005) and Carneiro et al. (2010) show that that the MTE is equal to

$$\beta^{MTE}(p) = \frac{\partial E(Y|P(Z) = p)}{\partial p} \qquad (1.45)$$

Thus we can estimate a nonparametric regression of Y on $P(Z)$, where $P(Z)$ is the propensity score or the probability that treatment is assigned, given Z. The estimate of the marginal treatment effect then is the derivative of this nonparametric estimator.

As a tool the MTE can be very useful. For example suppose we estimate the MTE for going to college as a function of different levels of p; and suppose that we find that the MTE is high for those with a low probability of attending college. This indicates that a policy that targets those with a low probability of attendance is likely to have high returns. In some circumstances, such an empirical finding may be interpreted as reflecting the presence of liquidity or other constraints of attending college. The difficulty with the MTE is the extent that the instruments Z can span a continuous support of the probability of being assigned to treatment between 0 and 1. It is generally difficult to identify instruments that satisfy the independence assumptions and have sufficient support. In practice many discrete instruments may serve that purpose.

3. THE RETURNS TO EDUCATION AND LABOR FORCE PARTICIPATION

3.1 Bias to the estimated returns when participation is ignored

We have emphasized the issue of endogenous education when estimating the returns. However, another equally important problem when estimating the returns is that of missing wages for nonworking individuals. Comparing the wages of workers can lead to biased results on the returns to education because those with missing wages are not selected randomly: suppose we measure the wage returns to college by

$$\Delta^{C/H} = E(\ln w | C, P = 1) - E(\ln w | H, P = 1)$$

If education affects participation in the labor market ($P = 1$) then the ability composition of those working with a college degree will be different from the ability composition for those working with a high-school degree even if education is exogenous for wages. This problem is important because the proportion of nonworkers can be very high. In the U.K., for example, in 2000 only 78% of men with statutory schooling and 85% of high school graduates worked. For women the respective figures are 60% and 75%.

A simple analysis based on Heckman's (1979) model will illustrate that ignoring nonparticipation is likely to lead to an underestimate of the returns to education. The intuition is simple: if education increases participation the composition of the workers with a higher level of education will be worse than the composition of the workers with lower levels of education, where participation is lower. This intuitive analysis is based on many strong assumptions. For example, when individuals sort into educational groups by comparative advantage it is no longer obvious how the bias will go. One way of understanding the potential amount of bias is to use Manski's (1994) worst-case bounds.

Denote by $F(w|ed)$ the distribution of wages for the entire population with education level ed, irrespective of work status. Assume for simplicity that education itself is exogenous. The concept here is that each individual has some wage they would earn were they to work; however this wage is not observed when the individual is not employed. Hence $F(w|ed)$ is not itself observed. Instead we observe $F(w|ed, P = 1)$, where $P = 1$ denotes those working. The two are related by

$$F(w|ed) = F(w|ed, P = 1) \Pr(P = 1|ed) + F(w|ed, P = 0) \Pr(P = 0|ed)$$

where $F(w|ed, P = 0)$ is not observed. This implies that

$$F(w|ed, P = 1) \Pr(P = 1|ed) \leq F(w|ed) \leq F(w|ed, P = 1) + \Pr(P = 0|ed)$$

which implies that the width of the bounds for the unconditional distribution of wages is $\Pr(P = 0|ed)$, giving a potentially very large range for the order statistics (median, quartiles, etc.) of the wage distribution and leaving all the order statistics below $\Pr(P = 0|ed)$ and above $\Pr(P = 1|ed)$ unidentified. Moreover without restrictions on the support of wages it is not possible to bound the mean of wages corresponding to $F(w|ed)$, without other information or restrictions. This means that the wage returns to education are unidentified and those based on comparing order statistics, such as the medians, can lie in very wide ranges. Although this is definitely not a novel point it is often overlooked when estimating returns to education.

3.2 Accounting for nonparticipation

The original way of dealing with the issue was that of correcting wages for selection into employment as in Gronau (1974) and Heckman (1974, 1979) and many others that followed. Heckman and Honoré (1990) provided an in-depth analysis of identification in a Roy model that includes the simple selection model. Heckman (1990), Ahn and Powell (1993), and Das, Newey, and Vella (2003) developed further identification results. The literature on selectivity corrected wage equations is vast and we will not discuss it further here.

Alternatively we discuss recent developments on using bounds to account for selection when estimating the distribution of wages or more specifically the returns to education. In an earlier section we illustrated the use of bounds for allowing for the endogeneity of wages. Here we discuss the approach of Blundell, Gosling, Ichimura, and Meghir (2007) (henceforth BGIM) who develop bounds that allow us to control for the effects of selection into work.

Worst-case bounds are generally too wide to be useful, other than to illustrate that without any assumptions it is very difficult to say anything. Thus BGIM obtain tighter bounds by using three different restrictions. In the first they assume that the distribution of wages of workers either stochastically dominates the unobserved one of nonworkers or at least has a higher median than that of nonworkers. The idea here is that there is positive selection into the labor market. Under the stronger stochastic dominance restriction the lower bound to the distribution of wages increases and we obtain that

$$F(w|ed, P=1) \leq F(w|ed) \leq F(w|ed, P=1)\Pr(P=1|ed) + \Pr(P=0|ed)$$

This restriction is never testable. In addition it does not follow from economic theory, particularly if we do not condition on wealth. Indeed it is possible that higher wage individuals have higher reservation wages because they are on average wealthier; this would lead to a violation of the stochastic dominance assumption. On the other hand there is circumstantial evidence, presented in BGIM, that there is positive selection into the labor market, even when we do not condition on wealth.

An alternative and non-nested set of restrictions relates to the use of instruments. The idea is the same as the one presented earlier for the case of endogenous education. Denote the instrument by Z. Note that while the observed distribution of wages for workers $F(w|Z, ed, P=1)$ will depend on Z in general, the population distribution of wages $F(w|ed)$ will not, by assumption. Then BGIM show the bounds to be[29]

$$\max_z \{F(w|Z=z, ed, P=1)\Pr(P=1|Z=z, ed)\}$$
$$\leq F(w|ed) \leq$$
$$\min_z \{F(w|Z=z, ed, P=1)\Pr(P=1|Z=z, ed) + \Pr(P=0|Z=z, ed)\}$$
(1.46)

In the above expression we search over different values of z to identify the tightest bounds. These may not necessarily be where $\Pr(P=1|Z=z, ed)$ is maximized, unless it goes to one. In contrast to the case with stochastic dominance this restriction has some testable implications because its violation can lead to the bounds crossing, that is, to the lower bound being higher than the upper bound; this provides a means of testing for the validity of the exclusion restriction, although note that it may be possible for the restriction to be false and still the bounds may not cross. Hence the test may not have power one against the null that wages are independent of the instrument (see Section 2.6 for more on bounds for endogenous education).

---

[29] See Blundell, Gosling, Ichimura, and Meghir (2007), Equation 8.

Manski and Pepper (2000) originally presented the idea of monotone instrumental variables. In this case it is no longer assumed that wages are independent of the instrument but that the mean of wages is monotonic in the instrument. BGIM extend this idea to the entire distribution by assuming that

$$F(w|Z = z', ed) \leq F(w|Z = z, ed) \qquad \forall w, z, z' \text{ with } z < z'$$

This then implies the following bounds *conditional* on some value of the instrument $z1$

$$F(w|Z = z_1, ed) \geq F^l(w|Z = z_1, ed) \equiv$$
$$\max_{z > z_1} \{F(w|ed, Z = z, P = 1) \Pr(P = 1|Z = z, ed)\}$$
$$F(w|Z = z_1, ed) \leq F^u(w|Z = z_1, ed) \equiv$$
$$\max_{z > z_1} \{F(w|ed, Z = z, P = 1) \Pr(P = 1|Z = z, ed) + \Pr(P = 0|Z = z, ed)\}$$

By averaging over all possible values of z we can then obtain bounds to $F(w|ed)$ that are consistent with the monotonicity assumption. These take the form

$$E_z[F^l(w|z, ed)] \leq F(w|ed) \leq E_z[F^u(w|z, ed)]$$

where E_z denotes the expectation with respect to the distribution of z. As in the case of the exclusion restrictions, these bounds can cross if the monotonicity restriction is not valid. Moreover, it is possible to combine the monotonicity assumption with positive selection, such as stochastic dominance.

This procedure bounds the distribution of wages. This allows us to bound some quantiles as discussed above, but not means without support conditions on the distribution of wages. Bounding differences in the order statistics can give us a measure of the wage returns to education; this is done as in Equation 1.41. As an indication of the results that one can obtain, Table 1.1 presents results on bounds to the returns to college versus high school estimated by BGIM for men in the U.K. These use both the monotonicity restriction and the assumption that the median wage of workers is higher

Table 1.1 Bounds to the Returns to College Relative to High School By Cohort, Males, U.K

Birth Cohort	Age	Bounds(%)
1965	30	23–
1955	30	18–23
1945	35	17–20
1935★	45	16
1925★	55	44

★Point Estimate obtained
Source: BGIM, Figure 13.

of that which nonworkers would earn. The instrument used is the income that an individual would have if they did not work; this is determined by the benefit system in place at the time and the demographic structure of the household. Interestingly BGIM report that the instrument they use is rejected when used as an exclusion restriction based on the test for crossing bounds. This may reflect the fact that characteristics determining out-of-work income may be related to wages. The weaker monotonicity restriction allows these factors to be correlated with wages, so long as the distribution of wages is monotonically related to out-of work-income. Indeed, the monotonicity restriction is not rejected. The reported returns correspond to different ages, because older cohorts are not observed at younger ages. These bounds are quite tight and in some cases lead effectively to point estimates. This illustrates the point that identification may be obtained without having to assume that participation rates are 1 for a set of values of the instrument Z.

3.3 Nonparticipation and endogeneity

The discussion in this chapter has dealt with the implications of endogeneity of education when estimating returns and separately with the implications of nonparticipation. Both these issues are very important and ignoring them can cause bias. It is thus important to deal with both issues simultaneously, although this is not always done in the empirical literature.

From a parametric viewpoint the obvious way to proceed would be to extend the model presented earlier for educational choice to one that also allowed for labor force participation. Two examples of such models are Keane and Wolpin (1997) and Adda, Dustmann, Meghir, and Robin (2009) among others. In these models individuals decide on their educational attainment; subsequently during their labor market career individuals also decide (among other choices) whether to work or not. Within this context the models can be enriched further by allowing for endogenous accumulation of human capital in work (experience) as in Eckstein and Wolpin (1989) and the papers mentioned above among others, and by allowing for search frictions as in Adda et al. (2009) as well as earlier papers including, for example, Wolpin (1992). In these integrated models the issue of endogeneity of education and labor force participation is treated in a comprehensive, albeit fully parametric way. Nonparametric approaches, either to point estimation or to just bounds, have not been implemented in practice to our knowledge and neither has a comprehensive analysis of identification taken place. However, preliminary unpublished calculations by Hide Ichimura and Costas Meghir suggested that bounds would be too wide to be informative, even if we were to assume that only those expecting to gain from education actually attended. Finding suitable restrictions that would make such an approach informative would be an important advance.

To provide a brief illustration of how the model of Section 2.2 can be generalized to allow for nonparticipation we rewrite the value functions for the period of working life in period (age) t as[30]

$$V_t^{WJ}(X_{it}, \tau_i^J) = w_{it}^J + \beta Emax\left[V_{t+1}^{WJ}(X_{it+1}, \tau_i^J), V_{t+1}^{0J}(X_{it+1}, \tau_i^J)\right] \quad \text{value when working,} \quad J = S, H, C$$

$$V_t^{0J}(X_{it}, \tau_i^J) = b(X_{it}) + \xi_{it} + \beta Emax\left[V_{t+1}^{WJ}(X_{it}, \tau_i^J), V_{t+1}^{0J}(X_{it}, \tau_i^J)\right] \quad \text{value when not working,} \quad J = S, H, C$$

$$\log w_{it}^J = m^J(X_{it}) + \tau_i^J + \varepsilon_{it}^J \quad \text{wages for education level} \quad J = S, H, C$$

$$X_{it+1} = X_{it} + P_{it} \quad \text{experience}$$

(1.47)

In Equation 1.47, X_{it} represents experience, which here is defined as the number of periods working in the labor market. We have introduced a flow value for leisure, $b(X_{it}) + \xi_{it}$ which is stochastic and depends on experience, possibly reflecting the level of benefits dependent on past wages, or contributions to some unemployment insurance fund. Wages are assumed to depend on work experience and education J but on on age. The decision to work is

$$P_{it} = 1\left(V_{it}^{WJ} > V_{it}^{0J}\right)$$

Experience X_{it} is endogenous, because it is an accumulation of past work decisions, which depend on the unobserved heterogeneity component τ_i^J. The terminal value function could be specified as in Equation 1.10, where X now represents experience at the time when we stop having information on wages. To complete the model one needs to specify the stochastic properties of the shocks ε and ξ including their distribution. Because of the finite life nature of the model, the value functions depend on age t as well as on experience. Thus the model is solved backwards from the terminal point to the point where the education decisions are made. The work value functions (V^{WJ}, $J = S, H, C$) are evaluated at zero experience when solving for the education choice. In this model it is assumed that all education decisions are made at the beginning of the life cycle, but there is no reason why we cannot further generalize the model to include the possibility of returning to full-time education after a period of work. Finally, note that the return to education, as seen at the beginning of the life cycle, will be generalized now to include the effect of education on the length of work spells.

Estimation will be similar to that discussed in Section 2.3 with the important modification that we need to model the probability of working in each period and we need to account for the fact that wages are observed for workers only. Assuming for

---

[30] Recall that the education levels are S for statutory, H for high school, and C for college.

simplicity that ε and ξ are i.i.d. normal, the likelihood contribution for an observed career of T_i periods, conditional on education and on unobserved heterogeneity, becomes

$$L_i^J \equiv L(w_{is...}w_{iT_i}|J_i, \tau_i, X_i, \theta)$$
$$= \prod_{t=1}^{T_i} \left[g^J(w_{it}|X_i, \tau_i^{J_i}) \Pr(P_{it}=1|X_i, \tau_i^{J_i}, w_{it})\right]^{P_{it}=1} \quad (1.48)$$
$$\times \left[\int_{u} g^J(w|X_i, \tau_i^{J_i}) \Pr(P_{it}=0|X_i, \tau_i^{J_i}, w)dw\right]^{P_{it}=0}$$

The construction of the rest of the likelihood follows as in Section 2.3. In particular Equation 1.16 completes the likelihood function including the step relating to educational choice. The unobserved heterogeneity is integrated out and the likelihood for the whole sample is put together as in Equation 1.17. The joint distribution of $G(F, \tau)$ accounts for the endogeneity of education in wages and participation over the subsequent periods of the life cycle.

Finally, we have already discussed the difficulties relating to nonparametric identification of such models, even without endogenous participation. Obviously with participation being endogenous, matters do not become easier because we would now need to also identify the distribution of the shocks to leisure ξ as well as the distribution of the shocks to wages. In practice many of these aspects will be specified parametrically. However, identification is aided by the presence of exogenous variation at the time of education choice. For example, continuous (or even discrete) variables that affect the costs of education and vary exogenously across individuals can provide credible exogenous sources of identification. Attanasio, Meghir, and Santiago (2009) argue that the use of a randomized experiment with, say, educational incentives, as in the PROGRESA conditional cash transfer program in Mexico, can serve such a purpose.

4. EDUCATION POLICY AND THE ESTIMATED RETURNS TO EDUCATION

We have argued that it is hard to interpret results from estimating wage equations without a theoretical foundation. The need for models is reinforced when we consider scaling up human capital policies. Consider, for example, the impact of a school subsidy for children from low-income families.[31] Estimating the impact of such a policy on a

---

[31] An example of such a policy is the Education Maintenance allowance in the U.K., a subsidy to 16-year-olds for post-compulsory school attendance, evaluated by Dearden, Emmerson, Frayne, and Meghir (2009). This is a conditional cash transfer offered to pupils who complete statutory education at 16 and whose family's income is low, on condition they remain in full-time education At the time the policy was evaluated in 1999–2001, the amount received was at a maximum when the family earned less than $20,800 a year and thereafter declined linearly up until the family income reached $48,000, which was the eligibility threshold. Based on a pilot/control comparison, the estimated effect of the policy was to increase post-compulsory school participation by 6–7 percentage points for eligible children.

small scale is insufficient for understanding its longer term effects, even if we can estimate the wage returns to education for those induced into education due to the policy. Among other issues, we need to know the mechanism through which the subsidy acted: was the increase primarily due to a distortion of incentives or due to the alleviation of liquidity constraints? Second, we need to know what the general equilibrium effects are. The latter include: i. the effect of changes in the supply of skill on skill prices, which can feed back onto the decision to obtain the extra education; ii. the potential dilution of education quality as the resources are spread out more thinly; and iii. the peer effects of keeping more of the 16-year-olds in school, which could change the composition of the classrooms as well as the cultural norms. Allowing for all of this is a tall order and it will be hard, to say the least, to build a credible model that will be able to capture all these elements. One needs to make some realistic choices of which of these aspects are likely to be of first-order importance. We will briefly discuss dealing with the changes in human capital prices as a result of the increased supply of educated workers due to the subsidy. Important work in this field of general equilibrium models with heterogeneous agents has been carried out by Heckman, Lochner, and Taber (1998), Lee (2005), Lee and Wolpin (2006), and Gallipoli, Meghir, and Violante (2008).[32]

Start with the model in Section 2.2 and assume this has been estimated on data either collected as part of the experimental pilot or from observational survey data. This is the first building block. Since the problem has been set up as a life cycle one, to solve for equilibrium one needs to set it up as an overlapping generations model. However, since the environment is stationary the problem to be solved for each generation is identical. Thus for any given set of human capital prices we can solve the individual problem and then account for the number of individuals in each education group at each point in time.

The next step is to estimate the production function of the form presented in Section 2.1. Heckman, Lochner, and Taber (1998), for example, estimate a production function with two human capital inputs: less than college and college, while Gallipoli et al (2008) allow for three human capital inputs, as in the model of Sections 2.1 and 2.2. Both allow for one factor of capital. The estimated production function and the assumption of competitive labor markets allow us to derive relative human capital prices for each group as as function of employed human capital. Both authors estimate substitution elasticities for the human capital inputs that imply quite a lot of sensitivity of relative prices to changes in supplies.[33]

---

[32] Gallipoli et al (2008) also considers other important issues, such as the role of parental transfers liquidity constraints.
[33] This may be controversial because in an open economy with more goods than factors, trade can lead to factor price equalization. If this was really the case then policies that changed the supply of human capital would not affect human capital prices and would not be subject to such general equilibrium effects. Nevertheless, factor price equalization is either a very slow process or is prevented by other mechanisms.

Simple policy simulation would then compare the baseline outcomes (essentially the data) to the results from a simulated new steady state arising as a result of implementing a new policy such as an educational subsidy. The simulation based on the model described here would allow for the effect of changes in individual incentives; for the impact of funding the subsidy by raising taxation through, say, income taxes, which would compress the effects of education on wages; and for the effect of changes in the return to education induced by a new equilibrium in the labor market as supplies change.

The point is that all these effects can be potentially important and the results can be sensitive to the assumed environment and the specification of the model. Heckman, Lochner, and Taber (1998) show that the GE effects can almost neutralize the effects of a policy. Lee (2005) has a different model specification where the feedback effects from GE are small. This shows that the results can be sensitive to important modeling choices and that we do need to know all the components of the model to acquire a good understanding of what the policy will achieve. Just estimating the wage returns to education, even when we can do so based on a partial model, is useful but is only part of the story as far as design of policy is concerned.

5. ESTIMATION OF SCHOOL INPUT EFFECTS

Variation in the return to observed schooling comes from many sources, one of the most important of which is the quality of education. A growing body of research investigates the effects of various educational inputs, and the proliferation of administrative and survey data facilitates such analyses. Similar to research on school attainment, endogenous choices and unobserved heterogeneity complicate efforts to identify variable effects. Empirical models must explicitly or implicitly account for the interrelated choices of families, teachers, administrators, and policy makers to avoid contamination from confounding factors.

In this section we discuss selected papers covering four topics that have generated substantial interest in education research in order to highlight key empirical and methodological issues including the treatment of the multiple decisions that determine the allocation of educational inputs. These areas are class size effects, teacher quality, housing market capitalization of school quality, and the effects of choice and accountability. The selected papers use a variety of approaches and types of data, and we emphasize implications of the specification choices. Methods discussed include the use of observed characteristics as controls, various types of IV techniques including regression discontinuity and lottery generated quasirandom assignment, difference-in-differences and large-scale fixed effects specifications, hierarchical linear modeling (HLM), and structural discreet choice models. As in the previous section, we highlight the explicit and implicit assumptions regarding the underlying choice framework as they relate to both the identification and interpretation of variable effects. Prior to considering these four topics we describe a model of housing choice that highlights many of the determinants of family location decisions and then discuss some general issues related to learning and the accumulation of human capital. The latter discussion focuses on empirically relevant issues pertinent to much education research.

5.1 Housing choice[34]

Consider the location equilibrium of a household that resides at location d. Ignoring mobility costs, the household will be in equilibrium at location d if:

$$d^* = argmax_d E \int_H \left[U(X_\tau^d, SQ_\tau^d, O_\tau^d | w^d, f, \kappa_d, p_d) d\tau \right] \text{ for } d \in \{d\}$$

where expected utility is accumulated over the relevant planning horizon, H, and the location, d^*, is chosen once and for all (for simplicity) compared to all d.[35] Each location is associated with a wage w_d, preferences for such a location k_d, prices p_d (which include house prices), a set of local amenities O and school quality SQ. Utility may depend on individual abilities f, that drive wages. They also depend on a vector of household consumption, on labor supply and on demographics, all of which have all been maximized given location.[36] Hence $U(.)$ represents indirect utility given location. Largely static variants of this lie behind general theories of urban location decisions, the quality of local public services, and the demand for local government services (cf. Straszheim (1987); Tiebout (1956); Wildasin (1987)).

In the simplest models, a household optimizes across all of the feasible locations within its choice set given complete information for all periods. Yet life cycle changes, unexpected shocks, or incorrect predictions move families out of equilibrium and often lead to relocation. For example, households may decide to relocate because of changes in expected lifetime income, family structure (additions of children, divorce or remarriage), perceptions of the quality of local public services including schools, the distribution of employment opportunities, or other factors. Even in the absence of prediction error, rising income may reduce borrowing constraints and expand opportunities. Note further that moving costs introduce inertia into the decisions, so that at any point in time a household might drift away from its current utility maximizing location and might not move until a time when the utility loss from d^* compared to the next best alternative becomes large.

A much more complete model of location choice is developed by Kennan and Walker (2009) and shows the complexity of such decision making. Developing this in a general equilibrium framework and understanding the interaction between amenities, labor market opportunities, and preferences is at the heart of understanding how individuals end up choosing school quality as a function of preferences and

---

[34] This section draws from Hanushek, Kain, and Rivkin (2004).
[35] See Kennan and Walker (2009).
[36] We are being vague about household formation so as not to complicate the notation.

abilities as well as prices. This simple model highlights some of the main impediments to the estimation of school and teacher effects. First, it is quite difficult to account for all the factors that lead families to make different location and school choices. Second, even with panel data to account for student or family fixed effects, changes sizeable enough to induce geographic moves are likely also to have direct effects on outcomes. This raises immediate questions about the validity of exogeneity restrictions in panel data analyses.

5.2 Learning dynamics

The cumulative nature of knowledge acquisition introduces an additional complication into the estimation of school and teacher effects, and we now consider specification issues directly related to the modeling of the dynamics of knowledge retention in a data generating process driven by the multiple dimensions of choices that determine the distribution of teacher and school characteristics. In order to highlight the specification issues related to assumptions regarding the rate of knowledge depreciation we assume no heterogeneity in school input effects. Equation 1.49 models the outcome of student i in year t as a function of a school input S, a vector of control variables X, a time varying student effect α_{it} that captures unobserved student heterogeneity other than differences resulting from S and X, and an error term e that represents all other determinants of A including measurement error in the outcome variable and unobserved school, community, and family influences.

$$A_{it} = \alpha_{it} + \beta X_{it} + \delta S_{it} + e_{it} \tag{1.49}$$

The variables X and S have t subscripts, because many studies make use of panel data that contain multiple measures of family and school variables. In other cases including research on earnings, earnings in year t are regressed on family and school characteristics measured during childhood.

If S is orthogonal to α and e, estimation of Equation 1.49 produces consistent estimates of δ. In reality, OLS estimation of Equation 1.49 is unlikely to produce consistent estimates given limited information available and the complex processes that determine the distribution of school and teacher characteristics. These include 1) family location and schooling decisions that are part of the previously discussed process of life-cycle optimization of utility; 2) utility maximizing choices of schools and districts by teachers and other school personnel; 3) purposeful matching of students and teachers in classrooms; and 4) the political and judicial processes that determine school finances and a range of laws that affect the allocation of resources and students among classrooms, schools, and districts.

Although confounding factors and consequent omitted variables bias tend to be the primary issue considered in the discussion of the merits of most empirical approaches, other measurement and specification errors also threaten estimation of Equation 1.49.

As we discuss below, complications introduced by test-measurement error have received considerable attention in studies of teacher and school effects and related policies including merit pay and NCLB accountability.[37]

Another frequently discussed specification issue is the appropriate treatment of the history of family and school inputs given life cycle utility optimization. As Cunha, Heckman, and Schennach (2010), Cunha and Heckman (2008), and Todd and Wolpin (2003) emphasize, the development of cognitive and noncognitive skills is a cumulative and complex process and the failure to account for the history of inputs can lead to biased estimates of the effects of variables of interest. Limited availability of historical data on parental, school, and community inputs and the endogeneity of parental inputs impede efforts to estimate the full life-cycle model, leading to the use of lagged achievement measures and student fixed effects to account for the history of parent, community, and school input effects. Such methods fail to capture the nuances of skill development processes involving endogenous parental behavior in which there appear to be sensitive periods during childhood for parental investments in both types of skills (Cunha and Heckman, 2008).

Nonetheless, the value-added and fixed effect methods may account for the aggregate effects of the history of inputs, and it is informative to examine the implications of imposing various assumptions on the rate of knowledge depreciation. Therefore we assume no confounding family or other factors including endogenous responses to realized school quality, and describe the implications of five commonly used approaches using a simple model of achievement for student i in grade G in which a constant proportion $(1-\theta)$ of knowledge is lost each year ($0 \leq \theta \leq 1$), the effect and variance of SC (a particular school characteristic) do not differ across grades, the covariance of SC across grades is constant, and the error is orthogonal to SC in all periods.

$$A_{iG} = \beta \sum_{g=0}^{G} \theta^{G-g} SC_g + error \qquad (1.50)$$

First consider an OLS regression of achievement in grade G on SC with no control for prior achievement and thus likely to be subject to the influences of confounding factors. In this case the error includes effects of all past values of the school characteristic:

$$A_{iG} = SC_G \beta_{level} + \beta \sum_{g=0}^{G-1} \theta^{G-g} SC_g + error \qquad (1.51)$$

---

[37] The arbitrary normalization of test scores also complicates estimation, as monotonic transformations may lead to very different findings. Cunha and Heckman (2008) discuss this issue.

and[38]

$$E(\hat{\beta}_{level}) = \beta + \beta\rho\left(\sum_{g=0}^{G-1}\theta^{G-g}\right)\frac{1}{var(SC)} \quad (1.52)$$

where ρ is the covariance of the school characteristic in grades i and j that is assumed not to vary by number of years or grades apart.

In general, the magnitude of any bias depends on both θ and ρ. Not surprisingly, bias decreases along with the rate of decay and approaches zero as θ approaches zero. In the special case of random assignment experiments, IV, or other methods that isolate the component of the school characteristic in grade G that is uncorrelated with the school characteristic in other grades, this specification produces unbiased estimates of β regardless of θ.

Any correlation between the current and past values of the school characteristic complicates interpretation of the estimate and limits the generalizability of the findings. The estimate would reflect some weighted average of current and depreciated past effects, where the weighting depends upon the often unknown serial correlation in the school characteristic. Given the substantial demographic differences in school mobility rates by race, ethnicity, and family income, estimates would tend to be higher for students in stable schools even if the true effects were either similar for all students or higher for those in more turbulent environments.[39]

More compelling approaches use multiple years of test score results to account for student heterogeneity. One such approach is the student fixed effects model without a control for lagged achievement. Taking first differences of Equation 1.49 (subtracting A_G-1 from A_G) to remove any student fixed error component gives:

$$A_{iG} - A_{iG-1} = (SC_G - SC_{G-1})\beta_{f.e.} + \beta\left[\theta SC_{G-1} + \sum_{g=0}^{G-2}\theta^{G-g} - \theta^{G-(g+1)}SC_g\right] + error$$
$$(1.53)$$

In this case[40]

$$E(\hat{\beta}_{f.e.}) = \beta - \beta\theta/2 \quad (1.54)$$

In contrast to the simple levels model, the fixed effect specification produces an estimate of the school characteristic effect that is biased toward zero as long as the rate of decay (1-θ) does not equal one. Notice that the magnitude of the bias does not depend upon the value of correlation of the school characteristic across grades, ρ.

---

[38] Given the assumption that θ is a constant, the expected value can be calculated using the omitted variables bias formula treating the terms in the summation as a single variable.

[39] Hanushek, Kain, and Rivkin (2004) describe mobility differences in Texas elementary schools.

[40] Here the term in brackets is treated as the single omitted variable. Notice that the assumption of a constant covariance regardless of the number of grades between grades i and j mean that the covariance between $(SC_G - SC_{G-1})$ and SC_g equals zero for all values of g less than G-1.

A second approach uses prior year test score to account for student heterogeneity by subtracting it from current year score and using the test score gain as the dependent variable. This model is a special case of the value added model of test score in grade g regressed on test score in grade g-1 and the school characteristic in which θ is assumed to equal 1. This model is often preferred to the unrestricted value added model, because the inclusion of an imprecisely measured lagged endogenous variable as a regressor can introduce other types of specification error including errors in variables and endogeneity bias.[41] Here achievement in grade g minus achievement in grade g-1 is regressed on the school characteristic in grade G.

$$A_{iG} - A_{iG-1} = SC_G \beta_{gain} + \beta \sum_{g=0}^{G} (\theta^g - \theta^{g-1}) SC_{G-g} + error \quad (1.55)$$

and[42]

$$E(\hat{\beta}_{gain}) = \beta - \beta \frac{(1-\theta^G)\rho}{var(SC)} \quad (1.56)$$

The magnitude of any bias depends on both θ and ρ. In the case of θ, the problem is that the violation of the assumption of no knowledge depreciation means that the higher the lagged score the higher is the over-estimate of expected test score in the current year. Not surprisingly given the structure of the model, bias decreases as the true value of θ increases and disappears if there is no loss of knowledge from year to year, that is, when $\theta=1$. As is the case with the levels model, the use of a value added framework, random assignment experiments, IV, or other methods that isolate the component of the school characteristic in grade G that is uncorrelated with the value of the characteristic in other grades produces unbiased estimates of β regardless of the true value of θ; if ρ equals zero the error introduced by the mis-specification is orthogonal to the school characteristic and does not introduce bias.

As is the case with the model with lagged achievement, the inclusion of a student fixed effect does not eliminate the specification error to the gains model. Taking first differences of Equation 1.55 (subtracting $A_{G-2} - A_{G-1}$ from $A_G - A_{G-1}$) to remove any student fixed effect in gains gives the fixed effect in gains model.

$$(A_{iG} - A_{iG-1}) - (A_{iG-1} - A_{iG-2}) =$$
$$(SC_G - SC_{G-1})\beta_{f.e.gain} + \beta\left[(\theta-1)SC_{G-1} + \sum_{g=2}^{G}(\theta^g - 2\theta^{g-1} + \theta^{g-2})SC_{G-g}\right] + error$$
$$(1.57)$$

---

[41] Numerous studies use test score gain as the dependent variable including Rivkin, Hanushek, and Kain (2005) and Harris and Sass (2009); both papers discuss the model in some detail.

[42] Given the assumption that cov(SC_i, SC_j) is constant regardless of the number of grades apart, all terms cancel except for one grade G − 1 term and one grade 0 term.

and[43]

$$E(\hat{\beta}_{f.e.gain}) = \beta + \beta(1-\theta)/2 \qquad (1.58)$$

Similar to the case for levels, bias in the fixed effect in gains specification is of the opposite sign as any bias in the gains model without student fixed effects, and the magnitude of the bias does not depend upon the value of ρ. Notice that the bias is the same magnitude but the opposite sign for the two fixed effects models in cases where $\theta = 0.5$.

In summary, this simple education production function model illustrates that the violation of a strong assumption regarding the rate of knowledge depreciation introduces bias in fixed effects models regardless of the magnitude of ρ and in models without fixed effects as long as the magnitude of ρ does not equal zero. This provides some rationale for the use of models including those with student fixed effects in which the value of θ is not constrained to equal zero or one.[44]

Of course the dynamics of noncognitive and cognitive skill formation necessitate the use of richer empirical models to control for potentially confounding family and community influences. Cunha and Heckman (2008) argue in favor of the use of a latent variable framework to account for the endogeneity of parental inputs and multiplicity of potential proxies for family background. Although their interest in the pattern of family effects differs from our focus on school inputs, the issues of endogenous parental behavior and student heterogeneity along multiple dimensions have direct relevance to the identification of school input effects given the possibility of parental responses to realized teacher quality, class size, and other school inputs and potential nonrandom sorting of students into schools and classrooms on the basis of cognitive and noncognitive skills.

Another important issue is the scale of the test scores. This is arbitrary and any monotonic transformation provides the same information. However, this raises two related issues: first there is no reason to expect that linearity and additivity of fixed effects or other unobservables, such as the one postulated in Equations (1.49, 1.50, 1.51 or 1.55) has to be valid for the particular scale in use. Second, the comparison of changes in test scores is not invariant to monotonic transformations: for example, the statement that the change in test scores was larger for some group than for another is not invariant to monotonic transformations of the scores. One way around this problem is to find a natural cardinalization or anchoring of the test scores.[45] This in itself raises interesting questions, because test scores are an aggregation of answers to many different questions and also provide the benchmark for the teacher to evaluate her of success. As a result, the way test scores are arrived at may affect teacher incentives.

---

[43] Given the assumption that cov(SC_i, SC_j) is constant regardless of the number of grades apart, all terms cancel except for one grade G − 1 term and one grade 0 term.

[44] Nerlove (1971), Nickell (1981), Arellano and Bond (1991), and Hsiao (2003) discuss estimation of fixed effects models with a lagged dependent variable and biases that can arise from within groups estimation.

[45] See Cunha, Heckman and Schennach (2010).

Suppose for example that test scores were calculated in order to maximize their predictive power with respect to future wages, academic attainment, or other outcome. Then the objective for teachers could be defined as aligned with such longer term outcomes, and the scores could be anchored in that metric. This would not eliminate complications introduced by nonlinearities, but at least it would fix the metric and define clearly the meaning of the linearity assumption. The difficulty is of course that we often do not have a clearly measured link between the test scores at hand and an outcome variable let alone agreement on what that outcome variable should be.

5.3 Estimation of class size effects

Similar to the case of the return to schooling, the benefits of smaller classes may vary along several dimensions including initial class size, student characteristics, the school environment, and the nature of the comparison. Yet little of the empirical work on class size is grounded in a conceptual model of class size effects that points toward particular types of heterogeneity. Rather, analyses typically provide average effects or effects that differ by demographic group or grade. If there is substantial heterogeneity in the benefits of smaller classes, samples drawn from different populations would be expected to produce different estimates of average effects for all students or even students in a particular demographic group. Estimates would also be expected to differ on the basis of whether or not the differences in class size used to identify a coefficient are related to differences in unobserved teacher quality resulting from either teacher preferences for smaller classes or any expansion in the number of teaching positions necessary to reduce class size.

We begin this section by outlining a model of the relationship between learning and class size and then discuss six studies of class size effects that use a range of methods and types of data. The model allows for heterogeneity by student ability and the level of disruptive behavior in a classroom and can incorporate general equilibrium effects resulting from changes in teacher quality. Recent research finds evidence of heterogeneous class size effects along the achievement distribution, and Lazear (2001) highlights differences in the level of disruption as a likely explanation for why lower income students appear to realize larger benefits from smaller classes.[46]

5.3.1 Model[47]

Equation (1.59) models learning for student i in classroom c in school j as a function of the amount of classroom time available for learning and the value of that time in terms of the quality of the teaching and relevance of the material, plus all other student, community, and school factors:

---

[46] Ding and Lehrer (2005), Konstantopoulos (2008), and McKee, Rivkin and Sims (2010) all find that the benefits of smaller classes appear to increase with achievement.
[47] The discussion is drawn from McKee, Rivkin and Sims (2010).

$$learning_{icj} = \rho(d)_{cj}^{n} q(n,a)_{icj} + X_{icj} \qquad (1.59)$$

where ρ is the proportion of time a student is not disrupting the class; d is the classroom average propensity to disrupt the class; q is the value of a unit of instructional time; n is class size; a is an index of ability[48] and X is a vector of other student, community and school factors.

The term $\rho(d)_{cj}^{n}$ is drawn from Lazear (2001) and represents the share of class time not lost to disruption by any of the n students in the room, while the term $q(n,a)_{icj}$ models the value of a unit of instructional time as a function of both class size and academic preparation. Variation in classroom behavior, d, and academic preparation, a, provide two dimensions of potential heterogeneity in the benefit of smaller classes. Importantly, all students in a classroom experience the same amount of instructional time, but the value of instructional time may vary by ability due to targeting of the curriculum, the distribution of teacher effort, and student heterogeneity.

In order to illustrate the ways in which disruption and academic preparation may affect the benefits from class size reduction, we take the derivative of Equation 1.1 with respect to n and then again with respect to d (Equation (1.60)) and a (Equation (1.61) below):

$$\frac{\partial^2 learning}{\partial n \partial d} = \left\{ [\rho(d)]^{n-1} \frac{\partial \rho(d)}{\partial d} \right\} \left\{ (n \ln(\rho(d)) + 1) q(n,a) + n \frac{\partial q(n,a)}{\partial n} \right\} \qquad (1.60)$$

Equation (1.60) illustrates the relationship between the propensity to disrupt class and the benefit of class size reduction.[49] The product of the two relationships in curly brackets determines the sign of the cross-partial derivative of learning with respect to n and d. The first is negative, as the derivative of ρ with respect to d is assumed to be negative (a higher average propensity to disrupt reduces the share of time available for learning), while the second is ambiguous and depends on the magnitudes of the various terms; $\frac{n \partial q(n,a)}{\partial n}$ is assumed to be negative: the quality of instructional time declines as class size increases for a number of reasons including more difficulty differentiating the curriculum to account for variation in academic preparation. $q(n,a)$ is positive and the product of $ln(\rho)$ and n lies between 0 and -1, so $n ln(\rho) + 1$ is also positive.[50]

Thus the relationship between the benefits of class size reduction and the degree of disruption (d) thus depends upon the magnitudes of two counteracting effects. First, as Lazear (2001) points out, at lower values of ρ reduced class size has a larger effect on

---

[48] Ability represents a one-dimensional index of academic skill and is not meant to refer to innate differences.
[49] The derivative of learning with respect to class size (n) equals $[\rho(d)]^{n} ln(\rho(d)) q(n,a) + [\rho(d)]^{n} \frac{\partial q(n,a)}{\partial n}$. Taking the derivative of this relationship with respect to d produces Equation (1.60) and with respect to a produces Equation (1.61).
[50] At a value of ρ below 0.95, nln(ρ) + 1 becomes negative, but at such a low value of ρ the share of class time available for instruction is well below 50%.

the share of time available for learning and thus a larger effect on achievement. Second, at lower values of ρ any improvement in the quality of instruction time due to smaller classes has a lower overall impact, because classrooms with lower values of ρ have less time for learning.

Equation (1.61) illustrates the relationship between initial achievement and the benefit of class size reduction:

$$\frac{\partial^2 learning}{\partial n \partial a} = [\rho(d)]^n \left\{ ln(\rho(d)) + \frac{\frac{\partial^2 q(n,a)}{\partial n \partial a}}{\frac{q(n,a)}{\partial a}} \right\} \quad (1.61)$$

As is the case with disruption, the relationship between the benefit of class size reduction and initial achievement cannot be signed *a priori* in this framework. Here the sum of the two relationships in curly brackets determines the sign of the cross-partial derivative of learning with respect to n and a. The first term, roughly the average disruption of a single student, is negative, while the ratio can be positive or negative depending upon the relationship between achievement and the quality of instruction and the relationship between achievement and the change in the quality of instruction as class size falls.

In sum, the pattern of heterogeneous effects along both dimensions cannot be predicted *a priori*. Moreover, differences in district policies may produce variation across districts in the distribution of treatment effects across each of these dimensions. Finally, any accompanying changes in teacher quality may affect both the quality of instruction and level of disruption per student (changes in teacher skill at managing the classroom), and any such affects may vary by school characteristics.

5.3.2 Discussion of empirical analyses

Table 1.2 lists the six studies that we consider and describes their methods, data, and findings. The studies use a range of empirical methods to account for potential confounding factors including controls for observables, regression discontinuity, and fixed effects, and various types of administrative, survey, and experimental data. Importantly, these different approaches also alter the interpretation of the parameter estimates.

Pong and Pallas (2001) use TIMSS data on the mathematics achievement of 13-year-olds in nine countries to estimate the effects of class size on achievement and the degree to which curriculum and classroom instruction mediate those effects. In order to explicitly account for the multi-level structure of the data that has test score and family background measured at the individual level and class size and other school characteristics measured at the school level, the paper uses hierarchical linear modeling (HLM) estimation methods.[51] The inclusion of a random school effect in the empirical model accounts for the fact that class size is a school level variable.

---

[51] See Raudenbush and Bryk (2002) for a comprehensive description of HLM including two- and three-level random effects models.

Table 1.2 Selected Research on Class Size Effects

	Method	Interpretation	Data	Findings
Dearden, Ferri, and Meghir (2002)	Matching	Ceteris paribus effect plus effect of differences in supply of teacher quality related to class size	U.K. National Child Development Study	Smaller classes increase future wages of women but not men
Pong and Pallas (2001)	Hierarchical linear modelling	Ceteris paribus effect plus effect of differences in supply of teacher quality related to class size	TIMMS	Little evidence of class size effect on achievement
Card and Krueger (1992)	State and cohort fixed effects	Ceteris paribus effect plus any change in state average teacher quality related to changes over time in average class size	U.S. Census PUMS	Smaller classes increase return to education in labor market
Rivkin, Hanushek, and Kain (2005)	Student, school by grade, and school by year fixed effects	Ceteris paribus effect	Texas public school administrative data	Smaller classes increase achievement in 4th and 5th grade; effects slightly larger for low income students
Angrist and Lavy (1999)	Regression discontinuity	Ceteris paribus effect	Israeli public school administrative data	Smaller classes increase achievement in 5th grade
Krueger (1999)	Random assignment experiment	Ceteris paribus effect	Tennessee STAR experimental data	smaller classes increase achievement in early grades; larger effect for lower income students

The results reveal little evidence of a significant negative relationship between class size and achievement in any of the countries; in fact the class size coefficients are as likely to be positive as negative. Note that the study does not account for student heterogeneity explicitly with either student fixed effects or measures of prior achievement, and it includes only a handful of family characteristics as controls. The fact that the inclusion of a small number of other school level variables tends to reduce the magnitude of the positive coefficients provides evidence that confounding variables introduce upward bias. Moreover, the cross-sectional estimator used in this analysis in combination with the local nature of teacher labor markets means that class size effects capture any related differences in teacher quality: teacher quality may be lower in schools with smaller classes because of the need to hire additional teachers, or teacher quality may be higher in schools with smaller classes because higher wealth communities can afford both smaller classes and higher teacher salaries.

Although the random effects provide a standard error correction to the clustering of students in schools, the validity of random effects models in general and HLM models as a special case rests in the assumption of orthogonality between the included variables and random effects. Given the limited number of covariates and multiple dimensions of choices that generate the distribution of class size, this assumption is likely to be violated in this case. Fixed effects provides an alternative to random effects that does not require the orthogonality assumption, but fixed effects do not provide a plausible approach in this case because of the absence of class size variation within schools and the assumption of linearity.[52]

Dearden, Ferri, and Meghir (2002) use rich longitudinal data that follow all subjects living in Great Britain who were born during the week of March 3–9, 1958 to estimate the effects of the pupil-teacher ratio at age 11 and at age 16 on educational attainment and wages for men and women. Equation (1.62) models log wage as a function of a time varying student effect α that captures unobserved differences among students, a vector X of family and community characteristics, the primary and secondary school pupil teacher ratios PPT and SPT, other included components of school and peer group quality in primary and secondary school PS and SS, and a random error.

$$w_{iy} = \alpha_{iy} + \beta X_{iy} + \delta_p PPT_i + \delta_s SPT_i + \lambda_p PS_i + \lambda_s SS_i + e_{iy} \qquad (1.62)$$

If the two pupil teacher ratio variables were uncorrelated with e and α, OLS would yield unbiased estimates of δ_p and δ_s. But as noted above, the endogeneity of family choice of school and the dependence of school finance on a number of factors including family demographics in combination with existing evidence on peer, teacher, and

---

[52] Blundell and Windmeijer (1997) show that the random and fixed effect multilevel estimators are equivalent when group sizes (in this case number of students per school) are large. However, the number of students in classrooms and schools is not large enough to eliminate the bias introduced by correlation between the random effects and included variables.

school effects on achievement strongly suggest that typically available variables contained in X and S will not account adequately for potentially confounding factors, thereby introducing bias into OLS estimates of δ_p and δ_s based on cross-sectional data.

However, the array of test results available in the longitudinal data along with extensive information on schools and communities permits the inclusion of both earlier test scores as controls for unobserved heterogeneity α and a set of school and community variables to account for potentially confounding factors captured by the error.[53] In addition, the use of the pupil-teacher ratio at the school level rather than the size of individual classes circumvents potential bias introduced by the purposeful allocation of students into classes. Although a portion of the between-school variation in the pupil-teacher ratio results from differences in the numbers of special education teachers and additional financing for disadvantaged populations, the included test scores and school variables should account for much of the variation in school circumstances.

It is not possible to prove that even an extensive set of controls fully accounts for all confounding factors. Altonji, Elder, and Taber (2005) discuss selection on observables and unobservables and develop an informal method for assessing the probability that selection on unobservables introduces substantial bias. In this case the estimates show little sensitivity to changes in the specifications, suggesting that selection on unobservables is unlikely to introduce substantial bias.

Error in the measurement of the pupil-teacher ratio provides an additional potential source of bias in many studies such as this where there is only a single snapshot of school characteristics to represent the school environment for a number of years. The use of a class size in a particular grade likely introduces attenuation bias, though the similar limitations in the measurement of controls also introduce bias that may amplify or offset the bias resulting from the measurement of class size. Given the relatively small size of the sample and noisiness of the wage measure, it may be difficult to identify small but educationally and economically meaningful effects such as the effects of the pupil-teacher ratio on educational attainment which are insignificant statistically but large enough to be meaningful for education policy.

In terms of interpretation, the use of pupil-teacher ratio does introduce some uncertainty, as reduction achieved through the addition of special education or intervention teachers is likely to produce a different effect on average achievement and have different implications for the educational attainment and earnings distributions than a reduction brought about by the hiring of additional classroom teachers. Therefore the estimates capture differences of the type experienced by students in the March, 1958 cohort. Moreover, if a lower pupil-teacher ratio increased the supply of teacher quality to a school, the estimated benefit of smaller classes will incorporate class size induced differences in teacher quality given the absence of information on teachers.

---

[53] This approach is a form of matching on observable characteristics.

Concerns about omitted variables bias even in rich specifications have contributed to the expanded use of instrumental variable and fixed effect methods to account for unobserved influences. Card and Krueger (1992) provide a prominent example of an analysis with little or no information on family background that uses fixed effects for both the state of birth and state of residence to account for unobserved influences on earnings that could contaminate estimates of the pupil-teacher effect on the return to schooling. The two-step procedure begins by estimating separate returns to education for each cohort-state combination from a regression of log (wage) on state of birth dummy variables, state of residence dummy variables, education by region interactions, and separate education variables for each cohort-state of birth combination. Then the coefficients on the separate education terms are regressed on the cohort-state average pupil-teacher ratio, the cohort-state average teacher salary, and the cohort-state average school year length. Note that the use of cohort average school characteristics mitigates the measurement error introduced by a single snapshot, though any heterogeneity in class size effects by grade raises questions about the interpretation of coefficients on characteristics that aggregate information across elementary and secondary grades.

The fixed effects model uses interstate movers and within state variation over time in school inputs to identify variable effects. Three key assumptions underlying the analysis are 1) school quality affects earnings via the return to education only; 2) selective migration does not contaminate the estimates; and 3) unobserved school or community factors are not related to the pupil-teacher ratio. Betts (1995) and Heckman, Layne-Farrar, and Todd (1996) raise questions about the first assumption, and Heckman, Layne-Farrar, and Todd (1996) document evidence of selective migration.[54] In terms of Equation (1.62), selective migration introduces bias by leading to a correlation between unobserved heterogeneity (represented by α in Equation (1.62)) and the school quality measures thereby violating the exogeneity condition required for identification.

Finally, Hanushek, Rivkin, and Taylor (1996) show that the use of information aggregated to the state level can affect the magnitude of any omitted variables bias. Aggregation may dampen or exacerbate any specification error depending upon the structure of the covariance between the omitted variable, the school variable of interest, and the outcome. For example, if the omitted factors were to vary only at the level of aggregation (such as would be the case if these are state policy factors) and the factors were positively related to school quality and negatively related to class size, aggregation would tend to amplify the omitted variables bias. Note that the oft-asserted concern that aggregate measures of school inputs introduce measurement error because of the difference between actual school values and the state average is incorrect regardless of

---

[54] Betts (1995) investigates the effect of school resources using the NLSY and fails to find a significant relationship between wages and the pupil-teacher ratio for various parameterization of the pupil-teacher ratio effect.

whether outcome data are aggregated to the level of aggregation of the school input measures. Rather, aggregation alters the variation used to identify the estimates and does not introduce bias if the relationship between the outcome and input are linear and there are no other specification errors.[55]

This paper also uses the pupil-teacher ratio, and therefore the estimates provide information on differences produced by similar underlying variation in instructional staff. However, changes in the number and potentially the quality of teachers likely accompany state average changes in the pupil-teacher ratio, conditional on salary. Therefore these estimates capture both the direct benefit of a lower pupil-teacher ratio and any offsetting effects resulting from the expansion of the teaching force, the latter of which almost certainly depends upon labor market factors specific to the place and time period.

In contrast to the earnings papers that relate school inputs in childhood to earnings as an adult, the three achievement analyses investigate the effects of class size on end-of-year achievement. In order to account for unobserved school and neighborhood factors and student differences, Rivkin, Hanushek, and Kain (2005) model test score gain as a function of class size, teacher experience and education, family characteristics, and full sets of student, school by year, and in some cases school by grade fixed effects. Equations (1.63) and (1.64) divide this model in two in order to highlight the school fixed effects:

$$A_{iGst} - A_{iG-1,s',t-1} = SC_{Gst}\beta_{gain} + \alpha_i + e_{iGst} \tag{1.63}$$

$$e_{iGst} = \omega_s + \xi_G + \psi_t + \rho_{Gt} + \pi_{sG} + \varphi_{st} + \tau_{sGt} + \varepsilon_{iGst} \tag{1.64}$$

where SC is a vector of the school characteristics and α is a student fixed effect. Equation (1.64) decomposes the error term into a number of school, grade, and year components and a random error. The first three terms are fixed school (ω), grade (ξ), and year (ψ) effects, the next three terms (ρ, π, φ) are second-level interactions among these three components, the seventh term (τ) is the third-level interaction, and the final term (ε) is a random error.

The school fixed effect (ω) captures time invariant differences in neighborhoods and schools, many of which are likely related to both achievement and class size. These include school facilities, public services, community type, and working conditions that influence teacher supply. The grade, year, and year-by-grade fixed effects (ξ, ψ, ρ) account for statewide trends in class size and achievement by grade and year and other factors including changes in test difficulty.

Because school quality may vary over time and by grade for each school, Equation (1.64) also includes interactions between school and both grade and year.

---

[55] Theil (1954) examines aggregation in a linear framework.

The school-by-grade component (π) captures any systematic differences across grades in a school that are common to all years, and the school-by-year (φ) term accounts for systematic year-to-year differences that are common to all grades in a school. The school-by-grade fixed effects account for school or district specific influences on the quality of instruction that might vary by grade, such as curriculum or information technology.

The school-by-year fixed effects remove in a very general way not only school-specific performance trends but also idiosyncratic variation over time in school administration and in neighborhood and local economic conditions that likely affect mobility patterns including such things as the introduction of school policies or local economic or social shocks. For example, an economic shock that reduces neighborhood employment and income is absorbed and will not bias the estimates; nor will a shock to local school finances or the quality of the local school board, because each of these would affect all grades in a school.

The seventh term, τ, is the full three-way interaction between school, grade, and year; it cannot be included in the estimation, because there would be no class size variation remaining. Ignoring this three-way interaction means that grade specific variation over time in school average teacher quality or other achievement determinants could potentially bias the estimates if also correlated with class size. Yet the nontrivial costs of switching schools, the presence of multiple children in a family, and the fact that teacher assignments and other relevant aspects of school decisions are typically not known until immediately prior to the beginning of school year reduce the likelihood that changes over time in school and teacher quality for specific grades are systematically linked with yearly changes in class size through parental behavioral responses.

In this framework, the remaining variation in class size comes from differences across classrooms at a point in time and differences in the pattern of grade average class sizes experienced by adjacent cohorts in a school that come from changes in policy regarding the allocation of resources among grades, students movement among schools, and natural demographic variations in cohort composition. In terms of differences across classrooms, the potential for nonrandom allocation of students such as the placement of more difficult-to-educate students in smaller classes raises concerns about the validity of such variation, and the use of grade average class size in this study avoids the introduction of selection bias from this channel. In terms of differences in the pattern of grade average class size among adjacent cohorts, an identifying assumption in a number of studies that make use of cohort differences is that either raw cohort differences or differences remaining following the removal of school specific trends over time are not correlated with confounding factors. This approach builds on the intuition that students close in age in the same school have many similar experiences including similar quality teachers. Therefore this structure identifies the ceteris paribus class size effect, holding constant other school factors.

Despite the multiple levels of school fixed effects, unobserved student heterogeneity might introduce bias, possibly through the linkages between academic preparation and either the number of new entrants or cohort size. The use of achievement gain as dependent variable and inclusion of student fixed effects should, however, account for differences related to both student movement among schools and enrollment differences among adjacent cohorts.

Although the fixed effect in gains specification accounts for primary confounding factors, the use of achievement gain as dependent variable in a student fixed effects model biases the coefficients away from zero as discussed above. Moreover, the multiple fixed effects likely exacerbate any error in the measurement of class size, and the estimates are sensitive to the elimination of observations with class size values that appear to be incorrect. Finally, the exogeneity assumption that the remaining errors are orthogonal to class size may be violated if within a school, differences in class size across cohorts are related to unobserved differences in teacher quality or time varying student factors that affect achievement.

Angrist and Lavy (1999) use a regression discontinuity, instrumental variables approach based on Maimonides Law to identify class size effects on 4th and 5th grade achievement in Israel. Regression Discontinuity (RD) is a quasi-experimental method that uses a discontinuity in the probability of treatment to identify the local average treatment effect (LATE) and avoid bias introduced by nonrandom selection into treatment. Hahn, Todd, and Van der Klaauw (2001) describe identification conditions and estimation using an RD design, and we review their work prior to discussing the Angrist and Lavy estimates of class size effects.

Equation (1.65) presents a simple model of the effect of treatment x on outcome y for individual i:

$$y_i = \alpha_i + x_i \beta_i$$
$$\alpha_i \equiv y_{0i}$$
$$\beta_i \equiv y_{1i} - y_{0i}$$
(1.65)

where y_{0i} is the outcome without treatment and y_{1i} is the outcome with treatment. Hahn, Todd, and Van der Klaauw begin by considering the case of a homogeneous treatment effect where $\beta_i = \beta$. Let z take on a continuum of values where the conditional probability

$$f(z) = E[x_i|z_i = z] = Pr[x_i = 1|z_i = z]$$
(1.66)

is discontinuous at $z_i = z_0$. Note that this is commonly referred to as a fuzzy RD design where other unobserved variables also affect the probability of treatment; the sharp design can be treated as a special case in which assignment to treatment is a deterministic function of z.

The key assumption required for identification is that $E[\alpha_i|z_i = z]$ is continuous in z at z_0, which is justified by the belief that persons close to the threshold are similar. The authors prove that β is nonparametrically identified as long as this assumption holds, the positive and negative limits for the probability of treatment exist at z_0, and the probability of treatment is discontinuous at z_0.

Hahn, Todd and Van der Klaauw turn next to identification when treatment effects are heterogeneous. They first prove that the local average treatment effect at z_0 is nonparametrically identified if the assumptions from the constant treatment effect case outlined in the previous paragraph are satisfied, the average treatment effect at z_i, $E[\beta_i|z_i = z]$, is continuous at z_0, and x_i is independent of β_i conditional on z_i near z_0.

The authors point out that the assumption that x_i is independent of β_i conditional on z_i near z_0 assumes that the anticipated gains from treatment do not affect the probability of receiving treatment, a strong assumption that may well be violated in practice. Therefore the authors, drawing from Imbens and Angrist (1994), establish the identification of the local average treatment effect at z_0 under an alternative set of conditions that allows selection into treatment on the basis of prospective gains without the strong assumption of conditional independence. Specifically, they consider the case where treatment assignment is a deterministic function of z for each observation i, but the function is different for different groups or persons. Given this supposition, Hahn, Todd, and Van der Klaauw describe the specific assumptions necessary for identification of the local average treatment effect at z_0.

The authors then turn to estimation and propose the use of local linear nonparametric regression (LLR) methods rather than standard kernel estimators, based on work by Fan (1992) showing that the LLR estimator has better boundary properties than the standard kernel estimator. They derive the asymptotic distribution of the RD treatment effect estimator based on LRR in the Appendix to the paper.

We now turn back to the class size application of RD based on Maimonides Law. This rule prohibits class sizes larger than 40 meaning that if schools desire to have class size of at least 40 an increase in enrollment from 40 to 41 reduces average class size from 40 to 20.5, and increase in enrollment from 80 to 81 reduces average class size from 40 to 27, and so on. The authors argue that the use of predicted class size based on the rule as an instrument for class size along with flexible controls for enrollment effects produces consistent estimates of class size effects on 4th and 5th grade achievement, and the pattern of observed class sizes largely corresponds to that which would be predicted by Maimonides Law. As is the case with the study by Rivkin, Hanushek and Kain (2005), these estimates are aimed at capturing the pure effect of smaller classes holding all other factors constant. In this case the estimates can be interpreted as weighted averages of local average treatment effects across the various boundaries, where the weights reflect the numbers of schools that contribute to identification by having enrollment that places it at a particular boundary.

There are reasons to be concerned that the identification conditions described in Hahn, Todd and Van der Klaauw (2001) could be violated. First, the paper shows that many schools add classes prior to enrollment reaching a multiple of 40 and districts may manipulate enrollment among schools in order to comply with the rule. Consequently the assumption that expected achievement in the absence of the small class is continuous at the boundary may be violated, as schools with enrollments just above boundaries may differ systematically from those just below. Moreover, the basic models combine the effects of changes in class size around the boundaries and intra-boundary changes, and intra-boundary class size variation may well be correlated with unobserved determinants of achievement. Restricting identification to comparisons across boundaries by limiting the sample to schools with enrollment that is first within five students and then within three students of a boundary leads to fluctuation in the estimates, and the increasingly small samples also reduce precision. Moreover, such selection may be endogenous because of the way the system is actually administered in practice.

In contrast to the other five papers based on observational data, Krueger (1999) uses data generated by a random assignment experiment designed to uncover the benefits of smaller classes. In an ideal experiment in which both students and teachers were randomly assigned to class types, mean achievement comparisons between treatment and control groups would produce unbiased estimates, and family background, teacher, and school information could be included to reduce sampling error. However, nonrandom movement between treatment and control groups and nonrandom attrition from the sample potentially introduces selection bias. Although the use of initial random assignment as an instrument for actual class type can produce LATE estimates, subject to the monotonicity assumption, selective attrition provides a more vexing problem.

Similar to the two other class size papers, the Tennessee STAR experiment is designed to produce estimates of the direct benefit of smaller classes ignoring any change in the quality of instruction. This potentially diverges from the benefit that would be realized in a large-scale class size reduction that requires substantial expansion of the teaching force.[56]

5.4 Estimation of teacher value-added

The passage of No Child Left Behind requiring that states test students annually and build comprehensive data systems has expanded opportunities to estimate teacher productivity as measured by value-added to student achievement. The repeated test scores and tracking of students and teachers through time enable researchers to account for

---

[56] Jepsen and Rivkin (2009) estimate the effects of changes in teacher experience and certification that accompanied class size reduction in California, but a lack of data impedes efforts to learn more about the magnitude, timing, and distribution of any decline in teacher quality.

differences among students and schools that could impede efforts to identify teacher value-added. In this section we examine methods used to estimate teacher value-added in five papers listed in Table 1.3. The first four papers estimate effectiveness for each teacher using regression models that account for potential confounding factors in different ways, while the final paper estimates the variance in teacher quality on the basis of the pattern of school average achievement.

Despite the steps taken to account for confounding factors in these and other papers, Rothstein (2009) and others have begun to raise concerns about the methods used to measure teacher quality. These critiques argue that sorting on unobservables that vary over time, endogenous parental response to teacher quality, test measurement error, and other failings introduce bias to estimates of teacher value-added and estimates of the variance in teacher value-added.

In order to highlight the issues of bias and sampling error that are addressed in each of these papers, Equation (1.67) decomposes the estimate of teacher value-added for teacher j in year y as the sum of the true teacher effect (assumed not to vary over time), the confounding student contribution (subscript i), the confounding peer contribution (subscript p), the confounding school contribution (subscript s), and random sampling error (subscript n):

$$\hat{t}_{jy} = t_j + \hat{\varepsilon}_{iy} + \hat{\varepsilon}_{py} + \hat{\varepsilon}_{sy} + \hat{\varepsilon}_{ny} \qquad (1.67)$$

Estimates of teacher value-added deviate from the true teacher effect, but if the expected values of each of the four error terms are zero unobserved differences in student, peer, and school characteristics would not introduce bias. Regardless, the variance of $\hat{t}_{jy}$ incorporates the true variance in teacher quality plus the variances of the other terms. Thus estimation of the variance in teacher value added must address complications related to both bias and sampling error, and the methods frame the interpretation of the estimates.

Aaronson, Barrow, and Sander (2007) use lagged achievement and observed characteristics to account for unobserved student heterogeneity and school fixed effects to control for school and peer differences that would otherwise be captured by the teacher effects; experience controls are not included, meaning that the estimated effects combine fixed differences across teachers and differences related to experience. The school fixed effects are omitted from some models, because in addition to accounting for confounding school factors they also soak up any systematic sorting by quality of teachers into schools. Importantly, the school fixed effects do not mitigate bias resulting from sorting into classrooms on the basis of unobserved time varying or even fixed differences in the rate of learning not captured by the included lagged achievement measures.

Rockoff (2004) takes a different approach to accounting for unobserved heterogeneity; it includes student fixed effects but not measures of prior achievement, implicitly imposing the strong assumption of no knowledge depreciation over time. It also

Table 1.3 Selected Research on Variance in Teacher Quality

Paper	Method	Data	Findings
Aaronsen, Barrow, and Sander (2007)	Value-added model; teacher fixed effects; school fixed effects in some models; observed student characteristics	Chicago Public Schools administrative data	Significant variation in teacher quality including variation by experience
Rockoff (2004)	Achievement model; teacher fixed effects; student and school by year fixed effects; teacher experience; observed student and school characteristics	New Jersey school district administrative data	Significant variation in teacher quality, conditional on experience
Ballou, Sanders, and Wright (2004)	First estimate separate teacher specific residual test score gains for each subject and grade; then produce a single quality estimate for each teacher based on the variance-covariance structure of these residual gains	Administrative data	Significant variation in teacher quality including variation by experience
Kane and Staiger (2008)	Regress difference in average test scores for two teachers in a school randomly assigned to classrooms on earlier year difference in Empirical Bayes estimates of value-added for the same pair	Experimental and nonexperimental data for a small number of Los Angeles public schools	Significant variation in teacher quality in nonexperimental and experimental data; do not reject the hypothesis that nonexperimental estimates are unbiased
Rivkin, Hanushek, and Kain (2005)	Compare cohort differences in test score gains with share of teachers who are different in the respective cohorts in a school	Texas public school administrative data	Significant variation in teacher quality within schools

includes school by year fixed effects to eliminate any between-school variation including systematic differences in teacher quality. Finally, it controls for teacher experience in order to isolate fixed differences in teacher effectiveness.

Ballou, Sanders, and Wright (2004) uses a sequential process to estimate teacher effects purged of the influence of student heterogeneity. First, it regresses test score gain on a vector of student characteristics and teacher fixed effects separately by grade and subject. Rather than simply treating the estimated teacher fixed effects as estimates of teacher quality in a particular subject and grade, it combines information from different subjects and grades in order to produce a single quality estimate for each teacher. This is accomplished in the following steps: 1) use the student demographic variable coefficients obtained from the teacher fixed effect models to subtract the contributions of the student variables from test score gain; and 2) use the variance/covariance structure of teacher average residual test score gains for all grades and subjects to produce a single quality estimate for each teacher. Note that although the use of teacher fixed effects in the first stage eliminates bias introduced by sorting into classrooms on the basis of the included variables, omitted student factors introduce bias if students sort into schools or classrooms on the basis of unobserved factors.

The authors claim that the insensitivity of the estimates to the inclusion of the student covariates provides evidence that the use of multiple tests accounts for the confounding effects of unobserved heterogeneity, but this finding is not surprising given that the limited set of covariates explains little of the achievement variation within classrooms, accounts for little of the heterogeneity among students, and may well be unrelated to unobserved confounding variables. The strong implicit assumptions about the nature of sorting among schools and classrooms, about the contributions of school and peer effects, about the covariance of teacher effectiveness across subjects and years, and about the manner through which knowledge accumulates through time are unlikely to be satisfied, and this may introduce substantial bias. The fact that the estimates were far more sensitive to the introduction of peer characteristics than to student level controls suggests that unobserved school differences and systematic student sorting by school may present particular problems.

Recognizing the threat of student sorting both within and between schools to the estimation of teacher value-added, Kane and Staiger (2008) use experimental data generated by a random assignment study of the National Board for Professional Teaching Standards Certification Program to investigate the validity of nonexperimental estimates of teacher value-added. In the study, pairs of teachers are identified in each school, one with and the other without certification, and classrooms are randomly assigned to the pairs. The difference in average test scores of the classrooms is regressed on the difference in empirical Bayes estimates of value-added for the pair of teachers based on data from earlier years in order to examine the validity of the estimation based on nonexperimental data.[57] The hypothesis test is based on the estimate of β in the regression of average achievement in teacher j's classroom on VA, the empirical Bayes value-added estimate for teacher j:

$$\bar{A} = \beta VA_j + \varepsilon_p \qquad (1.68)$$

It is the structure of the empirical Bayes estimator that underlies the hypothesis test. Specifically, VA_j equals the random effect estimate for teacher j multiplied by

$$a = \frac{\sigma_t^2 + \sigma_{\bar{i}}^2 + \sigma_{\bar{p}}^2 + \sigma_{\bar{s}}^2 + 2\sigma_{t,\bar{i}}^2 + 2\sigma_{t,\bar{p}}^2 + 2\sigma_{t,\bar{s}}^2}{\sigma_t^2 + \sigma_i^2 + \sigma_p^2 + \sigma_s^2 + 2\sigma_{t,i}^2 + 2\sigma_{t,p}^2 + 2\sigma_{t,s}^2} \qquad (1.69)$$

Note that the bars in the numerator indicate that the terms capture the persistent components of individual, peer, and school variation among teachers.[58] Thus the magnitude of a determines the extent to which the estimate for teacher j is shrunk toward the grand mean teacher quality of zero: the lower the ratio of the persistent components to the total variance the more the estimate is shrunk toward zero.

The expected value of β equals

$$\frac{\text{cov}(\bar{A}_j, VA_j)}{\text{var}(VA_j)} = \frac{\sigma_t^2}{a\left(\sigma_t^2 + \sigma_i^2 + \sigma_p^2 + \sigma_s^2 + 2\sigma_{t,i}^2 + 2\sigma_{t,p}^2 + 2\sigma_{t,s}^2\right)}$$

$$= \frac{\sigma_t^2}{\left(\sigma_t^2 + \sigma_{\bar{i}}^2 + \sigma_{\bar{p}}^2 + \sigma_{\bar{s}}^2 + 2\sigma_{t,\bar{i}}^2 + 2\sigma_{t,\bar{p}}^2 + 2\sigma_{t,\bar{s}}^2\right)} \qquad (1.70)$$

If there were no persistent differences in student, peer, or school components across teachers not accounted for in the model, then all terms following σ_t^2 would equal 0, and the ratio would equal 1. This suggests a test of the null hypothesis of $\beta=1$ as a specification test: rejection of the null hypothesis would provide evidence in support of the presence of nonrandom sorting on unobservables. Kain and Staiger report estimates that range from roughly 0.75 to 1.1 in their preferred specifications that control for student heterogeneity with lagged test scores. Importantly, none of these estimates are significantly different from 1, which is consistent with the hypothesis that sorting on unobservables does not confound the estimates of teacher value-added based on observational data.

It should be noted that the test does have some limitations. First, given the small sample size, even if the 95% or even 90% confidence interval for β contains 1, it also contains values that are much smaller than 1 that would be evidence of sorting on unobservables. Second, if there is compensatory assignment of better teachers to more difficult students, the covariance terms would be negative and would offset some of the

---

[57] See Morris (1983) for a discussion of the empirical Bayes estimator.
[58] To simplify we set the covariances among the individual, peer, and school factors equal to zero.

persistent variation in student, school, or peer differences among teachers not captured by the model, potentially pushing the estimate toward 1. Finally, the small group of schools in which principals agreed to permit classes to be randomly assigned to teachers is unlikely to be representative, meaning that evidence of the validity of value-added estimates with this sample may not generalize beyond this sample.

The final paper by Rivkin, Hanushek, and Kain (2005) avoids the question of sorting within classrooms altogether by focusing on cohort differences in achievement gains within schools. Specifically, the approach builds on the notion that if schools select teachers from a pool with substantial variation in quality, higher teacher turnover should lead to larger differences in test score gains between adjacent cohorts as fewer students in a cohort have a teacher who also taught the other cohort. Equation (1.71) represents average achievement gain in grade g in school s for cohort c as an additive function of grade average student (γ) and teacher (θ) fixed effects, a school fixed effect, and the grade average error:

$$\Delta \bar{A}^c_{gs} = \bar{\gamma}^c_{gs} + \bar{\theta}^c_{gs} + \delta_s + \bar{v}^c_{gs} \tag{1.71}$$

Taking the difference between adjacent cohorts c and c' in the differences of grade average gains in achievement in grades g and g-1 for the sample of students who remain in the school in both grades, eliminates all fixed student and family differences, leaving only cohort-to-cohort differences in the grade average difference in teacher quality and time varying student and school factors (contained in v) as determinants of the difference in the pattern of achievement gains.

$$\left(\Delta \bar{A}^c_{gs} - \Delta \bar{A}^c_{g's}\right) - \left(\Delta \bar{A}^{c'}_{gs} - \Delta \bar{A}^{c'}_{g's}\right) =$$
$$= \left[\left(\bar{\theta}^c_{gs} - \bar{\theta}^c_{g's}\right) - \left(\bar{\theta}^{c'}_{gs} - \bar{\theta}^{c'}_{g's}\right)\right] + \left[\left(\bar{v}^c_{gs} - \bar{v}^c_{g's}\right) - \left(\bar{v}^{c'}_{gs} - \bar{v}^{c'}_{g's}\right)\right] \tag{1.72}$$

Squaring this difference yields a natural characterization of the observed achievement differences between cohorts as a series of terms that reflect variances and covariances of the separate teacher effects plus a catchall component e that includes all random error and cross product terms between teacher and other grade specific effects.

$$\left[\left(\Delta \bar{A}^c_{gs} - \Delta \bar{A}^c_{g's}\right) - \left(\Delta \bar{A}^{c'}_{gs} - \Delta \bar{A}^{c'}_{g's}\right)\right]^2 = \left(\bar{\theta}^c_{gs}\right)^2 + \left(\bar{\theta}^c_{g's}\right)^2 + \left(\bar{\theta}^{c'}_{gs}\right)^2 + \left(\bar{\theta}^{c'}_{g's}\right)^2$$
$$- 2\left(\bar{\theta}^c_{gs}\bar{\theta}^{c'}_{gs} + \bar{\theta}^c_{g's}\bar{\theta}^{c'}_{g's}\right) + 2\left[\left(\bar{\theta}^c_{gs}\bar{\theta}^{c'}_{g's} - \bar{\theta}^c_{gs}\bar{\theta}^c_{g's}\right) + \left(\bar{\theta}^c_{gs}\bar{\theta}^{c'}_{g's} - \bar{\theta}^{c'}_{gs}\bar{\theta}^{c'}_{g's}\right)\right] + e \tag{1.73}$$

Under assumptions that formally characterize the notion that teachers are drawn from common distributions over the restricted time period of the cohort and grade observations, the expectation of Equation (1.73) yields:

$$E\left[\left(\Delta \bar{A}^c_{gs} - \Delta \bar{A}^c_{g's}\right) - \left(\Delta \bar{A}^{c'}_{gs} - \Delta \bar{A}^{c'}_{g's}\right)\right]^2 = 4\left(\sigma^2_{\theta_s} - \sigma^2_{\theta^c_s \theta^{c'}_s}\right) + E(e_s) \quad (1.74)$$

where $\sigma^2_{\theta_s}$ is the variance of teacher quality in school s and $\sigma^2_{\theta^c_s \theta^{c'}_s}$ is the covariance in teacher quality across cohorts in a school.

Equation (1.74) provides the basis for estimation of the within-school variance of teacher quality over the sample of students that remain in the same school for both grades. The left-hand side is the squared divergence of the grade pattern in gains across cohorts, which is regressed on the proportion of teachers in a school that are different in cohort c' than in cohort c. In order to account for different in the number of teachers and place all schools on a common metric, the proportion different must be divided by the number of teachers per grade, and the coefficient on this proportion divided by four provides the estimate of the within-school variance in teacher quality. Only unobserved, time-varying factors systematically related to teacher turnover can introduce bias, and sensitivity testing suggests that any such biases are negligible.

As previously noted, the use of test score gain likely introduces some upward bias, though violation of the strong assumption that true teacher effectiveness never varies over time and errors in the measurement of both the number of teachers in a grade and turnover both bias the estimates toward zero. Moreover, the estimates based on this approach ignore all between-school differences in the quality of instruction. A limitation of this aggregate approach for policy is the absence of value-added estimates for individual teachers.

Finally the issue of scale for the test scores reappears in this literature. Many studies of teacher value-added rely on a specific test score scale and are based on comparing gains, which are not invariant to monotonic transformations. Moreover, the empirical strategy of differencing out heterogeneity relies on the assumption of linearity for the particular score at hand. This issue raises questions about the robustness of the results to changes of scale and merits attention during sensitivity testing given the absence of an agreed upon metric to anchor the results. Moreover, this concern supports the use of more flexible parameterization of prior achievement as controls.

One source of bias for all approaches to the estimation of teacher value-added or the variance in teacher quality is the endogenous intervention of parents and schools. Todd and Wolpin (2003) and Dearden, Ferri, and Meghir (2002) discuss the likelihood that the amount of time and money dedicated to academic support is likely to depend on the quality of instruction. Cullen, Jacob, and Levitt (2006) find mixed evidence regarding the effect of winning a lottery to choice into a specific school on parent involvement, but individual teacher quality may induce a stronger parental response. Though inspiring teachers can potentially induce parents to become more involved, parental intervention to compensate for lower quality instruction is more likely. In addition to influencing parental behavior, teacher quality may also affect the amount of intervention support allocated by the school. For example, reading or mathematics specialists may spend additional time in classrooms with less effective teachers.

Such compensatory intervention by school staff and parents would tend to biased value-added estimates toward the school mean and estimates of the within-school variance in teacher quality toward zero due to the negative correlation between teacher quality on the one hand and both the school and parent components on the other. Even the random assignment of classrooms to teachers does not mitigate the impact of this type of endogenous response to realized quality, and any such biases would not be detected in the specification test proposed by Kane and Staiger (2008). Therefore in the absence of controls for parental and school interventions such as the quantity and quality of family and school support in specific subjects, teacher value-added estimates capture both classroom teacher effects and the contributions of other sources of academic support.

5.5 Estimation of the housing market capitalization of school quality

The belief that the quality and cost-effectiveness of local public schools affect housing values provides a key underpinning for the notion that competition among localities fosters higher quality public services; this issue is the focus of Chapter 10. Yet the non-random sorting of families into communities, multitude of public services provided, and difficulty controlling for all housing and neighborhood amenities impede efforts to empirically test the relationship between housing prices and school quality. Recent work has attempted to overcome these difficulties by focusing on comparisons of houses on opposite sides of school attendance zone boundaries. The validity of school quality capitalization models with boundary fixed effects rests in large part on the assumption that unobserved determinants of housing prices vary continuously at the boundary and are virtually uncorrelated with school quality differences between houses on opposite sides of the boundary. This is the continuity assumption described in Hahn, Todd, and Van der Klaauw (2001). If it is satisfied, differences in school quality would account for any discontinuity in housing prices at the school attendance zone or school district boundary, and boundary fixed effects models would generate consistent estimates of the relationship between measured school quality and price at the boundary.

Table 1.4 lists three papers that utilize somewhat different boundary fixed effect models. Despite their differences, each finds that accounting for unobserved neighborhood differences substantially reduces the estimated relationship between house price and school average test score. Although remaining concerns about bias introduced by unobserved differences in housing quality, the characteristics of immediate neighbors, or the quality of other amenities remains an important issue, a key methodological question is what exactly underlies any relationship between the measures of school quality and the house price.

Table 1.4 Selected Research on Boundary Fixed Effect Estimates of Housing Market Capitalization of School Quality

Paper	Comparison	Method	Data	Findings
Black (1999)	Attendance zone boundaries within school districts	Relate differences in school average test score to house price differences across boundaries, controlling for observables	House price data and information on school achievement for districts in Massachusetts	Evidence of housing market capitalization of test scores
Bayer, Ferreira, and McMillan (2007)	Attendance zone boundaries within school districts	Relate differences in school average test score to house price differences using reduced form and discreet choice boundary fixed effects models	House price data, restricted U.S. Census demographic data and information on school achievement for districts in San Francisco Bay Area	Inclusion of neighborhood demographic characteristics reduces the estimated effect of test score; evidence of heterogeneity in willingness to pay for school quality
Gibbons, Machin, and Silva (2009)	Local education authority boundaries and empirically determined attendance zone boundaries within local education authorities	Relate differences in school average test score to house price differences across boundaries, controlling for observables	U.K. administrative data sources and census data	Evidence of housing market capitalization of school value-added and average achievement

Black (1999) calculates differences in mean house prices on opposite sides of school attendance zone boundaries and investigates whether the differences are systematically related to the differences in test scores in the respective schools, adjusted for a set of observed housing characteristics. Only boundaries in which both attendance zones lie in the same city and school district are included, so this method holds constant the property tax rate, district administration, the quality of city public services, and other amenities that do not vary within the narrow boundaries. The focus on close neighbors also has the advantage of accounting for the effects of factors that change over space such as proximity to parks, police and fire stations, and public transportation.

One potential threat to the identification of the capitalized value of higher test scores is the possibility that the parsimonious set of housing variables fail to capture quality differences that may be related to test scores; higher income families may both select the house in the higher test score zone and spend more on home renovation, introducing an upward bias in the estimate of the capitalized value of higher scores. Any failure of the included characteristics to capture dimensions of housing quality that are related to school average test score including the demographic characteristics of neighbors will lead to a nonzero within boundary covariance between the error and test score and introduce bias. The direction of the bias would likely be negative if unobserved housing quality were higher on the low test score side of the boundary, consistent with heterogeneous preferences regarding education, and would likely be positive if higher income households tended to live in the higher test score side of boundaries.

An important limitation of this approach is the inability to disentangle the contributions of peers from that of the quality of the provision of public education per tax dollar spent. The restriction that boundaries lay within as opposed to between school districts mitigates biases potentially introduced by confounding factors across district boundaries at a cost of eliminating any impact of district policies or resource use on house prices. As the district controls principal and staff hiring, curricular decisions, and capital investments, this is a major drawback, making it more likely that student demographic characteristics play a primary role in the determination of the desirability of an attendance zone.

Bayer, Ferreira, and McMillan (2007) embed a boundary fixed effects approach in a model of neighborhood choice using restricted U.S. Census data that provides rich information on the characteristics of neighbors. The finding that the inclusion of neighborhood socio-demographic characteristics roughly cuts in half the estimated effect of school average test score even in models with extensive controls for average student characteristics suggests that some of what appears to be preference for school or peer quality is actually a preference for neighbor demographics. Importantly, average test score is likely to be a poor proxy for school effectiveness in raising achievement, and a more accurate measure of school value-added would likely provide a clearer picture of the value placed on more effective schools.

The difference in neighborhood characteristics on opposite sides of the boundaries suggests the existence of heterogeneous preferences regarding education, and this is precisely what is shown by the structural estimation of willingness to pay for school quality and other neighborhood characteristics. The discrete choice model incorporates heterogeneity in the willingness to pay for higher test scores and other house characteristics and neighborhood amenities. It should be noted that the focus on within-district comparison of attendance zones prevents differences in district quality from being capitalized into higher house prices in both the hedonic price and discrete choice regressions.

The additional structure requires the satisfaction of a number of assumptions including 1) place of work is exogenous; 2) housing characteristics more than three miles from any house have no direct effect on the residents; 3) the included neighborhood characteristics account fully for sorting across boundaries; 4) school average test scores and other school characteristics control fully for differences in school quality; and 5) the multinomial logit IIA assumptions. Concerns can be raised by each of these assumptions, but the underlying assumption of no variation in the weighting of different aspects of school quality merits additional attention in a framework that emphasizes heterogeneity in preferences. The possibility of variation in the quality of instructing students from different points in the achievement distribution or different backgrounds cannot be dismissed, and this model may misinterpret that as differences in willingness to pay for an amenity whose quality does not vary by student or family characteristics.

Gibbons, Machin, and Silva (2009) use boundary fixed effect hedonic models to estimate capitalized values of both school effectiveness, as measured by test score gain, and school composition, as measured by initial test score, for a sample of British students. In contrast to the two other papers, this paper focuses on boundaries between local authorities, which perform many of the same functions as U.S. school districts. Therefore local authority actions that affect achievement gain are captured in the estimates. Moreover, test score gain would appear to provide a better measure of school value-added than average test score.

Because of the absence of school attendance zones within local authorities, the authors had to construct a method for measuring the quality of schooling associated with each housing unit. They used the empirical distribution of school attendance to define a set of overlapping school attendance zone boundaries, meaning that many houses were located in more than one attendance zone. Subsequently school characteristics were computed for each house as a weighted average of the initial test score and test score gain for schools in all the relevant attendance zones.

A concern about this approach to measuring school quality is the fact that families are assumed to respond to the same test score and gain information that their actual location decisions help to determine (for example through peer effects). This problem holds for all the papers using test score information and relates to the aforementioned possibility that test scores capture differences in unobserved quality of neighbors or neighborhood amenities. It is quite difficult to distinguish whether 1) test score differences reflect differences in school quality; 2) test score differences result from sorting on the basis of school reputations; and 3) test score differences result from sorting on the basis of other amenities including the characteristics of residents. In fact each of these channels could contribute to test score differences across boundaries.

The use of measures of school quality less directly related to family characteristics would mitigate this problem, but input measures historically explain little of the variation in school effectiveness. The estimation of school value-added controlling for observed and unobserved student heterogeneity would provide a better measure of school quality with which to estimate the capitalization of school effectiveness into housing prices.

5.6 Estimation of the effects of competition, choice, and accountability

Recent expansions in public school choice and the growth of accountability systems in many countries have altered the public school environment, but the effects of such programs have proven elusive to estimate because of both the manner in which the programs have been introduced and the difficulty accounting for student and family heterogeneity related to different choices. A number of methods have been used to identify choice and accountability effects, including instrumental variables, difference-in-differences and lottery outcomes as instruments for school enrollment. Table 1.5 provides examples of three of these methods used in studies of choice and accountability. The study of catholic-public school quality differences by Neal (1997), the study of accountability system effects on achievement by Hanushek and Raymond (2005), and the investigation of open enrollment effects by Cullen, Jacob and Levitt (2006) provide examples of these three methods.

The endogeneity of the decision to attend private school introduces a difference between students in public and private school that biases estimates of sector differences in quality unless the unobserved heterogeneity is fully accounted for. Consider the following two-equation model. In the first equation achievement A is a function of a school sector indicator variable P (equal to 1 for catholic school and 0 for public school), a vector of family and community characteristics X, and an error u. In the second equation the unobserved propensity to attend private school P^* is a function of a vector of family and community characteristics Z and an error e. If $P^* > 1$ students attend catholic school and $P = 1$; otherwise students attend public school and $P = 0$.

$$A_i = P_i \delta + X_i \beta + u_i$$
$$P_i^* = Z_i \gamma + e_i \qquad (1.75)$$

OLS estimation of the top equation is likely to produce an upward biased estimate of δ and overstate the catholic school–public school quality differential, because the expected value of the error u is likely to be higher for students attending private school.

Table 1.5 Selected Research on Choice and Accountability

Paper	Method	Data	Findings
Hanushek and Raymond (2005)	Difference-in-differences	National Assessment of Educational Progress	Accountability increases achievement
Neal (1997)	Estimate catholic school effects using catholic church adherents as a share of the county population and number of catholic secondary schools per square mile as instruments	NLSY	Effects on educational attainment from catholic school attendance are significant for urban minorities, modest for urban whites, and negligible for suburban students
Cullen, Jacob, and Levitt (2006)	Use lotteries for over-subscribed schools to identify benefits of open enrollment in Chicago public schools	Chicago Public School District administrative data	Attendance at a non-neighborhood school does not significantly increase achievement

A solution to this problem is the identification of an instrument that belongs in Z but not X, that is, it affects the probability of attending private school but otherwise does not affect achievement.[59]

Neal (1997) argues that catholic church adherents as a share of the county population and the number of catholic secondary schools per square mile provide valid instruments for the estimation of δ, because they affect the money (first instrument) or time (second instrument) costs of attending catholic school but are otherwise unrelated to A. Although religious affiliation may be a stronger predictor of catholic school attendance, Neal argues that it is not a valid instrument because of the possibility that it is directly related to achievement. For example, families may choose to become catholic in order to send a child to a catholic school.

The argument that personal religious affiliation is likely related to confounding factors while the county mean share of individuals with a particular religious affiliation is not related to those factors appears tenuous, as it seems likely that students in more heavily catholic counties with more catholic schools per square mile are more likely to have family backgrounds and even tastes similar to the average catholic. This would introduce a nonzero correlation between these instruments and u and bias estimates of δ. Moreover, the share of Catholics in the county population and number of catholic schools may be directly related

---

[59] See Heckman (1979) for a comprehensive treatment of nonrandom selection.

to the quality of public schools by affecting both the level of tax support for the public schools and the involvement of community members in public school affairs. Such a correlation would also introduce an upward bias into the estimate catholic–public school gap.

Finally, as Neal points out, this approach relies on the assumption that the residential choice is exogenous with respect to the quality of public and catholic schools. Given the previously discussed evidence that families appear to sort partly on the basis of preferences regarding education, this assumption may well be violated. If the choice is between living in School District A and attending catholic school and living in School District B and attending public school, county composition is likely to be related to the quality of the public schools. The measurement of the instrument at the county level and the inclusion of a number of demographic characteristics likely mitigate the potentially problematic impact of sorting, though many metropolitan areas include multiple counties and included demographic variables may not capture salient differences among families and communities.

In terms of interpretation, this IV approach rules out consideration of general equilibrium effects of the presence of catholic schools affecting the quality of local public schools either through competitive pressures or financial support. Rather it identifies the race-specific average catholic–public school difference in school value-added based on county differences in catholic religiosity. Given housing constraints faced by blacks in many metropolitan areas during the late 1970s, the arguments justifying the empirical approach seem stronger for blacks than for whites.

Cullen, Jacob and Levitt (2006) investigate choice entirely within a single public school district (open enrollment) through comparisons of lottery winners and losers. The use of lottery outcomes circumvents problems introduced by the fact that those who apply to non-neighborhood schools differ from nonapplicants, and winners who decide to accept admission differ from those who decide not to accept admission.

Estimation of the following OLS specification generates estimates of the benefits of open enrollment:

$$A_{ia} = Win\_Lottery_{ia}\delta + Lottery_a \Gamma + + X_i \beta + u_{ia} \qquad (1.76)$$

where *Win_Lottery* is a dummy variable equal to 1 if application a for student i was a lottery winner and *Lottery* is vector of lottery fixed effects that indicates to which lottery the observation refers (there are 194 different lotteries, and students may participate in more than one). In this model the estimate of δ is the weighted average of the regression adjusted difference in mean outcomes for winners and losers of the various lotteries. In the absence of selective attrition from the sample or contamination of the lotteries, the lotteries produce an unbiased estimate of δ. Note in general, the problems introduced by selective attrition on unobservables are likely to grow in importance the larger the perceived differential in quality between the default public school on the one hand and the lottery charter or private school on the other.

The possibilities of participating in multiple lotteries and not attending a lottery school even if you win the lottery affect the interpretation of δ. Choosing to participate in more lotteries raises the probability of winning and the probability of not attending a particular lottery school even if you win that lottery. If the treatment is defined as the average effect of attending the lottery school, the estimate of δ captures the intention to treat effect on applicants. The authors also provide an alternative explanation: the average impact of having a school in the choice set for students who expressed an interest. Note that as the number of choices and lotteries perstudent rise, one would expect a decrease in the benefit to winning as fewer students would take up the opportunity to attend the lottery school and the next-best alternative for losers would tend to be closer in expected match quality to the lottery school.

Importantly, this and other lottery based analyses provide no information on either the general equilibrium effects of choice on the overall distribution of school quality or the specific factors that account for any positive or negative effects. Because the lottery analyses compare the outcomes of winners and losers, the estimates ignore any district wide increases or decreases in school quality. In terms of the sources of any differences between those attending non-neighborhood and neighborhood schools, the lotteries do not provide information on the contributions of teachers, facilities, curriculum, or peers.

The limitations of lottery based analyses in terms of public policy are perhaps most severe in cases where the set of lottery school spaces is small relative to the total number of students. The fact that participants in such lotteries are a selective sample means that students in schools made up entirely of lottery winners will also constitute a selective group. Consequently a finding that winners of lotteries to charter or private schools outperform the losers who end up primarily at neighborhood schools could be driven entirely by differences in the peer composition. If that is the case, program expansion would tend to diminish the average benefits to lottery winners as the lottery sample became less select, and the benefits of attending a charter or private school would decline to zero if all students were to attend such schools.

Hanushek and Raymond (2005) use a difference-in-differences framework to analyze the effect of accountability on the level and distribution of achievement. In contrast to school choice, analyses where endogenous decisions on the part of families complicate the estimation, empirical studies of accountability effects must address issues related to the political decision to adopt an accountability regime at a particular time. Adoption affects all districts in a state, and it is likely that adoption is related to other contemporaneous policy changes such as a decision to add resources that also affect outcomes. Identification of accountability effects requires the construction of valid counterfactuals for accountability regimes.

Equation (1.77) describes state average achievement (A) in year y as a function of an indicator for an accountability regime C, a vector of a characteristic X that varies by state and year, and a composite error that includes a year effect α, a state effect τ and random term ε that varies by state and year.

$$A_{sy} = C_{sy}\delta + X_{sy}\beta + \alpha_y + \tau_s + \varepsilon_{sy} \tag{1.77}$$

Consider the following four possible estimators of the accountability effect. The first uses cross-sectional data for a single year, and identifies the accountability effect as the mean achievement difference between states with and without accountability systems. Clearly myriad differences among states would introduce a correlation between C and τ and contaminate the estimate.

The second uses time-series data for a single state that implemented an accountability system during the sample period. This method identifies the accountability effect as the mean achievement difference between periods following adoption and periods prior to adoption. In this case, any changes over time would confound the estimated accountability effect by introducing a correlation between C and α.

The third method uses panel data on states and a state and year fixed effects specification with a dummy variable for whether or not a state has an accountability program in year y. The fixed effects explicitly account for differences among states common to all years τ and all differences among years common to all states α. Identification relies on the assumption that changes over time in states that do not change accountability status provide a valid counterfactual estimate of what would have occurred in states that transition to an accountability system. This assumption that the covariance between C and ε equals zero would be violated if adoption of an accountability system were correlated with other changes that affect educational outcomes, perhaps including changes in the political system, economic circumstances, and so on.

The fourth method used by Hanushek and Raymond adds a state specific time trend to account for state specific changes over time that could bias estimates of δ; the paper also measures accountability by the share of the previous four years covered by an accountability system. In this framework the accountability effect is identified by within-state deviations from the time trend related to the adoption of an accountability system and differences in the timing of accountability adoption across states. Although the addition of a state-specific time trend controls for trends over time that could confound the estimates, it does not account for discontinuous time-varying factors including those related to the decision to enact an accountability structure. Even with long time series and polynomial trends the possibility remains that accountability program adoption would not be the only factor contributing to a discontinuous change in achievement around the time of program adoption.

Interpretation is complicated by a number of factors including heterogeneity in accountability programs, uncertainties in the time pattern of effects following program adoption, and the extent to which the adoption of accountability programs led to changes in other factors that affect achievement, including the amount of resources devoted to education. Hanushek and Raymond control for school spending, but to the extent that accountability increases the return on investments in education, the magnitude of the effect varies with school spending. Therefore a specification that restricts the effect to be constant when it is in fact interwoven with the level of spending will provide an incomplete picture of the overall effects. In addition, the long-run effects may include any impact on the quality and distribution of the stock of teachers, while effects in the short run operate largely through other mechanisms.

6. CONCLUSIONS

Estimation of the return to schooling or school input effects must account for the complications introduced by the myriad choices made by families, teachers, administrators, politicians, judges, or other actors. Approaches to estimation range from structural models derived explicitly from theory to experimental and quasi-experimental methods based on randomized trials, rule changes, policy changes, lotteries, or other source of variation. Although these methods may appear as almost polar opposites in terms of their reliance on theory and explicit assumptions about behavior, closer inspection says otherwise. Rather, conditions for identification and parameter interpretation in most cases require assumptions about some aspects of the underlying choice framework. Importantly, such assumptions appear to take on greater importance as the models become more flexible and comprehensive. As we highlight in Sections 1–4, identification of the return to schooling in models that allow for heterogeneous returns and multiple dimensions of unobserved heterogeneity require assumptions about the processes underlying the choice of schooling level. Similarly, efforts to estimate differences in teacher quality require assumptions regarding the mechanisms through which teachers and students are matched. In addition, they also require assumptions about the behavior of parents in response to observed instructional quality in order to identify teacher effects on learning.

The proliferation of elementary and secondary school administrative data facilitates the use of panel data methods that can account for confounding factors introduced by purposeful choices. Moreover, the linking of these data with information on wages, involvement in the criminal justice system, and vital statistics will enable researchers to follow children from birth to adulthood. This expands the range of questions that can be addressed but also introduces additional choices and behaviors that must be accounted for. More complicated conceptual and empirical models will be required to identify treatment effects in these settings.

Although there are many directions to expand and improve upon existing work, four specific areas come to mind based upon existing findings and recent methodological developments. The first is improved treatment of individual heterogeneity along multiple dimensions including noncognitive skills; the second is the incorporation of endogenous parental responses into estimates of school input effects or teacher quality; the third is an enhanced understanding of the linkages among school and teacher effects across years and classrooms including the effects of heterogeneity in preparation on the distribution of teacher effort and learning; and the fourth is a greater integration of differences in school quality into models of education choice and the returns to schooling. In terms of the fourth, access to elementary and secondary school quality may be an important determinant of heterogeneous returns to schooling and differences in education choices, and the incorporation of such differences would enhance our understanding of the ways in which various policy changes that alter schooling choices are likely to affect the distribution of achievement, academic attainment, and future earnings.

Serious progress along these dimensions is likely to require additional data on the years prior to kindergarten entry, individual skills and behaviors, the allocation of academic support within schools, and parental time and financial support for learning. The combining of administrative and survey data sets would appear to be a particularly promising way of building a data set with the elements necessary to gain a much better understanding of the distribution of teacher and school effects and the underlying choice frameworks that contribute to the distribution of achievement and future earnings.

REFERENCES

Aaronson, D., Barrow, L., Sander, W., 2007. Teachers and Student achievement in the Chicago Public High Schools. Journal of Labor Economics 25 (1), 95–135.

Abbring, J.H., Heckman, J.J., 2007. Econometric Evaluation of Social Programs, Part III: Distributional Treatment Effects, Dynamic Treatment Effects, Dynamic Discrete Choice, and General Equilibrium Policy Evaluation. In: Heckman, J.J., Leamer, E.E. (Eds.), first ed. Handbook of Econometrics 6, Elsevier, (chapter 72).

Acemoglu, D., Angrist, J., 1999. How Large are the Social Returns to Education? Evidence from Compulsory Schooling Law. NBER Working Papers 7444.

Adda, Dustmann, Meghir, Robin, 2009. Career Progression and Formal versus On-the-Job Training. IFS Working Paper.

Ahn, H., Powell, J., 1993. Semiparametric Estimation of Censored Selection Models with Nonparametric Selection Mechanism. Journal of Econometrics 58, 3–29.

Altonji, J., Matzkin, R., 2005. Cross Section and Panel Data Estimators for Nonseparable Models with Endogenous Regressors. Econometrica 73 (4), 1053–1102.

Altonji, J.G., Elder, T.E., Taber, C.R., 2005. Selection on Observed and Unobserved Variables: Assessing the Effectiveness of Catholic Schools. Journal of Political Economy 113 (1), 151–184.

Angrist, J.D., Krueger, A.B., 1991. Does Compulsory School Attendance Affect Schooling and Earnings? The Quarterly Journal of Economics 106 (4), 979–1014 MIT Press.

Angrist, J., Lavy, V., 1999. Using Maimonides' Rule to Estimate the Effect of Class Size on Scholastic Achievement. Quarterly Journal of Economics 114 (2), 533–575.

Arellano, M., Bond, S., 1991. Some tests of specification for panel data: Monte Carlo evidence and an application to employment equations. The Review of Economic Studies 58, 277–297.

Attanasio, O., Meghir, C., Santiago, A., 2009. Education choices in Mexico: using a structural model and a randomized experiment to evaluate PROGRESA. IFS/EDEPO Working Paper.

Ballou, D., Sanders, W., Wright, P., 2004. Controlling for Student Background in Value-added Assessment of Teachers. Journal of Educational and Behavioral Statistics 29 (1), 37–66.

Bayer, P., Ferreira, F., McMillan, R.A., 2007. A Unified Framework for Measuring Preferences for Schools and Neighborhoods. Journal of Political Economy 115 (4), 588–638.

Betts, J.R., 1995. Does School Quality Matter? Evidence from the National Longitudinal Survey of Youth. Rev. Econ. Stat. 77 (2), 231–250.

Black, S.E., 1999. Do Better Schools Matter? Parental Valuation of Elementary Education. Quarterly Journal of Economics 114 (2), 577–599.

Blundell, R.W., Gosling, A., Ichimura, H., Meghir, C., 2007. Changes in the Distribution of Male and Female Wages accounting for employment composition using bounds. Econometrica 75 (2), 323–363.

Blundell, R.W., Powell, J., 2004. Endogeneity in Semiparametric Binary Response Models. The Review of Economic Studies 71 (3), 655–679.

Blundell, R., Windmeijer, F., 1997. Cluster Effects and Simultaneity in Multilevel Models. Health Economics Letters 6, 439–443.

Bound, J., Jaeger, D.A., Baker, R.M., 1995. Problems with Instrumental Variables Estimation When the Correlation Between the Instruments and the Endogenous Explanatory Variable is Weak. Journal of the American Statistical Association 90 (430), 443–450.

Cameron, S.V., Heckman, J.J., 1998. Life Cycle Schooling and Dynamic Selection Bias: Models and Evidence for Five Cohorts of American Males. The Journal of Political Economy 106 (2), 262–333.

Card, D., 1995. Using Geographic Variation in College Proximity to Estimate the Return to Schooling. In: Louis, N., Christofides, E.K.G., Swidinsky, R. (Eds.), Aspects of Labour Market Behaviour: Essays in Honour of John Vanderkamp. University of Toronto Press, Toronto, pp. 201–222.

Card, D., 2001. Estimating the Return to Schooling: Progress on Some Persistent Econometric Problems. Econometrica 69 (5), 1127–1160.

Card, D., Krueger, A.B., 1992. Does School Quality Matter? Returns to Education and the Characteristics of Public Schools in the United States. Journal of Political Economy 100 (1), 1–40.

Carneiro, P., Heckman, J.J., Vytlacil, E., 2010. Evaluating Marginal Policy Changes and the Average Effect of Treatment for Individuals at the Margin. Econometrica 78 (1), 377–394.

Chernozhukov, V., Hong, H., 2003. An MCMC Approach to Classical Estimation. Journal of Econometrics.

Chesher, A., 2003. Identification in Nonseparable Models. Econometrica 71 (5), 1405–1441.

Chib, S., 2001. Markov Chain Monte Carlo methods: computation and inference. In: Heckman, J.J., Leamer, E.E. (Eds.), first ed. Handbook of Econometrics 5, Elsevier, pp. 3569–3649 (Chapter 57).

Cullen, J.B., Jacob, B.A., Levitt, S., 2006. The Effect of School Choice on Participants: Evidence from Randomized Lotteries. Econometrica 74 (5), 1191–1230.

Cunha, F., Heckman, J.J., 2008. Symposium on Noncognitive Skills and Their Development: Formulating, Identifying and Estimating the Technology of Cognitive and Noncognitive Skill Formation. J. Hum. Res. 43 (4), 738–782.

Cunha, F., Heckman, J.J., Schennach, S., 2010. Estimating the Technology of Cognitive and Noncognitive Skill Formation. Econometrica, NBER Working Paper 15664, forthcoming.

Darolles, S., Florens, J.P., Renault, E., 2002. Nonparametric instrumental regression. GREMAQ, University of Social Science, Toulouse, Working Paper.

Das, M., Newey, W.K., Vella, 2003. Nonparametric Estimation of Sample Selection Models. Review of Economic Studies 70, 33–58.

Dearden, L., Emmerson, C., Frayne, C., Meghir, C., 2009. Conditional Cash Transfers and School Drop out Rates. J. Hum. Res. 44 (4), 827–857 (Fall).

Dearden, L., Ferri, J., Meghir, C., 2002. The Effect Of School Quality On Educational Attainment And Wages. Rev. Econ. Stat. 84 (1), 1–20.

Ding, W., Lehrer, S., 2005. Class Size and Student Achievement: Experimental Estimates of Who Benefits and Who Loses from Reductions. Working paper.

Eckstein, Z., Wolpin, K., 1989. Dynamic Labour Force Participation of Married Women and Endogenous Work Experience. Review of Economic Studies 56 (3), 375–390.

Florens, J.P., Heckman, J.J., Meghir, C., Vytlacil, E., 2008. Identification of treatment effects using control Functions in models with continuous, endogenous Treatment and heterogeneous effects. Econometrica 76 (5), 1191–1206.

Gallipoli, G., Meghir, C., Violante, G., 2008. Equilibrium Effects of Education Policies: A Quantitative Evaluation. mimeo University of British Columbia.

Gibbons, S., Machin, S., Silva, O., 2009. Valuing School Quality Using Boundary Discontinuities. Spatial Economics Research Centre, LSE, SERC Discussion Papers 0018.

Griliches, Z., 1977a. Education, Income, and Ability: Rejoinder. Journal of Political Economy 85 (1), 215.

Griliches, Z., 1977b. Estimating the Returns to Schooling: Some Econometric Problems. Econometrica 45 (1), 1–22.

Gourieroux, C., Monfort, A., Renault, E., 1993. Indirect Inference. Journal of Applied Econometrics 8, S85–S118 Supplement: Special Issue on Econometric Inference Using Simulation Techniques.

Gronau, R., 1974. Wage Comparisons–A Selectivity Bias. The Journal of Political Economy 82 (6), 1119–1143.

Hahn, J., Todd, P., Van der Klaauw, W., 2001. Identification and Estimation of Treatment Effects with a Regression-Discontinuity Design. Econometrica 69 (1), 201–209.

Hanushek, E.A., Kain, J.F., Rivkin, S.G., 2004. Disruption versus Tiebout Improvement: The Costs and Benefits of Switching Schools. Journal of Public Economics 88 (9–10), 1721–1746.

Hanushek, E.A., Raymond, M.E., 2005. Does School Accountability Lead to Improved Student Performance? J. Policy Anal. Manage. 24 (2), 297–327.

Hanushek, E.A., Rivkin, S.G., Taylor, L.L., 1996. Aggregation and the Estimated Effects of School Resources. Rev. Econ. Stat. 78 (4), 611–627.

Harmon, C., Walker, I., 1995. Estimates of the Economic Return to Schooling for the United Kingdom. Am. Econ. Rev. 85 (5), 1278–1286.

Harris, D.N., Sass, T.R., 2009. The Effects of NBPTS-Certified Teachers on Student Achievement. J. Policy Anal. Manage. 28 (1), 55–80.

Heckman, J.J., 1974. Shadow Prices, Market Wages, and Labor Supply. Econometrica 42 (4), 679–694.

Heckman, J.J., 1979. Sample Selection Bias as a Specification Error. Econometrica 47, 153–162, [326, 336].

Heckman, J.J., 1990. Varieties of Selection Bias. Am. Econ. Rev. 80, 313–318 Papers and Proceedings of the Hundred and Second Annual Meeting of the American Economic Association.

Heckman, J.J., Honoré, B., 1990. The Empirical Content of the Roy Model. Econometrica 58, 1121–1149.

Heckman, J.J., LaLonde, R., Smith, J., 1999. The Economics and Econometrics of Active Labour Market Programmes. In: Ashenfel-ter, O., Card, D. (Eds.), Handbook of Labour Economics 3a, North-Holland, Amsterdam, pp. 1865–2097.

Heckman, J., Layne-Farrar, A., Todd, P., 1996. Human Capital Pricing Equations with an Application to Estimating the Effect of Schooling Quality on Earnings. Rev. Econ. Stat. 78 (4), 562–610.

Heckman, J.J., Lochner, L., Taber, C., 1998. Explaining Rising Wage Inequality: Explanations With A Dynamic General Equilibrium Model of Labor Earnings With Heterogeneous Agents. Review of Economic Dynamics, Elsevier for the Society for Economic Dynamics 1 (1), 1–58.

Heckman, J.J., Lochner, L., Todd, P., 2003. Fifty Years of Mincer regressions. IZA Discussion Paper No. 775.

Heckman, J.J., Navarro, S., 2007. Dynamic discrete choice and dynamic treatment effects. Journal of Econometrics 136, 341–396.

Heckman, J., Robb, R., 1985. Alternative methods for evaluating the impact of interventions. In: Heckman, J., Singer, B. (Eds.), Longitudinal analysis of labor market data, Econometric Society monograph series. Cambridge University Press, New York.

Heckman, J., Sedlacek, G., 1985. Heterogeneity, Aggregation, and Market Wage Functions: An Empirical Model of Self-selection in the Labor Market. Journal of Political Economy 93 (6), 1077–1125.

Heckman, J.J., Urzua, S., Vytlacil, E., 2006a. Understanding Instrumental Variables in Models with Essential Heterogeneity. Rev. Econ. Stat. 88 (3).

Heckman, J.J., Urzua, S., Vytlacil, E., 2006b. Instrumental Variables in Models with Multiple Outcomes: The General Unordered Case. mimeo University of Chicago.

Heckman, J.J., and Vytlacil, E.J., 1998. Instrumental Variables Methods for the Correlated Random Coefficients Model: Estimating the Average Rate of Return to Schooling when the Return is Correlated to Schooling. J. Human Res. 33, 974–987.

Heckman, J.J., Vytlacil, E., 2005. Structural Equations, Treatment Effects, and Econometric Policy Evaluation. Econometrica 73 (3), 669–738.
Hsiao, C., 2003. Analysis of Panel Data, second ed. Cambridge University Press.
Imbens, G.W., Angrist, J.D., 1994. Identification and Estimation of Local Average Treatment Effects. Econometrica 62 (2), 467–475.
Imbens, G., Newey, W., 2009. Identification and Estimation of Triangular Simultaneous Equations Models Without Additivity. Econometrica 77 (5), 1481–1512.
Jepsen, C., Rivkin, S., 2009. Class Size Reduction and Student Achievement: The Potential Tradeoff between Teacher Quality and Class Size. J. Hum. Res. 44 (1), 223–250.
Kane, T.J., Staiger, D.O., 2008. Are Teacher-Level Value-Added Estimates Biased? An Experimental Validation of Non-Experimental Estimates. Harvard University (mimeo March).
Katz, L., Murphy, K., 1992. Changes in relative wages, 1963–1987: Supply and demand factors. Quarterly Journal of Economics 107, 35–78.
Keane Michael, P., Wolpin, K.I., 1997. The Career Decisions of Young Men. The Journal of Political Economy 105 (3), 473–522.
Kennan, J., Walker, J.R., 2009. The Effect of Expected Income on Individual Migration Decisions. University of Wisconsin working paper.
Kitagawa, T., 2010. Testing for Instrument Independence in the Selection Model. CEMMAP working paper, February 2010.
Konstantopoulos, S., 2008. Do Small Classes Reduce the Achievement Gap Between Low and High Achievers, Evidence from Project STAR? Elementary School Journal 108, 275–291.
Krueger, A.B., 1999. Experimental Estimates Of Education Production Functions. The Quarterly Journal of Economics 114 (2), 497–532.
Lazear, E., 2001. Educational Production. Quarterly Journal of Economics 116 (3), 777–803.
Lee, D., 2005. An Estimable Dynamic General Equilibrium Model of Work, Schooling and Occupational Choice. International Economic Review 46, 1–34.
Lee, D., Wolpin, K., 2006. Intersectoral Labor Mobility and the Growth of the Service Sector. Econometrica 47, 1–46.
Lerman, S., Manski, C., 1981. On the Use of Simulated Frequencies to Approximate Choice Probabilities. In: Manski, C., McFadden, D. (Eds.), Structural Analysis of Discrete Data with Econometric Applications. MIT Press, Cambridge, pp. 305–319.
Magnac, T., Thesmar, D., 2002. Identifying Dynamic Discrete Decision Processes. Econometrica 70 (2), 801–816.
Manski, C., 1994. The Selection Problem. In: Sims, C. (Ed.), Advances in Econometrics, Sixth World Congress1, Cambridge University Press, Cambridge, U.K., pp. 143–170, [327,329,331].
Manski, C., Pepper, J., 2000. Monotone Instrumental Variables: With Application to the Returns to Schooling. Econometrica 68, 997–1010, [327,332].
McFadden, D., 1989. Method of Simulated Moments for Estimation of Discrete Response Models Without Numerical Integration. Econometrica 57 (5), 995–1026.
McKee, G., Rivkin, S., Sims, K.R.E., 2010. Disruption, Achievement and the Heterogeneous Benefits of Smaller Classes. NBER working paper number.
Meghir, C., Palme, M., 2005. Educational Reform, Ability, and Family Background. Am. Econ. Rev. 95 (1), 414–424.
Meghir, C., 2006. Dynamic Models for Policy Evaluation. In: Blundell, R., Newey, W.K., Persson, T. (Eds.), Advances in economics and econometrics: theory and applications, 9th World Congress of the Econometric Society. UCL, London.
Mincer, J., 1958. Investment in Human Capital and Personal Income Distribution. Journal of Political Economy 66 (4), 281–302.
Mincer, J., 1974. Schooling, Experience, and Earnings. NBER Press, New York.
Morris, C., 1983. Parametric Empirical Bayes Inference: Theory and Applications (with discussion). Journal of the American Statistical Association 78, 47–65.
Neal, D., 1997. The Effects of Catholic Secondary Schooling on Educational Achievement. Journal of Labor Economics, Part 1 15 (1), 98–123.

Nerlove, M., 1971. Further evidence on the estimation of dynamic economic relations from a time series of cross sections. Econometrica 39 (2), 359–382.

Newey, W., Powell, J., 2003. Instrumental Variable Estimation of Nonparametric Models. Econometrica 71 (5), 1565–1578.

Newey, W., Powell, J., Vella, F., 1999. Nonparametric Estimation of Triangular Simultaneous Equations Models. Econometrica 67 (3), 565–603.

Nickell, S., 1981. Biases in dynamic models with Fixed effects. Econometrica 49 (6), 1417–1426.

Pakes, A., Pollard, R., 1989. The Asymptotic Distribution of Simulation Experiments. Econometrica 57, 1027–1057.

Pong, S., Pallas, A.M., 2001. Class Size and Eighth-Grade Math Achievement in the United States and Abroad. Educational Evaluation & Policy Analysis 23 (3), 251–273.

Raudenbush, S.W., Bryk, A.S., 2002. Hierarchical linear models: Applications and data analysis methods, second ed. Sage, Thousand Oaks, CA.

Rivkin, S.G., Hanushek, E.A., Kain, J.F., 2005. Teachers, schools, and academic achievement. Econometrica 73 (2), 417–458.

Robert, C.P., Casella, G., 1999. Monte Carlo Statistical Methods. Springer Verlag, New York.

Rockoff, J.E., 2004. The impact of individual teachers on student achievement: Evidence from panel data. Am. Econ. Rev. 94 (2), 247–252.

Rothstein, J., 2009. Student sorting and bias in value added estimation: Selection on observables and unobservables. NBER Working Paper number 14666.

Roy, A.D., 1951. Some Thoughts on the Distribution of Earnings. Oxford Economic Papers, New Series 3 (2), 135–146.

Rust, J., 1987. Optimal Replacement of GMC Bus Engines: An Empirical Model of Harold Zurcher. Econometrica 55, 999–1033.

Rust, J., 1994. Structural Estimation of Markov Decision Processes. In: Engle, R., McFadden, D. (Eds.), Handbook of Econometrics 4, North Holland, Amsterdam, pp. 3081–3143.

Staiger, D., Stock, J.H., 1997. Instrumental Variables Regression with Weak Instruments. Econometrica 65 (3), 557–586.

Straszheim, M., 1987. The Theory of Urban Residential Location. In: Mills, E.S. (Ed.), Handbook of Regional and Urban Economics. North-Holland, Amsterdam, pp. 717–757.

Su, C., Judd, K., 2008. Constrained Optimisation Approaches to Estimation of Structural Models. Mimeo Stanford.

Theil, H., 1954. Linear Aggregation of Economic Relations. North Holland Publishing Co.

Tiebout, C.M., 1956. A Pure Theory of Local Expenditures. The Journal of Political Economy 64 (5) (Oct.), 416–424.

Todd Petra, E., Wolpin, K.I., 2003. On the Specification and Estimation of the Production Function for Cognitive Achievement. Economic Journal F3–F33.

Vytlacil, E., 2002. Independence, Monotonicity, and Latent Index Models: An Equivalence Result. Econometrica 70 (1), 331–341.

Vytlacil, E.J., 2006. Ordered Discrete-Choice Selection Models and Local Average Treatment Effect Assumptions: Equivalence, Nonequivalence, and Representation Results. Rev. Econ. Stat. 88 (3), 578–581.

Wildasin, D.E., 1987. Theoretical Analysis of Local Public Economics. In: Mills, E.S. (Ed.), Handbook of Regional and Urban Economics. North-Holland, Amsterdam, pp. 1131–1178.

Willis, R., Rosen, S., 1979. Education and Self Selection. Journal of Political Economy 87, S7–S36.

Wolpin, K.I., 1992. The Determinants of Black-White Differences in Early Employment Careers: Search, Layoffs, Quits and Endogenous Wage Growth. Journal of Political Economy 100 (3), 535–560.

CHAPTER 2

The Economics of International Differences in Educational Achievement☆

Eric A. Hanushek* and Ludger Woessmann[†]

*Stanford University, University of Texas at Dallas, NBER, and CESifo
[†]University of Munich, Ifo Institute for Economic Research, CESifo, and IZA

Contents

1. Introduction	91
1.1 Unique advantages of cross-country data on cognitive skills	93
1.2 Concerns with the use of cross-country data on cognitive skills	94
1.3 Scope of this analysis	95
2. Economic Motivation	96
3. International Tests of Educational Achievement	98
3.1 Overview of available international testing and participation	98
3.2 Validity of international sampling and testing	105
4. Determinants of International Educational Achievement	111
4.1 International evidence on education production functions	111
4.2 Student and family background	116
4.3 School inputs	126
4.3.1 Evidence across countries	126
4.3.2 Evidence within different countries	132
4.4 Institutions	138
4.4.1 Accountability	139
4.4.2 Autonomy	146
4.4.3 Competition from private schools	148
4.4.4 Tracking	153
4.4.5 Preprimary education system	157
4.4.6 Additional results	158
4.5 Conclusions on the determinants of international educational achievement	158
5. Economic Consequences of International Educational Achievement	160
5.1 Cognitive skills and individual labor-market outcomes	160
5.2 Cognitive skills and the distribution of economic outcomes	168

We are grateful to participants at the Handbook of the Economics of Education conference at CESifo in Munich in September 2009 for valuable discussion and comments. Woessmann gratefully acknowledges the support and hospitality provided by the W. Glenn Campbell and Rita Ricardo-Campbell National Fellowship of the Hoover Institution, Stanford University, as well as support by the Pact for Research and Innovation of the Leibniz Association. Hanushek has been supported by the Packard Humanities Institute. Lukas Haffert provided capable research assistance.

    5.3 Cognitive skills and macroeconomic growth ... 171
        5.3.1 Aggregate measures of cognitive skills ... 172
        5.3.2 Evidence on the role of cognitive skills in economic growth ... 174
        5.3.3 Causation in a cross-country framework ... 182
        5.3.4 Expanding country samples by regional tests from developing countries ... 184
        5.3.5 Basic skills, top performance, and growth ... 187
        5.3.6 IQ models ... 187
    5.4 Conclusions on the economic impact of differences in cognitive skills ... 190
6. Conclusion and Outlook ... 191
References ... 192

Abstract

An emerging economic literature over the past decade has made use of international tests of educational achievement to analyze the determinants and impacts of cognitive skills. The cross-country comparative approach provides a number of unique advantages over national studies: It can exploit institutional variation that does not exist within countries; draw on much larger variation than usually available within any country; reveal whether any result is country-specific or more general; test whether effects are systematically heterogeneous in different settings; circumvent selection issues that plague within-country identification by using system-level aggregated measures; and uncover general-equilibrium effects that often elude studies in a single country. The advantages come at the price of concerns about the limited number of country observations, the cross-sectional character of most available achievement data, and possible bias from unobserved country factors like culture.

This chapter reviews the economic literature on international differences in educational achievement, restricting itself to comparative analyses that are not possible within single countries and placing particular emphasis on studies trying to address key issues of empirical identification. While quantitative input measures show little impact, several measures of institutional structures and of the quality of the teaching force can account for significant portions of the large international differences in the level and equity of student achievement. Variations in skills measured by the international tests are in turn strongly related to individual labor-market outcomes and, perhaps more importantly, to cross-country variations in economic growth.

JEL classification: I20, O40, O15, H40, H52, J24, J31, P50

Keywords

Human Capital
Cognitive Skills
International Student Achievement Tests
Education Production Function

"If custom and law define what is educationally allowable within a nation, the educational systems beyond one's national boundaries suggest what is educationally possible."
        Arthur W. Foshay (1962) on the first pilot study of international student achievement

1. INTRODUCTION

Virtually all nations of the world today realize the research and policy value of student performance data that come from testing the cognitive skills of students. While there is wide variation across nations in testing—differing by subject matter, grade level, purpose, and quality of testing—the idea of assessing what students know as opposed to how long they have been in school has diffused around the world, in part at the instigation of international development and aid agencies. Somewhat less known is that comparative cross-national testing has been going on for a long time. Nations participated in common international assessments of mathematics and science long before they instituted national testing programs. These common international assessments provide unique data for understanding both the importance of various factors determining achievement and the impact of skills on economic and social outcomes.

International consortia were formed in the mid-1960s to develop and implement comparisons of educational achievement across nations. Since then, the math, science, and reading performance of students in many countries have been tested on multiple occasions using (at each occasion) a common set of test questions in all participating countries. By 2010, three major international testing programs are surveying student performance on a regular basis: the Programme for International Student Assessment (PISA) testing math, science, and reading performance of 15-year-olds on a three-year cycle since 2000, the Trends in International Mathematics and Science Study (TIMSS) testing math and science performance (mostly) of eighth-graders on a four-year cycle since 1995, and the Progress in International Reading Literacy Study (PIRLS) testing primary-school reading performance on a five-year cycle since 2001. In addition, regional testing programs have produced comparable performance information for many countries in Latin America and Sub-Saharan Africa, and international adult literacy surveys have produced internationally comparable data on the educational achievement of adults.

In a variety of cases, these international assessments actually substitute for national testing. The international testing provides information on educational outcomes where otherwise only small, unrepresentative samples of outcome data are available. Indeed, the simplest of international comparisons has spurred not only governmental attention but also immense public interest as is vividly documented by the regular vigorous news coverage and public debate of the outcomes of the international achievement tests in many of the participating countries. For example, the results of the first PISA study made headlines on the front pages of tabloids and more serious newspapers alike: the *Frankfurter Allgemeine Zeitung* (Dec. 4, 2001) in Germany titled "Abysmal marks for German students", *Le Monde* (Dec. 5, 2001) in France titled "France, the mediocre student of the OECD class", and *The Times* (Dec. 6, 2001) in England titled "Are we not such dunces after all?"

These international assessments, which are generally embedded within a larger survey of individual and school attributes, are ultimately valuable in providing direct measures of human capital. The idea that individual skills are important in a wide variety of economic and social circumstances is generally captured under the blanket term of human capital. Since the influential work of Schultz (1961), Becker (1964), and Mincer (1970), the concept of human capital has pervaded many economic analyses.[1] But the challenge has consistently been to find explicit measures that could be used in empirical analysis. Simply identifying, for example, differences in the labor-market outcomes for individuals as human capital does not provide a useful empirical structure. The invention of Mincer (1970, 1974) was to pursue the empirical power of defining human capital in terms of school attainment, an easily measured factor that almost certainly related to skill development and human capital. This idea has subsequently dominated most thinking about human capital such that school attainment is often taken virtually as a synonym for human capital.

The fundamental problem with this development is that it very frequently ignores other elements of skill development that will generally be related to school attainment. For example, a large body of work, generally under the rubric of educational production functions, focuses on the concomitant influence of families in the skill development of children. Moreover, much of the concern about governmental investments in schooling, particularly in developed countries, focuses on issues of differential quality. Both of these factors and other omitted elements are very likely to be related to the school attainment of individuals.[2] While there has been considerable research aimed at getting consistent estimates of the rate of return to school attainment, little of this has addressed issues of systematic omitted determinants of human capital.[3]

Much of our motivation for the analysis described in this paper comes from the conclusion that cognitive skills, identified by test scores such as those incorporated into the international assessments, are good measures of relevant skills for human capital. Thus, in looking at the impacts of human capital on economic outcomes, instead of attempting to identify all of the relevant determinants of differences in individual or aggregate skills, we simply begin with measures of cognitive skills as our indication of human capital. Along the way, however, we also discuss the alternatives to this along with providing evidence about the appropriateness of different measures.

The research based on the international assessments goes in two different directions: research designed to understand the underlying determinants of cognitive skills and

---

[1] As traced by Kiker (1968), the antecedents of human capital analysis go much farther back including Petty (1676 [1899]) and Smith ([1776] 1979), but the idea went dormant with the arguments against it at the beginning of the twentieth century by Alfred Marshall (1898).

[2] For general discussions of these issues, see Hanushek (2002) and Hanushek and Woessmann (2008). For the quality-attainment relationship, see Hanushek, Lavy, and Hitomi (2008).

[3] For an evaluation of alternative approaches to estimation of returns to schooling, see Card (1999, 2001). The interpretation of such estimates as an internal rate of return is discussed in Heckman, Lochner, and Todd (2006, 2008). The more general interpretation of the determinants of human capital is found in Hanushek and Woessmann (2008) and Hanushek and Zhang (2009) along with the discussion below.

research focused on the consequences of skill differences. Our purpose here is to review and evaluate both lines of research employing international assessments. While generally not appreciated, perhaps because of the recent upsurge in work, an extensive body of research exploiting the international dimensions of these assessments has already accumulated.

1.1 Unique advantages of cross-country data on cognitive skills

International achievement data, developed and refined over the past half century, were not collected to support any specific economic research agenda. But, as we shall discuss below, there are a number of research and policy agendas that are uniquely amenable to analysis because of the existence of such data. Indeed, it is somewhat peculiar to have a handbook chapter focus on specific data as opposed to issues of economic methodology or substantive research and policy areas. We argue, however, that such data have made it possible for economists to address a range of fundamental questions that previously resisted satisfactory analysis. And, because the extent and nature of international achievement data still remain largely unknown, it is important to evaluate the advantages and disadvantages of these data in understanding a variety of significant research and policy questions.

In terms of understanding the determinants of educational achievement, the international data have at least six unique advantages over research restricted to single countries or states. First, the data permit exploitation of variation that only exists across countries. For example, systematic institutional variation between countries as found with differences in the competitiveness and flexibility of teacher labor markets, forms of accountability systems, the extent of a private school sector, or the structure of student tracking simply does not exist within most countries. Or, the existence of central exit exams is a national characteristic in nearly all countries, so that the effect of central exams cannot be estimated using national data in these countries unless their status changes over time. The lack of within-country institutional variation makes an empirical identification of the impact of many institutional features of school systems impossible when using national datasets.

Second, even where within-country variation exists, variations across countries in key institutional factors and in characteristics of the schools and population are frequently much larger than those found within any country. From an analytical viewpoint, using such international variation generally implies increased statistical power to detect the impact of specific factors on student outcomes.

Third, the international achievement data based on the same data collection process provides an opportunity to examine comparable estimates of the determinants and consequences of educational achievement for a diverse set of countries. Such research can thus throw light on whether a result is truly country-specific, applies more generally, or is simply a spurious result from a particular within-country sample.

Fourth, and related to the previous point, international evidence can identify systematic heterogeneity in effects that differ across countries. For example, such comparative research can delve into why class-size effects on achievement are heterogeneous across countries, perhaps leading to deeper insights about, say, the interaction between curriculum or teacher training and classroom processes.

Fifth, even where within-country variation exists, for example, in the case of public and private schools operating within the same system, comparisons of student achievement are often subject to severe selection problems. Students who choose to attend a private school may differ along both observable and unobservable dimensions from students taught in neighborhood public schools. While it is possible to control for some differences in student, family, and school characteristics when estimating the effects of institutional structures, thereby comparing students who are observationally equivalent, such estimates may still suffer from selection on unobserved characteristics. By aggregating the institutional variables to the country level, it is possible to circumvent these selection problems—in effect measuring the impact of, for example, the share of students in a country attending private schools on student achievement in the country as a whole. Such cross-country evidence will not be biased by standard issues of selection at the individual level.

Sixth, uncovering general equilibrium effects is often impossible in a single country but sometimes feasible across countries. For example, the presence of private schools may influence the behavior of nearby public schools with which they compete for students. As a result, simple comparisons of private and public schools may miss an important part of the effects of greater private involvement in education. Aggregated measures of the institutional feature can solve the problem: By comparing the average performance of systems with larger and smaller shares of private schools, the cross-country approach captures any systemic effect of competition from private schools.

Research into the consequences of differences in cognitive skills has similar advantages. For example, while the implications of human capital development for macroeconomic outcomes—including, importantly, economic growth—can potentially be investigated with time-series data for individual countries, historical data are effectively limited to school attainment with no information on the cognitive skills that we emphasize here. On the other hand, variations in cognitive skills across different economies can, as we describe below, effectively get at such fundamental questions. Similarly, investigating whether features of the structure of economic activity affect the individual returns to skills is very difficult within a single economy with interlocking labor and product markets.

1.2 Concerns with the use of cross-country data on cognitive skills

With these research advantages also come concerns and disadvantages. Three stand out. First, the relevant variations are frequently limited by the number of countries with both assessment and other common data. Second, even though each of the assessments collects substantial amounts of ancillary survey information at the individual level, virtually all are single cross-sectional designs with no ability to track individuals.[4] Third, there is frequently a concern that unmeasured "cultural" factors are important in various processes of interest. Each of these make the identification and estimation of cross-country models difficult and limit the range of analyses currently possible.

Further, while not specific to this cross-country work, some inherently difficult data and modeling problems also remain. The focus of this chapter is measures of educational achievement—skills that are expressed in test scores—rather than quantitative measures of educational attainment. For reasons of availability, the focus of our skill measurement is just on cognitive skills, opening up possible concerns about other skills such as noncognitive skills. The systematic measurement of such skills has yet to be possible in international comparisons. Furthermore, the research covered refers to basic general skills that are generally learned through the end of secondary school, leaving aside programs of higher education and specific vocational skills. Apart from data availability, this focus is also dictated by a need for international comparability where measures of any quality aspects of higher education are generally unavailable.[5]

1.3 Scope of this analysis

The standards of evidence throughout empirical economics have changed in recent years, sometimes dramatically. The character of change also enters directly into our consideration of cross-country analyses. The analytical designs employed in the cross-country analyses we discuss have developed over time in a way that parallels much of the related micro-econometric work within individual countries. The initial publications of comparative tests across nations by the organizations that conducted the different studies tended to report bivariate associations. Subsequent analyses performed multiple regressions in the form of educational production functions and cross-country growth regressions that tried to address the most obvious perils of bias from intervening factors by adding corresponding control variables. While initial studies estimated international educational production functions at the aggregate country level, subsequent studies exploited the full variation of the international micro data.

---

[4] Recent work in a few countries has built within-country follow-ups into the PISA testing; see Section 5.1 below.
[5] A couple of attempts have been made to analyze differences among universities, but these are generally limited. There are academic rankings of the world's research universities by the Center for World-Class Universities, Shanghai Jiao Tong University, based on measures of university research (for 2010, see http://www.arwu.org/, accessed September 7, 2010). A 2007 professional ranking by the Ecole des Mines de Paris considered graduates who were CEOs at Global Fortune 500 countries (see http://www.ensmp.fr/Actualites/PR/EMP-ranking.html, accessed January 12, 2008). Neither would appear to provide very general measures of higher education outcomes in different countries, and each also is subject to the same concerns that human capital is developed in more places than just schools.

More recently, several studies have started to employ econometric techniques such as instrumental-variable, regression-discontinuity, differences-in-differences, and different sorts of fixed-effects specifications in order to come closer to identification of causal relationships in the international data on educational achievement. This applies both to the identification of causal effects within countries and to the challenge of overcoming possible bias from unobserved country heterogeneity—for example, in terms of cultural differences—in cross-country estimation. While these developments are far from complete at this time, we emphasize the issues of identification and interpretation in much of the discussion below.

We limit the coverage of this chapter to studies that make cross-country comparisons. Based on this criterion, we cover only studies that estimate the same specification for different countries or estimate a cross-country specification. Studies that use the international survey data for analysis within a single country will be referenced only insofar as they are directly relevant for the internationally comparative approach.

The next section provides a brief economic motivation to frame the subsequent discussions. Section 3 gives an overview and critical assessment of the different available international datasets on educational achievement. Section 4 surveys the literature on the determinants of international educational achievement, covering both evidence within different countries and evidence across countries and covering family background, school resources, and institutional structures as three groups of possible determinants. Section 5 surveys the literature on the economic consequences of international educational achievement, covering both individual labor-market outcomes and macroeconomic growth. The final section presents some overall conclusions along with a discussion of how the data and research could be improved.

2. ECONOMIC MOTIVATION

A wide variety of analyses motivate the discussions here. They are most easily described as models falling under the rubric of human capital, although that nomenclature has become so widely used that it does not provide any clear description.

In general terms, the literature reviewed in Section 5 considers economic outcomes as determined by human capital—or relevant skills—and a variety of other factors. The canonical case, which we deal with extensively here, is where the economic outcome is individual labor-market earnings. (More generally, relying on some underlying models of markets, earnings might reflect the productivity of individuals in that labor market). This simple view is expressed by:

$$O = \gamma H + X\beta + \varepsilon \tag{2.1}$$

where O is the outcome of interest, H is human capital, X is a vector of other determinants of the outcome, and ε is a stochastic term. In the standard labor-market view of earnings determination, everything is measured at the individual worker level, O is simply individual earnings, and X includes such things as labor-market experience of the worker, gender, and health status.

The empirical issue is how to measure human capital, or H. Almost without comment, it is now commonplace simply to substitute school attainment, S, for human capital and to proceed with estimation of the underlying model. This approach is reinforced by the ubiquitous availability of measures of school attainment, a common addition to population censuses, household surveys, and other specialized data collections in nations around the world.

Assuming that school attainment is a measure of human capital, however, requires a series of strong assumptions, ones that conflict with other well-developed lines of research. Most relevant, analyses of educational production functions have considered the outcomes of schools within a broader model of production. Specifically, these models identify skills as being affected by a range of factors including family inputs (F), the quality and quantity of inputs provided by schools (qS), individual ability (A), and other relevant factors (Z) which include labor-market experience, health, and so forth as in:

$$H = \lambda F + \phi(qS) + \eta A + \alpha Z + v \qquad (2.2)$$

The schooling term combines both school attainment (S) and its quality (q).

Human capital is, however, not directly observed. To be verifiable, it is necessary to specify the measurement of H. Estimating versions of Equation (2.2), the literature reviewed in Section 4 concentrates on the cognitive-skills component of human capital and considers measuring H with test-score measures of mathematics, science, and reading achievement. The use of measures of cognitive skills has a number of potential advantages. First, achievement captures variations in the knowledge and ability that schools strive to produce and thus relate the putative outputs of schooling to subsequent economic success. Second, by emphasizing total outcomes of education, these models incorporate skills from any source—families, schools, and ability. Third, by allowing for differences in performance among students with differing quality of schooling (but possibly the same quantity of schooling), they open the investigation of the importance of different policies designed to affect the quality aspects of schools.

The implications of this perspective for the estimation of Equation (2.1) are immediately obvious. Estimation that incorporated just school attainment (S) would yield biased estimates of the impact of human capital except in the most unlikely event that S is actually uncorrelated with the other determinants of skills.

The issues are perhaps most relevant when considering aggregate outcomes. In considering the impact of human capital on aggregate output or on economic growth, comparing a year of schooling across countries implies assuming that the learning per year is equivalent, say, from Hong Kong to South Africa. Few people would think that is a reasonable assumption.

We investigate the value of international measures of achievement for the analysis of both Equations (2.1) and (2.2). For some estimation and analysis, international data are clearly not needed. For example, the extensive study of educational production functions has for the most part been conducted entirely within countries. Our focus here is very specific. We wish to consider analyses that are not possible within single countries or that provide extended analytical possibilities when put in an international framework. For example, as we discuss later, a variety of educational institutions are constant within individual countries—such as the use of early tracking systems—and thus are not susceptible to analysis within individual countries. Alternatively, understanding differences in economic growth across countries requires reliable cross-country data.

3. INTERNATIONAL TESTS OF EDUCATIONAL ACHIEVEMENT

The beginning of international testing was a series of meetings in the late 1950s and early 1960s when a group of academics met to design an international testing program.[6] An exploratory study in testing mathematics, reading comprehension, geography, science, and nonverbal ability was conducted in 1959–1962 (cf. Foshay (1962)). This led to the first major international test in 1964 when 12 countries participated in the First International Mathematics Study (FIMS). This and a series of subsequent assessments were conducted in a set of nations voluntarily participating in a cooperative venture developed by the International Association for the Evaluation of Educational Achievement (IEA). The continuing IEA efforts have been more recently matched by an ongoing testing program from the Organisation for Economic Co-operation and Development (OECD).

3.1 Overview of available international testing and participation

These international testing programs, and related ones that we discuss below, are marked by some common elements. They involve a group of voluntarily participating countries that each pay for their participation and administer their own assessments (according to agreed-upon protocols and sampling schemes). Since they involve individual country policy decisions to participate, the set of participating countries has differed across time and even across subparts of specific testing occasions. Additionally, the different tests differ somewhat in their focus and intended subject matter. For example, the IEA tests, of which the most recent version is the Trends in International Mathematics and Science Study (TIMSS), are developed by international panels but are related to common elements of primary and secondary school curriculum, while the OECD tests (Programme in International Student Assessment, or PISA) are designed to measure more applied knowledge and skills.[7] The range of subject matters tested

---

[6] See "A Brief History of IEA" at http://www.iea.nl/brief_history_of_iea.html [accessed August 23, 2009].

[7] A separate analysis of coverage and testing can be found in Neidorf, Binkley, Gattis, and Nohara (2006).

varies across time, with assessments in math and science being supplemented by reading tests.[8] Third, until recent testing, little effort has been made to equate scores across time. Finally, the testing has been almost exclusively cross-sectional in nature, not following individual students' change in achievement.[9]

Along with the assessments of cognitive skills, extensive contextual information and student background data have been provided by related surveys. The motivation for this is using the international databases to address a variety of policy issues relevant to the participating countries.

The IEA and OECD tests have the broadest coverage and have also adapted regular testing cycles. Table 2.1 provides an account of their major international tests with an indication of age (or grade level) of testing, subject matter, and participating countries. By 2007, there were 15 testing occasions, most of which include subparts based upon subject and grade level.[10]

The major IEA and OECD testing programs have expanded dramatically in terms of participating countries. While only 29 countries participated in these testing programs through 1990, a total of 96 countries had participated by 2007. Three additional countries participated in 2009, and another three additional countries plan to participate in 2011, raising the total number of countries ever participating in one of these international tests to 102. Only the United States participated in all 15 testing occasions, but an additional 17 countries participated in 10 or more different assessments. Figure 2.1 shows the histogram of participation on the IEA or OECD tests between 1964 and 2007, divided by OECD and other countries. From this figure, it is clear that the depth of coverage is much greater for developed than for developing countries. Further, much of the participation in one or two different test administrations occurs after 2000. On the other hand, those countries participating eight or more times have now accumulated some information on intertemporal patterns of performance with testing going back to the early 1990s or before.

At the same time, a number of more idiosyncratic tests, some on a regional basis, have also been developed. These tests have been more varied in their focus, development, and quality. And they have in general been used much less frequently in analytical work. Table 2.2 provides basic information on these additional assessments, although most of the remaining portion of this chapter concentrates on the information

---

[8] There have also been some other studies of foreign languages, civic education, and information technology. These have involved smaller samples of countries and in general have not been repeated over time. We do not include these in our discussions, in part because they have not been analyzed very much.

[9] The Second International Mathematics Study (SIMS) of the IEA did have a one-year follow-up of individual students that permitted some longitudinal, panel information, but this design was not repeated. Recent innovations have permitted development of panel data by individual countries.

[10] See Mullis, Martin, Kennedy, and Foy (2007), Mullis, Martin, and Foy (2008), and Organisation for Economic Co-operation and Development (2007) for details on the most recent cycle of the three major ongoing international testing cycles.

Table 2.1 International Tests of Educational Achievement: IEA and OECD Student Achievement Tests

	Abbr.	Study	Year	Region	Subject	Age[a,b]	Countries[c]	Organiz.[d]	Scale[e]
1	FIMS	First International Mathematics Study	1964	World	Math	13,FS	11	IEA	PC
2	FISS	First International Science Study	1970–71	World	Science	10,14,FS	14,16,16	IEA	PC
3	FIRS	First International Reading Study	1970–72	World	Reading	13	12	IEA	PC
4	SIMS	Second International Mathematics Study	1980–82	World	Math	13,FS	17,12	IEA	PC
5	SISS	Second International Science Study	1983–84	World	Science	10,13,FS	15,17,13	IEA	PC
6	SIRS	Second International Reading Study	1990–91	World	Reading	9,13	26,30	IEA	IRT
7	TIMSS	Third International Mathematics and Science Study	1994–95	World	Math/Science	9(3+4), 13(7+8),FS	25,39,21	IEA	IRT
8	TIMSS-Repeat	TIMSS-Repeat	1999	World	Math/Science	13(8)	38	IEA	IRT
9	PISA 2000/02	Programme for International Student Assessment	2000+02	World	Math/Science/Reading	15	31+10	OECD	IRT
10	PIRLS	Progress in International Reading Literacy Study	2001	World	Reading	9(4)	34	IEA	IRT
11	TIMSS 2003	Trends in Internat. Mathematics and Science Study	2003	World	Math/Science	9(4),13(8)	24,45	IEA	IRT

12	PISA 2003	Programme for International Student Assessment	2003	World	Math/Science/Reading	15	40	OECD	IRT
13	PIRLS 2006	Progress in International Reading Literacy Study	2006	World	Reading	9(4)	39	IEA	IRT
14	PISA 2006	Programme for International Student Assessment	2006	World	Math/Science/Reading	15	57	OECD	IRT
15	TIMSS 2007	Trends in Internat. Mathematics and Science Study	2007	World	Math/Science	9(4), 13(8)	35, 48	IEA	IRT

Notes:
[a] Grade in parentheses where grade level was target population.
[b] FS = final year of secondary education (differs across countries).
[c] Number of participating countries that yielded internationally comparable performance data.
[d] Conducting organization: International Association for the Evaluation of Educational Achievement (IEA); Organisation for Economic Co-operation and Development (OECD).
[e] Test scale: percent-correct format (PC); item-response-theory proficiency scale (IRT).

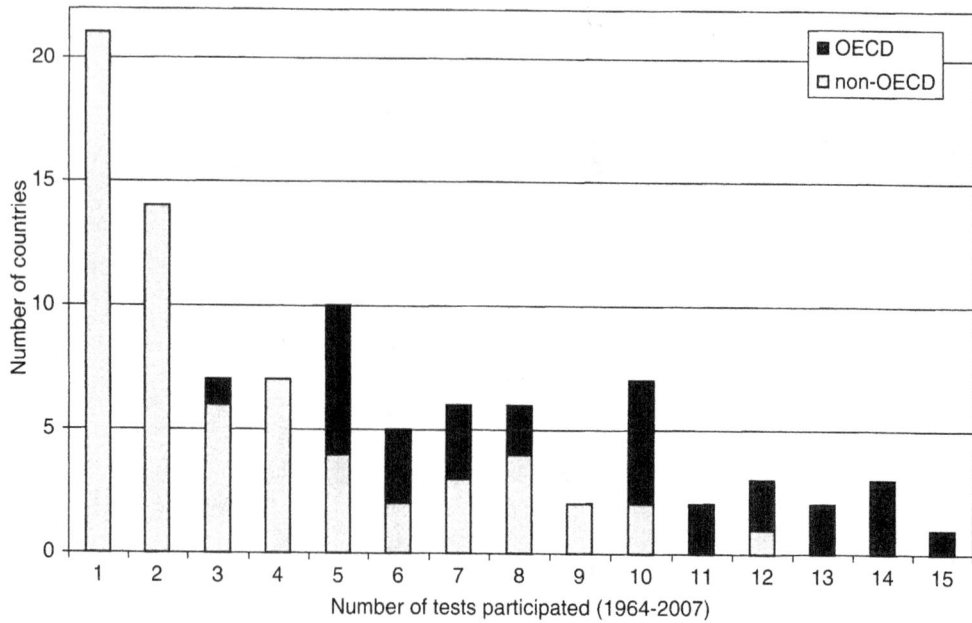

Figure 2.1 Participation in international student achievement tests of IEA and OECD through 2007. Notes: Number of tests in which a country has participated in the following 15 IEA and OECD tests: FIMS, FISS, FIRS, SIMS, SISS, SIRS, TIMSS, TIMSS-Repeat, PISA 2000/02, PIRLS, TIMSS 2003, PISA 2003, PIRLS 2006, PISA 2006, TIMSS 2007. Total number of participating countries: 96.

from tests in Table 2.1. Of the 10 additional testing occasions, six are regional tests for Latin America (ECIEL, LLECE, SERCE) or Africa (SACMEQ I and II, PASEC). As discussed below, the IEA and OECD tests may be too difficult for many students in the developing countries of Latin America and Africa, thus providing unreliable information about performance variations. These regional examinations use tests that are more appropriate to the countries of the region.

The remaining assessments and surveys cover a broader set of countries but are somewhat different in focus from those in Table 2.1. The International Assessment of Educational Progress (IAEP) I and II are tests constructed to mirror the National Assessment of Educational Progress (NAEP) that has been used in the United States since 1970 and that aligns to the United States school curriculum, a design that may limit international comparability. The International Adult Literacy Survey (IALS) and the Adult Literacy and Life Skills Survey (ALLS) have a very different structure involving sampling of adults in the workforce.[11] The IALS survey data in particular have been

---

[11] The OECD has currently also embarked on a new endeavor, the Programme for the International Assessment of Adult Competencies (PIAAC), which will update and expand the adult testing, in terms of both the scope of the test and the number of participating countries. This assessment is scheduled to be administered in 2011.

Table 2.2 International Tests of Educational Achievement: Additional Testing

	Abbr.	Study	Year	Region	Subject	Age[a,b]	Countries[c]	Organiz.[d]	Scale[e]
1	ECIEL	Programa de Estudios Conjuntos para la Integración Económica Latinoamericana	1975–76	Latin America	Reading/ Science	(1, 4, 6, FS)	7	ECIEL	PC
2	IAEP-I	International Assessment of Educational Progress I	1988	OECD	Math/ Science	13	6	IAEP	PC
3	IAEP-II	International Assessment of Educational Progress II	1990–91	World	Math/ Science	10,14/ 9,13	13,19/13,18	IAEP	PC
4	IALS	International Adult Literacy Survey	1994–98	World	Prose/ Document/ Quantitative Literacy	16–65	20	OECD	IRT
5	SACMEQ I	Southern and Eastern Africa Consortium for Monitoring Educational Quality	1995–98	Southern and Eastern Africa	Math/ Reading	(6)	7	IIEP/ SACMEQ	IRT
6	PASEC	Programme d'Analyse des Systèmes Educatifs des Pays de la CONFENEM	1996+98 +2001	Francophone Sub-Saharan Africa	Math/ Reading	(2),(5)	6	CONFE- NEM	PC
7	LLECE	Primer Estudio Internacional Comparativo	1997	Latin America	Math/ Reading	(3),(4)	11	LLECE	IRT

Continued

Table 2.2 International Tests of Educational Achievement: Additional Testing—cont'd

	Abbr.	Study	Year	Region	Subject	Age[a,b]	Countries[c]	Organiz.[d]	Scale[e]
8	SACMEQ II	Southern and Eastern Africa Consortium for Monitoring Educational Quality	1999–2004	Southern and Eastern Africa	Math/ Reading	(6)	14	SACMEQ /IIEP	IRT
9	ALLS	Adult Literacy and Life Skills Survey	2002–06	OECD	Prose/ Document Literacy/ Numeracy	16–65	5	OECD	IRT
10	SERCE	Segundo Estudio Regional Comparativo Explicativo	2006	Latin America	Math/ Science/ Reading	(3),(6)/ (6)/(3),(6)	16/9/16	LLECE	IRT

Notes:

[a] Grade in parentheses where grade level was target population.
[b] FS = final year of secondary education (differs across countries).
[c] Number of participating countries that yielded internationally comparable performance data.
[d] Conducting organization: Estudos Conjuntos de Integração Ecônomica da América Latina (ECIEL); International Assessment of Educational Progress (IAEP); Organisation for Economic Co-operation and Development (OECD); UNESCO International Institute for Educational Planning (IIEP); Southern and Eastern Africa Consortium for Monitoring Educational Quality (SACMEQ); Conférence des Ministres de l'Éducation des Pays ayant le Français en Partage (CONFENEM); Laboratorio Latinoamericano de Evaluación de la Calidad de la Educación (LLECE).
[e] Test scale: percent-correct format (PC); item-response-theory proficiency scale (IRT).

used in a variety of studies about the consequences of education and cognitive skills (and will be discussed below in that context).

Given the different test designs, can results be compared across countries? And can the different tests be aggregated? Interestingly, the TIMSS tests with their curricular focus and the PISA tests with their real-world application focus are highly correlated at the country level. For example, the simple correlations between the TIMSS 2003 tests of 8th graders and the PISA 2003 tests of 15-year-olds across the 19 countries participating in both are 0.87 in math and 0.97 in science; they are 0.86 in both math and science across the 21 countries participating both in the TIMSS 1999 tests and the PISA 2000/02 tests. There is also a high correlation at the country level between the curriculum-based student tests of TIMSS and the practical literacy adult examinations of IALS (Hanushek and Zhang (2009)). Tests with very different foci and perspectives tend to be highly related, suggesting that they are measuring a common dimension of skills (see also Brown, Micklewright, Schnepf, and Waldmann (2007)). As discussed below, the consistency lends support to aggregating different student tests for each country in order to develop comparable achievement measures. It is also encouraging when thinking of these tests as identifying fundamental skills included in "human capital."

As an example of the different international tests, Table 2.3 provides comparative information on country performance on the major worldwide tests of math at the lower secondary level. The more recent tests have been normed to have a mean of 500 and standard deviation of 100. But, because the group of countries going into the norm differs and because there is no attempt to equate scores across time, it is not possible to say that a country with an average of 510 in one year and 515 in another has improved or not. We return to this issue below.

3.2 Validity of international sampling and testing

The available international tests of educational achievement are not without criticism. In particular, despite the stringent technical standards and extensive efforts of quality assurance by the international testing organizations (e.g., Organisation for Economic Co-operation and Development (2009)), in principle differences in sample selectivity across countries clearly have the potential to undermine the validity of specific country rankings on the tests. While critics of international educational comparisons argue that results may be influenced by differences in the extent to which countries adequately sample their entire student populations (e.g., Rotberg (1995); Prais (2003)), others disagree with the view that sample selection is a major source of bias in international achievement comparisons (e.g., Baker (1997); Adams (2003)).

In any case, the extent to which such sample selection affects results of econometric analyses that use the international test score data (rather than just leading to mismeasurement of country mean performance) depends on whether it is idiosyncratic or

Table 2.3 Performance on Selected International Student Achievement Tests

Code	Country	FIMS 1964	SIMS 1980–82	TIMSS 1995	TIMSS-Repeat 99	PISA 2000/02	TIMSS 2003	PISA 2003	PISA 2006	TIMSS 2007	Adjusted average[a]
ALB	Albania					381					378.5
DZA	Algeria									387	
ARG	Argentina					388			381		392.0
ARM	Armenia						478			499	442.9
AUS	Australia	27.0		530	525	533	505	524	520	496	509.4
AUT	Austria			539		515		506	505		508.9
AZE	Azerbaijan								476		
BHR	Bahrain						401			398	411.4
BEL	Belgium	43.4	52.8	546	558	520	537	529	520		504.1
BIH	Bosnia and Herzegovina									456	
BWA	Botswana						366			364	357.5
BRA	Brazil					334		356	370		363.8
BGR	Bulgaria			540	511	430	476		413	464	478.9
CAN	Canada		50.9	527	531	533	532	532	527		503.8
CHL	Chile				392	384	387		411		404.9
CHN	China										493.9
COL	Colombia			385					370	380	415.2
HRV	Croatia								467		
CYP	Cyprus			474	476		459			465	454.2
CZE	Czech Rep.			564	520	498		516	510	504	510.8
DNK	Denmark			502		514		514	513		496.2
EGY	Egypt						406			391	403.0
SLV	El Salvador									340	
EST	Estonia						531		515		519.2
FIN	Finland	37.7	48.2		520	536		544	548		512.6

Code	Country										
FRA	France	30.0					511	496		504.0
GEO	Georgia	53.5	538		517				410	
DEU	Germany	36.3	509		490		503	504		495.6
GHA	Ghana					276			309	360.3
GRC	Greece		484		447	586	445	459		460.8
HKG	Hong Kong–China	49.9	588	582	560		550	547	572	519.5
HUN	Hungary	54.6	537	532	488	529	490	491	517	504.5
ISL	Iceland		487		514		515	506		493.6
IND	India									428.1
IDN	Indonesia			403	367	411	360	391	397	388.0
IRN	Iran, Islamic Rep.		428	422		411			403	421.9
IRL	Ireland		527		503		503	501		499.5
ISR	Israel	45.6	522	466	433	496	466	442	463	468.6
ITA	Italy			479	457	484		462	480	475.8
JPN	Japan	63.5	605	579	557	570	534	523	570	531.0
JOR	Jordan			428		424		384	427	426.4
KAZ	Kazakhstan									
KOR	Korea, Rep.		607	587	547	589	542	547	597	533.8
KWT	Kuwait		392						354	404.6
KGZ	Kyrgyzstan							311		
LVA	Latvia		493	505	463	508	483	486		480.3
LBN	Lebanon					433			449	395.0
LIE	Liechtenstein				514		536	525		512.8
LTU	Lithuania	37.9	477	482		502		486	506	477.9
LUX	Luxembourg				446		493	490		464.1
MAC	Macao–China						527	525		526.0
MKD	Macedonia			447	381	435				415.1
MYS	Malaysia			519		508			474	483.8
MLT	Malta								488	

Continued

Table 2.3 Performance on Selected International Student Achievement Tests—cont'd

Code	Country	FIMS 1964	SIMS 1980–82	TIMSS 1995	TIMSS-Repeat 99	PISA 2000/02	TIMSS 2003	PISA 2003	PISA 2006	TIMSS 2007	Adjusted average[a]
MEX	Mexico					387		385	406		399.8
MDA	Moldova, Rep.				469		460				453.0
MNE	Montenegro								399		
MAR	Morocco				337		387			381	332.7
NLD	Netherlands	30.6	58.1	541	540		536	538	531		511.5
NZL	New Zealand		46.4	508	491	537	494	523	522		497.8
NGA	Nigeria		33.4								415.4
NOR	Norway			503		499	461	495	490	469	483.0
OMN	Oman									372	
PSE	Palestinian Nat. Auth.						390			367	406.2
PER	Peru					292					312.5
PHL	Philippines				345		378				364.7
POL	Poland					470		490	495		484.6
PRT	Portugal			454		454		466	466		456.4
QAT	Qatar								318	307	
ROU	Romania			482	472		475		415	461	456.2
RUS	Russian Fed.			535	526	478	508	468	476	512	492.2
SAU	Saudi Arabia						332			329	366.3
SRB	Serbia						477	437	435	486	444.7
SGP	Singapore			643	604		605			593	533.0
SVK	Slovak Rep.			547	534		508	498	492		505.2
SVN	Slovenia			541	530		493		504	501	499.3
ZAF	South Africa			354	275		264				308.9
ESP	Spain			487		476		485	480		482.9
SWZ	Swaziland		33.9								439.8
SWE	Sweden	21.9	43.5	519		510	499	509	502	491	501.3
CHE	Switzerland			545		529		527	530		514.2
SYR	Syrian Arab Rep.									395	

TWN	Taiwan (Chinese Taipei)			585		585	549	598	545.2
THA	Thailand	42.7	522	467	432	417	417	441	456.5
TUN	Tunisia			448		359	365	420	379.5
TUR	Turkey			429		423	424	432	412.8
UKR	Ukraine							462	
GBR	United Kingdom	32.9	502	496	529	498	495	500	495.0
USA	United States	25.4	500	502	493	504	474	508	490.3
URY	Uruguay						422	427	430.0
ZWE	Zimbabwe								410.7

Notes: All scores refer to the mathematics test in lower secondary school. (FIMS, SIMS: age 13; TIMSS: grade 8; PISA: age 15).
[a] Average score on all international tests 1964–2003 in math and science, primary through end of secondary school (Hanushek and Woessmann (2009a)).

systematic and on the extent to which it is correlated both with (conditional) outcomes and determinants of the analyses. If sample selectivity is idiosyncratic, it simply introduces classical measurement error that works against finding statistically significant associations.[12] The same is true if sample selectivity is persistent across time but orthogonal to the (conditional) variable whose association with test scores is of interest. Only if it is correlated with the error term of the estimation equation does systematic sample selectivity introduce bias to econometric analyses.[13]

In order to test the extent to which this is true, Hanushek and Woessmann (2010b) draw on detailed information about sampling quality provided in the more recent international tests and estimate whether international differences in sample selection affect the outcomes of typical economic analyses. They show that countries having more schools and students excluded from the targeted sample (e.g., because of intellectual or functional disabilities or limited proficiency in the test language), having schools and students who are less likely to participate in the test (e.g., because of unwillingness to participate or absence on the testing day), and having higher overall school enrollment at the relevant age level indeed tend to perform better on the international tests. However, accounting for this sample selectivity does not affect the results of standard growth regressions and education production functions. This finding implies that the international variation in selectivity of student samples is not systematically related to the associations of interest in the economic analyses reviewed in this chapter.

The tests included in our analyses have been devised in an international cooperative process between all participating countries with the intent of making the assessments independent of the culture or curriculum in any particular country. Yet, another criticism that is sometimes raised against international comparisons of student achievement is that test items may be culturally biased or inappropriate for specific participating countries (e.g., Hopmann, Brinek, and Retzl (2007)). Adams, Berezner, and Jakubowski (2010) show that overall country rankings are remarkably consistent when countries are compared using just those PISA-2006 items that representatives of each specific country had initially expressed to be of highest priority for inclusion, and presumably most appropriate for their own school system.[14]

---

[12] The importance of this will be lessened in applications that use averages of performance across several tests, since the error variance is reduced by averaging.

[13] Studies such as Hanushek and Woessmann (2009a) that include country fixed effects deal with possible bias from systematic sampling errors by removing time-invariant factors for each country. They also show that changes in enrollment rates over time are uncorrelated with trends in test scores, diluting worries that differential changes in enrollment bias the results of economic analyses using test scores.

[14] From the opposite perspective, the IAEP comparisons (not employed here) were built on tests directly taken from the assessments used in the United States, but the results from these comparisons did not alter the low ranking of U.S. students (see Lapointe, Mead, and Phillips (1989)).

The summary is that international testing is now well-established and broadly accepted. The assessments, particularly in Table 2.1, plus their corresponding survey information form the basis for the cross-country analyses discussed here.

4. DETERMINANTS OF INTERNATIONAL EDUCATIONAL ACHIEVEMENT

In reviewing the economic literature on international educational achievement, this section focuses on its determinants and the next section on its consequences. After a brief introduction to the estimation of international education production functions, this section covers student background, school inputs, and institutional structures of the education system as three groups of factors determining achievement. Note that the analysis is weighted toward developed countries, largely mirroring the time pattern of participation where developing countries have until very recently participated infrequently. At the same time, since most international analyses of the determination of achievement rely just on the cross-sectional data, it might be expected that this balance will change in the near future.

4.1 International evidence on education production functions

As is the case in the majority of the literature on educational production, the basic model underlying the literature on determinants of international educational achievement resembles some form of the education production function:

$$T = a_0 + a_1 F + a_2 R + a_3 I + a_4 A + e \qquad (2.3)$$

which basically is a version of our Equation (2.2) applied to students currently in school. Here, T is the outcome of the educational production process as measured, for example, by test scores of mathematics, science, and reading achievement. The vector F captures facets of student and family background characteristics, R is a vector of measures of school resources, I are institutional features of schools and education systems, and A is individual ability.

When estimating equation (2.3) within different countries, studies based on international data face the same methodological challenges as studies restricted to a specific country (see Hanushek (1979, 2002) and Todd and Wolpin (2003) for key issues in empirical identification of education production functions). The fundamental challenge is that most inputs in the education production function are likely not to be exogenous in a statistical sense. Leading concerns derive from omitted variables, sample selection, and reverse causation. An important example of an omitted variable is student ability A, most dimensions of which tend to go unmeasured and are likely correlated with other inputs in important ways. An additional concern for research on most of the international tests is their cross-sectional structure that does not allow for panel or value-added estimation, so that temporally prior inputs are usually unobserved. School inputs will often be the outcome of choices of parents, administrators, and schools that are correlated with the error term of the production function. The same is true for some institutional characteristics. Given this substantial scope for endogeneity bias, least-squares estimates of Equation (2.3) need to be interpreted with great care, even when they control for a large set of observable input factors. This has led to the development of more elaborate techniques that try to draw on exogenous variation in the variables of interest.

In the following review of the literature, we will refer to the more descriptive studies only briefly and mostly focus on studies trying to address the key identification issues. There is, however, one specific instance of making cross-country comparisons of estimates obtained from performing the same estimation in different countries worth noting: If one is willing to make the assumption that any bias is constant across countries, then a cross-country comparison of estimates is feasible, even if interpretation of the size of each estimate is not.

The main challenges change when it comes to studies estimating cross-country associations. As discussed in the introduction to this chapter, there are both unique advantages and specific concerns with using cross-country data to estimate the determinants of educational achievement. At the most general level, cross-country estimation is able to get around the most pressing concerns of bias from selection but introduces new kinds of omitted variable concerns. Within-country variation is often subject to severe selection problems: For example, students who choose to attend a private school may differ along both observable and unobservable dimensions from students taught in neighborhood public schools. While many observable characteristics are often controlled for in econometric analyses, thereby comparing students who are observationally equivalent, within-country estimates may still suffer from selection on unobserved characteristics.[15] In cross-country analyses, one can aggregate the institutional variable of interest up to the country level, thereby circumventing the selection problem. In effect, the cross-country analysis then measures the impact of, for example, the share of students in a country attending private schools on student achievement in the country as a whole. Such cross-country analysis cannot be biased by standard issues of selection at the individual level, as patterns of sorting cancel out at the system level.

The main cost to this—apart from the limited degrees of freedom at the country level—is that unobserved heterogeneity at the country level may introduce new forms of omitted variable bias. For example, cultural factors such as "Asian values" may remain unobserved in the econometric model and correlate both with student outcomes and relevant inputs in the education production function. Education systems—and societies more generally—may also differ in other important dimensions

---

[15] There is, for example, an extensive literature within the U.S. on private school choice and the potential problems with student selection (see, for example, Coleman and Hoffer (1987); Coleman, Hoffer, and Kilgore (1981); Neal (1997); Altonji, Elder, and Taber (2005)).

unobserved by the researcher. To address such concerns, the main results of cross-country studies should be checked for robustness to including obvious correlates of the cultural factors as control variables at the country level. Another robustness check is to draw only on variation within major world regions by including regional (continental) fixed effects. More fundamentally, some cross-country studies have started to adopt new techniques directly developed to address such issues of identification in particular contexts, and these studies will be the main focus of the following review.

Early studies that employ the international student achievement tests to estimate similar education production function within different countries include Heyneman and Loxley (1983) and Toma (1996). Early studies using the cross-country variation of international tests to estimate international education productions on country-level observations include Bishop (1997), Hanushek and Kimko (2000), and Lee and Barro (2001). The first economic study to make use of the vast potential of the international micro data on students' achievement, family background, and school inputs and of the broad array of institutional differences that exists across countries to estimate extensive multivariate cross-country education production functions is Woessmann (2003b). While still subject to the prior issues of cross-country identification, employing the rich student-level data on background factors permits holding constant a large set of observable factors usually unavailable in national datasets.

Table 2.4 presents an example of estimation of an international education production function.[16] Using student-level data for 29 OECD countries from the 2003 cycle of the PISA test of 15-year-olds, the model expresses individual student achievement in math as a function of a large set of input factors. While this is a basic model that does not fully exploit the potential of the international data, the model specification already documents the rich set of background factors available from the student and school background questionnaires. Moreover, the international data display wide variation in many of the potential inputs to achievement, thus allowing for more precise estimation of any effects. At the individual level, the factors include student characteristics such as age, gender, immigration, and preprimary educational attendance and family-background measures such as socio-economic status, parental occupation, family status, and the number of books in the home. At the school level, the model includes resource measures such as class size and shortage of materials, instruction time, teacher education, community location, and institutional factors such as a set of measures of teacher monitoring and student assessment, different dimensions of school autonomy, and their interaction with accountability measures. At the country level, this basic model includes a country's GDP per capita, educational expenditure per student, the institutional factors of external exit exams, share of privately operated schools, and average government funding of schools.

---

[16] See Woessmann, Luedemann, Schuetz, and West (2009) for additional background and robustness analyses related to these estimates.

Table 2.4 An Example of an International Education Production Function: PISA 2003

	Coefficient	Standard error
STUDENT CHARACTERISTICS		
Age (years)	17.59***	(1.10)
Female	−17.36***	(0.64)
Preprimary education (more than 1 year)	5.61***	(0.70)
School starting age	−3.86***	(0.51)
Grade repetition in primary school	−35.79***	(1.41)
Grade repetition in secondary school	−34.73***	(1.65)
Grade		
7th grade	−47.18***	(4.07)
8th grade	−28.01***	(2.24)
9th grade	−12.49***	(1.34)
11th grade	−6.95***	(2.06)
12th grade	7.03	(4.83)
Immigration background		
First generation student	−9.05***	(1.54)
Non-native student	−9.04***	(1.64)
Language spoken at home		
Other national dialect or language	−23.74***	(2.85)
Foreign language	−8.38***	(1.67)
FAMILY BACKGROUND		
Living with		
Single mother or father	19.35***	(1.84)
Patchwork family	21.27***	(2.03)
Both parents	27.43***	(1.83)
Parents' working status		
Both full-time	−2.48*	(1.33)
One full-time, one half-time	6.74***	(1.06)
At least one full time	13.75***	(1.17)
At least one half time	8.42***	(1.13)
Parents' job		
Blue collar high skilled	0.43	(0.97)
White collar low skilled	2.86***	(0.93)
White collar high skilled	8.64***	(0.99)
Books at home		
11–25 books	5.55***	(0.98)
26–100 books	22.94***	(1.01)
101–200 books	32.78***	(1.12)
201–500 books	49.83***	(1.22)
More than 500 books	51.18***	(1.40)
Index of Economic, Social and Cultural Status (ESCS)	18.11***	(0.52)
GDP per capita (1,000 $)	−1.89*	(1.06)
SCHOOL INPUTS		
School's community location		
Town (3000–100,000)	3.23*	(1.53)
City (100,000–1,000,000)	10.78***	(1.89)
Large city with > 1 million people	7.90***	(2.38)

Table 2.4 An Example of an International Education Production Function: PISA 2003—cont'd

	Coefficient	Standard error
Educational expenditure per student (1000 $)	1.17***	(0.41)
Class size (mathematics)	1.47***	(0.07)
Shortage of instructional materials		
Not at all	−10.18***	(2.58)
Strongly	6.72***	(1.30)
Instruction time (minutes per week)	0.04***	(0.01)
Teacher education (share at school)		
Fully certified teachers	9.72***	(3.42)
Tertiary degree in pedagogy	6.57***	(2.01)
INSTITUTIONS		
Choice		
Private operation	57.59***	(8.36)
Government funding	81.84***	(22.33)
Accountability		
External exit exams	25.34*	(10.05)
Assessments used to decide about students' retention/promotion	12.19***	(1.63)
Monitoring of teacher lessons by principal	4.56***	(1.34)
Monitoring of teacher lessons by external inspectors	3.80***	(1.42)
Assessments used to compare school to district/national performance	2.13*	(1.26)
Assessments used to group students	−6.07***	(1.30)
Autonomy and its interaction with accountability		
Autonomy in formulating budget	−9.61***	(2.18)
External exit exams x Autonomy in formulating budget	9.14***	(3.12)
Autonomy in establishing starting salaries	−8.63***	(3.25)
External exit exams x Autonomy in establishing starting salaries	5.87	(3.98)
Autonomy in determining course content	0.18	(1.91)
External exit exams x Autonomy in determining course content	3.22	(2.86)
Autonomy in hiring teachers	20.66***	(2.25)
External exit exams x Autonomy in hiring teachers	−28.94***	(3.37)
Students	219,794	
Schools	8,245	
Countries	29	
R^2 (at student level)	0.390	
R^2 (at country level)	0.872	

Notes: Dependent variable: PISA 2003 international mathematics test score. Least-squares regressions weighted by students' sampling probability. The models additionally control for imputation dummies and interaction terms between imputation dummies and the variables. Robust standard errors adjusted for clustering at the school level in parentheses (clustering at country level for all country-level variables, which are private operation, government funding, external exit exams, GDP per capita, and expenditure per student). Significance level (based on clustering-robust standard errors): *** 1%, ** 5%, * 10%.
Source: Own calculations based on Woessmann, Luedemann, Schuetz, and West (2009), who provide additional background details.

While the cross-sectional nature of this estimation allows for a descriptive interpretation only, it is worth noting that many measures of students' individual and family background are systematically related to their achievement, as are several measures of the institutional structure of the school system. By contrast, the point estimate on class size, the classical measure of quantitative school inputs, is counterintuitive,[17] and the estimates on the more qualitative school inputs, while positive, are more limited than the background and institutional estimates. The model accounts for 39% of the achievement variation at the student level and for 87% at the country level. That is, while unobserved factors such as ability differences are important at the individual level, the model is able to account statistically for most of the between-country variation in academic achievement. These basic result patterns are broadly common to all studies of international education production functions estimated on the different international student achievement tests.[18] We will now discuss the literature on each of the three groups of determinants—student and family background, school inputs, and institutions—in greater detail.

4.2 Student and family background

The results of the international education production function just presented show strong associations of educational achievement with many measures of student and family background. Given the importance of learning and child development outside school, family inputs have long been viewed as a leading input in educational production. As a consequence, consideration of measures of family background is generally taken as the most rudimentary quality standard when analyzing effects of school inputs (cf. Hanushek (2002)). But the effects of different measures of student and family background are generally seen as having important interest in their own right, not least because they provide an indication of the equality of opportunity of children with different backgrounds (see this book's Chapter 3 by Björklund and Salvanes (2010)). When using international student achievement data to estimate the same basic specification in different countries, measures of equality of opportunity can be compared across countries for several dimensions such as social background, ethnicity and immigrant status, and gender. Moreover, estimates of how strongly student achievement depends on family background provide an indication of intergenerational mobility of a society. We first discuss evidence derived from estimation within different countries and follow with evidence across countries.

---

[17] The coefficient on country-level spending is very small. While it is statistically significant, identification here comes from a very particular margin, as the correlation between spending and per-capita GDP (whose coefficient is negative here) in this model is as high as 0.93. Other studies tend to find a significant positive coefficient on GDP per capita, but not on spending. See below for more extensive discussion.

[18] See Aghion et al. (2010) and Aghion (2008) for an example of an international education production function in higher education, using university rankings based on the Shanghai research ranking (see above).

Figure 2.2 depicts an example, based on Schuetz, Ursprung, and Woessmann (2008), of using international data to generate comparable estimates of the association between family background and educational achievement in different countries. By combining the 1995 TIMSS test with its 1999 repeat study, the study can draw on micro data for over 325,000 students from a total of 54 countries. For the OECD countries, the figure depicts the coefficient on books available in the student's household in a student-level regression predicting the average 8th-grade test score in math and science disaggregated by country. By controlling for the immigration status of student, mother, and father interacted with family background (as well as age, gender, and family status), the multivariate analysis ensures that the estimates are not driven by cross-country differences in the immigrant population, but reflect socio-economic differences in the nonmigrant population of each country.

The number of books in the students' home is used as a proxy for socio-economic background not only because cross-country comparability and data coverage are superior to such indicators as parental education, but also because books at home are the single most important predictor of student performance in most countries (Woessmann (2003b, 2008)). The sociological literature suggests books at home as a powerful proxy for the educational, social, and economic background of the students' families. Furthermore, Schuetz, Ursprung, and Woessmann (2008) corroborate the cross-country validity of the books-at-home variable by showing that the association between household income and books at home does not vary significantly between the six countries for which both income and books measures are available in the PIRLS dataset. At the same time, it is important to be clear about the interpretation. The consistency of the estimates across studies is not meant to imply that books in the home per se are causally related to achievement and that providing more books to families would raise student performance. Books in the home proxy systematic differences in parenting, home education, and home resources that are presumed to be causally related to performance. In other words, the specific measures are not causally related to achievement even if the underlying concept is.[19]

The association between the family-background measure and student achievement is statistically significant at the 1% level in every country in Figure 2.2. The size of the estimates indicates how much students' test scores, measured in percentage points of an international standard deviation, increase when raising the number of books at home by one category. For example, in England the difference in educational achievement between children of families with more than two bookcases of books and children of families with only very few books at home (the two extremes of the five available categories) is 1.15

---

[19] A similar interpretation but in a different context can be seen from the use of family income to proxy behavior and family outcomes (cf. Mayer (1997)). A similar point about the causal impact of parental education is made by Black, Devereux, and Salvanes (2005).

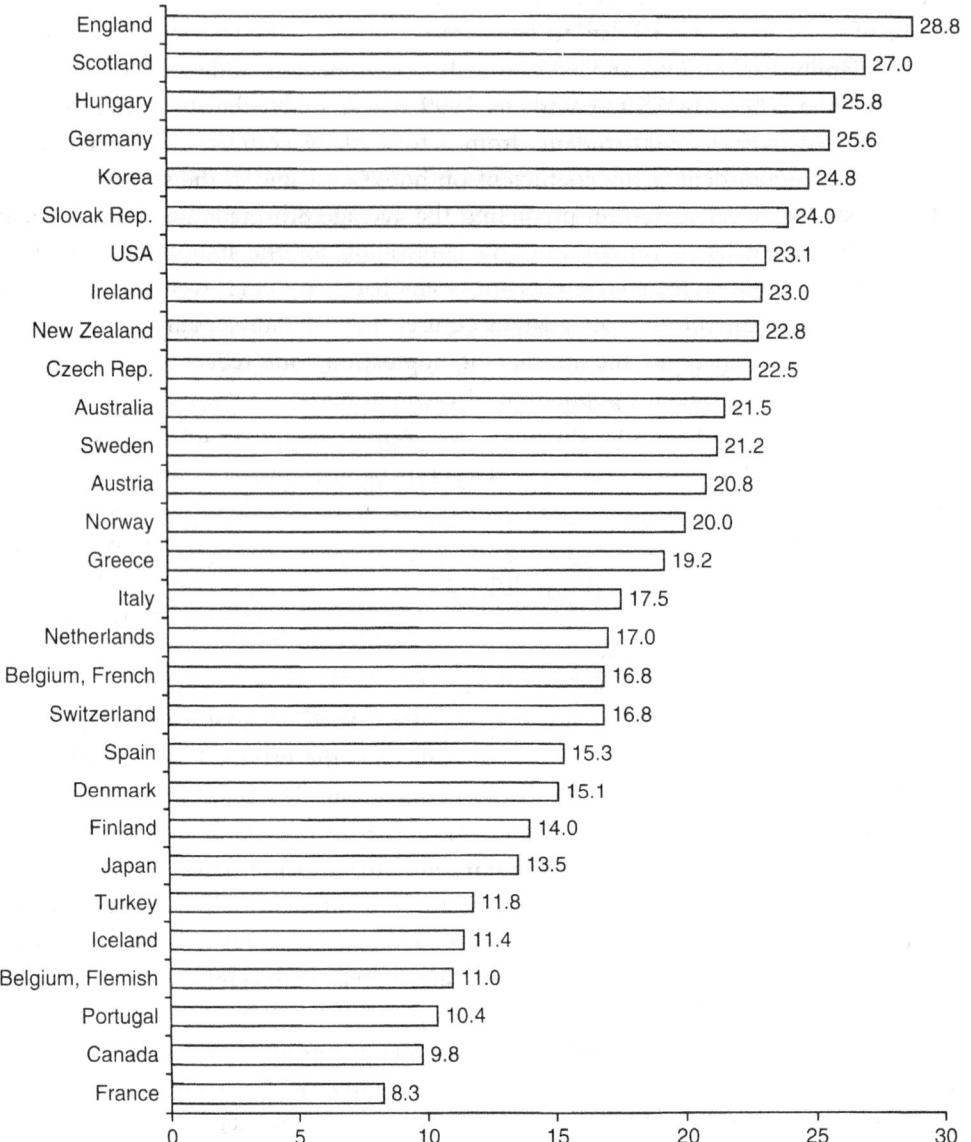

Figure 2.2 Family-background effects in different countries. Notes: Coefficient estimates from a student-level regression within each country of the mean of math and science performance in the TIMSS-95 and TIMSS-Repeat international tests on books at home, which is a categorical variable with five categories. Regressions control for age, gender, family status, student born in country, mother born in country, father born in country, interactions between the three immigration variables and books, and a dummy for the second test cycle. All estimates are statistically significantly different from zero at the 1% level. *Source*: Based on Schuetz, Ursprung, and Woessmann (2008), Table 3.

standard deviations, or more than three times what students on average learn during a whole school year.[20] While the estimated family-background effect differs substantially across countries, the socio-economic difference equals roughly one grade-level equivalent even in France, the OECD country with the lowest estimate. The United States falls in the top quarter of OECD countries in terms of the impact of socio-economic differences on achievement, whereas Canada belongs to the group of countries with the least impact. A natural interpretation is that educational opportunity is less equally distributed where the impact of family background on achievement is strong. By estimating the same association in 54 countries, the study provides an index of inequality of educational opportunity that permits comparisons of the intergenerational educational mobility across countries. Obviously, specific country results may be sensitive to the specific background measure and TIMSS dataset. On the other hand, analytical results on the cross-country association of education policies with equality of opportunity are consistent when using an index of socio-economic status as an alternative background measure and when estimated with the PISA dataset (Woessmann, Luedemann, Schuetz, and West (2009)).

Table 2.5 provides a detailed overview of studies using international tests to estimate the association between several student background measures and educational achievement in different countries. Education production functions that include several measures of student and family background in a way comparable across countries have been estimated for groups of countries in East Europe (Ammermueller, Heijke, and Woessmann (2005)), East Asia (Woessmann (2005a)), West Europe and the United States (Woessmann (2008) using TIMSS, Peterson and Woessmann (2007) using PISA), and Latin America (Woessmann (2010a)). Special attention to the relative performance of students with immigration background in different countries is given in Entorf and Minoiu (2005) and Schnepf (2007). Zimmer and Toma (2000) and Ammermueller and Pischke (2009) focus on effects of peers' background on student achievement in different countries. Bedard and Dhuey (2006) and Sprietsma (2010) analyze the effect of relative school starting age. Wolter and Coradi Vellacott (2003) look at sibling rivalry in different countries. Jenkins, Micklewright, and Schnepf (2008) calculate measures of between-school social segregation in different countries. Another recent paper that uses international test score data - from TIMSS 1999 and TIMSS 2007 - to estimate the association of student achievement with measures of family background such as gender, immigrant status, and parental background factors is Freeman, Machin, and Viarengo (2010). In each case, these studies make use of the cross-country structure of the data to compare the size of the association of the specific background measure with student achievement across countries. In general, the studies find that educational achievement differs substantially by student and family background within the separate countries, but also that there is

---

[20] On these tests, one grade-level equivalent equals roughly 35% of a standard deviation (see Schuetz, Ursprung, and Woessmann (2008)).

Table 2.5 Within-Country Studies on Student Background and Educational Achievement

Study	Dataset	Countries	Topic of investigation	Measure(s) of student background	Measure of achievement	Estimation method	Results
Zimmer and Toma (2000)	SIMS	Belgium, France, New Zealand, Canada, U.S.	Peer effects in private and public schools	Peers' mean test score, share of high-/low-ability students in classroom	Math, age 13–14	Value-added, country and school-type fixed effects	Positive peer effect; gains from high-quality peers stronger for low-ability students; mixed results on school types
Ammermueller, Heijke, and Woessmann (2005)	TIMSS	Czech Rep., Hungary, Latvia, Lithuania, Slovak Rep., Slovenia, Romania	Educational production in transition countries	Immigration, family status, parental education, books at home, community location	Math + science, grade 7+8	Cross-section WCRLR	Substantial effects of family background; larger in more (Czech Rep., Slovak Rep., Hungary, Slovenia) than in less advanced group (Lithuania, Latvia, Romania)
Woessmann (2005a)	TIMSS	Hong Kong, Japan, Singapore, South Korea, Thailand; France, Spain, U.S.	Educational production in East Asian countries	Immigration, family status, parental education, books at home, community location	Math (+ science), grade 7+8	Cross-section WCRLR	Strong family-background effects in Korea and Singapore; more equitable outcomes in Hong Kong and Thailand
Woessmann (2008)	TIMSS	17 West European countries + U.S.	Educational production in West Europe	Books at home, parental education, immigration, family status, community location	Math (+ science), grade 7+8	Cross-section WCRLR, quantile regression	Strong associations; aggregate size similar in Europe and U.S.; France, Flemish Belgium most equitable; Britain, Germany least; equity unrelated to mean performance
Bedard and Dhuey (2006)	TIMSS, TIMSS-R	10 for grade 3+4, 18 for grade 7+8	Effects of relative school starting age	Relative age	Math + science, grade 3+4 + 7+8	IV (instrument: age assigned by cutoff date)	Significant and sizeable effects of relative school starting age on performance at ages 9 and 13
Wolter and Coradi Vellacott (2003)	PISA	Belgium, Canada, Finland, France, Germany, Switzerland	Sibling rivalry	No. of siblings, ISEI, parental education and employment, immigration and family status	Reading, age 15	Cross-section WCRLR	Effects of number of siblings relevant in all six countries, but to a different extent; effects concentrated in subgroup low-SES families
Schuetz, Ursprung, and Woessmann (2008)	TIMSS, TIMSS-R	54 countries	Equality of opportunity	Books at home	Mean math + science, grade 8	Cross-section WCRLR	Significant family-background effect in all countries; considerable variation; large effects in Britain, Hungary, Germany; relatively small effects in France, Canada

Study	Data	Topic	Variables	Outcome	Method	Findings
Peterson and Woessmann (2007)	PISA	France, Germany, Great Britain, U.S.	Equality of opportunity	Books at home, parental job and employment, immigration status, family status	Math, age 15	Cross-section WCRLR	Family background strongly linked to educational performance; largest in Germany and U.S., slightly smaller in Great Britain, even smaller in France
Entorf and Minoiu (2005)	PISA	Australia, Canada, Finland, France, Germany, New Zealand, Sweden, U.K., U.S.	Immigration policy	Immigration status, ISEI index	Reading, age 15	Cross-section OLS	Socio-economic effect highest in Germany, U.K., U.S.; lowest in Scandinavia, Canada; migrant disadvantage larger in Continental Europe than in traditional immigration countries; language spoken at home a key factor
Schnepf (2007)	PISA, TIMSS, TIMSS-R, PIRLS	10 OECD countries with share of foreign born > 10%	Immigrants' disadvantage in high immigration countries	Immigration status, language spoken at home, measures of socio-economic background	math, age 15; math, grade 8; reading, grade 4	Cross-section OLS	Immigrants fare best compared to natives in English-speaking countries and worst in Continental Europe; language skills, socio-economic background, and school segregation as determinants of immigrant gap
Jenkins, Micklewright, and Schnepf (2008)	PISA + PISA 2003	27 countries	Social segregation in schools	ISEI index	—	Calculation of summary indices of segregation	Between-school segregation high in Austria, Belgium, Germany; low in Nordic countries, Scotland; middle in England, U.S.; higher where student selection by schools, but not with more private schools or parental choice
Woessmann (2010a)	PIRLS	Argentina, Colombia, Turkey, Macedonia; Germany, Greece, Italy, England	Educational production in Latin America	Immigration, books at home, parental education, job, employment, and income, community location	Reading, grade 4	Value-added WCRLR model (controlling for preschool performance)	Family background strongly related to student performance; relatively large in Argentina and small in Colombia

Continued

Table 2.5 Within-Country Studies on Student Background and Educational Achievement—cont'd

Study	Dataset	Countries	Topic of investigation	Measure(s) of student background	Measure of achievement	Estimation method	Results
Ammermueller and Pischke (2009)	PIRLS	France, Germany, Iceland, Netherlands, Norway, Sweden	Peer effects	Peers' index of books at home	Reading, grade 4	Cross-section WCRLR, school fixed effects, IV (instrument: students' for parents' report)	Modestly large peer effects; measurement error important; selection introduces little bias
Sprietsma (2010)	PISA 2003	16 countries	Effects of relative school starting age	Relative age	Math + reading, age 15	Cross-section, school random effects	Significant effect of relative school starting age in 10 out of 16 countries; relevant channels are probabilities of starting school too late, grade retention, and grade skipping

Notes: Student is the level of analysis in all studies. SES = socio-economic status. WCRLR = weighted clustering-robust linear regression. OLS = ordinary least squares. IV = instrumental variable. ISEI = international socio-economic index of occupational status. See Tables 2.1 and 2.2 for acronyms of datasets.

substantial variation in the influence of families across countries. Section 4.4 below reviews studies that relate such measures of equity of educational achievement to institutional differences in the education systems across countries.

When estimating the association between socio-economic background and economic achievement, the literature has been generally interested in overall associations, irrespective of their origin. Methodologically, most of the cross-country literature on background effects so far is thus descriptive in nature. At the same time, not much headway has been made on the underlying causal mechanisms, such as the relative roles of nature and nurture in these associations. However, lacking obvious reasons to assume that natural transmission differs across countries, cross-country comparisons can be interpreted in terms of differences in the extent to which societies achieve more or less equal educational opportunities. Differences in the estimates across countries can thus still be correlated with different national features to estimate relevant policy parameters (see below).

As the studies covered in Table 2.6 testify, the strong association between students' socio-economic background and their educational achievement is also confirmed in cross-country studies, estimated both at the country level (Lee and Barro (2001)) and at the student level (Woessmann (2003b) using TIMSS, Fuchs and Woessmann (2007) using PISA).[21] (Table 2.6 reports results on family backgrounds and school inputs together because most studies estimating cross-country associations deal with both at the same time.) On more particular subjects, Gunnarsson, Orazem, and Sánchez (2006) use variation across Latin American countries in the LLECE test to estimate the effect of child labor on student achievement. They exploit cross-country variation in truancy regulations to identify exogenous variation in the opportunity cost of children's time in a cross-country instrumental variable model. McEwan and Marshall (2004) and Ammermueller (2007) perform decomposition analyses of the variation between two countries to estimate the extent that family-background measures can account for achievement difference between Cuba and Mexico and between Finland and Germany, respectively.

For questions of specific background factors, the literature has also used more elaborate identification techniques. For example, Bedard and Dhuey (2006) use the variation created by national cutoff dates for school enrollment to derive exogenous variation in relative school starting ages. The relative school starting age assigned by national cutoff date is consequently used as an instrument for the actual relative school starting age of the students.[22] Zimmer and Toma (2000) make use of the specific structure of the SIMS study that included a one-year follow-up to estimate value-added models when analyzing

---

[21] Jürges and Schneider (2004) employ a two-step approach to first estimate country fixed effects and then relate them to country-level measures in TIMSS.
[22] This strategy identifies effects of *relative* maturity at school entry. Leuven, Lindahl, Oosterbeek, and Webbink (2010) is a study of the effect of *absolute* age at starting school. Bedard and Dhuey (2006) also indicate that the cross-country pattern of results suggests that relative age effects may be less persistent in countries with limited ability-differentiated learning groups during the primary grades. We will discuss the topic of tracking below.

Table 2.6 Cross-Country Studies on Student Background, School Inputs, and Educational Achievement

Study	Dataset	No. of countries	Level of analysis	Topic of investigation	Measure of inputs	Measure of achievement	Estimation method	Results
Hanushek and Kimko (2000)	FIMS, FISS, SIMS, SISS, IAEP-I+II	70 country-cohorts	Country	Production of student achievement	Student-teacher ratios, expenditure, adult schooling	Math + science	Cross-section OLS	Positive effect of education of parents on student performance; no effects of school resources
Lee and Barro (2001)	FIMS, FISS, FIRS, SIMS, SISS, SIRS, IAEP-I+II	58	Country	Determinants of schooling quality	Student-teacher ratios, spending per student, teacher salaries, length of school year	Math, science + reading, repetition + dropout rates	Panel SUR regression, fixed effects	Strong relation between family background and school outcomes; positive and significant impact of school resources
Woessmann (2003b)	TIMSS	39	Student	Effects on student performance	18 background measures, 12 resources and teachers, 26 institutional	Math + science	Cross-section WCRLR	Strong effects of family background and institutional arrangements; far more important than resources
Jürges and Schneider (2004)	TIMSS	23	Student, country	Sources of student achievement	14 groups of student, teacher, class, school measures, 2 national	Math	Cross-section OLS, IV, kernel density	Positive effects of family background, teacher characteristics, and school resources
McEwan and Marshall (2004)	LLECE	2 (Cuba, Mexico)	Student	Explaining Cuban-Mexican gap	Parental education, books at home, school, teacher and peer characteristics	Math + Spanish	Blinder-Oaxaca decomposition	30% of achievement gap explained; family and peer characteristics play a role, school characteristics not
Fertig and Wright (2005)	PISA	30	Student	Class-size effects	Class size	Reading	Cross-section OLS	Class-size estimates get negative and significant only at high aggregation levels, indicating aggregation bias

Study	Dataset	Countries	Level	Topic	Inputs	Output	Method	Main findings
Gunnarsson, Orazem, and Sánchez (2006)	LLECE	10	Student	Effects of child labor	Intensity of working outside the home	Math + language, grade 3+4	Cross-section, IV	Significant negative effect of child labor on student achievement
Afonso and St. Aubyn (2006)	PISA 2003	25	Country	Efficiency of expenditure	Teachers per students, time spent in school	Avg. of math, reading, science, problem solving	DEA, Tobit, bootstrap	Substantial inefficiencies in most countries; nondiscretionary inputs (GDP and parental education) account for large part
Fuchs and Woessmann (2007)	PISA	31	Student	Effects on student performance	13 groups of student measures, 5 resources and teachers, 10 institutional, interactions	Math, science, + reading	Cross-section WCRLR, IV	Background, resources, teachers, and esp. institutions all significantly associated with achievement; models account for >85% of between-country variation
Ammermueller (2007)	PISA 2000	2 (Finland, Germany)	Student	Explaining Finish-German gap	Parents' education, books at home, teacher characteristics	Reading	Oaxaca-Blinder, Juhn-Murphy-Pierce decomposition	Finish-German gap not explained by different backgrounds; Finland uses resources more efficiently
Dolton and Marcenaro-Gutierrez (2010)	TIMSS+R +03, PISA +03 +06	39	Country	Effects of teacher pay	Teacher salaries (absolute, relative), other teacher variables	Math, science + reading	Panel with country fixed effects	Absolute and relative teacher salary positively related to achievement

Notes: SUR = seemingly unrelated regression. WCRLR = weighted clustering-robust linear regression. OLS = ordinary least squares. IV = instrumental variable. DEA = data envelopment analysis. See Tables 2.1 and 2.2 for acronyms of datasets.

peer effects. More rudimentarily, Woessmann (2010a) draws on retrospective reports on preschool performance by parents in the PIRLS study to estimate quasi-value-added models. In estimating peer effects, Ammermueller and Pischke (2009) assume that classes within primary schools are randomly formed and accordingly employ school fixed effects estimation. They also address measurement error issues by instrumenting the parent-reported variable by the same variable reported by the student.

In sum, measures of student and family background prove to be key factors in international education production functions. A significant association of students' academic achievement with the socio-economic background of their families is evident in all countries around the world. The variation in this association across countries, however, suggests that differences in education policies might be an important element in differences in equality of opportunity, a topic to which we return below.[23]

4.3 School inputs

When moving from family to school determinants of educational achievement, the topic most intensively researched are the inputs available in schools (Hanushek (2006)). As exemplified in the international education production function shown in Table 2.4, measures of school inputs include expenditure per student, class size, availability of instructional material, and teacher characteristics. The studies reviewed in Table 2.6 reveal that in general, the cross-country association of student achievement with resources tends to be much weaker than with socio-economic backgrounds.

4.3.1 Evidence across countries

When looking across countries, the most straightforward starting point is the simple association between the aggregate financial measure of average expenditure per student and average achievement. Figure 2.3 presents the international association between cumulative spending per student from age 6 to 15 and the average math achievement of 15-year-olds on the 2003 PISA test. Without considering the strong outliers of Mexico and Greece, there is no association between spending levels and average achievement across countries.[24] At the most basic level, countries with high educational spending appear to perform at the same level as countries with low expenditures.

---

[23] While our focus is on the effects of cognitive skills, other related work has delved into cross-country differences in participation in higher education and its relationship to family background (see, for example, Orr, Schnitzer, and Frackmann (2008)). The transition into higher education has at the same time been shown to be closely related to student achievement.

[24] With the two outliers, there is a weak positive association as long as other effects are ignored. Taken literally, the full-sample association suggests that $60,000 per student in additional expenditure (a quadrupling of spending in the low-spending countries) is associated with about a half standard deviation improvement in scores. However, once a country's GDP per capita is controlled for, the cross-country association between student achievement and expenditure loses statistical significance and even turns negative, suggesting that the bivariate association is driven by the omitted factor of average socio-economic status.

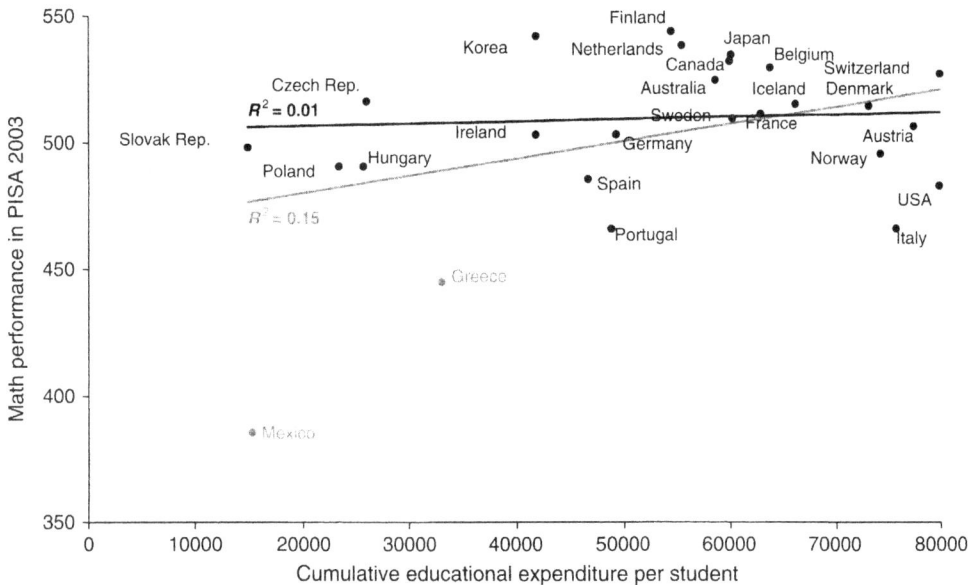

Figure 2.3 Expenditure per student and student achievement across countries. Notes: Association between average math achievement in PISA 2003 and cumulative expenditure on educational institutions per student between age 6 and 15, in U.S. dollars, converted by purchasing power parities. Light line: regression line for full sample. Dark line: regression line omitting Mexico and Greece. *Source*: Woessmann (2007a).

This picture has been evident in many other waves of the different international achievement tests (e.g., Woessmann (2002), Section 3.2, for the 1995 TIMSS test). Furthermore, in most cases the lack of a significant positive cross-country association between expenditure per student and educational achievement holds up when numerous other determining factors such as family background and school features (including instruction time) are accounted for in a regression framework. Hanushek and Kimko (2000) and Lee and Barro (2001) perform country-level regressions using different tests and Woessmann (2003b) and Fuchs and Woessmann (2007) perform student-level microeconometric regressions using TIMSS 1995 and PISA 2000, respectively.

As discussed above, such cross-sectional analysis has to be interpreted cautiously, even when controlling for a large set of factors. There may be reverse causality, and unobserved country differences—for example, cultural traits or institutional and political factors—may be correlated with both inputs and outcomes. As a first step to address such worries, one can look at within-country variation over time (Table 2.7). By looking at changes in inputs and outcomes, one can rule out unobserved level effects. Thus, Gundlach, Woessmann, and Gmelin (2001) calculate changes in expenditure and

Table 2.7 Within-Country Studies on School Inputs and Educational Achievement

Study	Dataset	Countries	Level of analysis	Topic of investigation	Measure of school inputs	Measure of achievement	Estimation method	Results
Heyneman and Loxley (1983)	FISS, ECIEL, national datasets	29 countries	Student	Educational production in low-income countries	Up to 20 measures, differing by dataset	Science (math in few countries), primary school	Cross-section analysis of variance explained by sets of measures	School and teacher quality predominant influence on student learning; resources more closely related to student performance in developing countries
Michaelowa (2001)	PASEC	Burkina Faso, Cameroon, Cote d'Ivoire, Madagascar, Senegal	Student	Educational production in Francophone Sub-Saharan Africa	Teacher, classroom, and school characteristics, national expenditure per student	Mean of math + French, grade 5	HLM, pooled across countries	Many measures, such as textbooks and teacher education, significantly associated with student performance; no positive association with smaller classes
Gundlach, Woessmann, and Gmelin (2001)	FIMS, FISS, SIMS, SISS, TIMSS	11–17 OECD countries	Country	Change in schooling productivity in OECD countries	Expenditure per student	Math + science, different grades	Longitudinal measurement of skills and expenditures	Real expenditure per student increased substantially in most countries in 1970–1994; student performance remained constant at best; productivity decline larger in many countries than in U.S.
Gundlach and Woessmann (2001)	SIMS, SISS, TIMSS	Hong Kong, Japan, Singapore, South Korea, Philippines, Thailand	Country	Change in schooling productivity in East Asia	Expenditure per student	Math + science, different grades	Longitudinal measurement of skills and expenditures	Real expenditure per student increased substantially in most countries in 1980–1994, mostly due to decrease in student-teacher ratios; student performance did not change substantially
Hanushek and Luque (2003)	TIMSS	37 countries	Classroom	Effects of class size and teacher characteristics	Class size, teacher experience and education	Math, ages 9+13	Cross-section OLS	Limited evidence of effects of school inputs; cross-country differences hard to explain systematically; no evidence of stronger effects in developing countries
Woessmann and West (2006)	TIMSS	11 countries	Student	Class-size effects	Class size	Math + science, grades 7+8	Cross-section WCRLR, school fixed effects (using between-grade variation), IV	Sizable beneficial effects of smaller classes rejected in 8 countries; only in Greece, Iceland; noteworthy effects only in countries with low teacher salaries; conventional estimates severely biased

Study	Dataset	Countries	Level of analysis	Topic	Resource measures	Outcome measures	Method	Main findings
Woessmann (2005b)	TIMSS	17 West European and U.S.	Student	Class-size effects	Class size (shortage of materials, instruction time)	Math, grades 7+8	Cross-section WCRLR, school fixed effects, IV, RD	No statistically and economically significant class-size effect in any country; small statistically significant effects only in Iceland, Norway, Spain
Ammermueller, Heijke, and Woessmann (2005)	TIMSS	7 East European (see Table 2.5)	Student	Educational production in transition countries	Class size, shortage of materials	Math + science, grades 7+8	Cross-section WCRLR, school fixed effects, IV	No causal class-size effects; in some countries, positive association with teacher experience and education and with sufficient reported materials
Woessmann (2005a)	TIMSS	5 East Asian + 3 (see Table 2.5)	Student	Class-size effects in East Asia	Class size, shortage of materials, teacher background	Math (+ science), grades 7+8	Cross-section WCRLR, school fixed effects, IV	No causal class-size effects; not much evidence of positive association with other school inputs
Ammermueller and Dolton (2006)	TIMSS/R/2003, PIRLS	England, U.S.	Student	Student-teacher gender interaction	Teacher gender	Math + science, grades 4+8; reading, grade 4	Cross-section WCRLR, student fixed effects (across subjects)	Some evidence of positive interaction effects of student and teacher gender in 8th-grade math in England in 2003, but not U.S. and most other specifications
Woessmann (2010a)	PIRLS	2 Latin American + 6 (see Table 2.5)	Student	Educational production in Latin America	Class size, instructional time, shortage of materials or staff	Reading, grade 4	Value-added WCRLR model (controlling for preschool performance)	No consistent evidence of association between student performance and schools' resource endowments
Bratti, Checchi, and Filippin (2008)	PISA 2003	24 countries	Student	Cooperative vs. competitive learning approach	OECD index of students' reports of cooperative and competitive attitudes toward learning	Math, age 15	Pooled cross-section CRLR with country fixed effects, quantile regressions	Positive association with individual competitive learning attitude (higher in comprehensive systems) and with school-average cooperative learning attitude (higher in tracked systems)
Altinok and Kingdon (2009)	TIMSS 2003	33–45 countries	Student	Class-size effects	Differences in class size across subjects	Math + science, grade 8	Cross-section WCRLR, school and student fixed effects (across subjects), IV	Few class-size effects; small significant negative effects only in 10 countries, positive in 6; larger in developing countries and with low teacher quality

Notes: WCRLR = weighted clustering-robust linear regression. HLM = hierarchical linear model. OLS = ordinary least squares. IV = instrumental variable. RD = regression discontinuity. See Tables 2.1 and 2.2 for acronyms of datasets.

achievement for individual OECD countries from 1970–1994, and Gundlach and Woessmann (2001) for individual East Asian countries from 1980–1994.[25]

The results, depicted in Figure 2.4, suggest that educational expenditure per student has increased substantially in real terms in all considered OECD countries between the early 1970s and the mid-1990s, and in all considered East Asian countries except the Philippines between the early 1980s and the mid-1990s.[26] Yet, comparing test scores over the same time intervals suggests that no substantial improvement in average

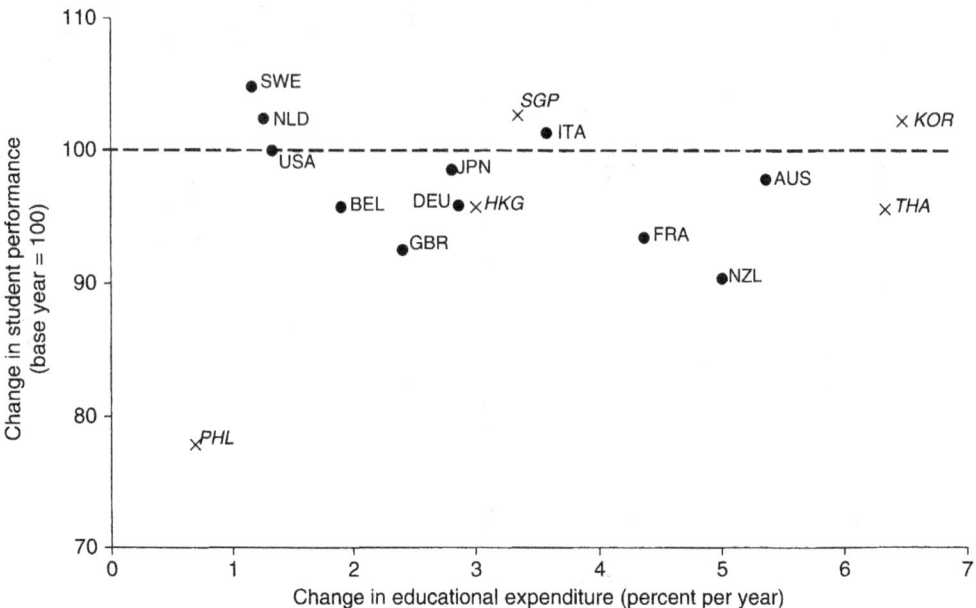

Figure 2.4 Change in expenditure per student and in student achievement over time. Notes: Data for OECD countries (circles) refer to 1970–1994, data for East Asian countries (X's) to 1980–1994. Change in student performance: students' average educational performance in math and science in 1994 relative to base year. Change in educational expenditure: average annual rate of change in real educational expenditure per student in percent. Country abbreviations: Australia (AUS), Belgium (BEL), France (FRA), Germany (DEU), Hong Kong (HKG), Italy (ITA), Japan (JPN), Netherlands (NLD), Philippines (PHL), Singapore (SGP), South Korea (KOR), Sweden (SWE), Thailand (THA), United Kingdom (GBR), United States (USA). Source: Based on Gundlach, Woessmann, and Gmelin (2001) and Gundlach and Woessmann (2001).

---

[25] Achievement data from the international tests at the two respective points in time are linked using U.S. longitudinal achievement data. Increases in educational expenditure are adjusted not only for average inflation, but also for the so-called "Baumol effect" of increasing costs in service sectors with constant productivity. Three different approaches of calculating price deflators for the schooling sector that account for this effect are averaged in the depiction of Figure 2.4. For details, see Gundlach, Woessmann, and Gmelin (2001), Gundlach and Woessmann (2001), and Woessmann (2002), Section 3.3.

[26] Gundlach and Woessmann (2001) show that the resource expansion in the East Asian countries mostly results from government decisions to raise the number of teachers per student.

student achievement has occurred in any of these countries. Combining the time-series evidence on resources and achievement, it is fair to conclude that substantial increases in real school expenditure per student did not lead to improvements in student outcomes in most of the sampled OECD and East Asian countries. In fact, the experience of many countries is much bleaker than what had been termed the "productivity collapse in schools" in the United States (Hanushek (1997)).[27]

Apart from the aggregate expenditure measure, the cross-country variation has also been used to analyze specific resource inputs in cross-sectional analysis (see Table 2.6 for details). Expenditure per student is an encompassing measure of school inputs which considers not only personnel costs but also material costs. But international comparisons of expenditure may be hampered by the problem of choosing an appropriate exchange rate (Figure 2.3 uses conversion by purchasing power parities). Because personnel costs make up more than three quarters of total expenditure in nearly all countries, class size lends itself particularly well as a nonmonetary input measure for international comparisons which determines a large part of total expenditure. However, using class size instead of expenditure per student yields the same general picture as in Figure 2.3. Regression analyses that control for family background measures come to similar results. At the country level, Lee and Barro (2001) find a positive effect of smaller student-teacher ratios, but Hanushek and Kimko (2000) find no such relationship.[28] However, country-level analysis may suffer from aggregation bias (Hanushek, Rivkin, and Taylor (1996)), as Fertig and Wright (2005) show that the probability of finding statistically significant and correctly signed class-size effects increases with the level of aggregation. Student-level analyses that use data on the actual size of the class of the tested students, rather than ratios of teachers to students at some level, tend to find counterintuitive signs of the coefficient on class size that are often statistically significant (e.g., Woessmann (2003b); Fuchs and Woessmann (2007); Table 2.4 above).

The latter studies also take indicators of the shortage of instructional material, usually reported by school principals, into account. Shortage of material tends to be negatively associated with student outcomes. Measures of instruction time also tend to be significantly related to achievement. By contrast, in multivariate analyses the availability of computers at school is not related to student outcomes, and intensive computer use is negatively related to test scores (Fuchs and Woessmann (2004)).

---

[27] One potential explanation for this bivariate longitudinal pattern might of course be that students' family background might have deteriorated on average. Students may increasingly be lacking many of the basic capabilities required for a successful education and may thus be increasingly expensive to educate. Such effects may play a significant role in countries with a large inflow of immigrant students or with rising levels of poverty. But on average, parents in the considered countries have been enjoying higher incomes and better education over time, and the number of children per family has declined. Hence by the later periods, children may actually start schooling with better basic capabilities than before. These issues, however, await thorough econometric analysis.

[28] Using country-level data for data envelopment analysis, Afonso and St. Aubyn (2006) find indications of substantial inefficiencies in the use of teachers per student in most countries.

In the student-level studies, measures of teacher education tend to show positive associations with student achievement in cross-country analyses. Drawing on information from teacher background questionnaires in TIMSS, Woessmann (2003b) finds positive associations of student achievement with teacher experience and female gender and a negative one with teacher age. In their country-level analysis, Lee and Barro (2001) find a positive effect of teacher salary levels. Similarly, Woessmann (2005b) reports a significant positive coefficient on a country-level measure of teacher salary when added to an international student-level regression. Dolton and Marcenaro-Gutierrez (2010) pool country-level data from international tests from 1995–2006 to show that teacher salaries—both when measured in absolute terms and relative to wages in each country—are positively associated with student achievement, even after controlling for country fixed effects.

In sum, the general pattern of the cross-country analyses suggests that quantitative measures of school inputs such as expenditure and class size cannot account for the cross-country variation in educational achievement. By contrast, several studies tend to find positive associations of student achievement with the quality of instructional material and the quality of the teaching force. While these cross-country associations reveal to what extent different input factors can descriptively account for international differences in student achievement, studies that focus more closely on the identification of causal effects have reverted to using the within-country variation in resources and achievement. This literature is most advanced for the estimation of class-size effects. In the following, we discuss three approaches that have been suggested to estimate causal class-size effects on international data: a combination of school fixed effects with instrumental variables, a regression discontinuity approach that makes use of variation stemming from maximum class-size rules, and a subject fixed effects approach.

4.3.2 Evidence within different countries

The initial within-country studies, reviewed in Table 2.7, have used conventional least-squares techniques to focus on developing countries and their comparison to developed countries, a particular advantage of using international data. Relying on data from early international tests, Heyneman and Loxley (1983) suggested that school resources tend to be more closely related to student achievement in developing countries than in developed countries. Hanushek and Luque (2003) did not corroborate this conclusion using the more recent TIMSS data. Michaelowa (2001) uses the regional PASEC data to provide conventional evidence for five countries in Francophone Sub-Saharan Africa.[29]

---

[29] Using PIRLS data, Woessmann (2010a) estimates a quasi-value-added model, controlling for retrospective information on preschool performance, for primary-school students in two Latin American and several comparison countries.

The problem with such conventional estimates is that resources in general, and class sizes in particular, are not only a cause but also a consequence of student achievement or of unobserved factors related to student achievement. Many features may lead to the joint and simultaneous determination of class size and student achievement, making class size endogenous to student achievement. For example, schools may reduce class sizes for poorly performing students and policymakers may design compensatory funding schemes for schools with large shares of students from poor backgrounds (see West and Woessmann (2006) for international evidence). In both cases, class sizes are allocated in a compensatory manner, biasing the class-size coefficient upwards. In contrast, policymakers may also have high-performing students taught in special small classes to support elite performance. Likewise, parents who particularly care for the education of their children may both make residential choices to ensure that their children are taught in schools with relatively small classes and support their children in many other ways, leading them to be relatively high performers. In these cases, class sizes are allocated in a reinforcing manner, biasing the class-size coefficient downwards. In short, parents, teachers, schools, and administrators all make choices that might give rise to a noncausal association between class size and student achievement even after controlling extensively for family background. Conventional estimates of class-size effects may thus suffer from endogeneity bias, the direction of which is ambiguous *a priori*.

To identify causal class-size effects, two quasi-experimental strategies have been applied to the international test data (cf. Woessmann (2005b)). The first quasi-experimental approach draws on exogenous variation in class size caused by natural fluctuations in the size of subsequent student cohorts of a school (similar to Hoxby (2000)). In this case, the quasi-experiment results from the idea that natural fluctuations in student enrollment lead to variations in average class size in two adjacent grades in the same school. Natural birth fluctuations around the cut-off date that splits students into different grade levels occur randomly. Therefore, they lead to variation in class size that is driven neither by students' educational achievement nor by other features that might jointly affect class size and student achievement.

Woessmann and West (2006) develop a variant of this identification strategy that exploits specific features of the TIMSS database. The sampling design of the first TIMSS study, which tested a complete 7th-grade class and a complete 8th-grade class in each school, enables them to use only the variation between two adjacent grades in individual schools. This strategy aims to exclude biases from nonrandom between-school and within-school sorting through a combination of school fixed effects and instrumental variables using grade-average class sizes as instruments. The rationale of this approach is as follows. Any between-school sorting is eliminated in a first step by controlling for school fixed effects, restricting the analysis solely to variation within individual schools. Within schools, the allocation of students to different classes in a grade may also be nonrandom. Within-school sorting is filtered out in a second step by instrumenting actual class size by the average class size in the relevant grade in each school. Within-school variation in class size is thus used only insofar as it is related to variation in average class size between the 7th and 8th grade of a school. The identifying assumption is that such variation is not affected by student sorting but reflects random fluctuations in birth-cohort size between the two grades in the catchment area of each school. Thus, causal class size effects are identified by relating differences in the relative achievement of students in 7th and 8th grade within individual schools to that part of the between-grade difference in class size in the school that reflects between-grade differences in average class size.

Figure 2.5 illustrates the basic intuition behind this identification strategy for the example of math achievement in Singapore. The top panel indicates that class-average test scores are *positively* associated with class size, as is the case in most countries—likely reflecting ability sorting of students between and within schools. The middle panel plots the achievement difference between the 7th-grade and 8th-grade class in each school against the same grade difference in class size, which is equivalent to including school fixed effects in a regression framework. Overcoming effects of between-school sorting by removing any difference in overall achievement levels between schools, the size of the positive correlation is reduced substantially, but remains statistically significant. The reduction suggests that poorly performing students tend to be sorted into schools with smaller classes in Singapore. The final step of the identification strategy, illustrated in the bottom panel, additionally eliminates any effects of within-school sorting by using only that part of the between-grade variation in actual class sizes that can be predicted by variation in grade-average class sizes. The picture suggests that class size has no causal effect on student achievement in math in Singapore. Rather, weaker students seem to be consistently placed in smaller classes, both between and within schools.

Woessmann and West (2006) implement this identification strategy in microeconometric estimations of education production functions for 11 countries around the world.[30] In line with Figure 2.5, their results suggest that conventional estimates of class-size effects tend to be severely biased. They find sizable beneficial effects of smaller classes in Greece and Iceland, but reject the possibility of even small effects in four countries and of large beneficial effects in an additional four countries. Additional specification tests support the identifying assumption that students and teachers are not systematically sorted between grades within individual schools. There are no systematic differences at all in the observable characteristics of students or teachers between the two grades in schools in which one of the two adjacent grades has substantially larger average class sizes than the other; there are no systematic differences in the estimated class-size

---

[30] Additional evidence based on the same identification strategy for countries in West Europe, East Europe, and East Asia is presented in Woessmann (2005b), Ammermueller, Heijke, and Woessmann (2005), and Woessmann (2005a), respectively.

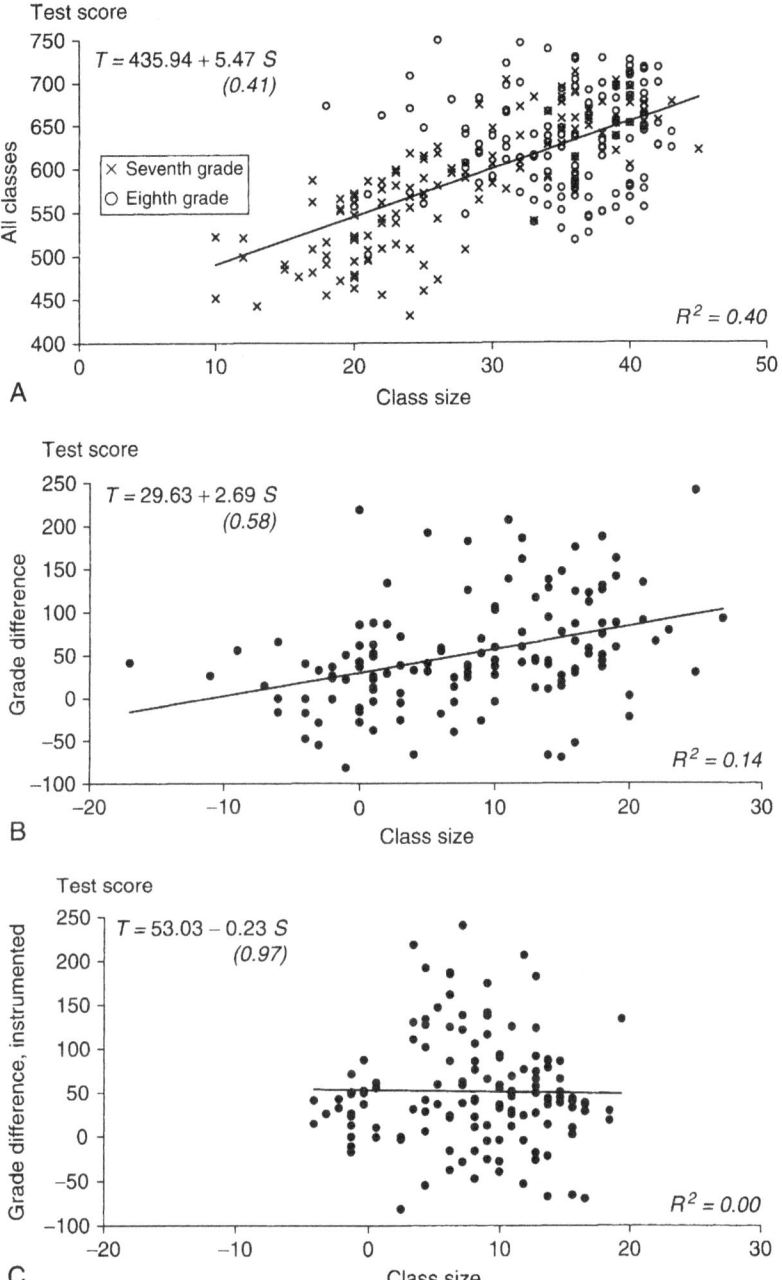

Figure 2.5 Identifying class-size effects: Singapore as an illustrative example. *Source:* Woessmann (2007a).

effects between expanding, stable, and contracting schools; and there are no systematic differences in the estimated class-size effects between countries where 7th grade is the first grade of a particular school and countries where it is not, so that grade-average class sizes might have been adjusted based on schools' experience with the particular students.

The basic pattern of results is corroborated by a second quasi-experimental identification strategy based on rule-induced discontinuities. Following the study by Angrist and Lavy (1999) for Israel, Woessmann (2005b) exploits the fact that many countries have maximum class-size rules that induce a nonlinear association between the number of students in a grade of a school and average class size. In particular, the association has sharp discontinuities at multiples of the maximum class size that can be exploited to identify variation in class sizes that is exogenous to student achievement. The TIMSS data suggest that 10 West European school systems implement national maximum class-size rules reasonably strictly and with enough sharpness to enable an empirical implementation of this instrumental variable strategy.[31] In all 10 countries, results from identification by rule-induced discontinuities rule out the possibility of large causal class-size effects in lower secondary school. The only statistically significant, but small estimates are, again, in Iceland and, marginally, in Norway.

Woessmann (2005b) shows that these results are robust to several specification tests. Some models control for peer effects, in terms of the mean achievement and family background of each student's classmates, to exclude bias from peer sorting. Controlling for any continuous association between grade enrollment and student achievement by adding enrollment in the specific grade and its squared term as additional controls does not lead to substantive changes in results. When applying the specification to a discontinuity sample of students whose grade enrollment is within a margin of plus or minus five or six students of the rule-based discontinuities, so that identification does not come from observations far off the discontinuities, the instrument gets weak in about half the countries, while results remain robust in the other half. Excluding especially large schools in each country (of a size three or four times the maximum class size) does not lead to a substantive change in results.[32]

However, as discussed by Woessmann (2005b), some reservations remain with this regression-discontinuity identification strategy (cf. also Urquiola and Verhoogen (2009)). In particular, intentional exploitations of the rule by systematic between- and within-school choices might lead to remaining endogeneity in the rule discontinuity approach. Thus, it is possible that parents and schools "play the system": parents particularly keen to ensure low class sizes for their children may make their enrollment decisions—and school principals their acceptance decisions—on the basis of expected class

---

[31] The 10 West European school systems that employ maximum class-size rules are: Denmark, France, Germany, Greece, Iceland, Ireland, Norway, Spain, Sweden, and Switzerland.
[32] The size of the induced discontinuity in class size is smaller when grade enrollment is larger.

size, and those decisions may be related to student achievement. Still, in the end both quasi-experimental identification strategies come to a very similar pattern of results. Moreover, the source of the potentially remaining biases differs in the two cases, adding confidence that any remaining bias in each strategy is of second-order magnitude.

Both identification strategies reach the conclusion that class size is not a major force in shaping achievement in lower secondary school in any of the countries considered. There is no single country for which any of the specifications showed a statistically significant and large class-size effect. In every case where one of the methods leads to a reasonably precise estimate, a large effect size can be ruled out with considerable statistical confidence. There is only one country, Iceland, where results create confidence that a causal class-size effect exists. However, in both specifications the estimates are relatively small and estimated precisely enough to reject the possibility of a large effect.

The unique value of cross-country research, however, lies in analyses of whether the cross-country differences in estimated class-size effects are systematically related to underlying features of the school systems. Such analyses can improve our understanding of the particular circumstances under which class sizes matter or not. Although causal class-size effects are small at best in all the countries considered, there are still differences across countries. The international evidence shows that the estimated effect size does not vary systematically for children from differing family backgrounds or for countries with different levels of average achievement, economic development, average class size, or educational spending (Woessmann and West (2006); Woessmann (2005b)). But the existence of class-size effects is systematically associated with the salary and education level of the teaching force. In both studies, class-size effects were detected only in countries with relatively low teacher salaries and education. The pattern is similar within countries in which the education level of teachers varies. In these countries, the estimated class-size effect tends to be larger in classes that are taught by teachers with lower education. Interpreting average teacher salary and teacher education as proxies for average teacher quality, the results suggest that relatively capable teachers do as well when teaching large classes as when teaching small classes. By contrast, less capable teachers do not seem to be up to the job of teaching large classes, while doing reasonably well in small classes. Consequently, the pattern of international effect heterogeneity suggests that class-size effects occur only when the quality of the teaching force is relatively low.

A third approach to the identification of causal class-size effects tries to avoid bias from nonrandom sorting of students by using variation within individual students. If the same student is taught two different academic subjects in differently sized classes, the within-student between-subject variation can be used for identification (cf. Dee (2005); Dee and West (2008)). The inclusion of student fixed effects, implemented by differencing across subjects, effectively excludes bias from subject-invariant student, family, and school characteristics, observable and unobservable. Unobserved characteristics that vary by subject and are correlated with class size, such as subject-specific fast-track or enrichment classes or teacher characteristics, could, however, still bias this research design. Altinok and Kingdon (2009) implement this identification strategy to estimate class-size effects in up to 45 countries using TIMSS 2003 data, which provide test scores in math and science for each student. Their results provide little support for class-size effects, with only few countries showing significant and sizeable positive effects of smaller classes. Analyzing the cross-country variation in class-size effects, they confirm that class-size effects are larger where teacher qualifications are lower, and also find indication of larger class-size effects in developing countries.

Beyond class-size effects, Ammermueller and Dolton (2006) use the same cross-subject identification strategy to estimate the effect of teacher-student gender interaction in England and the United States using TIMSS and PIRLS data. In most specifications (with the exception of one in England), they find little evidence of a significant effect of the interaction between student and teacher gender on student achievement. Schwerdt and Wuppermann (2009) use the same cross-subject identification with student fixed effects to identify the effects of teaching practices on TIMSS data in the United States. Recently, Lavy (2010) applies the cross-subject identification strategy to estimate effects of instruction time in the PISA 2006 data. At a more descriptive level, Bratti, Checchi, and Filippin (2008) use the PISA data to estimate the association of student achievement with cooperative and competitive attitudes toward learning at the individual and school level.

All in all, the international evidence on the role of school inputs in educational production provides little confidence that quantitative measures of expenditure and class size are a major driver of student achievement, across and within countries. Studies using different methods to identify causal class-size effects consistently find no strong effects of class size in most countries. The cross-country pattern suggests that class size is a relevant variable only in settings with low teacher quality. Descriptive evidence suggests that measures of the quality of inputs and, in particular, teachers are more closely related to student outcomes. However, research in this area awaits more work to identify the underlying causal links.

4.4 Institutions

Motivated by the poor results on school inputs, research has increasingly focused on whether nonresource institutional features of school systems affect student outcomes. In this topic, the particular opportunity of cross-country research comes into play: The chief advantage of the international comparative approach stems from its ability to exploit the substantial variation in national education policies across countries (cf. Woessmann (2007b)). By contrast, within-country studies are usually restricted to analysis of much more limited variation in institutional structure. Moreover, by drawing on wider and long-established institutional variation between countries, the international approach can capture general-equilibrium effects of institutional settings, which will not necessarily be the case when a specific educational reform is introduced only on a small scale, or only very recently. Such long-term general-equilibrium effects are usually the ones that economic theory stresses as being particularly important, because persistent institutional changes will alter incentives and thus behavior. By changing prices, available alternatives and competitive pressures for other market participants will have effects on market outcomes beyond the people specifically treated.

Since cross-country studies can address the most obvious issues of selection into treatment by using average measures of institutions at the systemic level, the main challenge for the identification of causal effects lies in unobserved country heterogeneity. Institutions may be correlated with other, unobserved country characteristics that are related to student achievement. While still in its infancy, several methods have been developed to address this problem, tailored to specific worries related to each specific institution. As will be discussed below, the range includes fixed effects for world regions to eliminate the most basic cultural differences; within-country identification where different education systems exist within one country (holding constant differences in language, legal structures, and cultures); differences-in-differences models that identify effects from changes between grades within each country; and the use of historical instruments that gave rise to arguably exogenous variation in institutional structures today.

The following review is structured around five institutional features that have attracted the most attention in the international literature so far: accountability measures, school autonomy, competition and private involvement, school tracking, and the preprimary education system. It closes with more explorative studies into education beyond the school level, public sector institutions, and less formal, cultural features of societies. Tables 2.8–2.10 provide details on the individual studies analyzing institutional features. Table 2.8 reports evidence within different countries, and the other two tables report cross-country evidence. Given that different institutional features tend to be related both to the level and to the equity of outcomes, Table 2.9 focuses on achievement levels, and Table 2.10 on the equity of achievement.

4.4.1 Accountability

Analyses of the impact of curriculum-based external exit exam (CBEEE) systems illustrate the unique power of international production function estimates to address important policy-relevant issues.[33] By signaling student achievement to potential employers on the labor market and institutions of higher education, external school-leaving exams increase students' rewards for learning as well as parents' scope for

---

[33] We concentrate on accountability for achievement that comes through exit exams, because understanding this topic requires analyses spanning jurisdictions with and without such institutions, making it a natural topic for use of international assessments. Of course, many analyses of accountability systems in general have proceeded within individual countries; see Hanushek and Raymond (2004) and Figlio and Loeb (2010).

Table 2.8 Within-Country Studies on Institutions and Educational Achievement

Study	Dataset	Countries	Level of analysis	Topic of investigation	Measure of institutions	Measure of achievement	Estimation method	Results
Bishop (1995), ch. 6	IAEP-II	Canada, U.S.	Student	Effect of curriculum-based external exams	Central exams, type of school	Math + science	Cross-section	External exams positively associated with student achievement; also with student, parental, and teacher behavior
Toma (1996)	SIMS	Belgium, France, New Zealand, Ontario (Can.), U.S.	Student	Effects of public funding and private schools	Type of school (public/private)	Math, beginning and end of school year	Value-added achievement model	Positive effect of private schools; funding not significantly associated with performance; governmental control over private schools negative factor
Vandenberghe and Robin (2004)	PISA	9 countries	Student	Private vs. public education	Type of school (public/private)	Math, science, + reading	Cross-section, IV, Heckman two stages, PSM	Significant positive association of private schools with achievement in some but not all countries
Corten and Dronkers (2006)	PISA 2000	19 countries	Student	Low-SES students and private schools	Governance and funding of school	Math + reading	MLM	Slight advantage of private government-dependent schools, no significant differences between public and private-independent schools
Dronkers and Robert (2008)	PISA 2000	22 countries	Student	Public and private schools	Governance and funding of school	Reading	MLM	Better performance of government-dependent private schools explained by better school climate
Cascio, Clark, and Gordon (2008)	IALS	13 countries	Country	Age profile of literacy and university education	Average years of university education	Share of population with high-level literacy	Cross-section	High correlation between literacy gains into adulthood and university graduation rate

Notes: SES = socio-economic status. IV = instrumental variable. PSM = propensity score matching. MLM = multilevel modeling. See Tables 2.1 and 2.2 for acronyms of datasets.

Table 2.9 Cross-Country Studies on Institutions and Levels of Educational Achievement

Study	Dataset	No. of countries	Level of analysis	Topic of investigation	Measure of institutions	Measure of achievement	Estimation method	Results
Bishop (1995), ch. 4	IAEP-II	15–21	Country	Effects of CBEEE	CBEEE	Math, science, + geography	Cross-section OLS	Student achievement and teacher salaries higher in CBEEE countries; differences in qualifications and spending not significant
Bishop (1997)	TIMSS, IAEP-II	39, Canada	Country, School	Effects of CBEEE	CBEEE	Math + science	Cross-section OLS	Large effect of CBEEE on student achievement; effects on parent, teacher, administrator behavior
Woessmann (2003b)	TIMSS	39	Student	Effects on student performance	Seven different categories	Math + science	Cross-section WCRLR	Large effects of institutional arrangements such as external exit exams, school autonomy, and private competition; far more important than resources
Woessmann (2003a)	TIMSS+ TIMSS-R	39, 38 (54)	Student	Effects of central exit exams	Central exit exams	Math + science	Cross-section WCRLR	Performance of students higher in systems with central exams; positive interaction with autonomy
Woessmann (2005c)	TIMSS+ TIMSS-R + PISA	39, 38 (54), 32	Student	Heterogeneity of central exam effect	Central exit exams, school autonomy	Math + science	Cross-section WCRLR, quantile regression	Substantial heterogeneity of central exam effects along student, school, and time dimension
Bishop (2006), ch. 3	PISA	41	Country	Effects of MCE and CBEEE	CBEEE	Math, science + reading	Cross-section OLS	Positive effects of CBEEE on student achievement; do not affect school attendance
Fuchs and Woessmann (2007)	PISA	31	Student	Effects on student performance	CBEEE, autonomy, private schools	Math, science, + reading	Cross-section WCRLR, IV	Institutional variation accounts for a quarter of between-country achievement variation; external exams interact positively with autonomy; positive effect of private operation
Sprietsma (2003)	PISA 2003	8	Student	School choice, school selectivity, and student performance	School choice, schools' student selection	Math, reading + science	Cross-section, MLM, quantile regression	Regional intensity of school choice and school selectivity positively related to student achievement; similar effect for low and high performing students

Continued

Table 2.9 Cross-Country Studies on Institutions and Levels of Educational Achievement—cont'd

Study	Dataset	No. of countries	Level of analysis	Topic of investigation	Measure of institutions	Measure of achievement	Estimation method	Results
Woessmann (2009b)	PISA	29	Student	Public vs. private school funding and operation	Private operation and funding	Math + reading	Cross-section WCRLR	Negative effects of public operation on student achievement; positive effect of public funding
Woessmann, Luedemann, Schuetz, and West (2009), ch. 2-6	PISA 2003	29, 37	Student	Accountability, autonomy, and choice	Several measures of accountability, autonomy, choice	Math + science	Cross-section WCRLR	Positive effects of several accountability measures on student performance and on role of autonomy; positive effects of share of privately operated schools and of government funding
Falch and Fischer (2008a)	SIMS, SISS, IAEP-II, TIMSS, TIMSS-R, +2003, PISA +2003	19–72	Country	Effect of welfare state on student achievement	Government consumption, social expenditures, tax progressivity	Average math + science	Panel with country fixed effects	Negative association of redistributive government activities with student achievement
Falch and Fischer (2008b)	SIMS, SISS, IAEP-II, TIMSS, TIMSS-R, PISA	24	Country	Effect of decentralization on student achievement	Public sector decentralization	Average math + science	Panel with country fixed effects	Positive association of government spending decentralization with student performance
West and Woessmann (2010)	PISA 2003	29	Student	Effect of competition from private schools on student achievement	Share of privately operated schools	Math, science, + reading	Cross-section WCRLR, IV (instrumenting private school share by historical Catholic share)	Positive causal effect of share of privately operated schools on student achievements, negative effect on costs
Schuetz (2009)	PISA 2003	38	Student	Effect of preprimary education on later educational achievement	Characteristics of preprimary education system	Math	Cross-section WCRLR, country fixed effects, (DiD)	Positive association of preprimary attendance with test scores; systematically stronger in countries with higher spending, larger shares of privately managed institutions, and higher training and relative pay of educators in preprimary system

Notes: CBEEE = curriculum based external exit exams. MCE = minimum competency exams. WCRLR = weighted clustering-robust linear regression. OLS = ordinary least squares. IV = instrumental variable. MLM = multilevel modeling. DiD = differences in differences. See Tables 2.1 and 2.2 for acronyms of datasets.

Table 2.10 Cross-Country Studies on Institutions and Equity of Educational Achievement

Study	Dataset	No. of countries	Level of analysis	Topic of investigation	Measure of institutions	Measure of achievement	Measure of equity	Estimation method	Results
Hanushek and Woessmann (2006)	PISA, PIRLS, TIMSS	45	Country	Early tracking and inequality	Age of first tracking	Math, science, + reading	Standard deviation in test scores	Pooled data, DiD	Significant effect of early tracking on inequality; no clear effect on mean performance
Schuetz, Ursprung, and Woessmann (2008)	TIMSS+ TIMSS-R	54	Student, country	Equality of opportunity	Age of first tracking, preschool enrollment and duration	Mean math + science	Dependence of test scores on books at home	Cross-section WCRLR, country fixed effects	Late tracking and preschool duration reduce impact of family background; inverted U-shaped effect of preschool enrollment; no tradeoff with efficiency
Ammermueller (2005)	PISA, PIRLS	14	Student	Institutions and educational opportunities	Number of school types, instruction time, private school share, autonomy	Reading	Dependence of test scores on student background variables	Pooled data, WCRLR, DiD	Significant negative effect of number of school types and share of private schools on equality of opportunity; positive effect of instruction time
Brunello and Checchi (2007)	IALS, PISA 2003	17, 32	Student	School tracking and equality of opportunity	Age of first selection, length of tracking, share of vocational education	Competences and other indicators	Dependence of test scores on parental education; coefficient of variation in test scores	Cohort study, OLS, probit, multinomial logit	Mixed results; tracking reinforces family-background effects on formal education but weakens them on learning on the job
Waldinger (2006)	PISA +2003, TIMSS, PIRLS	8–14 (DiD), 29 (cross-section)	Student	Tracking and family background	Grade of first tracking	Math + reading	Dependence of test scores on parental background variables	Pooled cross-section data, DiD	Tracking does not increase impact of family background after controlling for pretracking differences; but small samples
Guiso, Monte, Sapienza, and Zingales (2008)	PISA 2003	32–37	Student/ country	Gender differences	Cultural attitudes, female political empowerment	Math + reading	Gender gap in test scores	Cross-section	Girls' lag in math eliminated in more gender-equal societies

Continued

Table 2.10 Cross-Country Studies on Institutions and Equity of Educational Achievement—cont'd

Study	Dataset	No. of countries	Level of analysis	Topic of investigation	Measure of institutions	Measure of achievement	Measure of equity	Estimation method	Results
Woessmann, Luedemann, Schuetz, and West (2009), ch. 7	PISA 2003	27	Student	Accountability, autonomy, and choice	Several measures of accountability, autonomy, choice, and tracking	Math	Dependence of test scores on PISA index of ESCS	Cross-section WCRLR	Public funding, private operation, and later tracking reduce impact of family background; accountability measures mostly equity-neutral
Schneeweis (2010)	TIMSS, TIMSS-R, +2003, PISA +2003	62, 167 country-years	Student/country	Educational institutions and integration of migrants	Ethnic segregation, preprimary enrollment, school starting age, instruction time, external exams	Math + science	Unexplained test score gap of immigrants	Blinder-Oaxaca decomposition, pooled WLS, country fixed effects	Institutions account for 20% of immigrant disadvantage; esp. preprimary education, young school starting age, low classroom segregation, instruction time
Fryer and Levitt (2010)	TIMSS 2003, PISA 2003	17–47	Country	Gender differences	Female economic and political opportunities	Math	Gender gap in test scores	Cross-section	Correlation of gender gap with societal gender inequality not robust to including Muslim countries

Notes: ESCS = economic, social, and cultural status. WCRLR = weighted clustering-robust linear regression. OLS = ordinary least squares. DiD = differences in differences. See Tables 2.1 and 2.2 for acronyms of datasets.

monitoring the education process, so that they can be understood as an accountability device. (See Bishop (2006) for a discussion of the underlying theoretical concepts.)

Students in countries that have external exit-exam systems very consistently perform significantly and substantially better on the international student achievement tests than students in countries without external exit-exam systems (see Table 2.9). Using country-level data, John Bishop has shown this for the 1991 IAEP math, science, and geography tests (Bishop (1995), section 4), the 1991 SIRS reading test (Bishop (1999)), the 1995 TIMSS math and science tests (Bishop (1997)), and the PISA 2000 reading, math, and science tests (Bishop (2006), section 3). Microeconometric cross-country analyses that extensively control for family-background and school-input factors at the student level have confirmed this result for the 1995 TIMSS tests (Woessmann (2001, 2003b)), the 1999 TIMSS-Repeat tests (Woessmann (2003a)), the 2000 PISA tests (Woessmann (2005c); Fuchs and Woessmann (2007)), and the 2003 PISA tests (Woessmann, Luedemann, Schuetz, and West (2009); see Table 2.4). Taken as a whole, the existing cross-country evidence suggests that the effect of external exit exams on student achievement may well be larger than a whole grade-level equivalent, or between 20% and 40% of a standard deviation of the respective international tests.[34]

Beyond external exit exams, student achievement in PISA 2000 is also positively associated with teachers' monitoring of student progress by regular standardized tests (Fuchs and Woessmann (2007)). Richer data on additional accountability mechanisms available in PISA 2003 (documented in Table 2.4) reveal positive associations of student achievement with accountability measures aimed at teachers, such as internal and external monitoring of teacher lessons, and with accountability measures aimed at schools, such as assessments used to compare them to district or national achievement (Woessmann, Luedemann, Schuetz, and West (2009)).

Given the cross-sectional nature of identification, possible unobserved country heterogeneity related to the existence of external exit exams is a concern. To exclude the possibility that external exit exams just capture general cultural features of different world regions, Woessmann (2003a) shows that results are robust to a regional fixed effects specification that controls for indicators of nine world regions. To ensure that the results do not capture other features of centralization, results also prove robust to including controls for the centralization of school curricula and textbook approval, the share of central government financing, and ethnolinguistic fractionalization as a proxy for the homogeneity of a country's population.

Substantial cultural biases are also ruled out by the fact that the same positive association between central exams and student achievement is found within countries where some regions have external exam systems and others do not. Such cross-regional

---

[34] Schneeweis (2010) finds that across countries, central exit exams are negatively related to the achievement gap between migrants and natives.

studies exist for Canadian provinces (Bishop (1997)), German states (Jürges, Schneider, and Büchel (2005); Woessmann (2010b)), and U.S. states (Bishop, Moriarty, and Mane (2000). Woessmann (2010b) even shows that the estimated size of the effect of external exit exams does not differ significantly between the sample of German states and the sample of OECD countries. To probe causality further, Jürges, Schneider, and Büchel (2005) apply a differences-in-differences approach to the German TIMSS 1995 data that exploits the fact that in some secondary-school tracks, the states with central exit exams have them in math but not in science, finding smaller but still substantial effects.[35]

Woessmann (2005c) exploits the student-level variation within each country to analyze whether external-exam effects are heterogeneous along several dimensions in quantile regressions and interacted specifications. Results using the TIMSS, TIMSS-Repeat, and PISA tests suggest that the effect tends to increase with student ability but does not differ with most family-background measures. It increases during the course of secondary education and with regular standardized examination. Furthermore, as discussed below, the effects of external exams are complementary to several dimensions of school autonomy.

4.4.2 Autonomy

Another institutional feature that is sometimes argued to exert positive effects on student outcomes is school autonomy, because local decision-makers tend to have superior information. On the other hand, in decision-making areas where their interests are not strictly aligned with improving student achievement, local decision-makers may act opportunistically unless they are held accountable for the achievement of their students (see Woessmann (2005c) for a discussion in a principal-agent framework).

The school background questionnaires of the international tests allow deriving measures of school autonomy in several different decision-making areas. The general pattern of results (cf. Table 2.9) is that students perform significantly better in schools that have autonomy in process and personnel decisions (Woessmann (2003b); Fuchs and Woessmann (2007); Woessmann, Luedemann, Schuetz, and West (2009)). These decisions include such areas as deciding on the purchase of supplies and on budget allocations within schools, hiring and rewarding teachers (within a given budget), and choosing textbooks, instructional methods, and the like. Similarly, students perform better if their teachers have both incentives and the possibility to select appropriate teaching methods. By contrast, school autonomy in budget formation and teacher autonomy over the subject matter to be covered in class—two decision-making

---

[35] This approach assumes that there are no spillovers between achievement in math and in science. Jürges and Schneider (2010) find positive effects of central exit exams on student achievement, but negative effects on self-reported student attitudes toward math, across German states.

areas that are likely subject to substantial opportunism but little superior local knowledge—are negatively associated with student achievement.

The international evidence also points to a significant interaction of the effect of school autonomy with the extent of accountability in the school system (as previously found in Table 2.4). In some areas, autonomy is negatively associated with student achievement in systems that do not have external exit exams, but the association turns positive when combined with external-exam systems. Reflecting coefficient estimates from a student-level international education production function using the combined TIMSS and TIMSS-Repeat data, Figure 2.6 depicts school autonomy over teacher salaries as one such example. School autonomy over teacher salaries is *negatively* associated with student achievement in systems without external exams. However, in line with the arguments above, the average level of student achievement is higher in systems with external exams. But what is more, the association between school autonomy and student achievement turns completely around in systems with external exams: Salary autonomy of schools is *positively* associated with student achievement in external-exam systems. The estimates in Figure 2.6 are expressed in percentages of a standard deviation on the international test scores, suggesting that the achievement difference

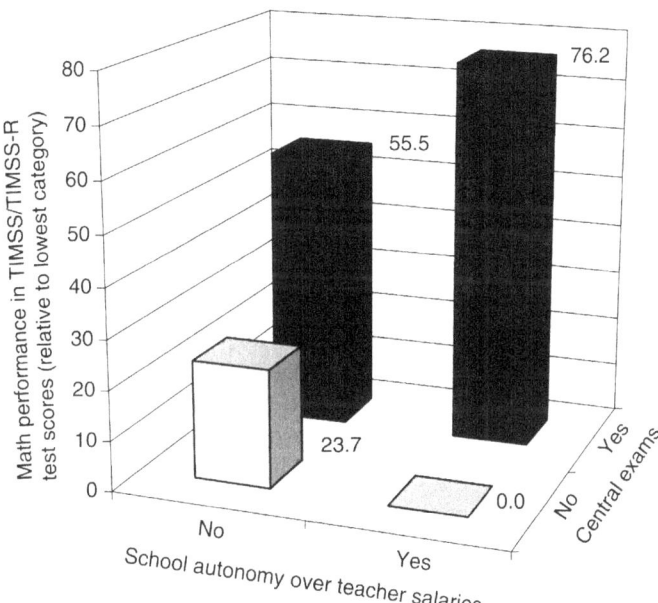

Figure 2.6 External exams, school autonomy, and student achievement across countries. Notes: Performance difference between the four categories relative to the lowest category which is set equal to zero. Based on a cross-country student-level multiple regression using the combined TIMSS and TIMSS-Repeat micro databases that extensively controls for family background, school inputs, and other institutional features. *Source*: Woessmann (2005c).

between the best and worst institutional setting amounts to three quarters of a standard deviation, a huge effect compared to other educational interventions. Evidence from PISA 2000 corroborates this interaction pattern (Fuchs and Woessmann (2007)). Similar positive interactions between external exams and school autonomy have also been found for such decision-making areas as school autonomy in determining course content and teacher influence on resource funding, among others (see Woessmann (2005c) for details).

In light of economic theory, this pattern of results is intuitively appealing. It indicates that local autonomy can lead to worse student outcomes if schools do not face incentives to focus attention on these outcomes. By contrast, when external exams hold schools accountable for student achievement, school autonomy leads to better outcomes. However, methodologically the existing empirical evidence on school autonomy is descriptive and awaits additional work that tries to more explicitly identify exogenous variation in school autonomy.[36]

4.4.3 Competition from private schools

A third institutional feature that has been researched using international data is the relative performance of publicly and privately operated schools and the competition introduced by the latter. (For a general overview of school competition, see Hoxby (2003) and Rouse and Barrow (2009)).

A first approach is to estimate differences in student achievement between public and private schools in each country, after controlling extensively for student and school background information. The PISA school background questionnaire provides specific school-level information on public versus private management and financing. Public school management is defined as schools managed directly or indirectly by a public education authority or governing board appointed by government or elected by public franchise, whereas private school management is defined as schools managed directly or indirectly by a nongovernment organization, for example churches, trade unions, or businesses. The share of public funding of each school is reported as the percentage of total school funding coming from government sources (at different levels), as opposed to such private contributions as fees and donations.

Looking across all countries (Table 2.8), private school management tends to be positively associated with student achievement, with a difference to publicly operated schools of 16–20% of an international standard deviation in the three subjects in PISA 2000 (Fuchs and Woessmann (2007)). A similar result is found in PISA 2003 (Woessmann, Luedemann, Schuetz, and West (2009)). The pattern is not uniform across countries, however, as revealed when estimating the effect within countries (Woessmann

---

[36] At the level of higher education, Aghion et al. (2010) and Aghion (2008) provide descriptive evidence that university autonomy is associated with better outcomes in terms of research rankings.

(2009b)). Toma (1996) (see also Toma (2005)) similarly estimates the effect of private school operation in five countries using the 1981 SIMS, noting that the positive effect of private provision is independent of whether the countries tend to finance the schools publicly or not. Estimating the effect of private school operation in eight countries in PISA 2000, Vandenberghe and Robin (2004) find positive effects only in some countries, but they do not account for differences in the source of school funding. Using the same database and distinguishing between privately operated schools that do and do not depend on government funding, Corten and Dronkers (2006) find a positive association of the achievement of students with low socio-economic status with private government-dependent schools, but no significant differences between public and private-independent schools. Dronkers and Robert (2008) find that the better performance of government-dependent private schools can be accounted for by a better school climate.

Using school-level variation of public-private operation in a pooled sample of countries, Woessmann, Luedemann, Schuetz, and West (2009) find positive interactions between private school operation and the average extent of autonomy that schools have in a country. Privately operated schools perform better if schools in the system are autonomous in formulating the budget and in staffing decisions, suggesting that the incentives created by parental choice of private schools work particularly well if (private and public) schools in the system have autonomy to respond to the parental demands. Furthermore, they show that the association of student achievement with two measures of external accountability—the monitoring of teacher lessons by external inspectors and assessment-based comparisons of schools to national performance—is stronger in privately operated schools than in publicly operated schools. Private schools may thus benefit particularly from the accountability created by external inspection and performance comparisons with other schools.

Given the problem of nonrandom selection into private versus public schools within a country, these results based on microlevel variations within countries should be interpreted with caution. While many features of self-selection will be held constant by the extensive family-background controls that most of the studies contain, possible unobserved student heterogeneity may still raise concerns of selection bias. Because issues of self-selection cancel out at the country level, the cross-country estimation approach provides the possibility to address selection concerns by measuring private schooling as a share at the country level. In addition, in contrast to most within-country studies, studies that measure private-school shares at the country level are able to capture general-equilibrium effects that may arise from private competition. If the existence of private alternatives exerts competitive pressure on nearby public schools, both private and public schools may perform at a higher level due to larger private shares. Consequently, there may be important effects of private schools at the system level even if there is no performance difference between private and public schools at the school level.

Studies that include country-level measures of private school operation (Table 2.9) consistently find a strong positive association with student achievement (see Woessmann (2003b) for TIMSS 1995; Woessmann (2009b) for PISA 2000; and Woessmann, Luedemann, Schuetz, and West (2009) for PISA 2003). At the same time, the measure of private funding shares available in PISA is negatively associated with student achievement. This pattern is depicted in Figure 2.7 and Table 2.4, which show that students in countries that combine relatively high shares of private operation with relatively high shares of public funding perform highest among the different operation-funding combinations, while students in countries that combine public operation with private funding perform lowest. On average, the difference between the countries at the first and ninth decile on the international distribution—60 percentage points in terms of private operation and 45 percentage points in terms of government funding—can account for roughly 0.35 standard deviations in educational achievement each.

The results point toward the importance of distinguishing between the operation and funding dimensions of private involvement. Without public funding, poor families may be constrained in their choices because they do not have the financial means to

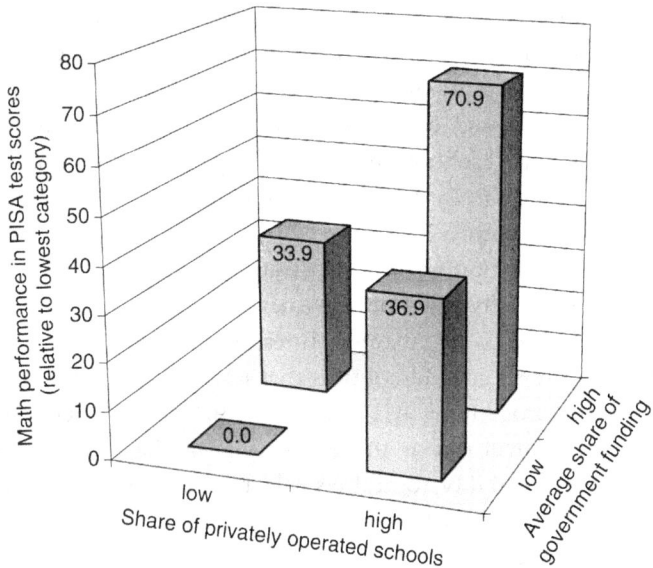

Figure 2.7 Private operation, public funding, and student achievement across countries. Notes: Performance difference between the four categories relative to the lowest category which is set equal to zero. Based on a cross-country student-level multiple regression using the PISA 2003 micro database that extensively controls for family background, school inputs, and other institutional features. "Low" and "high" refer to the 1st and 9th decile on the international distribution of the two variables (0% and 60% in the case of private operation and 55% and 100% in the case of government funding). *Source*: Woessmann, Luedemann, Schuetz, and West (2009).

opt for private schooling. In this case, public funding may help families to exert their choices in terms of privately managed schools. The fact that public funding is positively associated with student achievement may thus also point to positive performance effects of school choice and competition. This line of reasoning is consistent with evidence in Woessmann (2009b) showing that at the school level, the advantage of privately operated schools over publicly operated schools is particularly strong in countries with large shares of public funding. It is also in line with the finding of Woessmann, Luedemann, Schuetz, and West (2009), who show that students in countries where public funding is equalized between privately and publicly operated schools perform significantly better than students in countries where privately operated schools receive less government funding than publicly operated schools. Thus, a level playing field between public and private schools in terms of government funding may be an important ingredient for the competitive effects of private schools to emerge.

Beyond choice created by private schools, Woessmann, Luedemann, Schuetz, and West (2009) do not find significant associations on average of student achievement with proxies for choice among public schools, such as the share of students in a country who do not attend their school because it is the local school and who report that they attend their school because it is better than alternatives. But within urban areas where there are schools to choose from, reduced local attendance and increased choice of better schools are associated with better student achievement. Using subnational regional variation in PISA 2003, Sprietsma (2008) finds a positive association of student achievement with the regional average of students reporting to attend their school because it is known to be a good school, which is interpreted as a measure of quality-based school choice.

Combining German state-level data with data for OECD countries, Woessmann (2010b) shows that the association of private school shares with student achievement is not statistically different between the sample of German states and the sample of OECD countries. The result suggests that the international finding is not driven by major cultural differences between countries.

But there are additional challenges to causal identification of the effect of private competition. Omitted variables may be correlated with both the extent of private schooling and student achievement, such as factors related to the demand for private schooling or institutional or policy factors that affect its supply. Moreover, even well-controlled comparisons of countries or regions with small and large private sectors will be biased to the extent that low-quality public schools increase demand for private schooling as a substitute. To address these concerns, West and Woessmann (2010) develop an instrumental variable identification that exploits the fact that resistance of the Catholic Church to the state schooling emerging in the nineteenth century has repercussions for the size of the private school sector today. This historical source of variation can be used as a natural experiment to identify exogenous variation in private school competition. The instrumental-variable specification uses the share of Catholics in 1900—interacted with an indicator for Catholicism not being the state religion, as Catholics had no need to opt out of the state school system if the Church could control it—as an instrument for current private-school shares. The historical nature of the instrument allows controlling directly for any effect that the current Catholic share has on student achievement.

Estimating richly controlled student-level international education production functions on the PISA 2003 data, West and Woessmann (2010) confirm a significant positive effect of the share of privately operated schools on student achievement in math, science, and reading. The fact that the current share of Catholics, a control in some of their model, is negatively related to student achievement suggests that distinctive cultural features of traditionally Catholic countries are unlikely to be driving the results. The validity of the identification is additionally corroborated by the fact that Catholic shares are historically related to lower literacy and lower GDP per capita. To account for other possible channels through which the historical prevalence of Catholicism might be related to student outcomes today, the models also control for current GDP per capita and educational spending per student. Additional specification tests show that other current outcomes that might be conceived to be related to historical Catholicism, such as the decentralization of school policy decision-making, public social spending, and income inequality, are in fact uncorrelated with historical Catholic shares. West and Woessmann (2010) also show that much of the positive effect of private school shares accrues to students in public schools. This suggests that the overall effect is not simply due to privately operated schools being more effective, but rather reflects general-equilibrium effects of private competition. Finally, private competition is also found to reduce educational expenditure per student in the system, so that the better educational outcomes are obtained at lower cost.

As the overview in Table 2.10 shows, a topic that emerged only relatively recently in the international literature is the question to which extent institutional features of the school systems can account for differences in the equity (rather than level) of student achievement across countries. A consistent pattern in this literature is that shares of privately operated schools and shares of public funding are not only associated with higher levels of student achievement, but also with a reduced dependence of student achievement on socio-economic background. This has been shown both for the books-at-home indicator of family background in TIMSS and TIMSS-Repeat (Schuetz, Ursprung, and Woessmann (2008)) and for an index of socio-economic background in PISA 2003 (Woessmann, Luedemann, Schuetz, and West (2009), chapter 7).[37] In addition, Woessmann, Luedemann, Schuetz, and West (2009) find that

---

[37] Ammermueller (2005) finds a negative association of the share of private schools with his measure of equality of opportunity, but this may be due to the fact that the model does not control for public versus private funding of schools.

a higher difference between private and public schools in the share of government funding is negatively associated not only with average student achievement, but also with equality of educational opportunity.

4.4.4 Tracking

Another institutional feature of school systems that has been discussed mostly in terms of the equity of student outcomes is tracking. Here, tracking is meant to refer to the placement of students into different school types, hierarchically structured by performance. Such school placement policies are variously called tracking, streaming, ability grouping, or selective (as opposed to comprehensive) schooling. From a theoretical viewpoint, the effects of educational tracking are controversial: Depending on the nature of peer effects assumed, homogeneous classes may contribute to optimal learning situations for all students through focused curricula and adequate progress, or weaker groups may be systematically disadvantaged if they are separated early on.[38] Countries differ widely in the age at which they first track children into different types of schools. In the majority of OECD countries, tracking takes place at the age of 15 or 16, with no tracking until grade 9 or 10. In contrast, some countries undertake the first tracking at the age of 10. Again, this international variation lends itself particularly well to analyze the effects of the institutional feature of tracking (cf. Woessmann (2009a)).

Hanushek and Woessmann (2006) develop an international differences-in-differences approach to identify the causal effect of early tracking in a cross-country setting (see Table 2.10). The basic idea starts with the fact that in *all* countries, students are taught in a uniform school type for the first four years of schooling. Therefore, a comparison of the *change* in the variance of educational outcomes between 4th grade and the end of lower-secondary school between countries with and without early tracking can provide information on possible impacts of tracking. The analysis takes out the general level of inequality and considers only the change in inequality that occurs after 4th grade to determine the effect of early tracking. This method basically involves an investigation of the relationship depicted in Figure 2.8. The figure shows the inequality in reading achievement in 4th grade (in PIRLS) and at age 15 (in PISA 2003) for all countries that participated in both studies, measuring educational inequality by the standard deviation in student test scores. The essence of the analysis is to compare the *change* in inequality that occurs from primary to lower-secondary school between countries with and without educational tracking during this period. When looking at the change between the achievement dispersion in PIRLS and PISA, that part of the inequality measured at the end of lower-secondary school that already existed in 4th grade is eliminated. The change is indicated by the lines that connect the two

---

[38] Here we concentrate entirely on tracking that occurs between schools, that is, where children are sorted into separate schools. Many countries of the world, including the U.S., pursue tracking within schools but not generally across schools. For more on within-school tracking, see Betts (2010).

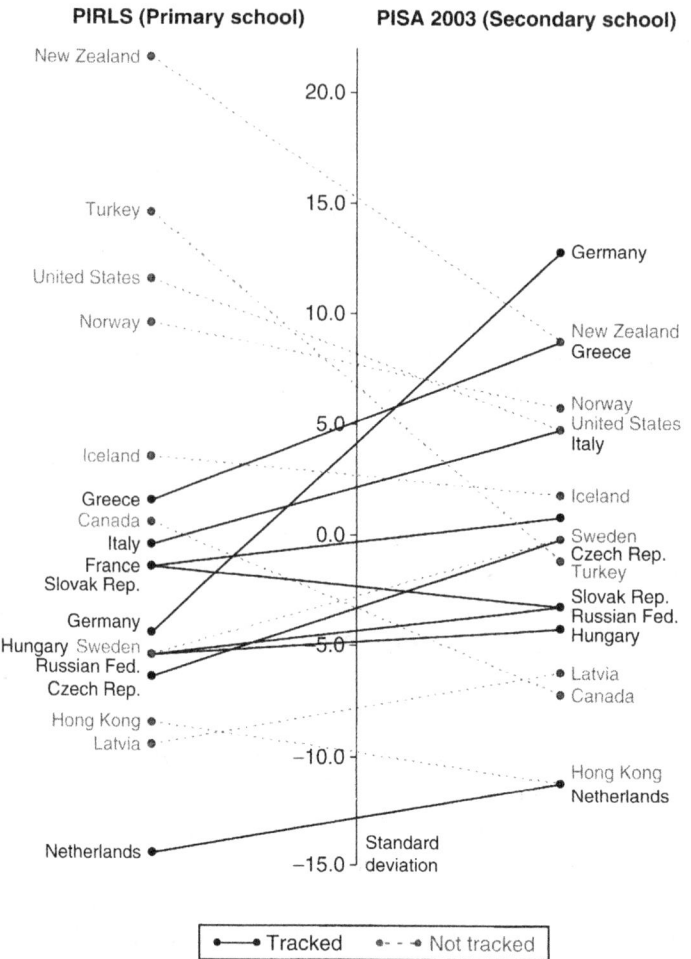

Figure 2.8 Educational inequality in primary and secondary school. Notes: Dispersion of student achievement measured as standard deviation of test scores in primary school (PIRLS) in comparison to lower-secondary school (PISA 2003), in both cases measured as difference to the international mean of national standard deviations in each test. The lines indicate the change in performance dispersion from primary to lower-secondary school. The dark solid lines indicate school systems that track their students into different school types before the age of 16, while the light dashed lines refer to those school systems that do not track their students by this age. *Source*: Based on Hanushek and Woessmann (2006).

points of each country. For countries with early tracking, solid connecting lines are used, while dashed lines indicate countries without early tracking. It is clearly visible that nearly all black solid lines point upward whereas nearly all red dashed lines point downward: In countries with early tracking, inequality increases systematically, whereas it decreases in countries without tracking.

Hanushek and Woessmann (2006) confirm this graphic depiction in country-level econometric estimates based on a differences-in-differences approach: The difference between countries with and without early tracking is investigated in terms of the difference in inequality between primary and lower-secondary school. The results show that early tracking systematically increases the inequality of student achievement. In total, their analyses take into account eight pairs of tests in primary and secondary schools, combining a total of 176 country observations. In contrast to the results on inequality, the results on achievement levels are less clear. But there is little evidence that early tracking increases the achievement level. To the contrary, in the most comprehensive model there is a marginally significant negative effect of early tracking on the average achievement level. When evaluating achievement at different percentiles of the performance distribution, not even for the best 5% of students is there a positive effect of early tracking.

While this investigation considers the dispersion of student achievement, Schuetz, Ursprung, and Woessmann (2008) investigate the more direct measure of inequality of opportunity outlined above: the extent to which individual student achievement depends on the family background of the student. At a more descriptive level, the effect of early tracking on equity is identified by the interaction of the country-level measure of early tracking with the student-level measure of family background in a student-level model with country fixed effects. The measure of inequality of opportunity familiar from Figure 2.2 above is found to be significantly smaller, the later the tracking age of students. If tracking is postponed by four years, for example, the impact of family background on student achievement is smaller by one quarter of the entire impact of the family background averaged across the OECD countries. In a model without country fixed effects, the association between early tracking and the average achievement level is statistically insignificant and negative.

The same association between tracking and equality of opportunity is found in a related study using PISA 2003 data (Woessmann, Luedemann, Schuetz, and West (2009), chapter 7). Using the Index of Economic, Social, and Cultural Status (ESCS) provided by the PISA study as an alternative measure for family background, the qualitative results are the same: The association between test scores and family background is significantly smaller, the higher the age of first tracking. This association is depicted in Figure 2.9: In countries with earlier tracking, the achievement difference between children with different socio-economic backgrounds is considerably larger. As the figure reveals, this effect arises primarily from the fact that children with low socio-economic status in countries without early tracking perform considerably better. At the same time, children from families with a relatively high socio-economic status perform at approximately the same level. Accordingly, the effect of later tracking on the average achievement level is again positive, albeit not statistically significant.

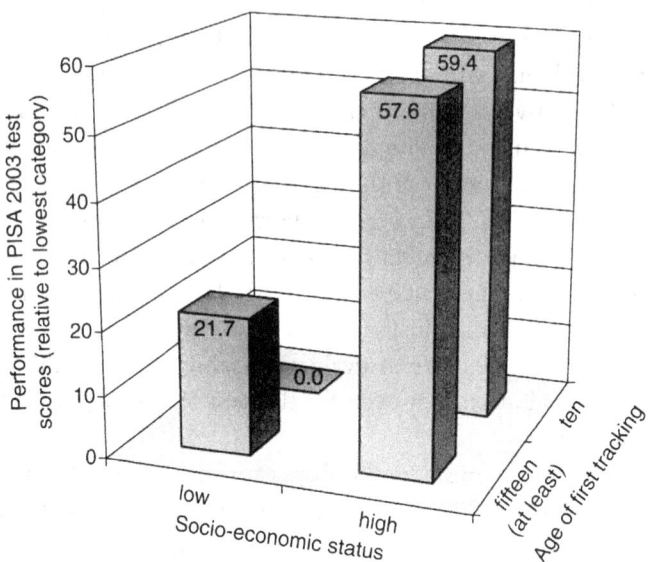

Figure 2.9 Tracking and socio-economic status in PISA. Notes: Performance difference between the four categories relative to the lowest category which is set equal to zero. Based on a cross-country student-level multiple regression using the PISA 2003 micro database that extensively controls for family background, school inputs, and other institutional features. Low and high socio-economic status correspond to the 25th and 75th percentile of the PISA ESCS index, respectively. *Source*: Based on Woessmann, Luedemann, Schuetz, and West (2009).

In terms of the equity effects, Ammermueller (2005) reports similar results for the number of school types (rather than the age of first tracking) based on the international PIRLS and PISA data. Waldinger (2006) uses a combination of the approach of Hanushek and Woessmann (2006) and Schuetz, Ursprung, and Woessmann (2008) and tends to find statistically insignificant results, but this may be largely due to limited degrees of freedom in samples of only 8–14 countries and a less informative tracking measure. Brunello and Checchi (2007) use the international approach described here for results beyond school age, finding that tracking increases the effect of family background on earnings in the labor market. Using a similar approach, Schneeweis (2010) finds some indication that an index of between-school social segregation, presumably partly caused by early tracking, is positively associated with the achievement gap between migrants and natives across countries.

Using system-level data, Woessmann (2010b) pools German states (most of which track after 4th grade, but some of which track after 6th grade) with OECD countries in a sample of 42–54 observations. Results indicate that the negative association between early tracking and the measure of inequality of educational opportunity (the slope of the socio-economic gradient) is statistically indistinguishable between the sample of German states and the sample of OECD countries. This shows that the cross-country association cannot be accounted for by such country-level omitted factors as differences in culture, language, or legal background.

4.4.5 Preprimary education system

The fact, discussed above, that student achievement is strongly associated with family background is suggestive of the idea that learning in the formative years before formal schooling is important for ultimate academic achievement. Consequently, student achievement toward the end of compulsory school is not only related to features of the school system, but also to preschool education (see the conceptual discussion in Cunha, Heckman, Lochner, and Masterov (2006) and Blau and Currie (2006) for a general review of the empirical literature). In line with this reasoning, Schuetz, Ursprung, and Woessmann (2008) find a positive association of student achievement in 8th grade (in TIMSS and TIMSS-Repeat) with the usual duration of the preschool cycle in a country.

Schuetz (2009) uses the individual-level information on preprimary attendance available in PISA 2003 to show that preprimary attendance is positively associated with achievement at age 15 in most countries. She goes on to exploit the fact that the size of this association varies substantially across countries. She estimates a cross-country student-level specification with country fixed effects and interactions between individual preprimary attendance and country-level indicators of the quality of preprimary education. She finds that the achievement advantage of students who attended preprimary education over those who did not is positively associated with country-level measures of per-student spending in preprimary education, of the share of preprimary institutions being privately operated, and of the training level and relative pay of preprimary teachers. Thus, indicators of institutions and structural quality of preprimary education systems can account for variation in the estimated coefficients on preprimary attendance across countries. While the study is descriptive in the sense that individual preprimary attendance may not be conditionally random, the estimators of interest are unbiased by selection decisions as long as the selection process is the same in all countries. In this sense, under the assumption that enrollment in preprimary education follows the same rules in all countries, interacted specification can be interpreted as an international differences-in-differences approach.

In terms of equity, using the interacted specification described above, Schuetz, Ursprung, and Woessmann (2008) show that the association between socio-economic background and 8th-grade student achievement is negatively related to the duration of preprimary education in a country. Furthermore, the thus measured equality of educational opportunity follows an inverted U-shaped relationship with preschool enrollment: The association between the books-at-home measure of socio-economic background and TIMSS student achievement increases up to a preprimary enrollment rate of 60%

in a country and decreases beyond that threshold. This result pattern may indicate that initially children who are otherwise advantaged attend preprimary education. Only once most of a country's children attend preprimary institutions does preprimary attendance increase equality of educational opportunity for children from lower socio-economic backgrounds. Using a similar approach to focus on equality of educational opportunity between native and migrant children, Schneeweis (2010) finds that the migrant achievement gap is negatively associated with preprimary enrollment across countries.

4.4.6 Additional results

Apart from the five institutions discussed so far—accountability, autonomy, competition, tracking, and preprimary system—descriptive studies have also looked beyond school age and into less formal institutional settings of societies. Cascio, Clark, and Gordon (2008) focus on the education system beyond the school level by observing age profiles of literacy into adulthood using the IALS adult achievement test. They show that countries with higher university graduation rates have larger literacy gains into adulthood. Falch and Fischer (2008a, 2008b) focus on institutional structures of a country's public sector in general and find student achievement to be negatively associated with redistributive government activities and positively associated with government spending decentralization, although their panel identification from short-term variation in the government measures on immediate student achievement warrants further investigation.

Guiso, Monte, Sapienza, and Zingales (2008) show a negative country-level association of the achievement gap between boys and girls in PISA 2003 with several indicators of a gender-equal culture such as indices of cultural attitudes toward women, female economic activity, and women's political empowerment. However, Fryer and Levitt (2010), after replicating their main finding on the PISA 2003 data, show that it does not hold when including a group of Middle Eastern countries in a country-level analysis of the TIMSS 2003 data.

These suggestive findings warrant further rigorous testing.

4.5 Conclusions on the determinants of international educational achievement

The economic literature on determinants of international differences in educational achievement has applied two main approaches. The first approach exploits the cross-country variation for identification of cross-country associations. The second approach estimates the same association within different countries in order to enhance understanding of whether a factor's importance differs systematically in different settings. Part of the existing work is descriptive in nature, estimating the association of student achievement with certain factors after controlling for the rich set of possible inputs into educational production available in the international background data. But quasi-experimental work has been developed to identify some of the underlying causal mechanisms both in the cross-country and in the within-country approach.

On family background and school inputs, the international results tend to mirror the existing national evidence on educational production. Many dimensions of students' family background are important factors for their educational achievement. At the same time, it is hard to find evidence of substantial positive effects of most resource inputs, in particular class sizes and expenditure levels. Among school inputs, there is somewhat more indication of positive effects of measures capturing teacher quality, such as (in an international setting) teacher education. A particular opportunity of the international research is that it can unveil whether certain effects differ systematically across countries, such as class-size effects or the equality of educational achievement for students with different family or migration backgrounds. For example, the international pattern suggests that significant class-size effects are only present in systems with relatively low teacher quality. This result raises the cost-effectiveness question of whether student achievement is best served by reducing class size or by increasing the low teacher quality even in the countries where class-size effects are present.

The second particular opportunity of the international research is the substantial institutional variation that exists across countries. The international evidence on education production functions suggests that schools matter for student outcomes, but not so much in terms of traditional inputs. Instead the impact of schools comes through teacher quality and institutional structures that determine incentives. Institutional features of school systems can account for a substantial part of the cross-country variation in student achievement. In the school system, institutions that tend to be associated with higher achievement levels include accountability measures like external exit exams, school autonomy in process and personnel decisions (if combined with accountability), private-school competition, and public financing. Later tracking, public funding, and private operation are systematically related to the equality of student outcomes. While some of the evidence is descriptive, convincing causal identification has been developed that support the results on external exit exams, private-school competition, and tracking. Also beyond the school system, institutions of the preschool and post-school education systems are related to international differences in educational achievement. In particular, more extensive preprimary education systems relate to more equalized student achievement for children from different family and migration backgrounds, and measures of preprimary quality tend to be related to the size of the preprimary effect.

As more and more countries participate in the international tests, the opportunities grow for future research on the determinants of international educational achievement. With the additional variation, the international research will be able to draw on more experience with different institutions and start to analyze additional specific features beyond the broad concepts of institutional structures analyzed so for. There is also considerable scope for future research to advance identification in quasi-experimental research settings. Furthermore, as more regular tests with reasonable comparability over time become available, a panel structure of international tests emerges that provides longitudinal information within countries. This will allow future research to exploit educational reforms in different countries over time. A limiting factor remains the lack of individual-level panel data in the international tests.

5. ECONOMIC CONSEQUENCES OF INTERNATIONAL EDUCATIONAL ACHIEVEMENT

Turning to the economic consequences of educational achievement, the international achievement data permit several types of studies that are impossible when relying on skill information for a single country. First, at the individual level it is possible to investigate whether the translation of skills into earnings differs across a range of countries. While there are many studies of schooling and earnings within individual countries, it is impossible to make reliable comparisons across countries without common skill measures for the different countries. And without such comparisons, it is not possible to understand how economic institutions and market forces affect the returns to skills. Second, it is impossible to understand fully how these same forces enter into the determination of earnings distributions of countries. While it is possible to trace the evolution of the income and earnings distributions over time within a country, it is very difficult to understand how differences in the structure of the country's economy enter into the observed distributional outcomes. Finally, effects of labor-force skills on aggregate economic outcomes essentially demand cross-country data so that outcomes can be related to varying structures. Work on each of these areas is evaluated in the subsequent sections.

5.1 Cognitive skills and individual labor-market outcomes

Evaluating the impact of cognitive skills on individual earnings has always been difficult because of data availability issues. Most work in earnings determination has relied just on school attainment—in large part because individual earnings and school attainment are frequently collected together in population censuses. Thus, for example, the world survey of Psacharopoulos and Patrinos (2004) provides estimates of basic Mincer earnings functions for 98 separate countries.[39] But it is much less common to measure both

---

[39] The model of earnings determination by Mincer (1970, 1974) relates the logarithm of earnings to years of schooling, potential experience, potential experience squared, and possibly other control variables; see Equation (2.4) below. The coefficient on school attainment is frequently interpreted as the rate of return to a year of schooling, although this interpretation is challenged by Heckman, Lochner, and Todd (2006, 2008). In our analysis below, we do not interpret the common estimates as a rate of return but instead simply think of them as the earnings gradient that is associated with schooling or higher cognitive skills.

cognitive skills and labor-market outcomes within the same survey.[40] Cognitive skills are typically measured for students in school, and thus generally before any labor-market outcomes can be observed. The most common joint measurement of skills and wages comes from panel data that covers both schooling periods and subsequent labor-market experiences, and these are invariably available for just individual countries.[41]

One innovation in international surveys is to sample adults of different ages instead of using a school-based or cohort-based design. The first international survey of this type was the International Adult Literacy Survey (IALS), a set of surveys and tests given to 20 countries between 1994 and 1998. This focus was very different than the school-based international tests because it considered a labor force centered survey that covered adults (age 16–65). The tests employed were also unique, covering several functional areas including: Prose Literacy—the knowledge and skills needed to understand and use information from texts including editorials, news stories, poems, and fiction; Document Literacy—the knowledge and skills required to locate and use information contained in various formats, including job applications, payroll forms, transportation schedules, maps, tables, and graphics; and Quantitative Literacy—the knowledge and skills required to apply arithmetic operations, either alone or sequentially, to numbers embedded in printed materials, such as balancing a checkbook, calculating a tip, completing an order form, or determining the amount of interest on a loan from an advertisement. They were designed to be very practical.[42]

All of the existing comparative analyses rely on data from the IALS survey (Table 2.11).[43] By linking labor-market outcomes to comparably measured cognitive skills, direct international comparisons and analyses are possible.[44]

---

[40] We focus exclusively on cognitive skills, although others have pointed to the role of noncognitive skills. Noncognitive skills, while seldom precisely defined, include a variety of interpersonal dimensions including communications ability, teamwork skills, acceptance of social norms, and the like. Along such a line, Samuel Bowles and Herbert Gintis and more recently James Heckman and his co-authors have argued that noncognitive skills are very important for earnings differences. The early work along these lines includes Bowles and Gintis (1976) and Bowles, Gintis, and Osborne (2001). This is extended in a variety of ways in Cunha, Heckman, Lochner, and Masterov (2006) and Heckman, Stixrud, and Urzua (2006). Nonetheless, no consistent international data have been available on noncognitive skills.

[41] Because of our focus on international comparative analyses, we do not review the work related to individual countries. For a review of the role of cognitive skills on earnings determination within individual countries, see Hanushek and Woessmann (2008).

[42] The tests on the IALS surveys are identified as being very practical, but they have been shown to be closely related to the PISA scores for individuals. For individual performance on the prose literacy scale, the correlation with PISA is 0.85 (Yamamoto (2002)).

[43] The follow-on Adult Literacy and Life Skills Survey (ALLS), conducted in 2002–06, has not been used, in part because only five countries participated. A second follow-up by the OECD, the Programme for the International Assessment of Adult Competencies (PIAAC), promises an expansion of participating countries when it is initially administered in 2011.

[44] Other researchers have used single-country samples from IALS to investigate labor-market issues, but we do not include them in our evaluation of the cross-country uses of the data. See, for example, Oosterbeek (1998), McIntosh and Vignoles (2001), and Edin and Gustavsson (2008).

Table 2.11 Studies on Cognitive Skills and Individual Labor-Market Outcomes

Study	Countries	Topic of investigation	Measure of achievement	Measure of labor-market outcome	Estimation method	Results
Denny, Harmon, and Redmond (2000)	Great Britain, Ireland, Northern Ireland	Impact of functional literacy on earnings	Prose, document, and quantitative literacy	Hourly earnings	Cross-section log-linear maximum likelihood	Literacy has a role, but formal education dominant factor in determining earnings; positive interaction between literacy and years of schooling in Great Britain
Denny, Harmon, and O'Sullivan (2004)	21 countries	Impact of years of schooling and basic skills on earnings	Mean of prose, document, and quantitative literacy	Hourly earnings	Cross-section log-linear OLS	Skills have significant effect on earnings, highest in English-speaking countries; excluding skill measures significantly biases return to years of schooling upwards
Leuven, Oosterbeek, and Ophem (2004)	15 countries	International differences in skill wage differences	Mean of prose, document, and quantitative literacy	Differing earnings concepts, mostly gross annual	Demand and supply analysis, cross-section	Model of skill supply and demand successfully explains cross-country differences in wage differentials between skill groups
Kahn (2004)	Canada, New Zealand, Switzerland, U.S.	Skills of immigrants and employment	Mean of prose, document, and quantitative literacy	Employment probability	Cross-section	Immigrants had lower cognitive skills than natives in each country, largest gaps in U.S., small in Canada and New Zealand; controlling for skills, male immigrants in U.S. no less likely to be employed than natives, while other immigrants less likely to be employed
Kahn (2007)	Canada, Finland, Italy, Netherlands, Switzerland, U.K., U.S.	Impact of employment protection laws on employment	Mean of prose, document, and quantitative literacy	Permanent or temporary job	Cross-section, differences-in-differences multinomial logit	Controlling for skill levels, employment protection laws do not interact with probability to have job, but decrease probability to have permanent rather than temporary job for low-skilled workers
Hanushek and Zhang (2009)	13 countries	Returns to years education after adjusting for school quality	Quality-adjusted years of schooling; mean of prose, document, and quantitative literacy	Annual earnings from employment	Cross-section log-linear OLS	Cognitive skills and quality-adjusted years of schooling both have significant positive effects on earnings; returns to quality-adjusted education higher than traditional Mincer estimate, but bias more than offset by accounting for nonschool influences

Notes: IALS is the dataset used in all studies. OLS = ordinary least squares.

The clearest example of the possibilities can be found in Leuven, Oosterbeek, and Ophem (2004). They consider a simple question of whether underlying supply and demand for skills could explain the pattern of observed wage differentials in countries. This work was partly motivated by an earlier study by Blau and Kahn (1996), which suggested that returns to school attainment across countries did not reflect supply and demand conditions. Leuven, Oosterbeek, and Ophem (2004) use the skill measures from the IALS survey for 14 countries. By comparing the relative demand for skill categories across industries in each country to the aggregate supply of these skill groups, they find that wage patterns are indeed consistent with a simple supply-demand model, at least for lower and intermediate skill categories. This analysis highlights the necessity of having cross-country information to address questions about overall economic structures.

The typical international study of individual earnings emulates wage determination models employed in studies of individual economies, although here the interpretation becomes more difficult because of concerns about quality differentials. By far the most common model of individual earnings is the "Mincer earnings model," which can be thought of as a specialized form of Equation (2.1). In this, the standard estimation model takes the form:

$$y = b_0 + b_1 S + b_2 Exp + b_3 Exp^2 + b_4 W + v \quad (2.4)$$

where Exp is labor-market experience, W is a vector of other measured factors affecting incomes, and y is labor-market earnings, typically measured in logarithms. One can think of this as estimating Equation (2.1) where S is simply substituted as the measure of human capital (H). But, according to Equation (2.2), the estimated return to a year of schooling (b_1) is biased through the correlation of S with F, A, and any omitted elements of Z; examples of such correlation would be predicted in standard optimizing models of the choice of years of schooling (e.g., Card (1999); Glewwe (2002)). Recognizing this, significant attention has concentrated on ability bias arising from the correlation of school attainment with A and from other selection effects having to do with families and ability (see Card (1999)).

One set of typical estimates of earnings models adds test-score measures to the Mincer model in Equation (2.4) explicitly to control for ability differences. The international versions of these can be found in Denny, Harmon, and Redmond (2000) and Denny, Harmon, and O'Sullivan (2004). Their focus is largely on how inclusion of IALS test scores in Equation (2.4) alters the estimates of b_1.

The second issue beyond general concerns about omitted variables bias in Equation (2.4) is that most formulations of Mincer models assume that school quality is either constant or can be captured by addition of direct measures of school quality such as school resources in Equation (2.4). One extended version is to assume that cognitive skills is a measure of school quality—leading to estimating models that either add cognitive skills to Equation (2.4) or interact cognitive skills with school attainment.

But both approaches neglect the importance of nonschool influences on cognitive skills, particularly from the family. These factors have been well-documented within the literature on education production functions, and recognition of them provides the backdrop for the formulation in Equation (2.2).[45] If the vector of other factors, W, in the earnings model includes the relevant other influences on human capital from Equation (2.2), the estimate of b_1 would be simply $\phi\gamma$ (as long as school quality is constant).[46] Unfortunately, rich information about other determinants of skills outside of school attainment is seldom available, because this requires data about factors contemporaneous with schooling and long before observed labor-market data are available. While a number of ingenious approaches have been used, including, for example, exploiting the common experiences of twins, it is seldom plausible to conclude that the other factors in Equation (2.2) have been adequately controlled, leading to the interpretation of b_1 as the combined influence of school and correlated but omitted other influences.[47] As such, b_1 is a reduced-form coefficient that will give biased estimates of the potential impact from a policy designed to change school attainment alone.

An alternative conceptual approach is simply to take the measure of cognitive skills as a direct measure of human capital. While this appears similar in some ways to the classic estimation of Mincer equations except that cognitive skills (C) are employed instead of school attainment (S), it has some potential advantages, because it implicitly subsumes the various (unmeasured) determinants of human capital in Equation (2.2).

This suggests the following modification of Equation (2.4), which is a reduced-form equation that combines influences of cognitive factors through the channels of C and S:

$$y = b'_0 + b'_1 S + b'_2 Exp + b'_3 Exp^2 + b'_4 W + b'_5 C + v' \qquad (2.5)$$

In this formulation, estimation of Equation (2.5) with the inclusion of C yields an implication that the coefficient on S (i.e., b'_1) would reflect the impact of human capital

---

[45] See, for example, the discussion in Hanushek (1979).
[46] While Equation (2.2) highlights measurement error and its sources, the historical treatment has concentrated almost exclusively on simple misreporting of years of schooling, as opposed to potential omitted variables bias from neglecting (correlated) components of the true skill differences contained in H. See, for example, Ashenfelter and Krueger (1994). In our context, simple survey errors in S are a relatively small part of the measurement errors and omissions in specifying human capital.
[47] In terms of Equation (2.2), studies using schooling and income differences of twins (see Card (1999)) assume that school quality differences are relatively unimportant or unsystematic so that quantity of schooling, S, is the central object. Then, if ability, family circumstances, and other factors affecting skills are relatively constant across twins, differences in schooling can be related to differences in earnings to obtain an unbiased estimate of γ. Of course, the key question remaining is why S differs across otherwise identical twins who presumably face identical investment payoffs. Other instrumental variable approaches have also been introduced to deal with the endogeneity of schooling, but they frequently will suffer if human capital evolves from nonschool factors as in Equation (2.2).

differences that are not captured by C.[48] Yet, for the same reasons discussed previously, b'_1 would not be simply $\phi\gamma$. It is still biased by other omitted determinants of C, such as the family, described in Equation (2.2).

It is important to note, nonetheless, that finding a direct effect of schooling on earnings to be zero ($b'_1 = 0$) after conditioning on cognitive skills is not the same as saying that school attainment does not matter. It merely says that the impact of school comes entirely through the impact on cognitive skills, so that schooling that does not raise cognitive skills is not productive. In general, the impact of school attainment is:

$$\partial y/\partial S = b'_1 + b'_5(\partial C/\partial S) \qquad (2.6)$$

What does this mean in an international context? First, as discussed previously, it does not make much sense to combine the estimates of earnings models across countries, because it is inappropriate to assume that the rate of learning during a year of school is the same across countries. It also implies that it is difficult to compare international returns to school attainment, since the estimated returns are dependent on country-specific elements including school quality, the importance of other determinants of skills, and the rewards for differing levels of schooling.

The pattern of returns to cognitive skills across countries can be seen from estimating Equation (2.5) for the sample of countries in the IALS survey. Hanushek and Zhang (2009) provide estimates of b'_5 for 13 separate countries, which exhibit wide variation, as shown in Figure 2.10. Each standard deviation of test performance is associated with almost 20% higher annual earnings in the U.S. but less than 5% in Sweden and is actually insignificantly different from zero in Poland. (Note, however, that the Polish survey was conducted in 1994, and its economy had yet to adjust completely from the fall of communism.)

The IALS survey permits direct investigation of the importance of omitted factors from Equation (2.2) when estimating Mincer models. Obtaining unbiased estimates of the return to school attainment within different countries has consumed considerable attention, but little work has actually combined the determinants of achievement with the estimation of Equation (2.4). Figure 2.11 illustrates the impact on estimated schooling parameters from including information about an individual's family background and cohort-specific measures of health and ability.[49] From this figure, it is apparent that the average returns to attainment fall significantly (from 0.071 to 0.044) while the variation across countries is also lessened considerably. These adjustments

---

[48] Heckman and Vytlacil (2001) go further to argue that it is not possible to separate school attainment and achievement because they are so highly correlated. The importance of this depends, however, on the specific data samples and questions being investigated.

[49] One element of the analysis in Hanushek and Zhang (2009) is the adjustment of school attainment for variations in school quality over time (for each country separately). They find that many countries have had significant changes in quality (generally improvements in quality) over time, but the U.S. is an exception to this.

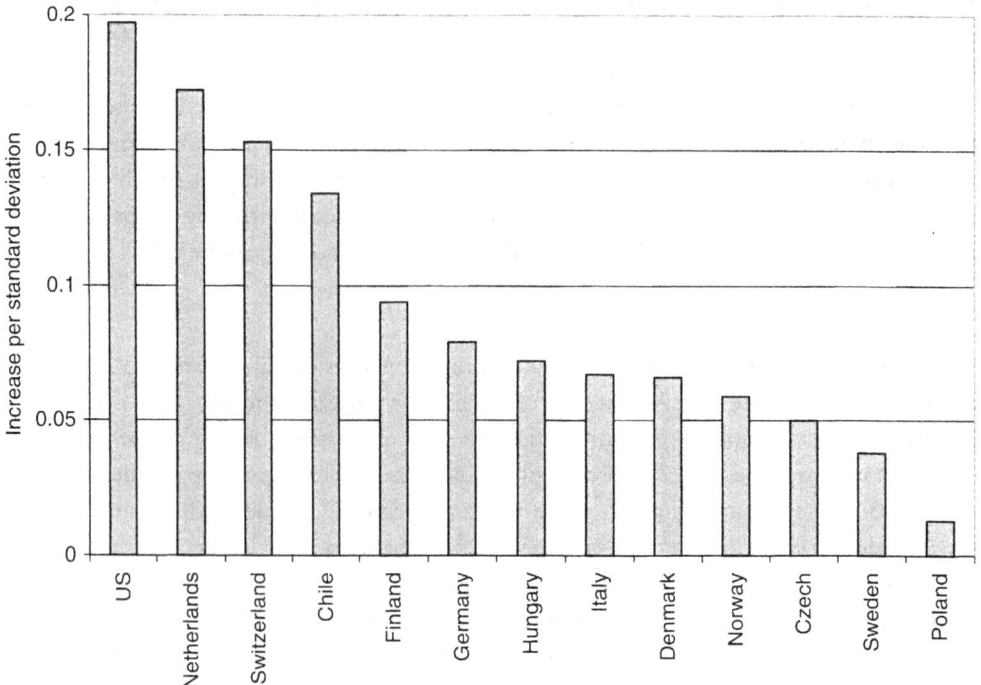

Figure 2.10 Returns to cognitive skills, International Adult Literacy Survey. *Source*: Hanushek and Zhang (2009).

are also more significant than is typical in the literature concerned with the estimation of returns to schooling (Card (1999)).

The study of substantive economic policy issues is also aided by having international data for individuals with comparable skills. In work consistent with the discussion here, Kahn (2004) takes cognitive skills measured by IALS test scores as a consistent measure of human capital and focuses directly on inter-country differences in immigrants. His comparison of the labor-market employment rates of immigrants in four different developed countries shows variations in labor-market assimilation (that largely remain unexplained). In a second international study, Kahn (2007) defines skill categories of workers by the IALS cognitive-skills tests in order to look at the distributional impacts of varying employment protection laws across countries—a subject that cannot be easily researched within countries because of the uniformity of the laws within a country. He finds that low-skill workers are pushed from permanent jobs to temporary jobs by more stringent employment protection laws.[50]

---

[50] Similar impacts are also seen for youth and for immigrants in the seven countries analyzed (Canada, Finland, Italy, the Netherlands, Switzerland, the United Kingdom, and the United States).

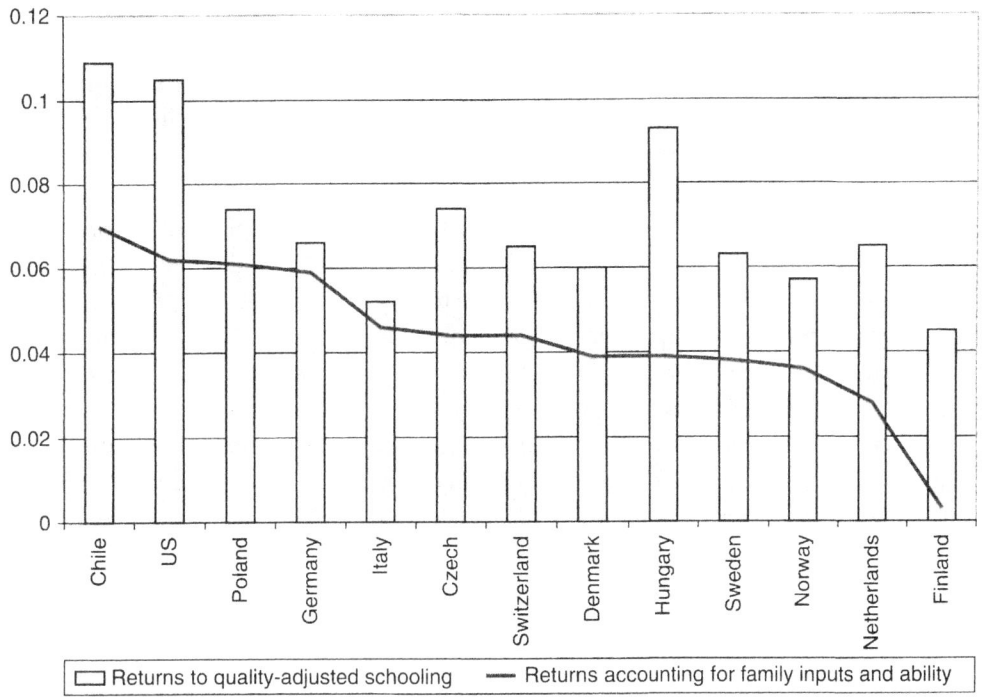

Figure 2.11 Impact of controlling for family inputs and ability on returns to schooling. *Source*: Hanushek and Zhang (2009).

Finally, while it is too early to see the full range of possibilities, some individual countries have followed earlier PISA test takers or have merged data from PISA with other existing data such as that from country registers. These studies, because they build on either the PISA-2000 or the PISA-2003 data and have relatively short transitions since age 15 when the students were tested, have looked largely at school transitions and movements into first jobs.[51] A common finding of these studies is that performance on the international tests is predictive of entry into higher education. Nevertheless, since these have been the uncoordinated work of individual countries, there is neither consistent data outside of PISA nor any commitments to continue these datasets into the future. Thus, these uses appear to be idiosyncratic to individual countries and do not easily support cross-country analyses.

---

[51] See, for example, studies in Canada (Knighton and Bussière (2006); Bushnik, Barr-Telford, and Bussière (2004)), Denmark (Jensen and Andersen (2006); Humlum, Kleinjans, and Nielsen (2010)), and Switzerland (Bertschy, Cattaneo, and Wolter (2009)). Follow-up data collection is also being developed in Australia and in the Czech Republic, although analyses using these data are currently unavailable. See also the summary of databases and analyses in Organisation for Economic Co-operation and Development (2007), p. 300.

5.2 Cognitive skills and the distribution of economic outcomes

One implication of the impact of cognitive skills on individual earnings is that the distribution of those skills in the economy will have a direct effect on the distribution of income. Cognitive skills by themselves do not of course determine the full distribution, because other factors such as labor-market institutions, taxes, and the like enter. But the importance of skills is becoming increasingly evident.

Very suggestive evidence on the impact of skills on the income distribution comes from Nickell (2004). Nickell, using the IALS data, considers how differences in the distribution of incomes across countries are affected by the distribution of skills and by institutional factors including unionization and minimum wages. While union coverage is statistically significant, he concludes that "the bulk of the variation in earnings dispersion is generated by skill dispersion" (page C11).[52]

The impact of the skill distribution across countries is shown dramatically in Figure 2.12 which is derived from a simple comparison of the dispersion of wages and the dispersion of prose literacy scores (each measured as the ratio of the 90th to

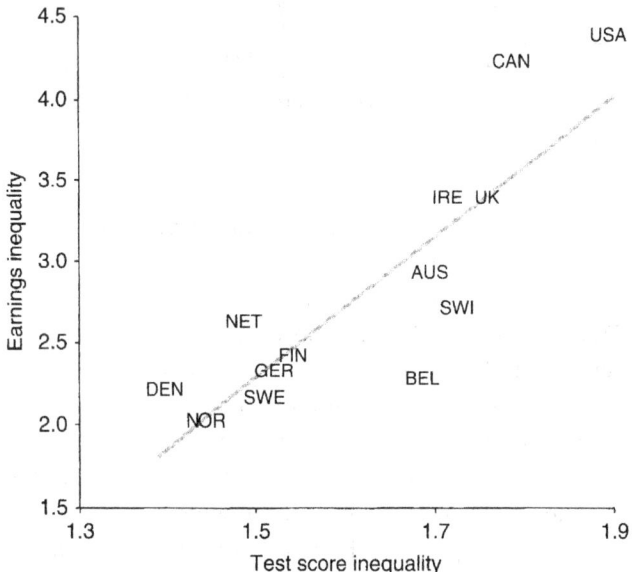

Figure 2.12 Inequality of test scores and earnings. Notes: Measure of inequality is the ratio of 9th decile to 1st decile in both cases; test performance refers to prose literacy in the International Adult Literacy Survey. *Source*: Based on Nickell (2004).

---

[52] Bedard and Ferrall (2003) similarly find a positive cross-country association between test-score inequality measured at age 13 and wage inequality of the same cohort measured later in life. De Gregorio and Lee (2002) find a (somewhat weaker) positive association between inequality in years of schooling and income inequality.

the 10th percentile). The tight pattern around the regression line reflects a simple correlation of 0.85 (which is not affected by including the other institutional factors).

There are of course many reasons to be concerned about this aggregate descriptive comparison, and other authors have pursued more systematic analysis of the variation in earnings using the micro data. Table 2.12 lists three existing studies that contrast the distribution of earnings in the U.S. with that in one or more other countries and that employ IALS data to define the underlying distribution of skills. Blau and Kahn (2005) provide the most comprehensive study where the U.S. is compared to nine other countries, and earnings are decomposed following the general approach of Juhn, Murphy, and Pierce (1993). They reach two general conclusions that provide a useful link to the previous analyses of earnings determination.[53] First, variations in cognitive skills are indeed a component of the observed earnings distribution, explaining 3–13% of variations in earnings depending on gender and the specific distributional measure, but they are not the dominant determinant. Second, differences in prices, that is, the rewards to differences in skills, explain a considerably larger part of the observed variation: 28–55%.

The results of the decomposition into skills and prices by Blau and Kahn (2005) are consistent with the relatively small explanatory power of skills in the more restricted analyses of Freeman and Schettkat (2001) and Devroye and Freeman (2001) and lead to questions about how to interpret Figure 2.12. The argument of Nickell (2004) is that skill distributions and not labor-market institutions are the dominant determinant of earnings variations, but this conflicts with the analyses of micro data from the same survey.

The reconciliation of Figure 2.12 with the micro analyses is straightforward at one level. The results from the previous section described differences in returns to cognitive skills and school attainment (Figures 2.10 and 2.11). These prior results show vividly that the prices of skills vary widely across countries. Moreover, there is a strong positive association of the estimated returns for cognitive skills in Figure 2.10 and the magnitude of test-score inequalities in Figure 2.12. Thus, the skill differences and the price differences reinforce each other to yield the almost linear relationship of skill variations and earnings variations in Figure 2.12.

The deeper question revolves around what aspects of labor markets lead to these price differences, which in turn appear so important in explaining earnings distributions. The analysis of Leuven, Oosterbeek, and Ophem (2004) focused on how the relative supplies and demands for skills were key, while Blau and Kahn (2005) suggest that other institutional features of the labor markets may be as important if not more

---

[53] A third conclusion of Blau and Kahn (2005) is the suggestion that a significant effect of school attainment (while also conditioning on cognitive skills) in their statistical analysis introduces some question about the use of cognitive skills as the only index of human capital as done by Leuven, Oosterbeek, and Ophem (2004).

Table 2.12 Studies on Cognitive Skills and Distribution of Labor-market Outcomes

Study	Dataset	Countries	Topic of investigation	Measure of achievement	Measure of labor-market outcome	Estimation method	Results
Freeman and Schettkat (2001)	IALS	Germany, U.S.	Skill compression and wage distribution	Quantitative literacy (numeracy)	Income, employment	Cross-section log-linear OLS	More compressed distribution of skills in Germany explains only modest proportion of higher wage compression compared to U.S.
Devroye and Freeman (2001)	IALS	Germany, Netherlands, Sweden, U.S.	Inequality in skills and in earnings	Mean of prose, document, and quantitative literacy	Annual earnings	Cross-section log-linear OLS	Skill inequality explains only small part of cross-country differences in inequality
Bedard and Ferrall (2003)	FIMS, SIMS	11 countries	Dispersion in test scores and in wages	Math	Annual wages	Aggregate correlations and OLS	Significant positive cross-country association of Gini coefficients of test scores at age 13 with Gini coefficients of cohorts' later wages
Blau and Kahn (2005)	IALS	9 countries	Inequality of skills and of earnings	Mean of prose, document, and quantitative literacy	Weekly earnings	Cross-section, Juhn-Murphy-Pierce decomposition	Greater skill dispersion in U.S. plays a part in explaining higher wage inequality, but relatively modest

Notes: OLS = ordinary least squares. See Tables 2.1 and 2.2 for acronyms of datasets.

important.[54] Moreover, the variations in skills themselves may feed back into the character of the labor market and the observed skill prices.

These analyses underscore the value of expanding the international component of various investigations of labor markets. The role of supply and demand conditions, of market institutions, and of governmental policy in determining skill prices and distributional issues remains a rather open and fertile ground for further investigation—and it has obvious ramifications for a variety of actively discussed governmental policies.

5.3 Cognitive skills and macroeconomic growth

Macroeconomists have long been interested in the factors that contribute to the growth of nations. Economists have considered the process of economic growth for much of the last 100 years, but most studies remained as theory with little empirical work.[55] Over the past two decades, economists linked analysis much more closely to empirical observations and in the process rediscovered the importance of growth.

Human capital has been a central focus of much of the recent growth modeling, and it is a standard element of any empirical work. The empirical macroeconomic literature focusing on cross-country differences in economic growth has overwhelmingly employed measures related to school attainment, or years of schooling, to test the predictions of growth models.[56] Initial analyses employed school enrollment ratios (e.g., Barro (1991); Mankiw, Romer, and Weil (1992); Levine and Renelt (1992)) as proxies for the human capital of an economy. An important extension by Barro and Lee (1993, 2001, 2010) was the development of internationally comparable data on average years of schooling for a large sample of countries and years, based on a combination of census and survey data.

The vast literature of cross-country growth regressions has tended to find a significant positive association between quantitative measures of schooling and economic growth.[57] But, average years of schooling is a particularly incomplete and potentially misleading measure of education for comparing the impacts of human capital on the economies of different countries. It implicitly assumes that a year of schooling delivers

---

[54] Note that Nickell (2004) attempted to address the issue of other institutional features with simple cross-country regressions that added unionization and minimum-wage restrictions and concluded that it was just the skill distribution that was important. In the formulation of Leuven, Oosterbeek, and Ophem (2004) or of Blau and Kahn (2005), however, the linear model would be inappropriate since the returns to skills are themselves a function of features of the labor market, including possibly the employment restrictions.

[55] For an account of the historical development, see Barro and Sala-i-Martin (2004). The associated empirical work concentrated on within-country analyses are found in Solow (1957), Jorgenson and Griliches (1967), and Denison (1985). A concise review of alternative models and the associated empirical testing can be found in Hanushek and Woessmann (2008).

[56] The earliest studies used adult literacy rates (e.g., Azariadis and Drazen (1990); Romer (1990)) but these data cover a limited number of countries and are error prone.

[57] For extensive reviews of the literature, see, e.g., Topel (1999), Temple (2001), Krueger and Lindahl (2001), Sianesi and Van Reenen (2003), and Pritchett (2006).

the same increase in knowledge and skills regardless of the education system. For example, a year of schooling in Peru is assumed to create the same increase in productive human capital as a year of schooling in Japan. Additionally, this measure assumes that formal schooling is the primary (sole) source of education and, again, that variations in nonschool factors—such as included in Equation (2.2)—have a negligible effect on education outcomes and human capital. This neglect of cross-country differences in the quality of education and in the strength of family, health, and other influences is probably the major drawback to employing such attainment measures of schooling. It also highlights the potential role for using the international data on cognitive skills described in Section 3, above.

The empirical inconsistencies arising from explaining growth with school attainment are well-described in Pritchett (2004, 2006). In simplest terms, positive trends in schooling attainment around the world and especially in developing countries have not been matched by changes in growth rates, suggesting problems with either the underlying conceptual model or with the measurement of human capital.

5.3.1 Aggregate measures of cognitive skills

A clear way to deal with the human capital measurement issues is to introduce information from the international achievement tests, paralleling the use of the cognitive-skills measures in the IALS surveys in analyzing patterns of earnings determination. There are two issues that are important in developing suitable data for macroeconomic analyses. First, each of the testing situations is a separate activity with no general attempt to provide common scaling. Second, the relevant feature for considering growth is clearly the skills of the labor force of a nation, but the international tests described previously provide data on the current school population.

The aggregation of prior test information to create a composite for each country involves empirical calibration.[58] To understand the basic approach, we sketch the approach in Hanushek and Woessmann (2009a) that was used to produce the score aggregates in the final column of Table 2.3 and that enters into several of the recent cross-country analyses.[59]

As shown in Table 2.1, there are data from international student achievement tests on 12 major international testing occasions before 2005. The individual testing situations contain separate tests in different subjects and at different age groups. These

---

[58] Empirical scaling as described here relies upon information about the overall distribution of scores on each test to compare national responses. This contrasts with the psychometric approach to scaling that calls for calibrating tests through use of common elements on each test. More recent testing, such as the PISA tests by the OECD, are constructed so that they can be consistent over time through using common questions to link tests in different years. A few of the available studies use data from a single testing occasion and thus do not have to aggregate scores; see Lee and Lee (1995), Coulombe, Tremblay, and Marchand (2004), and Coulombe and Tremblay (2006).

[59] This construction builds on earlier attempts to develop consistent aggregates as found in Hanushek and Kimko (2000) and Barro (2001). Altinok and Murseli (2007) present a different approach but the details are unclear.

testing occasions yield 36 separate test-subject-age observations, each providing internationally comparable performance data for between 11 and 45 participating countries. Most of the tests were conducted by the IEA, with the exception of the OECD-conducted PISA tests. Hanushek and Woessmann (2009a) describe in detail a methodology for making the separate testing data comparable, which we sketch here.

The methodology involves adjusting both the level of test performance and the variation of test performance through two data transformations. Because the United States has both participated in all of the international tests and has maintained its own longitudinal testing (the National Assessment of Educational Progress, or NAEP), the U.S. international performance over time can be calibrated to this external standard—thus benchmarking each of the separate international tests to a comparable level. This provides a relative comparison of countries taking each test over time, but it is also necessary to establish the variance on the tests so that direct compatibility of countries taking different tests can be established. The calibration of the dispersion of the tests relies on holding the score variance constant within a group of countries with stable education systems (defined in terms of secondary school attendance rates) over time. For this, Hanushek and Woessmann (2009a) use the 13 OECD countries who had half or more students completing upper secondary education around the beginning of international testing in the 1970s as the "stable" country group and standardize variances to their group performance on the 2000 PISA tests.

These two normalizations of the separate test data provide the basis for comparing and aggregating the available test data. The simple average of the transformed mathematics and science scores over all the available international tests in which a country participated provides the most straightforward combination of the data. The test instruments yield a total of 77 countries, indicated in the final column of Table 2.3, that have ever participated in any of the 12 international student achievement tests in mathematics and science through 2003.[60] We scale scores to a mean of 500 with a student-level standard deviation of 100 among the OECD countries (the same scale currently used by PISA).

This procedure of averaging performance over a 40-year period is meant to provide a consistently measured proxy for the educational performance of the whole labor force, because the basic objective is not to measure the skills of students but to obtain an index of the skills of the workers in a country. If the quality of schools and skills of graduates are roughly constant over time, this averaging is appropriate and uses the available information to obtain the most reliable estimate of skills. If on the other hand there is changing performance, this averaging will introduce measurement error of

---

[60] The latest rounds of PISA results, conducted in 2006 and released in December 2007 and in 2009 for release in December 2010, are not contained in our aggregations which were developed to analyze growth over the 1960–2000 period. There are five countries participating in PISA 2006 that had never participated on a previous international test. Likewise, the 2006 round of the PIRLS primary-school reading test includes three additional participants without prior international achievement data.

varying degrees over the sample of economic data. (The analysis in Hanushek and Woessmann (2009a) shows some variation over time, but its importance will clearly depend on the analytical approach and questions—a subject discussed below.)

The precise scaling on the transformed metric is of course subject to considerable noise, in particular for the early tests and for countries performing far below the international mean. The tests are usually not developed to provide reliable estimates of performance in the tails of the achievement distribution, which would be relevant for very poorly performing countries. However, the rough pattern across countries of overall performance should not be severely affected by the rescaling.

5.3.2 Evidence on the role of cognitive skills in economic growth

Empirical analyses building on aggregate measures of cognitive skills have reached dramatically different conclusions than most of the prior growth analysis built on school attainment measures of human capital. Table 2.13 displays the range of studies that have considered the impacts of cognitive skills. On the whole, these contributions to empirical growth research demonstrate that better measures of human capital alter the assessment of the role of education and knowledge in the process of economic development dramatically.

Using the data from the international student achievement tests through 1991 to build a measure of labor force quality, Hanushek and Kimko (2000)—first released as Hanushek and Kim (1995)—find a statistically and economically significant positive effect of the cognitive skills on economic growth in 1960–1990 that dwarfs the association between quantity of schooling and growth.[61] Thus, even more than in the case of education and individual earnings, ignoring differences in cognitive skills very significantly misses the true importance of education for economic growth. Their estimates suggest that one country-level standard deviation higher test performance would yield around one percentage point higher annual growth rates. (The country-level standard deviation is roughly equivalent to half of the individual-level standard deviation on the PISA scale.)

Table 2.13 provides short descriptions of the array of currently available models of cognitive skills and economic growth. This area is rapidly expanding, but it is valuable to assess where it currently stands.

---

[61] Their estimates employ a statistical model that relates annual growth rates of real GDP per capita to the measure of cognitive skills, years of schooling, the initial level of income, and a wide variety of other control variables (including in different specifications the population growth rates, political measures, openness of the economies, and the like). Hanushek and Kimko (2000) find that adding the international achievement test measures to a base specification including only initial income and educational quantity boosts the variance in growth of GDP per capita among the 31 countries in their sample that can be explained by the model from 33 to 73%. The effect of years of schooling is greatly reduced by including cognitive skills, leaving it mostly insignificant in alternative specifications. At the same time, adding the other factors leaves the effects of cognitive skills basically unchanged. Their basic formulation is also applied in much of the work described below.

Study	Dataset	No. of countries	Topic of investigation	Measure of achievement	Measure of macroeconomic outcome	Estimation method	Results
Hanushek and Kimko (2000)	FIMS, FISS, SIMS, SISS, IAEP-I, IAEP-II	31 (projected to 80)	Effect of labor-force quality on growth	Average score of all tests, math + science, different age levels	Growth rate of real GDP per capita, 1960–90	Cross-section growth regressions with different controls	Strong and robust effect of quality of labor force on growth; strong increase in explained growth variance; school quantity tends to lose significance
Lee and Lee (1995)	FISS	17	Effect of education on growth	Science, secondary school	Growth rate of real GDP per worker, 1970–85	Cross-section growth regressions, controlling for initial GDP	Significant effect of student achievement score on growth rate, ratio of physical investment to GDP, and lower fertility rate
Barro (2001)	FIMS, FISS, FIRS, SIMS, SISS, SIRS, IAEP-I, IAEP-II	23–43	Effect of education on growth	Average score of all tests, math, science + reading, different age levels	Growth rate of real GDP per capita, 1965–95 (10-year averages)	10-year-interval panel regressions by 3SLS with lagged instruments (scores as single cross-section), several controls	Significant effect of test scores, esp. science, on growth; quality of schooling much more important than quantity
Gundlach, Rudmar, and Woessmann (2002)	Hanushek and Kimko (2000), with extended imputations	(131)	Accounting for differences in level of development	Average score of all tests, math + science, different age levels	Output per worker, 1990	Development accounting (covariance decomposition)	Quality-adjusted measure of human capital accounts for 45% of variation in output per worker in global sample, and for whole variation in OECD sample
Woessmann (2003c)	Hanushek and Kimko (2000), with extended imputations	29 (–132)	Comparison of different measures of human capital	Average score of all tests, math + science, different age levels	Output per worker, 1990	Development accounting (covariance decomposition)	Quality-adjusted human capital accounts for 60% of variation in output per worker in 64-country sample with nonimputed data
Bosworth and Collins (2003)	Hanushek and Kimko (2000), with extended projections	31, projected to 84	Determinants of economic growth	Average score of all tests, math + science, different age levels	Log change in real output per worker, 1960–2000	Cross-section growth regressions with several controls	Significant effect of educational quality on growth, but sensitive to conditioning on quality of government institutions
Coulombe and Tremblay (2006)	IALS	14	Effect of literacy scores on growth	Synthetic time series of literacy of labor-market entrants 1960–1995, derived from age distribution of IALS test	Growth rate of real GDP per capita/worker, 1960–95 (5-year averages)	5-year-interval panel regressions with country (and time) fixed effects and different controls; test scores sometimes instrumented by years of schooling	Significant effect of literacy scores on growth; outperform years of schooling; stronger effect of women's than men's literacy

Continued

Table 2.13 Studies on Cognitive Skills and Macroeconomic Growth—cont'd

Study	Dataset	No. of countries	Topic of investigation	Measure of achievement	Measure of macroeconomic outcome	Estimation method	Results
Ramirez, Luo, Schofer, and Meyer (2006)	Hanushek and Kimko (2000)	38	Student achievement and growth	Average score of all tests, math + science, different age levels	Growth rate of real GDP per capita, 1970–90 and 1980–2000	Cross-section growth regressions with controls	Some effects of achievement on growth, but sensitive to East Asian countries and time period
Hanushek and Woessmann (2008)	FIMS, FISS, FIRS, SIMS, SISS, SIRS, TIMSS, TIMSS-R, PISA, PIRLS, TIMSS 2003, PISA 2003	50	Effect of cognitive skills on growth	Average score of all tests, math + science, different age levels; also, share of students reaching thresholds	Growth rate of real GDP per capita, 1960–2000	Cross-section growth regressions with different controls	Strong and robust effect of cognitive skills on growth, both in developing and developed countries; positive interaction with economic institutions; strong increase in explained variance; years of schooling lose significance; separate effects of low– and high-achievers
Jamison, Jamison, and Hanushek (2007)	Hanushek and Woessmann (2008)	43–54	Effect of education quality on growth	Average score of all tests, math, different age levels	Growth rate of real GDP per capita, 1960–2000; infant mortality rates, 1960–2000	Cross-section growth regressions with different controls; HLM of 10-year interval panel level model (but time-invariant test scores)	Mechanism by which education affects per-capita income is likely through increasing rate of technological progress; significant effect of education quality on rate of decline in infant mortality
Altinok (2007)	FIMS, FISS, SIMS, SISS, IAEP-I+II, TIMSS/-R+ 2003, LLECE, PASEC, PISA+ 2003, SACMEQ	"Approx. 120"	Effect of schooling quality on growth	Math + science, secondary school, averaged and as panel	Growth rate of real GDP per capita, 1965–2005 (10-year averages)	10-year-interval panel regressions with time fixed effects and controls, OLS with country fixed effects and GMM	Positive effect of schooling quality on growth in panel framework with large number of countries
Ciccone and Papaioannou (2009)	Hanushek and Kimko (2000), as extended in Bosworth and Collins (2003)	21–41	Effect of education on structure of production	Average score of all tests, math + science, different age levels	Growth rate of value added and employment at country-industry level, 1980–1999	Cross-section growth regressions at industry level with country and industry fixed effects, effects identified by interaction with industry-level schooling intensity	Positive interaction between schooling quality and industry-level schooling intensity in predicting industry growth, indicating that countries with greater schooling quality shifted production structure to schooling-intensive industries; effect stronger in open economies

Appleton, Atherton, and Bleaney (2008)	FIMS, FISS, FIRS, SIMS, SISS, SIRS, IAEP-I+II, TIMSS/-R	24–41	Effect of schooling quality on growth	Average math, science + reading, as panel	Growth rate of real GDP per capita over differing 5-year periods between 1960 and 2004	Growth regressions using lagged test scores, with controls, pooled cross-section; country fixed effects	Significant effect of lagged test scores on subsequent 5-year growth, quantitatively smaller than in averaged long-run models
Hanushek and Woessmann (2009a)		50–52	Causal effect of cognitive skills on growth	Average score of all tests, math + science (jointly and separately, also reading), different age levels; also, share of students reaching thresholds	Growth rate of real GDP per capita, 1960–2000 and subperiods	Cross-section growth regressions with controls; IV and LIML (instrumenting test scores by system features); DiD comparing earnings of home-educated to U.S.-educated immigrants in U.S.; model in changes over time	Remarkably stable association between cognitive skills and growth across specifications, time periods, country samples; IV and DiD models confirm causality: significant effects of cognitive skills originating in institutional features of school systems; home-country skills affect earnings of U.S. immigrants; effect of change in skills over time on change in growth paths
Hanushek and Woessmann (2009b)	LLECE, SERCE, Hanushek and Woessmann (2008)	59, 16 Latin American countries	Reasons for disappointing growth in Latin America	Average score of different tests, math + science, different age levels; math + reading, grades 4+6	Growth rate of real GDP per capita, 1960–2000	Cross-section growth regressions with several controls	Low cognitive skills account for poor Latin American growth in global perspective; significant effect of cognitive skills measured by regional tests on intra-regional growth variation

Notes: GDP = gross domestic product. HLM = hierarchical linear model. GMM = general method of moments. IV = instrumental variable. LIML = limited information maximum likelihood. DiD = differences in differences. See Tables 2.1 and 2.2 for acronyms of datasets.

The most current picture in Hanushek and Woessmann (2008, 2009a) expands the international student achievement tests from 31 countries in Hanushek and Kimko (2000) to 50 countries and uses more recent data on economic growth that extends the modeling to the longer time period (1960–2000).[62] The basic result is reported in the second column of Table 2.14 and depicted graphically in Figure 2.13. After controlling for the initial level of GDP per capita and for years of schooling, the test-score measure of math and science skills features a statistically significant effect on the growth in real GDP per capita for 1960–2000.[63] According to this specification, test scores that are larger by one standard deviation (measured at the student level across all OECD countries in PISA) are associated with an average annual growth rate in GDP per capita that is two percentage points higher over the whole 40-year period. This quantitative result is virtually identical to that in Hanushek and Kimko (2000).

When cognitive skills are added to a model that just includes initial income and years of schooling (the first column of Table 2.14), the share of variation in economic growth explained by the model (the adjusted R^2) jumps from 0.25 to 0.73. As shown in the top of Figure 2.14, quantity of schooling is statistically significantly related to economic growth in a specification that does not include the measure of cognitive skills, but the association between years of schooling and growth turns insignificant and its marginal effect is reduced to close to zero once cognitive skills are included in the model (see the bottom of Figure 2.14). In other words, school attainment has no independent effect over and above its impact on cognitive skills. The result remains the same when the measure of years of schooling refers to the average between 1960 and 2000, rather than the initial 1960 value (the third column of Table 2.14). In the different specifications, there is evidence for conditional convergence in the sense that countries with higher initial income tend to grow more slowly over the subsequent period.

Several intervening studies have since found very similar results (see Table 2.13). Another early contribution, by Lee and Lee (1995), found an effect size similar to Hanushek and Kimko (2000) using data from the 1970–71 First International Science Study on the participating 17 countries, also leaving quantitative measures of education with no significant effect on growth. Using a more encompassing set of international

---

[62] While more countries have test data, 50 are included in the analyses of economic growth. Twenty-five countries are not included in the growth database due to lack of data on economic output or because they drop out of the sample for a standard exclusion criterion in growth analyses (15 former communist countries, three countries for which oil production is the dominant industry, two small countries, three newly created countries, and two further countries lacking early output data). Two further countries (Nigeria and Botswana) turn out to be strong outliers in the growth regressions and are therefore dropped from the sample (see Hanushek and Woessmann (2009a)). The source of the income data is version 6.1 of the Penn World Tables (cf. Heston, Summers, and Aten (2002)), and the data on years of schooling is an extended version of the Cohen and Soto (2007) data which is developed from Barro and Lee (1993, 2001).

[63] Another recent set of international tests has focused on reading. While the reliability of these measures is an issue, consideration of them in addition to or instead of the math and science tests does not change the basic results (see Hanushek and Woessmann (2009a)).

Table 2.14 Cognitive Skills Versus Years of Schooling in Growth Regressions

	(1)	(2)	(3)[a]	(4)[b]	(5)[c]
Cognitive skills		1.980	1.975	1.666	1.239
		(9.12)	(8.28)	(5.09)	(4.12)
Years of schooling 1960	0.369	0.026	0.024	0.047	−0.049
	(3.23)	(0.34)	(0.78)	(0.54)	(0.66)
GDP per capita 1960	−0.379	−0.302	−0.298	−0.255	−0.310
	(4.24)	(5.54)	(6.02)	(3.12)	(5.73)
No. of countries	50	50	50	50	45
R^2 (adj.)	0.252	0.728	0.728	0.706	0.797

Notes: Dependent variable: average annual growth rate in GDP per capita, 1960–2000. Regressions include a constant. Test scores are average of math and science, primary through end of secondary school, all years (divided by 100). *t*-statistics in parentheses.
[a] Measure of years of schooling refers to the average between 1960 and 2000.
[b] Specification includes dummies for eight world regions.
[c] Specification includes additional controls for openness, property rights, fertility, and tropical location.
Source: Hanushek and Woessmann (2009a).

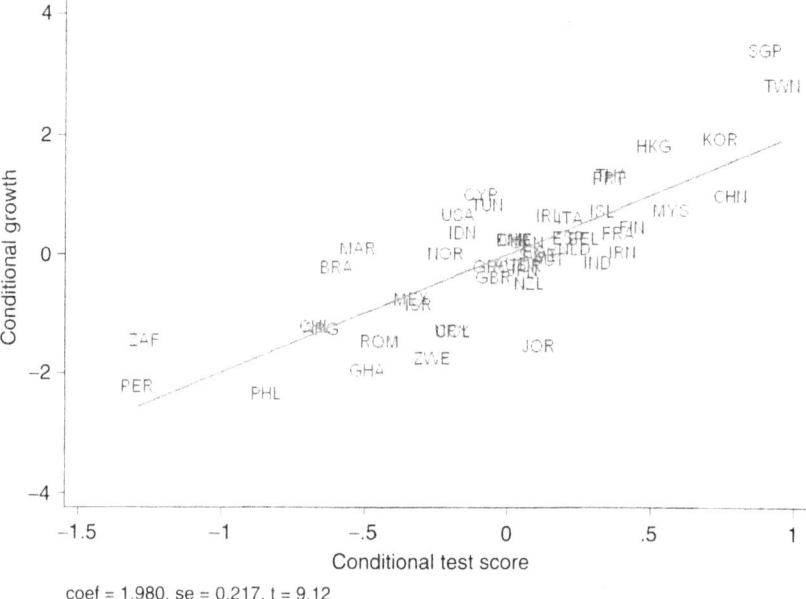

coef = 1.980, se = 0.217, t = 9.12

Figure 2.13 Cognitive skills and economic growth. Notes: Added-variable plot of a regression of the average annual rate of growth (in percent) of real GDP per capita in 1960–2000 on the initial level of real GDP per capita in 1960, average years of schooling in 1960, and average test scores on international student achievement tests. *Source*: Hanushek and Woessmann (2008).

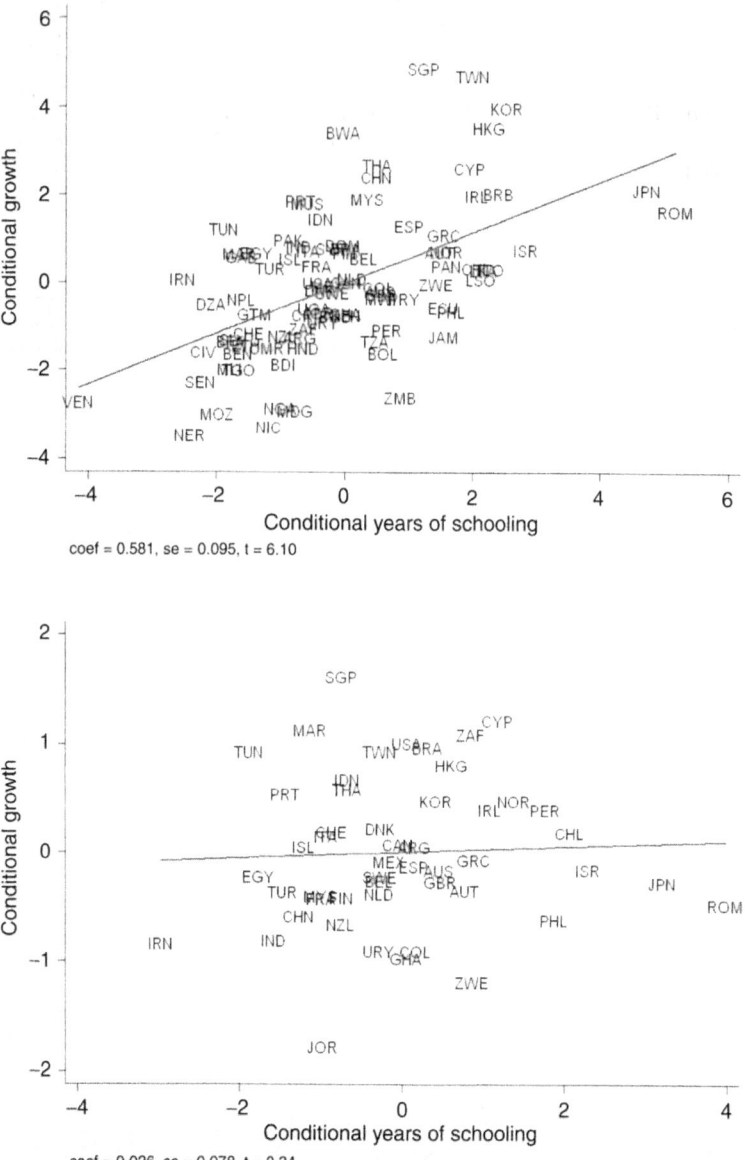

Figure 2.14 Years of schooling and economic growth without and with test-score controls. Notes: Added-variable plot of a regression of the average annual rate of growth (in percent) of real GDP per capita in 1960–2000 on the initial level of real GDP per capita in 1960 and average years of schooling in 1960. The bottom panel additionally controls for average test scores on international student achievement tests, whereas the top panel does not. Source: Based on Hanushek and Woessmann (2008).

tests, Barro (2001) also finds that, while both the quantity of schooling and test scores matter for economic growth, measured cognitive skills are much more important. Employing the measure of cognitive skills developed by Hanushek and Kimko (2000) in a development accounting framework, Woessmann (2002, 2003c) finds that the share of cross-country variation in levels of economic development attributable to international differences in human capital rises dramatically when cognitive skills are taken into account. Building on Gundlach, Rudman, and Woessmann (2002), this work analyzes output per worker in 132 countries in 1990. The variation that can be attributed to international differences in human capital rises from 21% to 45% once the international achievement measures are taken into account, and to over 60% in samples with reasonable data quality.

Extensions of the measure of Hanushek and Kimko (2000) and its imputation in Woessmann (2003c) are also used in the cross-country growth regressions by Bosworth and Collins (2003) and in the cross-country industry-level analysis by Ciccone and Papaioannou (2009). Both also find that measured cognitive skills strongly dominate any effect of schooling quantity on growth.[64] Coulombe and Tremblay (2006) use test-score data from the International Adult Literacy Survey (see Section 5.1 above) in a panel of 14 OECD countries, confirming the result that the test-score measure outperforms quantitative measures of education.[65] Jamison, Jamison, and Hanushek (2007) extend the Hanushek and Kimko (2000) analysis by using the mathematics component of the transformed and extended tests in Hanushek and Woessmann (2009a), replicating and strengthening the previous results by using test data from a larger number of countries, controlling for a larger number of potentially confounding variables, and extending the time period of the analysis. Using the panel structure of their growth data, they suggest that cognitive skills seem to improve income levels mainly though speeding up technological progress, rather than shifting the level of the production function or increasing the impact of an additional year of schooling.[66]

The collection of existing studies strongly suggests that cognitive skills are closely related to the long-run growth rates for countries. While there is some variation, the existing studies also indicate a consistency in the quantitative magnitude of effects. Simulation exercises show that this magnitude means that relatively small improvements in the skills of a nation's labor force can have very large effects on long-run economic well-being (Hanushek and Woessmann (2010a)).

---

[64] Note that Bosworth and Collins (2003) cannot distinguish the effect of cognitive skills from the effect of quality of government institutions. The analysis in Hanushek and Woessmann (2008) shows, however, that they can be separated when we use our new measure of cognitive skills that also extends the country sample by several additional data points on international test scores.

[65] Additional details of this study can be found in Coulombe, Tremblay, and Marchand (2004).

[66] A novel element of the work by Jamison, Jamison, and Hanushek (2007) is investigation of the impact of cognitive skills on changes in health outcomes across countries, which can be taken as another indicator of the welfare on nations. They find that cognitive skills have a strong impact on the decline of infant mortality rates.

5.3.3 Causation in a cross-country framework

Work on cross-country growth analysis has been plagued by legitimate questions about whether any truly causal effects have been identified, or alternatively whether the estimated statistical analyses simply pick up a correlation without causal meaning. Perhaps the easiest way to see the problems is early discussion of how sensitive estimated growth relationships were to the precise factors that were included in the statistical work and to the country samples and time periods of the analyses (Levine and Renelt (1992); Levine and Zervos (1993)). The sensitivity of the estimated models provided prima facie evidence that various factors were omitted from many of the analyses.

Whether or not the impact of cognitive skills is a causal relationship is indeed a very important issue from a policy standpoint. It is essential to know that, if a country managed to improve its achievement in some manner, it would see a commensurate improvement in its long-run growth rate. Said differently, if the estimates simply reflect other factors that are correlated with test scores, a change in test scores may have little or no impact on the economy (unless the other factors also changed). Indeed, analysis of prior estimates of school attainment have been identified as possibly reflecting reverse causality; that is, improved growth leads to more schooling rather than the reverse (Bils and Klenow (2000)).

It is difficult to develop conclusive tests of causality issues within the limited sample of countries included in the analysis. Nonetheless, Hanushek and Woessmann (2009a) provide initial analyses of the issue of causality between cognitive skills and growth. That study pursues a number of different approaches to ruling out major factors that could confound the results and that could lead to incorrect conclusions about the potential impact. While none of the approaches addresses all of the important issues and while each approach fails to be conclusive for easily recognized reasons, the combination of approaches eliminates a number of common concerns about the identification of a causal relationship.

First, in an extensive investigation of alternative model specifications, different measures of cognitive skills, various groupings of countries, and specific subperiods of economic growth, the consistency of the alternative estimates—both in terms of quantitative impacts and statistical significance—indicate a robustness of estimates that is uncommon to most cross-country growth modeling. These specifications consider the timing of tests and growth in detail.[67] To tackle the most obvious reverse-causality issues, one specification separates the timing of the analysis by estimating the effect of scores on tests conducted until the early 1980s on economic growth in 1980–2000.

---

[67] For example, Ramirez, Luo, Schofer, and Meyer (2006) suggest that if one looks at the recent period (1980–2000) and also drops the East Asian countries, math and science is no longer significant. However, Hanushek and Woessmann (2009a) show that the coefficient on test scores is virtually the same in their basic results as when the sample is restricted to 1980–2000 and dropping East Asian countries. Their study, which relies on the cognitive skills measures from Hanushek and Kimko (2000), is likely to suffer from a combination of measurement issues and small sample problems.

In this analysis, available for a smaller sample of countries only, test scores predate the growth period. Results are even stronger than using the measure based on all tests.[68] In addition, reverse causality from growth to test scores is also unlikely because of the results of education production functions, discussed above, that indicate additional resource in the school system (which might become affordable with increased growth) do not relate systematically to improved test scores.

The only substantial effect on the estimates is the inclusion of various measures of economic institutions (security of property rights and openness of the economy). Including measures of economic institutions, suggested for example by Acemoglu, Johnson, and Robinson (2005), does lead to a reduction in the estimated impact of cognitive skills by about one third. However, as Glaeser, La Porta, Lopez-de-Silanes, and Shleifer (2004) argue, there is a good case that human capital causes better institutions as opposed to the opposite. Thus, one could consider the estimate with institutional measures as a lower bound on any achievement effects. This estimate remains highly significant and very substantial. Furthermore, in the sample of OECD countries, where there is more limited variation in these broad institutions, the reduction is much smaller at 15%, and the institutional measures do not enter significantly.[69]

Second, an instrumental variable specification traces the impact on growth of just the variations in achievement that arise from the previously identified institutional characteristics of each country's school system (exit examinations, autonomy, and private schooling).[70] This estimated impact is essentially the same as reported in the OLS regressions, lending support both to the causal impact of more cognitive skills and to the conclusion that schooling policies can have direct economic returns.

Third, one major concern is that countries with good economies also have good school systems—implying that those that grow faster because of the basic economic factors also have high achievement. To deal with this, immigrants to the U.S. who have been educated in their home countries are compared to those educated just in the U.S. Since it is the single labor market of the United States, any differences in labor-market returns associated with cognitive skills cannot arise because of differences in the economies of their home country. Looking at labor-market returns, the cognitive skills seen in the immigrant's home country lead to higher incomes—but only if the immigrant was educated at home. Immigrants from the same home country schooled in the U.S. receive no return to home-country quality. This differences-in-differences approach rules out

---

[68] Similarly, the studies by Altinok (2007) and Appleton, Atherton, and Bleaney (2008) use initial test scores to predict subsequent growth in a panel framework, confirming significant growth effects of cognitive skills.

[69] Hanushek and Woessmann (2008) also find a positive interaction between cognitive skills and institutional measures, suggesting that good institutional quality and good cognitive skills can reinforce each other in advancing economic development.

[70] The statistical analysis employs an instrumental variable strategy that relies upon changes in achievement induced by school structure. Its major limitation is that the instruments tend to be weak, given the small number of countries that is included.

the possibility that test scores simply reflect cultural factors or economic institutions of the home country.[71] It also provides further support to the potential role of schools to change the cognitive skills of citizens in economically meaningful ways.

Finally, perhaps the toughest test of causality is reliance on how *changes* in test scores over time lead to *changes* in growth rates, thereby eliminating possible bias from any time-invariant country-specific economic and cultural factors. Figure 2.15 relates the gains in test scores over time to the gains in growth rates over time, revealing a consistent and strong positive association.[72] As with the other approaches, this analysis must presume that the pattern of achievement changes has been occurring over a long time, because it is not the achievement of school children but the skills of workers that count. Nonetheless, the consistency of the patterns and the similarities of magnitudes of the estimates to the basic growth models is striking (see Hanushek and Woessmann (2009a)).

Again, each approach to providing a deeper look at the issue of causation is subject to some real uncertainty. The simple conclusion from the combined evidence is that differences in cognitive skills lead to economically significant differences in economic growth. Nonetheless, further investigations of the causal structure of growth relationships provide an obvious field for further research. The approach in Hanushek and Woessmann (2009a) is to employ standard microeconomic approaches to the investigation of causation in the context of cross-country models. Alternative approaches could provide additional information. Similarly, expanded data samples or different model specifications may prove useful.

5.3.4 Expanding country samples by regional tests from developing countries

A limiting factor in some of the prior analyses is the size of the samples, which in turn is dictated by past participation in the international testing programs. This issue is especially important when looking at developing countries and at different economic regions of the world. Latin America, for example, has been a perennial concern because of its low growth and its inability to show continued development, but Latin American countries are very lightly represented in the prior testing programs.

While progress has been made, disappointment has been growing with Latin American development strategies built on schooling because expansion of school

---

[71] Two potential problems arise in this analysis. First, it just looks at labor-market returns for individuals and not the aggregate impact on the economy of achievement differences. Second, those who migrate at a young enough age to be educated in the U.S. might differ from those who migrate at later ages; while effects of the migration age that are the same across countries are held constant in the regression, cross-country differences in age-migration patterns that are related to the quality of the home-country education system would affect the results.

[72] Only 12 OECD countries have participated in international tests over a long enough period to provide the possibility of looking at trends in test performance over more than 30 years. The analysis simply considers a regression of test scores on time for countries with multiple observations (allowing for student age and subject of tests). The trends in growth rates are determined in a similar manner: annual growth rates are regressed on a time trend. The plot provides the pattern of slopes in the test regression to slopes in the growth-rate regression. Hanushek and Woessmann (2009a) consider more complicated statistical relationships, but the overall results hold up.

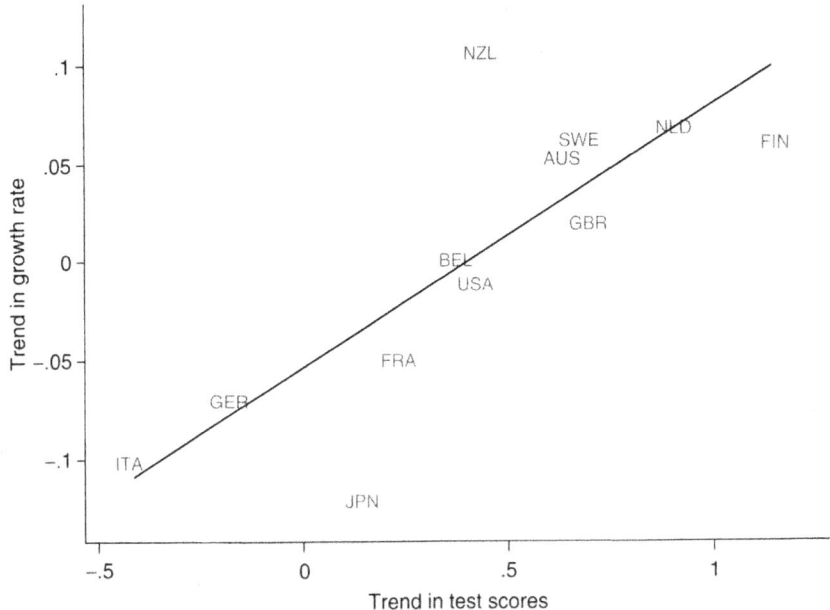

Figure 2.15 Trends in educational achievement and trends in growth rates. Notes: Scatter plot of trend in the growth rate of GDP per capita from 1975–2000 against trend in test scores for countries whose test scores range back before 1972. *Source*: Own depiction based on the database derived in Hanushek and Woessmann (2009a).

attainment has not guaranteed improved economic conditions (Easterly (2001)). In 1960, adult school attainment in Latin America was surpassed only by OECD countries and was significantly ahead of East Asia, Sub-Saharan Africa, and the Middle East and North Africa (MENA) region. Still, economic growth in Latin America since 1960 has lagged so much behind growth in East Asia and MENA that Latin American income per capita, which was considerably above the other three regions in 1960, has by now been overtaken by East Asia and MENA, leaving only Sub-Saharan Africa behind.

The poor growth performance of Latin America despite its relatively high initial schooling level remains a puzzle by conventional thinking. While economic research on Latin American growth has given much attention to institutional and financial factors (e.g., Edwards, Esquivel, and Márquez (2007) or Fernández-Arias, Manuelli, and Blyde (2005)), the basic puzzle remains unresolved.

To compare countries within the region, Hanushek and Woessmann (2009b) make use of regional measures of cognitive skills that were designed specifically for Latin American countries. Regional achievement tests from the Laboratorio Latinoamericano de Evaluación de la Calidad de la Educación (LLECE) were conducted in 1997 and in 2006 (see Table 2.2). Together, the two tests cover all 16 Latin American countries usable in analyses of national growth, which is an important expansion compared to the seven Latin American countries that ever participated in a worldwide test. Neither of the two tests is perfect for such analyses, because they measure performance just in early grades and because both are very recent. Nonetheless, these regional tests offer the possibility of explaining the large differences in growth among the countries of Latin America.

Their results using the regional test data support the important role of cognitive skills in understanding Latin American growth. These test scores are statistically and quantitatively significant in predicting economic growth differences in intra-regional growth regressions. They increase the explanatory power of standard growth models considerably and render the effect of years of schooling insignificant. Also in Latin America, schooling appears relevant for economic growth only insofar as it actually raises the knowledge that students gain as depicted in tests of cognitive skills.

Hanushek and Woessmann (2009b) also splice the regional test information into the worldwide tests discussed above. Results of the worldwide regressions extended to 59 countries confirm the consistent effect of cognitive skills. They can even resolve the Latin American growth puzzle: The poor growth performance of Latin American countries can be fully accounted for by their poor performance on student achievement tests.

This analysis suggests that an even wider set of student assessments—those included in Table 2.2—can be usefully employed to understand fundamentals of the aggregate economies. The expansion of sampling, in this case to regional economies with limited participation in past tests, permits more detailed analysis than previously possible.

While part of the sampling problem is automatically being dealt with through the continued expansion from new countries added to the PISA and TIMSS programs, other issues of the appropriateness of those tests and of the ancillary survey data suggest that these other data sets should not be neglected. For example, Sub-Saharan Africa is only minimally included in prior testing. Furthermore, the worldwide tests may simply be too difficult for the typical student in many countries in Latin America and Sub-Saharan Africa. Because test efficiency requires the international assessments to focus testing time on discriminating performance in the vicinity of the international mean, there may not be sufficient test questions that reliably distinguish performance at the level of many developing countries. This limits the power of these tests in discriminating performance at low levels and makes intra-regional comparisons in these regions unreliable. Splicing regional tests into the worldwide tests therefore provides a viable option to expand international analysis to countries far below the mean of OECD countries.[73]

---

[73] The value of regional testing programs could also be expanded substantially by ensuring that the assessments included specific linking questions with PISA and/or TIMSS. This practice would permit each country to ascertain where it stands in the world achievement rankings.

5.3.5 Basic skills, top performance, and growth

The modeling efforts to date have concentrated most attention on mean achievement and on the implications of overall differences in human capital. However, this sidesteps important questions facing education officials in many countries. Some argue in favor of elitist school systems which focus on the top performers as potential future managers of the economy and drivers of innovation. This approach, for example, appears to match the historic policies of India, with a set of premier engineering schools coexisting with a large illiterate population. Others favor more egalitarian school systems to ensure well-educated masses that will be capable of implementing established technologies. This approach would coincide with development policies such as the Education for All initiative (UNESCO (2005)) that concentrate on raising the skills of all to minimal levels. Do these choices have a discernible effect on aggregate economic performance?

To capture these differences in the distributional patterns of the test-score performance in different countries, Hanushek and Woessmann (2009a) use the micro data from each of the international assessments to calculate measures of the share of students in each country who reach at least basic skills as well as those who reach superior performance levels. Specifically, they use performance of at least 400 test-score points on the PISA international scale—one standard deviation below the OECD mean—as the threshold of basic literacy and numeracy and one standard deviation above the OECD as the measure of superior performance. They then employ these alternative measures of skill distribution instead of mean performance in their cross-country growth models.

Their analysis suggests that both measures of the test-score distribution are significantly related to economic growth, either when entered individually or jointly. Both the basic-skill and the top-performing dimensions of educational performance appear separately important for growth.

These early results, however, still leave open a series of analytical and policy questions. For example, while these models indicate the relative impacts of improving the different levels of performance, policies built upon these would have to use other information about the costs or feasibility of changing people at the different skill levels.

5.3.6 IQ models

An alternative perspective is that IQ differences among nations are driving the results described previously. The potential difference from the preceding analysis is the common view that IQs are fixed and not subject to schooling or environmental influences. If true, this would suggest both that IQ measures might more accurately represent the relevant cognitive skills and the analytics of them might be less prone to the types of identification issues discussed. This fixed-factor view, often related to ideas of the high degree of heritability of IQs, of course is not the uniform view of researchers in the area. Indeed, in the economics literature, Goldberger and Manski (1995) and Heckman (1995) have clear analyses showing that families and schools have strong effects on measured IQ.[74] Thus, the most reasonable interpretation of IQ studies is that they apply an alternative measure of cognitive skills to the international assessments previously described.

All studies of the economic impacts of IQ are based on the international IQ scores compiled by Lynn and Vanhanen (2002, 2006).[75] They have assembled data from specific national samples using a variety of measurement instruments. The earliest work by Weede and Kämpf (2002) mimics that of the work described previously (see Table 2.15). Similar to the analyses of cognitive skills, IQ differences have a strong and significant effect on growth rates even allowing for differences in school attainment. Jones and Schneider (2006) provide a series of robustness analyses, similar to Sala-i-Martin, Doppelhofer, and Miller (2004) with the addition of the Lynn and Vanhanen (2002) measures of IQ. They demonstrate that the IQ has a strong predictive power with economic growth. They also show that the measures are very strongly correlated with the labor-force quality measures of Hanushek and Kimko (2000). Ram (2007) estimates models similar to the augmented neoclassical production functions of Mankiw, Romer, and Weil (1992). The general conclusion is that school attainment appears less relevant when IQ measures (again from Lynn and Vanhanen (2002)) are included in the analysis. Finally, Jones and Schneider (2010) use IQ measures of skills to account for variations in immigrant wages, similar to the analyses of Hanushek and Kimko (2000) and Hanushek and Woessmann (2009a). They conclude that IQ is a powerful predictor of wages and, relatedly, that it explains a significant portion of earnings differences across countries.

The real question with these analyses is what exactly is being measured. The underlying IQ scores by country come from an idiosyncratic collection of national data that relies on specialized samples for specific cohorts and subsets of the population.[76] Thus,

---

[74] Much of this recent discussion in the economics literature came in response to Herrnstein and Murray (1994), who argued that the labor-market relationships to relatively fixed IQ measures had strong implications for social policy. Much of the discussion is, of course, outside of economics. While there is ongoing controversy to how genetics and environment are seen as influencing IQ (see, for example, the exchange by Rose (2009) and Ceci and Williams (2009)), it is clear that environment can have substantial impact on measured IQ (e.g., Turkheimer et al. (2003)). Another source of discussion is the so-called "Flynn effect" where political scientist James Flynn noted that IQ scores had been rapidly rising in many nations around the world over the twentieth century. For discussions of this, see Dickens and Flynn (2001) and Flynn (2007), both of which argue that aggregate societal factors can affect the measured national data.

[75] Their analyses of economic outcomes relate the level of GDP per capita to IQ scores. It is difficult to see these analyses in level form as identifying the impact of skills. Their data series, however, have been used extensively in other analyses.

[76] As Hunt and Wittmann (2008) point out, concerns with the data include that values for the majority of countries are derived from an unclearly specified method drawing on data from nearby countries and that most data points are not derived from representative samples. For example, the value for Ethiopia is based on the IQ scores of a highly selected group that had emigrated to Israel, and the value for Equatorial Guinea, the lowest IQ estimate in the data, refers to a group of children in a home for the developmentally disabled in Spain.

Table 2.15 Studies on IQ and Macroeconomic Growth

Study	Dataset	No. of countries	Topic of investigation	Measure of achievement	Measure of macroeconomic outcome	Estimation method	Results
Weede and Kämpf (2002)	Predecessor of Lynn and Vanhanen (2002) IQ database	97	IQ and growth	Average national IQ	Growth rate of real GDP per capita, 1965–1990	Cross-section growth regressions with controls	Significant effect of IQ measure on growth; outperforms quantitative measures
Jones and Schneider (2006)	Lynn and Vanhanen (2002) IQ database	51	IQ and growth	Average national IQ	Growth rate of real GDP per capita, 1960–1992	Bayesian Averaging of Classical Estimates of 1330 cross-section growth regressions using 21 control variables	Significant and robust effect of IQ measure on growth; outperforms quantitative measures
Ram (2007)	Lynn and Vanhanen (2002) IQ database	98	IQ and growth	Average national IQ	Growth rate of real GDP per working age person, 1960–1985	Cross-section growth regressions with controls	Significant effect of IQ measure on growth; outperforms quantitative measures
Jones and Schneider (2010)	Lynn and Vanhanen (2006) IQ database	59, 87	IQ, wages, and levels of development	Average national IQ	Immigrant wages in the U.S. by country of origin	Cross-section wage regressions; coefficient used in cross-country development accounting	Country-average IQ measure predicts immigrant wages in U.S.; differences in average IQ account for 1/6 of international differences in log GDP

Notes: GDP = gross domestic product.

the question that arises is how much measurement error there is in an underlying skill dimension. Hunt and Wittmann (2008) provide a direct analysis (albeit in terms of the level of GDP per capita) of the empirical value of IQ scores versus PISA scores. They conclude that PISA scores are better predictors of GDP per capita than the Lynn and Vanhanen (2002) measures of IQ. Lynn and Mikk (2007, 2009) confirm the very high correlations between IQ scores and either TIMSS or PISA scores. More importantly, this analysis questions whether the simple relationships estimated in Lynn and Vanhanen (2002) are causal (as Lynn and Vanhanen (2002) assert).

The conclusion from the various models of the impact of national IQ scores on economic outcomes is that IQ provides another potential measure of cognitive skills. If accurate, the Lynn and Vanhanen IQ data provide for a considerable expansion of the sample sizes, reaching 113 nations (Lynn and Vanhanen (2006), Appendix 1). Nonetheless, most of the analyses would suggest that this measure is noticeably more error prone than the international test data stressed here. Additionally, rather than capturing innate differences, they are amenable to family and school influences—opening a similar set of identification issues as discussed here (but not addressed in these analyses).

5.4 Conclusions on the economic impact of differences in cognitive skills

The international data on the individual returns to cognitive skills begin to paint an interesting picture of the value of human capital in the labor market—a picture going beyond the common but misleading view that only schooling attainment matters. First, while labor markets in a broad set of countries clearly reward individuals with higher skill as measured by assessments of math and science, the rewards do appear to vary significantly across countries. The underlying determinants of these differential rewards remain an important but unanswered question. Second, variations in skills within countries have clear impacts on the distribution of incomes. Here again, while the facts are relatively clear, the interaction of skills and rewards—which is a fundamental determinant of the distributional outcomes—is much less understood.

The results of growth modeling that employ measures of national cognitive skills strongly suggest that the basic human capital model is very relevant for aggregate outcomes. Variations in skills measured by international math and science tests are strongly related to variations in economic growth, and they solve many of the difficult measurement problems with the more traditional school attainment measures.

At the same time, there are many issues to be addressed in future work. Clearly the limitations of having just cross-country variations for a limited number of countries raise uncertainties with the results. Most importantly, given the myriad differences among nations, confirming any causal impact is difficult. Each of these issues is high on the research agenda, particularly given the rapid expansion of test information from expanded new testing opportunities.

6. CONCLUSION AND OUTLOOK

The economic literature on international educational achievement has expanded our understanding of the determinants and economic consequences of international educational achievement tremendously. Considering that, with few antecedents, this literature is only a decade old, it has clearly covered a lot of ground and made remarkable progress. In doing so, it has exploited the possibilities opened up by the international data to raise fundamental questions, ones not amenable to any simple within-country analysis. For example, this work highlights the crucial role of educational achievement in understanding the vast international differences in economic well-being. It also begins to suggest some key factors that account for the immense international differences in educational achievement.

At the same time, by the very nature of the limited degrees of freedom in cross-country identification, it can mostly reveal broad patterns. At the very least, a lot of the details of specific implementation issues related to any policy application obviously must be left for national approaches.

Given its infancy, there is obviously still considerable scope for future advances in the economic literature on international evidence on educational achievement. Clear directions forward include exploring further the institutional variation and making more use of regional information, yielding larger numbers of independent observations. Interesting extensions could also go beyond general schooling to cover topics in vocational and higher education.

A topic unexplored by economists is also the international tests in nontraditional subjects, such as foreign languages, civic education, and information technology. More generally, some of the rich background information contained in the international studies could be explored further, and part of it may provide information on relevant noncognitive skills. For example, recent work by Falck and Woessmann (2010) attempts to derive measures of entrepreneurial intentions from the international background data, and chapter 6 in Woessmann, Luedemann, Schuetz, and West (2009) explores such measures of noncognitive outcomes as student morale and commitment, nondisruptive behavior, disciplinary climate, and tardiness. Further information on noncognitive skills may be derived from the international background questionnaires. As a more distant outlook, international testing of noncognitive skills would be an obvious challenge.

Methodologically, further exploration of quasi-experimental settings in the international data should be high on the agenda. When analyzing determinants of educational achievement, building panel datasets from the more extensively emerging international tests could help in this regard and allow the evaluation of educational reforms in different countries.

In the more distant future, it is tempting to envision what research will be able to do with the sort of achievement data that will be available in 20 to 30 years from now. The number of participating countries is as high as 57 in both PISA 2006 and TIMSS

2007. In PISA 2009, 70 countries participated. In 2011, 51 countries, including 23 not participating in PISA 2009, are scheduled to participate in TIMSS. For PISA 2012, another 10 new additional countries are scheduled to participate. With these sets of comparable achievement data for extensive samples of countries being linked to subsequent economic growth, and with the emerging long panels of regular achievement data for large samples of countries, the outlook for future research in the economics of international differences in educational achievement is clearly bright.

REFERENCES

Acemoglu, D., Johnson, S., Robinson, J.A., 2005. Institutions as a fundamental cause of long-run growth. In: Aghion, P., Durlauf, S.N. (Eds.), Hand. Econ. Growth. North Holland, pp. 385–472.

Adams, R.J., 2003. Response to "Cautions on OECD's recent educational survey (PISA)" Oxford Rev. Educ 29 (3), 377–389.

Adams, R.J., Berezner, A., Jakubowski, M., 2010. Analysis of PISA 2006 preferred items ranking using the percentage correct method. Organisation for Economic Co-operation and Development, OECD Education, Working Paper 46.

Afonso, A., St. Aubyn, M., 2006. Cross-country efficiency of secondary education provision: A semi-parametric analysis with non-discretionary inputs. Econ. Model. 23 (3), 476–491.

Aghion, P., 2008. Higher education and innovation. Perspektiven der Wirtschaftspolitik 9 (Special Issue), 28–45.

Aghion, P., Dewatripont, M., Hoxby, C.M., Mas-Colell, A., Sapir, A., 2010. The governance and performance of universities: Evidence from Europe and the US. Econ. Policy 25 (61), 7–59.

Altinok, N., 2007. Human capital quality and economic growth. Université de Bourgogne: Institute for Research in Education (IREDU) IREDU, Working Paper DT 2007/1.

Altinok, N., Kingdon, G., 2009. New evidence on class size effects: A pupil fixed effects approach. Centre for the Study of African Economies, University of Oxford, CSAE Working Paper WPS/2009-16.

Altinok, N., Murseli, H., 2007. International database on human capital quality. Econ. Lett. 96 (2), 237–244.

Altonji, J.G., Elder, T.E., Taber, C.R., 2005. Selection on observed and unobserved variables: Assessing the effectiveness of Catholic schools. J. Polit. Econ. 113 (1), 151–184.

Ammermueller, A., 2005. Educational opportunities and the role of institutions. Centre for European Economic Research, Mannheim, ZEW Discussion Paper 05-44.

Ammermueller, A., 2007. PISA: What makes the difference? Explaining the gap in test scores between Finland and Germany. Empir. Econ. 33 (2), 263–287.

Ammermueller, A., Dolton, P., 2006. Pupil-teacher gender interaction effects on scholastic outcomes in England and the USA. Centre for European Economic Research, Mannheim, ZEW Discussion Paper 06-060.

Ammermueller, A., Heijke, H., Woessmann, L., 2005. Schooling quality in Eastern Europe: Educational production during transition. Econ. Educ. Rev. 24 (5), 579–599.

Ammermueller, A., Pischke, J.S., 2009. Peer effects in European primary schools: Evidence from the Progress in International Reading Literacy Study. J. Labor Econ. 27 (3), 315–348.

Angrist, J.D., Lavy, V., 1999. Using Maimondides' rule to estimate the effect of class size on scholastic achievement. Q. J. Econ. 114 (2), 533–575.

Appleton, S., Atherton, P., Bleaney, M., 2008. International school test scores and economic growth. University of Nottingham: Centre for Research in Economic Development and International Trade Credit Research Paper 08/04.

Ashenfelter, O., Krueger, A.B., 1994. Estimates of the economic return to schooling from a new sample of twins. Am. Econ. Rev. 84 (5), 1157–1173.

Azariadis, C., Drazen, A., 1990. Threshold externalities in economic development. Q. J. Econ. 105 (2), 501–526.
Baker, D.P., 1997. Surviving TIMSS: Or, everything you blissfully forgot about international comparisons. Phi Delta Kappan 79 (4), 295–300.
Barro, R.J., 1991. Economic growth in a cross section of countries. Q. J. Econ. 106 (2), 407–443.
Barro, R.J., 2001. Human capital and growth. Am. Econ. Rev. 91 (2), 12–17.
Barro, R.J., Lee, J.W., 1993. International comparisons of educational attainment. J. Monetary Econ. 32 (3), 363–394.
Barro, R.J., Lee, J.W., 2001. International data on educational attainment: Updates and implications. Oxford Econ. Pap. 53 (3), 541–563.
Barro, R.J., Lee, J.W., 2010. A new data set of educational attainment in the world, 1950-2010. National Bureau of Economic Research, NBER Working Paper 15902 (April).
Barro, R.J., Sala-i-Martin, X., 2004. Economic Growth, second ed. The MIT Press.
Becker, G.S., 1964. Human Capital: A Theoretical and Empirical Analysis, with Special Reference to Education, first ed. National Bureau of Economic Research.
Bedard, K., Dhuey, E., 2006. The persistence of early childhood maturity: International evidence of long-run age effects. Q. J. Econ. 121 (4), 1437–1472.
Bedard, K., Ferrall, C., 2003. Wage and test score dispersion: some international evidence. Econ. Educ. Rev. 22 (1), 31–43.
Bertschy, K., Cattaneo, M.A., Wolter, S.C., 2009. PISA and the transition into the labour market. Labour: Rev. Lab. Econ. & Ind. Relations 23 (special issue), 111–137.
Betts, J., 2010. The economics of tracking in education. In: Hanushek, E.A., Machin, S., Woessmann, L. (Eds.), Handbook of the Economics of Education. Elsevier.
Bils, M., Klenow, P.J., 2000. Does schooling cause growth? Am. Econ. Rev. 90 (5), 1160–1183.
Bishop, J.H., 1995. The impact of curriculum-based external examinations on school priorities and student learning. Int. J. Ed. R. 23 (8), 653–752.
Bishop, J.H., 1997. The effect of national standards and curriculum-based examinations on achievement. Am. Econ. Rev. 87 (2), 260–264.
Bishop, J.H., 1999. Are national exit examinations important for educational efficiency? Swed. Econ. Pol. Rev. 6 (2), 349–398.
Bishop, J.H., 2006. Drinking from the fountain of knowledge: Student incentive to study and learn—Externalities, information problems, and peer pressure. In: Hanushek, E.A., Welch, F. (Eds.), Handbook of the Economics of Education. North Holland, pp. 909–944.
Bishop, J.H., Moriarty, J.Y., Mane, F., 2000. Diplomas for learning, not seat time: The impact of New York Regents examinations. Econ. Ed. Rev. 19 (4), 333–349.
Björklund, A., Salvanes, K.G., 2010. Education and family background: Mechanisms and policies. In: Hanushek, E.A., Machin, S., Woessmann, L. (Eds.), Handbook of the Economics of Education. Elsevier.
Black, S.E., Devereux, P.J., Salvanes, K.G., 2005. Why the apple doesn't fall far: Understanding intergenerational transmission of human capital. Am. Econ. Rev. 95 (1), 437–449.
Blau, D.M., Currie, J., 2006. Pre-school, day care, and after-school care: Who's minding the kids? In: Hanushek, E.A., Welch, F. (Eds.), Handbook of the Economics of Education. North-Holland, pp. 1163–1278.
Blau, F.D., Kahn, L.M., 1996. International differences in male wage inequality: Institutions versus market forces. J. Polit. Econ. 104 (4), 791–837.
Blau, F.D., Kahn, L.M., 2005. Do cognitive test scores explain higher U.S. wage inequality? Rev. Econ. Stat. 87 (1), 184–193.
Bosworth, B.P., Collins, S.M., 2003. The empirics of growth: An update. Brookings Pap. Eco. Ac. (2), 113–206.
Bowles, S., Gintis, H., 1976. Schooling in Capitalist America: Educational Reform and the Contradictions of Economic Life. Basic Books.
Bowles, S., Gintis, H., Osborne, M., 2001. The determinants of earnings: A behavioral approach. J. Econ. Lit. 39 (4), 1137–1176.

Bratti, M., Checchi, D., Filippin, A., 2008. Should you compete or cooperate with your schoolmates? Institute for the Study of Labor, IZA Discussion Paper 3599.

Brown, G., Micklewright, J., Schnepf, S.V., Waldmann, R., 2007. International surveys of educational achievement: How robust are the findings? J. R. Stat. Soc. A 170 (3), 623–646.

Brunello, G., Checchi, D., 2007. Does school tracking affect equality of opportunity? New international evidence. Econ. Policy 22 (52), 781–861.

Bushnik, T., Barr-Telford, L., Bussière, P., 2004. In and Out of High School: First Results from the Second Cycle of the Youth in Transition Survey. Statistics Canada.

Card, D., 1999. The causal effect of education on earnings. In: Ashenfelter, O., Card, D. (Eds.), Handbook of Labor Economics. North-Holland, pp. 1801–1863.

Card, D., 2001. Estimating the return to schooling: Progress on some persistent econometric problems. Econometrica 69 (5), 1127–1160.

Cascio, E., Clark, D., Gordon, N., 2008. Education and the age profile of literacy into adulthood. J. Econ. Perspect. 22 (3), 47–70.

Ceci, S.J., Williams, W.M., 2009. Should scientists study race and IQ? Yes: The scientific truth must be pursued. Nature 457 (February 12), 788–789.

Ciccone, A., Papaioannou, E., 2009. Human capital, the structure of production, and growth. Rev. Econ. Stat. 91 (1), 66–82.

Cohen, D., Soto, M., 2007. Growth and human capital: good data, good results. J. Econ. Growth 12 (1), 51–76.

Coleman, J.S., Hoffer, T., 1987. Public, Catholic, and Private Schools: The Importance of Community. Basic Books.

Coleman, J.S., Hoffer, T., Kilgore, S., 1981. Questions and answers: Our response. Harvard Educ. Rev. 51 (4), 526–544.

Corten, R., Dronkers, J., 2006. School achievement of pupils from the lower strata in public, private government-dependent and private government-independent schools: A cross-national test of the Coleman-Hoffer thesis. Educ. Res. & Evaluation 12 (2), 179–208.

Coulombe, S., Tremblay, J.F., 2006. Literacy and growth. Top. Macroecon 6 (2) article 4.

Coulombe, S., Tremblay, J.F., Marchand, S., 2004. Literacy Scores, Human Capital and Growth across Fourteen OECD Countries. Statistics Canada.

Cunha, F., Heckman, J.J., Lochner, L., Masterov, D.V., 2006. Interpreting the evidence on life cycle skill formation. In: Hanushek, E.A., Welch, F. (Eds.), Handbook of the Economics of Education. Elsevier, pp. 697–812.

De Gregorio, J., Lee, J.W., 2002. Education and income inequality: New evidence from cross-country data. Rev. Income Wealth 48 (3), 395–416.

Dee, T.S., 2005. A teacher like me: Does race, ethnicity, or gender matter? Am. Econ. Rev. 95 (2), 158–165.

Dee, T., West, M., 2008. The non-cognitive returns to class size. National Bureau of Economic Research, NBER Working Paper 13994 (May).

Denison, E.F., 1985. Trends in American Economic Growth, 1929–1982. The Brookings Institution.

Denny, K., Harmon, C., O'Sullivan, V., 2004. Education, earnings and skills: A multi-country comparison. Institute for Fiscal Studies, IFS Working Paper 04/08.

Denny, K., Harmon, C., Redmond, S., 2000. Functional literacy, educational attainment and earnings: Evidence from the International Adult Literacy Survey. Institute for Fiscal Studies, IFS Working Paper 00/09.

Devroye, D., Freeman, R.B., 2001. Does inequality in skills explain inequality in earnings across advanced countries?. National Bureau of Economic Research, NBER Working Paper 8140.

Dickens, W.T., Flynn, J.R., 2001. Heritability estimates versus large environmental effects: The IQ paradox resolved. Psychol. Rev. 108 (2), 346–369.

Dolton, P., Marcenaro-Gutierrez, O.D., 2010. If you pay peanuts do you get monkeys? A cross country analysis of teacher pay and pupil performance. Royal Holloway College, University of London Mimeo.

Dronkers, J., Robert, P., 2008. Differences in scholastic achievement of public, private government-dependent, and private independent schools: A cross-national analysis. Educ. Policy 22 (4), 541–577.

Easterly, W., 2001. The Elusive Quest for Growth: An Economist's Adventures and Misadventures in the Tropics. The MIT Press.
Edin, P.A., Gustavsson, M., 2008. Time out of work and skill depreciation. Ind. Labor Relations Rev. 61 (2), 163–180.
Edwards, S., Esquivel, G., Márquez, G. (Eds.), 2007. The Decline of Latin American Economies: Growth, Institutions, and Crises. University of Chicago Press.
Entorf, H., Minoiu, N., 2005. What a difference immigration policy makes: A comparison of PISA scores in Europe and traditional countries of immigration. Ger. Econ. Rev. 6 (3), 355–376.
Falch, T., Fischer, J.A.V., 2008a. Does a generous welfare state crowd out student achievement? Panel data evidence from international student tests. CESifo Working Paper 2383 (September).
Falch, T., Fischer, J.A.V., 2008b. Public sector decentralization and school performance: International evidence. Norwegian University of Science and Technology, Department of Economics NTNU Working Paper 4/2008 (October).
Falck, O., Woessmann, L., 2010. School competition and students' entrepreneurial intentions: International evidence using historical Catholic roots of private schooling. Harvard University Program on Education Policy and Governance, Working Paper PEPG 10-01.
Fernández-Arias, E., Manuelli, R., Blyde, J.S. (Eds.), 2005. Sources of Growth in Latin America: What is Missing?. Inter-American Development Bank.
Fertig, M., Wright, R.E., 2005. School quality, educational attainment and aggregation bias. Econ. Lett. 88 (1), 109–114.
Figlio, D., Loeb, S., 2010. School accountability. In: Hanushek, E.A., Machin, S., Woessmann, L. (Eds.), Handbook of the Economics of Education. Elsevier.
Flynn, J.R., 2007. What Is Intelligence?: Beyond the Flynn Effect. Cambridge University Press.
Foshay, A.W., 1962. The background and the procedures of the twelve-country study. In: Foshay, A.W., Thorndike, R.L., Hotyat, F., Pidgeon, D.A., Walker, D.A. (Eds.), Educational Achievement of Thirteen-Year-Olds in Twelve Countries: Results of an International Research Project, 1959–61. Unesco Institute for Education.
Freeman, R.B., Machin, S., Viarengo, M., 2010. Variation in educational outcomes and policies across countries and of schools within countries. National Bureau of Economic Research, NBER Working Paper 16293 (August).
Freeman, R.B., Schettkat, R., 2001. Skill compression, wage differentials, and employment: Germany versus the U.S. Oxford Econ. Pap. 53 (3), 583–603.
Fryer, R.G., Levitt, S.D., 2010. An empirical analysis of the gender gap in mathematics. AEJ: Applied Economics 2 (2), 210–240.
Fuchs, T., Woessmann, L., 2004. Computers and student learning: Bivariate and multivariate evidence on the availability and use of computers at home and at school. Brussels Economic Review 47 (3/4), 359–385.
Fuchs, T., Woessmann, L., 2007. What accounts for international differences in student performance? A re-examination using PISA data. Empir. Econ. 32 (2–3), 433–462.
Glaeser, E.L., La Porta, R., Lopez-de-Silanes, F., Shleifer, A., 2004. Do institutions cause growth? J. Econ. Growth 9 (3), 271–303.
Glewwe, P., 2002. Schools and skills in developing countries: Education policies and socioeconomic outcomes. J. Econ. Lit. 40 (2), 436–482.
Goldberger, A.S., Manski, C.F., 1995. Review article: The bell curve by Herrnstein and Murray. J. Econ. Lit. 33 (2), 762–776.
Guiso, L., Monte, F., Sapienza, P., Zingales, L., 2008. Culture, math, and gender. Science 320 (5880), 1164–1165.
Gundlach, E., Rudman, D., Woessmann, L., 2002. Second thoughts on development accounting. Appl. Econ. 34 (11), 1359–1369.
Gundlach, E., Woessmann, L., 2001. The fading productivity of schooling in East Asia. J. Asian Econ. 12 (3), 401–417.
Gundlach, E., Woessmann, L., Gmelin, J., 2001. The decline of schooling productivity in OECD countries. Econ. J. 111 (471, May), C135–C147.

Gunnarsson, V., Orazem, P.F., Sánchez, M.A., 2006. Child labor and school achievement in Latin America. World Bank Econ. Rev. 20 (1), 31–54.
Hanushek, E.A., 1979. Conceptual and empirical issues in the estimation of educational production functions. J. Hum. Resour. 14 (3), 351–388.
Hanushek, E.A., 1997. The productivity collapse in schools. In: Fowler, W.J. (Ed.), Developments in School Finance, 1996. National Center for Education Statistics, pp. 185–195.
Hanushek, E.A., 2002. Publicly provided education. In: Auerbach, A.J., Feldstein, M. (Eds.), Handbook of Public Economics. Elsevier, pp. 2045–2141.
Hanushek, E.A., 2006. School resources. In: Hanushek, E.A., Welch, F. (Eds.), Handbook of the Economics of Education. North Holland, pp. 865–908.
Hanushek, E.A., Kim, D., 1995. Schooling, labor force quality, and economic growth. National Bureau of Economic Research, NBER Working Paper 5399 (December).
Hanushek, E.A., Kimko, D.D., 2000. Schooling, labor force quality, and the growth of nations. Am. Econ. Rev. 90 (5), 1184–1208.
Hanushek, E.A., Lavy, V., Hitomi, K., 2008. Do students care about school quality? Determinants of dropout behavior in developing countries. J. Human Capital 1 (2), 69–105.
Hanushek, E.A., Luque, J.A., 2003. Efficiency and equity in schools around the world. Econ. Educ. Rev. 22 (5), 481–502.
Hanushek, E.A., Raymond, M.E., 2004. The effect of school accountability systems on the level and distribution of student achievement. J. Eur. Econ. Assoc. 2 (2–3), 406–415.
Hanushek, E.A., Rivkin, S.G., Taylor, L.L., 1996. Aggregation and the estimated effects of school resources. Rev. Econ. Stat. 78 (4), 611–627.
Hanushek, E.A., Woessmann, L., 2006. Does educational tracking affect performance and inequality? Differences-in-differences evidence across countries. Econ. J. 116 (510), C63–C76.
Hanushek, E.A., Woessmann, L., 2008. The role of cognitive skills in economic development. J. Econ. Lit. 46 (3), 607–668.
Hanushek, E.A., Woessmann, L., 2009a. Do better schools lead to more growth? Cognitive skills, economic outcomes, and causation. National Bureau of Economic Research, NBER Working Paper 14633 (January).
Hanushek, E.A., Woessmann, L., 2009b. Schooling, cognitive skills, and the Latin American growth puzzle. National Bureau of Economic Research, NBER Working Paper 15066 (June).
Hanushek, E.A., Woessmann, L., 2010a. The High Cost of Low Educational Performance: The Long-Run Economic Impact of Improving PISA Outcomes. Organisation for Economic Cooperation and Development.
Hanushek, E.A., Woessmann, L., 2010b. Sample selectivity and the validity of international student achievement tests in economic research. Econ. Lett. (in press).
Hanushek, E.A., Zhang, L., 2009. Quality-consistent estimates of international schooling and skill gradients. J. Human Capital 3 (2), 107–143.
Heckman, J.J., 1995. Lessons from the bell curve. J. Pol. Econ. 103 (5), 1091–1120.
Heckman, J.J., Lochner, L.J., Todd, P.E., 2006. Earnings functions, rates of return and treatment effects: The Mincer equation and beyond. In: Hanushek, E.A., Welch, F. (Eds.), Handbook of the Economics of Education. North Holland, pp. 307–458.
Heckman, J.J., Lochner, L.J., Todd, P.E., 2008. Earnings functions and rates of return. J. Human Capital 2 (1), 1–31.
Heckman, J.J., Stixrud, J., Urzua, S., 2006. The effects of cognitive and noncognitive abilities on labor market outcomes and social behavior. J. Lab. Econ. 24 (3), 411–482.
Heckman, J.J., Vytlacil, E., 2001. Identifying the role of cognitive ability in explaining the level of and change in the return to schooling. Rev. Econ. Stat. 83 (1), 1–12.
Herrnstein, R.J., Murray, C.A., 1994. The Bell Curve: Intelligence and Class Structure in American Life. Free Press.
Heston, A., Summers, R., Aten, B., 2002. Penn World Table Version 6.1. University of Pennsylvania, Center for International Comparisons at the University of Pennsylvania (CICUP).

Heyneman, S.P., Loxley, W., 1983. The effect of primary school quality on academic achievement across twenty-nine high and low income countries. Am. J. Sociol. 88 (6), 1162–1194.

Hopmann, S.T., Brinek, G., Retzl, M. (Eds.), 2007. PISA Zufolge PISA: Hält PISA, Was Es Verspricht? PISA According to PISA: Does PISA Keep What It Promises? LIT Verlag.

Hoxby, C.M., 2000. The effects of class size on student achievement: New evidence from population variation. Quart. J. Econ. 115 (3), 1239–1285.

Hoxby, C.M., 2003. School choice and school competition: Evidence from the United States. Swed. Econ. Pol. Rev. 10 (3), 9–65.

Humlum, M.K., Kleinjans, K.J., Nielsen, H.S., 2010. An economic analysis of identity and career choice. Econ. Inq. forthcoming.

Hunt, E., Wittmann, W., 2008. National intelligence and national prosperity. Intelligence 36 (1), 1–9.

Jamison, E.A., Jamison, D.T., Hanushek, E.A., 2007. The effects of education quality on mortality decline and income growth. Econ. Educ. Rev. 26 (6), 772–789.

Jenkins, S.P., Micklewright, J., Schnepf, S.V., 2008. Social segregation in secondary schools: How does England compare with other countries? Ox. Rev. Educ. 34 (1), 21–38.

Jensen, T.P., Andersen, D., 2006. Participants in PISA 2000 – four years later. In: Northern Lights on PISA 2003. Nordic Council of Ministers, Copenhagen, pp. 239–248.

Jones, G., Schneider, W.J., 2006. Intelligence, human capital, and economic growth: A bayesian averaging of classical estimates (BACE) approach. J. Econ. Growth 11 (1), 71–93.

Jones, G., Schneider, W.J., 2010. IQ in the production function: Evidence from immigrant earnings. Econ. Inq. 48 (3), 743–755.

Jorgenson, D.W., Griliches, Z., 1967. The explanation of productivity change. Rev. Econ. Stud. 34 (3), 249–282.

Juhn, C., Murphy, K.M., Pierce, B., 1993. Wage inequality and the rise in returns to skill. J. Pol. Econ. 101 (3), 410–442.

Jürges, H., Schneider, K., 2004. International differences in student achievement: An economic perspective. Ger. Econ. Rev. 5 (3), 357–380.

Jürges, H., Schneider, K., 2010. Central exit examinations increase performance... but take the fun out of mathematics. J. Popul. Econ. 23 (2), 497–517.

Jürges, H., Schneider, K., Büchel, F., 2005. The effect of central exit examinations on student achievement: Quasi-experimental evidence from TIMSS Germany. J. Eur. Econ. Assoc. 3 (5), 1134–1155.

Kahn, L.M., 2004. Immigration, skills and the labor market: International evidence. J. Popul. Econ. 17 (3), 501–534.

Kahn, L.M., 2007. The impact of employment protection mandates on demographic temporary employment patterns: International microeconomic evidence. Econ. J. 117 (521), F333–F356.

Kiker, B.F., 1968. Human Capital: In Retrospect. University of South Carolina.

Knighton, T., Bussière, P., 2006. Educational outcomes at age 19 associated with reading ability at age 15. Culture, Tourism and the Centre for Education Statistics Research papers. Statistics Canada (June).

Krueger, A.B., Lindahl, M., 2001. Education for growth: Why and for whom? J. Econ. Lit. 39 (4), 1101–1136.

Lapointe, A.E., Mead, N.A., Phillips, G.W., 1989. A World of Differences: An International Assessment of Mathematics and Science. Educational Testing Service.

Lavy, V., 2010. Do differences in school's instruction time explain international achievement gaps in math, science, and reading? Evidence from developed and developing countries. National Bureau of Economic Research, NBER Working Paper 16227 (July).

Lee, D.W., Lee, T.H., 1995. Human capital and economic growth: Tests based on the international evaluation of educational achievement. Econ. Lett. 47 (2), 219–225.

Lee, J.W., Barro, R.J., 2001. Schooling quality in a cross-section of countries. Economica 68 (272), 465–488.

Leuven, E., Lindahl, M., Oosterbeek, H., Webbink, D., 2010. Expanding schooling opportunities for 4-year-olds. Econ. Educ. Rev. 29 (3), 319–328.

Leuven, E., Oosterbeek, H., van Ophem, H., 2004. Explaining international differences in male skill wage differentials by differences in demand and supply of skills. Econ. J. 114 (495), 466–486.

Levine, R., Renelt, D., 1992. A sensitivity analysis of cross-country growth regressions. Am. Econ. Rev. 82 (4), 942–963.

Levine, R., Zervos, S.J., 1993. What we have learned about policy and growth from cross-country regressions? Am. Econ. Rev. 83 (2), 426–430.

Lynn, R., Mikk, J., 2007. National differences in intelligence and educational attainment. Intelligence 35 (2), 115–121.

Lynn, R., Mikk, J., 2009. National IQs predict educational attainment in math, reading and science across 56 nations. Intelligence 37 (3), 305–310.

Lynn, R., Vanhanen, T., 2002. IQ and the Wealth of Nations. Praeger Publishers.

Lynn, R., Vanhanen, T., 2006. IQ and Global Inequality. Washington Summit Publishers.

Mankiw, N.G., Romer, D., Weil, D., 1992. A contribution to the empirics of economic growth. Q. J. Econ. 107 (2), 407–437.

Marshall, A., 1898. Principles of Economics. 1, Macmillan and Company.

Mayer, S.E., 1997. What Money Can't Buy: Family Income and Children's Life Chances. Harvard University Press.

McEwan, P.J., Marshall, J.H., 2004. Why does academic achievement vary across countries? Evidence from Cuba and Mexico. Edu. Econ. 12 (3), 205–217.

McIntosh, S., Vignoles, A., 2001. Measuring and assessing the impact of basic skills on labor market outcomes. Oxford Econ. Pap. 53 (3), 453–481.

Michaelowa, K., 2001. Primary education quality in francophone Sub-Saharan Africa: Determinants of learning achievement and efficiency considerations. World Dev. 29 (10), 1699, 1695.

Mincer, J., 1970. The distribution of labor incomes: A survey with special reference to the human capital approach. J. Econ. Lit. 8 (1), 1–26.

Mincer, J., 1974. Schooling, Experience, and Earnings. NBER.

Mullis, I.V.S., Martin, M.O., Foy, P., 2008. TIMSS 2007 International Mathematics Report: Findings from IEA's Trends in International Mathematics and Science Study at the fourth and Eighth Grades. TIMSS & PIRLS International Study Center, Lynch School of Education, Boston College.

Mullis, I.V.S., Martin, M.O., Kennedy, A.M., Foy, P., 2007. PIRLS 2006 International Report: IEA's Progress in International Reading Literacy Study in Primary Schools in 40 Countries. TIMSS & PIRLS International Study Center, Lynch School of Education, Boston College.

Neal, D., 1997. The effect of Catholic secondary schooling on educational attainment. J. Labor Econ. 15 (1), 98–123.

Neidorf, T.S., Binkley, M., Gattis, K., Nohara, D., 2006. Comparing Mathematics Content in the National Assessment of Educational Progress (NAEP), Trends in International Mathematics and Science Study (TIMSS), and Program for International Student Assessment (PISA) 2003 Assessments. National Center for Education Statistics (May).

Nickell, S., 2004. Poverty and worklessness in Britain. Econ. J. 114 (494), C1–C25.

Oosterbeek, H., 1998. Unravelling supply and demand factors in work-related training. Oxford Econ., Pap. 50 (2), 266–283.

Organisation for Economic Co-operation and Development, 2007. PISA 2006: Science Competencies for tomorrow's World. 1, OECD Analysis.

Organisation for Economic Co-operation and Development, 2009. PISA 2006 Technical Report. OECD.

Orr, D., Schnitzer, K., Frackmann, E., 2008. Social and Economic Conditions of Student Life in Europe: Synopsis of Indicators, Final Report, Eurostudent III 2005–2008. W. Bertelsmann Verlag GmbH & Co.

Peterson, P.E., Woessmann, L., 2007. Introduction: Schools and the equal opportunity problem. In: Woessmann, L., Peterson, P.E. (Eds.), Schools and the Equal Opportunity Problem. MIT Press, pp. 3–27.

Petty Sir, W., 1676. Political arithmetic. In: Hull, C.H. (Ed.), The Economic Writings of Sir William Petty. Cambridge University Press, pp. 233–313.

Prais, S.J., 2003. Cautions on OECD's recent educational survey (PISA). Oxford Rev. Educ. 29 (2), 139–163.

Pritchett, L., 2004. Access to education. In: Lomborg, B. (Ed.), Global Crises, Global Solutions. Cambridge University Press, pp. 175–234.
Pritchett, L., 2006. Does learning to add up add up? The returns to schooling in aggregate data. In: Hanushek, E.A., Welch, F. (Eds.), Handbook of the Economics of Education. North Holland, pp. 635–695.
Psacharopoulos, G., Patrinos, H.A., 2004. Returns to investment in education: a further update. Educ. Econ. 12 (2), 111–134.
Ram, R., 2007. IQ and economic growth: Further augmentation of Mankiw-Romer-Weil model. Econ. Lett. 94 (1), 7–11.
Ramirez, F., Luo, X., Schofer, E., Meyer, J., 2006. Student achievement and national economic growth. Am. J. Educ. 113 (November), 1–29.
Romer, P., 1990. Human capital and growth: Theory and evidence. Carnegie-Rochester Conference Series on Public Policy 32, 251–286.
Rose, S., 2009. Should scientists study race and IQ? No: Science and society do not benefit. Nature 457 (February), 787–788.
Rotberg, I.C., 1995. Myths about test score comparisons. Science 270 (5241), 1446–1448.
Rouse, C.E., Barrow, L., 2009. School vouchers and student achievement: Recent evidence and remaining questions. Annual Rev. Econ. 1, 17–42.
Sala-i-Martin, X., Doppelhofer, G., Miller, R.I., 2004. Determinants of long-term growth: A Bayesian averaging of classical estimates (BACE) approach. Am. Econ. Rev. 94 (4), 813–835.
Schneeweis, N., 2010. Educational institutions and the integration of migrants. J. Popul. Econ. forthcoming.
Schnepf, S.V., 2007. Immigrants' educational disadvantage: An examination across ten countries and three surveys. J. Popul. Econ. 20 (3), 527–545.
Schuetz, G., 2009. Does the quality of pre-primary education pay off in secondary school? An international comparison using PISA 2003. Ifo Institute for Economic Research, Ifo Working Paper 68.
Schuetz, G., Ursprung, H.W., Woessmann, L., 2008. Education policy and equality of opportunity. Kyklos 61 (2), 279–308.
Schultz, T.W., 1961. Investment in human capital. Am. Econ. Rev. 51 (1), 1–17.
Schwerdt, G., Wuppermann, A.C., 2009. Is traditional teaching really all that bad? A within-student between-subject aproach. CESifo, CESifo Working Paper 2634.
Sianesi, B., Van Reenen, J., 2003. The returns to education: Macroeconomics. J. Econ. Surv. 17 (2), 157–200.
Smith, A., [1776] 1979. An Inquiry into the Nature and Causes of the Wealth of Nations. Clarendon Press.
Solow, R.M., 1957. Technical change and the aggregate production function. Rev. Econ. Stat. 39 (3), 312–320.
Sprietsma, M., 2008. Regional school choice and school selectivity: How do they relate to student performance? Evidence from PISA 2003. Eur. J. Comparative Econ. 5 (2), 133–156.
Sprietsma, M., 2010. The effect of relative age in the first grade of primary school on long-term scholastic results: International comparative evidence using PISA 2003. Educ. Econ. 18 (1), 1–32.
Temple, J., 2001. Growth effects of education and social capital in the OECD countries. OECD Economic Studies 33, 57–101.
Todd, P.E., Wolpin, K.I., 2003. On the specification and estimation of the production function for cognitive achievement. Econ. J. 113 (485), F3–F33.
Toma, E.F., 1996. Public funding and private schooling across countries. J. Law Econ. 39 (1), 121–148.
Toma, E.F., 2005. Private schools in a global world: 2004 presidential address. South. Econ. J. 71 (4), 693–704.
Topel, R., 1999. Labor markets and economic growth. In: Ashenfelter, O., Card, D. (Eds.), Handbook of Labor Economics. Elsevier, pp. 2943–2984.
Turkheimer, E., Haley, A., Waldron, M., D'Onofrio, B., Gottesman, I.I., 2003. Socioeconomic status modifies heritability of IQ in young children. Psychol. Sci. 14 (6), 623–628.
UNESCO, 2005. Education for All: The Quality Imperative, EFA Global Monitoring Report. UNESCO.

Urquiola, M., Verhoogen, E., 2009. Class-size caps, sorting, and the regression-discontinuity design. Am. Econ. Rev. 99 (1), 179–215.

Vandenberghe, V., Robin, S., 2004. Evaluating the effectiveness of private education across countries: A comparison of methods. Labour Econ. 11 (4), 487–506.

Waldinger, F., 2006. Does tracking affect the importance of family background on students' test scores?. London School of Economics, Mimeo.

Weede, E., Kämpf, S., 2002. The impact of intelligence and institutional improvements on economic growth. Kyklos 55 (3), 361–380.

West, M.R., Woessmann, L., 2006. Which school systems sort weaker students into smaller classes? International evidence. Eur. J. Polit. Econ. 22 (4), 944–968.

West, M.R., Woessmann, L., 2010. 'Every Catholic child in a Catholic school': Historical resistance to state schooling, contemporary private competition, and student achievement across countries. Econ. J. 120 (546), F229–F255.

Woessmann, L., 2001. Why students in some countries do better: International evidence on the importance of education policy. Edu. Matters 1 (2), 67–74.

Woessmann, L., 2002. Schooling and the Quality of Human Capital. Springer.

Woessmann, L., 2003a. Central exit exams and student achievement: International evidence. In: Peterson, P.E., West, M.R. (Eds.), No Child Left Behind? The Politics and Practice of School Accountability. Brookings Institution Press, pp. 292–323.

Woessmann, L., 2003b. Schooling resources, educational institutions, and student performance: The international evidence. Oxford B. Econ. Stat. 65 (2), 117–170.

Woessmann, L., 2003c. Specifying human capital. J. Econ. Surv. 17 (3), 239–270.

Woessmann, L., 2005a. Educational production in East Asia: The impact of family background and schooling policies on student performance. Ger. Econ. Rev. 6 (3), 331–353.

Woessmann, L., 2005b. Educational production in Europe. Econ. Policy 20 (43), 446–504.

Woessmann, L., 2005c. The effect heterogeneity of central examinations: evidence from TIMSS, TIMSS-Repeat and PISA. Edu. Econ. 13 (2), 143–169.

Woessmann, L., 2007a. International evidence on expenditure and class size: A review. In: Brookings Papers on Education Policy 2006/2007. Brookings Institution, pp. 245–272.

Woessmann, L., 2007b. International evidence on school competition, autonomy and accountability: A review. Peabody J. Educ. 82 (2–3), 473–497.

Woessmann, L., 2008. How equal are educational opportunities? Family background and student achievement in Europe and the United States. Zeitschrift für Betriebswirtschaft 78 (1), 45–70.

Woessmann, L., 2009a. International evidence on school tracking: A review. CESifo DICE Report – Journal for Institutional Comparisons 7 (1), 26–34.

Woessmann, L., 2009b. Public-private partnerships and student achievement: A cross-country analysis. In: Chakrabarti, R., Peterson, P.E. (Eds.), School Choice International: Exploring Public-Private Partnerships. The MIT Press, pp. 13–45.

Woessmann, L., 2010a. Families, schools, and primary-school learning: Evidence for Argentina and Colombia in an international perspective. Appl. Econ. 42 (21), 2645–2665.

Woessmann, L., 2010b. Institutional determinants of school efficiency and equity: German states as a microcosm for OECD countries. Jahrbücher für Nationalökonomie und Statistik/J. Econ. Stat. 230 (2), 234–270.

Woessmann, L., Luedemann, E., Schuetz, G., West, M.R., 2009. School Accountability, Autonomy, and Choice around the World. Edward Elgar.

Woessmann, L., West, M.R., 2006. Class-size effects in school systems around the world: Evidence from between-grade variation in TIMSS. Eur. Econ. Rev. 50 (3), 695–736.

Wolter, S.C., Coradi Vellacott, M., 2003. Sibling rivalry for parental resources: A problem for equity in education? A six-country comparison with PISA data. Swiss J. Sociol. 29 (3), 377–398.

Yamamoto, K., 2002. Estimating PISA students on the IALS prose literacy scale. Educational Testing Service Mimeo. (Summer).

Zimmer, R.W., Toma, E.F., 2000. Peer effects in private and public schools across countries. J. Policy Anal. Manag. 19 (1), 75–92.

CHAPTER 3

Education and Family Background: Mechanisms and Policies

Anders Björklund* and Kjell G. Salvanes**

*Stockholm University and IZA
**Norwegian School of Economics and Business Administration, CEE, CESifo and IZA

Contents

1. Background and Motivation	202
2. How Important Is Family Background for Final Educational Attainment?	204
3. Theory: A Taxonomy of Effects	211
4. How the Family Affects the Child	216
4.1 Nature and nurture	216
4.2 The causal effect of parental education on their offspring	220
4.2.1 Framework	*221*
4.2.2 Adopted children	*222*
4.2.3 Twins as parents	*222*
4.2.4 Natural experiments	*223*
4.2.5 Discussion of results	*223*
4.2.6 Comparison across methods	*232*
4.3 Money and time as parental inputs	233
4.3.1 Early learning: critical periods and dynamic complementarities	*233*
4.3.2 Family size and birth-order effects	*234*
5. What Education Policy Can Do at Different Stages of the Educational Career: Lessons from Research on Reforms	236
5.1 Maternity leave and preschool reforms	237
5.2 Comprehensive school reforms and tracking	239
6. Conclusions	241
Acknowledgements	243
References	243

Abstract

In every society for which we have data, people's educational achievement is positively correlated with their parents' education or with other indicators of their parents' socio-economic status. This topic is central in social science, and there is no doubt that research has intensified during recent decades, not least thanks to better data having become accessible to researchers.

The purpose of this chapter is to summarize and evaluate recent empirical research on education and family background. Broadly speaking, we focus on two related but distinct motivations for this topic. The first is *equality of opportunity*. Here, the major research issues are: How important a determinant of educational attainment is family background, and is family background—in the broad sense that incorporates factors not chosen by the individual—a major, or only a minor, determinant of educational attainment? What are the mechanisms that make family background important? Have specific policy reforms been successful in reducing the impact of family background on educational achievement?

The second common starting point for recent research has been the *child development* perspective. Here, the focus is on how human-capital accumulation is affected by early childhood resources. Studies with this focus address the questions: What types of parental resources or inputs are important for children's development, why are they important, and when are they important? In addition, this literature focuses on exploring which types of economic policy, and what timing of the policy in relation to children's social and cognitive development, are conducive to children's performance and adult outcomes. The policy interest in this research is whether policies that change parents' resources and restrictions have causal effects on their children.

JEL classification: I21, J13, J24

Keywords

Intergenerational Mobility
Sibling Correlations
Education
Education Reform

1. BACKGROUND AND MOTIVATION

In every society for which we have data, people's educational achievement is positively correlated with their parents' education or with other indicators of their parents' socio-economic status. This pattern has fascinated many scholars, with early seminal contributions in sociology by, for example, James Coleman (1966) in the so-called Coleman report, and in economics by, for example, Gary Becker (1964). The topic has also arisen frequently in policy debates, and most democratic societies have adopted policies aimed at reducing the impact of family background on educational attainment. Although the topic is classical and central in social science, there is no doubt that research in this area has intensified during recent decades and even during the past few years, not least thanks to better data having become accessible to researchers.[1] The purpose of this chapter is to summarize and evaluate recent research on education and family background.

To put this research into perspective, it is useful to make a distinction between two different, though related, motivations for the study of educational attainment and family background. One common starting point is *equality of opportunity*. Here, family background is relevant because the individual has not chosen her family background and thus cannot be held accountable for any impact of family background on her status during adulthood. Therefore, the more important family background is—for instance, as

---

[1] See Björklund and Jäntti (2009) and Black and Devereux (2010) for recent reviews of intergenerational transmission of income and education. Blanden, Gregg and MacMillan (2010) and Erikson and Goldthorpe (2010) offer an illuminating discussion of the relative merits of intergenerational income and class mobility.

measured by parental education—for final educational achievement, the less equality of opportunity there is.[2] This reasoning has motivated many education policy reforms that aim to reduce the association between educational attainment and family background. Indeed, it has often been claimed that some reforms might enhance equality as well as efficiency. Perhaps the most notable example is the elimination of credit constraints for young people's educational decisions. For instance, if ability is distributed more evenly in the population than the availability of resources for funding education, there is clearly an argument for reducing credit constraints for the poor. Without well-functioning credit markets, many productive investments in human capital might not take place.

This kind of reasoning raises several research questions. A first basic question is: How important a determinant of educational attainment is family background? Is family background—in the broad sense that incorporates factors not chosen by the individual—a major, or only a minor, determinant of educational attainment? The great policy interest in this topic has motivated studies of whether specific policy reforms have been successful in reducing the impact of family background on educational achievement.

The second common starting point for recent research has been a *child development* perspective. Here, economists consider the parents as major actors who combine their resources and invest in their children's future earnings capacity via the children's educational attainment.[3] More generally, this literature has as its starting point the position that there are determinants of children's outcomes such as: 1) parents' choices, in terms of investment in the production of children's human capital (as well as other circumstances and choices); 2) the choices that children make given the investment parents have undertaken; and 3) policies the government undertakes in determining the environment for parents and children.

Studies with this focus address the questions of what type of parental resources or inputs are important for children's development, why they are important and when they are important (see, for instance, Conti, Heckman, and Zanolini (2009) and Currie (2009)). This literature also focuses on which types of economic policy, and what timing of policy in relation to children's social and cognitive development, are conducive to children's performance and adult outcomes. The policy interest in this research is whether policies that change parents' resources and restrictions have causal effects on their children. A common example is whether reforms that raise the educational attainment of women (mothers) have

---

[2] Of course, there is not necessarily a one-to-one link between the typical statistics on the role of family background, such as intergenerational correlations and equality of opportunity. For instance, Jencks and Tach (2006) make the point that the typical statistics on the role of family background measure the fraction of total inequality that is attributed to family background. Thus, for example, obvious improvements in equality of opportunity might reduce both the nominator and the denominator of the statistic, with ambiguous overall effects on the statistic. Further, all sources of family background effects do not violate norms of equality of opportunity equally. Jencks and Tach (2006) argue that causal effects of parental income strongly violate such norms. This argument underscores the importance of learning what mechanisms underlie the impact of family background. See also Roemer (1998) for a normative approach to equality of opportunity. Another strand of the equality literature focuses on the importance of economic incentives in modifying the degree of social mobility; perfect intergenerational mobility is clearly not optimal (Phelan (2006); Atkeson and Lucas (1992)).

[3] See Haveman and Wolfe (1995) for a general overview of this literature emphasizing a whole set of child outcomes. See Oreopoulos and Salvanes (2010) for a recent overview and analysis.

effects on their children. Other examples are the appropriate timing of parents' investments in children's outcomes and the complementarity of investments at different periods for children. In addition, much of the recent program-evaluation literature has focused particularly on the effectiveness of targeted programs for deprived children.

The intention of this chapter is thus to offer a summary and evaluation of the literature based on both these viewpoints and on these two important strands of the literature. In Section 3.2, we commence by addressing the question of how important family background—in the broad sense of incorporating both the family and the neighborhood—is for inequality of final educational attainment. We perform this analysis by investigating sibling correlations that tell us how much of the inequality in educational attainment is accounted for by factors that siblings share. Our conclusion is that, in all countries for which we have data, more than 50% of the variation in years of schooling can be attributed to factors shared by siblings. We argue that this is a sizable percentage that should motivate the search for a deeper understanding of what these factors are. On the other hand, the explanatory power of parental education is much lower, generally below 20%.

Given the importance of family background in explaining educational outcomes, we sketch a conceptual framework in Section 3, describing mechanisms that may explain children's outcomes. In Section 4, we provide an overview of the literature on the different types of inputs into the family production process for human capital for the next generation. After presenting the literature on the importance of nature and nurture, we focus our attention on the attempts in the literature to evaluate the causal effect of parental inputs. Further, a special focus is given to the recent literature on the causal effect of parental education on children's education. Then, we discuss other types of parents' investments, including resources in terms of time and money, as well as fertility decisions that indirectly determine resources available, such as family size and the birth order of children. In Section 5, we present results from the recent literature on economic reforms that target children's outcomes. In this section, we focus on the different policy instruments that governments use to establish the general environment for parents' and children's decisions. In particular, we offer an overview of the results with regard to family and education policies that affect parents' resource use or inputs in the family production function, and which provide an environment for children's educational choices. The chapter ends with concluding remarks in Section 6.

2. HOW IMPORTANT IS FAMILY BACKGROUND FOR FINAL EDUCATIONAL ATTAINMENT?

The purpose of this section is to demonstrate the importance of family background factors for educational attainment in modern societies. At the outset, we want to stress two major limitations in our exposition. First, we focus on final educational attainment, which is natural from an equality-of-opportunity point of view. However, intermediate outcomes such as grades and test scores are often useful when analyzing the timing of educational interventions. Our framework below is relevant for such outcomes as well. See Hanushek and

Woessman (2010, section 4.2) for an introduction to test scores and family background. Second, to keep the exposition simple, we apply years of schooling as our measure of final educational attainment.

Our point of departure is the fact that a sibling correlation is a broad measure of family background and neighborhood factors. To see this, consider years of schooling, S_{ij}, of sibling j in family i:

$$S_{ij} = a_i + b_{ij}, \quad (3.1)$$

where the family component, a_i, represents what siblings have in common, and the sibling-specific component, b_{ij}, denotes the effect of factors that are idiosyncratic to sibling j. Because the two components are orthogonal by construction, we can decompose the schooling variance as:

$$\sigma_S^2 = \sigma_a^2 + \sigma_b^2, \quad (3.2)$$

providing the following expression for the sibling correlation in education:

$$Corr(S_{ij}, S_{ij'}) = \rho_{SIB} = Cov(S_{ij}, S_{ij'})/\sigma_S^2 = \sigma_a^2/(\sigma_a^2 + \sigma_b^2). \quad (3.3)$$

Thus, the sibling correlation tells us what fraction of the total variance of years of schooling is attributable to factors that siblings share. Such factors can be of many different types, and include common genes, a common environment and the influence of one sibling on another. A common environment in turn includes the within-family environment as well as the neighborhood environment, including, for example, shared school quality. Although the shared family component captures many factors, it does not pick up all family background influences. For example, genetic traits not shared by siblings, differential treatment of siblings and time-dependent changes in the family, as well as neighborhood factors, will show up in the individual component, even though they are part of the individual's family and community background. Therefore, we must interpret the sibling correlation as *a lower bound* estimate of the impact of a broad set of family *and* neighborhood background factors.

How large is this lower bound in different countries? In Table 3.1, we have collected a set of estimated sibling correlations for different countries. Neglecting first correlations among twin siblings, we find that the correlations are generally quite large, typically in the range 0.40–0.60. The estimates are typically somewhat higher in the U.S. than in European countries. The lowest correlations are reported for former East Germany, where they are in the range 0.25–0.30. It is noteworthy, however, that the correlations were low for the early cohorts born around 1930, who grew up before the formation of the former German Democratic Republic. Further, for most countries, the estimates have been quite constant over time. For instance, Sieben, Huinink and de Graaf (2001) report that the decline in the Netherlands is not statistically significant. Some of the recent estimates for the U.S. are above 0.6, whereas those for Germany and the Netherlands fall in-between the U.S. and Nordic estimates. For the cases with separate estimates for brothers and sisters, there are no striking gender differences.

Table 3.1 Estimates of sibling correlations in years of schooling; standard errors in parentheses

Country	Study	Sibling definition	Cohorts	Brothers	Sisters	Mixed sex
Australia	Miller et al. (1995)	MZ twins				0.70 (n.a.)
		DZ twins				0.40 (n.a.)
Former West Germany	Sieben et al. (2001)	All siblings reported in survey	1919–21			0.39 (n.a.)
			1929–31			0.47 (n.a.)
			1939–41			0.48 (n.a.)
			1949–51			0.38 (n.a.)
			1954–56			0.40 (n.a.)
			1959–61			0.38 (n.a.)
Former East Germany	Sieben et al. (2001)	All siblings reported in survey	1929–31			0.30 (n.a.)
			1939–41			0.25 (n.a.)
			1951–53			0.24 (n.a.)
			1959–61			0.27 (n.a.)
Netherlands	Sieben et al. (2001)	All siblings reported in survey	1925–34			0.52 (n.a.)
			1935–44			0.46 (n.a.)
			1945–54			0.47 (n.a.)
			1955–64			0.45 (n.a.)
			1965–74			0.41 (n.a.)
Norway	Raaum et al. (2006)	Siblings identified in a census as living with the same mother	1946–55	0.42 (0.009)	0.46 (0.006)	
			1956–65	0.42 (0.008)	0.47 (0.008)	

Country	Study	Definition	Cohort			
Norway	Own estimates	Siblings defined in a census as living with the same mother	1932–38	0.40 (0.008)	0.43 (0.008)	0.40 (0.007)
			1938–44	0.41 (0.008)	0.46 (0.006)	0.41 (0.007)
			1950–56	0.42 (0.007)	0.48 (0.01)	0.42 (0.007)
			1956–62	0.40 (0.006)	0.43 (0.007)	0.41 (0.007)
			1962–68	0.40 (0.007)	0.43 (0.008)	0.40 (0.007)
Sweden	Björklund et al. (2009)	Full biological brothers	1932–38	0.46 (0.01)		
			1938–44	0.47 (0.01)		
			1944–50	0.47 (0.01)		
			1950–56	0.46 (0.01)		
			1956–62	0.46 (0.01)		
			1962–68	0.48 (0.02)		
Sweden	Isacsson (1999)	MZ twins				0.76 (n.a.)
		DZ twins				0.55 (n.a.)
United States	Ashenfelter and Rouse (1998)	MZ twins				0.75 (n.a.)
	Conley & Glauber (2008)	Same biological mother	1958–76	0.63 (0.07)	0.75 (0.07)	0.63 (0.05)
	Mazumder (2008)	Biological siblings in the same household	1957–69	0.62 (0.02)	0.60 (0.03)	0.60 (0.01)

From these results, we conclude that *a lower bound* on the share of variation in years of schooling that is attributable to common family and community background factors is between 40% and 65%. These percentages strike us as high. How important are the family and community factors that are *not* shared by siblings? We now discuss two sources of such nonshared factors, namely nonshared genes and so called birth-order effects.

According to standard genetic models, full biological siblings share only 50% of their genes, and each individual obtains 100% of his or her genes from his or her parents. Therefore, one approach would be to consider correlations among monozygotic (MZ) twins, or identical twins, so called because they have identical genes. One could argue that such correlations provide more reliable estimates of what we are looking for than do correlations of nontwin siblings. However, a caveat is that MZ twins might be particularly affected by interactions between themselves, and that such interactions might have no counterpart for nontwins and thus for the majority of the population. One could therefore argue that a correlation among MZ twins represents *a (potential) upper bound* on the share of variation in years of schooling that is attributable to family and community background.

In Table 3.1, we report some estimates for twins. These numbers are strikingly higher than those for the nontwins, in the range 0.70–0.76, suggesting that around 75% of the variation in years of schooling might be due to factors in the family and the community.

Is it likely that these correlations overstate the importance of family background because of an interaction between MZ twins that is not representative for the majority of the population? One way to shed some light on this issue would be to compare the correlations among dizygotic (DZ) twins with closely spaced—separated by, say, four years or less—full biological (but nontwin) siblings and with more widely spaced full biological siblings. The argument is that if interaction between the siblings is an important source of sibling similarity, we would expect higher correlations among DZ twins than among closely spaced full biological siblings, and even lower correlations among widely spaced siblings. Of course, other mechanisms, such as exposure to different shocks in the family and the neighborhood, might also create such a pattern. Nonetheless, similar correlations among these three sibling types would be suggestive of low interaction effects.

In Table 3.2, we report estimated sibling correlations for these three sibling types. For Norway and the U.S. we do not find any substantial differences between closely spaced and widely spaced siblings. This result suggests that, among nontwin siblings, it is permanent family background factors that are shared and not time-specific ones. For Norway, however, we find a substantial difference between closely spaced nontwin siblings and DZ twins. This result definitely suggests that there is more intensive interaction between twin siblings than between siblings in general, a result that in turn calls for care when using twins as a natural experiment in family background studies. We return to this issue when we discuss studies regarding nature-nurture decomposition in Section 4.1.

Yet another reason why the sibling correlation represents a lower bound estimate of family background factors not chosen by the individual is that the correlation only captures a common family component, which is shared by the siblings used in the estimation of the variance components. Recent research has shown that there is also a

Table 3.2 Comparisons of estimated sibling correlations among DZ twins, closely spaced full biological (nontwin) siblings and widely spaced full biological (nontwin) siblings; standard errors in parentheses

Country	Study	Cohorts	Sibling type	Brothers	Sisters	Mixed gender
Norway	Own estimates based on Norwegian register data	1946–65	DZ twins	0.54 (0.01)	0.59 (0.01)	0.49 (0.01)
			Closely spaced nontwins	0.41 (0.007)	0.42 (0.008)	0.39 (0.008)
			Widely spaced nontwins	0.40 (0.007)	0.43 (0.008)	0.39 (0.006)
			All siblings	0.40 (0.007)	0.42 (0.008)	0.39 (0.006)
United States	Conley & Glauber (2008)	1958–76	Closely spaced (twins excluded)			0.61 (0.05)
			Widely spaced			0.68 (0.06)

Note: By closely spaced siblings, we mean siblings with an age spread of four years or less.

systematic effect of birth order; see Section 4.3.2 for a longer exposition. Such an effect is not part of the common family component that is used to compute the sibling correlations above. Using Norwegian data on within-family variation, Black, Devereux and Salvanes (2005a) estimate that in families with two children, the second-born child has 0.4 years less schooling than the firstborn child and, in families with three children, the difference between the first-born and last-born children's schooling is as high as 0.6 years. Booth and Kee (2009), applying a different empirical strategy using British data, also find a significant birth-order effect with the same pattern, although lower in magnitude. These results demonstrate that the sibling correlations estimated above are lower bound estimates of the full impact of family background.[4]

Next, we turn to intergenerational correlations in years of schooling. To show that a sibling correlation is a broader measure of the importance of family and community background, we start by showing the formal relationship between a sibling and an intergenerational correlation. Because the individual component in Equation (3.1) is orthogonal to the family component, only the latter component can be related to parental education. Let this relationship be:

$$a_i = \beta S_i^p + z_i, \qquad (3.4)$$

where S_i^p is parental years of schooling in family i, and z_i denotes family factors that are orthogonal to parental years of schooling. Inserting (3.4) into (3.1), we obtain:

$$S_{ij} = \beta S_i^p + e_{ij}, \qquad (3.5)$$

---

[4] It strikes us as an important task to extend the conventional variance-component approach underlying estimates of sibling correlations to incorporate the role of birth-order effects.

where $e_{ij} = z_i + b_{ij}$, $Cov(S_i^p, e_{ij}) = 0$ and β is the intergenerational regression coefficient. In the case where we standardize years of schooling in both generations, β is also the intergenerational correlation coefficient. From (3.4), we have:

$$\sigma_a^2 = \beta^2 \sigma_{S^p}^2 + \sigma_z^2. \tag{3.6}$$

Dividing through by σ_S^2, we obtain:

$$\frac{\sigma_a^2}{\sigma_s^2} = \beta^2 \left(\frac{\sigma_{S^p}^2}{\sigma_s^2}\right) + \frac{\sigma_z^2}{\sigma_s^2} = \rho_{SIB} = \rho_{IG}^2 + \frac{\sigma_z^2}{\sigma_s^2}. \tag{3.7}$$

Thus, we find that the sibling correlation is a broader measure of the impact of family background than (the squared) intergenerational correlation because the sibling correlation also captures factors that are unrelated to parental schooling.

We now turn to Table 3.3, which contains a set of intergenerational correlations for different countries. We see that these are in the range from 0.30 (Denmark) to 0.46 (U.S.). Obviously, the square of these numbers gives us the share of variance that is explained statistically by parental schooling. Then, we obtain a range from 0.09 to 0.21. Thus, factors that are not even correlated with parental schooling dominate among the factors shared by siblings.

It would also be constructive to know whether the factors contributing to the high sibling correlations are to be found initially within the family or in the characteristics of the neighborhood where the children have grown up. Studies using an original approach by Solon, Page and Duncan (2000) indicate that the family is the most important factor. The approach is as follows. First, use data that identify whether individuals grew up in the same close neighborhood without belonging to the same family. Second, estimate a variance-component model with one component for the neighborhood and one orthogonal component for the individual. These variance components also

Table 3.3 Estimates of intergenerational correlations in years of schooling; standard errors in parentheses

Country	Estimate
Denmark	0.30 (0.029)
Finland	0.33 (0.027)
Norway	0.35 (0.016)
Sweden	0.40 (0.024)
Netherlands	0.36 (0.037)
Great Britain	0.31 (0.035)
United States	0.46 (0.023)

Source: Hertz et al. (2007), Table 7.

define a correlation among persons growing up in the same neighborhood. The neighborhood component will capture not only pure neighborhood effects but also some effects of the family. Because there is presumably a tendency for advantaged families to live in advantaged neighborhoods, the neighborhood component will be an upwardly biased estimate of true neighborhood effects. Thus, the neighborhood correlation is also an upward bounded estimate of a pure neighborhood correlation. If such an upper bound on the relative importance of neighborhood effects is low compared with a corresponding sibling correlation, one can infer that family factors are more important than neighborhood factors for observed sibling similarities.

In Table 3.4, we report results from three studies using this approach, for the U.S., Norway and Sweden. All three studies reveal the same pattern, namely that the upwardly biased neighborhood correlations are very low compared with the corresponding sibling correlation. The relatively largest neighborhood correlation is reported for the U.S., where it amounts to around 30% of the sibling correlation.

Three broad conclusions result from this section. First, something in the family background has sizable effects on final education. Factors shared by siblings account for at least 40% to 60% of the overall variation in years of schooling. This range is probably a lower bound estimate because siblings share only 50% of their genes with each other, but each individual obtains all of his or her genes from his or her parents. Further, differential effects, such as birth-order effects, are not taken into account by the sibling correlation approach. Such differential effects are obviously part of family background and not chosen by the individual. Second, parental years of schooling account for only a minor part of the factors that siblings share. Indeed, more than half of the factors that siblings share are not even correlated with parental years of schooling. Third, neighborhood effects account for, at most, around a third of the factors that siblings share. This shows that we should initially look for family rather than neighborhood factors to explore in more detail what are the most important factors that siblings share. From now on, we turn our focus to such family factors.

3. THEORY: A TAXONOMY OF EFFECTS

The economic literature on intergenerational transmission has emphasized the importance of family background for children's educational outcomes. In addition, as we have seen from Table 3.3, the raw intergenerational correlation in education between parents and children in most countries is high, with correlations varying between 0.30 and 0.50. The intergenerational persistence is also high for other outcomes and traits such as income, cognitive ability, being on welfare, and so on. What are the main reasons or mechanisms for this persistence in educational and other outcomes across generations?

To identify the main mechanisms for intergenerational transmission and assist in structuring further discussion in this chapter, we sketch a model inspired by Becker

Table 3.4 Comparisons of estimated sibling (SC) and neighborhood (NBC) correlations; standard errors in parentheses

Country	Study	Cohorts	Sibling (SC) and neighborhood correlation (NBC)		Brothers	Sisters	Mixed gender
Norway	Raaum et al. (2006)	1946–55	SC:		0.42 (0.01)	0.46 (0.01)	
			NBC:		0.11 (0.03)	0.10 (0.02)	
		1956–65	SC:		0.42 (0.01)	0.47 (0.01)	
			NBC:		0.06 (0.01)	0.07 (0.02)	
Sweden	Lindahl (2010)	1953	SC:		0.41 (0.02)	0.43 (0.02)	
			NBC:		0.08 (0.01)	0.05 (0.01)	
United States	Solon et al. (2000)	1952–60	SC:				0.51 (0.05)
			NBC:				0.15 (0.06)

and Tomes (1986). However, first, let us briefly review the main channels for transmission in a more descriptive way. The educational choices of children may be conditioned by several factors that may generate intergenerational correlations in education and therefore influence the overall intergenerational correlation in education:

1) Parents' educational choices may directly affect their children's choice to enter and complete higher education; parents' human capital raises the marginal productivity of children's education.
2) Parents may pass on unobserved genetic cognitive abilities along with other genetic traits.
3) Families' cultural backgrounds, including unobserved factors such as risk preferences, time preferences, and parenting skills, may affect children's choices.
4) Endowments, such as wealth or financial resources in general, may be passed on and give rise to transfers or borrowing constraints.
5) Public resources and more general public investments may directly affect or interact with parents' education and choices.

These are all broad mechanisms that have different implications for economic policies. Some of these channels can be affected by economic policies, whereas others cannot, and much emphasis has been placed on this distinction lately. The economics literature focuses on the role of parental education as the causal effect; thus, the role of human capital investments is central. However, if the correlation in education across generations is driven by a difference in inherited cognitive abilities, there is less room for economic policies, such as investments in expanding the education system. On the other hand, health policies targeting children at an early stage may be a promising approach to eliminating factors generated by genetics. Yet again, if financial constraints are the obstacle preventing children from poor economic or cultural backgrounds from reaping the economic and nonpecuniary gains from education, then subsidies to attend university or even easier access to high school and university will weaken the intergenerational transmission of education.

A simple sketch of a model in line with Becker and Tomes (1986), Caucutt and Lochner (2006), Checchi (2006, ch. 7), and Lochner (2009) will be helpful in identifying more carefully these different channels of persistence. The starting point is an overlapping-generations model, where parents are interested in developing their own current consumption and their offspring's human capital by investing in their schooling. In addition, parents may borrow or save in the form of debts or bequests for their children. Thus, parents may transfer resources to the next generation through bequests. In line with the informal discussion of mechanisms for transmission of schooling over generations, let the production function for a child's human capital, H^c, be:

$$H^c = f(H^p, A^c, S^c), \tag{3.8}$$

where H^p is parental human capital, A^c is the child's ability endowment that the child is born with and S^c is the child's years of schooling. S^c is chosen by the parents. It is important to note that we assume that the abilities of parents and children are correlated, and that parents' human capital and the child's ability both increase the productivity of going to school:

$$\partial^2 f/\partial S^c \partial H^p \geq 0; \partial^2 f/\partial S^c \partial A^c \geq 0. \tag{3.9}$$

Given these assumptions about the interaction effects in the offspring's human capital production, the implications for parental investments are as follows: 1) given investment at any level, a child obtains more human capital if his or her parents' schooling is higher or the child's ability is higher; and 2) more able children with more educated parents invest more in schooling. Hence, this assumes that parents' education has a direct effect on their children's productivity of investing and thus on how much children invest in human capital. For instance, expanding the parents' education levels through education reforms will have a spillover effect on their children's education levels. Note that Becker and Tomes (1986) assume that $df/dH^p = 0$.

The optimization problem, where parents allocate resources to their current consumption, C^p, and to their offspring's utility in terms of investments in human capital and bequests (W^c), is as follows:

$$\frac{MAXU}{W^p, S^c} = \left[U(C^p) + \alpha V(H^c, W^c) \right] s.t. \tag{3.10}$$

$$W^c = (1+r)(W^p + H^p - C^p - \gamma S^c) \geq -\overline{X}$$
$$H^c = f(H^c, A^c, S^c).$$

where α and γ are weights. The optimal solution for an unconstrained family is to invest in the offspring's schooling up to the point where the marginal value of the investment is equalized across generations. Where parents are not constrained by—and children's human capital investment does not depend on—parental wealth or earnings, there are two reasons or mechanisms for a positive correlation in schooling across generations:

1) Abilities are correlated across generations and they raise schooling for both parents and children
2) Parents' human capital has a direct effect on their children's schooling because it directly affects how productive the children are in terms of schooling

Translated to the nature–nurture framework, the first channel is mechanical and the talent in this sense comes from nature. In the Becker and Tomes (1986) model, this is the only mechanism. Because we allow for a direct effect of parents' human capital on the offspring's productivity in schooling, there is also another route for parental influence on the next generation's schooling.

Allowing for budget constraints, parents have to trade off their own consumption against investment in their children's consumption (Becker and Tomes, 1986). In this case, the wealth-constrained families—which are correlated with the low-education parents—may underinvest in their children's education. This implies that bright children from a poor, low-education background will invest too little in schooling. Families that are not wealth constrained will not underinvest. This therefore is a third channel for an observed intergenerational persistence in education, driven by the persistence among the low-education and low-income group.

A question that is connected to the effect of budget-constrained parents and that has been the focus of recent research is *how* parents are budget constrained. Is it the case that parents cannot afford to send their children to university because of budget limitations, or is it the case that children from low-income and low-education families are not well-prepared to attend university because of budget constraints impacting upon them much earlier than when they apply for university? This question is connected to the more general question of the timing of parents' investment in their children and has been the focus of many recent studies both theoretically and in empirical research (Cunha, Heckman, Lochner, and Masterov (2007); Cunha and Heckman (2007)). Therefore, not only parental investment *per se* but also the timing of investment is a channel for intergenerational persistence in education patterns.

As mentioned, other channels provide possible explanations for the observed intergenerational correlation. As we argued in Section 2, the sibling correlations are large and intergenerational correlation is only a fraction of the total effect of family background. One important part of interhousehold differences could be preferences for patience and risk aversion, which also affect schooling decisions for both parents and children (see Becker and Mulligan (1997)).

Further, a broader set of cultural influences on parents may be important and may be transferred to children. For instance, the fact that parents with higher education may be more aware of the value of the pecuniary and nonpecuniary advantages of education may mean that they put more pressure on their children to achieve more, or that they simply provide this necessary information to their children. Another example is that parenting skills more broadly that are obviously not genetic may be inherited within families across generations. A third example is that more educated parents are more aware of quality differences in primary and secondary schools, and may be more informed when choosing an area in which to live. This choice obviously is also influenced by parental economic resources. This type of selection of residential areas that are correlated with school quality, and the impact on whom the families interact with as peers, may lead to segregation, which may provide advantages in preparing children for schooling later. This type of preference, as well as skills preferences, may be correlated with the parents' education; of course, these preferences may in fact be influenced directly by education, but they may also be quite independent of education.

There may of course also be direct and indirect effects of public policy on the intergenerational relationship in education. In connection to the present model, in relation to budget constraints, parents will be affected both by the costs of schooling and by its benefits when deciding how much to invest in their children's education. Policies to lower the costs for university entry, for instance—which, in many countries, is a decision within the realm of local or central governments—affect the intergenerational persistence because lower entry costs increase the probability of attending higher education. Another route by which public policy can affect the intergenerational persistence in education is through the interplay with educational choices. For instance, if more educated parents are better informed about the benefits and quality of education, and there exist different tracks or different qualities of universities, policies toward strengthening (weakening) tracking would increase (decrease) educational persistence. It is not only education policies *per se* that are relevant. For instance, because the timing of parental investment seems to be very important, policies connected to families are also relevant, such as preschool programs, maternity leave, and other early invention policies such as the No Child Left Behind program in the U.S. Clearly, these types of programs have the potential to prepare children better for their later educational choices, depending on the alternatives they have available. In addition, different effects are expected depending on the age of the child and on whether he or she stays at home with his or her parents or attends day care during the preschool period.

In sum, a person's educational choices depend in general on his or her unobserved abilities or talent, the parents' abilities and education, the family cultural background and preferences, family financial resources, and public resources. Most of these factors exhibit intertemporal and intergenerational persistence and many of them are interrelated. A simple (and linear) version of the following equation is often used when estimating intergenerational transmission of education:

$$S^c = f(S^m, S^f, A^c, f^p, X^p), \qquad (3.11)$$

where a child's education, S^c, depends on both the mother's and the father's education, S^m and S^f, respectively, parent's unobserved ability inherited by the child, A^c, unobserved ability, parental child-rearing skills as well as on unobserved preferences for risk and time, f^p, as well as parental observed resources such as wealth and income, X^p. Public policies in terms of all types of preschool and school policies that alter the relative costs of education also influence educational choices.

To a large extent, the factors that influence a person's educational choice, and thus the persistence of education across generations, will determine the structure of the rest of this chapter. We start by discussing more directly how nature and nurture affect a child's educational choices, and then provide an overview of the empirical literature from which a linear version of the child's educational choice function is estimated.

4. HOW THE FAMILY AFFECTS THE CHILD

4.1 Nature and nurture

Parents obviously influence their children's school performance by transferring their genes to the children, but they also influence them directly them, via, for example, their parenting practices and the type of schools to which they send their children. It is common to talk about "nature" (genetic) and "nurture" (environmental transmission) as two broad categories of transmission mechanisms. Statements about the relative importance of nature and nurture are common in everyday discussions and there is a stream of research reports with such results. Although there are skeptics who doubt that there is much to learn from such decompositions, there seems to be a perennial interest in learning about the relative importance of transmission via nature and nurture in outcomes such as educational attainment.[5]

One research approach, which has its roots in quantitative genetics, uses correlations among relatives with different genetic and environmental connectedness to infer the relative importance of nature and nurture for the outcome of interest. In this section, we first describe this approach and report some of the results concerning schooling. We then continue with results from a more recent regression-based approach that has become increasingly popular in the social sciences.

Consider the following very simple model of educational attainment:

$$S = gG + eE + uU \tag{3.12}$$

where S denotes years of schooling, G denotes genetic factors, E denotes environmental factors that are shared between siblings, U denotes individual factors not shared by siblings and thus not correlated with either G or E, and g, e and u are the corresponding factor loadings. This model is very simple with its additive structure that rules out causal interaction effects between G and E. If we add the even stronger assumption that G and E are uncorrelated, we obtain the much-discussed decomposition of the variation in S into nature and nurture components. This decomposition is more transparent when S, G, E, and U are all standardized to have a mean of zero and a variance of one. Then, we obtain:

$$\text{var}(S) = 1 = g^2 + e^2 + u^2 \tag{3.13}$$

With information about the schooling correlation among certain family members, it is possible to infer the components of Equation (3.13). For example, the correlation between MZ twins, who have the same genes and are likely to share as many environmental factors as any siblings, gives us $g^2 + e^2$, because for them $Corr(G, G') = Corr(E, E') = 1$. For DZ twins, we can follow common genetic models and assume that half of their genes are shared, so $Corr(G, G') = 0.5$, and that their environmental influences are fully shared, giving us $Corr(E, E') = 1$, and thus $Corr(S, S') = 0.5g^2 + e^2$. These two sibling correlations therefore identify g^2 and e^2. A model that uses these strong assumptions is the prototypical model in much research on the influence of nature and nurture. As a matter of fact, we can now use the MZ and DZ correlations in Table 3.1 to illustrate this approach. The Australian MZ and DZ estimates imply that $g^2 = 0.60$, $e^2 = 0.10$, and $u^2 = 0.30$, whereas the Swedish estimates imply that $g^2 = 0.42$, $e^2 = 0.34$, and $u^2 = 0.24$.

With the same assumptions, it would be possible to identify these same components by using information on correlations among full (nontwin) siblings and half siblings who have been reared together. For full siblings, we have $Corr(S, S') = 0.5g^2 + e^2$, and for half siblings reared together, we have $Corr(S, S') = 0.25g^2 + e^2$.

In addition, it is possible to estimate g^2 separately from a correlation between identical twins who have been reared in different environments if we are willing to assume

---

[5] Goldberger (1979) offers a well-known and strong critique of the nature–nurture decomposition.

that these environments are independent and that the twin siblings were separated immediately after birth.[6] Such twin pairs are very rare. Even with a reasonable sample, one could strongly doubt that the necessary assumptions would be fulfilled. In a similar fashion, e^2 could be estimated using a correlation between adopted siblings who share only the same environment. Such sibling pairs are also rare and generally have not shared the same environment throughout their whole childhoods.

With information about estimates based on several sibling types, the underlying model becomes over-identified. In such cases, the typical approach is to choose the parameters that minimize the sum of squared errors between the sample moments and the fitted values of the sample moments. With estimates of more sibling types (or other family relationships), it is also possible to extend the model and make it more realistic.

Björklund, Jäntti and Solon (2005) use nine different sibling types: MZ twins, DZ twins, full siblings and half siblings, with all four of these types split into those siblings reared together and those reared apart, and adoptive siblings. All of the sibling types are derived from Swedish register data, including a representative sample of same-sex twins with zygosity information. Their outcome variable is long-run earnings, but the results are likely to be relevant for schooling as well. With nine sibling types at their disposal, they are able to test the assumptions of the underlying prototypical model; it was clearly rejected by the data. Of the more general models that impose weaker assumptions, they first show that the data did not reject the assumption of common genetic models that full biological siblings share 50% of their genes and half siblings share 25%. More surprisingly, when they allowed G and E to be correlated, and thus treated $Corr(G, E)$ as a parameter to be estimated, they found that this parameter was insignificant and did not lead to a nonrejected model. It is not possible to allocate such a variance component to either nature or nurture because it belongs to both. The only model not rejected by the data was one that allowed a different degree of shared environments for reared-together MZ and DZ twins and allowed the environments of siblings reared apart to be correlated. Using that model, Björklund, Jäntti and Solon estimate that $g^2 = 0.20$ and $e^2 = 0.16$ for brothers, whereas for sisters, the estimates were $g^2 = 0.13$ and $e^2 = 0.18$, suggesting that approximately equal importance should be assigned to genetic factors and shared environments as determinants of earnings. By contrast, the prototypical model yielded estimates of $g^2 = 0.28$ and $e^2 = 0.04$ for brothers and $g^2 = 0.25$ and $e^2 = 0.01$ for sisters.

In recent work, Cesarini (2010) follows and extends this approach with Swedish register data for men. He estimates variance components of alternative models using seven sibling types; he excludes MZ- and DZ-twins reared apart, which in Björklund, Jäntti and Solon had low weights due to small sample size. From our point of view, it is especially relevant that Cesarini not only considers income as outcome variable but also years of schooling, cognitive skills, and noncognitive skills. For income, his results are quite similar to the previous

---

[6] Indeed, the concepts prebirth and postbirth are more appropriate because, in these studies, there is no way to separate pure genetic effects from environmental effects in the womb and during delivery.

ones, namely that g^2 clearly dominates e^2 with the prototypical model but that the two components are more similar when more flexible assumptions are made about the degree of shared of environment. For years of schooling, however, the results are different in two respects. First, the correlations are generally stronger, suggesting a more important role of family background for schooling than for income. Second, all models suggest that nature is more important than nurture; for example, in a model in which the degree of genetic relatedness is estimated without any restrictions and nontwins reared together are allowed to share less environment than twins g^2 is estimated to 0.49 and e^2 to 0.21.

While Cesarini's results suggest that the genetic contribution to schooling inequality dominates the contribution of shared environment for MZ-twins (and other sibling types), our interpretation of these studies is that even the extended models rely on very strong assumptions and that the results generally are quite sensitive to these assumptions. Thus, the results must be interpreted with great care.

Another approach to examining the relative importance of nature and nurture is to start out with an intergenerational association between the educational attainment of parents and children, and make a distinction between biological parents, who transfer nature, and adoptive parents, who transfer nurture. This is a quite transparent approach, but it focuses only on the observed parental characteristics, which (as we saw in Section 2) account only for some 30% to 40% of factors shared by siblings. The variance-decomposition approach, however, focuses on factors shared by siblings, irrespective of whether they are observed factors.

In Table 3.5, we report estimates from this approach in recent studies by Plug (2004), Björklund, Lindahl and Plug (2006) and Sacerdote (2007).[7] Each column in the table reports results from two separate regressions of own birth and adoptive children. Björklund, Lindahl and Plug use Swedish register data on adopted children and their biological and adoptive parents to estimate models with both types of parents. For fathers, they find that the coefficients for the biological father and the adoptive father are significant and of equal magnitude. For mothers, both coefficients are also positive and significant, but the one for the biological mother is larger. Strikingly, for both fathers and mothers, the sum of the two coefficients is very close to the coefficient in regressions on families with own birth children.

In this comparison among parental variables, all are positive and generally significant and of about the same magnitude. Björklund, Lindahl and Plug (2006) also include interactions between adoptive and biological parents. The interactions are positive and significantly different from zero for mothers, but close to zero with very small standard errors for fathers. In this regression framework, as well as in the variance-decomposition framework discussed above, interaction effects imply that a straightforward decomposition into "nature" and "nurture" is not possible. Sacerdote's (2007) results are relevant here.

---

[7] See Scarr and Weinberg (1978), Sacerdote (2002) and Plug and Vijverberg (2003) for seminal contributions and Björklund, Jäntti, and Solon (2007) for more analysis along these lines.

Table 3.5 Estimated transmission coefficients in linear models with years of schooling for offspring and parents; standard errors within parentheses

	Sweden: native-born adoptees	U.S.: Korean-born adoptees	U.S.: all adoptees in Wisconsin data set
Own birth children	(1)	(2)	
Biological father	0.240 (0.002)		
Biological mother		0.243 (0.002)	0.315 (0.038)	0.538 (0.016)
Adoptive children			
Biological father	0.113 (0.016)		
Biological mother		0.132 (0.017)		
Adoptive father	0.114 (0.013)		
Adoptive mother		0.074 (0.014)	0.089 (0.029)	0.276 (0.063)

Sources: Swedish study: Björklund, Lindahl and Plug (2006); U.S. study of Korean-born adoptees: Sacerdote (2007); U.S. study of Wisconsin data: Plug (2004).

When he estimates separate intergenerational income coefficients for adopted and biological children in the same families, he obtains coefficients for adopted children that are about two-thirds of those for biological children.

What overall conclusions can be drawn from this research? Nature (or prebirth) factors and nurture (or postbirth) factors each account for at least one-third of the family associations. This holds both when the family background's share is assessed using sibling correlations and when it is measured using regression coefficients for biological and rearing parents' income or education. Therefore, any comprehensive theory for the impact of family background must incorporate both nature and nurture components. Any theory that focuses on only one of these will be incomplete. The conclusion about the substantive importance of both types of factors is reinforced by the possible presence of interactions between nature and nurture. It does *not* follow that policies can only affect the part of the family correlation that is associated with nurture. Most likely, different types of policies are needed to affect different sources of the family background impacts. Identifying these policies requires a quite different type of analysis.

4.2 The causal effect of parental education on their offspring

There is now a growing literature attempting to identify the *causal* effect of parental education on children's education, as well as on other adult outcomes. The question is whether higher parental education causally affects their children's own education, or whether there are other confounding factors, such as genetic or other prebirth effects that create the strong cross-sectional relationship between parents and children. Basically, this very recent literature estimates a linear version of Equation (3.11), where the focus is on using different natural experiments to tease out the causal effect of parental education, as opposed to other factors, in explaining the offspring's education. More precisely, this literature examines what the effect of parental education *per se* is in explaining children's schooling. Here, we summarize and discuss the recent approaches and results in this literature.

The recent literature has taken three approaches to identifying the intergenerational transmission of human capital by examining twins as parents, adoptees, and instrumental variables.[8] To help interpret the results from these three approaches, first we present the framework being used and then point out what the differences in approach may tell us about what is measured. We then summarize the results.

4.2.1 Framework

We start by presenting a generic reduced form intergenerational mobility model (see, for instance, Behrman and Rosenzweig, 2002) for educational achievement, where both parents potentially contribute to their children's outcomes. A linear version of Equation (3.11) is used, where we more explicitly split the inheritable unobserved factors in two parts:

$$S^c = \delta_1 S^m + \delta_2 S^f + \Gamma_1 h^m + \lambda_1 f^m + \Gamma_2 h^f + \lambda_2 f^f + \rho X + \varepsilon^c \qquad (3.14)$$

Here, S^c is the educational achievement of child and S^m and S^f represent the education of the mother and the father, respectively. The hs are the unobserved heritable endowments of both parents, whereas the fs represent the unobserved talents for child-rearing and parental skills. X is a vector of observed family-specific variables, such as family income, age of mother at birth, grandparents' education (to capture, for instance, inborn child-rearing skills of the parents), as well as child-specific demographic variables such as gender and year of birth. The parameters reflect the causal effects of parental schooling on children's schooling, conditioned on other observed family characteristics (from X), unobserved child-rearing abilities, and heritable endowments. However, in general, we cannot assume that the parents' schooling levels are independent of heritable endowments, child-rearing endowments, and assortative mating. Indeed, we would expect that parents' education is positively correlated with heritable endowments, child-rearing endowments, and assortative mating. Note also the difference here between the descriptive intergenerational correlations reported in Section 2 that capture the total correlation between offspring's and parents' education, and the causal effect as well as the impact of the omitted variables that are specified in Equation (3.14). Three different strategies are used in the literature to identify the causal effect of parental education on children's education. We now turn to a discussion of these strategies.

---

[8] There is also a small literature on the structural estimation of the intergenerational transmission of education; see Belzil and Hansen (2003).

4.2.2 Adopted children

Using adopted children provides an experiment based on children who do not grow up with their biological parents and adds the assumption that the children are randomly allocated to their nonbiological parents. Thus, within the sample of rearing parents and adopted children, there is no association between unobservable heritable endowments of parents and their adopted children ($\Gamma_1 = \Gamma_2 = 0$). Thus, Equation (3.14) is reduced to:

$$S^c = \delta_1 S^m + \delta_2 S^f + +\lambda_1 f^m + \lambda_2 f^f + \rho X + \varepsilon^c, \qquad (3.15)$$

where the confounding genetic effects in Equation (3.1) are eliminated. Compared to Equation (3.2), we see that the inborn child-rearing endowments for *both* parents remain. There are reasons to believe that these will provide an upward bias because of a positive correlation between the mother's education and child-rearing endowments, and because of assortative mating. In addition, notice that using adoptees hinges on the assumption of random allocation of children to nonbiological parents, that is, that the parents adopting children are not a strongly selected group of parents compared with the rest of the population. Further, it is expected that the age of the adopted child matters, as does whether the adopted child is foreign born and or from the same country as the parents. These conditions will differ across studies.

4.2.3 Twins as parents

Another strategy is to use the difference in educational attainment for children born to twin mothers (or fathers) and, in that respect, assess differences between children with (at least partly) the same heritable endowments. Taking the difference between the children of twin mothers, we obtain[9]:

$$\Delta S^c = \delta_1 \Delta S^m + \delta_2 \Delta S^f + \rho \Delta X + \Delta \varepsilon^c. \qquad (3.16)$$

This equation can be estimated separately for twin fathers and twin mothers. In the case of MZ twin mothers, $\Delta h^m = 0$. More generally, the effects both of genetic factors and of unobserved child-rearing endowments shared by twin sisters are eliminated by studying the difference between cousins with twin mothers. If fraternal twins are used instead of MZ twins, the genetic difference between the twins is likely to contribute to a nonzero correlation between differences of h and S. This may introduce an upward bias in the estimation of δ_1. Moreover, assortative mating may cause a correlation between the within-mothers' schooling differences and the unobserved endowments of the fathers. However, because assortative mating in education is likely to be positive, and we expect that heritable and nonheritable endowments are correlated, the inclusion of fathers' education levels may pick up at least some of the parts of h and f that are not differenced out.

Several issues arise with this approach if important assumptions are not met. Because the educational choices of the twin parents have to be different in order to identify

---

[9] This approach in economics follows the children of twins (COT) tradition in behavioral genetics (D'Onofrio (2005)).

parameters using this approach, the educational choices may not be random as is assumed. In this case, with unobserved heterogeneity between twins even if $\Delta h^m = 0$, it is commonly argued that family (grandparent) fixed effects estimates, do not necessarily reduce the bias since nonrandom unobserved heterogeneity remains (Griliches (1979); Bound and Solon (1999)). For instance, this nonrandomness in schooling choice for twins could come about through differences in f in our model if twins are treated differently by parents or if they are different by birth. Behrman and Rosenzweig (2004) argue that this type of heterogeneity can be explained by birth weight differences within MZ twins in the U.S.; this is also supported by Black, Devereux and Salvanes (2007a) using MZ twins for Norway. Measurement error introduces another possible problem when it comes to estimating a within-family fixed effects model. If misrepresentation of parental education is a serious problem in our analysis, it is well known that the attenuation bias from the classical measurement error in the variable on the right-hand side of the equation is inflated in fixed effects estimators, simply because noise constitutes a larger share of the observed schooling variation.[10] In fact, if the measurement error is corrected for by using an IV estimator for differences between twins, the ability bias in the IV may be exacerbated, as discussed thoroughly in Neumark (1999).

4.2.4 Natural experiments

The third approach to identifying causal effects is to use exogenous variations in parents' education as a natural experiment. For the case of the impact of mother's education we have:

$$S^m = \varphi Z + \varphi X + \upsilon, \qquad (3.17a)$$

$$S^c = \delta_1 S^m + \varphi X + \varepsilon, \qquad (3.17b)$$

where Z is the instrument used to identify the mother's education. Thus, we are attempting to isolate the pure effect of the mother's education on the child's education and control for unobserved factors. In the literature, mandatory education reforms for mothers and/or fathers have been used. Again, the same issue of assortative mating holds. In addition, the group most influenced by the mandatory school reforms that have extended education, is most likely at the bottom of the educational distribution. Most notably this implies that the results must be interpreted as local average treatment effects.

4.2.5 Discussion of results

In the light of the general framework, we now present the more recent contributions for the three different specifications. We also present results from two studies where

---

[10] If classical measurement errors are positively correlated within families (i.e., between siblings), the attenuation bias using fixed effects may not exceed that from OLS.

two or three different approaches are used with the same data set, in order to assess differences across methodologies.

In addition to inherent differences across specifications, as we have discussed, other issues exist when comparing results on intergenerational persistence across studies. For instance, there are differences in the studies in terms of whether the year of birth of the children and parents are included in order to control for trends in educational attendance over time. Also, some studies control for the grandparents' educational background in order to control as much as possible for persistence in inborn child-rearing skills.

More important, though, in terms of the effect on estimated intergenerational education parameters, is whether the spouse's education is included in order to control for the effect of assortative mating in education. Whether the spouse's education should be included or not depends on what policy experiment one has in mind. For instance, in an equation of the effect of the mother's education on the child's education where the spouse's education is included, one can obtain the answer to the question of whether the mother's education affects a child's education when assortative mating in education is controlled for. This experiment answers the question of whether it helps to increase a mother's education in order to increase a child's educational performance. If the spouse's education is not included, the experiment answers whether parental education increases a child's educational outcome, independent of whether the mechanism also operates through assortative mating. Both questions are relevant, but it is important to distinguish between them because the results sometimes differ substantially.

Another issue is, of course, which data set (country and number of observations) and time period are used in the study, as there may be differences in patterns across countries or across cohorts. Finally, different educational outcomes are being used in the studies.

In Table 3.6, we summarize the main results by identification strategy, and indicate the data period and data source, zygosity of twins, and other characteristics of the data set and specifications. More specifically, we indicate in a separate column whether assortative mating was controlled for. We start by presenting the results for studies using parents who are twins, reporting separate results for mothers and fathers who are twins. We present both cross-sectional results and within-parental-twin estimates.

All five studies for which we present results—two from the U.S. using the same data set and three from different Nordic countries—show a strong persistence in education across generations, as can be seen from the cross-sectional results. The intergenerational persistence is estimated to be higher in the U.S. than in Scandinavia, and it is also somewhat higher when a child's education is measured by his or her grades at the end of lower secondary school, compared with his or her completed education. One of the first papers to do this was Behrman and Rosenzweig (2002), who use data on pairs of identical twin parents to eliminate confounding genetic effects. Despite observing a positive correlation between the mother's education and the child's education, the authors find no effect between the

Table 3.6 Summary of results: causal effect of parental education; twins as parents, adoptees and IV studies; standard errors in parentheses

Authors	Data	Child's outcome	Assortative mating	Results OLS estimates		Difference estimator	
				Father (1)	Mother (2)	Father (3)	Mother (4)
	I. *Twins-as-parents studies*						
Behrman and Rosenzweig (2002)	U.S. Minnesota Twin Registry. MZ. 244 twin fathers and 424 twin mothers. Mean birth year parents 1946. Survey from 1983–1990.	Years of schooling	(no)	0.47 (0.05**)	0.33 (0.05**)	0.36 (0.16**)	−0.25 (0.15)
			(yes)	*0.33 (0.07**)*	*0.14 (0.05**)*	*0.34 (0.16**)*	*−0.27 (0.15)*
Antonovics and Goldberger (2005)	U.S. Minnesota Twin Register. MZ. 92 twin fathers and 180 twin mothers. Sample restricted to 18 and older and not in school. Survey from 1983–1990.	Years of schooling	(no)	0.49 (0.09**)	0.28 (0.09**)	0.48 (0.16)	0.03 (0.27)
			(yes)	0.50 (NA)	0.10 (NA)	0.48 (NA)	−0.003 (NA)
Holmlund, Lindahl, and Plug (2008)	Sweden Register Data. DZ. 5886 twin mothers and 4062 fathers. Parents born 1935–43. Children born before 1983 (at 23 or older).	Years of schooling	(no)	0.23 (0.001**)	0.28 (0.002**)	0.12 (0.03**)	0.06 (0.03**)
			(yes)	*0.15 (0.002**)*	*0.20 (0.002**)*	*0.11 (0.03**)*	*0.04 (0.03)*
Bingley, Christensen, and Jensen (2009)	Denmark Register Data. MZ. Children tested 2002–2006, aged 15–17.	GPA	(yes)	0.04 (0.02*)	0.07 (0.01**)	−0.04 (0.008**)	0.00 (0.008)
			(yes)	0.14 (0.02**)	0.11 (0.01**)	0.10 (0.04**)	0.01 (0.02)
Hægeland, Kirkebøen, Raaum, and Salvanes (2010)	Norway Register Data. DZ. Children tested 2002–2006, aged 15–17.	GPA	(no)	0.10 (0.001**)	0.10 (0.001**)	NA	NA
			(yes)	0.06 (0.001**)	0.07 (0.001**)	0.042 (0.022)	−0.004 (0.02)

Continued

Table 3.6 Summary of results: causal effect of parental education; twins as parents, adoptees and IV studies; standard errors in parentheses—cont'd

Authors	Data	Child's outcome	Assortative mating	Results			
				OLS estimates using own birth children		OLS estimates using adopted children	
				Father	Mother	Father	Mother
II. Adoption studies							
Dearden, Machin, and Reed (1997)	**U.K.** National Child Development Survey. 4030 own birth children and 41 adopted children. Birth year of child is 1958. Measured 1991.	Years of schooling	(no)	0.42 (0.02**)		0.356 (0.123**)	
Plug (2004)	**U.S.** Wisconsin Longitudinal Surevey. 1587 own birth and 610 adopted children. Birth year of mother is 1940, average birth year of adopted and birth child is 1969 and 1965. Measured 1992.	Years of schooling	(no)	0.39 (0.01**)	0.54 (0.02**)	0.27 (0.04**)	0.28 (0.10**)
			(yes)	0.30 (0.01**)	0.30 (0.02**)	0.23 (0.04**)	0.10 (0.08**)
Sacerdote (2007)	**U.S.** Holt International Children's Survey. 1051 own birth and 1256 adopted children from Korea. Average birth year adopted and birth child is 1975 and 1969. Measured 2003.	Years of schooling	(no)	NA	0.32 (0.04**)	NA	0.09 (0.03**)
Björklund, Lindahl, and Plug (2006)	**Sweden** Register data. 148 496 own birth and 7498 adopted children all born in Sweden. Mean birth year of adoptive mother is 1934. Mean birth year of child is 1966. Measured 1999.	Years of schooling	(no)	0.23 (0.00**)	0.24 (0.00**)	0.13 (0.01**)	0.11 (0.01**)
			(yes)	0.16 (0.00**)	0.16 (0.00**)	0.10 (0.01**)	0.06 (0.01**)

Study	Data	Outcome	(controls)					
Holmlund, Lindahl, and Plug (2008)	**Sweden** Register data. Measured 1999. 94 079 own birth and 2125 adopted children, all born in Sweden. Mean birth year of adoptive mother: 1932. Mean birth year for child: 1964. Measured 1999.	Years of schooling	(no) (yes)	0.24 (0.00★★) 0.17 (0.00★★)	0.24 (0.00★★) 0.16 (0.00★★)	0.11 (0.01★★) 0.09 (0.01★★)	0.07 (0.01★★) 0.02 (0.01★★)	
Hægeland, Kirkebøen, Raaum, and Salvanes (2010)	**Norway** Register Data. 588 Korean-born adopted. Less than 12 months old when adopted. Measured 2002–2006. Compared to cousins.	GPA	(no)	0.114 (0.012★★) *0.09 (0.013★★)*	0.091 (0.012★★) *0.06 (0.012★★)*	0.04 (0.012★★) *0.02 (0.01)*	0.031 (0.01★★) *0.02 (0.01★★)*	

III. IV-Studies Estimates

Study	Data	Outcome	(controls)					
Black, Devereux and Salvanes (2005b)	**Norway** Register data. 239 854/172 671 children. Parent cohort 1948. 1958. Reform 1960–1972.	Years of schooling	(no) (no)	0.22 (0.003★★) 0.21[1] (0.02★★)	0.24 (0.003★★) 0.21 (0.02★★)	0.03 (0.013) 0.04 (0.06)	0.08 (0.014) 0.02 (0.04★★)	
Chevalier (2004)	**U.K.** British Family Resource Surevey. 12 593 children aged 16–18 living at home. Birth year of parent is 1938–67. Measured 1994–2002. Reform in 1972.	Postcompuls. School attend.	(yes)	0.04 (0.00★★)	0.04 (0.00★★)	−0.01 (0.06★★)	0.11 (0.04★★)	
Oreopoulos, Page, and Stevens (2006)	**U.S.** Integrated Public Use Microdata Series. 711 072 children aged 7–15 living at home. Mean birth year of father is 1930. Mean birth year of child is 1960. Reforms 1950–70. Measured 1960–80.	Grade repetition (actual–normal)	(no)	−0.03 (0.00★★) −0.4[1] (0.00★★)	−0.04 (0.00★★) −0.4 (0.00★★)	−0.06 (0.01★★) −0.7 (0.01★★)	−0.05 (0.01★★) −0.6 (0.01★★)	

Continued

Table 3.6 Summary of results: causal effect of parental education; twins as parents, adoptees and IV studies; standard errors in parentheses—cont'd

Authors	Data	Child's outcome	Assortative mating	Results			
Maurin and McNally (2008)	**France** Register data. French Labor Force Survey. 5087 children aged 15 and living at home. Birth year of father is 1945–52. University reform in 1968. Measured 1990–2001.	Grade repetition (actual–normal)	(no)	−0.08 (0.00★★)		−0.33 (0.12★★)	
Carneiro, Meghir, and Parey (2007)	**U.K.** National Longitudinal Survey of Youth 1979. Cohort 1958 white children aged 12–14. Instruments used are local tuition fees, unemployment rates and wages.	Grade repetition (actual–normal)	(no)		−0.023 (0.005★★)	−0.028 (0.011★)	
Holmlund, Lindahl and Plug (2008)	**Sweden** Register data. Cohorts of parents 1935–1943. Children born prior to 1983 (at 23 or older). Reform 1950–1960.	Years of schooling	(no)	0.20 (0.006★★)	0.26 (0.009★★)	0.02 (0.061)	0.15 (0.074★)

[1]Results from a restricted sample using the lower part of the parental education distribution (less than 10(12) years of education).

mother's schooling and the child's schooling once one looks within female MZ twin pairs, thereby differencing out any genetic factors that influence children's schooling. The analogous fixed-effects exercise using male MZ twin pairs gives coefficients for the father's education that are about the same size as the OLS estimates. Results that do and do not control for assortative mating are presented, and do not differ greatly for this specification.

Antonovics and Goldberger (2005) question these results and suggest that the findings are somewhat sensitive to the coding and sampling of the data. As we can see from Table 3.6, the results do not really differ from Behrman and Rosenzweig's results; both indicate a positive effect of the father's education and no effect from the mother's education. The three papers using data from Sweden, Denmark, and Norway do partly resemble the U.S. studies, but there are some differences. Holmlund, Lindahl, and Plug (2008), studying DZ twins for mothers and fathers, find no effect of the mother's education on child outcomes when controlling for assortative mating, but they do find a positive effect of mother's education without this control (one-fourth of the effect from the OLS results). For the twin fathers' sample, they do find an effect of father's education (about one-half of the effect of the correlation).

Bingley, Christensen and Myrup Jensen (2009) study identical twins (as well as DZ twins) from the Danish Twins registry and several outcomes, such as grade point average (GPA) at the end of lower secondary school and completed education at 30 years of age (the latter results not presented here). Their results show no effect of mother's education on the GPA in 9th grade or on years of completed education (the latter effect is positive for parental cohorts born after 1945). Father's education is shown to have a significantly negative impact on children's GPAs, whereas it has a positive effect on years of education (although this is reversed for parental cohorts born after 1945, which show no effect of father's education on children's education). Further, when using DZ twins (not reported here), Bingley, Christensen and Myrup Jensen find a positive effect of mother's education on both educational outcomes (about half the size of the OLS results). Hægeland, Kirkebøen, Raaum, and Salvanes (2010) use DZ twin data from Norway with GPAs at the end of lower secondary school. With the same outcome and the same cohorts, these results are directly comparable to those of Bingley et al. (2009). For mother's education, there is no effect on children's education when using within twin mothers, independent of whether spouse's education is controlled for. This result resembles the previous papers, except for Bingley et al. for DZ twins. For fathers, the effect is about one-third of the OLS results but is not significant. Nonlinear effects are not found to be very important in these studies. For instance, Hægeland et al. test whether their results indicating no effect of mother's schooling are the result of power couples, such as parents who are both medical doctors. They find no support for this. They do not find any support for the theory that higher educated mothers who work more have a weaker effect on their children's education. This is supported by the literature for time use data, where the international finding is that more educated mothers spend more time with their children (Guryan, Hurst, and Kearney, 2008).

Dearden, Machin, and Reed (1997), Sacerdote (2002), and Plug (2004) are the first studies to use data sets of adoptees to control for heritable effects. They report results when estimating the impact of parental education on adoptee children's education and compare them to own birth children (or to other nonadoptee samples of parents/children). If children are randomly placed with adoptive parents, the relationship between parental education and child education cannot reflect genetic factors. They all find a positive coefficient for father's education for the adoptees and the coefficient falls only slightly below the cross-sectional effect for own children. Sacerdote (2002) and Plug (2004) find a strong positive effect for mother's education, although their coefficients are reduced to about one-half of the comparison groups of own children. Unfortunately, the sample sizes are quite tiny, especially for Dearden, Machin and Reed (1997) and Sacerdote (2002). Using a larger sample of Korean children adopted in the U.S., Sacerdote (2007) finds that the effect of mother's education on the adopted child's education remains important and is estimated to be about one-third of the effect for the comparison group.

Björklund, Lindahl, and Plug (2006) use Swedish adoptees placed in the years 1962–1966, and find a positive effect of adoptive fathers' education on their children's education, but the effect of adoptive mothers falls to between one-fifth and one-fourth of the own-children effect. The effect of mother's education becomes really small when assortative mating is controlled for. Holmlund, Lindahl, and Plug (2008) use both foreign-born and Swedish-born adoptees. For the Swedish-born adoptees, they find very similar effects as in Björklund, Lindahl and Plug (2006). It is notable that the effect of mother's education disappears when spouse's education is included. For foreign-born adoptees, the effect of parents' years of schooling on children's years of schooling is found to be much smaller than has been found in previous studies. When spouse's education is included, the effect is zero.

The authors also test the effect using a small sample of Korean adoptees, as in Sacerdote (2007), but the sample is too small to provide any significant result. Hægeland et al. use a sample of Korean adoptees in Norway and find significant effects of mother's education, even when spouse's education is included, amounting to about one-third of the size of the comparison group. For father's education, the effect is about the same, but it vanishes when spouse's education is included. Taken together, using the large register-based data sets for adopted children from the Nordic countries, the effect of parental education on children's education is relatively small compared with the earlier studies from the U.S. and U.K. using much smaller samples. The age at which children are adopted is found to be important in several of these studies, and Björklund, Lindahl and Plug (2006) find that selection is important when using information on education for both biological and adoptee parents for Swedish-born adopted children.

The third strategy attempting to identify the causal effect of parental education on their offspring's education is the instrumental variables approach. Black, Devereux, and Salvanes (2005b) focus on a mandatory school reform that took place over a 10-year period in Norway, where the reform was adopted in different years in different municipalities. In this way, the reform had the character of a social experiment that the authors use, in addition to municipality and cohort fixed effects, to identify the causal effect of parental education on the children's education. They find a positive causal effect of the father's education and no effect of the mother's education on their offspring's educational attainment.

Chevalier (2004) and Oreopoulos, Page, and Stevens (2006) use changes in compulsory schooling laws to identify the effect of parental education on children's educational outcomes. Chevalier uses a change in the compulsory schooling laws in Britain in 1957 and finds a large positive effect of a mother's education on her child's education, but no significant effect of paternal education. However, this paper suffers from the fact that the legislation was implemented nationwide; as a result, the identifying variation in parental education arises both from secular trends in education and from the one-off change in the law. Ignoring the existence of cohort effects may be a particular problem in this context, as less-educated individuals are more likely to have children while young and, therefore, in a sample of individuals with children of a certain age, older individuals are likely to have more education. Oreopoulos, Page, and Stevens (2006) use compulsory schooling legislation in the U.S., which occurred in different states at different times, to identify the effect of parents' educational attainment on children's educational attainment. They find that increasing the education of either parent has a significantly negative effect on the probability that a child will repeat a grade.

Carneiro, Meghir, and Parey (2007) use different instruments for the cost of schooling—for example, the distance to college—to assess the effect of parental education on their children's math and reading scores, as well as grade repetition on U.S. data. They find a positive effect of both parents' education for their children's math and reading scores at age eight, but no effect of mother's education on children's reading scores when children were 12–14 years.

Maurin and McNally (2008) use the change in the qualification level required for acceptance to universities in France in 1968, which occurred as a consequence of the student revolt in May of that year, to identify the effect of parental education on their children. They find that an increase in parental education reduced grade repetition for the children. Page (2006) uses the U.S. GI Bill for Veterans from World War II to identify the effect of paternal education on children's education and finds a positive effect. Holmlund, Lindahl, and Plug (2008) find results very much in line with Black, Devereux, and Salvanes (2005a) when they use a very similar Swedish mandatory education reform that took place 10 years before the Norwegian one. The study is also consistent with the small effects found when using education reforms as an instrument for education, although Black, Devereux, and Salvanes (2005a) find an effect of mother's education on attainment among sons and no effect of father's schooling.

4.2.6 Comparison across methods

In sum, all of the three approaches that attempt to identify the causal effect of parental education on their offspring's education find effects, although the strength of the effects differ across methodologies and countries and to some extent across cohorts. As we have seen, in general, the adoption approach measures the largest effects; up to one-half of the intergenerational correlation can be identified as causal. The twins-as-parents and IV approaches tend to yield weaker causal effects, particularly in regard to mother's education.

The recent papers by Holmlund, Lindahl, and Plug (2008) and Hægeland, Kirkebøen, Raaum, and Salvanes (2010) illustrate the findings across methodologies by using many complete cohorts of parents and children for Norway and Sweden and comparing methodologies across the same data sets. Devereux, Black, and Salvanes (2005a) present results for the third strategy for Norway. The twins-as-parents and adoptees approaches arrive at similar results for both countries, but with differences across the methods, which are also reflected in the previous literature.

Although there is a strong intergenerational correlation in schooling in Norway, even when controlling for a rich set of family background variables, including assortative mating, the effect of mother's education on children's education disappears when using the twins-as-mothers strategy, whereas using the twins-as-fathers strategy, the father's schooling is weaker but remains important. In the Swedish case, the result of mother's schooling is still important (about one-fourth of the descriptive associations) when assortative mating is *not* controlled for, but disappears when assortative mating is conditioned out. These results are also very similar for the IV approach. When restricting the samples of adopted children, both studies find a statistically significant effect of mother's education, but no effect for father's education. Thus, these results are in line with the evidence from the literature that different identification strategies matter, even when holding the country and period constant. It is also expected *a priori* that these two strategies will provide different results because they represent two ways of controlling for inherit ability differences. The twin strategy assumes that both unobserved inherited endowments and child-rearing endowments are differenced out, whereas the adopted children approach controls only for unobserved inherited endowments. In addition, the adoptees specification may suffer from nonrandom selection since there is a tendency that adoptee parents have higher education than in the rest of the population and other unobservables relevant for parenting skills be correlated with education and may not be controlled for.

This literature is still new and there is a need for new studies to attempt to understand the results. For instance, in general the causal effect of mother's education on children's education is much different than the correlation in education. In order to attempt to understand this result, the Norwegian study using twins and adoptees tested whether the fact that mothers with a higher education work more may explain the results of no or small effects of mother's education. They find no significant effect for this. This result is supported by time use studies showing that mothers with a higher education spend more time with their children.

4.3 Money and time as parental inputs

As Section 2 makes clear, family background is by far the most important factor explaining children's educational outcomes. However, it is also clear from Section 4.2 that parental education cannot explain all of children's educational outcomes. On balance, parental schooling in itself is important, but other factors in the socio-economic environment partly correlated with parental schooling are also important. The child development literature has focused on the broader effect of the childhood environment in general—including the prenatal environment for children—and outcomes for children. This literature focuses on other resources such as parental income, the timing of income, and the time use of parents. The emphasis in this literature is that there is a difference in children's outcomes as a result of growing up in different families (by parental education level, etc.) because parents invest differently in their children in terms of time and resources. Parents may invest differently across their children (gender differences/birth order) as well as in how many children they decide to have, thereby perhaps trading off quality for quantity. Some of these investments and family characteristics may be correlated with parental education and thus contribute to estimated intergenerational associations. Others may not be correlated but yet contribute to sibling similarity.

We provide an overview of some of this literature, focusing on particular aspects, without intending to provide a complete picture (see Almond and Currie (2010) and Conti, Heckman, and Zanolini (2009) for recent and extensive overviews of this literature on early investment in human capital and children's outcomes).

4.3.1 Early learning: critical periods and dynamic complementarities

The recent literature provides reasons to expect that the timing of parents' investment in children will have an effect on children's adult outcomes, independent of the level of investment. First, a wealth of evidence has documented differential accumulation of various skills across the lifetime of children (Heckman (2006); Knudsen, Heckman, Cameron, and Shonkoff (2006); Cunha and Heckman (2007); Heckman and Masterov (2007)). For instance, Cunha and Heckman (2007) note the presence of critical periods for investment in the development of certain skills. They note that the improvement of IQ and the aptitude to learn a language are stronger early on in life, although humans are able to develop and improve their vocabulary into their adulthood. This means that we may expect to find heterogeneity in the effect of income across the lifetime of the child. Further, a paper by Carneiro and Heckman (2003) distinguishes between short-term and long-term credit constraints that influence optimal investment in child human capital. They argue that the short-term income constraints facing parents at the time of their child's potential enrollment in college have no significant effect on child enrollment once the longer-term constraints are controlled for. Such long-term constraints are defined broadly in terms of family background characteristics, for example the parents' education level, their age at the birth of the first child, and other indicators of socio-economic status that are fixed across the child's life. The consequence of a lifetime of binding long-term credit constraints is that, by the time the child is of college age, he or she will not have developed the prerequisite skills for attending college.

Another aspect of the timing of investment in child human capital is that of dynamic complementarity in the manifestation of income in different periods across time into child skills. In their evaluation of the U.S. Head Start program, Currie and Thomas (1995) find that the initially positive effects of the program fade out, or reduce over time, for black children. Currie and Thomas (2000) argue that this is because the black children experienced a lower quality of postprogram education than the white children did. This suggests that investments across time are complementary in nature, whereby the marginal return to later (earlier) investment increases the level of early (late) investments. This literature is rapidly developing as documented by Almond and Currie (2010) and the papers by James Heckman and co-authors, which provide recent extensive overviews of contributions and directions for new research.

4.3.2 Family size and birth-order effects

The economics of the family suggests that children's success in general, and in particular their schooling, depends on childhood conditions. In particular, there is a strong focus in economics on the inter- and intra-familial differences in investment in children, leading to subsequent differences in adult outcomes. These observations have resulted in a well-established theoretical and empirical literature on the effects of both family size and birth order.

Family size may matter for schooling achievements because there may be a tradeoff between child quantity and quality (Becker (1964); Becker and Lewis (1973); Becker and Tomes (1976)). This theory develops a model in which there is an interaction between quality and quantity in the budget constraint, which leads to a tradeoff in the quality and quantity of children in a family. These models then predict that, with an exogenous increase in family size, there is a negative effect on child quality, as measured, for instance, by scholastic performance or other outcomes. The models assume that this effect is homogeneous across children within families.

There are also several hypotheses in the literature about the biological, economic, and psychological impacts of birth order (see Blake (1989) for seminal work and a summary of many of the earlier studies in this field). First, siblings may not receive an equal share of resources devoted to their education. Pecuniary or time resources may differ across siblings, for instance such that parents are able to devote more time to the eldest child relative to the younger siblings (Price, 2008). In addition, for higher birth-order children, there is a greater probability that the parents will be divorced, which may affect these children's development. Further, there may be biological differences resulting from birth order because of differing quality of prenatal care, or differences in the behavior of expectant mothers. There is also a tendency for children with a higher birth order to be born to older mothers, which may lead to a difference in support in the womb. Uncertainty regarding the rewards for having an extra child may also lead to an optimal stopping rule for parents. Parents continue to have more children if the first child is a good draw and then stop when there is a less favorable draw. Psychologists have provided several additional explanations and the "confluence" model by Zajonc (1976) has been very influential in explaining the effect of birth order on IQ, and thus subsequent schooling and earnings. This model has two elements: 1) a person's IQ is influenced by the average family environment, for instance, the average family IQ level; and 2) older children learn more from teaching younger children than younger children gain by being taught. In this way, Zajonc (1976) explains that intelligence falls with an increase in family size and that IQ falls off for the higher birth-order children.

The empirical literature that tests the hypothesis of whether there is a negative effect on adult outcomes of growing up in a large rather than a small family tends to find large negative associations, even controlling for socio-economic factors. However, the challenge is that family size may be endogenous and related to other unobserved parental characteristics affecting children's outcomes. In addition, birth order may confound family size. There are a couple of approaches to developing instruments for family size. A suggestion by Rosenzweig and Wolpin (1980) is to use twin births as compared to singletons. Alternatively, the sex composition of children may be used because it is well-documented that parents have strong preferences for variety and thus are more likely to have another child at any parity if the previous children are all the same sex (Angrist and Evans (1998)).

The results in this literature when controlling for birth order and instrumenting for family size is that the negative effect of family size on schooling and labor market outcomes disappears, although there is a strong cross-sectional association between children's outcomes and family size (Black, Devereux, and Salvanes (2005a); Black, Devereux, and Salvanes (2010)). This finding for Norway has been supported by several subsequent studies for different countries and several outcomes (Angrist, Lavy, and Schlosser (2006); Cáceres-Delpiano (2006); Conley and Glauber (2006)).

Testing for birth-order effects is also very challenging. Family size has to be controlled for because children with higher birth order are more likely to be born into larger families. Because higher rank children are more likely to be born in later years, Blake (1989) stresses the need to control for cohort effects. In addition, parent cohort effects have to be conditioned out because higher rank children are more likely to have older parents at birth. Finally, because parents differ across families, parental characteristics have to be controlled for. Thus, it is necessary to have multiple cohorts for each birth order so that one can control for cohort effects. Full fertility histories are also required so that one can control for the mother's age at each birth and the mother's age at the birth of the first child. In addition, parental characteristics such as mother's skills must also be controlled for, as they may also be correlated with birth order, conditional on the child and mother cohort.

The empirical literature tends to find negative effects of birth order: higher order siblings perform worse than older siblings on a set of outcome variables. Some of the earlier studies, such as Behrman and Taubman (1986), find small negative effects, whereas Hanushek (1992) finds a U-shape in outcomes for black children from large families. These studies use small samples and could not include parental and children cohort effects or a full set of family size indicators. More recent papers using large data sets that were able to properly control all these variables find significant and quite large negative effects on children's education, IQ, and other outcomes (Black, Devereux, and Salvanes (2005a, 2007b)).

5. WHAT EDUCATION POLICY CAN DO AT DIFFERENT STAGES OF THE EDUCATIONAL CAREER: LESSONS FROM RESEARCH ON REFORMS

Up to this point, we have stressed the literature focusing on the effect of parents' choices on children's educational outcomes: the choices regarding the quality and quantity of family resources or inputs devoted to children, and the effect of inherited capabilities. In addition, we made the distinction between parental choices and choices made by children, given the opportunities provided by parents. In this section, we focus on the different policy instruments that the government can use to set the general environment for parents' and children's decisions. Clearly, these policies or interventions may reduce the intergenerational persistence through economic policies affecting low socio-economic status (SES) children. More precisely, we give an overview of the results with regard to family policies and education policies that affect parents' resource use or inputs into the family production function, which provide the environment for children's educational choices.

One route by which public policy can affect intergenerational persistence in education is through the interplay with educational choices. For instance, if more highly educated parents are better informed about the benefits of education and the quality of education, and there exist different tracks or different qualities of universities, policies that strengthen (weaken) tracking would increase (decrease) educational persistence. It is not only education policies *per se* that are relevant. For instance, because the timing of parental investment appears to be very important, family-related policies are also highly relevant, such as preschool programs, maternity leave policies and other early invention policies, for example, the Head Start and Perry Preschool programs in the U.S. Clearly, these types of programs have the potential to prepare children better for later school choices, depending on the alternatives that are available to these children.[11] In addition, depending on the age of the child, different effects are expected depending on whether the child stays at home with his or her parents or attends day care before he or she reaches school age. Rules for the school starting age are another example of influential family-related policies.

5.1 Maternity leave and preschool reforms

A recent set of papers have focused on the impact of maternity leave policies not only on women's labor supply, but also on children's short-term and long-term outcomes. More specifically, the literature on changes in maternity leave policies focuses on the effects of parents' time with very young children, which can have both short-term effects on for instance health outcomes for children, and long-term effects on cognitive and labor market outcomes for adults. In particular, the literature attempts to condition out any income effect from maternity leave changes, and focuses on the time spent by the mother or father with the child in the first months after birth. In addition, there is a longer-standing literature that focuses on parental work and children's outcomes as a result of maternity leave policy. We also briefly discuss this latter literature (see Ruhm (2009) for a recent overview of this literature).

The theoretical results of parental time spent with children, and how this impacts on children's short-term and long-term outcomes by reducing market-based work or increasing maternity leave periods, are ambiguous (Becker and Tomes (1986); Blau and Hagy (1998)). On the positive side, it is expected that less work outside of home implies more time—and more quality time—spent with children and thus more investment in children's development. Longer periods away from the child may imply that both parents are less attached to the child, which may have long-term negative effects on the child. However, market-based work means increased income, leading to larger investment possibilities in both the short run and the long run. There are also potential gains or costs for the mother. Mandatory job-protected maternity leave, leading to a continuity of employment, may increase women's earnings and increase gender equality. However, staying out of the workforce may also harm mothers' present job roles and their earnings prospects because of a loss of human capital while taking care of children.

Given the ambiguous predictions from theory, the literature on the effect on children's *short-term* outcomes of parental work and of maternity leave is not conclusive. There is a literature on mother's employment on children's outcomes and a more specific literature on the effect of maternity leave policies as an exogenous variation to maternity employment, which thus impacts on children's outcomes. The results are inconclusive and they propose that more research and better methods of identification

---

[11] This literature is only briefly mentioned here because it has been recently reviewed in Almond and Currie (2010).

are needed to establish the causal effects of maternal employment and childcare use on children's outcomes (see Bernal and Keane (2006) for an overview). However, on balance, positive effects are found from spending more time with children in terms of breastfeeding benefits, improved child health, reduced behavioral problems and child mortality, and improved cognitive test scores (Baum (2003); Berger, Hill, and Waldfogel (2005); Ruhm (2000, 2004)).

Papers focusing on the effect of increasing parental leave on children's outcomes are rare. Several studies focus on short-term outcomes for children. Tanaka (2005) looks at variations in maternity leave across OECD countries. He finds that longer maternity leave has a small positive impact on the birth weight and mortality rates of infants. Baker and Milligan (2008, 2010) use variations in maternity leave legislation in Canada across provinces to establish a causal effect of maternity leave on children's outcomes. They find that there is no impact, or a very weak impact, on different measures of child development. Again, these studies focus on short-term outcomes of children. There are several issues in this literature concerning identifying causal effects of time spent with children, such as selection of parents working, controlling for the negative income effect of not working, and so on.

Only a few recent papers have begun to examine the long-term effects of mothers' work and maternity leave and carefully identify causal effects (Dustmann and Schönberg (2008); Carneiro, Løken, and Salvanes (2010); Liu and Nordström Skans (2010); and Rasmussen (2010)). These papers use data from four different countries and each arrives at different answers. There may be various reasons why the results differ. It is important when interpreting the results to note that the reforms that are studied differ in terms of the size of the extensions of mandatory education and also in terms of the timing of the extensions in the baby's life. Thus, the reforms were introduced under different conditions and therefore the alternatives for the children were different. More specifically, a change of maternity leave early in a child's life is more important than in a later period after birth. In addition, equally important for interpreting the results is the alternative: are there good day care centers available for the child's first year, and what are the child-rearing skills of the mother? The timing issue is connected to critical periods in development, as has been discussed. Whether breastfeeding is important is highly controversial in the medical literature and it remains an open question whether this is an important channel. Kramer and Kakuma (2004) undertake a review of most of the papers in the medical literature and are critical of most of the papers they review. However, they find support for the theory that breastfeeding appears to enhance cognitive development. For other outcomes such as health, the jury is still out. Dustmann and Schönberg (2008) assess outcomes such as wages and unemployment rates at the age of 23, and attendance at high-track schools when children are teenagers. Rasmussen (2010) uses a maternity leave reform in Denmark and finds no effect on medium-term outcomes such as test scores at age 15 or children's dropout rates from high school. The reform she assesses took place in the mid-1980s in Denmark, when it appears that high quality day care was highly accessible. Liu and Nordström Skans (2010) evaluate a reform taking place in the late 1980s in Sweden, which extended leave from 12 to 15 months, using test scores and grades at age 16 as outcomes. Carneiro, Løken, and Salvanes (2009) evaluate a maternity leave reform that occurred in Norway on July 1 1977 and extended the fully covered maternity leave period from 12 to 18 weeks. All of these papers use regression discontinuity or IV techniques, using the reform as the exogenous variation. Only the last of these papers finds effects on children's teenage outcomes. The high school dropout rate declined by 2.7 percentage points as a result of the increase in maternity leave; for children of less educated mothers, the effect was more marked, with the dropout rate decreasing by 5.2 percentage points. In contrast to the other studies, the latter study was able to identify eligible mothers only, and the characteristics of the reform allowed the authors to isolate the effect of the increase in the mothers' time with their children from the effect of the decrease in income from staying home. This literature on maternity leave and other family policy related to time use with children is still in its infancy and, as yet, results are only indicative.

5.2 Comprehensive school reforms and tracking

After World War II, several comprehensive school reforms took place in Europe that may have affected the intergenerational relationship in education (see Lechinsky and Mayer (1990) and Murtin and Viarengo (2010) for overviews). The expansion of compulsory schooling after World War II was considered an integral part of the development of welfare states in Europe and one of its explicit goals was to enhance equality of opportunity. In general, the two main components of these reforms consisted of an extension of the mandatory years of education, or a change in the school leaving age, and a change in the age of tracking. Basically, the reforms introduced nine mandatory years of schooling (or the school leaving age of 15 or 16), and all children were required to take the same academic track in lower secondary school. Tracking was thus postponed until the age of 15 or 16. These types of reforms are expected to have affected intergenerational mobility in different ways. A general way of thinking about this is to consider the public investment in prolonged schooling at the lower secondary level as an early investment in human capital that is complementary to later skills that are acquired (Cunha et al. (2007)). If this investment has a stronger effect on pupils with a disadvantaged background, we will expect that it may lead to a higher probability of completion of high school and university, and thus make completion of these degrees less dependent on family background. In this sense, the investment may lead to increased intergenerational mobility in education and, subsequently, in earnings (Restuccia and Urratia (2004)). One may also expect that staying longer in school will lead to a change in preferences for the value of schooling and in time preferences, leading to more investment in human capital, especially for children with less educated parents. Again, this may result in an increased university completion rate among the disadvantaged. Of course, it is an open question whether expansion of education in general will enhance equality of opportunity, as has been pointed out by several authors (see, for instance, Machin (2007) and Peterson and Woessmann (2007)). However, the particular focus here is on the comprehensive school reforms. A relevant U.S. reference is the high school reforms that took place during the decades prior to World War II (see Goldin and Katz (2003) and Oreopoulos (2005) for an overview of the effect of Canadian reforms).

Postponing the age of tracking may have a similar effect.[12] Positive spillovers, from more able or less disadvantaged students to those who were less able or came from more disadvantaged backgrounds, may lead to higher attendance rates at high school and university by the disadvantaged (Hoxby (2000)). In addition, if ability is measured with noise, early tracking may also be bad for the disadvantaged because they may be assigned to the wrong track (Brunello and Checchi (2006)).[13]

Several recent papers have analyzed the impact of these comprehensive school reforms, particularly in Europe and Scandinavia, on aspects related to the persistence of education across generations. Meghir and Palme (2005) and Aakvik, Salvanes, and Vaage (2010) analyze the effect on earnings and educational attainment of the comprehensive school reforms that took place in Sweden in the 1950s and Norway in the 1960s, respectively, where mandatory schooling was extended by two years and all students had to attend the same track. The reforms used in the studies were implemented as a natural experiment, with the new mandatory schools being adopted at different times in different municipalities. Both studies find support for a weakening of the effect of family background for disadvantaged pupils with parents with low educational attainment. Meghir and Palme (2005) also found increased earnings among pupils with disadvantaged backgrounds using the same Swedish reform.[14] Pekkarinen, Uusitalo, and Pakkala (2009) more directly assess the effect on the persistence in income across generations using a similar reform in Finland in the 1970s, but the focus of this reform was more explicitly on reduced tracking. They find support for a significant decrease in the intergenerational income elasticity (for fathers and sons) in Finland from about 0.29 to about 0.23. This is a quite strong effect, given that the standard result is that intergenerational income elasticity in the U.S. and U.K. is about 0.40 and about 0.20 in other Nordic countries and Canada (Björklund and Jäntti (2009)). Bauer and Riphahn (2006) results exploit differences in tracking across cantons in Switzerland, and also find support that later school tracking reduces persistence in persistence in schooling.

---

[12] See Betts (2010) for an extensive overview of the literature.
[13] See Duflo, Dupas, and Kremer (2008) and Guyon, Maurin, and McNally (2010) for recent analyses of changes in tracking and pupils' school performance.
[14] However, Nielsen, Sørensen, and Taber (2010) only find weak effects of college subsidies on college attendance in Denmark.

Several other papers evaluate related school reforms and the effect of school systems in other countries. Malamud and Pop-Eleches (2008) evaluate the effect of a 1973 Romanian reform that was similar to the Finnish reforms, and focus on the effect on low SES families. They do not find any effect for these groups on university degree completion, although more students from the low SES groups became eligible to undertake university courses. The reason the reform did not result in higher attendance rates at the universities was that new openings at the university level were not established. Dustmann (2004) finds a strong connection between parental background and the choice of children's secondary track in Germany, which strongly affected subsequent educational achievements and contributed to the low intergenerational mobility in education in Germany.

6. CONCLUSIONS

There is no doubt that, in recent years, the analysis of intergenerational mobility and the role of family background has become a very active research field in economics. This is not surprising because this analysis investigates issues of great scientific and policy interest, such as inequality of opportunity and child development. Recent research has also been spurred by the availability of new data; in some countries, household surveys have matured to cover more than one generation and researchers have been fortunate enough to obtain access to population-wide data sets based on administrative register information. Our review has not done full justice to what economists have done in this field, and even less to what has been done in other fields such as psychology and sociology. In our view, the new literature has provided a number of important insights and revealed useful research strategies for the future. However, the literature has also identified many gaps in our current knowledge about the role of family background in forming human capital accumulation in the next generation.

From an inequality-of-opportunity point of view, it is common to consider family background as a broad set of factors that the individual has not chosen him or herself and thus cannot be held accountable for in a normative sense. Thus, we want to gauge the overall importance of such factors. For this purpose, we started out by presenting sibling correlations in years of schooling. What makes such correlations particularly useful as omnibus measures of the role of family background is that they can be interpreted as the fraction of total inequality that can be attributed to factors shared by siblings. Our survey of sibling correlation estimates suggests that, in most modern societies, these fractions are in the range of 40% to 60%. Yet, these numbers represent lower bound estimates of the importance of family background because they do not take into account factors that are not shared by siblings. For example, the recent research that we discussed has shown that birth-order effects are more important than previously believed.

These numbers are nontrivial from an inequality-of-opportunity point of view. Thus, we want to know what underlies these numbers. To learn about this, recent research mainly offers analyses of intergenerational relationships between parental education and offspring's education (or income, in a related literature that we touch upon in our survey). These relationships, however, account for only about a third of what siblings have in common; the rest of the family component shared by siblings must be attributed to factors that are uncorrelated with parents' observed human capital. This result identifies one major gap in the literature, namely the factors shared by siblings that are uncorrelated with parents' education. These factors might represent unobserved parental skills and, from an inequality-of-opportunity point of view, it does not matter whether parental resources are observed or not. However, instead, they may mainly represent interaction among the siblings, with considerable between-family variations in effort, which in turn may not violate norms about equality of opportunity.

The analyses of intergenerational associations have provided more insights than simply providing information about the magnitude of the descriptive correlations. A sequence of recent studies have used novel methods and data to determine how much of the intergenerational correlations are causal, in the sense that a policy intervention that raises the education of one generation has an impact on the next generation. The conclusion that follows from our scrutiny of this literature is that, at most, half of the descriptive correlations can be considered as causal effects. This brings us even further away from the previously cited figure that 40–60% of the overall variation can be attributed to common family factors. One might conclude that these causal effects are small from an inequality-of-opportunity point of view. However, from a child-development perspective they might be considerable. Whether effects are small or large from such a perspective depends on the costs to achieve the specific education reform that is considered. Because the research suggests positive effects for children, there is one more benefit to consider in the social cost–benefit analysis of education reforms.

We have also examined some recent research on the relative importance of nature and nurture (or prebirth and postbirth factors). One strand of research has attempted to decompose the broad set of factors shared by siblings, whereas another strand has examined the more narrow intergenerational associations by means of a regression approach, which compares the relative magnitude of coefficients for biological and adoptive parents. Our examination stressed that the models using sibling types in particular rely on very strong assumptions that call for much caution in interpreting the conclusions. Nevertheless, the common conclusion from both approaches is that both nature and nurture are important and it is hard to find support for the view that one is particularly more important than the other. Thus, a comprehensive model of the role of family background should incorporate both early effects and effects that are accumulated throughout childhood.

In addition, we have stressed a recent wave of studies on the impact of policy reforms on intergenerational relationships and on outcomes for children with different socio-economic backgrounds. Typically, the studies in this genre exploit large data sets from a specific country as well as variations across regions, cohorts, and/or groups in exposure to the reform. We consider this research to be important because it addresses explicit policy questions and has a compelling research design. A common finding is that postponement of tracking until children are older has the potential to substantially reduce the intergenerational correlations. A critic of these studies might argue that the results are specific to one country and the period in time when the reform was implemented and, thus, that the studies do not have much external validity. While this is a valid argument, when the number of studies becomes larger and covers longer periods and more countries, it becomes possible to generalize the results.

However, it is striking that, to the best of our knowledge, no reform study has yet examined the impact of the broader set of factors shared by siblings. Instead, these studies have focused entirely on the intergenerational relationships. Thus, there is room for much future research along these lines. Such research would also assist the profession to improve upon the theoretical models that dominate the field today.

ACKNOWLEDGEMENTS

Björklund acknowledges financial support from the Swedish Council for Working Life and Social Research (FAS). Salvanes acknowledges the support from the Norwegian Research Council.

REFERENCES

Aakvik, A., Salvanes, K.G., Vaage, K., 2010. Measuring heterogeneity in the returns to education using an education reform. Eur. Econ. Rev. 54, 483–500.

Almond, D., Currie, J., 2010. Human capital development before age five. In: Card, D., Ashenfelter, O. (Eds.), Handbook of Labor Economics, (forthcoming).

Angrist, J.D., Evans, W.N., 1998. Children and their parents' labor supply: Evidence from exogenous variation in family size. Am. Econ. Rev. 88 (3), 450–477.

Angrist, J.D., Lavy, V., Schlosser, A., 2006. Multiple experiments for the causal link between the quantity and quality of children. MIT Working Paper 06–26.

Antonovics, K.L., Goldberger, A.S., 2005. Do educated women make bad mothers? Twin studies and the intergenerational transmission of human capital. Am. Econ. Rev. 95 (5), 1738–1744.

Ashenfelter, O., Rouse, C., 1998. Income, schooling, and ability: evidence from a new sample of identical twins. Q. J. Econ. 113 (1), 253–284.

Atkeson, A., Lucas, R.E., 1992. On efficient distribution with private information. Rev. Econ. Stud. 59, 427–453.

Baker, M., Milligan, K.S., 2008. Maternal employment, breastfeeding, and health: Evidence from maternity leave mandates. J. Health Econ. 27 (4), 871–887.

Baker, M., Milligan, K.S., 2010. Evidence from maternity leave expansion of the impact of maternal care on early child development. J. Hum. Resour. 45 (1), 1–32.

Baum, C.L., 2003. Does early maternal employment harm child development? An analysis of the potential benefits of leave taking. J. Labor Econ. 21, 609; 448.

Bauer, P.C., Riphahn, R., 2006. Timing of school tracking as a determinant of intergenerational transmission of education. Econ. Lett. 91, 90–97.

Becker, G., 1964. Human Capital. A Theoretical and Empirical Analysis, with Special Reference to Education. NBER.

Becker, G.S., Lewis, H.G., 1973. On the interaction between the quantity and quality of children. J. Polit. Econ. 81 (2), S279–S288.
Becker, G., Mulligan, C.B., 1997. The endogenous determination of time preferences. Q. J. Econ. 112 (3), 693–728.
Becker, G.S., Tomes, N., 1976. Child endowments and the quantity and quality of children. J. Polit. Econ. 84 (4), S143–S162.
Becker, G., Tomes, N., 1986. Human capital and the rise and fall of families. J. Labor Econ. 4 (3, pt 2), S1–S39.
Behrman, J.R., Rosenzweig, M.R., 2002. Does increasing women's schooling raise the schooling of the next generation? Am. Econ. Rev. 91 (1), 323–334.
Behrman, J.R., Rosenzweig, M.R., 2004. Returns to birth weight. Rev. Econ. Stat. 86 (2), 586–601.
Behrman, J.R., Taubman, P., 1986. Birth order, schooling and earnings. J. Labor Econ. 4 (3).
Belzil, C., Hansen, J., 2003. Structural estimates of the intergenerational education correlation. J. Appl. Econ. 18 (6), 679–690.
Berger, L.M., Hill, J., Waldfogel, J., 2005. Maternity leave, early maternal employment and child health and development in the US. Econ. J. 115, 29–47.
Bernal, R., Keane, J.M., 2006. The effect of maternal employment and child care on children's cognitive development. Northwestern University mimeo.
Betts, J., 2010. The economics of tracking in education. In: Hanushek, E., Machin, S., Woessmann, L. (Eds.), Handbook of the Economics of Education. vol. III. North Holland, (forthcoming).
Bingley, P., Christensen, K., Jensen, V.M., 2009. Parental schooling and child development: Learning from twin parents. The Danish National Centre for Social Research Working Paper 07:2009.
Björklund, A., Jäntti, M., 2009. Intergenerational income mobility and the role of family background. In: Salverda, W., Nolan, B., Smeeding, T. (Eds.), Oxford Handbook of Economic Inequality. Oxford University Press.
Björklund, A., Jäntti, M., Lindquist, M., 2009. Family background and income during the rise of the welfare state: Brother correlations in income for Swedish men born 1932–1967. J. Public Econ. 93, 671–680.
Björklund, A., Jäntti, M., Solon, G., 2005. Influences of nature and nurture on earnings variation: A report on a study of sibling types in Sweden. In: Bowles, S., Gintis, H., Osborne, M. (Eds.), Unequal Chances: Family Background and Economic Success. Russell Sage Foundation.
Björklund, A., Jäntti, M., Solon, G., 2007. Nature and nurture in the intergenerational transmission of socioeconomic status: Evidence from Swedish children and their biological and rearing parents. Berkeley Electronic J. Econ. Anal. Policy (Advances) 7 (2) article 4.
Björklund, A., Lindahl, M., Plug, E., 2006. The origins of intergenerational associations: Lessons from Swedish adoption data. Q. J. Econ. 121 (3), 999–1028.
Black, S.E., Devereux, P.J., 2010. Recent developments in intergenerational mobility. Forthcoming. In: Card, D., Ashenfelter, O. (Eds.), Handbook of Labor Economics.
Black, S.E., Devereux, P.J., Salvanes, K.G., 2005a. The more the merrier? The effect of family composition on children's outcomes. Q. J. Econ. 120 (2), 669–700.
Black, S.E., Devereux, P.J., Salvanes, K.G., 2005b. Why the apple doesn't fall far: Understanding intergenerational transmission of human capital. Am. Econ. Rev. 95 (1), 437–449.
Black, S.E., Devereux, P.J., Salvanes, K.G., 2007a. From the cradle to the labor market? The effect of birth weight on adult outcomes. Q. J. Econ. 122 (1), 409–439.
Black, S.E., Devereux, P.J., Salvanes, K.G., 2007b. Older and wiser? Birth order and IQ of young men. NBER Working Paper #13237.
Black, S.E., Devereux, P.J., Salvanes, K.G., 2010. The more the smarter? Family size and IQ. J. Hum. Resour. 45 (1), 33–58.
Blake, J., 1989. Family Size and Achievement. University of California Press.
Blanden, J., Gregg, P., MacMillan, L., 2010. Intergenerational persistence in income and social class: The impact of within-group inequality. Mimeo.
Blau, D.M., Hagy, A.P., 1998. The demand for quality in child care. J. Polit. Econ. 106, 104–145.
Booth, A.L., Kee, H.J., 2009. Birth order matters: the effect of family size on educational attainment. J. Popul. Econ. 22, 367–397.

Bound, J., Solon, G., 1999. Double trouble: On the value of twins-based estimation of the returns to schooling. Econ. Edu. Rev. 18, 169–182.

Brunello, G., Checchi, D., 2006. Does school tracking affect equality of opportunity? International evidence. IZA Discussion Paper No. 2348.

Cáceres-Delpiano, J., 2006. The impacts of family size on investment in child quality. J. Hum. Resour. 41 (4).

Carneiro, P., Heckman, J., 2003. Human capital policies. In: Heckman, J., Krueger, A. (Eds.), Inequality in America: What Role for Human Capital Policies. The MIT Press.

Carneiro, P., Løken, K., Salvanes, K.G., 2010. A flying start or no effect? Long-term consequences of Time investment in children during their first year of life. Norwegian School of Economics Discussion Paper 24/10, Norwegian School of Economics.

Carneiro, P., Meghir, C., Parey, M., 2007. Maternal education, home environment and the development of children and adolescents. IZA Discussion Paper Series no. 3072.

Caucutt, E.M., Lochner, L.J., 2006. Early and late human capital investment, borrowing constraints and the family. University of Western Ontario Working paper.

Cesarini, D., 2010. Family influences on productive skills, human capital and lifecycle income. Mimeo.

Checchi, D., 2006. The Economics of Education. Human Capital, Family Background and Inequality. Cambridge University Press.

Chevalier, A., 2004. Parental education and child's education: A natural experiment. IZA Discussion Paper no. 1153.

Coleman, J.S., Campbell, E.G., Hobson, C.J., McPartland, J., Mood, A.M., Weinfeld, F.D., York, R.L., et al., 1966. Equality of Educational Opportunity. US GPO.

Conley, D., Glauber, R., 2006. Parental educational investment and children's academic risk: Estimates of the impact of sibship size and birth order from exogenous variation in fertility. J. Hum. Resour. 41 (4), 722–737.

Conley, D., Glauber, R., 2008. All in the family? Family composition, resources, and similarity in socio-economic status. Research in Social Stratification and Mobility 26, 297–306.

Conti, G., Heckman, J.J., Zanolini, A., 2009. The developmental origins of health: Cognition, personality and education. 6th Annual Nestle International Nutrition Symposium.

Cunha, F., Heckman, J.J., 2007. The technology of skill formation. Am. Econ. Rev. 97 (2), 31–47.

Cunha, F., Heckman, J.J., Lochner, L.L., Masterov, D., 2007. Interpreting the evidence of life cycle skill formation. In: Hanushek, E., Welch, F. (Eds.), Handbook of the Economics of Education. 1, North-Holland.

Currie, J., 2009. Healthy, wealthy and wise: Socioeconomic status, poor health in childhood and human capital development. J. Econ. Lit. 47 (7), 87–122.

Currie, J., Thomas, D., 1995. Does Head Start make a difference? Am. Econ. Rev. 85 (3), 341–364.

Currie, J., Thomas, D., 2000. School quality and the longer-term effects of Head Start. J. Hum. Resour. 35 (4), 755–774.

Dearden, L., Machin, S., Reed, H., 1997. Intergenerational mobility in Britain. Econ. J. 107, 47–66.

D'Onofrio, B.M., 2005. The children of twins design. In: Everitt, B., Howell, D. (Eds.), Encyclopedia of Behavior Statistics. Wiley, pp. 256–258.

Duflo, E., Dupas, P., Kremer, M., 2008. Peer effects and the impact of tracking: Evidence from a randomized evaluation in Kenya. NBER WP No 14475.

Dustmann, C., 2004. Primary to secondary school transitions, parental characteristics and career patterns. Oxford Econ. Pap. 56, 209–230.

Dustmann, C., Schönberg, U., 2008. The effect of expansions in maternity leave coverage on children's long-term outcomes. IZA DP No. 3605.

Erikson, R., Goldthorpe, J.H., 2010. Income and class mobility between generations in Great Britain: The problem of divergent findings from the datasets of birth cohort studies. Brit. J. Sociol. (forthcoming).

Goldberger, A., 1979. Heritability. Economica 46 (184), 327–347.

Goldin, C., Katz, L.F., 2003. The origins of state-level differences in the public provision of higher education: 1890–1940. In: Belfield, C.R., Levin, H.M. (Eds.), The Economics of Higher Education. vol. 165. 624–629 Elgar Reference Collection. International Library of Critical Writings in Economics.

Griliches, Z., 1979. Sibling models and data in economics: Beginnings of a survey. J. Polit. Econ. 87 (5), S37–S64.
Guryan, J., Hurst, E., Kearney, M., 2008. Parental education and parental time with children. J. Econ. Perspect. 22 (3), 23–46.
Guyon, N., Maurin, E., McNally, S., 2010. The effect of tracking students by ability into different schools: A natural experiment. Centre for Economic Performance, London School of Economics Memo.
Hanushek, E.A., 1992. The trade-off between child quantity and quality. J. Polit. Econ. 100 (1), 84–117.
Hanushek, E.A., Woessman, L., 2010. The economics of international differences in educational achievement. In: Hanushek, E.A., Machin, S., Woessman, L. (Eds.), Handbook of the Economics of Education. Elsevier.
Haveman, R., Wolfe, B., 1995. The determinants of children's attainments: A review of methods and findings. J. Econ. Lit. 33 (4), 1829–1878.
Heckman, J., 2006. Skill formation and the economics of investing in disadvantaged children. Science 312, 1900–1902.
Heckman, J., Masterov, D., 2007. The productivity argument for investing in young children. NBER WP No. 13016.
Hertz, T., Jayasundera, T., Piraino, P., Selcuk, S., Smith, N., Veraschagina, A., et al., 2007. The inheritance of educational inequality: International comparisons and fifty-year trends. The B.E. J. Econ. Anal. & Policy (Advances) 7 (2) Article 10.
Holmlund, H., Lindahl, M., Plug, E., 2008. The causal effect of parent's schooling on children's schooling: A comparison of estimation methods. IZA DP No. 3630.
Hoxby, C., 2000. Peer effects in the classroom: Learning from gender and race variation. NBER Working Paper No. 7867.
Hægeland, T., Kirkebøen, L., Raaum, O., Salvanes, K.G., 2010. Why children of college graduates outperform their schoolmates: A study of cousins and adoptees. Norwegian School of Economics Discussion Paper 22/10.
Isacsson, G., 1999. Estimates of the return to schooling in Sweden from a large sample of twins. Labour Econ. 6, 471–489.
Jencks, C., Tach, L., 2006. Would equal opportunity mean more mobility? In: Morgan, S.L., Grusky, D.B., Fields, G.S. (Eds.), Mobility and Inequality: Frontiers of Research from Sociology and Economics. Stanford University Press.
Knudsen, E., James, I., Heckman, J., Cameron, J., Shonkoff, J.P., 2006. Economic neurobiological and behavioral perspectives on building America's future workforce. Proc. Natl. Acad. Sci. 103 (27), 10155–10162.
Kramer, M.S., Kakuma, R., 2004. The optimal duration of exclusive breastfeeding: A systematic review. Adv. Exp. Med. Biol. 554, 65–77.
Lechinsky, A., Mayer, K.U. (Eds.), 1990. The Comprehensive School Experiment Revisited: Evidence from Western Europe. Verlag Peter Lang.
Lindahl, L., 2010. A Comparison of family and neighborhood effects on grades, test scores, educational attainment and income—evidence from Sweden. J. Inequa., Forthcoming.
Liu, Q., Skans, O.N., 2010. The duration of paid parental leave and children's scholastic performance. B.E. J. Econ. Anal. & Policy 10 (1: Contributions) Article 3.
Lochner, L.J., 2009. Intergenerational transmission. In: Durlauf, S., Blume, L.E. (Eds.), The New Palgrave Dictionary of Economics. second ed. Palgrave Macmillan.
Machin, S., 2007. Education expansion and the intergenerational mobility in Britain. In: Woessmann, L., Peterson, P.E. (Eds.), Schools and the Equal Opportunity Problem. The MIT Press.
Malamud, O., Pop-Eleches, C., 2008. School tracking and access to higher education among disadvantaged groups. Columbia University Discussion paper.
Maurin, E., McNally, S., 2008. Vive la révolution! Long-term educational returns of 1968 to angry students. J. Labor Econ. 26 (1), 1–34.
Mazumder, B., 2008. Sibling similarities and economic inequality in the US. J. Popul. Econ. 21, 685–701.
Meghir, C., Palme, M., 2005. Education reform, ability and family background. Am. Econ. Rev. 95 (1), 414–424.

Miller, P., Mulwey, C., Martin, N., 1995. What do twins studies reveal about the economic returns to education? A comparison of Australian and U.S. findings. Am. Econ. Rev. 85 (3), 586–599.
Murtin, F., Viarengo, M., 2010. The expansion and conveyance of compulsory schooling in Western Europe: 1950–2000. Economica (forthcoming).
Neumark, D., 1999. Biases in twin estimates of the return to schooling. Econ. Edu. Rev. 18 (2), 143–148.
Nielsen, H.S., Sørensen, T., Taber, C., 2010. Estimating the effect of student aid on college enrollment: Evidence from a government grant policy reform. Am. Econ. J. Econ. Policy (forthcoming).
Oreopoulos, P., 2005. Canadian compulsory school laws and their impact on educational attainment and future earnings. Statistics Canada Research Paper No. 251.
Oreopoulos, P., Page, M.E., Stevens, A.H., 2006. Does human capital transfer from parent to child? The intergenerational effects of compulsory schooling. J. Labor Econ. 24 (4), 729–760.
Oreopoulos, P., Salvanes, K.G., 2010. How large are returns to education? Hint: money isn't everything. J. Econ. Perspect. (forthcoming).
Page, M.E., 2006. Father's education and children's human capital: Evidence from the World War II GI Bill. UC Davies Working Paper 06–33.
Pekkarinen, T., Uusitalo, R., Pakkala, S., 2009. School tracking and intergenerational income mobility: Evidence from the Finnish comprehensive school reform. J. Pub. Econ. 93, 965–973.
Peterson, P.E., Woessmann, L., 2007. Introduction: Schools and the equal opportunity problem. In: Woessmann, L., Peterson, P.E. (Eds.), Schools and the Equal Opportunity Problem. The MIT Press.
Phelan, C., 2006. Opportunity and social mobility. Rev. Econ. Stud. 73, 487–504.
Plug, E., 2004. Estimating the effect of mother's schooling on children's schooling using a sample of adoptees. Am. Econ. Rev. 94 (1), 358–368.
Plug, E., Vijverberg, W., 2003. Schooling, family background and adoption: Is it nature or nurture? J. Polit. Econ. 11 (3), 611–641.
Price, J., 2008. Quality time: The effect of birth order. J. Hum. Resour. 43 (1), 240–265.
Raaum, O., Sørensen, E.Ø., Salvanes, K.G., 2006. The neighborhood is not what it used to be. Econ. J. 116 (1), 278–300.
Rasmussen, A.W., 2010. Increasing the length of parents' birth-related leave: The effect on children's long-term educational outcomes. Labour Econ. 17 (1), 91–100.
Restuccia, D., Urratia, C., 2004. Intergenerational persistance of earnings: The role of early and college education. University of Toronto Memo.
Roemer, J.E., 1998. Equality of Opportunity. Harvard University Press.
Rosenzweig, M.R., Wolpin, K.I., 1980. Testing the quantity–quality fertility model: The use of twins as a natural experiment. Econometrica 48 (1), 227–240.
Ruhm, C.J., 2000. Parental leave and child health. J. Health Econ. 19, 931–960.
Ruhm, C.J., 2004. Parental employment and child cognitive development. J. Hum. Resour. 39, 155–192.
Ruhm, C.J., 2009. Maternal employment and child eevelopment. In: Crane, R.R., Hill, E.J. (Eds.), Handbook of Families and Work: Interdisciplinary Perspectives. University Press of America.
Sacerdote, B., 2002. The nature and nurture of economic outcomes. Am. Econ. Rev. 92 (2), 344–348.
Sacerdote, B., 2007. How large are the effects from changes in family environment? A study of Korean American adoptees. Q. J. Econ. 122 (1), 119–157.
Scarr, S., Weinberg, R., 1978. Educational and occupational achievements of brothers and sisters in adoptive and biological related families. Behavioral Genetics 24, 301–324.
Sieben, I., Huinink, J., de Graaf, P.M., 2001. Family background and sibling resemblance in educational attainment: Trends in the former FRG, the former GDR and the Netherlands. Eur. Socio. Rev. 17 (4), 401–430.
Solon, G., Page, M., Duncan, G., 2000. Correlations between neighboring children in their subsequent educational attainment. Rev. Econ. Stat. 82 (3), 383–392.
Tanaka, S., 2005. Parental leave and child health across OECD countries. Econ. J. 115, 7–28.
Zajonc, R.B., 1976. Family configuration and intelligence. Science 192, 227–236.

CHAPTER 4

Peer Effects in Education: How Might They Work, How Big Are They and How Much Do We Know Thus Far?

Bruce Sacerdote
Dartmouth College and NBER

Contents

1. Introduction and Overview	250
2. Models of Peer Effects	253
3. Identification of Peer Effects	256
3.1 Identification Using Excess Variance	258
4. Empirical Results on Peer Effects in Primary and Secondary Education	260
4.1 More on Nonlinear Effects and Tracking	265
4.2 Effects of Racial Composition	266
4.3 Effects Working through Classroom Disruption	267
5. Going Beyond Test Scores	268
6. Effects in Post-Secondary Education	269
7. Conclusions	271
References	273

Abstract

This chapter summarizes the recent literature on peer effects in student outcomes at the elementary, secondary, and post-secondary levels. Linear-in-means models find modest sized and statistically significant peer effects in test scores. But the linear-in-means model masks considerable heterogeneity in the effects experienced by different types of students. Using nonlinear models, one prevalent finding is larger peer effects in which high ability students benefit from the presence of other high ability students. Studies that stratify students by race and ability often find that students are affected both by the racial composition of their peers and by the achievement of their same-race peers. At the university level, several studies find modest sized effects from dormmate and roommate background on own academic performance. For both university and high school students, the measured peer effects on "social" outcomes such as drinking are larger than the effects on academic outcomes. Many authors find substantial peer effects in drinking, drug use, and criminal behavior. This chapter suggest areas for future investigation and data collection.

JEL classification: J0, I2

Keywords

Peer Effects
Social Networks

Education
Higher Education

1. INTRODUCTION AND OVERVIEW

Peer effects in education have recently received a great deal of attention from researchers: five of the most popular articles are cited collectively more than 2000 times.[1] The potential importance of peers in the educational process has long been noted with the influential Coleman Report (1966), Coleman (1968) being one well-known example. As educational researchers make halting progress toward a deeper understanding of the educational production function, many researchers and teachers have argued that peer composition is as important a determinant of student outcomes as other widely cited inputs including teacher quality, class size, and parental involvement. This chapter reviews the empirical evidence on peer effects in elementary, secondary and post-secondary education and concludes that within certain contexts and for certain outcomes, peer effects are indeed a powerful determinant of why students turn out the way they do.[2]

Motivating social scientists' interest in peer effects is not a difficult task. If peer influences are a major factor in generating outcomes that include test scores, college going, career choice, drug use, or teen pregnancy, then every parent, teacher, and policy maker will care about the size and nature of peer effects.[3] Epple and Romano (1998) show that the size and nature of peer effects have large implications for the sorting of students into schools and the distributional consequences of tuition voucher programs.

Defining what is meant by a *peer effect* is slightly more challenging. This chapter uses a broad definition of peer effects to encompass nearly any externality in which peers' backgrounds, current behavior, or outcomes affect an outcome. By limiting peer effects to externalities, market-based or price-based effects are excluded. For example if the families in a particular county contribute to a demand shock for private schooling which raises or lowers the dollar cost of private schooling to the individual, that is clearly a market-based effect and not a peer effect. Externalities that work through class size are also excluded.[4]

What are included as peer effects are any other externalities that spill over from peers' or peers' family background or current actions. For example, if a student's classmates have higher

---

[1] Google Scholar search of "peer effects and education."
[2] Epple and Romano (forthcoming) contains a comprehensive survey of theoretical models of peer effects and the implications of these models.
[3] Harris (1998) famously argued that it is *exclusively* peers and not parental nurturing that determines child outcomes. While her thesis is almost surely an overstatement, the papers reviewed in this chapter will suggest that for certain outcomes and certain student groups peers matter a great deal.
[4] The main reason for this exclusion is that most economists consider the class size literature and the peer effects literature to be addressing separate questions. Note that class size (like spending) may be an input that is relatively easily set by policy makers while peer achievement or peer racial composition may be more difficult to alter.

incoming ability and the student learns directly from her classmates, that is a peer effect. If the classmates have higher incoming ability and this enables the teacher to teach at a higher level or a more demanding pace, that is also a peer effect. If the student is disruptive and consumes more of the teacher's attention, thereby reducing her classmates' test scores, that too is a peer effect (Lazear (2001)). If the classmates' high current achievement motivates the student (through competition) to work harder, that is also a peer effect. If the student develops an interest in athletics or in shoplifting because of her peers, those are also peer effects. Manski (1993) defines endogenous effects as those that emanate from peers' current outcomes whereas exogenous effects are those that emanate from peers' backgrounds.

Suppose that a student's outcomes are improved because his peers' families are actively involved in insisting on teacher accountability or in finding a superstar principal. Such an effect is considered a peer effect, even though these influences can also be simultaneously classified as effects of teacher quality or principal quality. In short, there are a large number of channels through which peer effects might operate. Identifying the precise channel through which a given peer effect operates is a Herculean task and in many cases is asking too much of the data. But researchers have been successful both in demonstrating the existence of peer effects and measuring the magnitudes of some of these effects. Many of these same papers have suggested plausible mechanisms through which peer effects work.

In the last 15 years, economists have begun to provide credible measurement and identification on the nature and size of peer effects. One method frequently employed in modern studies is to rely upon some form of exogenous variation in the assignment of students to schools, classrooms, or dorms (in the study of peer effects at the university or college level). The other common method is use models with both school and student fixed effects in an effort to control for the nearly inevitable self selection of students into schools and classrooms. Below several dozen studies of both types are reviewed.

The picture that emerges is both fascinating and relatively coherent. At first glance, results from the myriad peer effects studies would seem to be all over the map. Within elementary and secondary schools, many studies find modestly large effects of peer background on own test scores (Hoxby (2000b), Vigdor (2006), Vigdor and Nechyba (2007), Betts and Zau (2004), Boozer and Cacciola (2001), Hanushek, Kain, Markman, and Rivkin (2003)). However, Burke and Sass (2008) find little evidence that the peer average background affects the average student's achievement. Angrist and Lang (2004) find that the busing of Metco students into suburban Boston schools has little effect on the test scores of students in the receiving schools. And Imberman, Kugler, and Sacerdote (2009) find only modest linear-in-means effects from the arrival of Katrina evacuees on achievement in receiving schools in Louisiana and Houston, Texas.

These apparently contradictory results can be reconciled if we accept Hoxby and Weingarth's (2005) argument that the *linear-in-means*[5] model of peer effects is not necessarily the right model nor is it the most interesting one. Instead one can allow for

---

[5] See below for definitions of the various models.

peer effects to differ by a student's own achievement and by whether changes in peer group composition are generated by adding students at the top, middle, or bottom of the ability distribution. Hoxby and Weingarth find that students at the bottom of the test score distribution benefit significantly from the addition to their classroom of students who are themselves at the 15th percentile of past test scores. Conversely, students at the top decile of the test score distribution benefit strongly from the addition of other classmates who are also at the top. Achievement for students in the middle tends to less affected by peer composition.

Burke and Sass (2008), Lavy, Paserman, and Schlosser (2007) and most recently Imberman, Kugler, and Sacerdote (2009) reinforce these findings. Lavy, Paserman, and Schlosser (2007) find that high ability high school students in Israel benefit from the presence of other high ability students. Burke and Sass find at most small effects in linear-in-means models, but large effects when they allow the effect to differ by own achievement and the type of peer group change contemplated. Imberman, Kugler, and Sacerdote use the unexpected arrival of Hurricane Katrina evacuees as a shock to peer groups and find that high achieving students benefit the most from the arrival of high achieving peers and are hurt the most by the arrival of low achieving peers.

The literature on peer effects in university and college settings also features an appearance of contradictory results which can be reconciled upon deeper examination. Many studies of peer effects in college rely on roommates and dormmates since these are often the peer groups which can be easily identified and in some cases there is quasi-random assignment of students to room and dorm groups. Sacerdote (2001), Zimmerman (2003), and Stinebrickner and Stinebrickner (2006) find that roommates' background and current achievement affect own achievement. Here current achievement is measured by college grade point average (GPA) and background is measured by incoming test scores and high school class rank or high school GPA.

Foster (2006) and Lyle (2007) find no evidence that roommates' or hallmates' background affects own college GPA. But the effects found in the original roommates studies are modest enough that it easy to believe that differences across institutional settings and differences across student bodies would either eliminate roommate and dormmate influences or make such influences difficult to detect. Using data from the U.S. Air Force Academy, Carrell, Fullerton, and West (2008) examine peer effects in an unusual context in which the full peer group is known and the institution forces a great deal of peer interaction. In that setting, they find large peer effects.

Perhaps the more interesting result from the literature on peer effects in higher education is the fact that while academic achievement (college GPA) is affected modestly by roommates and dormmates, the effects on more "social" outcomes are large. Duncan, Boisjoly, Kremer, Levy, and Eccles (2005) find that males who themselves binge drank in high school have a fourfold increase in their number of college binge drinking episodes (per month) when assigned a roommate who also reported binge drinking in high school.

Similarly Sacerdote (2001) finds that a student is much more likely to join a fraternity or sorority when surrounded by roommates or dormmates who join.

Finally, there is a burgeoning literature on peer effects in crime, drug use, and teenage pregnancy among high school and middle school students. Like the college literature on peer effects in social outcomes, the peer effects on drug use, criminal behavior, and teen pregnancy for these younger students are estimated to be quite large. (Gaviria and Raphael (2001), Case and Katz (1991), Kling, Ludwig, and Katz (2005)). For example, Gaviria and Raphael (2001) find that moving a student from a school in which 13% of the peers' parents have a drug problem to a school in which 40% of the parents have a drug problem increases the student's own drug use by 7 percentage points relative to a mean drug use rate of 14%.

2. MODELS OF PEER EFFECTS

The most commonly estimated model in the peer effects literature is the linear-in-means model in which the outcome Y is some function of a student's background characteristics, her peers' average background characteristics, and the student's peers' average outcome. More formally this can be written as:

$$Y_i = \alpha + \beta 1 * \overline{Y}_{-i} + \gamma 1 * X_i + \gamma 2 * \overline{X}_{-i} + \varepsilon_i \tag{4.1}$$

where Y_i represents the student's outcome, $\overline{Y}_{-i}$ represents her peers' average outcome, X_i is a vector of the student's background characteristics, and $\overline{X}_{-i}$ is a vector of her peers' average background characteristics. This model has the virtue of simplicity. Equation (4.1) encompasses both endogenous effects from the peers' current outcomes and exogenous effects from the peers' background. This model of course constrains the size of either peer effect ($\beta 1$ or $\gamma 2$) to be the same regardless of where the student falls within the distribution of student background or ability.

And by definition all peer effects work through the mean. Effects from any other aspects of the distribution of the peers' background are ruled out. For example, effects from mean-preserving increases in the variance of the peers' ability are assumed to be zero as are the potential effects that might work through the most able or least able peer.

Despite its popularity in use, there are two major problems with the linear-in-means model in practice. (These problems are pointed out most notably by Hoxby (2000b) and Hoxby and Weingarth (2005).) First, from a social welfare point of view the model is not that interesting since the model constrains the net effect from reassignment of peers to different classrooms or groups to be zero. Suppose that an exceptionally good student from classroom A is exchanged for an exceptionally bad student from classroom B. Assume the classrooms are of equal sizes. From a social welfare or total output prospective, the positive peer effects for the students in B are exactly offset by the negative peer effects for the students in classroom A.

Second, from an empirical point of view, researchers have found that peer effects are not in fact linear-in-means. If anything, there tend to be complementarities of the type that would support schools using various forms of tracking policies. Some of the available evidence suggests that the most able students benefit from having more high ability students around, while the least able students are actually harmed by adding high ability peers and removing lower ability peers. Hoxby and Weingarth (2005), Burke and Sass (2008), Lavy, Paserman, and Schlosser (2007), Cooley (2009), and Imberman, Kugler, and Sacerdote (2009) all find this form of complementarity in elementary and secondary schools using test scores as the outcome. Hanushek and Rivkin (2009) find that test score growth for high achieving black students is helped by increases in the proportion of whites in their school and grade. At the university level, Sacerdote (2001) finds some evidence that high ability students benefit each other more than high ability students benefit average or low ability students.

Fortunately Equation (4.1) can be expanded to allow both student i's position in the ability (or background characteristic) distribution to matter and to allow for different peer effects to stem from different possible changes to the peer group. The identification problems that plague nonlinear estimations are not much worse than the fundamental problems of identification inherent to the linear-in-means model. (See the next section for a discussion.)

Duncan et al. (2005) and Sacerdote (2001) take a very simple approach to testing for possible nonlinearities in peer effects. These two papers group student i into one of several possible categories and i's peers (in this case roommates) into categories and then include in the regression all possible interactions of student i's type and i's roommate's type. In the case of Duncan et al., student i binge drank in high school or did not, and i's roommate either binge drank in high school or did not, implying that there are four possible categories. The outcome investigated (i.e., the left-hand-side variable) is binge drinking episodes per month *in college*. In other words, Duncan et al. run the following regression:

$$Y_i = \alpha + \lambda 1 * (D_i = 0 * D_{-i} = 0) + \lambda 2 * (D_i = 1 * D_{-i} = 1) + \lambda 3 \\ * (D_i = 0 * D_{-i} = 1) + \varepsilon_i \tag{4.2}$$

Here Y_i is student i's number of binge drinking episodes per month in college and D_i and D_{-i} are dummies for whether i and i's roommate binge drank in high school. After running the regression, it is then a simple matter to hold student i's type constant and test whether student i has more drinking episodes in college with versus without a roommate who drank in high school. For example, testing whether $\lambda 2 = 0$ asks whether students who drank in high school have more episodes with a roommate who drank in high school versus without such a roommate.

Hoxby and Weingarth (2005) use a similar approach in testing for nonlinear peer effects among third through eighth grade students, but they have many more possible categories of student type and peer type. They divide students into deciles of past test score performance. They then interact student i's decile of previous score with the percent of i's peers (classmates) falling into each of the 10 deciles. This generates 100 interaction terms. The coefficients on these interaction terms allow the authors to test a wide variety of hypotheses about peer effects. For instance, one can ask whether high ability students benefit from being in a class with a higher proportion of high ability students. Similarly one can ask whether low ability (as measured by past test scores) students benefit the most from having classmates in the lowest, middle, or upper part of the test score distribution. And one can ask whether high ability classmates provide more externalities for students who are themselves at the lower, middle, or upper part of the test score distribution.

Hoxby and Weingarth provide a nice categorization of different possible theories of peer effects, as shown in Table 4.1.

A model is categorized as having homogenous effects if magnitude of the peer effect is constant for all student types i. Categorization is from Hoxby and Weingarth (2005) and Lazear (2001).

This provides a summary of possible ways in which peer effects in a classroom might work. Among the most discussed models are the bad apple model and the boutique model. In the bad apple model (Lazear (2001)), the most relevant peer effects are those provided by the least academically able or least disciplined student in the classroom. This student provides large negative externalities in several possible ways: The bad apple peer may cause so much commotion in the classroom as to distract the teacher and students from productive tasks. Or he may encourage additional raucous or disruptive behavior among other students. Or the bad apple may not be a discipline problem but he may simply have low ability and require extra teaching attention, thereby detracting from the experience of the other students.

Table 4.1 Possible models of peer effects

Model	Homogenous effects?	Description
Linear-in-means	Yes	Only the mean of peers background or outcomes matters
Bad apple	Yes	One disruptive student harms everyone
Shining light	Yes	One excellent student provides great example for all
Invidious Comparison	No	Outcomes are harmed by the presence of better achieving peers
Boutique/ tracking	No	Students perform best when surrounded by others like themselves
Focus	Yes	Classroom homogeneity is good, regardless of student i's ability relative to the homogenous classmates
Rainbow	Yes	Classroom heterogeneity is good for everyone
Single crossing	No	Positive effects from high ability classmate is weakly monotonically increasing in own ability

In the boutique model, students benefit from being around other students with a similar ability. One possibility is that a classroom with more homogeneity enables the teacher to customize the material and the pace of learning to that particular group of students. Another possible mechanism for the boutique model is that students can best learn from each other when the students are of similar ability or are working on similar material. The boutique model is perhaps the main justification behind tracking students into classroom by ability. Note that in the boutique model, the less able students are helped more by the presence of peers like themselves than they are helped by the presence of high ability peers.

Some of the other models are certainly possible from a theoretical point of view but may be less important from an empirical point of view. The rainbow model suggests that diversity of ability is good for all students. This notion seems contrary to the experience of many teachers and contrary to some (but not all) recent evidence on tracking. Furthermore the rainbow model can not explain why many if not most high schools in the U.S. use some form of tracking. The shining light model is interesting and is the opposite of the bad apple model. But it is somewhat more difficult to think of ways in which a great student could raise her classmates' achievement than it is to think of ways in which a terrible student could harm an entire classroom (Lazear (2001)). The invidious comparison model suggests that students are harmed by the presence of better students in the same classroom.

3. IDENTIFICATION OF PEER EFFECTS

As detailed in Manski (1993) and Brock and Durlauf (2001), the fundamental challenge for the peer effects literature is identification. One can imagine at least three reasons why running an OLS regression for Equation (4.1) would be problematic. First, since student i's outcome (Y_i) affects his peers' mean outcome ($\overline{Y}_{-i}$) and vice versa, $\beta 1$ is subject to endogeneity bias. Manski labeled this the reflection problem. Second, in most settings peers self select into peer groups or classrooms in a manner that is unobserved to the econometrician. Frequently there is positive selection in which similar people join or are assigned to the same group. This positive selection could cause substantial upward bias in the estimated magnitude of peer effects $\beta 1$ and $\gamma 2$. Manski labeled the influence of selection the *correlated effect*.

Third, Equation (4.1) includes effects that stem both from peers' average outcome ($\overline{Y}_{-i}$) and peers' average background characteristics ($\overline{X}_{-i}$). Manski labeled the former the endogenous effects and the latter exogenous (or contextual) effects. Separate identification of $\beta 1$ and $\gamma 2$ is difficult since peer background itself affects peer outcome. Even if one has exogenous variation in peer background characteristics (as in many of the roommates papers, such as Sacerdote (2001) and Zimmerman (2003) or as in Hoxby (2000b)), that does not imply that both coefficients are separately identified. Note that endogenous effects have the potential for social multipliers since a small change for student i will affect the peer group which will then reflect back to student I, and so on.

The modern peer effects literature has managed to overcome some but not necessarily all of these challenges. As noted in the introduction, the most commonly used approaches are 1) to include student level and/or school level fixed effects in an effort to control for selection into peer groups, and 2) to rely on some form of exogenous shock to peer-group composition. That said, most papers have one source of exogeneity and do not separately identify the exogenous and endogenous peer effects.

Hoxby (2000b) was one of the first papers to look for some exogenous shock to peer group composition. The key source of variation is idiosyncratic changes in the gender mix across cohorts within a given elementary school. Increases in the fraction of girls in the cohort lead to increases in mean peer test scores. Other papers within primary and secondary education also rely on exogenous shocks to peer group composition or more directly on random or quasi-random assignment of students to classrooms. Vigdor and Nechyba (2007) make the case that the assignment of students to classrooms within their sample of North Carolina schools is fairly random. Boozer and Cacciola (2001) use experimental variation from Project Star as a source of variation in peer ability.[6] Duflo, Dupas, and Kremer (2008) created a randomized experiment in which some students are assigned to tracked (i.e., more homogenous) classrooms and others are not. Peer ability is generally measured by using peers' prior test scores.

A group of papers at the university level relies on random assignment of roommates, dormmates, or squadron members to generate random variation in peer groups. These papers include Sacerdote (2001), Zimmerman (2003), Carrell, Fullerton, and West (2008), Foster (2006), Stinebrickner and Stinebrickner (2006), Lyle (2007), and Siegfried and Gleason (2006). The central identification in these papers stems from the idea that university policies generate random variation in the makeup of peer groups.

Removing or controlling for the selection of students into peer groups is an important step in being able to identify peer effects. As noted above, this is not the same as being able to separately identify β_1 and γ_2. Most of the above papers estimate the reduced form effects of changes in peer groups and do not tackle the question of whether the peer effects identified stem from exogenous or endogenous effects. In other words, most authors do not attempt to estimate the structural parameters β_1 and. Some authors including Boozer and Cacciola (2001), Case and Katz (1991), and Gaviria and Raphael (2001) assume that peer background does not enter directly (i.e., $\gamma_2 = 0$ or no contextual effects). Under this assumption, one can potentially identify the magnitude of endogenous effects.

Bramoullé, Djebbari, and Fortin (2009) show that one can identify both β_1 and γ_2 if one assumes that an individual's outcome is affected by that person's friends' background *but not* the background of the friends of the person's friends. Thus the

---

[6] Project STAR (Student Teacher Achievement Ratio) was a large scale randomized experiment carried out in 79 schools in Tennessee. Students were randomly assigned to a large (22–25) student classroom, a small (13–17) student classroom, or a large classroom with the addition of a full-time teacher aide.

background of the friends' friends (those with whom the individual does not have direct contact) can serve as an instrument for the friends' endogenous outcome.

A second approach to dealing with selection into peer groups has been to control for characteristics of individual students and schools. Often this means including student fixed effects and school fixed effects and identifying peer effects using cohort to cohort variation within school. The papers using this approach include Betts and Zau (2004) and Lavy, Paserman, and Schlosser (2007). Hanushek, Kain, Markman, and Rivkin (2003) include school-by-grade fixed effects and hence use classroom-to-classroom level variation within a school and grade. Burke and Sass (2008) include teacher fixed effects too. The basic concept in these papers is that the student, school, or school-by-grade fixed effects remove selection effects and allow the researcher to identify peer effects from idiosyncratic variation in peer ability. Again, in most of these papers the ability of classmates is generally calculated using peers' prior test scores. In the case of Lavy, Paserman, and Schlosser (2007), peer background is the average of a dummy variable for whether a classmate skipped or repeated a grade.

3.1 Identification Using Excess Variance

There is also a different methodology which uses the variance in mean outcomes across groups to detect the presence of social interactions (peer effects). Glaeser, Sacerdote, and Scheinkman (1996) show that imitation within groups generates more variation across group means than would be expected if individuals were making independent decisions.[7]

Graham (2008) uses excess variance plus experimental variation to estimate the size of peer effects within the Project Star data. Like the majority of papers described above, Graham is interested in estimating the reduced form effect of classmates' incoming ability which he labels γ. Keeping the notation consistent with Equation (4.1), Graham's reduced form is:

$$Y_i = \alpha + \gamma * \overline{X}_{-i} + \varepsilon_i \qquad (4.3)$$

where Y_i is student i's test score and $\overline{X}_{-i}$ are i's classmates' incoming scores. His insight is that social interactions will generate more between classroom level variation in the outcome Y than would be predicted given individual level heterogeneity in student ability.

In most settings one would be concerned that sorting into classrooms or teacher effects would also generate excess variance in mean outcomes at the classroom level. However, in the Project Star data, students are randomly assigned to small versus large classrooms and Graham is able to use this fact to difference out the excess variance that comes from sorting or teacher effects. Specifically he shows that a consistent estimate of γ^2 equals

$$\frac{E(G_c^b|small) - E(G_c^b|big)}{E(G_c^w|small) - E(G_c^w|big)} \qquad (4.4)$$

---

[7] The paper then proceeds to estimate the level of social interactions present in various forms of crime at the level of cities and police precincts.

where G_c^b and G_c^w are the between and within variance in outcomes for a classroom. In other words, an estimate of the social interaction parameter squared is the ratio of the between classroom to the within, where the between has been "inflated" by social interactions. And we first difference across the randomly assigned small versus big classroom category to account for nonsocial interaction factors which cause the between variation to be larger than the within.

Related to the Graham approach are the Glaeser and Scheinkman (2001) and Glaeser, Sacerdote, and Scheinkman (2003) papers which define the social multiplier as the ratio of the individual effect from an exogenous shock to the aggregate effect from the same exogenous shock. The intuition is that a small exogenous change at the individual level is magnified through the social interactions process to deliver the larger aggregate level coefficient. For a concrete example, think of the individual student level effect on achievement from giving some students extra teacher attention. Now consider a classroom level regression in which we calculate the effect on achievement from giving entire classrooms of students the additional teacher attention. If there are no social interactions (and no sorting into treatment status) the individual and aggregate coefficients should be the same and the social mutiplier is 1.0.

We suggest two related approaches for calculating the social multiplier. One is to simply take a ratio of an aggregate level coefficient to the corresponding individual coefficient. In the above example, the exogenous shift considered is an increase in teacher attention. At the individual level, one could regress test scores (Yi) on a dummy for receiving extra attention (Xi). This same regression could be run at the classroom level in which we regress classroom average test scores for classroom c, $\overline{Y}_c$ on the average number of students in c who received the treatment, that is, $\overline{X}_c$. The ratio of the classroom level coefficient to the individual level coefficient is by definition the social multiplier. Our second approach (which works well when there are many right-hand-side variables) is to use coefficients from an individual level regression to predict aggregate level outcomes. We then regress actual aggregate level outcomes on these predicted values and the coefficient from this second regression is the social multiplier.

Recovering the social interactions parameter from the social multiplier: Suppose we allow β to be the social interactions parameter, that is, the effect of average group level actions $\overline{Y}_{-i}$ on own action (Yi). If there is no sorting into groups and we take the aggregate coefficient for a sufficiently large group size N, then the social multiplier equals $1/(1-\beta)$. When there is sorting into groups based on an observable X, then we define $\sigma = \frac{Var(\overline{X})}{Var(X_i)}$ which is the share of total variation in X explained by variation at the group level. We show that as the group size gets large, the social multiplier converges to $1/[(1-\beta)\star(1+\sigma\beta)]$. Thus in either formulation, β can be calculated once the size of the social multiplier is known.

The social multiplier approach is useful for three reasons. First, it is easy to calculate and need not impose a specific functional form for peer effects. Second, for some research questions it delivers the parameter of direct interest to researchers or policy makers, namely if policy can exogenously induce one additional person to take action A, how many total people will take action A in equilibrium? Third, under some strong assumptions the social multiplier approach can take into account sorting into groups or locations.

4. EMPIRICAL RESULTS ON PEER EFFECTS IN PRIMARY AND SECONDARY EDUCATION

A major focus of the literature has been on peer effects in test scores for students in primary and secondary school. Table 4.2 shows estimated peer effects from a number of studies. The estimates encompass a large range. There are, however, two consistent themes: First studies using gender variation find larger effects. These studies generally conclude that increases in "percent female" help peer achievement through more channels than simply raising average classroom test scores. Second, there appear to be important nonlinearities. Several but not all studies find that reductions in peer heterogeneity improve outcomes and that students at the high end of the ability distribution experience the largest peer effects from high ability peers.

Hoxby (2000b) relies on random variation in the gender and racial makeup of peers to provide estimates of peer effects. She uses data from students in all Texas elementary schools in grades 3–6. Her outcome measure is performance on the Texas Assessment of Academic Skills (TAAS). Her strategy relies on the fact that within a school and grade level, cohort level variation in gender and racial composition is an unexpected shock to peer achievement. Girls on average score about a half a standard deviation higher than boys on the TAAS reading test, and hence changes in class composition do represent a significant shock to peer achievement.

Hoxby finds that a 10 percentage point rise in cohort percentage female is associated with boys reading scores being 0.04 to 0.08 test points higher. The positive effects of percent female on girls reading scores are similar in magnitude. Translating this into an effect of peer scores on own scores, she finds that an increase in the peer average reading score of 1.0 raises own reading score by 0.3 to 0.5 points.

When she performs a similar analysis (using gender variation) for math scores she finds a much larger peer effect coefficient of a 1.7 to 6.8 increase in own math score for every 1.0 increase in peer (cohort) average score. Because this figure is so large, she concludes that the effects of percent female likely work through additional channels beyond a simple increase in peer average test scores.

Hoxby also considers the effects of cohort level shocks to racial composition. She finds that peer effects are largest intra-race, meaning that altering the percentage black has the largest peer effect on black students.

Table 4.2 Peer effects in test scores for primary and secondary schools linear in means models

Paper	Sample	Identification	Effect of a 1.0 point move in average peer score**
Hoxby (2000b)	Texas Schools Project	Identified using within-school cohort-to-cohort variation in gender and racial makeup	using gender variation
	Grades 3–6		Reading: 0.3 to 0.5
			Math: 1.7 to 6.8
			Using racial variation
			(intra-group)
			Reading 0.68
			Math: 0.40
Lavy and Schlosser (2007)	Israeli primary, middle, high school students	Within-school variation in percent female	Matriculation exam score for males: 1.06; for females: 0.84
Whitmore (2005)	Tennessee elementary students in Project STAR	Random assignment of students to classrooms	0.60
Boozer and Cacciola (2001)	Tennessee elementary students in Project STAR	Instrument for peer mean using experimentally created variation	1st grade: 0.30
			2nd grade: 0.86
			3rd grade: 0.92
Angrist and Lang (2004)	Brookline students Iowa Test of Basic Skills. Grades 3,5,7	Effects of Metco students in Brookline, MA on non-Metco students	On all non-Metco[1] core IATB: 0.21
			On black non-Metco core IATB: 1.375

Continued

Table 4.2 Peer effects in test scores for primary and secondary schools linear in means models—cont'd

Paper	Sample	Identification	Effect of a 1.0 point move in average peer score**
Vigdor and Nechyba (2007)	North Carolina 5th graders	Limit sample to schools that appear to use quasi-random assignment; include school and year fixed effects and teacher effects	Reading: −0.10 Math: −0.12
Betts and Zau (2004)	San Diego public school students grades 2–11	Estimate effects on gains; include student fixed effects	Reading: 1.40 Math 1.9
Burke and Sass (2008)	Florida students grades 3–10	Student and teacher fixed effects	Reading: 0.014 to 0.068 Math: 0.04
Hanushek, Kain, Markman, and Rivkin (2003)	Texas Schools Project	Student fixed effects	Math: 0.17
Hoxby and Weingarth (2005)	Wake County North Carolina	Exogenous reassignments due to school desegregation	0.24^2
Ammermueller and Pischke (2006)	Students in Germany, France, Iceland, the Netherlands, Norway, and Sweden	School fixed effects	0.11
Carman and Zhang (2008)	Chinese elementary school students	Randomly assigned classrooms; teacher effects and student effects	Math: 0.40 English: −0.03 Chinese: 0.26
Lefgren (2004)	Chicago public schools grades 3 and 6	Uses school tracking policies as an instrument for peer ability	Math grade 6: 0.032 Reading grade 6: 0.027

**Most papers have standardized the test scores to be mean zero variance 1. This is not required, though, to compare coefficients across papers. The effects of racial composition from Hoxby (2000) are the effects on black students of changing the cohort's percentage black. Intra-race effects are larger than cross race effects. 1. Angrist and Lang's results are not statistically significant. These effects are translated by me into a peer effect coefficient using the calculation described in the text. 2. This is from Hoxby and Weingarth's baseline linear-in-means specification.

Lavy and Schlosser (2007) also find large effects from percent girls within a classroom and they also interpret these effects as working through more than simply increasing peer average test scores. The authors report effects on a wide range of outcomes. Table 4.2 is limited to reporting their effects on average scores on matriculation exams. For females the effect of percent female on average matriculation score has an effect of 5.3. Since females on average score about 6.3 points better, this implies a peer coefficient (β_1) of $5.3/6.3 = 0.84$. The corresponding calculation for males yields an estimated β_1 of 1.06.

Lavy and Schlosser's additional results suggest that much of the effect of percent female is working through reductions in classroom violence and disruption and through improvements in inter-student and student–teacher relationships.

Kramarz, Machin, and Ouazad (2008) have the complete census (National Register) of children in English public schools and identify peer effects using movers. For second graders the authors find that a 10% increase in the percentage of boys reduces test scores by 0.004 standard deviations.

Whitmore (2005) exploits experimental variation in Project Star to examine separately the effects from percent female and the effects from having higher achieving peers. She finds that each 1.0 randomly generated increase in peer percentile score raises a student's own percentile score by 0.6. And having a predominantly female class has an independent positive effect of 1.3 percentile points.

Boozer and Cacciola (2001) use the random assignment of peers in Project Star and argue that much of Project STAR's class size effect is working through peer effects. Their insight is that entry and exit from the classrooms in the experiment caused some peers to be treated longer than others and that this generates experimental variation in peer quality. The authors find coefficients on peers' mean test score of 0.30, 0.86, and 0.92 for the first, second, and third graders respectively.

Angrist and Lang (2004) use Boston's "Metco" busing program as an exogenous source of variation in peer ability. Their sample includes 443 Boston area schools, 141 of which receive Metco students. Their outcome measures are MCAS scores and Iowa Test of Basic Skills scores. Using all schools in their sample, they find that percentage Metco in a suburban school has no statistically significant effect on the non-bused (i.e., local) students in the school.

When the authors examine Brookline schools specifically and performance on the Iowa Test of Basic Skills, they find peer effects from Metco students which are negative in the point estimates though the estimates are not generally statistically significant. A 10% increase in percent Metco lowers the percentile ranking (for non-Metco students) on the IATB by a statistically insignificant 0.5 percentile points. This same change in percent Metco lowers peer average test scores by 2.4 percentile points. Together these numbers imply a peer effect coefficient of 0.21. Limiting the sample to just black non-Metco students yields a larger implied peer coefficient of $-3.3/-2.4 = 1.375$.

In a similar spirit, Imberman, Kugler, and Sacerdote (2009) examine peer effects of Hurricane Katrina evacuees on nonevacuee students in Houston and Louisiana. They find modest peer effects which are greatest for students at the lowest quintile of the test score distribution. As noted above, when they allow for nonlinearities, their estimated peer effects are much larger. If 10% of the school is composed of evacuees from the top quartile of the English Language Arts (ELA) test score distribution, "native" students from the top quartile of the test score distribution have an ELA test score gain of 0.2 standard deviations. These same high achieving native students experience a drop of 0.3 standard deviations in their ELA score in response to a 10% inflow of low achieving (bottom quartile) evacuees.

In addition to exploiting experiments and natural experiments, another method of identifying peer effects is to calculate the effects of peer test scores while including school, school by year, or student level fixed effects to control for the sorting of students into schools. Typically peer mean ability is measured as mean performance on a prior year's standardized test.

Betts and Zau (2004) use data from the San Diego Unified School district. They use test score gains as their dependent variable and they employ student level fixed effects to control for positive selection (tracking) of students into classrooms. They find a coefficient on the peer mean reading score of 1.4 and a coefficient on peer math score of 1.9. They also find some evidence of nonlinearities in which the average student is hurt more by low achieving peers than she is helped by high achieving peers.

Hanushek, Kain, Markman, and Rivkin (2003) utilize data from the Texas Schools Project. They use student gains in the TAAS as their dependent variable and they include student fixed effects. They find a peer effect coefficient ($\beta 1$) of 0.17 for math scores. Furthermore they find that the peer effect is similar across quartiles of a student's initial position in the test score distribution, though students in the highest quartile do show a smaller peer effect.

Burke and Sass (2008) follow a similar approach and include both student fixed effects and teacher effects. For math scores, they estimate that a 1.0 increase in peer mean achievement raises own achievement by 0.04. For reading, the effect varies from 0.014 to 0.068. But, when the authors allow the effects to vary by student type, the estimated effects are much larger. For example, elementary students in the lowest third of past performance experience a gain of 0.82 points for every 1.0 gain in peer achievement. Peer effects are somewhat smaller for students in the middle third of the distribution and smaller still for students in the highest third. As the authors note, these results suggest that tracking does not maximize total output of test scores, but rather high ability students should be spread among classrooms.

In contrast to some of the above studies, Vigdor and Nechyba's (2007) results call into question the methodology of using school fixed effects to identify peer coefficients. These authors have data on all North Carolina public school students during 1994/1995 through 2000/2001. Within that set, they include school and year fixed effects.

In their baseline "naïve" school fixed effects approach, Vigdor and Nechyba find that a 1.0 standard deviation increase in peer mean reading score yields a 0.05 to 0.07 standard deviation increase in a student's own reading score. The comparable effect for math is 0.06 to 0.08. Of equal interest, the authors find strong support for the hypothesis that increasing dispersion of peers mean scores *raises* own test score. However both of these results flip signs (and are negative and statistically significant) when the authors include teacher fixed effects. Furthermore, in a falsification exercise Vigdor and Nechyba find that 5th grade peers appear to improve 4th grade test outcomes in their baseline specification. These results lead the authors to conclude that simple measures of peer effects may actually be driven by teacher effects or by selection into classrooms.

Several additional studies estimate linear-in-means models outside the U.S. Ammermueller and Pischke (2006) use data encompassing six European countries and find an average coefficient on peer achievement ($\beta 1$) of 0.11. With a sample of Chinese elementary school students assigned randomly to classrooms, Carman and Zhang (2008) find coefficients of 0.4 for math scores, -0.03 for English scores, and 0.26 for Chinese scores. McEwan (2003) finds large effects from peers' background characteristics in a sample of 8th graders in Chile. Both Gibbons and Telhaj (2008) and Lavy, Silva, and Weinhardt (2009) find no evidence of linear-in-means effects for secondary school students in the U.K. Both of these papers use the full set of U.K. students at age 14 for several recent cohorts. They use Key Stage 2 national test scores (age 11) to measure peer inputs and Key Stage 3 national test scores (age 14) to measure outcomes.

4.1 More on Nonlinear Effects and Tracking

Hoxby and Weingarth (2005) proceed to a more general estimation of nonlinear effects. The authors rely on Wake County North Carolina's school reassignment policies which sought to even out disparities in average student backgrounds at each school. The authors instrument for actual peer groups using the peer groups that would be have been generated due to the reassignment rules. They allow the magnitude of peer effects to vary both by a student's *own position* in the test score distribution and by which part of the peer test score distribution is being increased. Specifically they interact own test score decile with the percentage of peers in each test score decile.

Hoxby and Weingarth find support for the boutique model of peer effects. Students in deciles 9 and 10 of the test score distribution benefit strongly from adding peers in the highest deciles. Students in the bottom decile benefit most from adding peers in deciles 2 and 3. The authors also find some evidence for the focus model, which is to say that students can be harmed by heterogeneity in their peers even when additional heterogeneity might be giving the student additional peers more like herself.

Cooley (2009) provides further evidence of large nonlinearities in peer effects. She finds that the magnitude of peer effects experienced by student *i* differs both by student i's race and by student i's achievement and by peers' level of achievement. And she finds that high achieving students benefit the most from high achieving peers. Gibbons and Telhaj (2008) find that test scores for low achieving students in the U.K. are harmed by the presence of high achieving students while upper-middle achieving students benefit from the presence of high achieving students.

Lavy, Silva, and Weinhardt (2009) reach slightly different conclusions about nonlinear peer effects. These authors find that all students are harmed by the presence of the lowest achieving peers (those in the bottom 5%). However, only high achieving girls are helped by the presence of other high achieving (top 5%) peers.

Many of the results on nonlinearities are consistent with a world in which tracking students into classrooms by ability raises total student output relative to a set of untracked classrooms. This seems quite plausible, particularly given that tracking has been a feature of school systems for so long despite its potential to appear anti-egalitarian. This pro-tracking result is somewhat at odds with what Burke and Sass (2008) found (namely that low ability students benefit the most from high average peer ability) and Vigdor and Nechyba's (2007) result that classroom heterogeneity raises scores.

Roughly half of the research addressing tracking specifically finds positive effects from the policy. Using an experiment in Kenya, Duflo, Dupas, and Kremer (2008) find that students in tracked classrooms experienced test score gains of 0.14 standard deviations relative to students in untracked classrooms. And the effect persists for at least one year following the elimination of the program. Lavy, Paserman, and Schlosser (2007) find that high achieving students benefit from the presence of other high achieving students in the classroom while the high achieving students do not help average students. On the other hand, Betts and Shkolnick (2000) find little support for benefits from tracking. Lefgren (2004) reaches the same conclusion using data on 3rd and 6th graders in the Chicago Public Schools. He uses tracking status as an instrument for peer group ability and he finds very small linear-in-means peer effects, and hence few benefits from tracking.

Peers may also influence the aspirations of students. Jonsson and Mood (2008) examine Swedish secondary school students and find that having very high achieving peers depresses the desire to attend university for average students.

4.2 Effects of Racial Composition

Peer effects may of course stem from peer characteristics other than measured achievement. The evidence suggests that peer racial composition is strongly correlated with own achievement. For example there is a burgeoning literature on "acting white" that posits that some black students may underachieve in order to fit in with their peers (Austen-Smith and Fryer (2005), Fordham and Ogbu (1986), Ogbu (2003)).[8] Fryer

---

[8] Cook and Ludwig (1997) do not find that average attitudes toward academic success differ between black and white students.

and Torelli (2010) find that a student's popularity is negatively associated with her academic grades for the highest achieving black students. They also find that the acting white effect does not exist in schools with a high proportion black, perhaps because the market for social interactions with other high achieving black students is thick in such schools.

Using data from the Texas Schools Project, Hanushek, Kain, and Rivkin (2009) find that black students' test scores are strongly decreasing in the fraction black in the school. To identify the effects of racial composition, they rely on variation in the fraction black within a school over time. A 10 percentage point increase in the fraction black is associated with own test scores that are roughly 0.02 standard deviations lower. The fraction black also affects test scores for white students but the coefficients are half as large. This makes sense if we believe that many more peer interactions take place within race than across race.[9] The authors point out that differences in racial makeup across Texas schools can account for 10–20% of the black-white test score gap. Hanushek and Rivken (2009) go on to show that the effects of racial composition are highly nonlinear. Black students in the top quartile of the achievement distribution (based on prior years' scores) are affected much more negatively by the school fraction black than are black students in the lower half of the test score distribution.

There are numerous channels through which peer effects from racial composition may occur. It is possible that teachers lower their expectations or the level at which they teach as the fraction black in a school rises. Or maybe there is an acting white effect for black students which increases as the proportion black rises.

4.3 Effects Working through Classroom Disruption

Lazear (2001) suggests that the most significant effects are negative ones emanating from disruptive peers and, as noted above, Lavy and Schlosser (2007) agree that disruption (or lack thereof) is a key mechanism. Perhaps the most innovative paper on this topic is Figlio (2005) which finds that the presence of boys with female sounding names increases classroom disruption and decreases test scores for students in that classroom. Similarly, Carrell and Hoekstra (2008) show that the classroom presence of children exposed to domestic violence raises classroom discipline problems and lowers math and reading test scores. Adding an additional troubled boy to a classroom raises the probability that another boy commits a disciplinary infraction by 17% and lowers test scores by two percentile points.

---

[9] Marmaros and Sacerdote (2006) and Mayer and Puller (2008) both measure the relative frequency of within- versus cross-race interactions.

5. GOING BEYOND TEST SCORES

The above studies document the existence of peer effects in test scores, though with considerable disagreement as to the magnitudes. Effects on nontest score outcomes for youth are quite possibly larger and the existence of such effects less controversial. Case and Katz (1991) instrument for peer average actions using peer family background and find large peer effects in drug use, gang membership, and criminal activity. For instance, when own drug use is the dependent variable, the effect of peer average drug use is 0.32.

Gaviria and Raphael (2001) perform a similar analysis using students in the same school and grade in the National Education Longitudinal Survey (NELS). They find strong peer effects in drug use, alcohol drinking, cigarette smoking, church going, and the likelihood of dropping out of high school. Their coefficient on peer group average drug use is 0.25. Kooreman (2003) finds a very similar coefficient when looking at the effect of classmate alcohol expenditure on own alcohol expenditure in a sample of Dutch students.[10]

Evans, Oates, and Schwab (1992) consider peer effects in teen pregnancy and dropping out of school. They find that naïve estimates of peer effects are overstated and that once they control for selection into peer groups their estimated effects disappear. Similarly Krauth (2005) finds that estimated peer effects on smoking are reduced by a factor of three once he controls for selection into friendship groups. His preferred estimator suggests that having an additional friend who smokes leads to a 5 percentage point increase in the prevalence of own smoking. Mihaly (2008) estimates that having one additional friend who smokes is associated with a 9 percentage point increase in own prevalence of smoking.

Eisenberg (2004) uses the Adolescent Health Survey and considers the experiment of a substance-using friend moving away (relocating). He finds that the moving away of a friend who uses marijuana leads to a 12% reduction in the probability of own marijuana use.

Argys and Rees (2008) look at the effects of having older peers in the same grade. Using NLSY97 data they examine students in grades 6–12 and find that having older peers increases the use of alcohol, marijuana, and cigarettes. Controlling for own age, being in the younger half of the peer group raises the likelihood of drinking by 3.5 percentage points.

Bobonis and Finan (2009) are able to use experimental variation from Mexico's PROGRESA program to measure the degree to which peer participation in school raises own participation. A 10 percentage point increase in peer participation raises own participation rates by 5 percentage points.

---

[10] Kooreman also finds large peer effects in time allocated to certain activities including studying and part-time jobs.

Kremer, Miguel, and Thornton (2009) is another paper that identifies peer effects by taking advantage of experimental variation in a developing country context. The experiment discussed in the paper gave girls financial incentives to perform well on exams. But the experiment also had large spillover effects on the boys in the same schools despite the boys not being eligible for the cash rewards. In the experimental treatment group, girls' scores rose on average by 0.29 standard deviations while (the ineligible) boys' scores rose by 0.16 standard deviations.

Some of the most interesting and convincing evidence on peer effects in social outcomes comes from the Moving to Opportunity (MTO) Experiment (Katz, Kling, and Liebman (2001) and Kling, Ludwig, and Katz (2005)). MTO randomly offered some low-income families an incentive to move to a census tract with a lower poverty rate than the initial census tract. Results from the experiment show that girls in families offered such a voucher showed decreased arrests for violent and property crimes while results for boys were more mixed.

6. EFFECTS IN POST-SECONDARY EDUCATION

Post-secondary education boasts its own literature on peer effects though the empirical approaches and outcomes examined differ a bit from the literature on younger students. A host of papers have utilized the random assignment of students into housing units in order to examine the effects of roommates, dormmates, and squadron members on own outcomes.

Sacerdote (2001) examines the effects of roommates and dormmates on college GPA and the likelihood of joining a fraternity. Roommate academic ability has a modest impact on own academic performance. For example, assigning a student a roommate who was in the top 25% of incoming admissions scores will raise the student's freshman year GPA by 0.06. Several other studies find either no effect from roommates on academic outcomes or modest effects. Foster (2006) finds no effect from randomly assigned roommates at the University of Maryland. Zimmerman (2003) finds that roommate verbal SAT matters more than math SAT. He finds that students are harmed somewhat by being assigned a roommate in the bottom 15% of the distribution. Hoel, Parker, and Rivenburg (2005) find strong nonlinear effects from roommates and no detectable effects from peers in the same classroom.[11] Stinebrickner and Stinebrickner (2006) shows that roommate ACT is less important than roommate high school GPA and that a peer effect on hours spent studying in college may be the mediating influence. Fletcher and Tienda (2008) find that college students benefit from having more peers who attended their same high school, presumably because such peers serve as a support network.

---

[11] Martins and Walker (2006) and Parker, Grant, Crouter, and Rivenburg (2008) also find no evidence of classroom peers on own grades.

Several other papers look for peer effects within squadrons at the U.S. Military Academy (Lyle (2007)) and U.S. Air Force Academy (Carrell, Fullerton, and West (2008)). These contexts are particularly interesting because the Academies enforce a great deal of interaction within squadrons. Lyle finds that there are peer effects in first year GPA, but that common shocks in the form of the upperclassmen in the squadron may account for half or more of the estimated "peer effect." Carrell, Fullerton, and West find large peer effects on first year GPA at the Air Force Academy and they attribute this finding to the unique setting in which the true peer group is well-measured.

Brunello, De Paola and Scoppa (2010) use data from a university in Italy and examine how course grades are influenced by peers enrolled in the same course. They find that a one standard deviation in classmate ability is associated with a 0.08 standard deviation increase in own grades.

A variety of the papers move beyond college GPA as the outcome of interest and find some very interesting and statistically significant effects of peers. Duncan, Boisjoly, Kremer, Levy, and Eccles (2005) use randomly assigned roommates to examine peer effects in drinking, marijuana use, and sexual activity. Among male students who binge drank in high school, assigning them a roommate who also binge drank in high school leads to a fourfold increase in the number of binge drinking episodes per month. There is no evidence of a comparable effect for females. The peer effects on number of sexual partners are smaller and not robust to changes in specification, and the peer effects on marijuana use are small and statistically insignificant. DeSimone (2007) finds that after controlling for selection into fraternity membership, being a fraternity member raises the frequency of binge drinking by 15 to 20 percentage points. And Wilson (2007) finds large peer effects in smoking.

In subsequent work, Duncan, Boisjoly, Kremer, Levy, and Eccles investigate whether having a minority roommate or a high income roommate affects student attitudes one year after initial room assignment. White students assigned a black roommate report support for affirmative action that is one half to two thirds of a standard deviation higher (on a four-point scale) than white students assigned nonblack roommates. More generally, students assigned minority roommates are more likely to report that they are comfortable interacting with people of a different race or ethnicity. Students assigned a high income roommate are one-third of a standard deviation less likely to support the statement that "wealthy people should pay more taxes."

Carrell, Malmstrom, and West (2008) examine peer effects in academic cheating at West Point. They find that adding a student who cheated in high school to the college class results in an additional 0.33 to 0.47 cheaters in the college cohort.

Finally, Sacerdote (2001) finds large peer effects in whether or not students join fraternities or sororities and large effects in which specific Greek organization that they join. If a roommate joins a fraternity, a student is 8% more likely to do so. Moving the student from a dorm in which no one joins to a dorm in which everyone joins raises the likelihood of the student joining a fraternity by 32%.

Perhaps most interesting from the perspective of labor economists is the question of whether peers are important in the career or job selection process. In Marmaros and Sacerdote (2002), we define an indicator for whether or not a student takes a high paying job, defined as finance, consulting or law, as her first job. We regress the student's outcome on the average outcome for the student's randomly assigned first-year dormmates and we find a statistically significant coefficient of 0.24. We also find that students rely heavily on their peers and their peers' parents in the job search process. Arcidiacono and Nicholson (2005) examine peer effects in specialty choice among medical students and they find little evidence of peer effects. De Giorgi, Pellizzari, and Redaelli (2007) find that a student's peers at Bocconi have a significant impact on choice of major. This paper uses the novel identification strategy of relying on the background of an individual's peers' peers as an instrument for the peers outcome (major choice).

Overall the literature on peer effects at the university level is fairly consistent. First, most authors find small peer effects in GPA from roommates. One key exception is the Air Force Academy study which is from a unique environment. Measured peer effects in GPA would likely be larger at other institutions if we knew the true peer group rather than limiting ourselves to roommates. There are much larger effects on social outcomes like drinking, cheating, and fraternity joining. And there is some evidence that peers are important for career choice. One next logical step may be the designing of experiments to see whether the peer effects measured in observational data can be exploited by university administrators to maximize GPA or some other objective. Carrell, Fullerton, and West (2009) find some nonlinearities in the peer effects at Air Force and they are currently running an experiment to see if the "optimal" allocation of cadets to squadrons improves GPA and physical fitness scores.

Another strand of the literature uses detailed data on interactions among university students to look for patterns of social interaction and to learn about the determinants of who is friends with whom. Marmaros and Sacerdote (2006) do this using email data and Mayer and Puller (2008) use Facebook.com data. The conclusions from the two studies are remarkably consistent. There is very strong same-race attraction in the determination of friendships, with black students being 10 to 20 times more likely to interact with another black students than a nonblack student. And proximity matters a great deal. Students who share a first-year dorm are four times more likely to interact than students who do not.

7. CONCLUSIONS

Recent years have brought a flurry of attention to the modeling and measurement of peer effects in education at the primary, secondary, and university levels. Within the university literature, there is a fair amount of agreement that peer effects from roommates and dormmates in determining GPA likely exist but are modest in size. In contrast, the peer effects in determining certain social outcomes (drinking, fraternity joining, political attitudes) are a fair bit larger and potentially peer effects are a major determinant of such outcomes.

The jury is still out on the exact size of peer effects in primary and secondary school test scores. The studies detailed in Table 4.2 encompass a fairly large range of estimates. However, many researchers agree that the linear-in-means model (the focus of Table 4.2) is probably not the most interesting model anyway. The more interesting question is whether there are nonlinearities that make policies like tracking of students into classrooms a really good or a really bad idea. Hoxby and Weingarth (2005) is the benchmark study in this regard, though many of the other studies discussed here also test for nonlinearities and in some cases find substantial nonlinear effects. For instance Burke and Sass (2008) find that low achieving students benefit more from high ability peers than do high achieving students, and Vigdor and Nechyba (2007) find that classroom heterogeneity is good for test scores.

There is broad agreement that increasing the number of girls in the classroom is associated with less disruption and higher test scores. And the effects are big enough that the effects likely work through more than just increases in peer mean scores. The result that more boys translates to more violence seems to fit with the personal experience of many authors, though fortunately does not point to any obvious policy prescription.

Most parents and students behave as if peer effects matter a great deal and the findings of the literature are consistent with this. As Winston and Zimmerman (2003) note, students are both consumers of the educational product and part of the production function. Tracking by ability is in such widespread use that it would not be surprising if future studies find more evidence that is consistent with the boutique and focus models, which imply benefits from tracking.

While directions for future research are not entirely obvious, the summary presented here may give us some hints. Additional data with exogenous assignment of students to classrooms would help clarify the size and nonlinear nature of peer effects in elementary and secondary school. Actual experiments will allow us to learn whether peer effects in observational data can truly be exploited by policy makers. And more work that identifies the true peer group, as opposed to the peer group we can measure may cause us to revise upward our estimates of the importance of peer effects.

There are several major questions that researchers and policy makers should address in the coming years. First, now that we have measured the existence and importance of peer effects for a variety of outcomes, how large are these peer effects relative to the influences of teacher quality, school quality, and home environment? Second, can measured peer effects actually be exploited by policy makers in order to increase total learning or to decrease criminal behavior or drug use? In researching peer effects have we been describing and studying an important policy tool or rather is this a part of human behavior that is worth understanding but not particularly relevant for policy? And following the Coleman Report's (1966) prescient writing, how much can we actually benefit disadvantaged students by changing the peer group with whom these students interact?

REFERENCES

Ammermueller, A., Pischke, J.S., 2006. Peer effects in European primary schools: Evidence from PIRLS. NBER Working Paper No. 12180.

Angrist, J.D., Lang, K., 2004. Does school integration generate peer effects? Evidence from Boston's Metco program. Am. Econ. Rev. 94, 1613–1634.

Arcidiacono, P., Nicholson, S., 2005. Peer effects in medical school. J. Public Econ. 89, 327–350.

Argys, L.M., Rees, D.I., 2008. Searching for peer group effects: A test of the contagion hypothesis. Rev. Econ. Stat. 90 (3), 442–458.

Austen-Smith, D., Fryer Jr., R.G., 2005. An economic analysis of "acting white." Q. J. Econ 120, 551–583.

Bayer, P., Pintoff, R., Pozen, D.E., 2005. Building criminal capital behind bars: Peer effects in juvenile corrections. Yale University Economic Growth Center Discussion Paper No. 864.

Betts, J.R., Morell, D., 1999. The determinants of undergraduate grade point average: The relative importance of family background, high school resources, and peer group effects. J. Hum. Resour. 34, 268–293.

Betts, J.R., Shkolnik, J.L., 2000. The effects of ability grouping on student achievement and resource allocation in secondary schools. Econ. Educ. Rev. 19, 1–15.

Betts, J.R., Zau, A., 2004. Peer groups and academic achievement: Panel evidence from administrative data. Unpublished manuscript.

Bhattacharya, D., 2009. Inferring optimal peer assignment from experimental data. J. Am. Stat. Assoc. 104 (486), 486–500.

Bobonis, G.J., Finan, F., 2009. Neighborhood peer effects in secondary school enrollment decisions. Rev. Econ. Stat. 91 (4), 695–716.

Boozer, M.A., Cacciola, S.E., 2001. Inside the black box of project star: Estimation of peer effects. Economic Growth Center Discussion Paper No. 832.

Bramoullé, Y., Djebbari, H., Fortin, B., 2009. Identification of peer effects through social networks. J. Econom. 150, 41–55.

Brock, W.A., Durlauf, S.N., 2001. Interactions-based models. In: Heckman, J., Leamer, E. (Eds.), Handbook of Econometrics. vol. 5. Elsevier Science, pp. 3297–3380.

Brunello, G., De Paola, M., Scoppa, V., 2010. Peer effects in higher education: Does the field of study matter?. Economic Inquiry. 48 (3), 621–634.

Burke, M.A., Sass, T.R., 2008. Classroom peer effects and student achievement. Calder Urban Institute Working Paper 18.

Carman, K., Zhang, L., 2008. Classroom peer effects and academic achievement: Evidence from a Chinese middle school. Unpublished manuscript.

Carrell, S.E., Fullerton, R.L., West, J.E., 2008. Does your cohort matter? Measuring peer effects in college achievement. NBER Working Paper No. 14032.

Carrell, S.E., Fullerton, R.L., West, J.E., 2009. Does your cohort matter? Measuring peer effects in college achievement. J. Labor Econ. 27 (3).

Carrell, S.E., Hoekstra, M.L., 2008. Externalities in the classroom: How children exposed to domestic violence affect everyone's kids. Unpublished manuscript.

Carrell, S.E., Malmstrom, F.V., West, J.E., 2008. Peer effects in academic cheating. J. Hum. Resour. 43, 173–207.

Case, A., Katz, L., 1991. The company you keep: The effects of family and neighborhood on disadvantaged youths. NBER Working Paper No. 3705.
Caucutt, E.M., 2001. Peer effects in applied general equilibrium. Econ. Theory 17, 25–51.
Caucutt, E.M., 2002. Educational vouchers when there are peer group effects-size matters. Int. Econ. Rev. 43, 195–222.
Coleman, J.S., 1966. Equality of educational opportunity. Washington: U.S. Govt. Print. Off., 1966. [summary report].
Coleman, J.S., 1968. Equality of educational opportunity. Equity & Excellence in Education 6 (5), 19–28.
Cook, P.J., Ludwig, J., 1997. Weighing the "burden of 'acting white'": Are there race differences in attitudes toward education? J. Policy Anal. Manag. 16, 256–278.
Cooley, J., 2009. Desegregation and the achievement gap: Do diverse peers help? WCER Working Paper No. 2008-7.
De Giorgi, G., Pellizzari, M., Redaelli, S., 2007. Be as careful of the books you read as of the company you keep: Evidence on peer effects in educational choices. IZA Discussion Paper No. 2833.
De Paola, M., Scoppa, V., 2009. Peer group effects on the academic performance of Italian students. Appl. Econ.
DeSimone, J.S., 2007. Fraternity membership and drinking behavior. NBER Working Paper No. W13262.
Dills, A.K., 2005. Does cream-skimming curdle the milk? A study of peer effects. Econ. Educ. Rev. 24, 19–28.
Ding, W., Lehrer, S.F., 2007. Do peers affect student achievement in China's secondary schools. Rev. Econ. Stat. 89, 300–312.
Duflo, E., Dupas, P., Kremer, M., 2008. Peer effects and the impact of tracking: Evidence from a randomized evaluation in Kenya. Unpublished manuscript.
Duncan, G.J., Boisjoly, J., Kremer, M., Levy, D.M., Eccles, J., 2005. Peer effects in drug use and sex among college students. J. Abnorm. Child Psych. 33, 375–385.
Duncan, G., Boisjoly, J., Kremer, M., Levy, D., Eccles, J.S., 2006. Empathy or antipathy? The impact of diversity. Am. Econ. Rev. 96 (5), 1890–1905.
Epple, D., Romano, R.E., 1998. Competition between private and public schools, vouchers, and peer-group effects. Am. Econ. Rev. 88, 33–62.
Epple, D., Romano, R.E., forthcoming. Peer effects in education: In: Benhabib, J., Bisin, A., Jackson, M. (Eds.), A survey of the theory and evidence. Handbook of Social Economics 1A, 1B, Amsterdam, North-Holland.
Eisenberg, D., 2004. Peer effects for adolescent substance use: Do they really exist? UC-Berkeley School of Public Health working paper.
Evans, W.N., Oates, W.E., Schwab, R.M., 1992. Measuring peer effects: A study of teenage behavior. J. Polit. Econ. 100, 966–991.
Falk, A., Ichino, A., 2006. Clear evidence on peer effects. J. Labor Econ. 24, 39–57.
Figlio, D.N., 2005. Boys named Sue: Disruptive children and their peers. NBER Working Paper No. 11277.
Fletcher, J.M., Tienda, M., 2008. High school peer networks and college success: Lessons from Texas. Mimeo.
Fordham, S., Ogbu, J., 1986. Black students' school success: Coping with the burden of "acting white" Urban Rev. 58, 54–84.
Foster, G., 2006. It's not your peers, and it's not your friends: Some progress toward understanding the educational peer effect mechanism. J. Public Econ. 90, 1455–1475.
Fryer Jr., R.G., Torelli, P., 2010. An empirical analysis of "acting white". J. Public Econ. 94 (5–6), 380–396.
Gaviria, A., Raphael, S., 2001. School-based peer effects and juvenile behavior. Rev. Econ. Stat. 83, 257–268.
Gibbons, S., Telhaj, S., 2008. Peers and achievement in England's secondary schools. SERC Discussion Paper 1.

Glaeser, E.L., Sacerdote, B., Scheinkman, J.A., 1996. Crime and social interactions. Q. J. Econ. 111, 507–548.

Glaeser, E., Scheinkman, J., 2001. Measuring social interactions. In: Durlauf, S.N., Young, H.P. (Eds.), Social dynamics, Washington, D.C. : Brookings Institution Press, Cambridge, Mass : MIT Press, 2001. pp. 83–132.

Glaeser, E.L., Sacerdote, B., Scheinkman, J., 2003. The social multiplier. J. Eur. Econ. Assoc. 1, 345–353.

Glewwe, P., 1997. Estimating the impact of peer group effects on socioeconomic outcomes: Does the distribution of peer group characteristics matter? Econ. Educ. Rev. 16, 29–43.

Graham, B.S., 2008. Identifying social interactions through conditional variance restrictions. Econometrica 76, 643–660.

Graham, B.S., Hahn, J., 2005. Identification and estimation of the linear-in-means model of social interactions. Econ. Lett. 88, 1–6.

Guryan, J., Kroft, K., Notowidigdo, M., 2007. Peer effects in the workplace: Evidence from random assignment in professional golf. NBER Working Paper No. 13422.

Han, L., Li, T., 2009. The gender difference of peer influence in higher education. Econ. Educa. Rev. 28 (1), 129–134.

Harris, J.R., 1998. The nurture assumption: Why children turn out the way they do. New York : Free Press.

Hanushek, E.A., Kain, J.F., Markman, J.M., Rivkin, S.G., 2003. Does peer ability affect student achievement? J. Appl. Econom. 18, 527–544.

Hanushek, E.A., Kain, J.F., Rivkin, S.G., 2009. New evidence about Brown v. Board of Education: The complex effects of school racial composition on achievement. J. Labor Econ. 27 (3), 349–383.

Hanushek, E.A., Rivkin, S.G., 2009. Harming the best: How schools affect the black-white achievement gap. J. Policy Anal. Manag. 28 (Summer), 366–393.

Henderson, V., Mieszkowski, P., Sauvageau, Y., 1978. Peer group effects and educational production functions. J. Public Econ. 10, 97–106.

Hoel, J., Parker, J., Rivenburg, J., 2005. A test for classmate peer effects in higher education. Reed College (September 2005). Unpublished manuscript.

Hoxby, C.M., 2000a. The effects of class size on student achievement: New evidence from population variation. Q. J. Econ. 15, 1239–1285.

Hoxby, C.M., 2000b. Peer effects in the classroom: Learning from gender and race variation. NBER Working Paper No. 7867.

Hoxby, C.M., 2002. The power of peers: How does the makeup of a classroom influence achievement. Education Next 2 (2), 56–63.

Hoxby, C.M., Weingarth, G., 2005. Taking race out of the equation: School reassignment and the structure of peer effects. Mimeograph.

Imberman, S., Kugler, A., Sacerdote, B., 2009. Katrina's children: Evidence on the structure of peer effects from hurricane evacuees. NBER Working Paper No. 15291.

Jonsson, J.O., Mood, C., 2008. Choice by contrast in Swedish schools: How peers' achievement affects educational choice. Soc. Forces 87 (2).

Kang, C., 2007. Classroom peer effects and academic achievement: Quasi-randomization evidence from South Korea. J. Urban Econ. 61, 458–495.

Katz, L.F., Kling, J.R., Liebman, J.B., 2001. Moving to opportunity in Boston: Early results of a randomized mobility experiment. Q. J. Econ. CXVI, 607–654.

Kawaguchi, D., 2004. Peer effects on substance use among American teenagers. J. Popul. Econ. 17, 351–367.

Kling, J.R, Ludwig, J., Katz, L.F., 2005. Neighborhood effects on crime for female and male youth: Evidence from a randomized housing voucher experiment. Q. J. Econ. CXX, 87–130.

Kooreman, P., 2003. Time, money, peers, and parents: Some data and theories on teenage behavior. IZA Discussion Paper No. 931.

Kramarz, F., Machin, S., Ouazad, A., 2008. What makes a test score? The respective contributions of pupils, schools, and peers in achievement in English primary education. INSEAD Working Paper Number 2008/58/EPS.

Krauth, B., 2005. Peer effects and selection effects on smoking among Canadian youth. Can. J. Economics 38 (3), 735–757.

Krauth, B.V., 2006. Simulation-based estimation of peer effects. J. Econom. 133, 243–271.

Kremer, M., Levy, D.M., 2003. Peer effects and alcohol use among college students. NBER Working Paper No. 9876.

Kremer, M., Miguel, E., Thornton, R., 2009. Incentives to learn. Rev. Econ. Stat. 91 (3), 437–456.

Lai, F., 2008. How do classroom peers affect student outcomes? Evidence from a natural experiment in Beijing's middle schools. Unpublished manuscript.

Lavy, V.M., Paserman, D., Schlosser, A., 2007. Inside the black of box of ability peer effects: Evidence from variation in high and low achievers in the classroom. Unpublished manuscript.

Lavy, V., Schlosser, A., 2007. Mechanisms and impacts of gender peer effects at school. NBER Working Paper No. 13292.

Lavy, V., Silva, O., Weinhardt, F., 2009. The good, the bad and the average: Evidence on the scale and nature of ability peer effects in schools. NBER Working Paper Series No. 15600.

Lazear, E.P., 2001. Educational production. Q. J. Econ. 116, 777–803.

Lefgren, L., 2004. Educational peer effects and the Chicago public schools. J. Urban Econ. 56, 169–191.

Lundborg, P., 2006. Having the wrong friends? Peer effects in adolescent substance use. J. Health Econ. 25, 214–233.

Lyle, D.S., 2007. Estimating and interpreting peer and role model effects from randomly assigned social groups at West Point. Rev. Econ. Stat. 89, 289–299.

Manski, C.F., 1993. Identification of endogenous social effects: The reflection problem. Rev. Econ. Stud. 60, 531–542.

Marmaros, D., Sacerdote, B., 2002. Peer and social networks in job search. Euro. Econ. Rev. 46 (4-5), 870–879.

Marmaros, D., Sacerdote, B., 2006. How do friendships form. Q. J. Econ. 121, 79–119.

Martins, P.S., Walker, I., 2006. Student achievement and university classes: Effects of attendance, size, peers, and teachers. IZA Discussion Paper No. 2490.

Mayer, A., Puller, S.L., 2008. The old boy (and girl) network: Social network formation on university campuses. J. Public Econ. 92, 329–347.

McEwan, P.J., 2003. Peer effects on student achievement: Evidence from Chile. Econ. Educ. Rev. 22, 131–141.

Mihaly, K., 2008. Peer effects of actual peers. Duke University Mimeo.

Parker, J., Grant, J., Crouter, J., Rivenburg, J., 2008. Classmate peer effects: Evidence from core courses at three colleges. Reed College Mimeo.

Powell, L.M., Tauras, J.A., Ross, H., 2005. The importance of peer effects, cigarette prices and tobacco control policies for youth smoking behavior. J. Health Econ. 24, 950–968.

Rivkin, S.G., 2001. Tiebout sorting, aggregation, and the estimation of peer group effects. Econ. Educ. Rev. 20, 201–209.

Robertson, D., Symons, J., 2003. Do peer groups matter? Peer group versus schooling effects on academic attainment. Economica 70, 31–53.

Sacerdote, B., 2001. Peer effects with random assignment: Results for Dartmouth roommates. Q. J. Econ. 116, 681–704.

Schneeweis, N., Winter-Ebmer, R., 2007. Peer effects in Austrian schools. Empir. Econ. 32, 387–409.

Siegfried, J.J., Gleason, M.A., 2006. Academic roommate peer effects. Unpublished manuscript.

Stinebrickner, R., Stinebrickner, T.R., 2006. What can be learned about peer effects using college roommates? Evidence from new survey data and students from disadvantaged backgrounds. J. Public Econ. 90, 1435–1454.

Trogdon, J.G., Nonnemaker, J., Pais, J., 2008. Peer effects in adolescent overweight. J. Health Econ. 27, 1388–1399.

Vigdor, J.L., 2006. Peer effects in neighborhoods and housing. In: Dodge, K.A., Dishion, T.J., Lansford, J.E. (Eds.), Deviant Peer Influences in Programs for Youth: Problems and Solutions. Guilford Press.

Vigdor, J.L., Nechyba, T.S., 2007. Peer effects in North Carolina public schools. In: Woessmann, L., Peterson, P.E. (Eds.), Schools and the Equal Opportunity Problem. The MIT Press, pp. 73–101.

Whitmore, D., 2005. Resource and peer impacts on girls' academic achievement: Evidence from a randomized experiment. Am. Econ. Rev. Papers and Proceedings 95 (2), 199–203.

Wilson, J., 2007. Peer effects and cigarette use among college students. Atlantic Econ. J. 35, 233–247.

Winston, G.C., Zimmerman, D.J., 2003. Peer effects in higher education. NBER Working Paper No. 9501.

Zabel, J.E., 2008. The impact of peer effects on student outcomes in New York City public schools. Education Finance and Policy 3, 197–249.

Zimmer, R.W., Toma, E.F., 2000. Peer effects in private and public schools across countries. J. Policy Anal. Manag. 19, 75–92.

Zimmerman, D.J., 2003. Peer effects in academic outcomes: Evidence from a natural experiment. Rev. Econ. Stat. 85, 9–23.

Zimmerman, D.J., Winston, G., 2004. Peer effects in higher education. In: Hoxby, C. (Ed.), College Choices: The Economics of Where to Go, When to Go, and How to Pay for It. University of Chicago Press.

CHAPTER 5

Teacher Compensation and Collective Bargaining

Michael Podgursky
University of Missouri – Columbia

Contents

1. Introduction	280
2. Studies of Relative Teacher Pay	281
3. Quantity versus Quality Tradeoffs	283
4. Comparing Teacher and Nonteacher Compensation	286
4.1 Public–private teacher compensation	288
5. Teacher Pay and Student Achievement	289
6. Structure of Teacher Compensation	290
6.1 Institutional framework: Single salary schedule	290
6.2 Confounding factors: Tenure and size of wage-setting units	296
6.3 Deferred compensation: Teacher pension incentives	298
7. Trends in Market-Based Pay	301
8. Teacher Collective Bargaining	305
9. Conclusion	309
Acknowledgements	310
References	310

Abstract

While compensation accounts for roughly 90% of K-12 instructional costs, there is little evidence of rational design in these systems. This chapter reviews the nature of teacher compensation systems in developed economies and research on their performance effects. Since these compensation schemes typically arise out of collective negotiations, this chapter also surveys the smaller literature on the effect of teacher collective bargaining on earnings and school outcomes.

JEL classification: I21, I22, J31, J32, J33, J45

Keywords

Teacher Compensation
Teacher Pay
School Finance
Teacher Collective Bargaining

1. INTRODUCTION

During the 2006–07 school year, the most current year for which national data are available, U.S. public schools spent $187 billion for salaries and $59 billion for benefits for instructional personnel. These compensation payments account for 55% of K-12 current expenditures and 90% of instructional expenditures (U.S. Department of Education (2009)). As large as these expenditures are, they do not fully capture the resources committed to K-12 compensation, since they do not include billions of dollars of unfunded liabilities of pension funds and retiree health insurance for teachers and administrators (Pew Center on the States (2010)). If productivity doubles for an input accounting for 1% of total cost, the overall social gain will be modest. However, given the large share of K-12 costs that arise from educator compensation, even small gains in efficiency can yield large social dividends.

There is ample reason to believe that significant efficiency gains can be found. Educator compensation "systems" are neither strategic nor integrated. In a well-run organization, the total compensation package—salaries, current and deferred benefits—would be structured with an eye toward overall firm performance. Tradeoffs between different types of salary and benefits would be carefully scrutinized. Not only the level, but the structure of salaries would take account of market benchmarks, as well as performance effects. In public education, however, overall teacher compensation arises not out of a rational planning process, but rather emerges as an amalgam of different components or "silos," reflecting pressures from different constituencies, legislative mandates, legacies from earlier vintages of collective bargaining agreements, and other institutional and political factors, with little or no consideration for overall efficiency. Neither starting nor senior salaries are market-based. In the United States, teacher pay is set by salary schedules that have evolved over decades of collective bargaining agreements or, in many nonbargaining states, legislative fiat. Base pay is augmented by various types of district or statewide salary supplements (e.g., coaching, career ladder). Deferred compensation in the form of retirement pay inhabits another silo altogether, with policy set by statewide pension boards often dominated by senior educators and administrators. Teacher compensation is the sum of all of these parts (plus fringe benefits such as health insurance, typically negotiated at the district level). There is no evidence that educator pay is market based or strategic in other developed nations. As compared to the U.S., teacher pay setting is usually more centralized, at a regional or prefectural level, often with differences by school level or type, but not market-driven.[1]

Concern over school performance and teacher quality is stimulating interest in more efficient and performance-oriented teacher compensation regimes. This, in turn, has stimulated research on the performance effects of teacher compensation and collective

---

[1] However, there is growing interest in market-based reforms of educator compensation. Experiments and pilot programs are under way in a number of countries. For surveys see Sclafani and Tucker (2006) and Podgursky and Springer (2007).

bargaining. This chapter provides a survey of several strands of this literature, with a focus on economic studies. Our discussion proceeds from a more aggregate, or "macro," perspective on overall levels and trends in teacher compensation to a more disaggregated, or "micro," discussion of the structure of teacher pay. First, we examine research on the overall level of teacher pay and possible quantity–quality tradeoffs with pay and staffing ratios. This is closely related to the issue of the overall decline in teacher quality associated with reduced labor market barriers for women. Then we turn our attention to the structure of teacher pay and the "single salary schedule," which is the primary determinant of teacher salaries in the U.S., and consider other institutional features of the labor market that exacerbate or dampen the effects of these salary schedules. We then examine the incentives produced by teacher retirement benefit systems. Since teacher compensation is largely structured by collective bargaining, it is appropriate to conclude the survey with a review of the small, but important, literature on the effects of collective bargaining on resource allocation in K-12 education. Given the central role of teachers in school performance and of compensation in K-12 school spending, we conclude that educator compensation is a surprisingly undeveloped area of education policy research. However, research can only progress in this area if education authorities create "regulatory space" for experimentation with teacher compensation models and permit their evaluation.

2. STUDIES OF RELATIVE TEACHER PAY

There has been a lively debate about the overall level of teacher salaries and a corollary discussion as to whether teachers are "underpaid." In the United States, this discussion has been related to the question of whether the elimination of labor market barriers for women (and the ensuing higher earnings opportunities) lowered the quality of the public school teaching workforce. The "crowding thesis" holds that, prior to advances in civil rights and anti-discrimination legislation, barriers to entry in other professions crowded well-educated and academically talented women into K-12 teaching positions. With the decline of discriminatory barriers in other professions such as accounting, management, law, and medicine, teachers who would have been pushed into teaching were now able to escape to other professions. In the absence of significant increases in relative pay for teachers, the relative quality of the teaching workforce fell.

One problem in examining long-term trends in teacher quality is that even rudimentary measures of teacher quality, such as test scores or academic credentials, are not available in a long time series. Several studies have taken up the empirical challenge of documenting the hypothesized secular decline in the relative quality of female teachers.[2] Several authors have made use of various waves of longitudinal studies to

---

[2] In theory, the same quality decline should have been observed in other "crowded" female dominated occupations such as nurses and librarians. We are unaware of any evidence in this regard.

examine long-term changes in the quality of the female teaching workforce. Corcoran, Evans, and Schwab (2004) draw on five different longitudinal surveys of high school graduation cohorts from 1957 to 1992 to document the decline in female teacher quality as measured by high school test scores. They find only a slight decline in the average academic quality of female teachers relative to the universe of female high school graduates. However, they find a substantial drop in the share of females in the highest academic quintile who become teachers. Interestingly, they find no such drop for male teachers. The female finding is replicated in Hoxby and Leigh (2004), who examine nine cohorts of the Recent College Graduates survey, spanning 1963 to 2000. They, too, find that the probability a new college graduate from the highest academic quintile (as measured by college selectivity) enters teaching falls from 20% to 4%—a much larger drop than any other quintile. Bacolod (2007a), examines several waves of the National Longitudinal Survey, and compares the probability of entry into teaching across different birth cohorts (1940–49 through 1960–69). She finds a sharp relative drop in the probability that high ability teachers (as measured by the Armed Forces Qualification Test, or AFQT) become teachers. (See also, Bacolod (2007b) for an analysis of further longitudinal data analysis.)

Although the sample sizes of teachers in each of these studies are modest, the findings are largely consistent with one another and are relatively robust to different measures of quality. Each of these studies find modest declines in the quality of teachers at the mean, but much sharper declines at the upper tails of the distribution. With the large increase in college attendance and completion rates for females between 1960 and 2000, the probability of a female graduate becoming a teacher declines over time, but the proportionate drop is greatest in the top ability quintiles. This is a nuanced version of the "overcrowding" thesis. Relative teacher quality at the median has not greatly declined. The major loss has been in the upper academic tail.

Given the paucity of data providing direct measures of teacher quality such as academic test scores, some researchers (Hanushek and Rivkin (1997); Lakdawalla (2006); Stoddard (2003)) treat relative teacher pay (e.g., teacher pay relative to all college graduates) as a measure of relative teacher quality. The most reliable of these pay measures is annual earnings data from the Dicennial Census. Using these Census data, Hanushek and Rivkin (2006, figure 1) compute the percent of college graduates earning less than the average teacher. For women, this percentage fell from roughly 55% in 1950 to 45% in 2000, with most of this decline occuring from 1950 to 1970. A similar pattern occurs for men, although they start from a much lower base. Note that these calculations of annual relative earnings take no account of current and deferred benefits, or annual hours of work, two issues we will consider in more detail below.[3]

The coincidence of the decline in relative teacher pay for females and the decline in the relative academic quality of teachers naturally leads many researchers to infer a

---

[3] Leigh and Ryan (2008) document a similar decline in academic skills for Australian teachers that coincides with a decline in teacher relative pay.

causal relationship from the former to the latter. Hoxby and Leigh (2004) provide a more comprehensive analysis of this issue by examining the roles of both the level of teacher pay relative to nonteacher earnings and the changes in dispersion of teacher pay within teaching. The insight here is that a high ability woman contemplating entry into a profession is likely less concerned with pay at the median than at the upper deciles. Thus, Hoxby and Leigh estimate an occupational choice model that decomposes the relative pay variable into several components: median female teacher pay, the dispersion of female teacher pay, male–female pay in nonteaching, and a trend (male) in nonteaching earnings. They highlight a factor often ignored in relative teacher pay discussion—a large compression of intrastate teacher pay that coincided with the rise of teacher collective bargaining. This had the result of producing a large compression of pay between the highest and lowest ability quintile of teachers. In their decomposition, they distinguish the "push" of wage compression from the "pull" of relative pay outside of teaching. They find that roughly 80% of the decline in the share of high ability candidates entering teaching is explained by the "push" of intrastate compression in teacher pay between 1963 and 2000.[4]

Several studies examine trends in earnings and measures of teacher academic quality in the U.K. Nickell and Quintini (2002) examine public sector pay and workforce quality from 1975 through 1999 based on two longitudinal surveys. They find clear evidence of slippage in the relative pay of both male and female teachers in the overall pay structure. This coincides with a significant decline in the level of academic ability for male teachers but not for female teachers. Chevalier, Dolton, and McIntosh (2007) provide a wider window on teacher quality by examining survey data on graduating cohorts of college students from 1960 through 1995 (surveyed six to seven years after graduation). They, too, find a larger quality decline for females. However, by 2002 (i.e., the 1995 cohort) teacher quality had actually improved vis-à-vis nonteachers.[5]

3. QUANTITY VERSUS QUALITY TRADEOFFS

Given that pay is set by governments and not by markets, a question arises as to how school districts have chosen to trade off the level of teacher pay with staffing ratios (i.e., the student-teacher ratio).[6] When spending per student rises by 10%, other things being equal, school administrators can raise teacher pay by 10% and hold staffing ratios constant, hold teacher pay constant and lower staffing ratios by 10%, or any

---

[4] Leigh and Ryan (2008) attempt a similar decomposition for Australian teachers over a smaller time span, 1983–2003. As noted in fn. 3, they find a similar decline in high ability males and females entering teaching. In their decomposition, relative pay rather than pay compression within teaching mattered much more. This is primarily due to the fact that little pay compression within teaching occurred over this time interval.

[5] See also Dolton (2006). International data on relative teacher salaries are reported in OECD (2001, 2009).

[6] Of course, if staffing ratios fall and relative teacher pay falls, applicant queues will fall as well. Whether, and to what extent, this lowers teacher quality is taken up below.

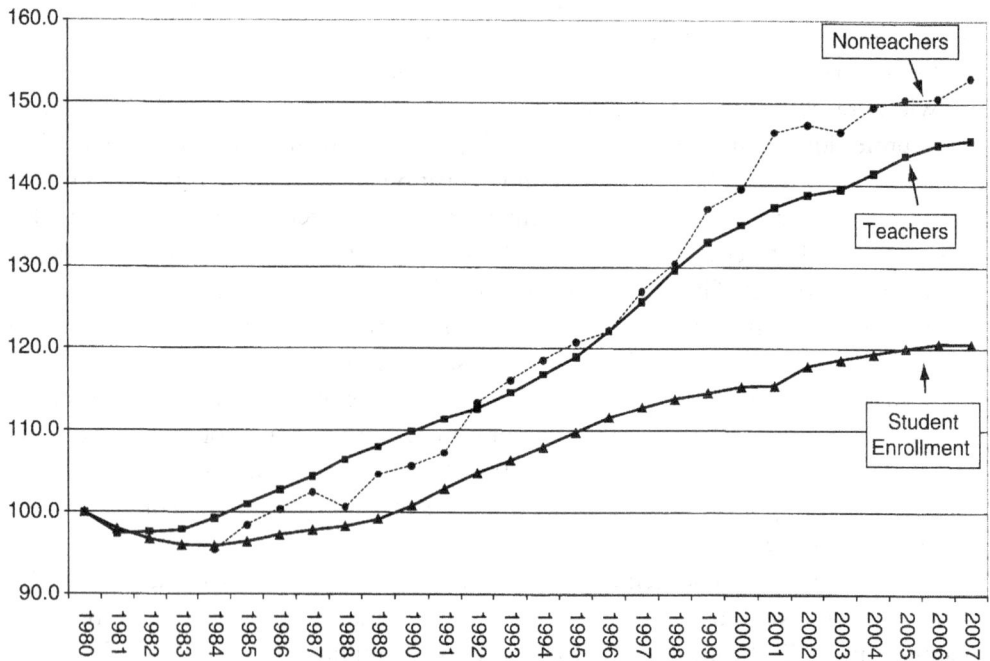

Figure 5.1 Student enrollment, teacher and nonteacher employment in U.S. public schools: Fall, 1980 to Fall, 2007. *Source:* U.S. Department of Education. National Center on Education Statistics. *Digest of Education Statistics.* Various years.

combination of the two that adds up to 10%. Figure 5.1 presents data for U.S. staff and enrollments in public schools, indexed to Fall 1980 levels. It clearly shows the dip in enrollments by the mid-'80s and the subsequent rise as the baby boom echo entered the school system. By 2007 enrollments had grown by 21%. The upper two lines show the level of teacher and nonteacher employment. Clearly the growth in staff far outstripped the growth in enrollments. Teacher employment grew by 46%, nonteacher employment grew by 53%, and the student-teacher ratio fell from 18.7 to 15.7 over the period. Over the same period, real spending per student grew on average by 2.3% per year. If the staffing ratio had been held constant, real teacher compensation could have grown by 78% over this period and would have produced an average 2007 teacher salary of $78,574. In fact, teacher salaries grew by only 7% over this period, and the average teacher salary was $52,578.[7] This is not a phenomenon unique to the U.S. (U.S. Department of Education (2009)). Lakdawalla (2006) presents data showing that student-teacher ratios have been falling at least since the 1950s in all of the major industrial nations.

---

[7] Our choice of 1980 as a benchmark is benign. Hanushek (1986, table 3) shows that the trend toward declining student-teacher ratio was underway at least several decades earlier—falling from 25.8 in 1960 to 19.0 by 1980.

This human resource policy on the part of school districts is perplexing, especially given complaints about low teacher pay and "teacher shortages" that have occurred in the U.S. and abroad. The universality of this trend begs parochial explanations. Several researchers have proposed economic explanations for this phenomenon. Flyer and Rosen (1997) argue that individualized attention by school staff and parent household time are substitutes in consumption. As family incomes and the shadow value of females' time rise, households substitute schooling for mother's time. They examine state level data and find that declines in the student-teacher ratio are positively associated with increases in the labor force participation of women.[8] However, we are aware of no data suggesting that more direct measures of substitutes for a mother's time, such as the length of the school day or school year, rose over time or in response to higher female labor force participation rates. Stoddard (2003) and Lakdawalla (2006) locate an explanation in K-12 education production. Rising skill premia economy-wide have increased the price of academically-skilled teachers. However, the relative productivity of academically skilled teachers in the K-12 education sector has not risen at the same rate. Thus, schools rationally substitute unskilled for skilled teachers and quantity over quality.

Anticipating our discussion of collective bargaining below, theories of "efficient contracts" in the general labor economics literature may also shed light on this phenomenon. In these models, unions value both higher earnings and more jobs and bargain to an efficient contract with employers that involves more jobs but lower wages as compared to a simple monopoly model (Ashenfelter and Brown (1986)).[9]

A common feature of the above analyses is the assumption of efficient, cost-minimizing behavior on the part of public school administrators. However, public schools have considerable monopoly power in local markets, and public school administrators operate in a political environment. Jobs are a reward that school boards and superintendents can distribute to purchase votes or otherwise expand political influence, which may lead public sector employers to favor more labor intensive production. Union dues income also rises with employment.[10] A public choice approach seems fruitful, but we are unaware of studies that have developed this line of inquiry regarding school staffing ratios.[11]

---

[8] However, there are no data suggesting that the school day or school year have increased over time.

[9] Ehrenberg and Smith (1991, p. 494) note express skepticism about the general relevance of these models, but note that teacher union contracts are one of the few examples where the union bargains over both earnings and employment (i.e., maximum class size).

[10] Teacher union dues in the United States are in dollars and not a percent of salaries. Thus an increase in dues revenue that arises from increases in teacher employment is automatic, whereas an increase arising from higher salaries requires a vote of the membership to raise per capita dues. This provides an incentive for union officials to favor lower staffing ratios over higher salaries. Hoxby (1996) finds a negative effect of teacher unionization on student-teacher ratios.

[11] Moe and Chubb (2009) provide an extensive discussion of teacher union efforts to resist adoption of computer-based instruction and distance learning technologies.

4. COMPARING TEACHER AND NONTEACHER COMPENSATION

As noted above, many researchers have examined the level and trend of teacher and nonteacher earnings (e.g., Hanushek and Rivkin, 1997; Stoddard, 2003; Allegretto, et al., 2004). Static or dynamic comparisons of salaries or compensation between teachers and other professionals present challenges. The implicit assumption is that the remuneration gap, however measured, is the relevant price for an individual considering teaching versus another career. Yet the differences in some pecuniary and nonpecuniary factors between teaching and other careers are large, and may not be stable over time, from one cohort to the next, or over a work career. The most obvious comparability problem concerns the much smaller number of annual work hours in teaching as compared to other professions. Data from the Bureau of Labor Statistics finds that the work week for teachers (on site) is considerably shorter than that for other professionals (37.1 hours for public school teachers versus 40.7 for management occupations in the private sector, U.S. Department of Labor (2008, tables 4 and 6)). A much bigger difference, however, is the annual weeks of work. The typical teacher contract in the U.S. calls for roughly 185 days of work, or only 37–38 annual weeks. Virtually all other professionals (except college professors) have 52-week contracts. Even adjusting for the fact that other professionals have paid time off and summer vacations, annual work hours (on site) are much lower for teachers (Podgursky and Tongrut (2006)). Data from 2006 find that annual hours on site for teachers average 1411 versus 2116 for managers—a gap of 705 hours annually (U.S. Department of Labor (2008)). At a minimum, this yields major savings on day care for women with young children.[12] Moreover, this annual hours gap may not have been stable over the longer term either, since the mix of nonteacher professions constituting the relevant opportunity set for females has shifted over time toward more time-intensive professions such as management, medicine, and law, as compared to clerks, librarians, and retail sales occupations.[13]

Teaching will tend to attract individuals who value short and predictable hours of work on site and long summer vacations. Women with young children or who plan to have children fit that description. In fact, Census data show that teachers have more (own) children than do other college-educated women in the workforce (Podgursky (2003)). Thus, it is not surprising that teaching is a female-dominated occupation and, unlike many other professions, increasingly so. Between 1961 and 2001, the most recent national data available in this series, the female share increased from 69% to 79% (U.S. Department of Education (2007, table 69)).

---

[12] The argument is sometimes made that work at home by teachers offsets this difference. The most extensive U.S. data on household time allocation is the American Time Use Survey (ATUS). A recent ATUS study examined work time allocation for full-time teachers and other professionals. Krantz-Kent (2008) found that more teachers were likely to report work at home during a weekday than other professionals. However, combining home and on-site work, teachers worked 24 minutes per weekday less than other professionals, and 42 fewer minutes on Saturdays. On Sundays teachers and other professionals worked about the same amount of time (roughly one hour).

[13] Nor is there evidence that most teachers who leave the profession earn more in their new occupations. See Stinebrickner, Scafini, and Sjodquist (2002), Podgursky, Monroe, and Watson (2004), Goldhaber and Player (2005).

Taylor (2008) highlights another important factor often overlooked in comparisons of teacher to nonteacher pay. She conducts an analysis of annual earnings gaps between teachers and nonteacher college graduates (with a rough control for annual hours of work). Taylor notes that teachers are spread throughout the country roughly in proportion to the population (i.e., wherever there are children). This contrasts with many professions routinely compared to teaching (e.g., medicine, management, engineering, accounting, advertising), which are more heavily concentrated in urban areas. She finds that, as compared to other college-educated workers, teachers are more heavily concentrated in (low-wage) rural areas. As a consequence, estimates of teacher–nonteacher earnings gaps are biased upward if detailed controls for locale type are omitted. Taylor reports an 8% teacher–nonteacher gap if geographic controls are omitted. This falls to just 5% when geographic controls are included. Unfortunately, she includes private school teachers in her definition of "teachers." Omitting private school teachers would nearly extinguish this gap.

The discussion above focuses on comparisons of teacher and nonteacher *salaries*. However, fringe benefits account for a large and growing share of professional compensation. Any attempt to understand the effects of compensation on recruitment and retention of teachers must take account of current and deferred benefits. While anecdotal evidence suggests that the fringe benefit package for public school teachers is relatively more generous than for comparable private sector professionals, until recently reliable national data on this issue were lacking. The Bureau of Labor Statistics of the U.S. Department of Labor has for some time been collecting data on employee benefit costs as part of its employer-based National Compensation Survey.[14] However, only recently have they begun to release some of these data at a level of disaggregation that would identify public school teachers.

Table 5.1 reports employer contributions for fringe benefits as a percent of earnings for teachers and private sector management and professionals. These are quarterly data starting in March 2004, the first quarter in which BLS released them, to the most recent available, March 2009. The BLS reports these on an hourly basis. The first thing to note is that the hourly pay for managers and professionals is roughly comparable to that of teachers. The major difference in annual salaries arises from a difference in annual hours of work. The BLS reports that the on-site work hours of public K-12 teachers are only 67% those of managers (i.e., 1411 versus 2116 hours). This hours gap is the primary explanation for the earnings gap.

Our focus, however, is on fringe benefits as a percent of salary. The BLS data are aggregated into three broad groups: insurance (primarily health insurance for current employees), retirement, and legally required (primarily Social Security). Comparisons of public school teachers and private sector professionals are complicated by the fact that roughly 30% of teachers are not covered by Social Security. For these teachers,

---

[14] The NCS is an establishment survey of employee salaries, wages, and benefits. It is designed to produce reliable earnings and benefit estimates at local levels, within broad regions, and nationwide (http://www.bls.gov/ncs/methodology.htm).

Table 5.1 Salary and fringe benefits: Teachers and private-sector managerial, professional, and technical jobs

March 2004	Teachers		Mgmt & Prof.	
	$/hr	%	$/hr	%
Salary	$35.92	100.00	$33.40	100.00
Insurance	$4.08	11.36	$2.43	7.28
Retirement and legally required	$4.99	13.89	$4.34	12.99
Total benefits	$9.07	25.25	$6.77	20.27
March 2009				
	$/hr	%	$/hr	%
Salary	$39.75	100.00	$40.30	100.00
Insurance	$5.77	14.52	$3.18	7.89
Retirement and legally required	$6.89	17.33	$5.32	13.20
Total benefits	$12.66	31.85	$8.50	21.09

Source: U.S. Department of Labor. Bureau of Labor Statistics. 2009, 2004.

then, legally required contributions are lower. However, because they are not covered by Social Security their public pension plans are more generous (more on this below). For this reason we have combined legally required and employer retirement contributions. The key point is that in 2004, the fringe benefit rate for public school teachers was five percentage points higher for public school teachers, and by 2009 the gap had widened to 10%. Thus, fringe benefits as a percent of salary are larger for teachers, and this gap has not been stationary, but widening, at least since 2004.[15]

4.1 Public–private teacher compensation

In areas other than K-12, public sector personnel managers often use private pay and benefits as a benchmark in setting government pay. In public administration, it is commonplace to undertake surveys comparing government and private sector pay. Indeed, one important function of compensation data collected by the Bureau of Labor Statistics is to provide private-sector as well as state and local benchmark data for Federal

---

[15] As noted above, the OECD now routinely reports international relative salary data for teachers, typically normed by GDP per capita (e.g., OECD (2009)). The U.S. ranks low in comparison to other developed countries by these measures, although spending per student ranks high. In part this reflects the low staffing ratios in the U.S. However, it should also be kept in mind that the fringe benefits for U.S. teachers compare very favorably to private sector employees. Other developed nations have national health insurance schemes, while the U.S. does not. This makes teacher health benefits relatively attractive. As noted in the text, the retirement benefits in relation to salary on average are also much higher for teachers.

wage-setting. Since 12% of teachers are employed in private schools, one might expect private sector compensation data to play a larger role in policy discussions concerning the adequacy of public school teacher pay. The two sectors compete for teachers, and mobility between the two is extensive. Data from the 1999–2000 School and Staffing Survey (SASS), national surveys of schools and teachers undertaken at regular intervals by the U.S. Department of Education's National Center for Education Statistics (NCES), show that 36% of full-time private and 13% of full-time public school teachers report some teaching experience in the other sector (Podgursky (2003)).

This cross-sector experience is hardly surprising since there are very few occupations or professions in which employment is entirely segmented in one or the other sector. It is not uncommon for many professionals to move from public to private sector employment over a work career, or from for-profit to nonprofit firms within the private sector. However, in spite of this mobility, comparisons of pay and benefits between public and private schools play little role in education policy discussions. There are legitimate objections to gross public–private teacher pay comparisons. First, many private schools have a religious orientation and are staffed by teachers of the same religious denomination. To the extent that such schools are advancing a religious mission, they and their teachers are not comparable to public K-12 schools. Second, private schools are generally more selective in admissions than public schools and, on average, have students with higher socio-economic status. To the extent that this results in better-behaved and more academically-motivated students in private school classrooms, it makes for a more attractive teaching environment. However, when religious-oriented and special emphasis (e.g., Montessori, special education) schools are eliminated from the private school sample, and public school teachers are limited to those in suburban low poverty districts, average private school pay is still well below that of the public schools at every level of experience. Benefit levels for private school teachers are lower as well (Podgursky (2003)). In spite of the lower pay and benefits, academic measures of teacher quality as well as principal evaluations are higher in private schools (Ballou and Podgursky (1998)).

5. TEACHER PAY AND STUDENT ACHIEVEMENT

An important strand of research on teacher compensation concerns the relationship between teacher pay and student performance. Surveys of the early education production function literature found little evidence of a strong positive effect of teacher pay on student achievement. Of 118 estimates reported in the literature, 73% were statistically insignificant, 20% were positive and significant, and 7% were negative and significant (Hanushek and Rivkin (2004)). A subset of "value-added," single state studies had 17 estimates of earnings. Of these, 82% were statistically insignificant and 18% were positive and significant. Two recent econometric studies of teacher effects cast further doubt on a positive wage effect. Jacob and Lefgren (2004) find no relationship between teacher pay and teacher performance in a large urban school district, and Hanushek, Kain, O'Brien, and Rivkin (2005) report no relationship between teacher productivity and changes in teacher pay for teachers who left a Texas school district. Contrary evidence is found in Loeb and Page (2000), who examine data from multiple Census years aggregated to the state level. They estimate the effect of changes in teacher relative pay on changes in dropout rates and college attendance and find significant effects. They estimate similar difference-in-difference models for California school districts and get comparable results.[16]

Ballou and Podgursky (1997) explore evidence concerning changes in teacher salaries and teacher quality during the 1980s. This period brackets the watershed year of 1983 in which President Ronald Reagan's National Commission on Excellence in Education issued its provocative report, *A Nation at Risk*. The furor in the wake of that report set in motion many efforts at education reform, along with substantial increases in spending per student and in relative teacher pay. However, there was wide variation across states with regard to pay increases. While nearly all measures of teacher quality rose over this period, these authors find no evidence that states with above average increases in teacher pay had above average increases in teacher quality, however measured. They identify a variety of structural factors in teacher labor markets such as tenure and single salary schedules, which dampen a quality response. Ballou (1996) finds no evidence that teachers with stronger academic credentials such as in-field majors or graduation from a selective college are favored in employer hiring decisions.[17] Ballou and Podgursky (1995, 1997) show that this weak return to quality, combined with other structural rigidities in the market for public school teachers, may actually discourage candidates from entering job queues in response to across-the-board pay increases.[18] Simulations over a wide range of parameters suggests that the quality elasticity of across-the-board pay increases, given such poor screening by employers, will be very low and possibly even negative.

6. STRUCTURE OF TEACHER COMPENSATION
6.1 Institutional framework: Single salary schedule

Salary schedules for teachers are a nearly universal feature of public school districts. Pay for teachers in public school districts is largely determined by these schedules. In large school districts the pay of thousands of teachers in hundreds of schools—from

---

[16] In general, aggregated studies have tended to find more positive effects of "inputs" on student achievement outputs than disaggregated student-level panel studies. For a discussion of this point see Hanushek, Rivkin, and Taylor (1996).
[17] Ballou finds that graduates from more selective institutions (conditional on certification) file as many applications as nonselective applicants, but are no more likely to be hired. Nor does he find evidence that "choosiness" by the former in applications is the explanation. Education majors are favored over academic majors as well.
[18] If all types of teachers of all quality types enter the labor market in response to an increase in relative pay, and schools are undiscriminating in either their hiring or firing, then the probability of getting a "good" teaching job for a high quality teacher may actually fall. This can act to lower the high quality share of the applicant labor pool, and hence average teacher quality.

kindergarten up to secondary teachers in math and science—is set by a single district schedule. The nearly universal use of salary schedules in public school districts is seen in data from the 1999–00 SASS. Ninety-six percent of public school districts accounting for nearly 100% of teachers report use of a salary schedule (Podgursky (2007)).

Table 5.2 provides an example of a salary schedule, in this case for Columbus, Ohio public school teachers. The rows and columns refer to years of experience and levels of teacher education, respectively. The pay increases associated with higher levels of education may be for training not associated with a teacher's actual classroom assignments. For example, it is not uncommon for teachers to earn remuneration for graduate credits and degrees in education administration while they are still employed full time as classroom teachers.

These teacher salary schedules are sometimes referred to as "single salary schedules," a term reflecting their historical development. Kershaw and McKean (1962) note that there were three phases in the historical development of teacher pay regimes. The first phase, which lasted roughly until the beginning of the twentieth century, saw teacher pay negotiated between an individual teacher and a local school board. As school

Table 5.2 2007–08 salary schedule for Columbus, Ohio public school teachers

Years Experience	Pre-License Bachelor's Degree	Bachelor's Degree	150 Hours and Bachelor's Degree	Master's Degree	Master' Degree Plus 30 Semester Hours
0	29,313	36,779	37,844	40,788	44,220
1	30,490	38,251	39,353	42,406	43,252
2	31,703	39,795	40,935	44,098	44,981
3	32,991	41,376	42,553	45,863	46,746
4	34,278	43,031	44,282	47,702	48,622
5	35,676	44,760	46,047	49,615	50,571
6		46,525	47,886	51,601	52,594
7		48,401	49,799	53,661	54,727
8		50,350	51,785	55,794	56,897
9		52,337	53,844	58,037	59,177
10		54,433	56,014	60,354	61,531
11		56,640	58,258	62,782	63,995
12		58,883	60,575	65,283	66,570
13		61,237	63,002	67,894	69,218
14		63,701	65,540	70,616	72,013

Source: Columbus Education Association.

districts consolidated and grew in size, this type of salary determination became increasingly unpopular with teachers. With consolidation and growth, the monopoly power of school districts in the labor market increased, and charges of favoritism were common. In response to these concerns, there was gradual movement toward the use of salary schedules that differed by grade level and position. "Typically the salaries differed from grade to grade, and high school salaries would inevitably be higher than those at the elementary level." (Kershaw and McKean (1962, p. 22)).

The third and current phase began in the 1920s and accelerated in WWII and the immediate post-war period. This is characterized by what is termed the "single salary schedule"—the current norm. An education commentator writing in the 1950s noted that "the distinguishing characteristic of the single salary schedule is that the salary class to which the classroom teacher is assigned depends on the professional qualifications of the teacher rather than the school level or assignment." Kershaw and McKean write, "The single salary schedule was regarded as bringing a feeling of contentment and *professionalism*. A teacher would no longer be an *elementary* teacher, but a *teacher*, a member on equal footing of the profession that included all teachers." By 1951, 98% of urban school districts employed the single salary schedule (Kershaw and McKean (1962, pp. 23, 25); see also Lieberman (1956, pp. 391–393)).

Since elementary school teachers were nearly all women whereas high school teachers were largely male, early struggles for a single salary schedule were seen by some commentators as an important part of feminist struggles for pay equity (Murphy (1990)). Eventually, the unification of schedules for elementary and secondary school teachers was embraced by the National Education Association as well as the American Federation of Teachers and embedded in collective bargaining agreements and, in some cases, state legislation.

These salary schedules for teachers contrast with the situation in most other professions. In medicine, pay of doctors and nurses varies by specialty. Even within the same hospital or HMO, pay will differ by specialty field. In higher education there are large differences in pay between faculty by teaching fields. Faculty pay structures in most higher education institutions are flexible. Starting pay is usually market-driven, and institutions will often match counter-offers for more senior faculty whom they wish to retain. Merit or performance-based pay is commonplace. Ballou and Podgursky (1997) and Ballou (2001) report generally similar findings for private K-12 education. Even when private schools report that they use a salary schedule for teacher pay, payments "off schedule" seem commonplace.[19]

---

[19] These salary schedules remain the primary determinant of U.S. teacher pay. As we will note below, some districts have begun to experiment with performance or market-based adjustments. This has been encouraged by several federal initiatives discussed below. Ballou (2001) finds that even when public schools report the use of performance bonuses, their effect on pay for recipients is very small. This is also seen in direct examination of performance pay plans actually enacted by districts (Podgursky and Springer (2007)).

Rigid salary schedules might have some efficiency rationale if the factors rewarded, teacher experience and graduate education, were strong predictors of teacher productivity. However, surveys of the education production literature find no support for a positive effect of teacher graduate degrees. Hanushek (2003) reports that, of 41 "value-added" estimates of the effect of education levels on teacher effectiveness (primarily Master's degrees), not a single study found a statistically significant positive effect. In fact, 10 of the studies found negative effects. Furthermore, teacher experience has little effect beyond the first few years (Hanushek and Rivkin (2004)).

If wages are not allowed to clear the labor market, then the market will clear in other ways ("You can't repeal the law of supply and demand.") We now consider some consequences of teacher salary schedules. First, the single salary schedule suppresses pay differentials by field. All teachers in a district with the same experience or education level earn the same base pay. Thus, a 2nd grade teacher will earn the same pay as a high school chemistry teacher. Given the major differences in human capital investments by teaching field (e.g., elementary education versus secondary physical science) it is almost certainly the case that nonteaching opportunity earnings differ greatly as well.

National data on teacher recruiting in Table 5.3 bear this out. These data are from the 1999–00 and 2003–04 SASS. These are assessments of market conditions by administrators who have recently recruited teachers in these fields. Respondents were asked to rate how difficult or easy it was to fill a vacancy in the field. In 2003–04, 75% of school administrators reported that it was "easy" to fill vacancies in elementary education, with fewer than 4% reporting it "very difficult" or that they could not fill the position. The situation changes dramatically when we turn to math, science, and special education, where a large share of districts reported it was "very difficult" or they were unable to fill a vacancy. Data in Table 5.4 show that this pattern also prevailed even in high poverty schools. While low poverty schools reported greater ease in recruiting, nonetheless 63% of high poverty schools reported it easy to fill vacancies in elementary education.[20]

In a market with flexible wages, earnings of elementary teachers would fall relative to science, math, and special education teachers. However, district salary schedules do not permit this relative wage adjustment to occur. Thus, the market "clears" in terms of quality rather than price. Numerous reports have documented the extent of "teaching out of field," or teachers practicing with substandard licenses in the fields of science, math, and special education, while over 95% of elementary school teachers are fully licensed in elementary education (U.S. Department of Education (2004b)).

---

[20] Further evidence on this point may be found in Goldhaber and Player (2005), who analyze the nonteaching earnings of former teachers by broad teaching field. Elementary school teachers on average earned less than secondary school teachers, and among former secondary teachers, those who taught in technical fields earned more than those in nontechnical fields.

Table 5.3 Recruitment difficulties by teaching field
How easy was it to fill the vacancy?

1999–00	Easy	Somewhat difficult	Very difficult	Could not fill
Elementary	67.6%	26.2%	5.5%	.7%
Social studies	70.0	24.7	4.7	.6
ELA	56.5	33.2	9.5	.8
Math	29.0	34.8	33.3	2.8
Biological science	34.0	38.5	26.2	1.3
Phys. science	31.7	35.7	30.2	2.4
Spec. ed.	25.5	35.8	32.8	5.8
2003–04				
Elementary	75.1	21.1	3.3	.5
Social studies	71.5	24.4	3.6	.4
ELA	59.0	32.9	7.1	1.1
Math	33.3	37.8	25.5	3.4
Biological science	34.9	44.2	19.0	1.9
Phys. science	34.6	37.7	25.3	2.4
Spec. ed.	29.1	41.8	25.7	3.5

Source: Schools and Staffing Surveys, various years.

Table 5.4 Recruitment difficulties by teaching field in high- and low-poverty schools

2003–04	Easy	Somewhat difficult	Very difficult	Could not fill
Elementary				
Low poverty (bottom 25%)	85.4%	13.0%	1.4%	.2%
High poverty (top 25%)	62.7	29.0	6.9	1.4
Math				
Low poverty (bottom 25%)	37.4	40.1	21.6	1.4
High poverty (top 25%)	31.1	29.4	32.5	7.1

Source: 2003–04 Schools and Staffing Surveys.

Policy makers and researchers tend to treat K-12 teachers as a single occupation. From a labor market perspective, this is probably not a very useful aggregation. The training, working conditions, and nonteaching opportunities of a 2nd grade teacher are very different from those of a high school chemistry teacher. Yet, for purposes of policy and in many research studies they are grouped into a single occupation: teachers. This is abetted in part by the collective bargaining process, which puts all teachers in a school district, regardless of the level of school or teaching field, into a single "bargaining unit." However, single salary schedules are the norm even in nonbargaining states.

A second problem with the single salary schedule is that it suppresses differentials by schools within districts. In larger urban districts dozens or even hundreds of schools are covered by the same salary schedule. The working environments for teachers often vary greatly between these schools. Some may even be dangerous places to work, whereas other schools are more pleasant and attractive worksites. Often teachers in the less desirable schools will be able to use their seniority to transfer to a more pleasant school, or they may simply quit at a higher rate. In either case, the result is that students in high poverty schools will on average have less experienced (and less educated) teachers. Because the salary schedule assigns lower pay to teachers with less experience within a school district, an unintended consequence of a district-wide salary schedule is lower spending per student in high-poverty schools (Roza and Hill, 2004; Roza, et al. (2007); Iaterola and Stiefel (2003)). High poverty schools will also have relatively more novice or inexperienced teachers. One fairly consistent finding in the "teacher effects" literature is that students taught by novice or inexperienced teachers have lower achievement gains than students with more experienced teachers (e.g., Hanushek, Kain, O'Brien, and Rivkin (2005); Aaronson, Barrow, and Sander (2007); Boyd, et al. (2006)). Lankford, Loeb, and Wyckoff (2002) examine the allocation of teachers in New York City and find that children in high poverty schools are more likely to be exposed to novice teachers. Again, this is an intra-NYC allocation problem—one that is clearly exacerbated by a uniform salary schedule across all schools. Podgursky (2009) examines an administrative data set with the universe of public elementary schools in Missouri. He finds that children in high poverty schools are more likely to be exposed to novice teachers, but this is entirely due to the intra-district allocation of teachers. To return to our market-clearing thesis, if the attractiveness of working conditions varies among schools within a district, then equalizing teacher pay disequalizes teacher quality. In order to equalize teacher quality, one needs to disequalize teacher pay.

A final consequence of single salary schedules is the equalization of pay regardless of teacher effectiveness. A consistent finding in the teacher value-added literature is that there is a very large variation in teacher effectiveness (e.g., Rivkin, Hanushek, and Kain (2005); Aaronson, Barrow, and Sander (2007)). Even within the same school building, some 4th grade teachers are much more effective at raising student achievement than other 4th grade teachers. Some teachers are harder working and elicit greater effort from students than others. Some teachers may be "burnt out" and simply putting in time until retirement (more on pension system incentives below). The single salary schedule suppresses differences between more effective and less effective teachers (however defined). Rewarding more effective teachers on the basis of performance would have two important consequences. The first is a motivation effect. Incumbent teachers would have an incentive to work harder to raise whatever performance measure is rewarded. In addition, over the longer term, performance pay would have a selection effect. It would draw teachers into the workforce who are relatively more effective at meeting the performance targets and would help retain such teachers as well (Podgursky and Springer (2007)). Equalizing teacher pay among teachers of different effectiveness lowers the overall quality and performance of the teaching workforce.

6.2 Confounding factors: Tenure and size of wage-setting units

The costs associated with teacher salary schedules are exacerbated by two other features of K-12 human resource policy: tenure and the size of wage-setting units (i.e., districts). Consider first the effect of teacher tenure. Even if experience *per se* does not raise a teacher's effectiveness, in principle a seniority-based wage structure might be efficient if less effective teachers are weeded out over time through contract nonrenewal. However, personnel policies in traditional public schools are not likely to produce such an effect. Teachers in traditional public school districts receive automatic contract renewal (tenure) after two to five years on the job. After receiving tenure, it is very difficult to dismiss a teacher for poor job performance, a finding that has been widely documented (Bridges (1992); Hess and West (2006)). Thus, the presence of teacher tenure laws and collective bargaining language, which further hampers dismissal of low-performing teachers, makes the economic costs associated with single salary schedules even greater.

Another factor that increases the cost of rigid district salary schedules is the size of wage-setting units. Other things equal, the larger the size of the unit, the greater the economic cost of rigid salary schedules. The wage-setting unit in private and charter schools is typically the school, whereas in traditional public schools wage-setting is at the district level. In fact, most personnel policy concerning teachers—the level and structure of teacher pay, benefits, and recruiting—is centralized at the district level in traditional public schools. This policy has two effects. First, it makes the market for teachers less flexible and less competitive. Rather than 10 "districts" each setting pay for 10 schools, a single employer sets pay for 100 schools. At least the 10 smaller districts could compete with one another and adjust their schedules to meet their own internal circumstances. A second consequence of large wage setting units is that the wage-setting process becomes more bureaucratic and less amenable to merit or market adjustments (Podgursky (2007)). Figure 5.2 illustrates the dramatic differences in the size of the wage and personnel units in traditional public and private schools. There are approximately 15,000 public school districts in the U.S. However, the size distribution of these districts in terms of teacher employment is very highly skewed. As a consequence, most teachers are employed in large school districts. One quarter of teachers in traditional public schools are employed in districts with at least 2100 full-time equivalent (FTE) teachers, and half of traditional public school teachers are in districts with at least 561 FTE teachers. Thus, the typical teacher finds herself in a large organization with standardized, bureaucratic wage-setting.

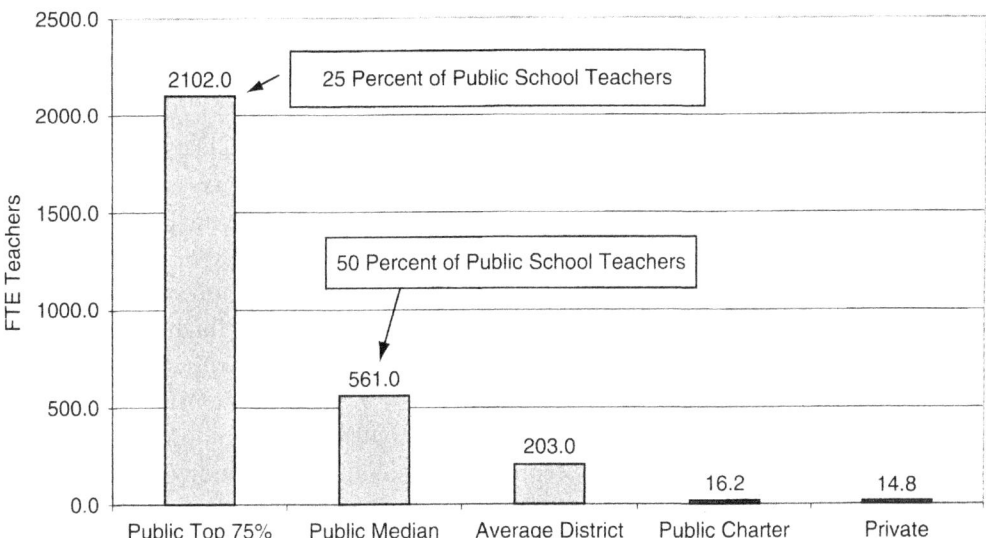

Figure 5.2 Size of wage-setting units in traditional public, charter, and private schools. *Source:* Podgursky (2007).

By contrast, the average charter school—an independent employer—employs just 16 FTE teachers, barely larger than the average private school (15 FTEs).

In principle, public school districts need not be so bureaucratic. They could adopt more decentralized systems of personnel policy, give school principals more control over teacher recruitment and pay, and adopt more of a team model. The fact that one observes wage-setting in private schools, including Catholic dioceses, following a more decentralized model suggests that there are few efficiency gains to be had from centralization of compensation. However, this highlights an important difference between traditional public and charter or private schools. The percent of teachers covered by collective bargaining agreements in charter schools is far lower than in traditional public schools; for private schools, it is virtually nil. Tabulations from the 1999–00 Schools and Staffing Surveys find that 70% of public school districts, employing 73% of teachers, have collective bargaining agreements covering their teachers. This contrasts with just 14% of charter schools (employing 18% of charter school teachers).[21] The absence of a binding collective bargaining agreement is an important source of personnel flexibility in private and charter schools. Teacher unions in general have been opposed to more flexible market or performance-based pay systems, although there are exceptions such as the widely-publicized

---

[21] The Schools and Staffing Surveys does not ask a collective bargaining question of private schools. However, we are aware of no private schools organized by the major teaching unions. Some Catholic dioceses negotiate agreements with Catholic teacher associations. However, these agreements are far less restrictive than anything negotiated in public schools, and Catholic school teachers do not have tenure.

Denver performance play plan. However, even in Denver, the plan is district-wide and not school-based (Podgursky and Springer (2007)). Collective bargaining laws, by defining the district as the "appropriate bargaining unit," have tended to push personnel policy and wage-setting to the district level and lock them there.

These types of salary schedules seem to be the norm in most OECD countries. However, some differences are apparent. It is not uncommon for secondary teachers to be on separate and higher salary schedules than primary teachers (Sclafani and Tucker (2006)). Another interesting effect arises as a consequence of the importance of rigorous high-stakes exams for college and high school placement. Some Asian countries have seen the development of a private, after-school market in test preparation. The most widely discussed is Japan, which has a private system of "juku" schools. Hagwon schools in South Korea are a similar phenomenon. While we are unaware of any systematic data on this, anecdotal evidence suggests that these schools are heavily staffed by moonlighting public school teachers. We do know that parents spend a good deal of money on them. Thus, while the public system has wages set bureaucratically, the private test-prep market is competitive and will likely tend to reward the most effective teachers in the key tested areas. Public school teachers and college students, contemplating their teaching and nonteaching options, will presumably take account of potential remuneration in these after-school markets as part of their teaching compensation package.[22]

6.3 Deferred compensation: Teacher pension incentives

Pensions have long been an important part of compensation for teachers in public schools. Traditionally, it has been argued, salaries have been relatively low, while pension benefits have been relatively high for teachers and others who spend their career in public service. This mix of current versus deferred income was rationalized by the contention that the public good was best served by the longevity of service that would be induced by these pension plans.[23] In recent decades, however, evidence has grown that many of these plans, both in the private and public sector, may actually have *shortened* rather than lengthened professional careers by encouraging early retirements.[24]

---

[22] The U.S. as well has a growing private and test preparation market, with national franchises such as Sylvan Learning Centers, Princeton Review, Kaplan, and Kumon, along with independent local firms. Unfortunately, the U.S. Department of Education does not collect data on these firms or their staff. Anecdotal evidence suggests that these firms do hire moonlighting and retired teachers as well as regular full-time staff.

[23] National Education Association (1995, p. 3). As this report points out, however, this purpose has "been lost for many in the mists of time," and "many pension administrators would be hard-pressed to give an account of why their systems are structured as is except to say that 'the Legislature did it' or 'It is a result of bargaining.'"

[24] Kotlikoff and Wise (1987) showed the incentives for early retirement in private defined benefit pension plans and argued that their spread in the post-war period contributed to declining labor force participation of older workers up to that time. More recently, Friedberg and Webb (2005) showed that the private sector shift toward defined contribution plans contributed to the rise of retirement ages since the 1980s. With regard to teachers, Harris and Adams (2007) find considerably higher rates of labor force exit at ages 56–64 than in comparable professions, as well as evidence that this is due to their pension coverage.

The cost side of teacher retirement benefits affects labor markets by driving a wedge between the amount paid by employers and the take-home pay received by teachers. In Ohio, for example, the combined contributions of teachers and school districts for retirement benefits have risen steadily from 10% in 1945 to 24% today. But even this large wedge falls well short of what is needed, and pension officials are recommending a phased increase to 29% to shore up funding for pensions and retiree health benefits. At this level, retiree benefits for teachers and other professionals would be consuming well over $1000 of the annual per student expenditures (Costrell and Podgursky (2007)). The costs of school retiree benefits (including "legacy" costs from unfunded benefits for previous retirees) consume a growing share of K-12 spending. Figure 5.3 reports employer costs for retirement and Social Security for teachers and private sector managers and professionals based on BLS benefit data discussed earlier. The gap in retirement benefit costs as a percent of salaries widened from 1.9% to 5.1% of earnings between 2004 and 2009. However, this understates the actual gap since the BLS data

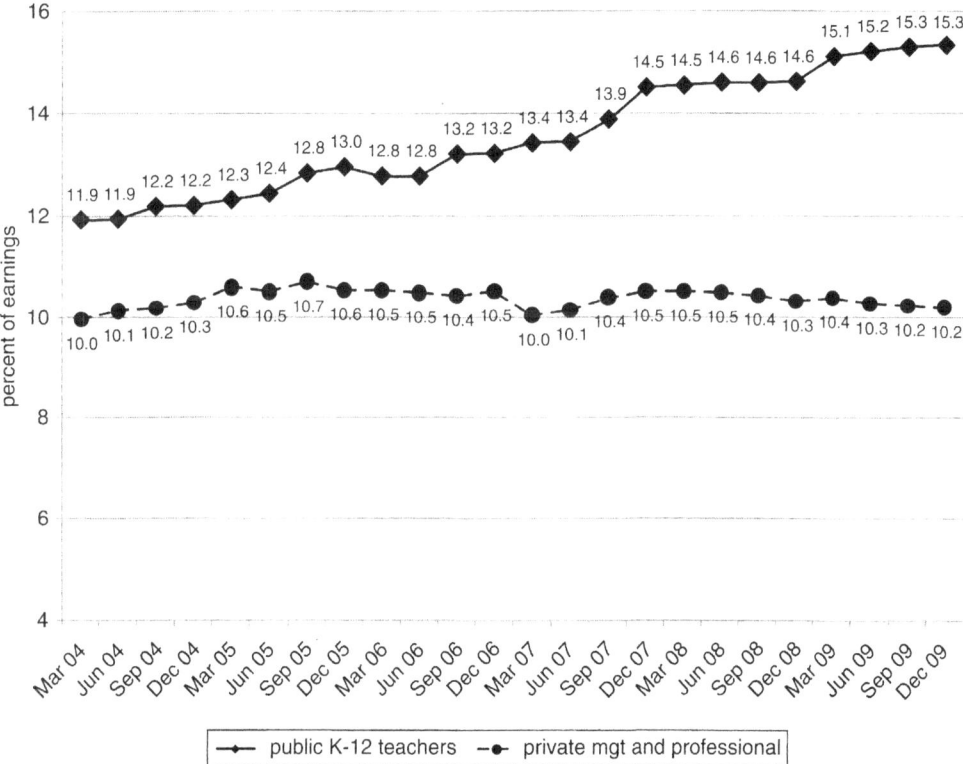

Figure 5.3 Employer contribution to public teacher and private professional retirement and Social Security as a percent of salary. *Source:* Costrell and Podgursky (2009c), updated.

do not include employer contributions for retiree health insurance, which are substantial in some states and districts, but have all but disappeared in the private sector.[25]

An important research question is the effect of these retirement benefits systems on the teaching workforce. Costrell and Podgursky (2009a) show that the pattern of pension wealth accrual in teacher defined benefit (DB) systems creates strong incentives to pull teachers to a given age and then push them out of the workforce afterward, with the push encouraging teachers to retire at relatively early ages by economy-wide standards. Figure 5.4 illustrates this point for a hypothetical female teacher who enters the profession at age 25 and teaches continuously in California.[26] The employer contribution rate is 12.77%, yet for most of a teacher's career, her annual accrual of pension wealth is below that. However, in certain years, the accrual of pension wealth has very sharp spikes. These are usually associated with earlier eligibility for regular benefits. For example, in the case of California, during her first 29 years on the job (up to age 54), on separation she would be unable to collect her pension until age 57. However, upon completion of her 30th year on the job (age 55) she can begin collecting the pension immediately. Thus, the spike in

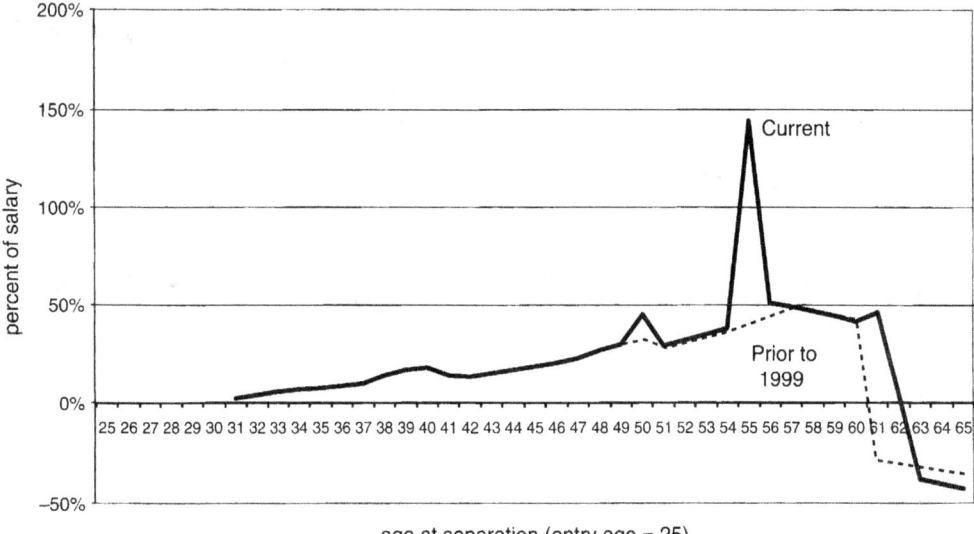

Figure 5.4 Deferred income per year as a percent of salary: California public school teachers (addition to pension wealth from an additional year of teaching)Age at separation (entry age = 25). *Source:* Costrell and Podgursky (2009a).

---

[25] Clark (2009). Since retiree health insurance is largely funded pay-as-you-go by districts and states, the BLS does not treat it as a benefit for *current* active teachers.

[26] The teacher's earnings rise along a typical California salary schedule (Sacramento). For other details, see Costrell and Podgursky (2009b).

pension wealth largely reflects the discounted value of two additional years of pension annuities. There is nothing unique about California. Costrell and Podgursky (2009b) show that these spikes exist in other teacher DB plans.

These pension systems also impose very large costs on mobile teachers. Costrell and Podgursky (2009a) consider the mobility costs of teacher pension systems in six state teacher pension systems. They show that teachers who work a full career in teaching but who transfer between systems ("movers") suffer huge losses of pension wealth as compared to "stayers." In their simulations, teachers who split a 30-year career evenly between two otherwise identical pension systems typically lose one half or more of their pension wealth as compared to an otherwise identical 30-year stayer.

It is difficult to discern an efficiency rationale for these spikes in pension wealth accrual. The fairly massive backloading of benefits might be justified if there were evidence of large returns to experience and important job specific human capital investments. However, the majority of value-added econometric studies of teacher effectiveness find that novice teachers (e.g., teachers with less than three years of experience) on average are less effective than more senior teachers, but thereafter the returns to experience level off quickly. There is little evidence that a teacher with 20 years experience is any more effective in the classroom than a teacher with 10 years experience. Ironically, the current pension system, by pushing many teachers into retirement at relatively young ages, actually raises the steady-state share of novice teachers in the workforce and thus lowers overall teacher effectiveness.

Do these pension incentives and penalties affect teacher behavior? A substantial literature in labor economics demonstrates that the incentives in pension systems matter, not only for the timing of retirement, but for labor turnover and workforce quality (Friedberg and Webb (2005); Asch, Haider, and Zissimopoulos (2005); Ippolito (1997); Stock and Wise (1990)). Unfortunately, little of this literature pertains to teachers. While there have been many studies of the effect of current compensation on teacher turnover (e.g., Murnane and Olsen (1990); Stinebrickner (2001); Hanushek, Kain, and Rivkin (2004); Podgursky, Monroe, and Watson (2004)), the econometric literature on teacher pensions is slender but expanding. Several papers find that the structure of teacher pension wealth accrual affects the timing of teacher retirement behavior (Furgeson, et al. (2006), Brown (2009); Costrell and McGee (2009)). Costrell and McGee (2009) use their model to explore what effect a smoother pension wealth accrual system (such as a defined contribution or cash balance plan) would have on teacher retirement. They find that smoother accrual would delay teacher retirement.

7. TRENDS IN MARKET-BASED PAY

Given the efficiency costs of rigid salary schedules described above and growing pressure on schools to raise performance, it is not surprising that interest in market and performance-based pay is growing. Several states and districts have implemented incentives to encourage experienced educators to teach in low-performing schools (Prince (2002)). Florida, Minnesota, and Texas have implemented state programs to encourage schools and districts to implement performance based pay systems for teachers. Congress has also provided an impetus through its Teacher Incentive Fund (TIF), a two-year, $200 million program to encourage states to set up pilot programs of teacher performance incentives (Podgursky and Springer (2007)). The administration has proposed another $200 million expansion in TIF in its current budget. Perhaps more importantly, implementation of performance pay is encouraged in "Race to the Top" state applications, wherein states compete for $4 billion in total awards for broad-based school reform initiatives (U.S. Department of Education (2010)).

The website of the National Center for Performance Incentives at Vanderbilt University tracks programs by state. Unfortunately, we do not have much "microeconomic" data on the actual implementation of these programs in schools, and state data systems generally do not capture these program details. Even states that have good data on teacher salaries and their components generally cannot break out teacher performance or incentive bonuses.

The best data currently available on national levels and trends is to be found in various waves of the Schools and Staffing Surveys (SASS). SASS is a large nationally representative sample of roughly 8000 public schools and 43,000 public school teachers.[27] There have been five waves of SASS, associated with five school years: 1987–88, 1990–91, 1994–95, 1999–00, and 2003–04. While SASS covers two decades of public school experience and has included various questions about performance and market-based pay, unfortunately, many of these survey questions have not been comparable over time. Thus, we focus attention on data in the most recent waves of the survey, which contain consistent items.

District administrators were asked whether they provided pay bonuses or other rewards for certain teacher characteristics or behaviors.[28] These are listed in the top rows of Table 5.5. The most common bonus is for professional development. In 2003–04, 36% of teachers were offered such a bonus. The next most common bonus among districts is NBPTS certification. In 2003–04, 18% of districts, accounting for 40% of teachers, offered some sort of bonus for NBPTS certification. This is also the most rapidly growing bonus, with the number of districts offering it growing by 10 percentage points between the 1999–00 and 2003–04 surveys.

Eight percent of districts, accounting for 14% of teachers, reported rewards for excellence in teaching. In 2003–04, 5% of districts (13% of teachers) had bonuses for

---

[27] SASS includes private schools and teachers as well. However, the focus of this study is on trends in public schools.
[28] "Does the district currently use any pay incentives such as a cash bonuses, salary increase, or different steps on a salary schedule to reward...?"

Table 5.5 Incidence of performance-based teacher compensation

District rewards following:	Teacher weighted (%)		
	1999–00	2003–04	change
NBPTS	22.9	39.8	17.0
Excellence in teaching	13.6	14.0	0.3
In-service professional development	38.8	35.9	−3.0
Teach in less desirable location	11.2	13.1	1.9
Teach in fields of shortage	23.6	25.3	1.7
Number of incentives			
None	39.2	31.1	−8.0
1 incentive	33.1	35.5	2.5
2 incentives	16.0	21.0	5.0
3 incentives	5.9	10.2	4.2
4 incentives	2.0	4.5	2.5
5 incentives	3.9	0.7	−3.2
Based on student achievement, were any schools in the district rewarded in any of the following ways?			
Cash bonus/addl. resources for school-wide activity	—	19.6	—
Cash bonus/addl. resources for teachers	—	15.4	—
Schools given nonmonetary forms of recognition	—	30.4	—

Source: Schools and Staffing Surveys, various years.

teaching in a less desirable location, and 12% of districts (25% of teachers) reported bonuses of some sort for teaching in shortage fields.[29] Table 5.5 also reports the number of incentives provided. Fifty five percent of districts (31% of teachers) provided no incentive rewards. This share has dropped between the 1999–00 and 2003–04 surveys. Two-thirds of teachers are employed in districts that provide one or more such incentives, and 15% of teachers are in districts providing three or more such incentives.

The first block of questions in Table 5.5 focuses on individual teacher bonuses. The next block of questions at the bottom of the table concerns school-wide bonuses. Some states and districts have begun to provide school-wide incentives for staff. Unfortunately,

---

[29] Interestingly, the rank order of district implementation of these incentives is nearly the opposite of teacher preferences, as reported in a recent study of Washington teachers by Goldhaber, DeArmond, DeBurgomaster (2007). Bonuses for teaching in a less desirable location were the most favored incentive (63%), followed by NBPTS (20%), shortage fields (12%), and performance pay (6%).

these questions were only asked in the 2003–04 survey. Of most interest for our purposes is the question concerning cash payments to teachers. Five percent of districts (15% of teachers) report cash bonuses or additional resources based on student achievement.

While all of the SASS surveys had questions on market and performance-based pay, few of the questions were consistently asked from one administration of the survey to the next. One block of questions that was nearly identical over the years concerned recruitment bonuses by field. This question asked district administrators whether they offered additional rewards in shortage fields, and in which teaching fields they are used. The results are presented in Table 5.6.

First, it is worth noting the sharp increase over the 16-year interval in the incidence of field-based incentives. In the first administration of SASS during the 1987–88 school

Table 5.6 Recruitment incentives by teaching field*
Reward to recruit/retain teachers in fields of shortage

	1987–88	1990–91	1993–94	1999–00	2003–04	change 1987–88 to 03–04
District provides incentive	11.3%	16.6%	18.7%	23.6%	25.3%	14.0%
Elementary	—	—	—	2.4	2.6	—
Special ed	6.7	11.8	13.4	14.3	20.6	13.9
English/language arts	—	—	—	5.3	4.2	—
Social studies	—	—	—	1.6	2.4	
Computer sci	1.4	2.9	1.3	3.4	3.4	2.0
Mathematics	5.2	5.8	3.9	8.9	15.7	10.5
Physical sciences	3.6	5.0	3.9	8.4	13.4	9.8
Biological sci	3.8	4.3	3.7	8.4	12.8	8.9
English as second lang.	3.3	7.6	8.1	11.1	15.5	12.2
Foreign lang.	2.4	3.1	2.4	5.3	9.4	7.0
Music or art	—	—	—	4.9	6.4	—
Vocational or technical educ.	—	4.7	3.2	8.0	7.3	—
Other fields	4.2	4.2	1.6	—	—	—

*"Does this district currently use any pay incentives to recruit or retain teachers to teach in fields of shortage?" Source: Schools and Staffing Surveys, various years. School District surveys.

year, only 7.5% of districts (11.3% of teachers) provided such incentives.[30] That share climbed to 12% of districts employing 25% of teachers by the 2003–04 school year. Consistent with the recruitment difficulty responses seen in Table 3, these recruitment incentives are most commonly used in the areas of special education, math, science, and English as a second language.

While similar quantitative survey data are lacking, available evidence suggests that government experiments in performance pay are growing in other developed nations as well (Sclafani and Tucker (2006); Springer and Balch (2009)).

8. TEACHER COLLECTIVE BARGAINING

Public school teachers, like state and local employees, are not generally covered by the National Labor Relations Act (NLRA), the legislation that regulates private sector collective bargaining in the United States. States have the option of permitting bargaining or not and setting the regulatory framework within which it occurs. In general, teacher collective bargaining largely followed the trend of public employee bargaining. In 1962 Wisconsin passed the first NLRA-type bargaining law for public employees (including teachers). Within the next five years, New York and Michigan passed similar laws. By 1974, 37 states had such bargaining laws. In 1974 roughly 22% of public school teachers were covered by collective bargaining agreements. That grew from over 60% by the mid-80s to 67% currently (Farber (2006)).

The institutional landscape changed dramatically as well. Prior to 1960, the National Education Association (NEA) was a professional association dominated by school administrators. Its ranks also included higher education faculty and administrators. It opposed collective bargaining and did not consider itself part of the labor movement (it was not then and has never been affiliated with the AFL-CIO). The American Federation of Teachers (AFT), the other major teacher organization, had a trade-union ideology, was part of the AFL-CIO, and actively sought to advance teacher collective bargaining. The base of strength for the AFT was (and is) in large urban school districts. However, as the AFT rode a wave of labor militancy and strikes during the 1960s to organize more and more schools, the NEA gradually shed its opposition to collective bargaining, as well as its school administrator membership, and effectively began competing with the AFT as a union. Along with teachers, both the NEA and AFT have thousands of K-12 school support personnel in their membership as well.[31]

---

[30] Note that these recruitment incentives can take the form of cash bonuses, higher pay, or higher initial placement on the salary schedule. The latter is more subtle, and thus less controversial, than explicit bonuses or differentiated pay structures.

[31] The NEA membership is over 2.7 million while the AFT has roughly 1.3 million members. Note that these membership figures include retired members, as well as education support personnel. Both unions have higher education members as well. (Kahlenberg (2006)).

Especially in larger school districts, both of these unions negotiate long and complex agreements that specify in detail not only what teachers will be paid, but also how staffing assignments will be made, the length of the work day and year, duty-free lunches, minutes of meetings or professional development time, how vacancies will be filled, maximum class sizes, and many other details about resource allocation in schools.[32] Furthermore, the due process procedures in the contract, combined with state statutes on teacher tenure, often make it very difficult to dismiss poor-performing teachers. Simple observation thus leads many observers to expect teacher collective bargaining to raise school costs and lower school productivity.

On the other hand, some observers note that many school managers are highly inefficient even in the absence of unions. Teacher unions, it is argued, can bring professionalism to a work environment in which it is often lacking. By providing greater worker "voice," unions may improve teacher productivity (Freeman and Medoff (1984)). Which of these effects dominates is an empirical point.

The episodic and clustered nature of the unionization process poses challenges for assessing its effect on teacher wages and school performance. In the interest of brevity, we will use the term "union teacher" to refer to a teacher whose terms of employment are determined by a union negotiated contract, and a "nonunion teacher," one who is not. Currently, nonunion teachers are primarily located in states that have not passed collective bargaining laws. The growth of teacher unionization in the U.S. was not smooth and incremental. Rather, it was characterized by episodic jumps in membership associated with state passage of such laws. The structure has stabilized now such that nonbargaining states are primarily located in the south.

Several papers have estimated cross-section models of teacher union effects on pay and student achievement (Baugh and Stone (1982); Eberts and Stone (1984)). Broadly, these studies find that unionization is associated with higher spending per student and teacher pay, and very modest increases in student achievement. However, it is difficult to have much confidence that these cross-section estimates identify causal effects of unions. There are two sources of cross-section variation in the union "treatment": within and between state variation. In both cases, it is very likely that there are omitted variables associated with teacher unionism and the outcome variables of interest (i.e., spending and student achievement). First, nonunion districts within a bargaining state have some characteristic (unmeasured) that has kept them nonunion—good labor management relations is one obvious candidate. These management skills can readily spill over to teacher quality and student achievement. Moreover, management may act in ways to preempt unionization, perhaps by raising pay. In the labor economics literature this is called a "threat effect" (Rosen (1969)).

---

[32] The collective bargaining agreement in the LA Unified school district (with appendices and supplements) is 348 single-spaced pages. The website of the National Center on Teacher Quality maintains a searchable database of the collective bargaining for 100 of the largest school districts in the U.S.: www.nctq.org. Goldhaber (2006) and Eberts (2007) are recent literatures reviews on the effect of teacher unions and school performance.

Cross-state variation in unionization is also a problem. Most of the cross-section variation in teacher unionization arises from differences in the legislative environment across states. Some states, like Texas, make collective bargaining illegal; others, like Ohio, mandate it. Thus, a cross-section achievement on unionization regression essentially becomes a regression on regions; students in southern states on average have lower achievement and their teachers are less likely to be unionized.

A more ambitious approach to estimating teacher union effects that attempts to address the problems of endogenieity and omitted variables is Hoxby (1996), who examines the effect of teacher collective bargaining on spending, school inputs, and school performance. Hoxby builds a large panel data set of school districts including teacher unionization information from 1972, '82, and '92 Census of Governments along with district data from several other sources. She addresses the endogeniety problem in two ways. First, she estimates difference-in-difference models on the input, spending, and performance variables. Second, she uses an IV for the change in unionism, using the passage of state collective bargaining laws as her instrument. She finds that unionism does, in fact, increase spending per student. Her estimated effect is 9.5%. Most of this increase goes to teacher salaries and a reduction in the student-teacher ratio. However, she also finds that collective bargaining reduces the productivity of these school inputs. The net effect is to lower school performance (as measured by dropout rates). She finds that the effects of teacher unions in raising inputs and lowering performance are more potent in metropolitan markets that are more competitive (with more school districts) than those that are more concentrated, which suggests that consumer residential choice can act as a check on union power.

Unquestionably, Hoxby (1996) has been the most widely cited study on teacher union effects. However, a recent study by Lovenheim (2009) argues that classification error in the measure of collective bargaining may be responsible for Hoxby's findings. Rather than using unionization measures from the Census of Governments, Lovenheim uses "hand collected" union election data from three mid-western states (Indiana, Iowa, Minnesota—chosen because they passed strong teacher collective bargaining laws in the 1970s). His data suggest that there are significant classification errors as compared to Census of Governments data for these three states. Given data on the timing of unionization by districts, he conducts an event history analysis, comparing the pre- and post-trends in the unionized districts. Unlike Hoxby, he finds little evidence that unions raise teacher pay or otherwise increase school spending. He finds no evidence that the teacher unions in his sample lower school productivity. He finds some weak results suggesting a positive union effect on the efficacy of student–teacher ratios.[33] On the whole, he finds little teacher union effect on outcomes or resource use.

---

[33] A conventional errors-in-variables model would suggest that the Hoxby estimates were biased toward zero. In an appendix to the paper, Lovenheim develops an extension of the classical model with a discrete regressor, drawing on work by Bound, Brown, Brown, and Mathiowetz (2001). He tests and rejects the hypothesis that the classification error is "nondifferential," the discrete analog of classical measurement error.

While the U.S. literature on teacher unions and school performance is slender, we could find almost no literature on this topic for other developed or developing countries. Kingdon and Teal (2008) estimate the effect of teacher union membership on pay and student performance in a sample of secondary schools in India. While the study is cross-section, they make use of the fact that the same student takes multiple tests and estimate a student fixed effect model. By construction, this model identifies a union–nonunion differential by teacher within the same school. They find a positive student effect in three of five subjects. (Whether this results from the fact that better teachers join unions or union membership raises teacher effectiveness cannot be ascertained.) This paper addresses a different issue from the question in the U.S. literature, which focuses on a school-wide union effect.

Some recent studies have examined the effect of teacher unions on the structure of earnings. Ballou and Podgursky (2001) examine the effect of teacher unions on the structure of teacher pay schedules. They find that pay schedules in unionized districts tend to be more backloaded (i.e., higher ratio of peak to starting pay) and more compressed (fewer years to hit peak). They also find evidence that backloading is higher in districts with an older teaching workforce whether or not the workforce is unionized (see also Babcock and Engberg, 1999). Goldhaber, et al. (2005) examine the effect of teacher unions on district use of various types of performance pay in several waves of the Schools and Staffing Surveys. They distinguish two competing hypotheses about performance pay and teaching. A "nature of teaching" thesis, most closely associated with Murnane and Cohen (1986), holds that performance pay is unsuited to K-12 teaching, whereas a "political cost" thesis, associated with Ballou (2001), holds that there is nothing inherent in teaching that precludes performance pay. The primary impediment is political opposition—largely from teacher unions. The Goldhaber, et al. evidence favors the "political cost" thesis.[34]

Koski and Horng (2007) is a cross-section study of the effect of union contract language on hiring and transfer on the concentration of low experience or poorly credentialed teachers in high poverty schools. They estimate their model on a sample of schools from California school districts from which they obtained contracts. The hypothesis tested is whether strong contract language facilitates the transfer of teachers away from high poverty schools within a district. They find no evidence that this is the case.

One as yet unexplored area of evidence for teacher union effects is charter schools. The union–nonunion landscape for traditional public schools in the U.S. has been stable for decades. Charter schools are another story. There are currently roughly 5000 charter schools in operation enrolling 1.5 million students.[35] The vast majority of

---

[34] Similar findings are reported in West and Mykerezi (2009). Lavy (2008) considers and dismisses a different variant of the "nature of teaching" hypothesis. He finds that women (who comprise roughly 80% of teachers) are no less likely to respond to or succeed in a performance pay system.

[35] These are from the website of the Center for Education Reform (www.edreform.com), which tracks charter schools state by state and up-to-date. The most recent data on charters available from the National Center for Education Statistics of the U.S. Department of Education are for school year 2003–04. They report 2179 charter schools with a total enrollment of 627,000 students. The number of charters and total enrollments is growing rapidly.

charter schools begin life nonunion. However, teacher unions have succeeded in organizing some of them. If that trend continues, there may be opportunities for school level studies of union effects.[36]

9. CONCLUSION

Human resource (HR) policy—the recruitment, retention, and motivation of employees—is increasingly recognized as a critical variable to the success of an organization. An integrated and coherent compensation policy is the central core of an efficient HR policy. In private and many public organizations, the compensation package is considered as a strategic whole and carefully designed to get the most HR return per dollar of compensation. By contrast, the compensation "system" in public K-12 education is much more fragmented and uncoordinated, with each piece perhaps responding to pressures from a particular constituency or inherited from an earlier collective bargaining agreement, but without systematic consideration of the logic or incentive effects of the whole.

Accountability pressures are forcing school districts to address the inefficiencies in this compensation system and rethink how they are spending roughly $250 billion annually for compensation of instructional personnel. Federal programs in the U.S. such as the Teacher Incentive Fund are encouraging states to experiment with performance and market-based pay. States such as Minnesota, Florida, and Texas have developed programs to encourage their districts to develop such programs. A number of large urban districts, most notably Denver, have taken important steps in this direction. Performance- and market-based incentives are much more common in charter schools and are expanding with the charter school base. Our examination of various waves of SASS find some evidence of growth in performance and market-based pay reform even among traditional public schools. Much less movement has occurred in the area of teacher pensions, and large unfunded liabilities for pensions and retiree benefits are likely to force reforms in this area as well.

Experience from the private sector and other government employment suggest that much trial and error, hopefully combined with evaluation, will be necessary to arrive at effective and workable systems. However, it is important for education authorities to create "regulatory space" within which these compensation reform experiments can be carried out and studied.

---

[36] Interesting evidence in this regard is Abdulkadiroglu, et al. (2009). This is a randomized study of Boston area charter and pilot schools (students were admitted to these schools by lottery). Charter schools were not covered by the teacher collective bargaining agreement while the pilot schools were. Although some work rules were relaxed, tenure, salary schedules, and many seniority provisions remained in place. The authors found large positive effects on student achievement in the charter schools but mixed and sometimes negative effects in the pilot schools.

ACKNOWLEDGEMENTS

The author wishes to thank Valeska Araujo, Martin Lueken, and Yi Du for helpful research assistance, and the National Center on Performance Incentives and CALDER for research support. The usual disclaimers apply.

REFERENCES

Aaronson, D., Barrow, L., Sander, W., 2007. Teachers and student achievement in Chicago high schools. J. Labor Econ. 25, 95–136.

Abdulkadiroglu, A., Angrist, J., Cohodes, S., Dynarski, S., Fullerton, J., Kane, T., et al., 2009. Informing the debate: Comparing Boston's charter, pilot, and traditional schools. NBER Working Paper No. 15549.

Allegretto, S., Corcoran, S., Mishel, L., 2004. How Does Teacher Pay Compare? Economic Policy Institute.

Asch, B., Haider, S.J., Zissimopoulos, J., 2005. Financial incentives and retirement: Evidence from federal civil service workers. J. Public Econ. 89, 427–440.

Ashenfelter, O., Brown, J., 1986. Testing the efficiency of employment contracts. J. Polit. Econ. 94, S40–S87.

Babcock, L., Engberg, J., 1999. Bargaining unit composition and the returns to education and tenure. Ind. Labor Relat. Rev. 12, 163–178.

Bacolod, M., 2007a. Do alternative opportunities matter? The role of female labor markets in the decline of teacher quality. Rev. Econ. Stat. 89, 737–751.

Bacolod, M., 2007b. Who teaches and where they choose to teach: College graduates of the 1990s. Educ. Eval. Policy An. 29, 155–168.

Ballou, D., 1996. Do public schools hire the best applicants? Q. J. Econ. 111, 97–134.

Ballou, D., 2001. Pay for performance in public and private schools. Econ. Educ. Rev. 20, 51–61.

Ballou, D., Podgursky, M., 1995. Recruiting smarter teachers. J. Hum. Resour. 30, 326–338.

Ballou, D., Podgursky, M., 1997. Teacher Pay and Teacher Quality. W.E. Upjohn Institute for Employment Research.

Ballou, D., Podgursky, M., 1998. Teacher recruitment and retention in public and private schools. J. Policy Anal. Manag. 17, 393–418.

Ballou, D., Podgursky, M., 2001. Returns to seniority among public school teachers. J. Hum. Resour. 37, 892–912.

Baugh, W.A., Stone, J., 1982. Teachers, unions, and wages in the 1970s: Unionism now pays. Ind. Labor Relat. Rev. 35, 368–386.

Boyd, D., Grossman, P., Lankford, H., Loeb, S., Wyckoff, J., 2006. How changes in entry requirements alter the teacher workforce and affect student achievement. Educ. Fin. Policy 1, 176–216.

Bridges, E., 1992. The Incompetent Teacher: The Challenge and Response. Routledge.

Brown, J., Brown, C., Mathiowetz, N., 2001. Measurement Error in Survey Data. Handbook of Econometrics. Vol. 5. North Holland, 3705–3843.

Brown, K., 2009. The Link between Pensions and Retirement Timing: Lessons from California Teachers. Department of Economics, University of Illinois at Urbana–Champaign.

Chevalier, A., Dolton, P., McIntosh, S., 2007. Recruiting and retaining teachers in the UK: An analysis of graduate occupational choice from the 1960s to the 1990s. Economica 74, 69–96.

Clark, R., 2009. Retiree health plans for public school teachers after GASB 43 and 45. Educ. Fin. Policy (forthcoming).

Corcoran, S., Evans, W., Schwab, R., 2004. Women, the labor market, and the declining relative quality of teachers. J. Policy Anal. Manag. 23, 449–470.

Costrell, R., McGee, J., 2009. Teacher Pension Incentives, Retirement Behavior, and Potential for Reform in Arkansas. Vanderbilt University National Center on Performance Incentives.

Costrell, R., Podgursky, M., 2007. Golden Peaks and Perilous Cliffs: Rethinking Ohio's Teacher Pension System. Thomas B. Fordham Institute.

Costrell, R., Podgursky, M., 2009a. Distribution of Benefits in Teacher Retirement Systems and Their Implications for Mobility. Vanderbilt University National Center on Performance Incentives.

Costrell, R., Podgursky, M., 2009b. Peaks, cliffs and valleys: The peculiar incentives in teacher retirement systems and their consequences for school staffing. Educ. Fin. Policy 4, 175–211.

Costrell, R., Podgursky, M., 2009c. Teacher Retirement Benefits. Education Next 9.

Dolton, P.J., 2006. Teacher supply. In: Hanushek, E., Welch, F. (Eds.), Handbook of the Economics of Education. North-Holland, pp. 1079–1161.

Eberts, R.W., 2007. Teacher unions and student performance: Help or hindrance? Future Child 17, 175–200.

Eberts, R.W., Stone, J., 1984. Unions and Public Schools: The Effect of Collective Bargaining on American Education. DC Heath.

Ehrenberg, R., Smith, R., 1991. Modern Labor Economics, fourth ed. Harper Collins.

Farber, H., 2006. Public and private sector union membership in the United States. In: Hannaway, J., Rotherham, A. (Eds.), Collective Bargaining in Education. Harvard Education Press.

Flyer, F., Rosen, S., 1997. The new economics of teachers and education. J. Labor Econ. 15, S104–S139.

Freeman, R., Medoff, J., 1984. What Do Unions Do? Basic Books.

Friedberg, L., Webb, A., 2005. Retirement and the evolution of pension structure. J. Hum. Resour. 40, 281–308.

Furgeson, J., Strauss, R., Vogt, W., 2006. The effects of defined benefit pension incentives and working conditions on teacher retirement decisions. Educ. Fin. Policy 1, 316–348.

Goldhaber, D., 2006. Are teacher unions good for children? In: Hannaway, J., Rotherham, A. (Eds.), Collective Bargaining in Education. Harvard Education Press.

Goldhaber, D., Hyung, J., DeArmond, M., Player, D., 2005. Why do so few public school districts use merit pay? J. Educ. Fin. 33, 262–289.

Goldhaber, D., Player, D., 2005. What different benchmarks suggest about how financially attractive it is to teach in public schools. J. Educ. Fin. 30, 211–230.

Hanushek, E.A., 1986. The economics of schooling: Production and efficiency in public schools. J. Econ. Lit. 24, 557–577.

Hanushek, E.A., 2003. The failure of input-based schooling policies. Econ. J. 113, F64–F98.

Hanushek, E.A., Kain, J.F., O'Brien, D.M., Rivkin, S.G., 2005. The market for teacher quality. NBER Working Paper No. 11154.

Hanushek, E.A., Kain, T., Rivkin, S.G., 2004. Why public schools lose teachers. J. Hum. Resour. 39 (2), 326–354.

Hanushek, E.A., Rivkin, S.G., 1997. Understanding the 20th century growth in U.S. school spending. J. Hum. Resour. 32, 35–68.

Hanushek, E.A., Rivkin, S.G., 2004. How to improve the supply of high quality teachers. In: Brookings Papers in Education Policy: 2004. Brookings Institution.

Hanushek, E.A., Rivkin, S.G., 2006. Teacher Quality. In: Hanushek, E., Welch, F. (Eds.), Handbook of the Economics of Education. North-Holland, pp. 1054–1078.

Hanushek, E.A., Rivkin, S.G., Taylor, L.A., 1996. Aggregation and the estimated effects of school resources. Rev. Econ. Stat. 78, 611–627.

Harris, D., Adams, S., 2007. Understanding the Level and Causes of Teacher Turnover: A Comparison with other Professions. Econ. Educ. Rev. 26 (3), 325–337.

Hess, F., West, M., 2006. A Better Bargain: Overhauling Teacher Collective Bargaining for the 21st Century. Kennedy School of Government, Program in Educational Policy and Governance.www.hks.harvard.edu/pepg/PDF/Papers/BetterBargain.pdf.

Hoxby, C., 1996. How teachers' unions affect education production. Q. J. Econ. 111, 671–718.

Hoxby, C., Leigh, A., 2004. Pulled away or pushed out? Explaining the decline in teacher aptitude in the United States. Am. Econ. Rev. 94, 236–240.

Iaterola, P., Steifel, L., 2003. Intradistrict equity and public education resources and reform. Econ. Educ. Rev. 22, 60–78.

Ippolito, R., 1997. Pension Plans and Employee Performance: Evidence, Analysis, and Policy. University of Chicago Press.

Jacob, B.A., Lefgren, L., 2004. The impact of teacher training on student achievement: Quasi-experimental evidence from school reform efforts in Chicago. J. Hum. Resour. 39, 50–79.

Kahlenberg, R., 2006. The History of Collective Bargaining Among Teachers. In: Hannaway, J., Rotherham, A. (Eds.), Collective Bargaining in Education. Harvard Education Press.

Kershaw, J.A., McKean, R.N., 1962. Teacher Shortages and Salary Schedules. A RAND Research Memorandum. RAND Corporation.

Kingdon, G., Teal, F., 2008. Teacher unions, teacher pay and student performance in India: A pupil fixed effects approach. CESifo Group Munich Working Paper No. 2428.

Koski, W.S., Horng, E.L., 2007. Facilitating the teacher quality gap? Collective bargaining agreements, teacher hiring and transfer rules, and teacher assignment among schools in California. Educ. Fin. Policy 2, 262–300.

Kotlikoff, L.J., Wise, D.A., 1987. The incentive effects of private pension plans. In: Bodie, Z., Shoven, J.B., Wise, D.A. (Eds.), Issues in Pension Economics. University of Chicago Press, pp. 283–336.

Krantz-Kent, R., 2008. Teachers' work patterns: When, where, and how much do U.S. teachers work? Mon. Labor Rev. 131 (March), 52–59.

Lakdawalla, D.N., 2006. The economics of teacher quality. J. Law Econ. 49, 285–329.

Lankford, H., Loeb, S., Wyckoff, J., 2002. Teacher sorting and the plight of urban schools. Educ. Eval. Policy An. 24, 37–62.

Lavy, V., 2008. Gender differences in market competitiveness in a real workplace: Evidence from performance-based pay tournaments among teachers. NBER Working Paper No. 14338.

Leigh, A., Ryan, C., 2008. How and Why has Teacher Quality Changed in Australia?. Aust. Econ. Rev. 41, 141–159.

Lieberman, M., 1956. Education as a Profession. Prentice-Hall.

Loeb, S., Page, M.E., 2000. Examining the link between teacher wages and student outcomes: The importance of alternative labor market opportunities and non-pecuniary variation. Rev. Econ. Stat. 82, 393–408.

Lovenheim, M., 2009. The effect of teachers' unions on education production: Evidence from union election certifications in three Midwestern states. J. Labor Econ. 24, 525–588.

Moe, T., Chubb, J., 2009. Liberating Learning: Technology, Politics, and the Future of American Education. Josey-Bass.

Murnane, R., Cohen, D., 1986. Merit pay and the evaluation problem: Why most merit pay plans fail and few survive. Harvard Educ. Rev. 56, 1–17.

Murnane, R., Olsen, R., 1990. The effects of salaries and opportunity costs on length of stay in teaching: Evidence from North Carolina. J. Hum. Resour. 25, 106–124.

Murphy, M., 1990. Blackboard Unions: The AFT and NEA 1900–1980. Cornell University Press.

National Education Association, 1995. Understanding Defined Benefit & Defined Contribution Pension Plans.

Nickell, S., Quintini, G., 2002. The consequences of the decline in public sector pay in Britain: A little bit of evidence. Econ. J. 112, F107–F118.

OECD, 2001. Teachers for Tomorrow's Schools. Organization for Economic Cooperation and Development.

OECD, 2009. Education at a Glance 2009. Organization for Economic Cooperation and Development. www.oecd.org/document/24/0,3343,en_2649_39263238_43586328_1_1_1_1,00.html.

Pew Center on the States, 2010. The Trillion Dollar Gap: Underfunded State Retirement Systems and the Roads to Reform.

Podgursky, M., 2003. Fringe benefits. Educ. Next 3, 73–76.

Podgursky, M., 2007. Teams versus bureaucracies: Personnel policy, wage-setting, and teacher quality in traditional public, charter, and private schools. In: Berends, M., Springer, M., Walberg, H. (Eds.), Charter School Outcomes. Lawrence Erlbaum Associates, Inc., pp. 61–84.

Podgursky, M., 2009. Market-based pay reform for teachers. In: Springer, M. (Ed.), Performance Incentives: Their Growing Impact on K-12 Education. Brookings Institution, pp. 67–86.

Podgursky, M., Monroe, R., Watson, D., 2004. Academic quality of public school teachers: An analysis of entry and exit behavior. Econ. Educ. Rev. 23, 507–518.

Podgursky, M., Springer, M., 2007. Teacher performance pay: A review. J. Policy Anal. Manag. 26, 909–950.

Podgursky, M., Tongrut, R., 2006. (Mis)-measuring the relative pay of teachers. Educ. Fin. Policy 1, 425–440.

Prince, C., 2002. Higher Pay in Hard-to-Staff Schools: The Case for Financial Incentives. American Association of School Administrators.

Rivkin, S.G., Hanushek, E.A., Kain, J.F., 2005. Teachers, schools, and academic achievement. Econometrica 73, 417–458.

Rosen, S., 1969. Trade union power, threat effects, and the extent of organization. Rev. Econ. Stud. 36, 185–196.

Roza, M., Guin, K., Gross, B., Deburgomaster, S., 2007. Do districts fund schools fairly? Education Next 7, 68–74.

Roza, M., Hill, P.T., 2004. How within-district spending inequalities help some schools to fail. In: Brookings Papers on Education Policy 2004. Brookings Institution.

Sclafani, S., Tucker, M., 2006. Teacher and Principal Compensation: An International Review. Center for American Progress (October).

Springer, M., Balch, R., 2009. Design Components of Incentive Pay Programs in the Education Sector. Vanderbilt University, National Center on Performance Incentives. (July).

Stinebrickner, T.R., 2001. A dynamic model of teacher labor supply. J. Labor Econ. 19, 196–230.

Stinebrickner, T.R., Scafidi, B., Sjodquist, D., 2002. Do Teachers Really Leave for Higher Paying Jobs in Alternative Occupations? Department of Economics, University of Western Ontario.

Stock, J., Wise, D., 1990. Pensions, the option value of work, and retirement. Econometrica 58, 1151–1180.

Stoddard, C., 2003. Why has the number of teachers per student risen while teacher quality has declined? J. Urban Econ. 53, 458–481.

Taylor, L.L., 2008. Comparing teacher salaries: Insights from the U.S. census. Econ. Educ. Rev. 27, 48–57.

U.S. Department of Education, National Center for Education Statistics, 2004. Qualifications of the Public School Teaching Force: the Prevalence of Out-of-Field Teaching. 1987–88 to 1999–00. NCES 2002603 (August).

U.S. Department of Education, National Center for Education Statistics, 2007. Digest of Education Statistics.

U.S. Department of Education, National Center for Education Statistics, 2009. Digest of Education Statistics.

U.S. Department of Education, 2010. Race to the top fund. www2.ed.gov/programs/racetothetop/index.html.

U.S. Department of Labor, Bureau of Labor Statistics, 2000. Employee benefits in state and local government, 1998. Bulletin 2531.

U.S. Department of Labor, Bureau of Labor Statistics, 2008. National compensation survey: Occupational earnings in the United States, 2007. Bulletin 2704.

West, L.K., Mykerezi, E., 2009. Effects of Teachers' Unions on Qualification-Specific and Incentive-Based Teacher Compensation. University of Minnesota.

CHAPTER 6

Licensure: Exploring the Value of this Gateway to the Teacher Workforce

Dan Goldhaber
University of Washington

Contents

1. Background	316
2. Theoretical Arguments for and Against Teacher Licensure	318
2.1 Consumer protection	318
2.2 Restriction of labor supply	319
3. Teacher Licensure Systems in the U.S. and Abroad	321
4. Empirical Evidence on the Impact of Teacher Licensure	325
4.1 The relationship between teacher licensure and teacher quality	326
4.2 Licensure requirements, labor supply, and the teacher workforce	331
4.3 Licensure requirements and hiring decisions	334
5. Concluding Thoughts	335
References	337

Abstract

Empirical research bears out the conventional wisdom that teacher quality is the key schooling resource influencing student achievement, so it is not surprising that policy makers attempt to influence it by regulating admission into the teacher labor market through licensure systems. Most of these systems require teachers to graduate from an approved teacher training institution and pass one or more tests, the notion being that these preservice requirements ensure a basic level of teacher competence. A criticism, however, is that these requirements dissuade talented individuals from attempting to become teachers, thereby lowering the quality of teachers in the workforce. It is shocking how little we actually know about key aspects of the teacher licensure–teacher quality equation. The great majority of the empirical literature on licensure speaks to one crucial link in the teacher licensure–teacher quality equation: the correlation between licensure requirements and student achievement. In general this literature suggests only weak links between specific licensure requirements and student achievement. Far less evidence exists on the impact of licensure on the pool of potential teachers, or who school district hiring officials would employ in the face of fewer requirements, or the absence of requirements altogether.

JEL classification: I21, J24, J44, J45, J48

Keywords

Teachers
Teacher Quality

Occupational Licensure
Labor Supply
Labor Market Requirements
Student Achievement

1. BACKGROUND

Empirical research bears out the conventional wisdom that teacher quality is the key schooling resource influencing student achievement (Aaronson, Barrow, and Sander (2007); Rivkin, Hanushek, and Kain (2005); Rockoff (2004)). It is not surprising therefore that policy makers attempt to influence teacher quality by regulating admission into the teacher labor market through teacher licensure systems. The idea behind licensure is a simple one: those who wish to become public school teachers ought to have a basic skill set related to teaching. This simple idea, however, does not necessarily mean that the licensing of prospective teachers will lead to better student outcomes. As described in this chapter, the efficacy of licensure systems is hotly debated, and the empirical evidence on the issue is mixed.

Teacher licensure (also commonly referred to as certification systems are found in many developed countries, but appear to be more common in nations that have less centralized control over teacher training (OECD (2005)).[1] These systems differ from country to country (and in the U.S. from state to state), but most require teachers to graduate from an approved teacher training institution (including having completed some preservice student teaching), and pass one or more licensure tests. One criticism of licensure systems is that they dissuade talented individuals from attempting to become teachers. Supporters of alternative pathways into the teaching profession contend that individuals may obtain the knowledge and skills necessary to be effective in the classroom in a variety of different ways (such as teaching in a private school), but that many licensure systems fail to recognize this. The requirements associated with these systems, such as having a degree from an approved teacher-training program, could severely limit the pool of potential teachers if individuals are unwilling to jump through what may be costly hoops. Those in mid-career, for instance, may be unwilling to bear the cost of an additional tuition expense or forgone earnings while obtaining the state-required degree necessary to get licensed. Unfortunately, the contentious debate about the extent to which licensure systems alter the potential pool of teachers takes place in the absence of much empirical evidence.

---

[1] Labor economists make a distinction between licensure and certification: Licensure is a requirement for the right to practice in a particular occupation, whereas certification is a voluntary credential whereby the government or a nonprofit professional association certifies that practitioners in a given occupation who have obtained certification have achieved demonstrated human capital investment levels (i.e., specific skills or knowledge).

On the flip side, supporters of licensure systems argue that these systems place a lower bound on the knowledge and skills individuals have prior to becoming a teacher, which is crucial as teachers work with a vulnerable population. This raises the issue of whether there is in fact a link between the knowledge and skills that individuals have demonstrated by successfully becoming licensed and teacher quality (as measured based on teacher contributions toward student achievement). It is only in the last decade or so that the links between licensure (or the components of licensure systems) and student achievement have been quantitatively explored, but a growing body of literature suggests that these links are tenuous at best. However, there are at least two qualifications to this conclusion: first, this literature is based almost entirely on student achievement as measured by performance on tests (e.g., state mandated assessments), and second, licensure is designed to set a lower bound on teacher quality. It is possible, at least in theory, that a licensure system has little or no impact (or even a negative effect) on the quality of the teacher workforce overall, while still serving the purpose of "weeding out" those individuals who would make very poor teachers if they were made eligible, and hired, to teach.

In many respects the debate over licensure comes down to a question of what local hiring authorities would do if left unconstrained by state regulation. Beyond the issue of how regulation affects the pool of those eligible to teach is whether licensure systems have an impact on which individuals would be *hired*. Local hiring authorities weigh various factors when making decisions and it is possible that licensure systems provide localities with information that could be used to make better hiring decisions. However, it is also conceivable that this information is superfluous; it may not add any relevant information to what local authorities would gather about candidates on their own. If this were true, and if licensure systems had no impact on the potential teacher applicant pool—an unlikely assumption—then one could imagine licensure having little impact on who is hired. In practice, licensure systems are likely to have distributional impacts since school systems vary in terms of the type of applicants they attract and their capacity to make judgments about prospective teachers.

This chapter describes what we know, both theoretically and empirically about teacher licensure. The remainder of the chapter is organized as follows. Section 2 describes the arguments for and against licensure in general and teacher licensure in particular, covering the theoretical ways in which licensure requirements might affect the teacher applicant pool, teacher hiring, and ultimately the quality of teachers who are in the classroom. Section 3 describes the licensure system in the U.S. and abroad. Section 4 examines empirical evidence linking licensure systems to student achievement on tests, paying particular attention to the econometric difficulties associated with assessing this relationship using nonexperimental data. Section 5 offers some concluding thoughts, focusing on our lack of knowledge about two key areas that determine the efficacy of teacher licensure systems: how licensure systems affect teacher applicant pools and the hiring preferences of localities.

2. THEORETICAL ARGUMENTS FOR AND AGAINST TEACHER LICENSURE

State regulation in the form of occupational licensure has grown significantly over the last several decades in the United States and, where we have reliable evidence, in other industrialized countries as well (Humphris, Kleiner, and Koumenta (forthcoming)).[2] Notwithstanding the prevalence of licensure in the workforce, there is actually little empirical evidence that this form of occupational regulation actually increases the overall quality of services, in education or in other sectors of the economy.[3] Some of the studies relating licensure to student achievement are described below, but first it is useful analyze the ways in which licensure can affect the quality of teachers in the workforce.

2.1 Consumer protection

The theory of licensure is relatively simple, resting on a consumer protection argument (Shapiro (1986)). For illustration, assume that teacher quality in the *population* falls along a continuum (teacher "quality" may mean different things to different people, but for the moment we leave it ambiguous since the analysis discussed below on the implications of a licensure system can be generalized for various definitions of teacher quality). Were it possible to directly observe teacher quality, we might wish to prohibit individuals who fall below some set quality level from employment in the teacher workforce. But, of course, it is not possible to directly observe teachers' quality prior to their being employed and practicing. Consequently, licensure requirements are established based on a set of observable characteristics (such as whether an individual holds a Baccalaureate degree or has passed a specified licensure exam) thought to be associated with teacher quality.[4]

As mentioned above, the potential upside of state regulation of the public sector teacher labor market is that it may protect consumers who have imperfect information about the quality of services they may wish to purchase, and who therefore might make consequential errors when hiring teachers. However, unlike many sectors of the economy where licensure exists, such as the medical and legal professions, in education the ultimate end-users of teacher labor services are students and their parents, but the purchasers of those services are local public school districts. This distinction is important as one might assume that those empowered to operate schools ought to have the competence to make good selections among teacher applicants. On the other hand, schools are a major source of employment in most communities and generally subject to political rather than market-based pressures, which raises concerns about patronage and nepotism.

---

[2] For example, in the United States in 2006, nearly 30% of workers reported a requirement of a government issued license in order to do their jobs (Kleiner and Krueger (2008)).

[3] For an overview of studies attempting to quantify the benefits of occupational licensing, see Kleiner (2000, 2008).

[4] The underlying assumption is that teacher candidates who fail to meet the minimum standards defined by these requirements will tend to be of worse quality than those who do meet the standards, and may be of such low quality as to be unsuitable for the classroom.

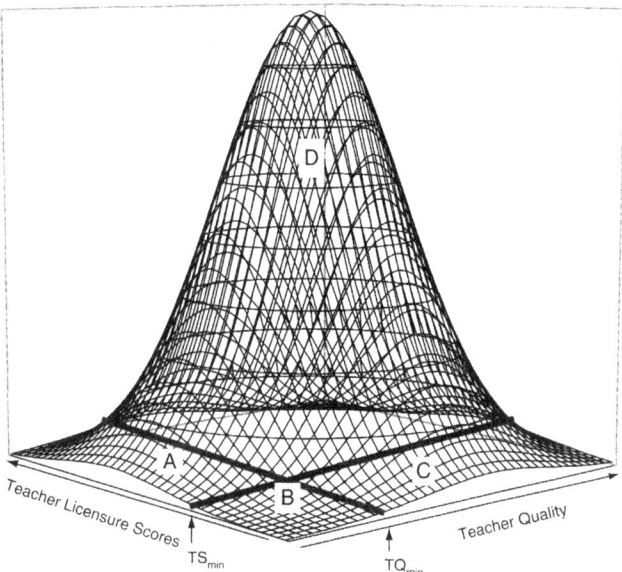

Figure 6.1 Joint normal distribution of teacher quality and teacher licensure scores.

2.2 Restriction of labor supply

There are at least two downsides associated with a teacher licensure system. The first is related to the fact that the state determines licensure requirements based on observable credentials, such as graduation from an approved program or passing a licensure test, rather than direct, but unobservable (at least for those who are not in the teacher workforce), measures of teacher quality. As a result, licensure requirements will invariably prevent localities from hiring at least some individuals who would have been effective teachers. Unless the requirements are perfect predictors of teacher ability in the classroom, this statement is true for any requirement or set of requirements. Conversely, the requirements will not screen out all those who would make for ineffective teachers, meaning there is still an important role that localities play in the teacher selection process.

This point is illustrated graphically in Figure 6.1, which shows the hypothetical relationship between licensure test scores (almost all states require teachers to pass licensure tests) and some purposely undefined measure of teaching quality.[5] Here it is assumed that both quality (measured on the x-axis) and teacher test performance (measured on the z-axis) have bell-shaped distributions; consequently the joint distribution of the two will be a bell-shaped mound (the y-axis) that represents the number of individuals (who are not necessarily allowed into the teacher labor market) with particular test-score–teacher quality combinations.

---

[5] See Goldhaber (2004) for a more comprehensive discussion of this issue.

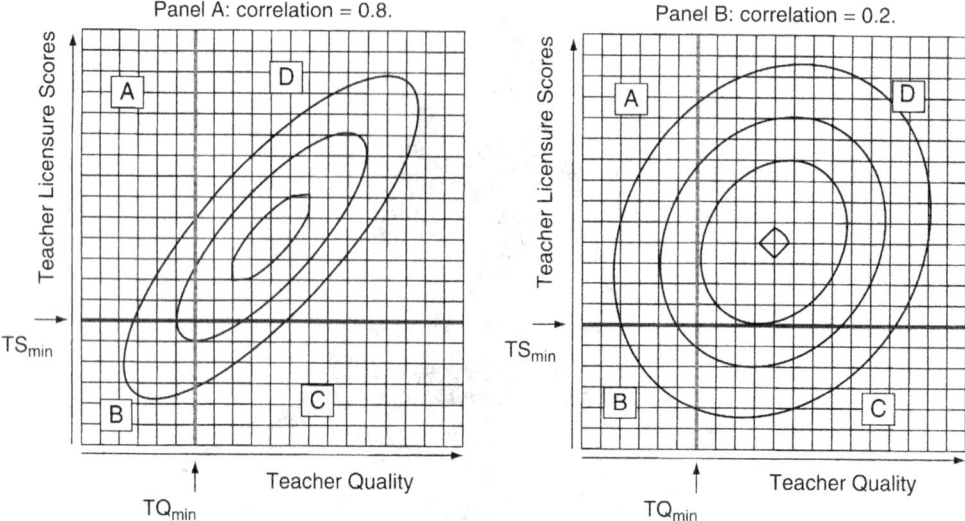

Figure 6.2 Correlation between teacher quality and teacher licensure scores determines prevalence of "false positives".

Teaching quality obviously cannot be directly observed for those who are not yet teaching or who will never teach. Thus, while policy makers might wish to exclude prospective teachers who fall below a set standard of quality (TQ_{min}) from participating in the labor market, they have to use a proxy for quality, like a licensure-test score. Setting a minimum cut-score (TS_{min}) will result, then, in both false positives and false negatives. Individuals in Quadrant A do well on the test, but would be low-quality teachers, represent false positives in the sense that they are allowed, by the state, into the teacher labor market despite the fact that they would be unacceptably low-quality teachers. Individuals in Quadrant C do poorly on the licensure test, but would, if allowed to teach, meet a state's minimum quality criteria. But, these individuals are prohibited from participating in the teacher labor market by their test performance. Finally, those individuals in Quadrants B and D represent true negatives and true positives, in the sense that they are correctly categorized, according to a state's teacher-quality standard, by their test performance.

The shape of the mound shows the number of individuals that will fall into the four quadrants, and depends on the correlation between unobserved teacher quality and licensure-test performance: the more closely the two are related, the fewer false positives and negatives. This is illustrated by Figure 6.2, which shows the mound as it would appear looking straight down from above, as on a topographical map, with the height of the mound represented by the ellipses in the diagram (the smaller ellipses represent higher points on the mound). Panel A of the figure shows a relatively strong correlation between teacher test performance and teacher quality, and Panel B shows a much weaker relationship between the two. The quadrants in the panels of this figure correspond with those in Figure 6.1, and depict once again that there are fewer false positives and false negatives in the case where a strong relationship exists between licensure-test performance and teacher quality.

In addition to directly screening out potentially effective teachers, licensure policies have a secondary impact: they will influence who chooses to enter the teacher labor market. Specifically, licensure requirements impose costs on prospective teachers and these costs will cause some potential teachers to opt for careers in other occupations, changing the distribution depicted by Figure 6.1.[6] Theory does not provide a clear indication of which individuals will opt not to pursue a career as a teacher (that is, which quadrant loses prospective teachers) as the decision to pursue a teaching career will depend on the cost to individuals of obtaining required credentials as well as the returns to participating in the teacher labor market relative to those of participating in other labor markets. But, it is clear that the imposition of more requirements to enter an occupation will restrict the supply of applicants, increasing wages and raising the cost of providing services (Kleiner (2000)).[7]

3. TEACHER LICENSURE SYSTEMS IN THE U.S. AND ABROAD

In the United States, teacher licensure is a state-level function; thus, while policy makers and researchers tend to treat licensure as if it represents a single system of requirements there are effectively 50 different systems in the U.S. That said, in broad terms, all states' systems share some common requirements for teachers to receive a "traditional" or "full" teaching credential: they always require college graduation and a background check, and typically require a minimum grade-point average, some combination of pedagogical (education-specific) and subject-matter course requirements, practice teaching, and passing one or more licensure tests. But delving beneath these broad categories shows that state requirements differ, sometimes substantially (see Table 6.1). For example, the primary source that compiles teacher requirements across states, the National Association of Directors of Teacher Education and Certification (NASDTEC), reports that as of 2005, just seven states require teachers to major in education. Twenty-eight states require that teachers take a basic skills exam to obtain a teaching certificate, 39 states require teachers to take a subject matter exam, and 27 states require a pedogagy-focused exam (NASDTEC (2010)). Moreover, broad test categories mask substantial variation in requirements, as licensure test achievement

---

[6] Individuals outside of the teacher workforce frequently cite licensure requirements as a reason for not seeking a teaching job; for example, only a minority of Teach for America teachers—an alternative certification route into the profession that allows individuals in some states to sidestep some traditional licensure requirements—report that they would have chosen to pursue a job in teaching if they had been required to enter the profession through a traditional route (Ballou and Podgursky (2000)).

[7] Kleiner and Krueger (2008) estimate that licensing raises wages, in the licensed workforce, by about 15%—an increase that is comparable to the impact of unionization.

Table 6.1 Variation in key licensure requirements across U.S. states

	State	Total number of states
Major in education[a]	ID, KY, MD, MO, NE, SC, SD	7
Examination prior to entering teacher education program[b]		
Basic skills test	AK, AR, CO, CT, DE, GA, IL, IN, IA, KY, LA, MO, NE, NV, NH, NM, NC, OH, SC, SD, TN, WA, WI	23
General knowledge test	FL, MO	2
Pedagogic skills test	NV, NM, SD	3
Subject matter test	CO, MO, NV, NH, NM, SD	6
Undergraduate studies[c]		
General education	AL, AK, AR, CO CT, DE, FL, HI, ID, IL, IN, IA, KS, KY, LA, MD, MA, MI, MO, MT, NE, NV, NH, NM, NY, NK, OH, PA, RI, SC, TN, UT, VT, VA, WA, WI, WY	37
Subject specific degree?	AL, AK, AZ, AR, CA, CO, CT, DE, FL, GA, HI, ID, IL, IN, IA, KS, KY, LA, MD, MI, MN, MO, MT, NE, NV, NH, NM, NY, ND, OH, OR, PA, RI, SC, SD, TN, UT, VT, VA, WA, WV, WI, WY	43
Pedagogy	AL, AK, AZ, AR, CA, CO, CT, GA, HI, ID, IL, IN, IA, KS, KY, LA, MD, MA, MI, MN, MO, MT, NE, NV, NH, NM, NY, ND, OH, OR, PA, RI, SC, SD, TN, UT, VT, VA, WA, WV, WI, WY	42
Examination prior to receipt of licensure[b]		
Basic skills	AL, AK, AR, CA, CT, DE, GA, HI, IN, LA, MD, MA, MI, MN, MO, NV, NH, NM, NY, OK, OR, PA, SC, TN, VT, VA, WA, WV	28

General knowledge	FL, HI, MO, NM, NY, OK, PA, TN	8
Subject matter	AL, AZ, AR, CO, CT, DE, FL, FA, HI, ID, IL, IN, KS, KY, LA, MD, MA, MI, MN, MO, NV, NH, NM, NY, NC, OH, OK, OR, PA, RI, SC, SD, TN, UT, VT, VA, WA, WV, WI	39
Pedagogic skills	AL, AZ, AR, CT, FL, HI, ID, IL, KS, KY, LA, MD, MN, NV, NM, NY, NC, OH, OK, PA, RI, SC, SD, TN, VA, WV, WY	27

[a]Source data are from NASDTEC (2010) Table B2.
[b]Source data are from NASDTEC (2010) Table G1.
[c]Source data are from NASDTEC (2007) Table B1.

thresholds can differ substantially from state to state; the "cut-score" threshold varies by more than a full standard deviation in states that utilize common licensure tests.[8]

Over the past two decades 47 states (as of 2008) have adopted a number of "alternative" routes into teaching (Peterson and Nadler (2008)). In theory, alternative licensure programs are designed to move individuals into the classroom more quickly and easily, based on the premise that it is possible to get more quality teachers by allowing them to bypass or postpone some of the requirements (particularly education-specific coursework) associated with traditional licensure programs. As is the case with traditional licensure, there is no single alternative licensure policy.

The number of individuals entering the teaching profession through alternative routes has grown considerably—roughly tripling from about 20,000 in 2001 to almost 60,000 in 2006 (Peterson and Nadler (2008))—but the extent to which individual states utilize alternative licensure as an important source of new teachers varies. States such as Texas and New Jersey have long relied on alternative programs as a major source of teachers, and in recent years 35–40% of new teachers in these states enter the system through an alternative route program (Feistritzer (2008)). In other states, alternative programs are primarily designed to allow localities facing "emergency" teacher shortage situations to hire teachers who haven't satisfied all the traditional pedagogical requirements for a year. However, if these *very same* requirements have not been satisfied after a set amount of time (typically a year), they are no longer eligible to teach. Thus, as Peterson and Nadler (2008) point out, it is not surprising that alternative routes are little used in some states since the requirements of many "alternative" route programs are virtually the same as those of traditional licensure programs. In short, many of the alternative programs that are on the books do not really lessen the time it takes for a college graduate to move into a teaching position (Rotherham (2008)), which is the main appeal of alternative route programs (Johnson, Birkeland, and Peske (2005)).

Reviews of documentation by the Organization for Economic Co-Operation and Development (OECD (2004), (2005), (2008)) on the teacher pipeline—broadly defined as the policies and systems that govern the movement of prospective teachers from secondary schools into the teacher labor force—suggests that most other developed countries tend to be less reliant on licensure as a means of regulating teacher quality (Goldhaber (2009)). The great majority of teachers, in both the U.S. and other OECD countries, enter the profession soon after having completed traditional teacher training, but a number of countries have no formal requirements beyond graduation from an approved teacher training institution (OECD (2005), Wang, Coleman, Coley, and Phelps (2003)).

The fact that many countries are less likely than the U.S. to rely on licensure is not surprising. Outside of the U.S., the pipeline to enter teaching is commonly narrowed

---

[8] They also vary in topic and substance depending on the grade level and subject area in which teachers intend to work.

at the point of entry into teacher training (Barber and Mourshed (2007)); in the U.S., where many teacher-training institutions effectively have open admissions policies, this narrowing tends to occur post-training. Some countries have few training providers, thus allowing for greater control over curricula. For example, one study compares various aspects of the teacher pipeline in the U.S. and seven other industrialized countries (Australia, England, Hong Kong, Japan, Korea, the Netherlands, and Singapore) and finds that it is only in the U.S. and Australia where the approval of the curriculum of teacher training resides at the state level as opposed to the national level (Wang et al. (2003)). Moreover, there are more than 1500 training providers in the U.S., a total that exceeds the number of providers in the other seven countries combined. Finally, there is some evidence that the training itself is more diverse in the U.S. than in other countries that have been studied (Schmidt (2008), Wang et al. (2003)).

Given the diversity of U.S. teacher training programs and the fact that the pipeline is not significantly narrowed at the point of entry, it is not surprising that the U.S. requires licensure as a final step toward teaching eligibility, while many other countries do not (Murnane and Steele (2007)).[9] In effect, other developed countries also regulate who enters the teacher workforce, they just do so at a different point in the teacher pipeline.[10]

4. EMPIRICAL EVIDENCE ON THE IMPACT OF TEACHER LICENSURE

As suggested above, in order to assess the general equilibrium consequences of licensure policies, one would need to know the answers to three separate but interrelated questions: 1) How do licensure requirements affect the propensity to pursue a career as a teacher? 2) How correlated are licensure requirements and teacher quality? 3) How does licensure impact the recruitment and selection of teachers by local school systems?

It could be argued that we have very little empirical evidence on questions 1 and 3, largely due to the fact that licensure systems are ubiquitous, so one cannot directly test how individuals or school systems would respond in their absence. However, there is far more empirical evidence—most, if not all, based on U.S. data—linking licensure to various measures of teacher quality. We start by reviewing this evidence, but note that the findings speak only to the issue of the correlation between licensure requirements and teacher quality. This will help determine the number of false positives and negatives (as depicted in Figure 6.2) that result from state imposed regulation, but, as described in Section 2, it is only one of the three issues that determines the impact of licensure on the quality of the teacher workforce as a whole.

---

[9] Unfortunately, the issue of occupational licensure has received relatively little academic attention (Humphris, Kleiner, and Koumenta (forthcoming)) so it is not clear whether the relative importance of licensure in the teaching profession in the U.S. is reflective of a relative importance of occupational licensure in the labor market or is unique to teaching.

[10] Interestingly, Germany appears to have a teacher development system that is quite similar to that of the U.S. (see Woessmann (2008)).

4.1 The relationship between teacher licensure and teacher quality

Many early studies of licensure predate the growth of specially designed alternative routes into teaching—like the Teach For America (TFA) program—and thus compare teachers who held a full teaching license to those who held a provisional or emergency license. These studies tended to focus on teacher attitudes and practices, with only a few measuring teacher quality based on student outcomes. In a widely cited 1985 review of licensure, Evertson, Willis and Zlotnik find that in 11 of the 13 studies reviewed, fully licensed teachers tend to be more effective than those who had not completed all the requirements for full licensure, leading the authors to conclude that "the available research suggests that among students who become teachers, those enrolled in formal preservice preparation programs are more likely to be effective than those who do not have such training." (p. 8). But this review reveals the state of the literature on teacher licensure at that time: of the 11 studies, only two are based on student outcomes; of these, one is an unpublished dissertation and the other did not separately identify the impact of licensure from teacher experience. As the authors themselves note, much of the research on teacher education "is often of dubious scientific merit" (p. 2), "investigations of teacher education do not represent a strong body of research" (p. 3), and the findings reported in the paper do "*not* add up to a defense of teacher preparation as it exists in most institutions" (p. 8).

More recent reviews of licensure-related studies (Walsh (2001a), (2001b) and Darling-Hammond et al. (2001)) reach radically difficult conclusions about the efficacy of licensure, but these reviews also suggest that the state of the art in the field had progressed very little over the 15 years since the 1985 Evertson et al. review.[11] Of the roughly 150 studies covered by these new reviews, few focus on student outcomes or utilize statistical techniques that allow for credible inferences.[12] Most of the studies included in these meta-analyses fail to meet accepted standards for academic rigor since they are not set in a value-added framework (Hanushek (1979)). For instance, more experienced and credentialed teachers tend to be matched to classes that include more high-achieving students from more affluent, well-educated families, and failure to account for this matching has been shown to lead to biased estimates of the effects of teacher characteristics on students.[13]

---

[11] An issue that is related to licensure is whether graduates who attend an accredited teacher preparation program, and as a consequence of attending such a program, are more effective teachers. The literature on this question is also sparse, as is pointed out in a recent report by the Education Commission of the States (see Allen (2003)).

[12] It can be argued that one should weigh studies that focus on student outcomes substantially more heavily than those that focus on a more intermediate measure of teachers (such as teaching practices), since no definitive links between these intermediate measures and student achievement are available.

[13] This point is particularly important when considering the effectiveness of different licensure policies. There is certainly pressure (which was made explicit by the No Child Left Behind Act of 2001) on schools to hire fully licensed teachers. Schools opting to employ teachers with an "alternative" or "emergency" license are likely doing so only because they are finding it difficult to hire those who have satisfied all of their state's traditional licensure requirements, and these same school systems are also likely to be serving students who are struggling academically.

Failure to adequately account for students' backgrounds might lead researchers to inadvertently interpret a correlational relationship between lack of full-licensure and low student achievement as a causal relationship. The need to account for students' backgrounds is illustrated by Goldhaber and Brewer (2000), which reports that students taught by fully licensed teachers tend to have higher *levels* of performance in math and science, but value-added models of student *growth* show few statistically significant differences in student achievement between students taught by teachers holding a full state license and those with an emergency credential, issued to those who have not met all the requirements to receive full licensure.

While the Goldhaber and Brewer study represents a methodological improvement over prior research on the impact of teacher licensure on student achievement, it is limited by data that included relatively few teacher observations within states (the authors utilized national data), so the specific definitions of a teacher being fully licensed versus the alternatives varied from one state to the next. More recent research on licensure has tended to exploit large administrative state databases and focus on the relative effects of fully licensed teachers versus those who hold a particular alternative credential, and/or the relationship between licensure requirements and student achievement. Table 6.2 summarizes some of the more recent studies.

It is important to note here that studies that focus on the relative value of any specific route into teaching should not be construed as generalized evidence on a link between licensure and teacher quality, since the specific requirements associated with alternative routes into the profession differ substantially from one another (Boyd et al. (2007)), both within and between states. Nor should it be interpreted as direct evidence about the value of pedagogical training (alternative licensure in some states bypasses certain pedagogical requirements, at least initially). There are both selection and training effects associated with a given route into the classroom, and one cannot easily parcel out the extent to which any differences in effectiveness between traditional and alternatively licensed teachers are a result of selection into a program versus differences in training.

Due to its prominence as an alternative pathway into the teaching profession, Teach For America (TFA) has received a great deal of research attention.[14] Most of the research on TFA suggests that teachers who enter the profession through this route tend to be at least as effective as other fully licensed teachers (e.g., Boyd et al. (2006), Glazerman et al. (2006), Kane, Rockoff, and Staiger (2007)), particularly at the secondary level (Xu et al. (2007)). One of the first studies to focus on the relative effectiveness of TFA teachers was conducted by Raymond, et al. (2001). They compared student outcomes of TFA and non-TFA teachers in the Houston Independent School District (HISD) between

---

[14] TFA, founded in 1990, focuses on recruiting talented recent college graduates who might not otherwise consider teaching, providing them with a relatively short (as compared to traditional teacher training) period of training, and placing them as teachers in needy schools throughout the country. TFA teachers commit to spending a minimum of two years in their assigned school.

Table 6.2 Selected studies linking teacher licensure to student achievement

Study	Data and methods	Licensure effect	Notes
Boyd, Grossman, Lankford, Loeb, & Wyckoff (2006)	Administrative district-level data/value-added regression model	Scaled score in Math test:	• Effects are relative to college-recommended teacher • Result for TFA teachers is negative for English achievement (−0.031★★)
		−0.012★ (individual evaluation)	
		−0.023★★ (teaching fellows)	
		0.007 (Teach for America—TFA)	
		−0.021★★ (temporary)	
		−0.021★★ (other)	
Clotfelter, Ladd, & Vigdor (2007)	Administrative state-level data/value-added regression model	Scaled test scores	• Student test scores are standardized to have a mean of zero and standard deviation of one
		0.018★ (licensure test score on math test)	
		0.011★ (licensure test score on reading test)	
Glazerman, Mayer, & Decker (2006)	Regional/metropolitan data/regression	Iowa Test of Basic Skills—effect size	• Students were randomly assigned to TFA teachers and non-TFA teachers
		0.15★ TFA versus non-TFA (math test)	
		0.03 TFA versus non-TFA (reading test)	
Goldhaber (2007)	Administrative state-level data/value-added regression model	Any teacher licensure test scale score on math	• Effects are relative to the bottom quintile of teacher licensure performance (quintile 1) • Pattern of results are similar for reading performance
		0.024★ (quintile 2)	
		0.028★★ (quintile 3)	
		0.033★★ (quintile 4)	
		0.047★★ (quintile 5)	

Study	Method	Results	Notes
Goldhaber & Brewer (2000)	National data/value-added regression model	Percentage points in math test: 1.29 (probationary in math) 0.58 (emergency in math) −1.26 (private school certification) −1.35 (not certified in subject)	• Effects are relative to standard certification • Pattern of results are similar for science examinations
Kane, Rockoff, & Staiger (2007)	Administrative district-level data/value-added regression model	No statistically significant differences between traditionally certified teachers and teaching fellows or uncertified teachers on students' math achievement	
Xu, Hannaway, & Taylor (2007)	Administrative state-level data/value-added regression model	TFA teacher effect (standard deviations): 0.10* (all subjects) 0.10* (math) 0.18* (science)	• Students assigned to TFA teacher did score significantly higher (0.2 of a standard deviation) than those assigned to traditionally certified teacher • More restrictive analyses (direct student-teacher link; TFA licensed in subject area; TFA versus traditional license pathways) show a similar pattern of results

*$p < 0.05$; **$p < 0.01$.

1996 and 2000. The authors used results on the TAAS exam to compare the performance of students with TFA teachers to students with traditional teachers. Their value-added analysis found consistently positive (though generally not statistically-significant) coefficients on the TFA variable, indicating that TFA teachers have a positive effect on student achievement in reading and math.

Some have criticized the Raymond et al. study for comparing TFA teachers to a set of other teachers that include both fully licensed and other unlicensed teachers (Laczko-Kerr and Berliner (2002), Darling-Hammond (2001)). These critiques raise the question of what the appropriate counterfactual comparison to TFA teachers might be. Some feel that the only appropriate comparison to make is between TFA teachers and traditionally licensed teachers. But, TFA teachers are placed by design in schools that have great difficulty hiring teachers, and for these schools the alternative to hiring TFA teachers is to hire teachers that are not fully licensed. For this reason, it can be argued that it is appropriate to make comparisons of TFA teachers to other teachers at the same schools, whether these teachers are traditionally licensed or not.

Decker et al. (2004) provide what is arguably the most convincing evidence on TFA to date. These researchers studied an experiment in which students were randomly assigned to TFA and non-TFA teachers, avoiding the potentially confounding problems associated with the matching of students and teachers based on *either observable or unobserved* student characteristics. Their results showed that students with TFA teachers did no worse in reading and did better in math than the students of non-TFA teachers: they found statistically significant positive effects in the growth of math scores and positive (but not significant) effects in the growth of reading scores. These results held whether the comparison teachers were novice or experienced teachers, though the sample sizes were too small to detect statistically significant effects.

The above TFA study is convincing because it is an experiment, but a number of other recent nonexperimental studies have been conducted that are both methodologically rigorous and include controls for licensure status. These studies rely on longitudinal state administrative data that include a large number of teachers and students who can be linked at the classroom- or grade-level and tracked over time. This data structure allows researchers to estimate models that include fixed student effects (e.g., Boyd et al. (2006), Goldhaber (2007), Harris and Sass (2008), Kane, Rockoff, and Staiger (2008)) or analyze data subsamples where students and teachers appear to be randomly matched in classrooms (Clotfelter et al. (2007)). Perhaps it is not surprising that these studies find differential effects, given that licensure provisions differ from state-to-state. But even in cases where research finds statistically significant positive effects on student achievement of having a teacher who is fully licensed relative to one who holds some type of alternative credential (see, for example, Clotfelter et al. (2007) and Goldhaber (2007) in North Carolina), the effects are modest and often do not hold up across empirical specifications (e.g., student fixed effects).

Moreover, one of the most interesting findings to emerge from these state-level studies is that, even when statistically significant differences occur between teachers who fall into different licensure categories, there is still a tremendous overlap in the estimated distributions of effectiveness of teachers in the different licensure categories. For example, Figure 6.3 shows the implications of this, based on the 2008 Kane et al. study on the relationship between a teacher's route into the classroom (e.g., traditional certification, TFA, Teaching Fellows Program) and student achievement on standardized tests.[15]

While statistically significant differences exist between some routes, none of these differences exceed 0.02 standard deviations of achievement. As suggested by the kernal density estimates of the teacher quality distribution for teachers who enter the profession through different routes, the differences between teachers within a particular category dwarf the average differences between categories. Specifically, the authors find the average difference in effectiveness between the most effective (those in the top quintile) and least effective (those in the bottom quintile) teachers within a particular category *is roughly 10 times* the average difference in performance between teachers who fall into different categories.[16]

In principal the finding of significantly overlapping teacher quality distributions suggests there is room for improvements in the quality of the teacher workforce. Some researchers advance the idea of relying less on licensure as a determinant of employment eligibility, suggesting instead that more individuals be permitted to initially enter the teaching profession, and that there be greater selectivity about who is allowed to remain in the profession (for example, Kane et al. (2008), Gordon et al. (2006), and Hanushek (2009)). However, the efficacy of such a policy shift depends on how changes in entry requirements would influence both the occupational and training decisions of individuals and the recruitment and selection decisions of institutions (schools). As described in the next subsection, we currently have very little empirical research from which to draw conclusions about these issues.

4.2 Licensure requirements, labor supply, and the teacher workforce

As described in Section 1, the labor economic theory suggests that regulation requiring prospective teachers to satisfy licensure provisions for employment eligibility increases the cost of entering teaching and decreases the *number* of individuals who will opt to pursue that occupational choice (Kleiner (2000)). The impact on the *quality* of teacher applicants is, however, ambiguous. The restriction of labor supply will increase teacher salaries, making the occupation relatively more attractive to individuals who face comparatively low costs associated with satisfying licensure regulations, and who would

---

[15] The author is grateful to Tom Kane for granting permission to use this figure.
[16] Goldhaber (2007) finds very similar results in a study focused on the relationship between licensure tests—a key licensure component—and student achievement.

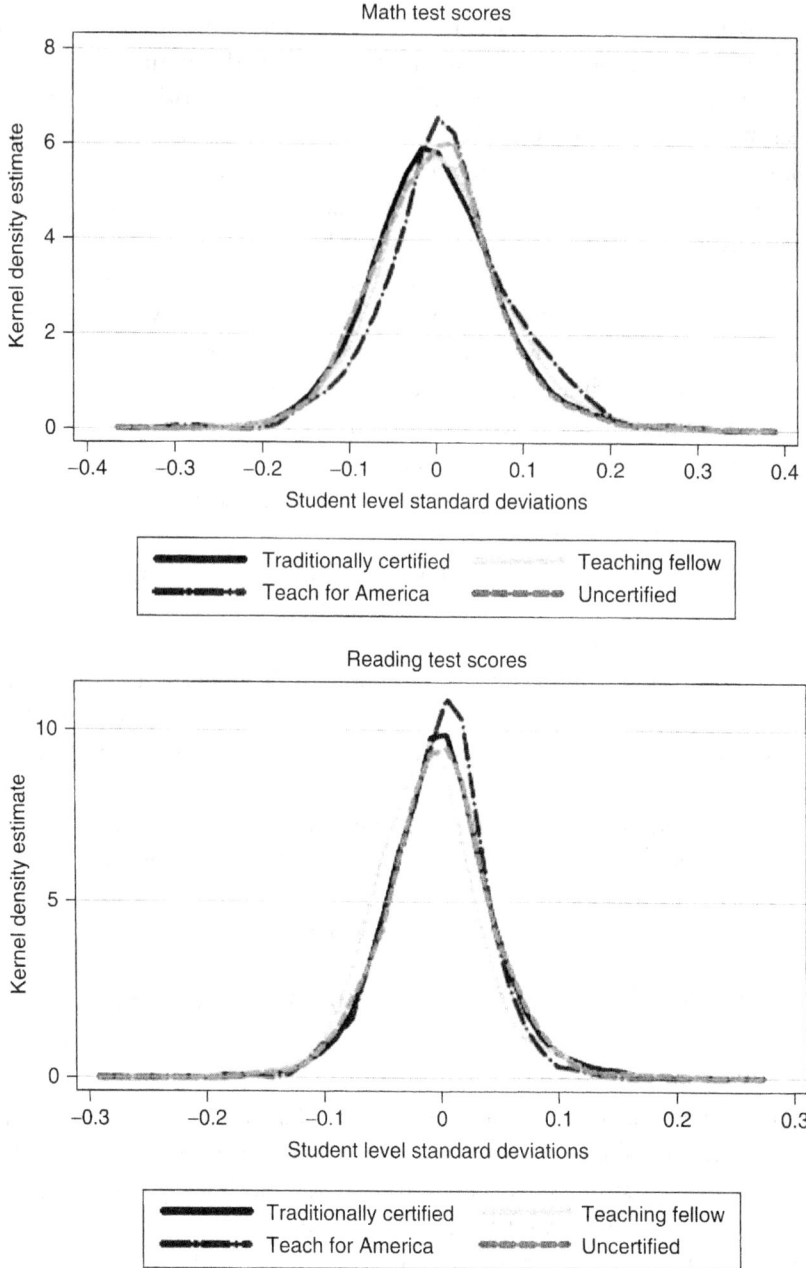

Figure 6.3 Variation in value-added within and between groups of teachers. *Source:* Kane et al. (2008).

earn more teaching than in other occupations. Several studies focused on occupational choice, for instance, find a relationship between anticipated future earnings and choice of major (see, for example, Berger (1988) and Dolton et al. (1989)).

The two major hurdles most often associated with obtaining a traditional teacher license are the requirement that individuals graduate from an approved teacher training institution with an approved degree (which may entail, for instance, a minimum number of pedagogical credit hours and/or field experiences) and that they achieve a specified standard on one or more licensure exams. Only a few labor market studies focus on the effects of these requirements on the number and type of individuals who opt to pursue a career in teaching.

Reback (2006) uses the National Educational Longitudinal Survey to examine the effect of reducing the entry cost of teacher licensure on the likelihood of pursuing a teaching career. He focuses on students who do not report an interest in teaching while in high school (in order to account for the likelihood that students pick their college according to the degree they intend to pursue) and who attend a selective college that has some type of education-related degree. He estimates that the probability of an individual pursuing an education degree increases substantially at the 135 most-selective colleges (according to Baron's U.S. rankings) if the education program can be completed within four years, but interestingly reduced entry costs have little impact on the probability of obtaining a teaching certificate (the dependent variable) in schools that are not among these 135 most-selective.

Reback's findings are not terribly surprising given that the cost in forgone earnings associated with satisfying some pedagogical requirements associated with licensure is likely to be quite high.[17] By contrast, for those who have the necessary degree, there is a relatively low *direct* cost associated with the other major hurdle associated with licensure systems: teacher licensure tests, which typically cost less than $200 for each test (Educational Testing Service (2008)). But while the great majority of test-takers pass the test the first time they take it—nearly 90% for those taking a commonly used Educational Testing Service-designed test (Gitomer and Latham (1999))—there is potentially a significant *indirect* cost associated with acquiring the knowledge necessary to pass these tests, and empirical evidence suggests that licensure-test requirements do have a considerable impact on the likelihood of pursuing a career as a teacher.

Hanushek and Pace (1995) use the *High School and Beyond Survey* to analyze the flows in and out of teacher training programs. One factor they find that influences the likelihood that individuals receive an education-focused Bachelor's degree (conditional on receiving a Bachelor's degree) is whether a state requires teachers to pass a licensure exam. In particular, they estimate that having such a requirement reduces

---

[17] This is especially true for lateral entrants into the labor market who might have to return to school despite already having a college degree.

the probability of prospective teachers (those who are enrolled in teacher training) from pursuing teacher preparation by about four percentage points.[18]

More recently, Angrist and Guryan (2008) utilize the *Schools and Staffing Survey* and focus on the relationship between licensure testing and the qualifications of the teacher workforce. This study assesses the combined impact of testing on occupational choice and school system selection since it is focused on teachers in the workforce. In particular, they examine whether testing is related to the selectivity of the college from which teachers graduate (based on the average SAT score of incoming freshman and Carnegie classifications) and whether teachers had an undergraduate degree in the subject in which they taught. They find some statistically significant results for the relationship between testing and undergraduate major (a positive relationship), but these are not robust across model specifications. And, they do not find any cases where there are statistically significant relationships between state testing requirements and the selectivity of the college from which teachers graduate.

Taken together, these studies suggest licensure requirements have little, or even negative, impacts on academic measures of the quality of individuals opting to pursue teaching as an occupation. Caution is appropriate, however, since all of these studies attempt to identify the impacts of licensure requirements based on cross-state or cross-institution variation and it is possible that the findings reflect unobserved factors correlated with both the propensity to pursue a career in teaching and either state or institution requirements.

4.3 Licensure requirements and hiring decisions

The final determinant of the impact of licensure policies on the quality of the teacher workforce is whether these policies affect hiring decisions. In theory, hiring authorities may be assisted by the information about prospective teachers that is conveyed by teacher licensure, and this may help them to make better hiring decisions. But, recall that, in the case where licensure requirements are strictly enforced, schools are precluded from hiring teachers who fail to satisfy them fully (e.g., those who fall into quadrants B and C on Figure 6.1). Thus, licensure requirements also constrain hiring authorities from hiring potentially competent teachers (those in quadrant C).

Since licensure systems are ubiquitous, we cannot know directly from empirical observation whether school systems would change recruitment and selection were regulation to be relaxed or, more specifically, whether they would make good decisions when given more freedom over whom they hire. Thus, evidence on this third determinant of the effects of licensure requirements on students—how they affect local hiring decisions—is both sparse and derived from either surveys, or research that focuses on individuals who ultimately are employed in different school districts. This observational data typically confounds the preferences of the districts and teachers because individuals are matched to both an occupation and to particular schools and districts,

---

[18] This represents a reduction of over 30%.

which makes it difficult to distinguish between the attributes that employers seek in job candidates and the preferences of individuals for an occupation (or, in the case of teachers, a particular school or district).

School surveys on hiring criteria from the late 1980s and early 1990s suggest that localities place an emphasis on education-specific credentials, like graduation from a state-approved teacher training institution, when making hiring decisions (Daugherty and Rossi (1996), Daugherty et al. (1997)). But there is also research suggesting that employee attributes valued in the private sector—for example, having attended a more selective college—are not as highly valued by the teacher labor market (Ballou (1996)). However, research based on administrative data on teachers in New York State suggests that localities are sensitive to the academic qualifications of applicants and have a preference for those from more-selective colleges and who score higher on licensure tests (Boyd et al. (2003)).[19] But these preferences over observable teacher attributes do not necessarily mean that school systems recruit more-effective teachers. Rivkin et al. (2005), for instance, focus on teachers in Texas who move from one district to another. They find some relationship between observable teacher characteristics (such as degree and licensure status) and the likelihood that teachers who hold an advanced degree or are fully credentialed "upgrade" their position (in terms of salary or the number of disadvantaged students they teach, for example) when they make a district move, but no significant relationship between direct measures of teacher effectiveness and school district characteristics.

5. CONCLUDING THOUGHTS

The impact of teacher licensure requirements on the quality of the teacher workforce is theoretically ambiguous. If the requirements do little to dissuade talented individuals from pursuing a teaching career, are strongly correlated with student achievement, and aid hiring officials in making decisions, then licensure systems are likely to be efficacious. However, to the extent that licensure requirements deter significant numbers of talented people from pursuing a teaching career, are not closely related to student achievement, and do little to improve the choices made by hiring officials, then such systems are likely to be both ineffective and costly.

The great majority of the empirical literature on licensure speaks to one crucial link in the teacher licensure–teacher quality equation: the correlation between licensure requirements and student achievement. In general the evidence suggests only weak links between the two, but the findings are not uniform across states. This is not terribly surprising since policy discussions tend to treat teacher licensure as if it is a *single*

---

[19] Some case study work suggests that when principals are given discretion over hiring teachers, they are often more concerned with the attitudes of prospective teachers and how they would fit within a school culture than measures of cognitive ability (see, for instance, DeArmond et al. (2008) and Harris et al. (2010)).

system, when in reality it is many different state-level systems. But, even when statistically significant effects are found in a state, there is significant overlap in estimates of teacher effectiveness across the licensure categories.

Less evidence is available on the impact of licensure requirements on the pool of potential teachers, so conclusions should be tempered. That said, the existing empirical work suggests (as theory would predict) that both pedagogical and testing requirements act to shrink the pool. This is not necessarily bad, as those who are dissuaded from pursuing a teaching career might not ultimately be effective teachers. Unfortunately, at least according to observable traits, the evidence suggests the teacher pipeline loses out on more academically capable individuals, and licensure testing policies in particular appear to have no positive impact on the academic caliber of the teacher workforce itself.

Even less is known about how school district hiring officials respond to changes in licensure requirements, or the absence of requirements altogether. The available evidence presents a mixed picture on whether district officials select the best candidates from their applicants. The mixed findings across states and time-periods may well represent reality, since hiring is likely to be dependent on school system recruitment and selection capacities and be sensitive to the political climate, labor market conditions, and the extent to which school systems face pressures from student outcome accountability systems. But, these findings should also be treated with caution, because of the scarcity of studies and because teacher quality is, at best, only weakly correlated with easily observable teacher attributes. Consequently, studies that focus on the teacher characteristics that school districts prefer may well miss whether districts actually favor individuals who are more successful in the classroom.

Given the diversity of the political, labor market, and accountability conditions across schools, districts, and states, it is conceivable that licensure systems have quite different impacts on different localities. For example, licensure regulations that greatly limit who is eligible to teach are unlikely to significantly impact the applicant pools of affluent school districts, since these districts often have numerous applicants for any open teaching position. On the other hand, school districts serving more disadvantaged students are far more likely to employ teachers who have not met all licensure requirements, therefore stricter enforcement of the requirements would surely have significant implications for teacher applications to those schools. Similarly, licensure systems may be quite beneficial in places where there are stronger motivations for inefficient (in terms of producing student learning) practices such as cronyism and patronage, whereas licensure is strictly limiting for systems that have the capacity and motivation to make good selections among applicants.

In terms of policy it is somewhat shocking how little we actually know about the impacts of teacher licensure systems. This is likely due, in part, to the fact that it is easy to promote and defend the notion that teachers should have minimal qualifications: the costs of having a truly poor teacher are immediately tangible to the public, whereas the costs of a licensure system in terms of investments in teacher-training and potential losses in the teacher pipeline are far more opaque. Regardless of the reason, our lack of knowledge about key aspects of the teacher licensure–teacher quality equation is unfortunate, since the current evidence on the links between licensure and student achievement does not provide much reassurance that licensure systems as currently constituted are effectively serving their intended purpose.

REFERENCES

Aaronson, D., Barrow, L., Sander, W., 2007. Teachers and student achievement in the Chicago Public High Schools. J. Labor Econ. 25 (1), 95–135.

Allen, M.B., 2003. Eight Questions on Teacher Preparation: What Does the Research Say?. Educational Commission of the States.

Angrist, J.D., Guryan, J., 2008. Does teacher testing raise teacher quality? Evidence from state certification requirements. Econ. Educ. Rev. 27 (5), 483–503.

Ballou, D., 1996. Do public schools hire the best applicants? Q. J. Econ. 111 (1), 97–133.

Ballou, D., Podgursky, M., 2000. Teacher unions and education reform: Gaining control of professional licensing and advancement. In: Loveless, T. (Ed.), Conflicting Missions? Teachers' Unions and Educational Reform. Brookings Institution, pp. 69–109.

Barber, M., Mourshed, M., 2007. How the World's Best-Performing School Systems Come Out on Top. McKinsey & Company. Available online at www.closingtheachievementgap.org/cs/ctag/view/resources/111 (accessed 16.01.09.).

Berger, M.C., 1988. Predicted future earnings and choice of college major. Review of 1988. Ind. Labor Relat. Rev. 41 (3), 418–429.

Boyd, D., Goldhaber, D.D., Lankford, H., Wyckoff, J.H., 2007. The effect of certification and preparation on teacher quality. Future Child 17 (1), 45–68.

Boyd, D., Grossman, P., Lankford, H., Loeb, S., Wyckoff, J., 2006. How changes in entry requirements alter the teacher workforce and affect student achievement. Educ. Financ. & Policy 1 (2), 176–216.

Boyd, D.J., Lankford, H., Loeb, S., Wyckoff, J.H., 2003. Analyzing the determinants of the matching public school teachers to jobs: Estimating compensating differentials in imperfect labor markets. NBER Working Paper No. 9878.

Clotfelter, C.T., Ladd, H.F., Vigdor, J.L., 2007. How and why do teacher credentials matter for student achievement?. NBER Working Paper No. 12828.

Darling-Hammond, L., 2001. The research and rhetoric on teacher certification: A response to "Teacher certification reconsidered" Educ. Policy Anal. Arch. 10 (36).

Darling-Hammond, L., Berry, B., Thoreson, A., 2001. Does teacher certification matter? Evaluating the evidence. Educ. Eval. Policy Anal. 23 (1), 57–77.

Daugherty, S., DeAngelis, K., Rossi, R., 1997. Credentials and tests in teacher hiring: What do districts require? In: Issue Briefs. U.S. Department of Education Office of Educational Research and Improvement.

Daugherty, S., Rossi, R., 1996. What criteria are used in considering teacher applicants? In: Issue Briefs. U.S. Department of Education Office of Educational Research and Improvement.

DeArmond, M., Gross, B., Goldhaber, D., 2008. Is it better to be good or lucky? Decentralized teacher selection in 10 elementary schools. CRPE Working Paper No. 2008–3.

Decker, P.T., Mayer, D.P., Glazerman, S., 2004. The effects of Teach for America on students: Findings from a national evaluation. Mathematica Policy Research Report.

Dolton, P., Makepeace, G., Van der Klaauw, W., 1989. Occupational choice and earnings determination—the role of sample selection and non-pecuniary factors. Am. Econ. Rev 94 (2), 230–235.

Educational Testing Service, 2008. Tests Directory > The Praxis Series: Teacher Licensure and Certification > Praxis I Overview. www.ets.org (accessed 28.07.08.).

Evertson, C.M., Hawley, W.D., Zlotnik, M., 1985. Making a difference in educational quality through teacher-education. J. Teach. Educ. 36 (3), 2–12.

Feistritzer, C.E., 2008. Alternative Teacher Certification: A State-by-State Analysis. National Center for Education Information.

Gitomer, D.H., Latham, A.S., 1999. The Academic Quality of Prospective Teachers: The Impact of Admissions and Licensure Testing. In: Giambattista, J. (Ed.), ETS.

Glazerman, S., Mayer, D.P., Decker, P.T., 2006. Alternative routes to teaching: The impacts of Teach for America on student achievement and other outcomes. J. Policy Anal. Manag. 25 (1), 75–96.

Goldhaber, D.D., 2004. Why do we license teachers? In: Hess, F., Rotherham, A., Walsh, K. (Eds.), A Qualified Teacher in Every Classroom: Appraising Old Answers and New Ideas. Harvard Education Press, pp. 81–100.

Goldhaber, D.D., 2007. Everyone's doing it, but what does teacher testing tell us about teacher effectiveness. J. Hum. Resour. 42 (4), 765–794.

Goldhaber, D.D., 2009. Lessons from abroad: Exploring cross-country differences in teacher development systems and what they mean for U.S. policy. In: Goldhaber, D., Hannaway, J. (Eds.), Creating a New Teaching Profession. Urban Institute Press.

Goldhaber, D.D., Brewer, D.J., 2000. Does teacher certification matter? High school teacher certification status and student achievement. Educ. Eval. Policy Anal. 22 (2), 129–145.

Gordon, R.J., Kane, T.J., Staiger, D.O., 2006. Identifying effective teachers using performance on the job. Brookings Institution, Hamilton Project White Paper.

Hanushek, E.A., 1979. Conceptual and empirical issues in the estimation of educational production functions. J. Hum. Resour. 14 (3), 351–388.

Hanushek, E.A., 2009. Teacher deselction. In: Goldhaber, D., Hannaway, J. (Eds.), Creating a New Teaching Profession. Urban Institute Press.

Hanushek, E.A., Pace, R.R., 1995. Who chooses to teach (and why)? Econ. Educ. Rev. 14 (2), 101–117.

Harris, D.N., Rutledge, S.A., Ingle, W.K., Thompson, C.C., 2010. Mix and match: What principals look for when hiring teachers. Educ. Financ. & Policy 5 (2), 228–246.

Harris, D., Sass, T., 2008. The effect of NBPTS-certified teachers on student achievement. Urban Institute, CALDER Working Paper 4.

Humphris, A., Kleiner, M.M., Koumenta, M., (forthcoming). How does government regulate occupations in the UK and US? Issues and policy implications. In: Marsden, D. (Ed.), Labor Market Policy for the 21st Century. Oxford University Press.

Johnson, S.M., Birkeland, S., Peske, H., 2005. A difficult balance: Incentives and quality control in alternative certification programs. Harvard Graduate School of Education, Project on the Next Generation of Teachers.

Kane, T.J., Rockoff, J.E., Staiger, D.O., 2007. Photo finish: Teacher certification doesn't guarantee a winner. Education Next 7 (1), 60–67.

Kane, T.J., Rockoff, J.E., Staiger, D.O., 2008. What does certification tell us about teacher effectiveness? Evidence from New York City. Econ. Educ. Rev. 27 (6), 615–631.

Kleiner, M., 2000. Occupational licensing. J. Econ. Perspect. 14 (4).

Kleiner, M., 2008. Enhancing quality or restricting competition? The case of licensing public school teachers. Paper prepared for the Bill and Melinda Gates Foundation.

Kleiner, M., Krueger, A., 2008. The prevalence and effects of occupational licensing. NBER Working Paper No. 14308.

Laczko-Kerr, I., Berliner, D.C., 2002. The effectiveness of "Teach for America" and other under-certified teachers on student academic achievement: A case of harmful public policy. Educ. Policy Anal. Arch. 10 (37).

Murnane, R.J., Steele, J.L., 2007. What is the problem? The challenge of providing effective teachers for all children. Future Child 17 (1), 15–44.

NASDTEC, 2007. NASDTEC KnowledgeBase Portal. Topical Table B1. National Association of State Directors of Teacher Education and Certification.

NASDTEC, 2010. NASDTEC KnowledgeBase Portal. Topical Tables B2 and G1. National Association of State Directors of Teacher Education and Certification.

OECD, 2004. The quality of the teaching workforce. In: Policy Brief. Organization for Economic Co-Operation and Development (February).
OECD, 2005. Teachers Matter: Attracting, Developing, and Retaining Effective Teachers. Organization for Economic Co-Operation and Development.
OECD, 2008. Education at a Glance 2008: OECD Indicators. Organization for Economic Co-Operation and Development.
Peterson, P.E., Nadler, D., 2008. What happens when states have genuine alternative certification? Education Next 9 (1), 70–74.
Raymond, M.E., Fletcher, S., Luque, J.A., 2001. Teach for America: An Evaluation of Teacher Differences and Student Outcomes in Houston, Texas. Stanford University: CREDO.
Reback, R., 2006. Entry costs and the supply of public school teachers. Educ. Financ. Policy 1 (2), 247–265.
Rockoff, J.E., 2004. The impact of individual teachers on students' achievement: Evidence from panel data. Am. Econ. Rev. 94 (2), 247–252.
Rivkin, S.G., Hanushek, E.A., Kain, J.F., 2005. Teachers, schools, and academic achievement. Econometrica 73 (2), 417–458.
Rotherham, A.J., 2008. Achieving Teacher and Principal Excellence: A Guidebook for Donors. Philanthropy Roundtable.
Schmidt, W., 2008. What we know about teacher preparation in other countries. The Urban Institute, Working Paper prepared for the Human Capital Project.
Shapiro, C., 1986. Investment, moral hazard, and occupational licensing. Rev. Econ. Stat. 13, 843–862.
Walsh, K., 2001a. Teacher Certification Reconsidered: A Rejoinder. Abell Foundation.
Walsh, K., 2001b. Teacher Certification Reconsidered: Stumbling for Quality. Abell Foundation.
Wang, A.H., Coleman, A.B., Coley, R.J., Phelps, R.P., 2003. Preparing teachers around the world. Policy Information Report: Educational Testing Service.
Woessmann, L., 2008. Enter the teacher labor force in Germany. The Urban Institute, Working Paper prepared for the Human Capital Project.
Xu, Z., Hannaway, J., Taylor, C., 2007. Making a difference? The effects of Teach for America in high school. The Urban Institute, CALDER Working Paper 17.

CHAPTER 7

The Economics of Tracking in Education

Julian R. Betts
UC San Diego and NBER

Contents

1. Introduction	342
2. Theoretical Foundations: Lessons for Various Empirical Approaches	344
2.1 Basic considerations	344
2.2 Potential for international and across-school variations in the meaning of tracking, and for mismeasurement	346
2.3 Endogeneity of tracking	347
2.4 A benchmark data generation process	348
3. Tracking and School Resources	349
4. Empirical Approaches to Estimating the Effects of Tracking	351
4.1 Traditional across- and within-school variation	351
4.1.1 Early work	351
4.1.2 Newer American research that uses nationally representative samples	352
4.2 Approaches that Use Geographical Variation	357
4.2.1 Geographic: Time difference in differences; natural experiments related to policy reforms	357
4.2.2 Geographic: Age difference in differences using international and subnational geographic variation	363
4.2.3 Other methods that use geographical variation in tracking	368
4.2.4 Endogeneity of tracking in international studies	370
4.3 Experiments with random assignment of students to treatment	371
5. Conclusion and Outline of a Possible Research Agenda for the Future	375
Acknowledgements	380
References	380

Abstract

Tracking refers to the practice of dividing students by ability or achievement. Students may be tracked within schools by placing them into different classrooms based on achievement, which is the typical practice in countries such as the United States or Canada. Alternatively, students could be streamed into different schools, with either vocational or academic emphases, as has been practiced commonly in Europe. Proponents of tracking argue that tracking can increase the efficiency of schooling by focusing on the needs of distinct groups of students. Opponents' main concerns relate to perpetuating and aggravating inequality. Evaluating effects of tracking on average student achievement and the distribution of achievement is difficult, in part because of variations from study to study and from country to country in the characteristics of the tracking system. Early work, largely in the United States and Britain, used variation across and within schools, and often found that tracking increased inequality in achievement. But more recent work in the United States has questioned these findings, suggesting that careful attention to endogenous placement of students into classrooms and endogenous use of tracking across schools changes results dramatically. Experimental studies on within-school tracking in the United States have produced mixed results, and one experiment in Kenya suggests that tracking can boost the achievement of both low-achieving and high-achieving students. A large body of work now uses geographical variation across regions, countries, grades, and time to identify the effects of tracking. These studies for the most part suggest that tracking aggravates inequality in outcomes. These results are fairly strong, and may be identifying the more dramatic effects that obtain when students are separated into vocational schools and more academically oriented schools, as opposed to the effects of within-school tracking. The paper concludes with an outline of how future research might better categorize and rigorously evaluate the real-world nuances of tracking.

JEL classification: I20, I21

Keywords

Tracking
Ability Grouping
Streaming
Pedagogy
Curriculum
Human Capital
Vocational Education

1. INTRODUCTION

Tracking refers to the tendency in many countries' public school systems to divide students by ability in some way. Students might be sorted into different classrooms within a school, or sorted into different schools. Definitions of tracking in the academic literature range from nothing more than ability grouping to more elaborate forms that divide students by academic achievement with the explicit intent of delivering a different curriculum, and using different pedagogical methods, for different groups of students. Countries differ widely on the degree to which they track students, and the age at which students begin to be tracked. Within-school ability grouping is common in the United States and Canada, while the practice of separating students into different flavors of schools at the secondary level, typically divided into academic versus vocational tracks, is or was the case in many European countries for at least part of the last half century.[1]

There are good reasons to believe that the within-school tracking prevalent in the United States should produce different effects than tracking into different types of schools as in Europe. Within-school tracking does not change one's peers at the school-wide level, or the overall demographics of schools, whereas these characteristics could change dramatically if students were streamed into two or more tiers of specialized schools. In a

---

[1] On the question of vocational education, Wolter and Ryan (this volume) review the related literature on apprenticeships.

system with within-school tracking, students should be able to move between tracks or ability groups relatively easily over time; they could be in a high track in one subject and a low track in another subject; mistakes could be fixed relatively easily. In contrast, a European style of tracking in which students are streamed into one of two or more styles of schools would be expected to be less flexible along each of these dimensions.

Proponents of tracking argue that it is economically efficient to group students by ability and perhaps by students' academic interests. By creating more homogeneous classrooms, in the case of tracking within a school, or more homogeneous schools, in the case of tracking across schools, in theory educators could tailor their pedagogical approaches for the given set of students. Separating students by initial achievement also opens up the possibility that school systems could tailor school resources to the given type of student. Examples of such resources include class size and teachers with certain types of qualifications.[2] At the secondary level, when students move beyond a focus on reading, writing, and arithmetic to coursework that helps to prepare them either for postsecondary education or for more vocationally oriented jobs, tracking can also save resources by teaching each student exactly what he or she needs to know. In the case of countries that have tracked students into one of several tiers of secondary schools, one can imagine that the savings from not having to replicate every possible course sequence in any one school could be substantial.

Opponents of tracking argue that it condemns students placed into the lower tracks to lower educational attainment, and therefore lower earnings in their adult years. They fear that tracking aggravates economic inequality and perpetuates economic disadvantage across generations. Opponents have also criticized the academic data with which students are categorized into tracks, fearing that standardized test scores are untrustworthy. Student misclassifications seem particularly likely when tracking decisions are made in early grades. Evidence from some countries suggests that track placement has at least as much to do with socio-economic status as with actual student achievement, implying that the efficiency gains from separating students by aptitude will dissipate if something other than achievement determines track placement. A final concern is that tracking changes the peer group of every student. The questions are whether those in the lower tracks suffer because of the reduced academic achievement of peers, and whether any such losses are counterbalanced by benefits to those in the higher tracks, whose peer group improves after tracking is implemented.

Tracking has generated heated political debate in many countries. The United Kingdom, which historically channeled students into three different types of schools based on a test administered to students when they were 11, began to move away from this system in

---

[2] As an example of why educators might want to customize the way they teach different groups of students, Finn and Achilles (1999) and Krueger (1999) show in the Tennessee class size reduction experiment that disadvantaged students tended to gain more from smaller class sizes. Betts, Zau, and Rice (2003) report that smaller classes at the elementary level are particularly beneficial to English learners, while Babcock and Betts (2009) present evidence that lower class size in elementary schools particularly benefits students who misbehave rather than the similar but distinct set of students who have low academic grades.

the 1960s, based on fears that the system generated and perpetuated inequality. But due to political opposition to "detracking," remnants of the three-tier approach still exist four decades later in the United Kingdom. Sweden reformed its system in the 1950s, ending the assignment of students at age 12 or 13 to different educational paths. Other Scandinavian countries have implemented similar reforms. In the United States, schools widely practice within-school tracking. Many American researchers tend to dislike tracking on the grounds that it robs students from disadvantaged neighborhoods of the chance to achieve their educational potential. For instance, a widely cited book by Oakes (1985, with a new edition in 2005) provides a strong critique of tracking as it exists in America.

This paper will study what we know about the effects of tracking on overall student achievement and the distribution of student achievement, using studies from many different countries. One of the central problems in this diverse literature is the typically loose definitions of tracking that are available in existing data-sets. Similarly, researchers face several definitional problems when identifying the ability level of individual classes. A second central problem has been the endogenous selection of students into different tracks. A third problem is that school systems or countries may endogenously select a tracking or nontracking approach. These problems have yet to be fully resolved.

2. THEORETICAL FOUNDATIONS: LESSONS FOR VARIOUS EMPIRICAL APPROACHES

This section provides a fairly general model of what determines student achievement, and then uses it to outline common pitfalls in empirical estimation of the effects of tracking. We will refer to this baseline model repeatedly when assessing strengths and weaknesses of various identification strategies used in the literature on tracking.

2.1 Basic considerations

To know what questions to pose about the economic consequences of tracking, we must begin with a clear idea of the factors that contribute to student learning, and how various forms of tracking might affect these basic factors. One can easily imagine an education production function that goes beyond the standard inputs of class size and teacher qualifications, and that in addition allows for multiple paths through which tracking might affect an individual student's achievement. The most obvious mechanism is that when a school adopts tracking within its classrooms, or a district adopts tracking across its schools, each student's peer group changes. Teaching style (pedagogy) and subject matter (curriculum) could also vary across classrooms when schools track, especially in secondary schools and in the European context, where in certain countries secondary students are streamed into entirely different types of schools. Examples of how pedagogical approaches might vary when tracking is used include variations in how the teacher divides her time, first, among students, and second, among whole-classroom, small group, and individual instruction.

We start with a production function for the test score for student i in country c, school s, with teacher r in grade g and year t, S_{icsrgt}. Assume that this test score depends on innate ability A_i (in a way that may vary with age), other personal traits X_{icgt}, a vector that implicitly contains an overall intercept, some key family characteristic F_{icgt}, a vector of teacher qualifications $QUAL_{icsrgt}$, teacher effort $QEFF_{icsrgt}$, which we index with i because the teacher may focus her efforts in a way that helps some students in the class more than others, class size $CLASS_{icsrgt}$, measures of the initial achievement and perhaps other traits of classroom peers, captured by $PEER_{icsrgt}$, a vector of variables indicating the curriculum being taught, captured by $CURR_{icsrgt}$, and a vector of variables indicating the pedagogical approach taken by the student's teacher PED_{icsrgt}. School level characteristics $SCHOOL_{icsgt}$ could matter. Finally, parents may purchase educational activities or materials for their child after school, $PRIV_{icgt}$. For example, many Japanese parents pay to send their children to after-school tutoring in private schools known as *juku*. It is likely that the entire past school history of the student affects his or her current score, but we omit these lags for the sake of simplicity:

$$S_{icsrgt} = f \begin{pmatrix} A_i, X_{icgt}, F_{icgt}, QUAL_{icsrgt}, QEFF_{icsrgt}, CLASS_{icsrgt}, \\ PEER_{icsrgt}, CURR_{icsrgt}, PED_{icsrgt}, SCHOOL_{icsgt}, PRIV_{icgt} \end{pmatrix} \quad (7.1)$$

Suppose that some schools use tracking. Then all of the determinants of achievement in Equation (7.1) apart from A_i, X_{icgt} and F_{icgt} are likely to be endogenous functions of both the overall use of tracking and the specific track to which a student i is assigned. With tracking, school administrators are able to alter all of the classroom and school characteristics. For instance, the use of tracking is likely to influence the qualifications of student i's teacher, and class size, because administrators now have the ability to tailor the resources devoted to students at different achievement levels. If teachers react differently to having more homogeneous groups of students in tracked schools or to higher or lower ability groups within tracked schools, teacher effort $QEFF_{icsrgt}$ will also depend on the use of tracking and perhaps student i's specific track. Peers, curriculum and pedagogical approaches adopted by the student's teacher could also depend upon the use of tracking. In countries such as Germany and Italy in which students are tracked into different types of secondary schools along the vocational college preparatory continuum, the vectors of school characteristics $SCHOOL_{icsgt}$ will also depend on tracking.

More subtly, if parents make decisions on how much to spend on private tutoring, $PRIV_{icgt}$, in response to the quality of schooling that is being provided for their children, this spending too could change once tracking was implemented. For instance, in a system without tracking, more affluent parents may spend considerably on private tutoring because they want to find ways to create a separating equilibrium in which their children obtain the top grades in school and gain either the best postgraduation jobs or admission to the best universities. Such spending might fall once tracking were introduced because parents viewed placement of their children into the upper track as a substitute for private tutoring. But less affluent parents may do the opposite if they perceived that once tracking was instituted, their children were likely to be placed in the lower tracks. Because affluent parents have greater financial resources than do less affluent parents, it is likely that the institution of tracking would lower overall parental spending on private educational resources.

This insight may hold implications for studies that use variations in tracking policy over time. If affluent parents seek a separating equilibrium that benefits their children, then they will increase private tutoring expenditures if tracking is ended. Presumably, then, this would bias down the estimated effects of tracking on both the equality of student outcomes and the overall level of student outcomes.

There are many complications we could add to the model. For example, one of the main concerns expressed in the empirical literature on tracking is that tracking in one grade affects student outcomes and the sorts of courses and teachers to which students have access in later grades. Thus each of the determinants of test scores in grade g in Equation (7.1) depend on tracking not only in that grade but in prior grades. The above production function is also ripe with possibilities for interactions between the various inputs on the right-hand side, and other types of nonlinearities.[3]

What decisions must a researcher make before attempting to estimate a version of the potentially complex production function implied by Equation (7.1)? Suppose that a longitudinal student-level data-set becomes available. Even if the data contained detailed information on peers, pedagogical approach, and so on, the endogeneity problems would be severe. In the student-level studies that have obtained information on the ability group to which a student has been assigned, researchers typically have estimated a reduced-form model that has not attempted to include controls for teachers' pedagogical methods, peer achievement and other endogenous factors, but instead has included either a simple control for whether tracking is used or an interaction between the use of tracking and the student's ability level, and some controls for overall school resources.

Similarly, the many studies that have used international variation in the use of tracking typically omit the many endogenous explanatory variables in Equation (7.1).

2.2 Potential for international and across-school variations in the meaning of tracking, and for mismeasurement

While this tendency to estimate reduced-form models makes sense, it does raise serious questions about what we mean by tracking. Especially in the many international studies in this literature, we are estimating an average treatment effect across what might be

---

[3] Nonlinearities raise concerns that aggregated analyses that average over large numbers of schools could be subject to aggregation biases. See Theil (1954) for an early examination of the issue of nonlinearities and Hanushek, Rivkin, and Taylor (1996) for a study specific to education production functions.

really quite different types of tracking between one country and another. For example, one country that tracks may stream students into different schools, with different types of teachers and other resources, and intentionally different curricula. In another country that uses tracking, tracking could be within-school, and it might give largely the same curriculum to different students, with similarly trained teachers, but use different pedagogical approaches for students in the various tracks.

Such differences in the meaning of tracking seem quite possible. A characterization of many European approaches to tracking is that they separate students into two or three different types of schools, each of which has a quite distinct curricular focus. American and Canadian schools are typified by informal tracking that rarely involves sending students to different types of schools. This will become an extremely important point to bear in mind when we consider studies that make international comparisons.

For instance, Brunello and Checchi (2007), similarly to other authors who compare tracking across countries, report that the age at first tracking in the United States is 18. This categorization is true only if one ignores the very strong within-school ability grouping and streaming that occurs as early as middle school. See, for example, Oakes (1985, 2005.)

2.3 Endogeneity of tracking

For both student-level within-country and international studies, even if we drop endogenous mediating variables such as teacher qualifications and teacher effort, the endogeneity of tracking itself remains an issue. Why do some schools within a country track, and why do some countries but not others track? The factors determining whether public schools track are likely to be quite complex, and in many cases these factors could affect achievement of students through other paths than tracking itself. For instance, the degree of competition from private schools may affect the probability that public schools within a region or country adopt tracking, as hypothesized by Epple, Newlon, and Romano (2002). Yet competition from private schools is likely to affect public school achievement through diverse channels in addition to whether public schools track. Societies that are more conservative in the sense of having less egalitarian social policies are more likely to use tracking to benefit the children of more affluent families. Societies that are more socially divided may seek out tracking as a way of separating students from different types of backgrounds. Racial mix, religious mix, and immigrant/native mixes could also influence the use of tracking.

Figlio and Page (2002) present results indicating a positive association between changes in American schools' use of tracking and changes in the socio-economic status of students. Their interpretation is that more affluent students seek out schools that track, although of course the causation could run in the opposite direction. They also find that county voting patterns, state graduation requirements, and the amount of public school competition are correlated with whether a given high school tracks.

For within-country studies, the endogeneity of tracking can become worse than in the case of international studies. First, families decide where to live, and so may opt into or out of a school with tracking through their locational choice. Second, if a dataset contains specific information on the track into which a student has been placed, it may be dangerous to condition on this information because this placement is itself endogenous.

On the other hand, across-country studies may suffer from greater omitted variable bias than studies using variation within a country, because of greater unobserved heterogeneity across countries than across areas within a country.

2.4 A benchmark data generation process

With these data concerns noted, it is useful to compare the production function in Equation (7.1) with the sort of model that is estimated in the majority of studies that have used variations in the use of tracking across geographic areas. The example below assumes that the geographic unit at which tracking is observed is countries, but the estimating equation would carry over to a case in which tracking varied by county or other geographic unit within a country.

We assume that we have no data on the range of endogenous variables in Equation (7.1) that schools might alter if they were able to use tracking. But we assume that some measure of overall school resources is available, without which omitted variable bias could be quite severe. We also reintroduce the idea briefly alluded to above that the entire history of a student's experience with tracking should affect his or her current achievement.

Consider the following data generation process, in which we observe the test score for student i in country c, in grade g and year t. Assume that this test score depends on personal traits X_{icgt}, a vector that implicitly contains an overall intercept, some key family characteristic F_{icgt}, some measure of the average school resources, such as spending per pupil, that student i experienced from kindergarten up to grade g, Q_{icgt}, and indicators for whether the student in each year and grade was in a tracked school (or lived in a country in which students were typically tracked in that year and grade), captured by indicator variables T_{icgt}, $T_{ic,g-1,t-1}$ and so on. We assume that the data generation process (d.g.p.) might be given by:

$$S_{icgt} = X_{icgt}\Phi + F_{icgt}\Pi + Q_{icgt}\gamma + T_{icgt}\lambda_g + T_{ic,g-1,t-1}\lambda_{g-1} + \ldots + T_{ic,1,t-g+1}\lambda_1$$
$$+ T_{icgt}F_{icgt}\rho_g + T_{ic,g-1,t-1}F_{ic,g-1,t-1}\rho_{g-1} + \ldots + T_{ic,1,t-g+1}F_{ic,1,t-g+1}\rho_1 \quad (7.2)$$
$$+ (\alpha_i + \alpha_c + \alpha_g + \alpha_t + \beta_{cg} + \beta_{ct} + \beta_{gt} + \delta_{cgt} + \varepsilon_{icgt})$$

The λ_k terms capture the average effects of having been tracked in grade k.[4] The model includes interactions between the tracking dummies T and the family characteristic F.

---

[4] Note that for simplicity we assume that the effects of being tracked in a given grade are permanent in the sense that they have the same impact on test scores in grade k and all later grades. If we allowed for deprecation of the effects slight complications which are well understood would be added. One could also imagine nonlinear effects on a student of being tracked for multiple years. These issues have yet to be studied empirically.

The ρ_k terms in Equation (7.2) capture the differential effects of tracking on different socio-economic groups, and thus are of interest to those focusing on whether tracking generates inequality in education outcomes. Some researchers exclude these terms in some of their models, so that in these simplified models the λ_k terms provide a measure of the overall efficiency effect of tracking, holding constant school resources Q_{icgt}.

A comparison of Equations (7.1) and (7.2) suggests that we may be missing some important explanatory variables, but that we have written the reduced form of a plausible data generation process. Researchers who typically estimate a variant of Equation (7.2) and who exclude endogenous regressors such as teacher qualifications and curriculum will thus also have sidestepped some severe issues of endogeneity bias.[5]

3. TRACKING AND SCHOOL RESOURCES

Before studying the effects of tracking on achievement, it is helpful to characterize how resources vary across tracks, and how countries themselves might vary in how they implement tracking systems.

Betts and Shkolnik (2000a) provide the first characterization using a large nationally representative U.S. data-set of the school resources assigned to students in five ability groups. They find that, relative to teachers of the top classes, teachers of the lowest ability classes tend to have less experience (12.3 years versus 15.0 years for the top classes) and to be less likely to hold a Master's degree (50% versus 69%). But conversely, class sizes are smaller for the bottom ability group (at about 19 students compared to about 26 students in the top ability group). It is possible that these smaller class sizes allow teachers to spend more time on individualized instruction. Evidence for such a correlation is provided in a separate study by Betts and Shkolnik (1999).

Betts and Shkolnik (2000a) also find some subtle differences in these patterns between schools at which principals claim ability grouping is used and schools at which principals claim ability grouping is not used. Most importantly, they find that only in schools with formal grouping do class size and teacher experience fall substantially for the bottom-ability classes.

Rees, Brewer, and Argys (2000) replicate these results using a separate nationally representative U.S. data-set. They report that grade 10 classes in history, math, science, and English tend to be smaller for below-average ability classes (by about 3 or 4 students), and that for math classes (only) students in low-ability classes are less likely to have a teacher with a Master's degree. They also report very small differences in

---

[5] For simplicity we have conditioned upon a student's past experience with tracking, but not upon past school resources. Researchers lack the detailed educational histories needed to do this, but sometimes condition upon a lagged score as a proxy for these past experiences. This imposes strong restrictions. An even more restrictive version of such a model models gains in achievement but does not include any lagged achievement scores as explanatory variables.

teacher experience across ability groups, but with a very weak pattern in which low-ability classes receive teachers with lower experience.

In contrast, Brunello and Checchi (2007, page 795) document large differences in pupil-teacher ratios experienced by students in different tracks in upper secondary grades in various European countries. They write that the largest differences in pupil-teacher ratio are in Germany, with 11.89 students per teacher in the general track and 21.25 students per teacher in the vocational track. Corresponding figures are, for Austria, 9.05 versus 14.51, for France, 6.75 and 14.67, and for Italy, 11.17 and 11.94. Conversely, though, they report calculations on total expenditures per student in vocational and academic tracks in Austria and find that the former is generally higher, which could perhaps arise due to the costs of on-the-job training components in the vocational tracks.

These pupil-teacher ratios are not the same thing as class size—actual class sizes will be larger because teachers typically have preparation time outside the classroom each day. But still, these figures show the opposite pattern to American schools in that class sizes appear to be larger in the vocational track in these European schools. However, the authors do not report on pupil-teacher ratios in the lower grades of secondary schools.

Perhaps in Europe it is politically more feasible to implement bigger resource differences by track because at the secondary level many European countries send different ability groups to different types of schools. Funding two or three types of schools differentially may be less visible (and objectionable) than would be the same resource differences implemented along different corridors of the same school, as would be required in the U.S style of within-school ability grouping.

In the following sections that evaluate the effects of tracking, it will be helpful to bear in mind the contrasts between the American and European versions of tracking. First, as mentioned in the previous section, American high schools tend to offer various tracks under the same roof, while the European approach more typically houses vocational and academic tracks under separate roofs. Second, as shown here, the differences in classroom resources in American high schools, as reported in two papers, are not large, and no ability group receives more of all resource types. But in four European countries pupil-teacher ratios are unequivocally larger in vocational schools at least in the higher grades. Countering this, though, is the finding that overall expenditures per pupil in Austria are higher on vocational education than in the academic track.

The overall sense that emerges is that European versions of tracking are more dramatic than the within-school tracking typical of countries such as the United States and Canada; when students are streamed into one of several distinct types of schools, overall resources, peers, pedagogy, and curriculum could vary dramatically. Further, with between-school tracking, students will presumably have less flexibility to move back and forth between tracks across grades, or across subjects in the same grade. This insight will prove useful in reconciling differences between the American and international literatures on the effects of tracking on student achievement.

4. EMPIRICAL APPROACHES TO ESTIMATING THE EFFECTS OF TRACKING

This section outlines the main approaches used thus far to estimate the effects of tracking. Each method is outlined, along with the main technical challenges in each case, and a review of findings.

4.1 Traditional across- and within-school variation

Many nonexperimental papers compare students in different tracks within a school or across schools. These regression-based studies typically use a sample of schools within a country or a smaller geographic area. In relation to the formulation in Equation (7.2) most of the terms in the error term are not accounted for by adding fixed effects, apart from dummies for grade level α_g. With one exception, this literature has taken the decision by schools to use tracking as exogenous. Typically but not always, researchers have assumed that the endogeneity of the student's track can be controlled for by including a sufficiently rich set of covariates. The papers in this section focus on within-school tracking, typically in American schools, which could be a quite distinct phenomenon from students being streamed selectively into one of a series of quite distinct types of secondary schools, as has occurred in many European countries.

4.1.1 Early work

Slavin (1987, 1990) assesses the large early literature, almost all of which was written by social scientists outside of economics. Researchers have typically estimated two types of equations, which aim to answer either the question of whether tracking affects efficiency of schools or the question of whether tracking contributes to inequality in outcomes. To answer the first question, researchers have compared overall achievement at schools with and without tracking, *ceteris paribus*. To study the second question, a single explanatory variable for tracking is typically replaced with the ability level of the class to which the student was assigned.

Slavin (1990) reviews 14 regression-based student-level studies of tracking in secondary schools. The studies he includes focus on American and to a lesser extent British schools. On the question of efficiency, Slavin shows that effect sizes in studies that compare tracking to nontracking schools vary but are typically close to zero. Somewhat more surprisingly, on the question of whether those in high, medium, and low-ability groups in schools with tracking perform differently from heterogeneously grouped students, he again finds no consistent patterns. Most of these studies involved anywhere from 1 to 28 schools. Thus, the often insignificant results could result from the low statistical power of the smaller studies. The most important exception to the characterization of the early literature as being small scale is Kerckhoff (1986), which studies a large sample of secondary school students in the United Kingdom. This paper concludes that there are small positive effects on average achievement, and that students in the high-ability classes had significantly higher test scores than students in the low-ability classes, after controlling for initial achievement.

Slavin (1987) provides a review of early work on tracking at the elementary school level. He reports that 13 correlational or regression-based studies typically find no overall effect of "comprehensive" (school-wide) ability grouping on achievement, and mixed evidence on whether students in higher-ability classes gain more than students in lower-ability classes. Again, many of these early studies use small samples, with eight using samples of under 1000 students, and most studying either a handful of schools or, in one case, two districts, one with and one without tracking. The two largest studies, one conducted in England and Wales and the other in New York City, reported no or slightly negative overall effects of ability grouping, and no evidence that high-ability groups perform better when they are in high-ability classes.

Slavin (1987) presents far more favorable evidence for two specific types of ability grouping in elementary schools. The first, known as the Joplin plan, allows for regrouping of students across grades for reading, with the grouping based on initial reading prowess. Eleven of 14 studies, including two experimental studies, suggested that this approach led to increases in average reading achievement, with the median effect size 0.45. Second, Slavin summarizes eight studies of within-class ability grouping, including five experimental studies. All but one study, which examines math, reading, and spelling, focus on mathematics. All studies suggested that within-class ability grouping led to an increase in average achievement. The studies differed on whether students in high- or low-ability classes gained more from this type of grouping.

Slavin's literature reviews have been quite influential, and were seen as a rebuttal to the claims by Oakes (1985, and also 2005), which were based on observation of individual schools, that in the United States tracking hurts low-performing students.

However, concerns about the papers reviewed by Slavin (1987, 1990) include not only small sample sizes but the very limited geographical range of the individual American studies, and limited attention to the endogeneity of group placement.

4.1.2 Newer American research that uses nationally representative samples

More recently, in the American literature, a number of papers have used far larger longitudinal data-sets than were available in the early studies. Moreover, these data-sets were also nationally representative. Hoffer (1992) studies math and science achievement of middle school students, and makes the important step of attempting to control for selectivity bias in the track to which each student is assigned, using propensity score methods. He finds that students placed in the upper group in schools that use ability grouping outperformed otherwise similar students in schools without tracking, while those placed in the low-ability groups underperformed. When he examines the overall effect on student achievement, tracking has no statistically significant effect. Thus, it would appear that tracking increases inequality without boosting efficiency.

Gamoran and Mare (1989) similarly use a nationally representative sample and, even after attempting to control for selectivity, find that in high schools tracking tends to increase inequality.

A paper by Argys, Rees and Brewer (1996) also yields results different from the general finding in Slavin's reviews of no or small effects. This paper uses Heckman selectivity corrections to control for assignment to track. In models of grade 10 math achievement, the authors report that tracking dramatically increases inequality, boosting scores of students in medium- and high-ability classes while lowering the achievement of students in the low-ability track. They find that tracking boosts average achievement slightly, by about 2%.

Betts and Shkolnik (2000a,b) introduce other approaches to studying tracking, again using a nationally representative set of secondary schools in the U.S., and raise concerns about bias in the approaches used by Argys, Rees, and Brewer (1996) and Hoffer (1992). Their first innovation is to reduce the selectivity bias problem inherent in comparing students in high-ability classes in schools with tracking to all students in heterogeneously grouped classrooms. They use reports by the principal on whether the school uses ability grouping, combined with reports that are available for *all* schools on the ability level of students in classrooms. This allows them to compare student outcomes in classes of a given ability level in tracking versus nontracking schools. They find little difference between outcomes for students in a class of given ability level between schools in which the principal reports the use of tracking and schools in which principals claim that tracking is not used.

Rees, Brewer, and Argys (2000) reinterpret the approach used in Betts and Shkolnik (2000a), arguing that if teachers in all schools are prepared to rate their classes' average ability level, then it must be the case that all schools use ability grouping. Thus, they argue, Betts and Shkolnik (2000a) are not comparing ability grouping to the absence of ability grouping, but instead are comparing formal ability grouping to informal ability grouping.

This is a reasonable interpretation of the approach adopted by Betts and Shkolnik (2000a), but the larger point in the Betts and Shkolnik (2000a) paper is that the meaningful effects on inequality reported by Hoffer (1992) and Argys, Rees, and Brewer (1996) reflect inadequate controls for endogenous placement of students into tracks.

Betts and Shkolnik marshall several pieces of evidence in this regard. Betts and Shkolnik (2000a) replicate the comparisons made by the aforementioned authors, by comparing achievement gains of those in a given track in schools with ability grouping to a control group consisting of *all* students at schools where ability grouping was not used. Like Hoffer (1992), who uses a subsample of the same data-set as Betts and Shkolnik, they find large positive and negative effects of being in a high-ability and low-ability class, respectively. But Betts and Shkolnik (2000a) express skepticism about the size of the effects. Figure 7.1 shows the 25th, 50th, and 75th percentiles of actual test scores in math by grade in their nationally representative sample, and superimposes on this (with dotted lines) the predicted test scores by grade of two hypothetical identical students who performed at the median level at the start of grade 7, but who were randomly assigned to the top and bottom ability groups in ensuing years. Betts and Shkolnik (2000a) conclude

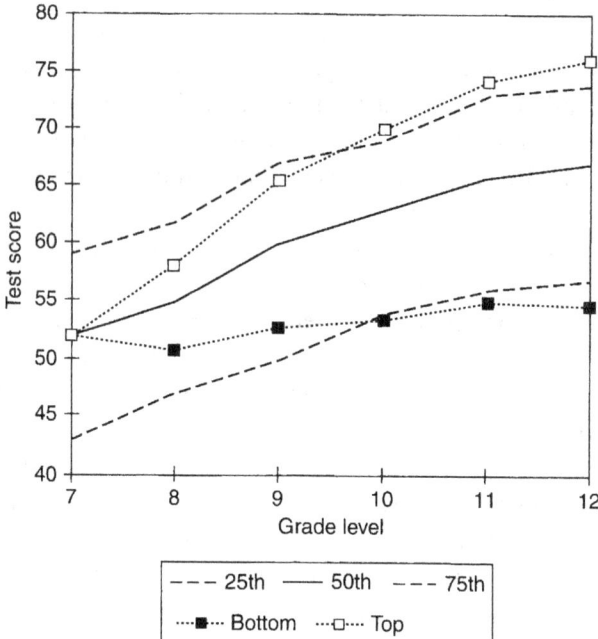

Figure 1 Actual range of test scores, and predicted scores of identical individuals placed in top and bottom classes. *Source:* Betts and Shkolnik (2000a).

that this rapid divergence between identical students predicted by standard models is far too big to be realistic. They reason that in their national sample the variance of test scores changes little across grades, and yet the vast majority of students (73%) in that sample are in schools that use ability grouping. They conclude that standard models do a poor job of controlling for unobserved differences among students.

The second piece of evidence that some of the earlier U.S. papers overstated the effect of tracking on inequality comes from models estimated by Betts and Shkolnik (2000a) that use Heckman selectivity corrections, propensity score, and instrumental variables approaches to control for endogenous group placement. They use as instruments students' lagged test scores, divided by average lagged scores in the students' school and grade, as well as school demographic variables, as predictors of the ability group to which the student is assigned. Once they use these explanatory variables and any of these three methods, the differential effects of ability grouping largely disappear. This does not appear to be due to weak explanatory power of the added instruments, which have considerable explanatory power in the first stage of the instrumental variables procedure.

Betts and Shkolnik (2000b) present other evidence that the approaches used by Hoffer (1992) and Argys, Rees, and Brewer (1996) almost surely do not control adequately for endogenous group placement. They point out a thoughtful robustness test used by Hoffer

(1992): instead of conditioning just on test scores from the previous year, he also conditions on test scores from two years earlier. Once he does this, the predicted gap between those in the high- and low-ability groups drops by about one half for math and one third for science. More to the point, although in his original model all three of his class ability levels were statistically significant, the only ability group coefficient that continues to be significant at the 5% level after adding the twice lagged test score is that for the low-ability group. This provides clear evidence that the norm in these papers of controlling for demographics and lagged achievement does a poor job of controlling for omitted ability bias: teachers assign students to ability groups based on a fuller knowledge of the student's actual achievement and motivation than can be gleaned by researchers who typically must rely upon a single noisy test score.

In the case of Argys, Rees, and Brewer (1996), Betts and Shkolnik (2000b) question this paper's implementation of Heckman selectivity corrections. First, none of the Inverse Mills terms is significant, indicating either that students are assigned randomly to ability groups (conditional on observables), which seems highly unlikely, or that the first-stage model of track placement lacks explanatory power. Second, they point out that the signs of the Inverse Mills terms are incorrect in that they suggest that students in the high-ability track were negatively selected, and that students in the low-ability track were positively selected.

In a similar vein, Figlio and Page (2002) use the same data as Argys, Rees, and Brewer (1996), and replicate their results fairly closely, but then question whether it makes sense to treat students' track placements as exogenous. Instead of attempting Heckman selectivity corrections, they replace the ability group variable with indicators for whether initial test scores of the individual student were in the bottom, middle, or top third of the grade 8 distribution. They find no effect of being in a tracked school for any of these three groups.

In a first in the literature, Figlio and Page (2002) use instrumental variables for the existence of tracking at the school, using county-level instruments. They report fairly good first-stage fit and if anything, their results support positive effects of tracking for students in the bottom of the initial test-score distribution and zero effects for students in the top two-thirds of the initial distribution.

Takeaway Lessons

Betts and Shkolnik (2000b) close with six observations for researchers who decide to undertake future nonexperimental work based on student/school level data on the effects of tracking. In brief, and with minor amendments, these are:

1. A student's classroom ability group is likely correlated with unobserved ability and motivation in regression-based studies. Therefore, unless adequate precautions are taken, the effects of tracking on inequality are almost surely overstated.
2. Informal ability grouping appears to be extremely common in American public schools, making it difficult to find a true "ungrouped" school.

3. Some studies such as Argys, Rees, and Brewer (1996) use as the comparison group classes that the teacher has labeled as "heterogeneous" ability. This is a very vague term that could mean different things to different teachers, and care must be used when using such definitions. (By the same reasoning, surveys that ask teachers to label the ability level of their class may not be particularly reliable, a point made by Rees, Brewer, and Argys (2000).)
4. Few U.S. studies at the secondary level make a clear distinction between simple ability grouping and ability grouping that is combined with differences in curriculum or pedagogy. The effects of the two types of ability grouping could be quite different.
5. We need to know more about whether and how secondary schools use ability grouping as an opportunity to tailor class size, teacher qualifications, and other inputs to the needs of students.
6. We know little about how schools group by ability within classrooms, especially at the secondary level.

Overall, this literature does not provide compelling evidence on either question: the overall effect of tracking on average achievement, or the effect of tracking on the distribution of achievement. Oakes (1985, 2005) writes powerfully about the disadvantages faced by students who are placed in lower tracks in American schools, and states that classroom observations indicate that students in low tracks spend less time on task in the classroom. Yet only a few studies in the quantitative literature find strong differential outcomes on standardized tests, and some of the papers that do find strong signs that tracking increases inequality appear to suffer from considerable omitted variable bias and endogeneity bias. Slavin (1990) notes that Oakes' observation that low-track students tend to spend less time on task, although legitimate, does not provide evidence that these differences are exacerbated by tracking. Rather, he writes: "Is this due to the poor behavioral models and low expectations in the low-track classes, or would low achievers be more off-task than high achievers in any grouping arrangement?". (Slavin, 1990, p. 474)

Again and again, the problem that crops up in the regression-based literature is the extreme difficulty social scientists face when attempting to estimate the counterfactual without tracking. Indeed, attempts by Betts and Shkolnik (2000a,b) and Figlio and Page (2002) to take into account the endogeneity of group placement suggests that tracking does not aggravate inequality in academic achievement, even though simpler models suggest it does.

A final observation is that with one exception this literature treats the use of tracking by a school as a decision that is exogenous with respect to student achievement. Any unobserved factors that are correlated with the use of tracking, and which are related to achievement, will bias the results of the papers reviewed above. Figlio and Page (2002) provide evidence that treating the existence of tracking at a school as endogenous can reverse earlier findings by Argys, Rees, and Brewer (1996) that tracking aggravates inequality.

4.2 Approaches that Use Geographical Variation

A large parallel literature avoids the difficult questions related to which individual schools track, who attends them, and the tracks chosen by individual students, and instead geographically aggregates schools, thus facilitating comparisons between one region and another or one country or another. Some papers do not aggregate across schools, but still use geographic variation in tracking policy. This literature focuses on between-school tracking in which students are streamed into vocational or academic schools. This approach to tracking could produce quite different effects than the within-school tracking discussed in the previous section.

4.2.1 Geographic: Time difference in differences; natural experiments related to policy reforms

Numerous countries or regions within countries have changed educational policies related to tracking. If it can be argued credibly that the change in tracking is exogenous with respect to student learning, and not correlated with any other (unmeasured) reforms to education policy, then one may have a plausible natural experiment for identifying the effects of the reform to tracking. Most of the studies to date have examined the phase-in or phase-out of tracking across regions of a single country.

This geographical identification approach holds some clear advantages over studies that make school-by-school comparisons. The international and subnational papers, through their use of geographic aggregation, mitigate concerns about the endogeneity of the decision to track at the school level, the endogenous assignment of individuals to specific tracks, and the endogenous choice by families of where to live. Obviously, the studies of regions within a country will reduce biases due to endogenous residential choice, but not as much as international studies, because families are free to move among regions within a country.

The difference-in-differences approach and its strengths and weaknesses are well-known. Referring to our d.g.p. in Equation (7.2), the typical paper in this literature explicitly includes dummy variables for geographic unit and time, removing the α_c and α_t from the error term. As always, the success of this approach depends on the assumption that trends between the control and treatment units (areas without and with tracking) must be the same, apart from differences directly resulting from tracking and other observables. Any correlation between the tracking variables and the error components β_{ct} and δ_{cgt} in Equation (7.2) will lead to bias. We will therefore pay attention to whether any other changes within geographic units may have occurred at the same time as the institution (or abolition) of tracking.

Meghir and Palme (2005) study student outcomes in the context of major policy changes in Sweden. Until roughly 1950, all students attended compulsory elementary schools up to sixth grade, at which point students with the best grades enrolled in junior secondary schools, which had a strong academic focus, with these students later articulating into upper secondary schools and ultimately, postsecondary education. Students in grade 6 who had lower grades were required to attend more basic compulsory schools, for either one or two additional years, and had the opportunity to attend vocational schools after that. Between 1949 and 1962, Sweden experimented with a new approach that implemented several reforms at the same time. Most relevant for our purposes, the reform ended placement into academic versus nonacademic tracks at the end of grade 6, and also introduced a national curriculum for all secondary students.

This reform did not require that all schools teach exactly the same material. Indeed, a three-level secondary school system was created, with academic, more basic academic, and vocational paths available at the student's discretion. Individual schools typically housed all three of these programs.

Notably, the reform also went further, increasing the minimum number of years of schooling required from seven or eight years (depending on the region) to nine years. Further, this increase in the school attendance requirement was buttressed by a financial stipend to families to make up for the lost labor-market earnings of adolescent family members who would have otherwise entered the labor market had the school attendance law not changed. As the authors point out it is impossible to know for sure which elements of the reform caused observed changes to students' earnings years after leaving school.

Meghir and Palme adopt a difference-in-differences approach that takes advantage of the fact that the reforms were phased in. They compare outcomes for two birth cohorts, the older of which was more likely to have experienced the old system. In addition they exploit variation across municipalities. (A national board selected which municipalities would implement the reform in a given year.) The key variable in their outcome model is an indicator for whether the person belonged to a combination of cohort and municipality (in grade 6), the members of which were subject to the new system. Outcomes include earnings and various measures of educational attainment.

They find that on average the reform was associated with an increase of 0.3 years of schooling completed. Students whose fathers had low education accounted for all of this gain. Most of the gain derives from the increase in the required years of school attendance, but attendance beyond the compulsory level also rose by 2.6 percentage points. Clearly, the increase in years of compulsory attendance induced much if not all of the increase in enrollment and attainment. It is not possible to infer whether the end of tracking contributed to these increases.

Meghir and Palme report a 1.4% increase in earnings that is associated with the reform package, but the change is not significant at conventional levels. Nonetheless, in the new regime earnings increased 3.4% for workers whose fathers had low education, and earnings increased by even more, 4.5%, for those whose fathers had low education but who themselves were of high ability. Conversely, the earnings of workers whose fathers were highly educated, and who were educated in the new system, fell by 5.6%. All of these subgroup effects were highly significant.

The key question for us is the degree to which the end of tracking, as opposed to the increase in compulsory schooling and the associated subsidy, could be responsible for any of these changes in earnings. The authors cite another paper which estimates that the return to one year of schooling in Sweden is 4.6%. If the observed earnings increases were all due to the observed increase in educational attainment, it would imply an 8.4% return to a year of education. One interpretation, if one accepts the outside estimate of the returns to a year of Swedish schooling, is that the reform package increased the returns to a year of schooling by 3.8%, perhaps by increasing school quality. But again, we cannot state whether any such increase in the returns to education emanates from the abolition of tracking rather than the other elements of the reform.

The finding that earnings of those whose fathers were highly educated fell is intriguing. One explanation might be that the increased heterogeneity of classrooms after the reform hurt the children of more highly educated parents, perhaps due to a weaker peer group for these children. But because the reform was implemented for entire municipalities at a time, we cannot rule out general equilibrium effects (namely, a drop in earnings induced by the increased supply of more educated workers). And as always in diff-in-diff models, a concern is that unobserved factors might have caused deviations in earnings between those who grew up in the treated areas and those who grew up elsewhere.

The United Kingdom acted in the 1960s to remove its system of tracking or "streaming" students into one of three levels of secondary education based on tests all students took at the age of eleven. On the surface this policy reform is cleaner than the Swedish reform because compulsory attendance laws did not change in the U.K. case. Still, some complications remained.

Numerous authors have studied the reforms in the U.K. Galindo-Rueda and Vignoles (2007) study a single cohort of students born in 1958, and thus do not implement a diff-in-diff estimator. Rather, their approach is to model test scores and years of schooling completed at age 16 as functions of control variables observed at ages 11 and 7, including test scores. The key explanatory variable is whether a student attended a noncomprehensive school, that is, a selective school, and in alternative specifications the number of years the student was in a selective school. Because some Local Education Authorities (LEAs) allowed comprehensive and selective (grammar) schools to coexist, the authors instrument the selective school indicator with the proportion of schools in the LEA that were comprehensive. Throughout, they use a propensity score matching approach in which they find that the political affiliation of the child's constituency is highly predictive of adoption of comprehensive schools. (Constituencies that elected a Conservative tended to be much slower to switch from grammar schools to comprehensive schools.)

Galindo-Rueda and Vignoles (2007) find that in their propensity score models, it matters whether they instrument the key explanatory variables related to attending selective schools. Without instruments, the results suggest positive effects of attending a selective school, and that students in the middle of the distribution gain the most. But the IV estimates, although supportive, are not statistically significant.

One of the more interesting findings of the paper is that including controls for achievement at age 11, right before students would enter the tracked system, greatly reduces the estimated effects of subsequent tracking. A natural interpretation is that selectivity bias has not been fully removed by the use of propensity scores. The authors develop a different interpretation, that in LEAs where selective grammar schools persisted, students had a stronger incentive to work hard before the age of 11 in the hope of entering a selective school at age 11. They buttress their theory by showing that LEAs that moved to a comprehensive system latest were the ones in which student achievement gains between ages 7 and 11 were higher.

Pischke and Manning (2006) reanalyze the data, and focus on the relative explanatory power of secondary school tracking on achievement gains between ages 11 and 16 (when the students were in secondary school) and the ages of 7 and 11. They conclude that because the "effect" of secondary tracking is of similar magnitude in these two age ranges, the elementary school effect cannot be real. Thus, they argue, selectivity bias must remain, even after they instrument for the date at which an LEA switches to comprehensive schools using political control of the county. However, it is conceivable that the gains in primary school could appear as large as the gains in secondary school, especially given that the tests at the different age groups are not vertically scaled.

It is not clear which story—incentive effects of secondary school tracking on primary school students (and their teachers), or selectivity bias—is the more important factor.

Pekkarinen, Uusitalo, and Kerr (2009) ask whether a move toward detracking in Finland in the 1970s is associated with changes in intergenerational income mobility. Their natural experiment appears to be very "clean." They examine a national school reform program implemented in phases between 1972 and 1977. In the preexisting system, students were placed into one of two tracks after four years of primary school. After the reform, the "civic schools" that had enrolled many students up to grade 8 or 9, and which provided a relatively vocational education, were abolished, as were most of the private secondary schools that enrolled students with strong academic aspirations. In their place, a nine-year comprehensive school for all students was implemented. (As before, after grade 9 students had an option to apply to upper secondary schools (the college-bound track) or vocational schools.) The reform was phased in over five years, with six broad regions being put on different timetables for reform.

Notably, by estimating models of sons' log earnings as functions of fathers' log earnings, the authors use a longer term outcome than test scores. They add interactions of father's log earnings with sets of dummy variables for cohort and region and with the crucial dummy variable indicating whether the region had already implemented detracking by the time the son was in the age range affected by the reform. These sets of dummy variables enter the equation directly and interacted with fathers' log earnings. The specific regressors are different from the set-up we provided in our sample data generation process in Equation (7.2) but the identifying assumption is essentially the same: there cannot have been variations in the correlation between fathers' and sons' earnings by region that varied over time differently across groups.

They find that the introduction of comprehensive schools from grades 5 through 9 is associated with a 20% reduction in the relation between sons' and fathers' earnings, implying a strong increase in income mobility that resulted from detracking.

One final but important note on all of the above papers is that they all use geographic variations *within a country* to identify the effects of tracking. To the extent that families endogenously choose where to live within the given country, any effects of tracking may simply reflect endogenous sorting.

Brunello and Checchi (2007) take a similar difference-in-differences approach, using geographical and time variation in tracking policies, but unlike the above papers they compare different countries. They focus on whether tracking accentuates the relation between family background and long-term education outcomes such as educational attainment, postsecondary enrollment, literacy, and labor market outcomes including employment, training and wages.

The authors' decision to examine longer-term outcomes than test scores makes this paper an important contribution. One concern in the many papers that examine patterns of inequality in test score is that the way in which test scores are scaled could easily create the appearance of increased inequality. With longer-term measures like earnings and educational attainment, we have cardinal measures for which inequality measures are more naturally defined.

Their model in fact goes a step beyond our d.g.p. in Equation (7.2) by including dummies for country interacted with cohort. Their specification, because it does not measure grade-by-grade performance, does not include a subscript for grade g. To facilitate comparisons with Equation (7.2) we use time t as an indicator for birth cohort:

$$S_{ict} = \beta_{ct} + X_{ict}\Phi + F_{ict}\Pi + Q_{ict}\gamma + F_{ict}Q_{ict}\Omega + T_{ict}F_{ict}\rho + (\alpha_i + \varepsilon_{icgt}) \qquad (7.3)$$

The random effect related to country and time, β_{ct}, is removed from the error term of Equation (7.2) and specifically included as a fixed effect, which of course also removes the random effects related to country and those related to time. Similarly, we have dropped the error terms related to grade given that the authors focus on outcomes measured, roughly speaking, at the end of school (age 16) or outcomes measured for young adults. For the same reason, the tracking dummy T_{ict} in Equation (7.3) is intended to capture the multiple-year effects expressed in Equation (7.2).

Another innovation in Equation (7.3) is that interactions between family background and a set of variables that are roughly analogous to measures of school quality Q_{ict} are included, to make sure that other variables in addition to tracking itself are not affecting the slope of the family background coefficients.[6]

The authors use two measures of tracking: "tracking length", that is, the number of years over which a student is likely to have been exposed to tracking; and the share of students in upper secondary schooling who are in vocational tracks. The first of these matches closely the tracking measures used by most other papers, while the latter variable is quite different, and merits scrutiny. A major concern is that the proportion of students in vocational education represents an endogenous outcome, the result of the interaction of the supply of student openings and demand for vocational schools, rather than a specific policy that could be argued to be exogenous.

Another concern is that the vocational education measure is prone to measurement error. For instance, Brunello and Checchi (2007) report that 0.0% of American high school students were in vocational education in 2002, (see their Table 1), on the grounds that virtually all students in the U.S. attend comprehensive schools. This misses the fact that tracking, including a robust vocational track, is a hallmark of American high schools. Levesque et al. (2008, Tables 2.1 and 2.2) report that although it is true that in the United States only 5.2% of high schools have a full Career and Technical Education focus, 88.1% of public high schools offer one or more occupational programs.

To be fair, this variable may not be measured with more error than the age at which students are first tracked, which is widely used throughout the literature.

Mainly because of our concern that the percent of students in vocational tracks is endogenous, in our summary of the results of Brunello and Checci (2007) below we will focus on the "length of tracking" variable.

Brunello and Checchi (2007) find that for the most part, when countries track at an early age, the influence of parental education on long-term outcomes is accentuated. This applies to measures of educational attainment (years of schooling and the probability of dropping out), and to earnings and the probability of employment. Interestingly, they find that tracking reduces the influence of parental education on adult literacy and the probability of receiving on-the-job training. (Their finding on on-the-job training is not necessarily counterintuitive—if less affluent students tend to take the vocational track, this may put them in line to receive more technical training once they launch their careers in jobs related to their upper secondary training.) Typically

---

[6] Brunello and Checchi (2007) in fact include some variables that we can directly interpret as measures of public school quality, such as the pupil-teacher ratio and expenditures on public education, as well as other variables measuring complementary or competing types of education: enrollment in private schools and enrollment in preschools.

however, the interaction of tracking and parental education is only sometimes statistically significant.[7]

4.2.2 Geographic: Age difference in differences using international and subnational geographic variation

Most international analyses of test scores and tracking have not used the Brunello and Checchi (2007) approach of exploiting changes within countries in tracking policies. This probably reflects the fact that there has been little variation in tracking policies over the short time spans over which international tests of achievement have been available.

A common approach to this lack of temporal variation has been to replace the time element in a standard diff-in-diff formulation with a grade element. That is, the difference in test score gains between a grade that is untracked and a grade that is tracked, between countries with and without tracking, could plausibly be used as an estimate of the effect of tracking on test scores (or on the effect of tracking on the link between family background and achievement).

Most of the papers in this genre ask whether countries that track at an early age have higher transmission of inequality intergenerationally. Several reasons for such a relationship seem evident. Perhaps parents have quite a lot of influence over track placement when their children are in the lower grades, but less influence in the higher grades because a school will have a much better grasp of a student's true achievement after several years. Alternatively suppose that more educated parents tend to have more success in placing their children in high tracks, regardless of grade.[8] Suppose further that educational outcomes diverge between students in high and low tracks, and that this divergence increases with the length of time that students are separated into different tracks.

This geographical identification approach, much like that in the previous section, provides a deft solution to concerns about the endogeneity of tracking policies at the school level and the endogenous placement of students into ability groups. But concerns remain about the reasons for why countries or regions differ in their tracking policies. Omitted variable bias could account for any correlation across regions in student achievement and the use of tracking. The potential for omitted variable bias is larger when using variation across disparate countries, rather than variation across regions within a country, to identify the effect of tracking.

---

[7] These results do not seem to hold when they instead model the inequality in earnings and literacy as a function of the dispersion within a country in family background. The former approaches seem more compelling because they use person-level observations.

[8] See Dustmann (2004) who documents a strong positive relation between parental education and children's secondary school track in Germany.

Hanushek and Woessmann (2006) provide a canonical example of this approach. They recognize that in their sample of countries, tracking never begins in primary grades and so there is some grade g^{min} below which tracking is never used. They use average test scores at the country level, for different grades, before and after tracking typically begins. The researchers have test scores available for a number of countries in grade g^H in year t and grade g^L in the year t' (which may be the same as t or in some instances earlier than t). They choose these grades such that in all countries $g^H > g^{min} > g^L$, so that achievement in g^L can be thought of as achievement in a grade before which any tracking has occurred. Then the average of these test scores, given the d.g.p expressed in Equation (7.2), are:

$$\bar{S}_{cg^Ht} = \bar{X}_{cg^Ht}\Phi + \bar{F}_{cg^Ht}\Pi + \bar{Q}_{cg^Ht}\gamma + T_{cg^Ht}\lambda_{g^H} + T_{c,g^H-1,t-1}\lambda_{g^H-1} + \ldots + T_{c,g^{minc},t-g^{minc}+1}\lambda_{g^{minc}}$$
$$+ T_{cg^Ht}\bar{F}_{cg^Ht}\rho_{g^H} + T_{c,g^H-1,t-1}\bar{F}_{c,g^H-1,t-1}\rho_{g^H-1} + \ldots + T_{c,g^{minc},t-g^{minc}+1}\bar{F}_{c,1,t-g^{minc}+1}\rho_{g^{minc}}$$
$$+ \left((\bar{\alpha}_i|g^H, t) + \alpha_c + \alpha_{g^H} + \alpha_t + \beta_{cg^H} + \beta_{ct} + \beta_{g^Ht} + \delta_{cg^Ht} + \bar{\varepsilon}^H_{cgt}\right)$$

(7.4)

where implicitly the tracking indicators equal one for all of the grades listed, and

$$\bar{S}_{cg^Lt'} = \bar{X}_{cg^Lt'}\Phi + \bar{F}_{cg^Lt'}\Pi + \bar{Q}_{cg^Lt'}\gamma$$
$$+ \left((\bar{\alpha}_i|g^L, t') + \alpha_c + \alpha_{g^L} + \alpha_{t'} + \beta_{cg^L} + \beta_{ct'} + \beta_{g^Lt'} + \delta_{cg^Lt'} + \bar{\varepsilon}^L_{cgt'}\right)$$

(7.5)

Note that the latter equation does not include any tracking terms because g^L is a grade at which no country c has started tracking. Note also that in Equation (7.4) tracking terms are added all the way down to the minimum grade at which country c begins to track, g^{minc}, and that this minimum grade varies from one country to another.

Hanushek and Woessmann (2006) model average test scores in one grade and year on average test scores in an earlier grade and nearby year, plus an indicator for early tracking ET_c. Let the regression coefficient on the test score in the earlier grade be denoted by b. By adding and subtracting b times the average score for grade g^L to the right-hand side of Equation (7.4), we gain a sense of what this regressor removes from the error term, and what biases likely remain:

$$\bar{S}_{cg^Ht} = b\bar{S}_{cg^Lt'} + ET_c\tau$$
$$+ \left\{ \begin{array}{c} (\bar{X}_{cg^Ht} - b\bar{X}_{cg^Lt'})\Phi + (\bar{F}_{cg^Ht} - b\bar{F}_{cg^Lt'})\Pi + (\bar{Q}_{cg^Ht} - b\bar{Q}_{cg^Lt'})\gamma - ET_c\tau \\ + T_{cg^Ht}\lambda_{g^H} + T_{c,g^H-1,t-1}\lambda_{g^H-1} + \ldots + T_{c,g^{minc},t-g^{minc}+1}\lambda_{g^{minc}} + \\ T_{cg^Ht}\bar{F}_{cg^Ht}\rho_{g^H} + T_{c,g^H-1,t-1}\bar{F}_{c,g^H-1,t-1}\rho_{g^H-1} + \ldots + T_{c,g^{minc},t-g^{minc}+1}\bar{F}_{c,1,t-g^{minc}+1}\rho_{minc} \\ \left[\begin{array}{c} ((\bar{\alpha}_i|g^h, t) - b((\bar{\alpha}_i|g^L, t'))) + \alpha_c(1-b) + (\alpha_{g^H} - b\alpha_{g^L}) + (\alpha_t - b\alpha_{t'}) \\ + (\beta_{cg^H} - b\beta_{cg^L}) + (\beta_{ct} - b\beta_{ct'}) + (\beta_{g^Ht} - b\beta_{g^Lt'}) \\ + (\delta_{cg^Ht} - b\delta_{cg^Lt'}) + (\bar{\varepsilon}_{cg^Ht} - b\bar{\varepsilon}_{cg^Lt'}) \end{array} \right] \end{array} \right\}$$

(7.6)

The early tracking indicator is included in the hope of picking up the average direct effects of tracking, that is, the λ terms, and the average family:tracking effects, that is, the ρ terms. Because different countries begin tracking in different grades $g^{\min_c}$, the regression coefficient τ should be interpreted as a weighted average of the effects of various years of tracking, which vary by country.

Above, the various terms inside the braces constitute the error term. Most of the terms in the braces will have non-zero expectation, and it seems likely that many of these components of the error term will be correlated with the early tracking indicator, thus biasing the coefficient estimate τ.

With roughly 16 country-pair observations, linear regression will of course choose b and τ to minimize the sum of squared residuals. Intuitively, if $b = 1$, then most of the components in the error term reduce to differences in the mean values of, for example, average personal characteristics, $\left(\bar{X}_{cg^H t} - \bar{X}_{cg^L t'}\right)$, and the country fixed effect α_c would be completely removed. In practice, this coefficient is unlikely to be 1. Therefore this approach is not quite the same as adding a country fixed effect to the model, and remains, at least to some degree, prone to bias due to omitted country characteristics α_c. The omitted country traits are likely to be correlated with the use of tracking.

Most importantly, it seems highly likely that differences in school resources across grades and years could be linked to tracking. That is, ET_c could be correlated with $\left(\bar{Q}_{cg^H t} - b\bar{Q}_{cg^L t'}\right)\gamma$. In particular, if countries that track early also tend to increase/decrease spending per pupil more between primary and secondary school, and if spending per pupil is positively related to test scores, then the coefficient on early tracking could be biased upward/downward. It is not easy to control for the school spending factor exactly: recall that when we average our d.g.p, Equation (7.2), across students, as in Equation (7.4) and (7.5), the $\bar{Q}_{cgt}$ terms refer to cumulative school resources enjoyed by the average student between kindergarten and grade g. As mentioned earlier, Brunello and Checchi (2007, page 795) document large differences in pupil-teacher ratios for students in different tracks in various European countries, with academic students implicitly attending smaller classes than do vocational students. As also mentioned earlier, the authors do not report on pupil-teacher ratios in earlier grades in secondary school, and they report that spending per pupil is actually higher in the vocational track in Austria. Thus, this does not establish that countries that track early tend to increase or decrease average resources disproportionately in higher grades, but it suggests that this is a possibility. The above concern applies not just to patterns of spending per pupil but to any other school characteristic that might change across grades (and/or tracks) such as teacher qualifications or class size.

Differences in the country/grade-specific error terms, $\left(\beta_{cg^H} - b\beta_{cg^L}\right)$, which in part will reflect the alignment between the test instrument and the curriculum taught in a given grade and country, could be strongly correlated with tracking. The difference in the country-year error terms, $(\beta_{ct} - b\beta_{ct'})$, could reflect gradual changes in the average curriculum between years t' and t, which could be correlated, but not causally, with early tracking. (This problem is smaller if t is close to t', which is the choice Hanushek and Woessmann make.) Finally, the term $\left(\delta_{cg}H_t - b\delta_{cg}L_{t'}\right)$ could reflect unobserved causes of changes in achievement growth across grades within a country, for instance variations in the preparation of teachers across grades over time, which we are liable to attribute to the existence of tracking.

Another approach to the problem of omitted variable bias is to use student-level data and to attempt to control for covariates. For example, Ammermüller (2005) studies reading achievement across countries in a model that examines the mediating influence of tracking on the effect of family background. He focuses on reading scores of students roughly in grade 9 and grade 4 across a set of countries, and like Hanushek and Woessmann (2006) exploits the fact that tracking does not begin until secondary school in his sample. His equation, using the above notation, translates roughly to:

$$S_{icgt} = \alpha_c + \alpha_g + X_{icgt}\Phi + Q_{icgt}\gamma + F_{icgt}(\Pi_c + \Pi_g) + T_{ic,9,t}F_{ic9t}\rho_9 \\ + \left(\alpha_i + \alpha_t + \beta_{cg} + \beta_{ct} + \beta_{gt} + \delta_{cgt} + \varepsilon_{icgt}\right) \quad (7.7)$$

where the main tracking variable used, $T_{ic,9,t}$, equals the number of types of schools at the secondary level in country c at time t, for those in grade 9, and equals 0 for those in grade 4. This model incorporates a number of innovations designed to reduce bias. Most notably, the model incorporates both country and grade fixed effects, which are brought out of the error term in parentheses. However, a cost of this approach is that estimates from this model cannot be used to infer the overall effects of tracking on efficiency because the country fixed-effect removes any levels effect of tracking.[9]

Similarly, Waldinger (2006) adopts a student-level strategy, while distinguishing between grades before and after tracking has started in a country. He also distinguishes between an indicator for whether the country c uses early tracking, ET_c, and an indicator for whether the actual grade is one by which tracking has started. In his sample, he simply defines a binary variable SECONDARY which equals one for secondary grades, which makes sense because only in secondary grades has tracking started. In terms of the above notation, the estimating equation is approximately represented by:

$$S_{icgt} = \alpha_c + \alpha_g + X_{icgt}\Phi + F_{icgt}\left(\Pi + \Pi_g + ET_c\eta + T_{icgt}\rho_g\right) + Q_{icgt}\gamma \\ + \left(\alpha_i + \alpha_t + \beta_{cg} + \beta_{ct} + \beta_{gt} + \delta_{cgt} + \varepsilon_{icgt}\right) \quad (7.8)$$

---

[9] There are two other notable features about this equation. First it allows for the effects of family background to vary separately by grade and by country, which we have signaled above by including two separate vectors of coefficients Π. Second, the controls for school resources are quite limited, including variables like instructional time but no overall measure of spending per pupil or pupil-teacher ratios. This increases the possibility of omitted variable bias.

This approach is similar to that of Ammermüller (2005) in that it removes country and grade fixed effects, and allows the family characteristics to have separate effects by grade (but not by country). Although this model does not go as far as that of Ammermüller (2005) in fully interacting family background with country fixed effects, the effect of family background on test scores is allowed to shift by an identical amount η for all countries that track at an early age. The coefficient of interest is ρ_g which captures the effects of tracking specifically in grade g. (Because there are only two grades in the model, there is a single parameter estimated for the differential effect of being in a secondary school in a country that begins to track in secondary school.)

4.2.2.1 Findings on Inequality

Most of these papers support the hypothesis that family background is more strongly related to student outcomes in countries that track students at an early age. Thus, tracking generates inequality. For instance, Hanushek and Woessmann (2006) find that in models of various measures of test-score inequality, early tracking is associated with significant increases in inequality in secondary school relative to primary school. Ammermüller (2005) finds that not all interactions between measures of family socio-economic status and the number of school types are statistically significant, but in roughly half the cases there was a significant relation supporting the idea that tracking increases the effect of family background. Most relevant was his uniform finding that parental education interacted with the number of school types was positively related to reading achievement in the higher (tracked) grades relative to the lower grades.

Waldinger (2006) finds an insignificant relation between parental education and whether the student was in a grade/country with tracking. (In Equation (7.8) the null that $\rho_g = 0$ is handily retained.) This finding is the opposite of the other studies noted above. However, η, the interaction between parental education and the use of early tracking, is routinely positive and highly significant. Similar results obtain when the background measure is based on books in the student's home.

There are at least three ways to interpret Waldinger's findings that $\rho_g = 0$ and $\eta > 0$. His own interpretation is that other studies that compare outcomes across countries failed to account for unobserved differences in the impact of family background across countries that do and do not track. Once one does take this into account by interacting family background with an indicator for whether the country as a whole tracks, there is no real increase in the importance of family background between untracked lower grades and tracked higher grades ($\rho_g = 0$). This explanation could be correct. But a remaining concern is that Equation (7.8) is in some ways a restricted version of Ammermüller's model, Equation (7.7), which allows for interactions between family background and a full set of country fixed effects. Yet this latter model, which should do an even better job of removing heterogeneity across countries in the effect of family background, finds that tracking does matter.

The two other explanations hearken back to the debate between Galindo-Rueda and Vignoles (2007) and Pischke and Manning (2006) in the context of the U.K. The conclusion of the former paper implies that perhaps the positive coefficients on the interaction between family background and whether the country as a whole tracks ($\eta > 0$) indicates that during their primary school careers, students are selected and groomed for the type of school track they will enter in their secondary school years. In this case identification from a difference in differences based on country-grade contrasts may not be a valid approach. Alternatively, the Pischke and Manning (2006) paper implies that perhaps the positive coefficient on η is another sign that fixed effect models cannot fully control for self-selection. The only difference is that Pischke and Manning (2006) focused on the selective nature with which jurisdictions in the U.K. switched to comprehensive schools; in the international setting the concern is that countries self-select into early tracking.[10]

4.2.2.2 Findings on Efficiency

The only international study that directly assesses the impact of tracking on school efficiency is the paper by Hanushek and Woessmann (2006). (The others, by adding a fixed effect for each country, cannot estimate the direct effect of a tracking policy on test scores because of lack of any variation within country of the tracking policy during the time frames they study.) Hanushek and Woessmann (2006) cannot reject the null of no overall effect on achievement.

4.2.3 Other methods that use geographical variation in tracking

Not all studies that exploit geographical variation fit into the two genres of difference-in-differences models discussed in the previous two sections.

A recent example is the work by Bauer and Riphahn (2006), which studies the correlation between parents' and children's education across Swiss cantons. (The cantons set the grade at which tracking begins.) The paper uses several measures of when tracking starts, to test for whether early tracking accentuates the intergenerational correlation between students' secondary school track and their parents' level of education. The approach is cross-sectional, examining secondary school students from the 2000 census.

In terms of the d.g.p. outlined in Equation (7.2), this approach virtually removes the random errors related to grade level α_g from the error term because all of the students are aged 17, and of course time variation α_t is removed as well because the

---

[10] Another explanation for why the Waldinger paper finds no significant effects of tracking is that the paper uses a smaller set of countries than some of the other papers that use this approach, thus perhaps lowering precision of the estimates.

data-set is a cross-section. But all of the components in the error term that relate to individuals i and region c remain. The main contribution that this approach makes to identification is that tracking is not measured at the level of the individual student or school, thus reducing concerns about endogeneity of tracking or students' individual tracks. But concerns remain about the potentially endogenous decision at the canton level of the grade at which to begin tracking, and the decision by families of the canton in which to reside. Similarly, the authors' model does not include any controls for school characteristics or demographics at the school or canton level. Given that a table in their paper shows that cantons that track at a later age tend to have more highly educated adult populations that spend a smaller share of public spending on education, omitted variable bias related to school resources and the geographical location (Q_{icgt} and α_c in Equation (7.2)) could affect the results.

The paper reports that tracking that starts at a later grade is associated with increased probability that children enroll in the secondary track that is considered "university-bound," regardless of parental education level. (The authors do not claim that this is a sign that late-tracking increases efficiency. Such a conclusion would be unwarranted because the models do not control for school resources.) Second, on the question of inequality, the results suggest that starting to track at a later age reduces relative differences by parental education in the probability that the student is in the highest secondary school track. Thus, a paper that geographically aggregates the tracking variable again finds that tracking aggravates inequality.

Woessmann (2010) uses a cross-section of 16 observations from German states and finds a negative relationship between the use of late tracking and the slope of the (positive) gradient between math test scores and the socio-economic status of the student.

Schutz, Ursprung, and Woessmann (2008) compile an unusually large set of 54 nations and test whether the link between students' math scores and books in the home, which is strongly positive, becomes weaker in countries that begin tracking at a later age. They find evidence favoring this idea. Although this paper does not use either of the difference-in-differences strategies typical of many of the international papers, and so risks omitted variable bias, it has roughly two to four times as many countries as in many of the earlier studies. Another worthwhile feature of this paper is that it explicitly controls for immigration in its estimate of the slope between test scores and family background.

Van Elk, van der Steeg, and Webbink (2009) study variations in the age at which secondary students in the Netherlands are placed into differentiated schools. They instrument the start of tracking using geographical variation in the relative supply of comprehensive and categorical schools. Their results suggest that when students are tracked at an earlier age, their average probability of participating in postsecondary education falls as a result.

4.2.4 Endogeneity of tracking in international studies

Further work might gainfully test for endogeneity of tracking in international studies, especially the approaches that do not use a time difference that exploits changes in tracking policy within countries.

One reasonably plausible scenario is that some social or political factor, unmeasured by the researcher, influences both the age at which tracking starts and the gradient of achievement with respect to family background (dS/dF) in the opposite direction. This could induce a spurious negative correlation between the two.

To make this issue concrete, consider immigration. Suppose that researchers used parental education as their measure of family background F, and calculated dS/dF without taking into account whether the parents were immigrants. Then countries with large numbers of immigrants might be observed to have higher dS/dF gradients, because parents with low education are likely also not to speak the native language fluently or know how best to negotiate public schools on behalf of their children. Suppressing the subscripts from the earlier models, we can express achievement S in a country as a function of family background F, and the average immigrant-to-population ratio I, where all of the a_j coefficients in the following model are positive:

$$S = a_1 + a_2 F + a_3 F * I - a_4 I \tag{7.9}$$

Thus $dF/dS = a_2 + a_3 I$ is an increasing function of a nation's immigrant-to-population ratio.

Consider next the evidence in Betts and Fairlie (2003) that in metropolitan areas in the United States, increases in the immigrant-to-population ratio among young people is associated with increases in the probability that natives enroll their children in private schools. If this relationship were causal, it is easy to imagine how native parents might also react to inflows of immigrants by seeking greater (or earlier) within-school ability grouping. Thus if T is our measure of age at which tracking starts, $dT/dI < 0$.

Putting this endogenous relationship of tracking to immigration together with the positive interaction between immigrant share and dS/dF, it becomes possible that models that don't take these relations into account would detect a noncausal negative relation between the age at which tracking begins and the achievement:family background gradient.

Notably, Schutz, Ursprung, and Woessmann (2008) take into account the immigration status of parents of individual students and allow for an interaction with their main measure of family background, and still find that countries that begin to track at a later grade have less inequality in achievement. It would still be worthwhile in this example to study whether the age at which tracking starts immigrant shares in the population is an endogenous function of immigration.

Another of the many possible socio-economic or political factors that could influence both tracking and the achievement:background gradient is political beliefs.

Galindo-Rueda and Vignoles (2007) and Pischke and Manning (2006), in the context of the U.K., and Figlio and Page (2002), in the context of the United States, present evidence that a local electorate that votes more conservatively is associated with use of tracking at an earlier age. Suppose that this pattern obtained internationally. Perhaps more conservative societies tend to prefer other policies that tend to strengthen the link between achievement and family background, for instance through policies related to housing segregation, or public subsidies for preschool. If these policies are not perfectly measured by the researcher, then even if there is no causal relation between tracking and the gradient between achievement and family background, the regression model is likely to suggest a positive relation between use of tracking and this gradient.

These examples are speculative, but are intended to illustrate the many ways that endogeneity of tracking, combined with omitted variable bias, could lead to incorrect inference. Much could be done to search for factors that explain variations across countries in tracking policies, and to explore, as in Schutz, Ursprung, and Woessmann (2008), what factors mediate the relationship between student outcomes and family background. Also, to the degree that omitted demographic and political variables are unchanging over time, international studies that exploit changes in tracking over time might reduce the potential for such problems.

4.3 Experiments with random assignment of students to treatment

As discussed above, comparisons across countries lead to concerns about major unmeasured differences that could bias results. Yet most existing within-country studies raise questions about why one school uses tracking and another does not, and whether unobserved characteristics of students are correlated with track placement. An additional concern in all of these studies is whether the definition of tracking is the same across schools or countries.

An apparent antidote to these problems would be to design an experiment in which schools were randomly assigned to tracked or nontracked status, and in which a consistent rule was used to assign students to classrooms in schools that tracked. Further, one would want to ensure that schools in the control group did not stealthily implement their own form of tracking, so that one could prevent substitution bias.[11] A properly executed experiment removes biases stemming from the correlation between tracking and the error terms in Equation (7.2) that arises in nonexperimental settings. It does this by randomly assigning treatment status, rendering the tracking variables in Equation (7.2) exogenous. But experiments are not without problems. External validity may be limited, in part because of the specificity of the experiment and in part because a small-scale and temporary experiment will not induce general equilibrium

---

[11] See section 5.2 of Heckman, LaLonde, and Smith (1999) for an overview of substitution bias in the context of evaluating government training programs.

effects. That is, experiments may not alter behavior or relative prices in the same way that a large-scale and permanent reform might.

Slavin (1987, 1990) reports that a total of 15 such experiments have been conducted in American secondary schools and that one experiment has been conducted in an American elementary school. These experiments were conducted from the 1920s through the early 1970s, after which time Slavin could find no new U.S. experiments.

More recently, a large-scale experiment has been conducted in Africa. We begin with that experiment and then discuss the 16 experiments conducted in the United States.

A recent paper by Duflo, Dupas, and Kremer (2008) studies a Kenyan experiment. World Bank funding allowed 121 elementary schools that had a single grade 1 class to receive an additional grade 1 teacher for an 18-month period. (In the second year of the program, the same cohort of students continued to participate in the program, and the additional teacher moved with these students to grade 2.) In one half of schools, a pretest administered by the local schools was used to rank students, and students were assigned in strict order to the high-ability and the low-ability classrooms. To create a control group against which to compare the students in the tracked schools, in the other half of schools students were randomly assigned to the two classrooms. As the authors point out, this second procedure guards against the concern expressed by Betts and Shkolnik (2000b) that in nonexperimental settings supposedly untracked classrooms and schools really are using ability grouping in some disguised form.

Tests in math and literacy were administered to the students 18 months after the arrival of the extra teachers. Also, in order to test whether any effects of tracking persisted, the students were tested a second time, one year after the program had ended.

The authors perform the standard tests to ensure that the control and treatment samples were similar, and that no students switched between classrooms.

The paper addresses several distinct questions. First, the authors examine whether the overall test scores in the schools with tracking are higher or lower after 18 months, which can be interpreted as a quite clean test of whether tracking has any impact on the efficiency of schools. Second, they examine whether tracking affects the distribution of test scores. Third, they use two different designs to study the impact of small and large variations in classroom peers. The chapter by Sacerdote in this volume covers the last two questions thoroughly, and we will instead focus mostly on the authors' analysis of the overall effect of tracking. Nonetheless, the authors' experimental design generates some compelling evidence about possible mechanisms through which tracking manifests its effects.

On the question of efficiency, the paper reports statistically significant increases in average test scores in the tracked schools of 0.175 standard deviations relative to the untracked schools, after controlling for covariates. Second, these effects largely persist a full year after the end of the program.

Third, on the question of tracking and inequality, the results stand in stark contrast to most of the inter-country literature. All ability groups, when defined by quartiles of initial test scores within schools, seem to gain equally from tracking. However, the coefficients on the ability/tracking interactions, while not nearing statistical significance, do hint that students in the higher quartiles may gain slightly more than students in the lower quartiles. Due to the lack of precision of these interactions, it is not clear whether the proper interpretation is that tracking benefited all groups equally or that tracking increased inequality slightly across student groups.

The paper also exploits the experimental design to infer the mechanisms through which tracking was helping students. The authors find evidence that small changes in peer groups affect achievement. Thus, some other factor must more than counterbalance the negative peer effect that students placed in the low-ability classes experience. The paper reports some evidence that teachers were able to take advantage of the smaller variance within their classrooms by focusing on the skills that students have yet to learn. Evidence backing this idea is that students in the lower ability tracked classroom show greater growth in simpler math concepts than their counterparts in untracked schools, while students in the higher ability classrooms improve relatively more in more advanced concepts. The implication is clear: lower-ability students appear to have gained from tracking—even though their peer group had lower achievement than if the school had not used tracking—because teachers can do a better job when they teach a more homogeneous group of students.

The paper also finds that teachers in tracking schools are more likely to come to work and to be in the classroom, although this result is limited to the upper-ability track and to civil-service teachers who had relatively secure employment. Recall the argument in the theoretical section above that under the existence of tracking, all other school resources experienced by the individual student could adjust, including teacher effort. It appears that teacher effort may indeed adjust, at least in this setting.

A commonly expressed concern about experiments is that although they may have high internal validity, their external validity, that is, applicability to other situations, is not always high. It seems apparent that extrapolation to developed countries is problematic. The average class size was around 46 after the experiment began. One sign of the large heterogeneity within each grade was the standard deviation in age of about 1.5 years. Still, these conditions may mimic quite well school conditions in other developing countries. Another concern about external validity is that the Kenyan experiment grouping was based on test results alone, whereas evidence from developed countries such as Germany and the United States suggest that socio-economic status plays an important role in group assignments as well.

To their credit, the authors also point out that randomly assigning teachers to classrooms may not mimic the real-life implementation of tracking.

A final concern about external validity is that by hiring contract teachers whose job security was far lower than the government teachers who typically teach in Kenyan schools, the experiment did not use a typical sort of teacher or a typical teacher contract, which raises questions about external validity not just for other countries but for Kenya itself. It might prove impossible to extend this system throughout Kenya without greatly altering the relative wages (and other aspects of employment of contract teachers and government teachers). This is a specific example of general-equilibrium effects that could arise if a system of tracking were implemented nationwide and permanently, rather than in selected schools for a predetermined (and quite short) period of time.

In comparing these results to the large number of studies that make international comparisons, reviewed in the previous section, it is also important to remember that these later studies examine the effects of tracking at the secondary level, not the effects of tracking in grades 1 and 2 as in the study by Duflo, Dupas, and Kremer (2008). Not only is there an age difference, but the types of tracking typical in the secondary school systems in Europe involved not just ability grouping but the exposure of students to quite distinct curricula and schools.

In conducting an experiment on tracking at the elementary level, the Duflo, Dupas, and Kremer (2008) paper seems to have only one precedent, even though there are many experiments that have been conducted in the U.S. at the secondary level. In one such experiment, Cartwright and McIntosh (1972) report that elementary school students in Hawaii were randomly assigned to heterogeneous classes, to ability grouping across grades, and to "flexible" grouping, in which students were grouped separately by subject, again with the possibility of putting students in different grades into the same classroom if their achievement levels were similar. The authors find slightly negative overall effects of either approach to tracking. However, with only 262 students in one school, all of whom were disadvantaged, the study may not generalize to other settings.

Slavin (1990) reviews 15 tracking experiments conducted in the United States in secondary schools. In six of these experiments, students were randomly assigned to tracked or untracked classrooms, with assignment to ability group being decided by students' initial test scores or grades. In the other nine experiments, students were prematched based on achievement, and then randomly divided into tracked or untracked classrooms. On the question of the overall effect of tracking on achievement, Slavin finds that four of the studies showed positive effects, two showed no effect, and nine showed negative effects. In most cases, the estimated effects were quite small to moderate, with an absolute effect size of 0.01 to 0.3 standard deviations. One outlier, a study of 240 students in Virginia, produced an effect size of -0.48 standard deviations by the end of a one-year experiment. The largest positive effect found, in a study of the math achievement of 148 students in Ohio, an effect of 0.28 standard deviations, resulting from a single semester of tracking.

All but three of these experiments conducted in secondary schools tested for differential effects on students in the various ability groups. Six of the 12 studies suggest that students in the high-ability group gained the most and that students in the low-ability group gained the least. However, four studies suggested that the high(est) ability group gained less than the other groups.

With two exceptions, each of the experiments lasted for one year. This of course, as in the Kenyan study, raises concerns that tracking could have a quite different effect if teachers believed that the tracking (or detracking, as the case may be) represented permanent reforms rather than ephemeral experiments.

One experiment which stands out both for the relatively large size of the student sample and the duration of the experiment is the work by Marascuilo and McSweeney (1972). In this experiment conducted in Berkeley, California, 603 students were randomly assigned to a high-medium-low system of ability grouping or to ungrouped social studies classes, and were tested with both standardized tests and tests created by the teachers involved in the experiment. The overall effect was -0.22 of a standard deviation, and evidence suggested that students in high-ability classes gained 0.14 of a standard deviation, while those in medium- and low-ability classes lost -0.37 and -0.43 of a standard deviation relative to their similar-ability counterparts in the control group. The same patterns obtained for the teacher-created test and the standardized test, although p-values were higher in the latter case (5% versus 10%, respectively).

Slavin (1990) cites an important limitation of the secondary school experiments: they did not allow schools to offer a different curriculum to students in the various ability groups. In the United States, secondary school tracking certainly does allow for curricular differences across grades, and so these experiments may not be at all representative of how tracking in U.S. secondary schools plays out. In particular, they may understate the differential effects on achievement.

5. CONCLUSION AND OUTLINE OF A POSSIBLE RESEARCH AGENDA FOR THE FUTURE

In spite of many decades of research, what we do not know about the effects of tracking on outcomes greatly exceeds what we do know. Our uncertainty reflects not only the usual methodological debates about causal inference, but also, and perhaps more fundamentally, quite poor measures of tracking combined with differences across countries in what tracking really means.

One always hopes to resolve any differences in findings by showing that they result largely from differences in method. Once one has ranked the methods, then the findings that emerge from the best method can be taken as the closest approximation to the truth. That approach does not apply readily in the case of tracking, because different methods have been used in different geographical contexts, and it is quite clear that definitions of tracking and ability grouping differ from one country to the next. Worse, existing measures of tracking do a rather poor job of identifying what these differences are, either between nations in the international studies, or between schools in national or local studies.

With these concerns in mind, what can we say about the various methods used to date and the empirical findings? Second, can we lay out some viable research paths for the future?

The largely American (and to a lesser extent, British) literature that examines tracking on a school-by-school basis offers the opportunity to control for confounding variables such as school resources, local area characteristics, and school demography. But these advantages come at a high cost—the need to control for the endogeneity of whether schools track and the track into which students are placed. The early literature, as reviewed by Slavin (1987, 1990) shows little evidence that the use of tracking affects the overall effectiveness of schools, or changes inequality in student outcomes. A number of more recent papers in the U.S. contradict that view, suggesting that tracking materially aggravates inequality. However, more recent papers find that once one controls for endogenous track placement, these large effects either become much smaller or disappear altogether (Betts and Shkolnik (2000a,b) and Figlio and Page, 2002). Figlio and Page (2002) also present some evidence that treating the use of tracking as endogenous can even generate the result that the use of tracking lessens inequality.

The bulk of recent work has instead focused on tracking at a regional or national level. This approach solves the problem of endogenous placement of students into tracks, and lessens but does not eliminate the problem of endogenous tracking policies. These advantages come at a cost, namely, the potential for very large omitted variable biases. Roughly speaking there have been three ways in which regional or national variation in tracking has been exploited. On the surface the most convincing approach has been to use changes in tracking policy over time, allowing a traditional differences-in-differences approach. Some of these studies have produced important hints that the decision to group students heterogeneously for longer periods of time leads to better outcomes for students from disadvantaged backgrounds. However, the two papers studying the transition to comprehensive secondary schools in the United Kingdom raise serious concerns that the date at which each jurisdiction adopted comprehensive schools is endogenous. Both find that even before the age at which tracking begins, in areas with tracking, young students progress more quickly than do students in other areas. Two logical explanations have been put forward—either the spectre of secondary school tracking induces primary school students to work harder, or the decisions on whether to track are endogenous, and existing methods fail to control for this endogeneity adequately.

The second large set of papers that uses regional variation in tracking does not use changes in tracking policy, but instead compares outcomes in grades before and after tracking begins. Because most of this research has added dummies for region, nothing can be concluded about the overall effect of tracking on achievement. However, one paper that uses a quasi difference-in-differences approach by regressing outcomes in high grades on outcomes in low grades suggests that the efficiency effects are near zero. What all of these papers can readily do is to address the inequality question. The papers fairly uniformly conclude that early tracking exacerbates differences in achievement that are correlated with family background. Here again, though, it may be that if countries track at the secondary level, this induces changes in behavior in primary schools. Such incentive effects raise questions about the validity of using primary school students as controls for secondary school students within a given country.

Third, some papers use cross-sectional variation but do not use variation in tracking policy across time or grade. These are useful papers but are particularly likely to suffer from omitted variable bias.

Another issue related to all of the international papers is that in some ways, even if student-level data are available, the true sample size is the number of countries, because this is the level at which tracking varies.

Finally, we have a large set of tracking experiments performed in the United States mostly before 1970, and one recent tracking experiment performed in Kenya. Taken as a whole, the former studies suggest no meaningful effects of tracking on overall achievement or on inequality in achievement. The recent Kenyan study suggests meaningful productivity gains from tracking, ostensibly due to the heightened effectiveness of teachers when they teach a more homogenous class, and no significant effects on inequality. All of the experiments raise concerns about external validity. The American experiments in secondary schools focused on changing peer groups, but did not change curriculum between treatment and control groups. The treatments typically were very short, about one year. The Kenyan experiment was a short-term experiment in which teachers were randomly assigned to classes, and the newly hired teachers lacked the job security of the other teachers. Moreover the population being studied, and average school resources, were starkly different from what one sees in European or North American schools.

To sum up, on the question of the overall efficiency effect of tracking, the school-level literature does not find big effects; only one of the international studies uses a specification that allows the efficiency question to be addressed, and finds no effect; experimental evidence from the U.S. suggests no large effect, and the Kenyan experiment does suggest a fairly large positive effect.

On the distributional question, some of the more recent school-level research in the United States suggests that tracking aggravates inequality. But the identification in these papers has been questioned, with later papers finding a smaller or insignificant effect.

The early school-level literature suggests no effect. The international and regional studies suggest that tracking aggravates inequality, which may in part reflect the effects of dividing students by school in many European countries. Finally, the relatively small experimental literature suggests there is no distributional effect.

The fact that the American literature tends to find less evidence that tracking generates inequality than does the international literature may reflect differences in resources. Brunello and Checchi (2007) cite evidence that different types of secondary schools in some European countries receive quite different resource packages, although the evidence does not uniformly suggest that more is spent on one track versus another. In the United States, where tracking occurs mainly within schools, evidence generated by Betts and Shkolnik (2000a) and corroborated by Rees, Brewer, and Argys (2000) point to quite small differences across ability groups in teacher qualifications and class size, and indeed, countervailing differences. Further, the European tradition of tracking often involves sending vocationally and academically tracked students to different schools, which further creates potential for differential outcomes. Put differently, the large effects on inequality that emerge from many of the international studies could be real, and could stand out more than in the American literature because of the relative lack of variation in school resources and curriculum across ability groups within America relative to that in some other countries.

In the end, definitional differences and poor measures of tracking likely have more to do with the lack of agreement in the literature than do differences in methodology. The American literature suggests that asking principals and teachers whether a school tracks can yield different answers. We also lack precise ways of asking teachers about the ability level of their classes. But perhaps the most glaring example of measurement issues is that in most international studies of tracking, American schools are listed as "late trackers" or, in some studies, are listed as started tracking at the university level. Yet the school-level U.S. literature finds evidence of widespread ability grouping and tracking, in the sense of students being grouped by achievement and taking different curricula, from grade 6 or the start of secondary school, forward. Canadian schools are similar in this regard. Thus, the papers that compare countries may in fact be comparing two distinct forms of tracking, across-school tracking, as is or was common in Europe, with within-school tracking, which occurs in some countries that have been mislabeled as "late trackers." Perhaps a better terminology is to drop the word "tracking" altogether, in favor of "within-school tracking" and "between-school-type tracking". In this case labeling the United States as starting "between-school tracking" after high school would be a clear and accurate statement.

A good starting point for further work would be to focus on better measurement. Surveys and observation at the school level would give us a far richer understanding of how tracking varies across areas. For example we need better information on whether tracking is mere ability grouping within grades, or curricular tracking;

grouping within versus across grades; overall grouping or separate grouping by subject; grouping within or between schools; grouping within or between classrooms in a school; grouping that leads to dramatic differences in the teachers, class size, and curriculum experienced by students in different groups, or grouping without much tailoring of school resources or curriculum.

Once we had this information we would be in a much better position to understand what facets of tracking are driving apparent differences in student outcomes across countries or regions within a country.

What about the methods themselves? Which should be the focus for the future?

Further work that measures tracking at the school level will not make important contributions unless it adopts methods to control for endogeneity of student placement and schools' decisions to track. Clearly, the measures of tracking need to improve. One rather expensive solution is to undertake detailed national studies involving surveys and classroom observation to document better the nuances of how tracking works in different locations. Another possible strategy is to avoid relying solely on principal or teacher surveys to infer the achievement level of each class, and instead to average some measure of achievement of students in a given classroom. This approach has recently become more feasible thanks to the growing number of panel data-sets in the United States that follow all students within a district, with details on classroom assignments.

In the international literature, better information on what tracking really is, careful thought about why countries vary in tracking policy, and a greater emphasis on finding policy innovations over time all would help convince readers that something close to causal is being measured.

The experimental literature has by far the best claim that it is isolating the causal effects of treatment. But it is easy to question the relevance of these experiments to the real world. What if the treatment is not a realistic portrayal of how tracking is actually implemented? Slavin (1990) expresses an important point: the many experiments in American secondary schools contrasted only the peer groups between treatment and control groups, while not allowing for the fundamental differences in curriculum that Oakes (1985, 2005) documents in American schools. Further, if teachers know that an experiment will last for only a year, and if the experiment omits other important real-world considerations, the external validity of the experiment falls into question.

This is why we need detailed studies of how tracking works in the real world in all sorts of variants. Then one could experimentally evaluate all of these real-world flavors of tracking.

If researchers succeeded in opening up the black box by documenting the details on how different areas implement tracking, this could allow for a set of quite realistic experiments. In the United States, given how prevalent tracking already is, one approach might be to sample a large number of school districts that had been documented to use different flavors of tracking, to use the status quo as the treatments, and then to use a random sample of schools to serve as a control group in which students were instead grouped heterogeneously.

One could imagine a series of experiments, each within a given country, in which some of the treatments were new, perhaps more radical, and borrowed from practices in other countries. For instance, European nations might experiment with more American-style within-school tracking, which could yield a test of whether the apparent effects on inequality of European-style streaming could be mitigated if streaming occurred within rather than across schools.

Ultimately, if the interventions were designed carefully, we might learn that in different forms, tracking can either increase or decrease efficiency, and can either increase or decrease inequality. The policy prescription would then emerge from our new, far more nuanced understanding of the many varieties of tracking.

ACKNOWLEDGEMENTS

I thank Ludger Woessmann for helpful updates regarding the European literature on tracking. I thank Rick Hanushek, Ludger Woessmann, Derek Neal, David Figlio, Jeff Smith, and Paul Ryan for helpful comments.

REFERENCES

Ammermüller, A., 2005. Educational opportunities and the role of institutions. Centre for European Economic Research Discussion Paper No. 05-44.
Argys, L.M., Rees, D.I., Brewer, D.J., 1996. Detracking America's schools: Equity at zero cost? J. Policy Anal. Manag. 15 (4), 623–645.
Babcock, P., Betts, J.R., 2009. Reduced-class distinctions: Effort, ability, and the education production function. J. Urban Econ. 65 (3), 314–322.
Bauer, P., Riphahn, R.T., 2006. Timing of school tracking as a determinant of intergenerational transmission of education. Econ. Lett. 91 (1), 90–97.
Betts, J.R., Fairlie, R.W., 2003. Does immigration induce "native flight" from public schools into private schools? J. Public Econ. 87 (5–6), 987–1012.
Betts, J.R., Shkolnik, J.L., 1999. The behavioral effects of variations in class size: The case of math teachers. Educ. Eval. Policy Anal. 21 (2), 193–213.
Betts, J.R., Shkolnik, J.L., 2000a. The effects of ability grouping on student achievement and resource allocation in secondary schools. Econ. Educ. Rev. 19 (1), 1–15.
Betts, J.R., Shkolnik, J.L., 2000b. Key difficulties in identifying the effects of ability grouping on student achievement. Econ. Educ. Rev. 19 (1), 21–26.
Betts, J.R., Zau, A., Rice, L., 2003. Determinants of Student Achievement: New Evidence from San Diego. Public Policy Institute of California. Available at www.ppic.org.
Brunello, G., Checchi, D., 2007. Does school tracking affect equality of opportunity? New international evidence. Econ. Policy 22 (52), 781–861.
Cartwright, G.P., McIntosh, D.K., 1972. Three approaches to grouping procedures for the education of disadvantaged primary school children. J. Educ. Res. 65 (9), 425–429.
Duflo, E., Dupas, P., Kremer, M., 2008. Peer effects and the impact of tracking: Evidence from a randomized evaluation in Kenya. NBER Working Paper 14475.
Dustmann, C., 2004. Parental background, secondary school track choice, and wages. Oxford Econ. Pap. 56 (2), 209–230.

Epple, D., Newlon, E., Romano, R., 2002. Ability tracking, school competition, and the distribution of economic benefits. J. Public Econ. 83, 1–48.

Figlio, D.N., Page, M.E., 2002. School choice and the distributional effects of ability tracking: Does separation increase inequality? J. Urban Econ. 51 (3), 497–514.

Finn, J.D., Achilles, C.M., 1999. Tennessee's class size study: Findings, implications, misconceptions. Educ. Eval. Policy Anal. 21 (2), 97–109.

Galindo-Rueda, F., Vignoles, A., 2007. The heterogeneous effect of selection in U.K. secondary schools. In: Woessmann, L., Peterson, P.E. (Eds.), Schools and the Equal Opportunity Problem. MIT Press, pp. 103–128.

Gamoran, A., Mare, R.D., 1989. Secondary school tracking and educational inequality: Compensation, reinforcement, or neutrality? Am. J. Sociol. 94 (5), 1146–1183.

Hanushek, E.A., Rivkin, S.G., Taylor, L.L., 1996. Aggregation and the estimated effects of school resources. Rev. Econ. Stat. 78 (4), 611–627.

Hanushek, E.A., Woessmann, L., 2006. Does educational tracking affect performance and inequality? Differences-in-differences evidence across countries. Econ. J. 116 (510), C63–C76.

Heckman, J.J., Lalonde, R.J., Smith, J.A., 1999. The economics and econometrics of active labor market programs. In: Ashenfelter, O., Card, D. (Eds.), Handbook of Labor Economics. North Holland, pp. 1865–2097.

Hoffer, T.B., 1992. Middle school ability grouping and student achievement in science and mathematics. Educ. Eval. Policy Anal. 14 (3), 205–227.

Kerckhoff, A.C., 1986. Effects of ability grouping in British secondary schools. Am. Sociol. Rev. 51 (6), 842–858.

Krueger, A.B., 1999. Experimental estimates of education production functions. Q. J. Econ. 114 (2), 497–532.

Levesque, K., Laird, J., Hensley, E., Choy, S.P., Forrest Cataldi, E., Hudson, L., 2008. Career and technical education in the United States 1990 to 2005. National Center for Education Statistics, U.S. Department of Education NCES 2008-035.

Marascuilo, L.A., McSweeney, M., 1972. Tracking and minority student attitudes and performance. Urban Educ. 6, 303–319.

Meghir, C., Palme, M., 2005. Educational reform, ability, and family background. Am. Econ. Rev. 95 (1), 414–424.

Oakes, J., 1985. Keeping Track: How Schools Structure Inequality. Yale University Press.

Oakes, J., 2005. Keeping Track: How Schools Structure Inequality, second ed. Yale University Press.

Pekkarinen, T., Uusitalo, R., Kerr, S., 2009. School tracking and intergenerational income mobility: Evidence from the Finnish comprehensive school reform. J. Public Econ. 93, 965–973.

Pischke, J., Manning, A., 2006. Comprehensive versus selective schooling in England in Wales: What do we know?. NBER Working Paper Series No. 12176. www.nber.org/papers/w12176.

Rees, D.I., Brewer, D.J., Argys, L.M., 2000. How should we measure the effect of ability grouping on student performance? Econ. Educ. Rev. 19 (1), 17–20.

Schutz, G., Ursprung, H.W., Woessmann, L., 2008. Education policy and equality of opportunity. Kyklos 61 (2), 279–308.

Slavin, R.E., 1987. Ability grouping and student achievement in elementary schools: A best-evidence synthesis. Rev. Educ. Res. 57 (3), 293–336.

Slavin, R.E., 1990. Achievement effects of ability grouping in secondary schools: A best-evidence synthesis. Rev. Educ. Res. 60 (3), 471–499.

Theil, H., 1954. Linear Aggregation of Economic Relations, Contributions to Economic Analysis, vol.7. North-Holland.

Van Elk, R., van der Steeg, M., Webbink, D., 2009. The effect of early tracking on participation in higher education. Centraal Planbureau, The Hague CPB Document No. 182.

Waldinger, F., 2006. Does tracking affect the importance of family background on students' test scores? London School of Economics. Unpublished manuscript.

Woessmann, L., 2010. Institutional determinants of school efficiency and equity: German states as a microcosm for OECD countries. Jahrbücher für Nationalökonomie und Statistik (J. Econ. Stat.) 230 (2), 234–270.

CHAPTER 8

School Accountability

David Figlio* and Susanna Loeb**
*Northwestern University, CESifo, and NBER
**Stanford University and NBER

Contents

1. Introduction	384
2. The Rationale for School-Based Accountability	386
3. The Nature of Accountability	388
3.1 The consequences of accountability	388
3.2 Scope and domains of accountability indicators	389
3.3 Measuring school performance	391
3.4 Exclusions	394
3.5 Subgroup identification	395
3.6 Time considered for rating schools	396
4. Accountability Might Not Improve School Performance	397
4.1 Improving measured, but not generalizable, achievement	397
4.2 Strategic behavior	399
4.3 Failure or inability to respond to incentives	401
5. Evidence on Student Outcomes	402
5.1 Differential effects of accountability	410
5.2 Early versus late adopters of accountability	411
5.3 Size and policy significance of the estimated effects	412
6. Accountability and Teacher Labor Markets	412
7. Directions for Future Research	416
References	417

Abstract

School accountability—the process of evaluating school performance on the basis of student performance measures—is increasingly prevalent around the world. In the United States, accountability has become a centerpiece of both Democratic and Republican federal administrations' education policies. This chapter reviews the theory of school-based accountability, describes variations across programs, and identifies key features influencing the effectiveness and possible unintended consequences of accountability policies. The chapter then summarizes the research literature on the effects of test-based accountability on students and teachers, concluding that the preponderance of evidence suggests positive effects of the accountability movement in the United States during the 1990s and early 2000s on student achievement, especially in math. The effects on teachers and on students' long-run outcomes are more difficult to judge. It is also clear that school personnel respond to accountability in both positive and negative ways, and that accountability systems run the risk of being counter-productive if not carefully thought out and monitored.

JEL classification: I21 I28 L15

Keywords

Accountability
Achievement
Education
NCLB

1. INTRODUCTION

School accountability—the process of evaluating school performance on the basis of student performance measures—is increasingly prevalent around the world. In the United States, accountability measures have become a centerpiece of both Democratic and Republican federal administrations' education policies, following the movement by individual states to introduce accountability systems in the 1990s. Centralized reporting of school-wide examination scores has occurred for over two decades in the United Kingdom (Burgess et al., 2005) and in Chile (Mizala, Romaguera and Urquiola, 2007). Most Western European and Latin American countries have had national assessment systems and some semblance of reporting for over a decade, and a new system is being unveiled at the time of writing in Australia.

Accountability in education is a broad concept that could be addressed in many ways, such as using political processes to assure democratic accountability, introducing market-based reforms to increase accountability to parents and children, or developing peer-based accountability systems to increase the professional accountability of teachers (and now, especially following the "Race to the Top" initiative of President Obama, using similar tools to evaluate, reward, and sanction individual teachers as well). The most commonly considered definition of accountability involves using administrative data-based mechanisms aimed at increasing student achievement.

We focus in this chapter on accountability systems that generate explicit or implicit rewards and/or sanctions to schools on the basis of aggregate student performance on standardized tests. We concentrate on accountability systems in which the school is the unit of analysis, rather than systems that demand higher standards of students or those that evaluate and compensate teachers based on their students' performance. The rewards and sanctions associated with accountability systems could be explicit, such as bonuses for educators in schools considered to be excellent or threats of restructuring or closing low-performing schools, and they could also be implicit—operating less through direct action by central decision-makers and more through community pressure on schools to improve. Thus, school accountability incentives can work through direct government action or through the provision of information. Accountability ratings help community stakeholders observe school performance. For example, school accountability ratings may affect the housing market in a community (Figlio and Lucas, 2004) and could influence private donations to schools (Figlio and Kenny, 2009). Figlio and Ladd (2007), in a previous survey of the school accountability literature, lay out many of the issues regarding school accountability; the present chapter summarizes these concepts and provides more detailed evidence on the effects of school accountability policies and programs.

The school accountability systems that we consider operate primarily within the traditional public school system and are based in large measure on student testing (Elmore, Abelmann, and Fuhrman, 1996; Clotfelter and Ladd, 1996; Carnoy and Loeb, 2002; Hanushek and Raymond, 2003). The most famous of these systems is the federal No Child Left Behind Act (NCLB), which became law in the United States in 2002. NCLB requires states to test students in reading and mathematics in grades three through eight, as well as in one high school grade. NCLB also requires science testing in at least one grade per traditional school level.[1] In addition, it requires states to determine what it means to be proficient on the state assessments and to evaluate schools based on whether their students, in aggregate and by subgroup, are progressing adequately toward an ultimate goal of 100% proficiency by 2014. This law was preceded in the United States by the Clinton Administration's 1994 Goals 2000: Educate America Act, though NCLB is more focused on school accountability than on standards, and exerts a stronger federal role in education policy than did previous accountability laws. Many U.S. states also had accountability initiatives in place before NCLB and even before the Goals 2000: Educate America Act, partially because the U.S. impetus for accountability emerged from a 1989 meeting between President George H.W. Bush and the set of state governors. Prior to NCLB, 45 states published report cards on schools and 27 rated schools or identified low-performing ones (Education Week, 2001). The state-based accountability movement pre-NCLB was strongest in the southern United States.[2]

The United States has not been alone in the introduction of school accountability; as noted above, English schools' performance has been reported since 1988. The most-developed accountability systems operate in the United States (both federally and at the individual state level), England, and Chile, and these are the systems on which the overwhelming majority of academic research has been based. Other countries vary in the degree to which they assess students, and whether they publicly report scores at the school level. In Latin America, for instance, scores are publicly reported in Brazil, Chile, Colombia, and Mexico (in some regions), and most

---

[1] Science testing is not, however, currently used for accountability purposes in every state.
[2] The concentration of early accountability efforts in the south was motivated by southern governors' desire to foster economic development; the fact that for historical reasons state governments in the south typically had more authority over education finance and governance than in other parts of the country and hence were in a position to impose accountability; and that teachers unions, which might have opposed accountability programs, were not a major factor in most southern states.

governments record school-level reports for internal purposes (Vegas and Petrow, 2008). Countries vary considerably in terms of the quality and fidelity of assessment practices: Brazil, Chile, Colombia, and Mexico rank at the top in Latin America in their present capacity for assessment (Ferrer, 2006). Other countries, such as Costa Rica, Cuba, Guatemala, and Panama, though they regularly test students and measure aggregate scores at the school level for internal purposes, rank much lower along the same metrics. Nonetheless, it is clear that many countries are developing capacities for conducting accountability systems, and the methodological and conceptual issues touched upon in this chapter will be important in any system design and implementation.

2. THE RATIONALE FOR SCHOOL-BASED ACCOUNTABILITY

The current school-based accountability movement emerged out of a desire, particularly seen in the United States and the United Kingdom beginning in the 1980s in the Reagan and Thatcher eras, to measure performance in the public and nonprofit sectors (Figlio and Kenny, 2009). In the United States, this movement aligned well with the broader standards-based reform movement both in terms of intent and substantive areas (O'Day and Smith, 1993). The objective of standards-based reform is to identify a set of clear, measurable, and ambitious performance standards for students across a number of core subject areas, to align curriculum to these standards, and to expect students to meet these high standards. A central component of standards-based reform is the assessment of students to ensure that they are meeting the expectations set out for them, to identify the schools that have students who are relatively successful (or unsuccessful) in meeting these expectations, and to encourage schools to improve student outcomes.

Accountability, in the context of standards-based reform, is part of a broader integrated policy package, providing incentives for students, teachers, schools, or districts to perform. The principal-agent problem, well-known to economists, provides a rationale for accountability: if stakeholders—be they parents, local firms, or policy makers—have difficulty monitoring the activities of schools, then educators might behave in a manner contrary to the interests of these stakeholders. In such a case, it would follow that more effective monitoring of educators could result in improved student outcomes.

The information content in school accountability systems can provide a powerful mechanism for overcoming the principal-agent problem. Assessing schools against the common metric of standardized student test scores provides policy makers and members of the general public with independent information regarding how well schools and school districts (and potentially teachers) are doing in comparison to their peers or to outside performance standards. Measuring and reporting school performance and attaching positive and negative consequences to meeting or failing to meet performance objectives provides incentives that encourage educators to concentrate on the subjects and materials that are being measured and to potentially alter the methods through which they educate students.[3] The measurement and reporting of a school's progress allows policy makers to assess how successful a school has been in meeting the state's achievement goals.

The school is not the only level at which accountability could be targeted. Some policy makers favor accountability for individual teachers—through, for example, merit or performance-based pay, as advocated by President Obama and others—rather than for schools; and some researchers have found evidence indicating that performance incentives for teachers can be beneficial for student outcomes (e.g., Lavy, 2007; Figlio and Kenny, 2007). Others view accountability at the school level as preferable both because it promotes collaboration among teachers and because schools have more opportunities than do individual teachers to enact the types of changes in resource allocation and practices that may be needed to raise student achievement (Ladd, 2001). Exclusive accountability at the school district level, instead of at the school or teacher levels, could mask the substantial heterogeneity in school performance observed across schools within a district. This is particularly the case in the larger school districts with dozens or hundreds of schools, though district level accountability has the benefit of allowing the reallocation of resources across schools in response to accountability incentives.

School accountability systems have the potential benefits of aligning effort with stakeholders' goals and providing information for improvement; however, they are limited by the fact that they can only measure a small number of the dimensions that stakeholders value. Rothstein, Jacobson, and Wilder (2008) demonstrate that educational stakeholders value a wide range of outcomes including not just academic performance and educational attainment but also areas such as citizenship, work ethic, and critical thinking. But school accountability systems generally do not cover even the full set of valued academic outcomes, instead often focusing solely on reading and mathematics performance, and the nontest measures like graduation rates or attendance rates are also crude proxies for the behavioral and attainment outcomes that stakeholders value. By focusing attention on the set of outcomes that are easily measurable, school accountability systems may lead some valued outcomes to be treated as more important than other valued outcomes.

The limitations of the outcome measures notwithstanding, school accountability can be successful in attaining its objectives if stakeholders value the information embedded within the accountability systems. A long line of papers, including work by Black (1999) and the papers summarized in the entry on real estate values by Black and Machin in Chapter 10 of this book, demonstrate that aggregate test score results are

---

[3] Such information may also facilitate improved monitoring by another important set of stakeholders in the education system, namely parents. Whether by complaining about poor performance or by threatening to withdraw their child from the school, parents could potentially use the publicly provided information on school performance to induce their children's schools to improve.

capitalized into real estate prices. Figlio and Lucas (2004) show that school accountability grades have major consequences for real estate valuation (even holding other measures of school effectiveness constant) demonstrating that the nature of the presentation of school accountability information is itself quite consequential, not only for parents of students but also for members of the general public in terms of their asset values. In recent work, Figlio and Kenny (2009) provide new evidence that suggests that school accountability measures influence voluntary contributions to public schools. Specifically, they find that schools that experience negative accountability information "shocks" lose financial support from parents and community members, while those that experience positive accountability information shocks gain financial support. These responses are particularly strong for schools serving minority students and lower-income families that might have lower levels of monitoring of schools than might other families, and are consistent with the findings from the psychology, charitable contribution, and marketing literatures, that stakeholders tend to wish to avoid "throwing good money after bad." In sum, the weight of the available evidence indicates that stakeholders of many stripes care deeply about the outcomes of school accountability systems, and this suggests that educators are likely to wish to respond as well.

3. THE NATURE OF ACCOUNTABILITY

How a school accountability system is designed can have a significant impact on the nature of and the strength of the incentives that schools face to raise student achievement in the tested subjects. Moreover the design can affect which students receive the most attention.

3.1 The consequences of accountability

School accountability systems can take two different approaches with regard to the consequences of accountability. One possibility is to include explicit rewards and/or sanctions for performance that exceeds or does not meet expectations. Examples of positive consequences for schools and educators in these systems may include increased resources or autonomy to spend these resources at the school level; and bonuses for educators in successful schools. Some accountability systems offer rewards to schools that are either exceeding stated expectations or moving strongly in the direction of doing so. On the flip side, accountability systems also frequently include explicit sanctions for schools not meeting expectations. Examples of these sanctions include the withdrawal of autonomy; requiring local education agencies to provide additional schooling options—either school choice or supplemental services—to students in these schools; and outright school restructuring or closure. Several studies, including Hanushek and Raymond (2005) and Dee and Jacob (2009), specifically identify systems with this more "consequential" accountability and provide evidence that these consequences appear to translate to improved student outcomes, suggesting that educators respond to the explicit consequential incentives.

School accountability systems may not need to have explicit consequences from central authorities to influence educator behavior, however. As mentioned above, central governments are only one of many monitors of school performance, and other performance monitors—parents and community members—may pack enough punch to influence educator behavior. The broader economics literature on the role of information on product quality (e.g., Figlio and Lucas, 2004; Jin and Leslie, 2003; Mathios, 2000) shows how strong information disclosure can be in influencing markets, and it is realistic to expect that a major source of consequences of school accountability would be community and local pressure provoked by increased accessibility of information. Black (1999) shows that school test scores are capitalized in housing prices, and Figlio and Lucas (2004) demonstrate that housing markets react even more to the information embedded in school accountability systems. The findings of these two studies have since been replicated in numerous settings in North America and Europe. Figlio and Kenny (2009) also show that parents and community members withhold financial support from schools that central governments say are performing poorly and offer more financial support to those that central governments say are performing well. This financial pressure, coupled with the other informal pressure that surely accompanies it, strongly suggests that even absent formal consequences of accountability, accountability systems may be effective in influencing educator behavior.

This last point is particularly important because it implies that accountability systems have the potential to be effective even when the threatened sanctions associated with poor performance are not viewed as credible. Accountability systems that set standards such that a massive fraction of schools would likely fail may be perceived as incredible by educators who do not believe that central authorities would shut down schools or fire educators on a grand scale. Indeed, there exist very few examples of large-scale implementation of the more draconian elements of some school accountability systems. Economic theory would indicate that educators, when faced with an incredible threat, would not react to those threats. But, if the less draconian consequences of school accountability systems, including those that come through community pressure as a result of reporting systems, are sufficient to generate educator responses, then it may be that the severe but less credible threats associated with an accountability system are unnecessary for generating educator responses. Of course, since there have been so few instances of large-scale implementation of these severe threats, there is little data to shed light on the degree to which more credible serious threats might impact educator behavior and school outcomes.

3.2 Scope and domains of accountability indicators

School accountability systems differ in the number and types of tests, or other performance indicators, they include. Central governments face important tradeoffs when determining how broad-based to make their accountability systems. In particular, systems that align accountability with a smaller set of outcomes tend to narrow the scope of the education provided to students. On the other hand, a broad set of outcomes is more difficult to measure reliably and may blur the focus of school and district personnel.

School accountability systems are intended to provide incentives for schools to generate higher performance in academic subjects, and indeed, schools appear to pay attention to the subject matter on which the tests are based. The available evidence strongly supports the conclusion that schools tend to concentrate their attention on the subjects tested and on the grades that have high stakes tests (Deere and Strayer, 2001; Ladd and Zelli 2002; Stecher et al., 2000). Other studies (e.g., Hamilton et al., 2005; Jones et al., 1999; Koretz and Hamilton, 2003; Linn, 2000; Stecher et al., 1998; and Stecher et al., 2000) show that teachers and schools tend to narrow the curriculum and shift their instructional emphasis from nontested to tested subjects, while earlier work by Shepard and Dougherty (1991) and Romberg et al. (1989) suggest that teachers focus more on tested content areas within specific subjects. In related work, Chakrabarti (2005) presents evidence that schools may concentrate their energies on the most easily-improved areas of instruction, rather than on subjects across the board.

This evidence on the narrowing of the curriculum in response to accountability implies that governments intent on school improvements along a wide variety of dimensions may wish to include a large number of subjects in the accountability system. However, increasing the scope of testing is costly, both in terms of financial costs and in terms of either the opportunity cost of foregone instructional time instead devoted to testing or the reliability of the test measures generated.

The scope and domain of accountability is also limited by the technology available to assess students' progress. Some subjects are simply more challenging to assess than are others. Given the well-established tendency of educators to focus their attention on the material most likely to be covered on the assessment, a behavior known commonly as "teaching to the test," it seems likely that educators will concentrate on the assessed components of difficult-to-assess subjects. Such a pattern of behavior could lead to attention redirected from the desired, but difficult to measure, knowledge and skills in favor of the less desirable, but easier to measure, aspects of a subject. A recent National Research Council panel (Wilson and Bertenthal, 2006) warns of this potential with regard to science assessment, as the members note how challenging it is to design a science assessment to tests students' scientific inquiry skills. It is therefore important to carefully consider the specific nature of assessments administered to students when deciding how broadly to base an accountability system.

There exists considerable heterogeneity across U.S. states in the substantive breadth of the state accountability system. While most states assess schools principally on the basis of reading, mathematics (and sometimes writing), some states administer a much farther-reaching set of tests for school accountability. Virginia, for example, tests students in more subjects, including science, U.S. and Virginia history, and social studies, and reports on end-of-course examinations in high school. Kentucky's core content areas identified for the basis of school accountability further include fine arts and humanities. Nebraska assesses schools on a narrower set of substantive areas, but at a greater depth, including portfolio reviews as part of the assessment.[4]

In principle, accountability systems could be expanded to incorporate other measures of school performance besides student performance on standardized tests. Hanushek and Raymond (2003) construct a hierarchy of nontest indicators of school performance, ranked on the basis of their relevance and likely alignment to objective measures of school progress. For instance, they argue that certain measures such as the drop-out rate, graduation rate, number of students in advanced courses, percent of students passing end-of-course exams, retention rate, student mobility, and suspension rate, are relatively closely related to student achievement. If schools are trading off these outcomes in order to increase measured and incentivized outcomes, accountability may be counter-productive (though Carnoy, Loeb and Smith, 2001, find no evidence of this tradeoff in Texas). Other variables, however, such as college entrance exam scores, course offerings, number of computers, number of noncredentialed teachers, parental satisfaction, school crime rate, principal mobility, or teacher mobility, are only weakly related to student achievement. To the extent that the goal of the accountability system is to increase student achievement, therefore, some of these measures would be more appropriate than others as elements of an accountability program. Some of these factors are already incorporated into many accountability systems. For example, graduation rates are part of NCLB's assessment of high schools, as well as those in numerous states. One shortcoming of this broader set of outcomes, however, is that they are more easily manipulated by school officials than achievement tests.

3.3 Measuring school performance

There have been two main approaches used to measure school performance on the basis of test scores. In "status" measures, a school's performance is judged based on levels of performance, such as the fraction of students attaining a given proficiency level or the average test score in the school. "Growth" measures, often called "gain scores" or "value-added" measures, evaluate schools on the degree to which their students improve in their test performance from one year to the next, or from fall to spring of a given school year. Growth measures can be technical complicated, and a thorough discussion of the issues is beyond the score of this chapter. The simplest of these measures averages year-to-year or fall-to-spring changes in test scores across all students in a school while more complicated measures regression-adjust test score changes for various student characteristics or take into account the variance in observed test score changes. The No Child Left Behind law in the United States is currently based on a status model of evaluating schools,

---

[4] At the time of writing, however, Nebraska was phasing out the portfolio review component of school accountability.

though the U.S. Department of Education has granted some states the ability to evaluate schools using a growth model. Proposals for reauthorization of the NCLB law being considered at the time of this writing would further expand the use of growth models in federal accountability evaluations in the United States.

The two types of approaches—status and growth—measure different outcomes and tend to generate different objectives and incentives for schools. Status-based systems that focus on the percent of students who achieve at proficient levels seek to encourage schools to raise performance at least to that level (Krieg, 2008; Neal and Schanzenbach, 2010). This approach is appealing to many policy makers because it sets the same target for all groups of students and because it encourages schools to focus attention on the set of low performing students who in the past may have received little attention. Status-based systems also have the advantage of being transparent.

The goal of the growth model approach is to encourage schools to improve the performance of their students independently of the absolute level of that achievement. Such an approach is appealing to many people because of its perceived fairness. It explicitly takes into account the fact that where students end up is heavily dependent on where they start and the fact that the starting points tend to be highly correlated with family background characteristics. At the same time, the use of the growth model approach may raise political concerns, both because the public may find the approach less transparent than the status approach and because some see it as a way of letting schools with low average performance off the hook.

Systems using status and growth models generate different incentives in part because they lead to different rankings of schools. Many schools deemed ineffective based on their aggregate performance levels may actually have quite high "value added" and vice versa (Clotfelter and Ladd, 1996; Ladd and Walsh, 2002; Kane and Staiger, 2002; and Stiefel et al., 2005). Some accountability systems (e.g., North Carolina's) encourage both high levels of performance and high test score growth, by including both levels and gains in the index of success for schools under the accountability system (Ladd and Zelli, 2002).

The status and growth approaches send different signals to schools about which students deserve more attention. Under a status-based system designed to encourage schools to raise student performance to some threshold level, the position of the threshold matters. A challenging performance threshold—one that would be consistent with the high aspirations of the standards-based reform movement, for example—would provide incentives for schools to focus attention on a larger group of students than would be the case with a lower threshold. Evaluating schools on the basis of "value added," by contrast, provides incentive for schools to distribute their effort more broadly across the entire student body. In such a system, however, schools may have an incentive to focus attention on the more advantaged students if the test score gains of those students are easier to increase, bringing up the average gains for the school (Ladd and Walsh, 2002; and Richards and Sheu, 1992).

Under either approach, random errors in the measurement of student performance can generate inconsistent rankings of schools over time—a factor that weakens incentives for improvement. The implications of measurement error are especially strong for small schools because the smaller the number of students in the school, the larger the school-wide average measurement error, and hence the less consistent the school's ranking is likely to be from one year to the next. Schools deemed to be improving at one point in time are often found to be declining the next year due to measurement error (Kane and Staiger, 2002). The problem of measurement error is exacerbated when schools are rated based on the growth model because it requires test scores for two years instead of one and both of these scores are measured with error. The danger is that personnel in such schools may receive such inconsistent signals from one year to the next that they have little incentive to respond in a constructive way. The policy relevant issue with measurement error is not whether there is any measurement error, there always is. The issue is whether this error is large enough to mask the signal that drives the incentives in the accountability system.

Neither the status nor the growth approach to measuring school performance perfectly captures school efficiency—the effectiveness with which schools use their resources to maximize student outcomes, given the students they serve. According to the "education production function" model, student achievement is determined by the characteristics of the student and his or her classmates, the school's resources (including the quantity and qualifications of the teachers), and the efficiency with which those resources are used. Because efficiency cannot be observed directly, it must be inferred from statistical analysis that controls both for the resources available to the school and the characteristics of the students being served (Stiefel et al., 2005). If the goal of an accountability system is to induce schools to use the resources they have more effectively, then, in principle, schools should be rated on their efficiency, not simply on the level or growth of their students' achievement. The problem is that the data requirements for such efficiency measures are often daunting and the statistical techniques can be complex (Ladd and Walsh, 2002; and Stiefel et al., 2005).

In contrast to a measure of school efficiency, the status and growth measures provide information on whether or not schools are meeting expectations for either the level of achievement or the growth in achievement with no attention to what accounts for that performance. Although inefficient use of available resources may be one reason for poor performance, another could well be that the resources available to the school are insufficient for the school to meet the accountability standard given the profile of the students in the school. In the latter case, it is neither fair nor likely to be productive for state or federal policy makers to hold the teachers or other school personnel responsible for the poor performance of the school's students (Ladd and Walsh, 2002). Thus, accountability and the financing of schools are closely intertwined.

3.4 Exclusions

Designers of accountability systems must also determine which students should be counted when evaluating student learning. It seems at first glance to be obvious that all students should be credited to a school—especially when accountability laws have names such as No Child Left Behind. But universal inclusion raises important questions about fairness and attribution. For instance, should a school be held responsible for the performance of a student who just arrived at the school a week prior or even a month prior to the test administration? Should schools be held responsible for students for whom testing is more challenging, or potentially less reliable, such as students with disabilities? The fact that these questions have no immediately obvious answer is evident in Florida's treatment of mobile students in successive iterations of its accountability system. When Florida introduced its system in 1999, the state included both those students who spent the full academic year and those who were recent in-migrants in its calculations of school grades. The following year the state amended its policies to include only students who had spent the full academic year up to testing in the school. These rule changes influenced the sets of schools identified as low- or high-quality (Figlio and Lucas, 2004). At the federal level, NCLB counts only those students who had spent the full year in the school toward school proficiency goals but still includes all students in the calculations of average proficiency rates for the purposes of public reporting. Transient students count for school *district* accountability under NCLB.

NCLB mandates that students with disabilities and English Language Learners be included in a school's aggregate proficiency counts, and these groups are specifically identified as separate subgroups of interest in the federal law. States, on the other hand, in implementing their own accountability systems, have diverging treatments of these students. Virginia, for instance, with an accountability system that predates NCLB, chose to include English Language Learners and students with disabilities in its calculations of school ratings, while Florida excludes all students with disabilities, even those who take tests, from the school-level aggregates used to measure performance. Florida schools, therefore, are subject to two different accountability treatments of these groups of students, one from the state level and one from the national level.

Policy makers face clear tradeoffs with respect to the treatment of these special populations. On the one hand, schools with large fractions of mobile and disabled students in many cases have a legitimate argument that holding them accountable for the academic achievement of such challenging-to-educate students puts them at an unfair disadvantage relative to other schools with fewer disabled students. On the other hand, excluding students on the basis of *classification* provides schools with less incentive to support these students as well as an incentive to selectively reclassify or move students in order to look better against performance metrics. The evidence is quite clear that schools have responded to accountability pressures by reclassifying low-performing students as students with disabilities (see, for example, Cullen and Reback, 2006; Deere and Strayer, 2001; Figlio and Getzler, 2007; and Jacob, 2005). Thus, while the incentives to reclassify are small under NCLB, such incentives may still exist under state policy.[5] NCLB (and other accountability systems that hold schools accountable for a disabled subgroup explicitly) also may provide incentives for schools to identify as disabled more marginal students so that the average proficiency rates amongst the school's disabled population increases. These incentives are all smaller under growth model accountability scenarios than under status model scenarios. Moreover, reclassification may not be detrimental; one can interpret the incentive effects of accountability with regard to disabled students as potentially providing incentives to correctly identify students as disabled, rather than to over-classify disability rates. Bokhari and Schneider (2009) find that accountability leads to increased prescription of psychostimulants, implying physician involvement in the identification of disabilities.

Accountability-based incentives for identifying students as special needs interact with other incentives embedded within the school finance system of a jurisdiction. Some U.S. states compensate school districts for disabled students on the basis of predicted—rather than actual—disability caseloads. In these cases, a district that reclassifies a student as disabled to avoid having that student counted for the purposes of accountability will generate higher costs for the district because it is responsible for the full costs of providing special services for the student. In places that compensate school districts for the extra costs of educating students who are specifically classified as disabled, in contrast, the finance system will exacerbate any incentives to over-classify students provided by the accountability system, and will also increase the incentives to correctly classify students in need of special education services. It is currently impossible to determine for certain the "correct" level of disability classification.

3.5 Subgroup identification

One purpose of accountability systems may be to focus attention on traditionally underperforming groups of students. Policy makers interested in doing so may explicitly require that schools meet certain performance targets for individual subgroups of students within a school's population. This focus on subgroups is central to federal accountability policy in the United States, as NCLB holds schools accountable not only for the performance of the full student body, but also for the performance of subgroups of students defined by their race, income, and disability status. Because of the small size of many subgroups, this subgroup requirement exacerbates the problems of measurement error highlighted by Kane and Staiger (2002). Nonetheless, NCLB requires such disaggregation on the grounds that it provides incentives for schools to pay attention to members of each subgroup and thereby prevents schools from leaving particular groups of children behind.

---

[5] Consistent with this conclusion, during the during the 1990s, Texas and North Carolina, both of which had highly touted state accountability systems, excluded increasingly large number of students from the NAEP tests, thereby biasing upward the observed gains in NAEP scores in those states (Amrein and Berliner, 2002; Braun, 2004).

States have the authority under NCLB to determine the minimum size of subgroups that are separately measured and reported, and states have set very different thresholds. Thresholds vary from five students in Maryland to as many as 50 to 200 students depending on the size of the school in Texas. Setting the size of the subgroup thresholds involves a clear policy tradeoff. On the one hand, a higher threshold increases the accuracy with which school performance is measured. On the other hand, a higher threshold means that large segments of a school's population could fall under the radar screen, an outcome that would be inconsistent with the goals of NCLB. A recent and highly publicized Associated Press analysis, for example, reported that 1.9 million students are not counted under their racial and ethnic subgroups, including more than one-third of Asian students and nearly half of Native American students (Bass, Dizon and Feller, 2006). A potential alternative to the subgroup requirement would be to focus special attention on the segment of the school's students that performed at a low level in the previous year and to track that group's growth. This segment would likely include a large fraction of the economically disadvantaged and racial minority students, and so might capture the spirit of the NCLB law without exacerbating the problem of measurement error.

The identification of subgroups, and the attendant issue of the size requirements for subgroup identification, influences the likelihood that a school will meet all of the annual yearly progress (AYP) criteria. When the subgroup size thresholds are low, the more racially heterogeneous schools will have more measured subgroups and will face greater risks of low accountability ratings compared to more homogeneous schools because any negative random error in any single subgroup is sufficient to lead to a negative rating for a school. Using national data, Stullich et. al. (2006) show that among schools that missed AYP in 2004, 23% missed because of the failure of a single subgroup and 18% missed because of insufficient achievement of two or more subgroups. Given the correlation between subgroups (e.g., those based on race and free lunch eligibility), one can reasonably assume that subgroup size requirements were responsible for anywhere from one-fifth to one-third of the failure to make AYP among the schools that missed it.

3.6 Time considered for rating schools

A final design issue is the relevant time period for accountability. Kane and Staiger (2002) demonstrate, both conceptually and with data, that substituting multiyear moving averages for year-by-year analysis considerably reduces the instability of the measures of school performance over time, and thereby provides schools with more consistent incentives to raise student performance. Accountability systems based on a single year of data (or growth from one year to the next), as is largely the case in both NCLB and state accountability systems, are far more likely to misjudge the performance of schools. Increasing the time period over which schools are evaluated reduces the measurement error and the incorrect classification of schools, though also requires more years of data to spot indications of improvement or decline.

Figlio (2004) simulates how permitting accountability to apply to periods longer than a year affects the set of schools likely to be sanctioned under the NCLB Act. His simulations show that the fraction of schools sanctioned under the year-by-year system is approximately 20% higher than it would be under a system based on a three-year time period. In addition, he demonstrates that shifting to the longer time period reduces the rate at which schools are likely to be sanctioned more for racially heterogeneous schools with multiple subgroups than for other schools. Thus, extending the time period to three years reduces the random variation within subgroups and allows for a more accurate picture of trends in student performance within a student category.

4. ACCOUNTABILITY MIGHT NOT IMPROVE SCHOOL PERFORMANCE

The preceding discussion predicts that school accountability programs will increase student achievement, although the magnitude of the predicted effects for particular groups of students or types of schools may well differ depending on how the system is designed. For several reasons, however, school accountability systems might not generate higher achievement.

4.1 Improving measured, but not generalizable, achievement

Monitoring provides incentives for those being monitored to appear as effective as possible against the metric being assessed. It is certainly possible, therefore, that educators could teach very narrowly to the specific material covered on the tests, and little or no generalizable learning outside of that covered on the test would take place (Koretz and Barron, 1998). This restriction on the domains of learning may not be a concern if the tests that come with high stakes for schools cover a wide range of material considered important by society; in fact, this "teaching to the test" may be desirable. On the other hand if the high-stakes tests reflect only a subset of the knowledge and skills desired by stakeholders, then teaching to the test could have negative consequences for students. Furthermore, educators can go further than teaching to the test, and teach test-taking strategies with little long-term benefit for students or even engage in outright cheating to appear better on the accountability examinations. For example, Jacob and Levitt (2003) show that a small fraction of Chicago teachers responded to accountability pressures in that city by fraudulently completing student examinations in an attempt to improve observed student outcomes.

A popular approach for determining the extent to which an accountability policy has resulted in generalized learning involves seeing whether gains observed on high-stakes tests are also observed using low-stakes tests with no particular consequences for schools or students. A natural test for that purpose is the National Assessment of Educational Progress (NAEP), which has been administered to a nationally representative random sample of students since the early 1970s and to representative samples of students in grades four and eight in most states since the 1990s. Because of its high profile and national scope, the NAEP has been widely employed in the studies described later in this chapter assessing the effects of accountability on student learning.

Observing a low-stakes test has considerable appeal, but it has at least two downsides. One downside is that students may not take a low-stakes test sufficiently seriously to do their best work. That said, this lack of effort would mainly introduce measurement error into the dependent variable of analyses of the effects of accountability on student outcomes and one might expect that a main consequence of using low-stakes tests to evaluate the effects of accountability is the imprecision associated with the estimates. Unless student effort differs from one administration of the low-stakes test to the next, changes in performance on the low-stakes test should provide a reasonable estimate of gains in student learning. A second downside to using low-stakes tests is that the high-stakes tests are often aligned to the standards valued by policy makers, while the low-stakes tests are not as aligned. Hence, findings of smaller effects of accountability when low-stakes tests are used to measure performance may simply reflect differences in the degree to which the two types of tests reflect the material that policy makers want to see covered.

The accountability experience in Texas illustrates the importance of this distinction between performance on high- and low-stakes tests. After a series of education reforms starting in the early 1980s, Texas introduced in 1990 a criterion-referenced testing program called the Texas Assessment of Academic Skills (TAAS) that was designed to shift the focus from minimum skills to higher-order thinking skills (Haney, 2000). By 1994, tests were being administered annually to all students in grades 3–8 and students had to pass a 10th-grade test to graduate. The state then used passing rates on the TAAS, along with dropout rates and student attendance rates, to hold individual schools accountable for their students' performance. Schools were held accountable not only for the overall pass rate in the school but also for the pass rates of four student subgroups: African Americans, Hispanics, whites, and economically disadvantaged students. Between 1994 and 1998, TAAS scores in both math and reading increased quite dramatically, suggesting that the accountability program had a large and positive impact on student achievement. Klein et al. (2000), however, showed that the large gains on TAAS did not translate into comparably large gains in the lower-stakes Texas NAEP scores. In general, the gains in NAEP scores were about a third the size of the gains in TAAS scores, though still meaningfully positive.

Further, the TAAS and NAEP results generate conflicting stories about how accountability affected racial achievement gaps in Texas. In particular, the gaps between blacks and whites based on the TAAS scores in fourth-grade reading and math and eighth-grade math decreased significantly between 1994 and 1998, while the comparable gaps based on the NAEP increased slightly (Klein et al., 2000). Similar patterns also emerge for Hispanics. Klein et al. speculate that the reasons for the differing patterns for TAAS and NAEP results is that Texas teachers may be teaching very narrowly to the TAAS and that the schools serving minority students may be doing so even more than other schools.

Additional evidence on whether the transferability of knowledge from high-stakes to low-stakes tests emerges from Jacob's 2005 study of accountability in Chicago. Jacob compared achievement gains for fourth and eighth graders in math as measured by scores on the district's high stakes test to those on a comparable, but low-stakes, test administered by the state of Illinois. Those comparisons show that gains for eighth graders generalized to the state test but that those for fourth graders did not.[6] In Florida, Figlio and Rouse (2006) find consistently smaller estimated effects of accountability on low-stakes tests than they do using high-stakes tests.

4.2 Strategic behavior

Teaching to the test is not the only mechanism through which schools might alter their behaviors in response to the incentives embedded within accountability systems. There exists considerable evidence that schools engage in strategies that artificially improve test scores by changing the group of students subject to the test. The most widely studied behavior of this type is the selective assignment of students to special education programs. As mentioned above, many studies show that schools tend to classify low-achievers as learning disabled in the context of accountability systems. Though there may be some debate about whether the greater rates of classification are undesirable in all cases, nonetheless, they highlight the possibility that schools are manipulating the testing pool specifically to inflate measured school performance. These decisions may have spillover consequences outside of education: Bokhari and Schneider's (2009) finding that school accountability policies enhances the use of psychostimulants suggests that there are health consequences of education policies. Likewise, Figlio's (2006) finding that some Florida schools changed their discipline and suspension patterns around the time of the testing in ways consistent with the goal of improving test-takers' average scores reinforces the concern that schools might engage in artificial improvements of student test performance, with possible significant ramifications for students involved.

Schools may engage in other types of strategic behavior that affect student performance. For example, Figlio and Winicki (2005) demonstrate that schools change their meals programs at the time of the tests in an apparent attempt to raise performance on high-stakes examinations, while Anderson and Butcher (2006) find that schools subject

---

[6] Data were not available for a comparable analysis of reading scores.

to accountability pressure are more apt than other schools to sell soft drinks and snacks through vending machines.[7] Finally, Boyd et al. (2008) illustrate how high-stakes testing in certain grades in New York altered which teacher taught in particular grades and schools.

Many of these behaviors are less likely to occur in growth model accountability systems than in status-based systems. The reason is that in the growth approach, the manipulative behavior that increases student achievement in one year would make it more difficult for the school to attain accountability goals the following year. No such tradeoff arises in status-based accountability systems. Indeed, Rouse et al. (2007) document a series of significant substantive responses with regard to instructional policies and practices as a consequence of Florida's school accountability system that assesses schools on the basis of student achievement growth.

In a federal system with multiple levels of accountability decision-making, states (or other subfederal units) may themselves respond strategically to federally imposed accountability pressures in ways antithetical to higher achievement. For example, at the same time that NCLB delegates to them the task of defining proficiency standards, it imposes penalties on schools and districts that fail to make adequate progress toward those standards. Consequently, states have incentives to set low proficiency levels. Peterson and Hess (2006) document the low level of concordance between their students' progress toward state-defined proficiency and their performance on the NAEP. States such as South Carolina that set very high standards for their students find themselves with large fractions of schools deemed in need of improvement, while states such as Texas that set low standards have few such schools. This interaction between state-set standards and the likelihood that their schools will face sanctions has the potential to lead, in Peterson and Hess's words, to a "race to the bottom" in terms of setting proficiency standards.

Another potentially adverse effect on achievement works through funding provisions. Under NCLB, districts that are sanctioned for low performance are required to use their federal Title I grants to pay for privately-provide supplemental services and for transportation for students who choose to opt out of failing schools. Figlio (2003) shows that the districts with the highest fractions of minority and low-income students are likely to lose the most Title I funding under this provision. Unless the district or the state replaces that funding with other revenue, NCLB could reduce the instructional resources available to students in those districts, which potentially could have adverse effects on student achievement.

---

[7] Anderson, Butcher, and Schanzenbach (2009) and Yin (2009) even find that school accountability systems have contributed to childhood obesity, though there is little evidence that the principal pathway through which this is happening is changes in school nutrition or food served in vending machines.

4.3 Failure or inability to respond to incentives

While the evidence mentioned above indicates that many school administrators and teachers are highly responsive to incentives,[8] some educators might not react to incentives—whether those incentives are in the form of bonuses, positive recognition, or negative sanctions—by changing their behavior in ways consistent with the goals of the accountability system. External incentives may be too small, for example, to override the professional judgments of teachers and school administrators, and if so, one may not see substantial changes in educator behavior as a result of the accountability system. Additionally, as Frey (2000) points out, if the extrinsic incentives associated with the accountability system crowd out the intrinsic motivations that attracted educators into teaching, one might observe stagnant or decreasing performance by students in a new accountability regime.

Schools personnel also might fail to incentives embedded within accountability systems if they lack the capacity to respond in ways desired by state or federal policy makers. Some schools may have insufficient resources to effect serious change in student outcomes, while others may lack the leadership required for significant change. Teachers may lack the necessary skills and knowledge to meet the expectations of an accountability system that requires rates of improvement far larger than historical experience has shown to be feasible, as is required under the initial iteration of NCLB. Thus, it could be that one of the major assumptions underlying standalone accountability programs—namely that teachers and schools are underperforming because of insufficient monitoring of their behavior—is incorrect. If school resources must be at a certain level to bring about positive performance improvements, or if principals and teachers have sufficient resources but lack the specific policy and practice knowledge necessary to implement highly successful instructional policy and practice changes, then accountability might not lead to meaningful improvements in student outcomes.

The lack of potential responsiveness to accountability could be exacerbated by the fact that accountability systems generally concentrate on shorter-term achievement improvements while many of the policies and practices that schools may wish to implement can take longer to bring to fruition. School accountability may solve one principal-agent problem by introducing a new one—educators may eschew the types of policies that might yield large-scale long-term success in favor of those that would be less successful in the longer term but might generate bigger boosts today.

Thus, despite the theoretical prediction that school accountability systems will improve student achievement—at least for certain segments of the school population—

---

[8] Recall that the responses to accountability are often substantive as well as potentially considered to be "gaming." Rouse et al. (2007) demonstrate that Florida schools engaged in a series of substantive changes in instructional policies and practices as a result of accountability incentives. Ladd and Zelli (2002), in a survey of elementary school principals in North Carolina, also find evidence that principal behaviors changed in line with state goals in the wake of accountability.

such gains are not a foregone conclusion. In some cases schools may focus on test scores to the exclusion of transferable knowledge or may end up with less funding for instruction. Potentially most important, schools may lack the knowledge and capacity to produce significant gains in student achievement.

5. EVIDENCE ON STUDENT OUTCOMES

Measuring the effects of test-based accountability systems on student achievement is not a simple task. When such systems are part of a larger standards based reform effort, it is difficult to separate the effects of the accountability system from those of other components of the reform package. In addition, researchers face the challenge of finding appropriate control groups to determine what would have happened to student achievement in the absence of the accountability system. In practice, researchers have used a variety of empirical strategies to address these challenges.

A few recent studies have tried to determine the achievement effects of NCLB. Given the difficulty of isolating the effect of NCLB from other concurrent changes, Wong, Cook, and Steiner (2009) use multiple approaches. First they compare the change in achievement in Catholic schools, not subject to NCLB, to the change in public schools since implementation. Second, they compare the growth in states with low proficiency standards and thus fewer schools failing to meet NCLB goals to those with higher proficiency standards. In both cases, they find positive effects of the accountability provisions on student achievement in the fourth and eighth grades. Using similar data from NAEP, Dee and Jacob (2009) compare states that had school-level accountability systems prior to NCLB to those that did not and find greater achievement gains in math for both fourth and eighth grade students in states that did not have assessment-based accountability at the school level prior to NCLB. They do not find corresponding gains in reading achievement. Cronin et al. (2005) use longitudinal data on students just before (2001–2002) and just after (2003–2004) NCLB was first implemented to assess the extent to which students are learning more after NCLB. They find higher achievement post NCLB especially on the math exams, but they find lower achievement gains over the course of the year; findings that are difficult to reconcile. Finally, Neal and Schanzenbach (2010) use a different approach comparing students who took the same test right before and right after NCLB was passed and found substantially higher scores among students in the middle of the achievement distribution. Table 8.1 summarizes the results of these four studies. Taken together, they provide some evidence that NCLB increased student test performance especially in math.

The short time-period since that federal law was implemented combined with the lack of variability in the law across states limits the conclusions that can be drawn from studies of NCLB. More compelling studies of how accountability affects student

Study	Data	Identification	Findings
Cronin et al. (2005)	Northwest Education Association longitudinal data	A comparison of achievement and student growth just prior (2001–2002) and just post (2003–2004) NCLB implementation.	0.05 and 0.01 standard deviations higher post NCLB fall scores in math and reading scores, respectively. 0.04 and .02 standard deviations lower post reform growth in math and reading respectively.
Neal and Schanzenbach, (2010)	Chicago public schools data	Compares students who took a high-stakes test under a new accountability system with students who took the same exam under low stakes in the year before the accountability system was implemented.	0.040, 0.073, 0.053, 0.093, 0.087, 0.080—5th grade reading gains between 2001 and 2002 for students in 3rd–8th decile of 3rd grade scores 0.080, 0.040, 0.060, 0.140, 0.107, 0.127, 0.080—5th grade math gains between 2001 and 2002 for students in 3rd–9th decile of 3rd grade scores
Dee and Jacob (2009)	Main NAEP state data: 1990–2007	A comparison of state-level achievement growth since NCLB implementation for states that did and did not have school accountability prior to NCLB.	0.23 and 0.10 standard deviation higher 4th and 8th grade math achievement by 2007, respectively. Estimates differ somewhat across specifications. No effect for 4th or 8th grade reading.
Wong, Cook and Steiner (2009)	Main NAEP state data and trend NAEP national data: 1990–2009	Comparison of (1) Catholic schools to public schools, (2) states with lower proficiency standard to states with higher proficiency standards, and (3) states with accountability systems that included school sanctions prior to NCLB and those that did not.	0.34 and 0.24 standard deviations higher gains for public school students than Catholic school students post-NCLB in 4th and 8th grade math, respectively. No effect for reading. 0.26 and 0.19 standard deviations higher gains for states with higher proficiency standards for 4th and 8th grade math. No effect for reading. 0.11 standard deviations higher 4th grade reading achievement for states with both higher proficiency standards and school sanctions.

achievement are based on the state and local accountability systems that preceded NCLB. This research includes district or state specific-studies as well as cross-state studies that measure achievement using the NAEP data. Researchers conducting district and state-specific studies have used a combination of state or district-wide trends in achievement along with trends or patterns in school and student level achievement in other comparable districts or states to sort out how the specific accountability system in that district or state affected student achievement. The main advantage of district and state studies is that the analysis is firmly focused on a specific, well-defined accountability system. Some of the studies, especially those for particular states, are hampered by the difficulty of predicting what would have happened to student achievement in the absence of the state's accountability system.[9]

Table 8.2 summarizes the results of state- or district-specific studies of the effects of accountability on student outcomes. The findings are, on average though not universally, positive. One set of papers describe trends in student achievement after districts or states implemented accountability measures. Richards and Sheu (1992) find positive trends in South Carolina following reform. Jacob (2005) also finds positive trends in both math and reading scores following accountability reforms in Chicago using a more sophisticated interrupted time series design, though these positive results are limited to the high-stakes test. Klein et al. (2000) compares high- and low-stakes tests in Texas following reform and similarly finds more positive results on the Texas state test than on the lower stakes NAEP, though even the low-stakes exam showed positive trends.

A second set of district-specific studies compares districts that implemented accountability reforms to other nearby jurisdictions. Ladd (1999) finds greater increases in pass rates in Dallas after the district implemented accountability than in other Texas districts. However, Smith and Mickelson (2000) find no difference in achievement trends between Charlotte-Mecklenburg and other North Carolina districts after accountability reforms.

The final set of district- or state-specific studies use variation in accountability pressures within a given system to identify effects. Figlio and Rouse (2006), Rouse et al. (2007), and Chiang (2007) all exploit discontinuities in school accountability grades and find positive effects of receiving low grades on student achievement gains with effects up to 0.20 standard deviations, though most between 0.05 and 0.10. Rockoff and Turner (2008) take a similar approach in New York City and find positive effects of accountability pressures associated with receiving a failing grade. Taken together the district- and state-specific studies, like the studies of NCLB, provide some evidence of a positive relationship between accountability and student achievement, though they are not universal in this conclusion.

---

[9] However, some studies (e.g., Figlio and Rouse, 2006; Figlio, 2006) focus not on overall achievement but rather on how specific provisions of Florida's accountability system affect student achievement.

Table 8.2 State-Specific or District-Specific Studies of the Effects of Accountability on Student Outcomes

Study	Data	Identification	Findings
Richards and Sheu (1992)	South Carolina data	Simple trends in student achievement and attendance following implementation of accountability	No comparison group. Upward trend in test performance but no change in attendance.
Ladd (1999)	Panel data for schools in large Texas cities from 1990–91 to 1994–95	Compares Dallas student outcomes to the outcomes of students in other districts after Dallas implements accountability system	After one year of program implementation Dallas pass rates increased by 15.5, 16.8 and 12.1 percentage points one, two and three years post implementation. Consistently positive effects for Hispanic and white 7th graders, but none for black students. The study does not provide information on pooled standard deviations for pass rates to compute effect sizes.
Klein et al. (2000)	Trends in State NAEP scores for Texas and in Texas state test scores (TAAS) separately for white, black and Latino students	Compares trends between 1992 and 1998 on NAEP and 1994 and 1998 on TAAS	0.13–0.15 increase on NAEP in 4th grade math compared to 0.31–0.49 increase in TAAS.
Smith and Mickelson (2000)	District average student outcomes from three North Carolina districts	Compares district average student outcomes in Charlotte-Mecklenburg after accountability implementation to those in two other North Carolina districts	No evidence of achievement effects.
Jacob (2005)	Student-level data from Chicago with low-stakes and high-stakes exam scores	Interrupted time series design	0.35 and 0.25 standard deviation increase on high-stakes in math and reading four years post reform. No effect on low-stakes exam.

Continued

Table 8.2 State-Specific or District-Specific Studies of the Effects of Accountability on Student Outcomes—cont'd

Study	Data	Identification	Findings
Figlio and Rouse (2006)	Student-level test scores from a subset of Florida districts	Compares schools with failing grade after change in accountability formula	0.20—effect of receiving an "F" in math on gains on the high-stakes test in the high-stakes grade (0.10 for all grades). 0.06 for low-stakes test in math for all grades.
Rouse et al. (2007)	Florida administrative data combined with a survey of all public schools	Uses regression discontinuity to estimate the effect of receiving an "F" grade on student achievement and school policy	0.099, 0.141, 0.069, 0.076—effect of receiving an "F" on high-stakes reading and math and low-stakes reading and math. 0.140, 0.212, 0.074, 0.122—effect one year later, respectively
Chiang (2007)	Florida administrative data	Regression discontinuity exploiting Florida's criteria for identifying schools that receive sanctions	0.11, 0.12—effect of attending F-graded school on reading and math after one year. 0.00 and 0.12 in year 2. 0.03 and 0.08 in year 3
Rockoff and Turner (2008)	New York City school-level data	Discontinuities in grade assignment across schools	0.10 and 0.05—effect of receiving an "F" relative to a "D" in math and ELA.

A final set of U.S. studies has sought to measure the effects of accountability by comparing achievement trends across states prior to NCLB. Table 8.3 summarizes these results. The cross-state studies make use of variation across states in the nature or timing of accountability systems. Although the conclusions are sensitive to how accountability policies are defined as well as to methodological considerations such as the determination of control groups, the findings of cross-state studies are likely to be less idiosyncratic and more generalizable than those that emerge from the analysis of a specific program. The earliest studies in this group compare states that implemented minimum competency exams or graduation exams. Fredericksen (1994) finds increases in test performance particularly for nine-year-olds following the implementation minimum competency exams, while Jacob (2001) finds increases in math and reading gains in states that implemented graduation exams.

The 1990s saw substantial increases in state accountability systems and a series of studies exploit this variation to estimate the effects of accountability (Amrein and Berliner, 2002, 2003; Carnoy and Loeb, 2002, 2005; Rosenshine, 2003; Braun, 2004; Hanushek and Raymond, 2005. Hanushek and Raymond, 2005) find that the introduction of an accountability system with consequences for schools during the 1990s raised eighth grade student test scores on the NAEP by about 3.2 scale points[10]. The study does not distinguish between effects on reading and on math. The effect is about a fifth of the 16.2 point standard deviation of average eighth grade scores across states, but would be a far smaller fraction of the deviation across individual students, which is the way effect sizes are more commonly measured in the education literature. Thus the effect is modest at best. This conclusion is similar to that reported by Lee (2006) based on his meta-analysis of 12 cross-state studies completed between 1994 and 2004.

In one of the first careful cross-state studies of accountability, Carnoy and Loeb (2002) show that the relationship between the strength of a state accountability system and student performance on NAEP math is stronger at the basic level than at the proficient level. Given that NCLB calls for performance at the proficient rather than the basic level, this finding suggests that even the strongest current state-level accountability systems may have little success in raising students to levels required under NCLB—except to the extent that states maintain proficiency levels far below the NAEP standards. Consistent with that conclusion, but inconsistent with findings by Hanushek and Raymond (2005), other studies indicate that even though high-stakes tests may be associated with gains in math scores at the fourth-grade level, they may not be associated with gains as students progress from fourth grade to eighth grade and, hence, as the students confront more challenging material.

---

[10] Even this study is not free from criticism. The study identifies the effects of accountability systems by making use of the variation in their time of introduction. The choice of specific starting dates for some of the states, including key states such Florida and North Carolina, raises some cause for concern. Hence, replications of this study would be useful.

Table 8.3 Cross-state Studies of the Effects of Accountability on Student Outcomes

Study	Data	Identification	Findings
Fredericksen (1994)	Long-term NAEP from 1978 and 1986	Difference-in-difference analysis of students in states that did and did not implement Minimum Competency Tests	0.22, 0.13—difference in gains between high-stakes and low-stakes states on 9-year-old math routine and nonroutine items 0.08, 0.12—difference in gains between high-stakes and low-stakes states on 13-year-old math routine and nonroutine items 0.02, 0.05—difference in gains between high-stakes and low-stakes states on 17-year-old math routine and nonroutine items
Jacob (2001)	National Educational Longitudinal Survey (NELS)	Models probability of dropping out of high school as a function of the state requiring graduation exams	0.04 and 0.001—effect of graduation exam on math and reading gains between 1998 (8th grade) and 1992 (12th grade)
Amrein and Berliner (2002)	Trend data on 18 states that implemented accountability programs	Simple trends in student achievement and attendance following implementation of accountability	No comparison group
Carnoy and Loeb (2002)	State NAEP data from 1996–2000	Rated state accountability policies on a scale from 0 to 5 and modeled test score growth as a function of accountability strength	0.78, 0.95, and 1.05; 0.80, 1.14, and 0.93—for a two-step move in accountability and the % white, black, and Hispanic students attaining basic skills and then proficiency on 8th grade math 0.10, 0.77, 0.54—relationship between a two-step move in accountability index and the % white, black, and Hispanic students attaining basic skills on 4th grade math assessment

Amrein and Berliner (2003)	State NAEP data from 1994–2000	Compare achievement gains between states that have and do not have high-stakes tests	1.2—effect of testing on 1996–2000 4th grade math gains
			No statistically significant effect on 1996–2000 8th grade math (positive and significant when all states are included)
			No statistically significant effect on 1994–1998 4th grade reading
Rosenshine (2003)	State NAEP data from 1994–2000	Compares achievement gains of states with and without high stakes testing	0.35 and 0.79—effect of high-stakes tests on 4th and 8th grade math gains between 1996 and 2000
			0.61—effect of high-stakes tests on 4th grade reading gains between 1994 and 1998
Braun (2004)	State NAEP math assessments from 1992–2000	Compares the achievement gains and cohort gains in states with high-stakes tests to other states	0.96 and 0.81—difference in 4th grade and 8th grade math gains between high- and low-stakes states (1992–2000)
			−0.67 and −0.31—difference in cohort gains (1992/96 4th grade to 1996/2000 8th grade math) between high- and low-stakes states
Hanushek and Raymond (2005)	State NAEP data from 1992–2002 combined with the timing of accountability	Compares cohort gains using 4th and 8th grade NAEP scores four years apart between states with and without accountability policies	0.22, 0.21, 0.09, 0.54—effect of states attaching consequences to school performance on NAEP gains in math and reading (overall, white, black, and Hispanic students)

Though no one approach or study is flawless and many inconsistencies remain, taken as a whole, the body of research on implemented programs suggests that school accountability improves average student performance in affected schools, at least in general. Experimental evaluations of test score reporting, such as Andrabi et al.'s (2009) new results from Pakistan, also support the notion that accountability can boost student outcomes.

While, in general, the findings of the available studies indicate achievement growth in schools subject to accountability pressure, the estimated positive achievement effects of accountability systems emerge far more clearly and frequently for mathematics than for reading. This pattern is particularly clear when the outcome measure is based on a national test, such as NAEP, but it also emerges in some of the district or state level studies such as Figlio and Rouse (2006). In part this pattern reflects the fact that some authors report results only for math, although that is presumably because of the smaller effects for reading. The larger effects for math are intuitively plausible and are consistent with findings from other policy interventions such as voucher programs (Zimmer and Bettinger, 2008) and tax and expenditure limitations (Downes and Figlio, 1998). Compared to reading skills, math skills are more likely to be learned in the classroom, the curriculum is well-defined and sequenced, and there is less opportunity for parents to substitute for what goes on the classroom (Cronin et al., 2005, p. 58).

One exception to this finding of larger effects for math emerges from Jacob's 2005 study of accountability in Chicago, where the positive effects for low performing students were somewhat stronger in reading than in math. This finding, however, is based on results from the district's high-stakes test rather than from a low-stakes test, and may well reflect the particular characteristics of Chicago's accountability system.

Several studies have documented that school accountability systems have had long-lasting effects on student test scores, even after the students have left the schools directly affected by accountability pressure. Rouse et al. (2007) and Chiang (2007) both show that student test scores, in mathematics and to a lesser degree in reading, are persistently higher for several years following a student's departure from an affected public school. This evidence provides support for the notion that the estimated test score responses to school accountability pressure, at least in Florida, are genuine.

5.1 Differential effects of accountability

The studies described above generate mixed results by racial group, with at least one study (Carnoy and Loeb, 2002) for the late 1990s finding larger effect sizes on passing rates at the basic level on NAEP for black and Hispanic students than for white students. Other studies with different outcome measures find different patterns. In particular, Hanushek and Raymond (2005) find essentially no effects of accountability on the eighth grade achievement of black students, but positive effects for Hispanic students, patterns that are consistent with early findings by racial group for seventh graders in Dallas (Ladd, 1999). Effects of accountability on racial achievement gaps are similarly mixed. The Hanushek and Raymond study finds that state accountability systems may have reduced the gap for Hispanics but raised it for blacks. The two recent national studies find little effect of NCLB on racially defined achievement gaps.

Some evidence from the district or state-specific studies suggests that the schools at the bottom of the performance distributions exhibit the greatest gains under an accountability system. This conclusion emerges from both Chicago (Jacob, 2005) and Florida (Figlio and Rouse, 2006). Working in the other direction is the finding from Cronin et al.'s (2005) national study that the effects of high stakes are greater for the higher scoring students. That said, there exists an emerging consensus that students whose scores are the most consequential for school accountability are those who gain the most, indicating that schools concentrate their energies on marginal students. Prominent examples of this evidence include Neal and Schanzenbach (2010), Reback (2008), and Krieg (2008) in the United States and Burgess et al. (2005), West and Pennell (2000), and Wiggins and Tymms (2002) in England.

The effects of accountability on students may also interact with other state policies. In particular, the theory of action behind accountability reforms is that school personnel will adjust their behavior to increase student achievement on the incentivized tests. However if local actors have little control over the education (e.g., over budget allocation or curriculum choice), they will be less able to respond to the new incentives. Loeb and Strunk (2007) using an approach similar to Carnoy and Loeb (2002) find far greater positive effects of accountability in states with greater local autonomy. This finding is consistent with more recent cross-national studies. A series of studies making use of international assessments—PISA and TIMSS—finds that countries in which schools have more autonomy experience improved test performance in the cases in which there are mandated external school exit examinations (Fuchs and Woessmann, 2007; Woessmann, 2003, 2005, 2007). Not surprisingly, school-level accountability incentives are more salient when schools have the discretion to respond.

5.2 Early versus late adopters of accountability

The evidence suggests that accountability systems generated larger effects on achievement in the late 1990s than in the early 1990s, although Carnoy and Loeb (2005) suggest that their effectiveness may now be declining. The larger estimated effects in the late 1990s relative to the early 1990s are consistent with the observation that the programs introduced in the late 1990s were typically more ambitious than those introduced earlier in the decade. The possibility that the size of the effects is now declining suggests either that accountability generates decreasing marginal returns over time within a state, or that the early state adopters were the most likely to benefit from accountability given their low initial test scores. A related potential explanation is that the early adopters were also more likely than later adopters—primarily those who introduced accountability in response to federal legislation—to embed their accountability systems in comprehensive standards based reform packages that included other elements such as additional funding or professional development for teachers. Although some of the studies control for certain elements of comprehensive reforms such as changes in funding, no study controls fully for all the components such as the development of organizational capacity, and investments in the capacity of teachers. In any case, both the recent decline and these possible explanations should be viewed as speculative at this time. More research would be useful.

5.3 Size and policy significance of the estimated effects

Tables 8.1 through 8.3 give an indication of the estimated size of the accountability effects. Dee and Jacob (2009) and Wong, Cook, and Steiner (2009) estimate effect sizes of up to 0.34 standard deviations for NCLB. Most of the other estimated effects range from no effect to up to 0.20 standard deviations. Judging the policy relevance and size of these effects is not easy. Achievement gaps between racial and ethnic groups and across income groups can be far larger than these gains, making the effects look small. On the other hand, these effects sizes are, in many cases, as great as a full standard deviation in teacher effectiveness as currently measured by value-added techniques (see Hanushek and Rivkin, 2010).

6. ACCOUNTABILITY AND TEACHER LABOR MARKETS

School reforms affect school personnel as well as students. Assessment-based accountability likely led to substantial changes in teachers' and principals' work lives, including increased scrutiny in the classroom, a more intense focus on student performance, and direct consequences for school funding and management. These changes, in turn, may affect career decisions about whether to join the profession, where to work, and, once working, whether to transfer to another school or to leave the profession. Likewise, accountability reforms may help administrators identify and replace ineffective teachers and principals.

As in any profession, turnover of personnel can be both beneficial and harmful. Turnover can be costly because recruitment and hiring takes time and resources away from a focus on instruction. Moreover as teachers leave they take with them specific human capital—an understanding of the school's instructional program, students, and community. New teachers need time and resources to develop these understandings. However, if the less-effective teachers leave and more effective teachers replace them, then turnover can benefit schools.

Accountability reforms can affect turnover and the cost of turnover through each of these mechanisms. They may simply either increase or reduce overall mobility. If teachers leave more or less as a result of accountability, the recruitment and hiring costs may increase or decrease. If accountability brings with it more school-specific human capital, then the cost of losing this knowledge may increase; while, if accountability leads to more similarity in the needed knowledge across schools then the cost of turnover may decrease. Finally, if accountability changes the composition of leavers, either encouraging more or less effective teachers to leave, then even the same level of turnover may be either more or less detrimental than it has been.

There are reasons to believe that accountability could change which teachers stay and which leave; and similarly, that it could affect who enters teaching. First, assessment-based accountability provides information on student performance that teachers can use to assess their own effectiveness and school leaders can use to assess their teachers' effectiveness. Teachers may be more likely to stay if they see themselves as benefiting their students. Moreover, with this information school leaders may put greater effort into keeping their best teachers and encouraging their less effective teachers to leave. Second, accountability reforms create pressure for school leaders to improve the achievement in their schools. This pressure may in turn lead these leaders to do more than they have done in the past to keep their best teachers and encourage their less effective teachers to leave. It may also lead these leaders to work harder to recruit more effective teachers. Finally, accountability may change who enters and who stays by changing the appeal of teaching differentially for more and less effective teachers. For example, if more effective teachers like the emphasis on test performance more than less effective teachers, then they might be relatively more likely to enter and stay than their less effective counterparts. The reverse could also be true.

While there are many reasons to believe that accountability polices could affect the teacher workforce, the research on the effects of accountability is relatively sparse. Ideally, we would be able to answer the following questions: Has accountability changed who enters teaching? Has accountability changed the mobility and attrition of teachers? Has accountability changed the mobility and attrition of teachers differentially across schools? Has accountability changed the mobility and attrition of teachers differentially for more or less effective teachers? We cannot answer any of these questions definitively but the extant research provides suggestive evidence.

Interview and survey research suggests that teachers feel pressure to deliver high student test scores (Barksdale-Ladd and Thomas, 2000; Hoffman, Assaf, and Paris, 2001). In addition, many teachers indicate that they view the high-stakes tests as an imposition on their professional autonomy, an invasion into their classrooms, a message that the state views them as incompetent, and a hindrance to professional creativity (Luna and Turner, 2001). However, teachers value cohesive, supportive work environments that acknowledge their efforts to promote student achievement (Johnson and

Birkeland, 2002; Luna and Turner, 2001; Heneman, 1998). Therefore, reforms, to the extent that they positively or negatively influence these aspects of the work place, will likely influence migration and attrition decisions. Disagreement with reforms is not one of the main reasons that teachers choose to leave. For example, analysis of a national survey of teachers in 2000, the Schools and Staffing Surveys, shows that less than 10% of teachers who leave indicate that disagreement with reforms was very important in their decision to leave, far below, for example the importance they place on salary for their attrition decisions. In addition, the proportion of teachers who indicate that reforms were important for them was no higher in states with stronger accountability systems (Loeb and Cuhna, 2007).

During the 1990s states varied substantially in the strength of their accountability systems. Just as Carnoy and Loeb (2002) and Hanushek and Raymond (2005) used this variation to try to identify the effects of accountability on student test performance, Loeb and Cuhna (2007) used it to try to identify the effects of accountability on teacher attrition. This cross-state analysis is constrained by the availability of national data. Yearly surveys of turnover, spanning the reform years, would be ideal; however, the only nationwide survey of teachers and turnover rates is the U.S. Department of Education's Schools and Staffing Surveys (SASS)—a nationally representative, random survey of U.S. districts, schools, and teachers—and its companion, the Teacher Follow-Up Survey (TFS). This study uses the 1993–94 and 1999–00 waves of SASS. In the year following each wave, sampled schools were recontacted to determine whether SASS-surveyed teachers had moved to a different school or left the teaching profession. A random sample of these "movers," "leavers," and "stayers" were administered the TFS. Unlike the similar studies of student test performance, this study finds no difference in turnover related to the introduction of state accountability system. The data used in this study are not ideal because they are based on survey responses instead of work history files, because there are only 50 states so the state-level variation in accountability has low power, and because there are a relatively low number of teachers in each state. However, it is the only study that we know that looks at the overall effect of accountability instead of the relative effect of accountability on one set of teachers in comparison to another.

Empirical research does provide evidence that accountability affects different groups of teachers differently. For example attrition appears higher in schools that are designated as low performing. Feng, Figlio, and Sass (2009) provide the most convincing evidence of this in a recent study of teachers in Florida. They exploit a rule change in Florida's school accountability system in the summer of 2002, and employ a similar identification strategy to that used by Rouse et al. (2007), Chiang (2007), and Figlio and Kenny (2009) in different contexts. Florida had graded every school in the state on a scale from "A" to "F" since the summer of 1999, based on proficiency rates in reading, writing, and mathematics. In 2002, the state changed its grading system to both recalibrate the acceptable student proficiency levels for the purposes of school accountability and to introduce student-level changes as an important determinant of school grades. Using student-level microdata to calculate the school grades that would have occurred absent this change, they show that over half of all schools in the state experienced an accountability "shock" due to this grading change. Some schools were shocked downward to receive a grade of F, which no school in the state had received the prior year of grading. They find that schools that experienced positive shocks showed a decrease in attrition (both movement to other schools in Florida and exit from the Florida public school system), while schools that experienced a negative shock saw an increase in attrition.

This recent study mirrors earlier results in North Carolina. Clotfelter, Ladd, Vigdor, and Diaz (2004) used the introduction of the state level accountability system in the 1996–97 academic year to assess the differential affect of accountability on low-performing and high-performing schools. In this system, students in kindergarten through 8th grade were tested each year and, using a combination of the average level of student achievement and the yearly change in average test scores, schools were ranked as "exemplary," "no recognition," or "low-performing." Low-performing schools fail to meet both the state-mandated standard for growth in test scores and have more than 50% of their students performing below grade level. Exemplary school meet both of these requirements and teachers in those schools are rewarded with a bonus of $1500. The paper finds that turnover increased in low-performing schools post-reform. For a typical teacher with 10 years of experience working in low-performing schools prior to the reform, the probability of leaving the school was approximately 17.6%. After the reform this increased to 19.1%. This 1.5 percentage point increase compares to a 0.5 percentage point increase for teachers who were not in low-performing schools. For new teachers, the change was 5.1 percentage points for low-performing schools and 0.8 percentage points for those in other schools. The increase in the probability of leaving was even greater for those low-performing schools labeled as such by the state. Following reform, low-performing schools saw a substantially greater increase in the turnover rate of their teachers than did higher performing schools.

A third study also provides support for the hypothesis that attrition is disproportional in low-performing schools as a result of reform. Sims (2009) finds that schools in California with subgroups large enough to qualify them for subgroup-based assessment are more likely to fail to meet annual yearly progress goals and are also more likely to see increased teacher attrition than similar schools with slightly smaller subgroups.

While these studies indicate that attrition increases in low-performing schools, this increase may not be detrimental if less effective teachers leave. Recent evidence across states shows that while both highly effective and less effective teachers leave schools, on average, less-effective teachers are more likely to do so (Boyd, Grossman, Lankford,

Loeb, and Wyckoff, forthcoming; Goldhaber, Gross, and Player, 2007; Hanushek, Kain, O'Brien, and Rivkin, 2005). Only the Feng, Figlio, and Sass paper has directly addressed the effects of accountability on the differential attrition of low-performing teachers. They find little clear relationship between the quality of teachers leaving and accountability pressures in schools that experienced positive shocks to their accountability grade. However, schools that experienced negative shocks, on average, loose more of their more effective teachers. Prior to the accountability system change, the average quality of those who left these schools was lower than the average quality of the stayers, in keeping with the work in other states. In contrast, after the negative shock, the average quality of leavers tended to be higher than that of stayers. In particular, these negatively shocked schools tended to lose more effective teachers to other schools in the same district. This result is particularly remarkable given the findings of an earlier paper, Rouse et al. (2007), which reports that downward-shocked schools experience larger test score gains the next year.

The research to date suggests that accountability has not dramatically changed the career choices of teachers overall, but that it has likely increased attrition in schools classified as failing relative to other schools. While increased attrition is not necessarily bad if the least effective teachers leave, the evidence suggests that it is not the least effective teachers who are leaving these schools. These results provide a warning of the potential difficulties of maintaining a stable high-quality workforce in schools classified as failing. However, the results are also not necessarily condemning of assessment-based accountability. Even in Florida, where some highly effective teachers left schools that received lower than expected scores, student outcomes actually improved, likely the result of school-level reforms (see Rouse et al., 2007). In New York State, Boyd et al. (2008) found that attrition did not increase more in grades with state-level standardized tests than in grades without these tests. In fact, attrition dropped in the tested grades and new teachers to the tested grade were on average more qualified than teachers in other grades. Even if testing is not necessarily appealing to teachers, schools were able to compensate teachers enough to increase the retention when needed. These results indicate that teacher compensation policies deployed in tandem with school accountability policies may influence the labor market implications of school accountability.

7. DIRECTIONS FOR FUTURE RESEARCH

In this chapter, we have identified design issues in developing test-based accountability systems for schools. We also have briefly described the benefits and costs of various choices inherent in the design of such systems. It is clear that there is no one ideal accountability system. The optimal system for one context and one set of policy goals is unlikely to be the optimal system for another context and another set of policy goals. Nonetheless, the research literature makes clear that these policy decisions have considerable consequences for the distribution of student learning, for teacher labor markets, and for housing markets. As a result, these policy decisions should be made very carefully.

Extant research tells us quite a bit about the intended and unintended consequences of accountability systems, particularly those implemented in the United States since the early 1990s. Yet, there exist a number of important directions for future research. At the time of writing, numerous states and localities have been experimenting with expansion of teacher accountability. It will be important to gauge the degree to which school accountability and individual teacher accountability programs jointly affect teacher performance and decisions. More generally, there exists very little information to date on the effects of accountability programs on teacher and principal labor markets, and it will be important to observe whether results seen in one setting are replicated in other settings. The data on accountability and education labor markets that do exist study the effects of accountability on the job decisions of incumbent teachers but do not speak to the question of whether accountability systems attract a different type of potential teacher than previously occurred.

In addition, and, perhaps most importantly, the research to date tells us relatively little about the ways in which school accountability affects outcomes other than the most easily-measured test scores. There have been very few attempts to explore the impacts of accountability on higher education or labor market outcomes, which would provide a longer-term view of whether school accountability programs achieve their goals of developing a better-educated workforce. Likewise, there have been a few studies linking school accountability to proximate health outcomes such as obesity; and we know of no attempts to link school accountability to measures of nonacademic outcomes such as civic engagement, voter participation, or crime. As school accountability systems mature, it should become more feasible to study the effects of test-based accountability on these long-term outcomes; outcomes which motivate much of the reforms.

REFERENCES

Amrein-Beardley, A., Berliner, D., 2002. High stakes testing, uncertainty and student learning. Educ. Policy Anal. Arch. 10 (18).

Amrein-Beardley, A., Berliner, D., 2003. Re-analysis of NAEP math and reading scores in states with and without high-stakes tests: Responses to Rosenshine. Educ. Policy Anal. Arch. 11 (25).

Anderson, P.M., Butcher, K.F., 2006. Reading, writing, and refreshments: Are school finances contributing to children's obesity? J. Hum. Res. 41 (3), 467–494.

Anderson, P.M., Butcher, K.F., Schanzenbach, D.W., 2009. The effect of school accountability policies on children's health. Working Paper. http://www.bus.lsu.edu/mcmillin/seminars/anderson_accountability.pdf.

Andrabi, T., Das, J., Khwaja, A.I., 2009. Report cards: The impact of providing school and child test scores on educational markets. Bureau for Research and Economic Analysis of Development, BREAD Working Paper No. 226.

Barksdale-Ladd, M.A., Thomas, K.F., 2000. What's at stake in high-stakes testing: Teachers and parents speak out. J. Teach. Educ. 51 (5), 384–397.

Bass, F., Dizon, N., Feller, B., 2006. Schools skirt "No Child Left Behind" rule. Associated Press, April 17.

Black, S., 1999. Do better schools matter? Parental valuation of elementary education. Q. J. Econ. 114 (2), 577–599.

Bokhari, F., Schneider, H., 2009. School accountability laws and the consumption of psychostimulants. Florida State University, Working paper.

Boyd, D., Grossman, P., Lankford, H., Loeb, S., Wyckoff, J., forthcoming. Who leaves? Teacher attrition and student achievement. Econ. Educ. Rev.

Boyd, D., Lankford, H., Loeb, S., Wyckoff, J., 2008. The impact of assessment and accountability on teacher recruitment and retention: Are there unintended consequences? Public Financ. Rev. 36, 88–111.

Braun, H., 2004. Reconsidering the impact of high-stakes testing. Educ. Policy Anal. Arch. 12 (1).

Burgess, S., Propper, C., Slater, H., Wilson, D., 2005. Who wins and who loses from school accountability? The distribution of educational gain in English secondary schools. University of Bristol, Working paper.

Carnoy, M., Loeb, S., 2002. Does external accountability affect student outcomes? A cross-state analysis. Educ. Eval. Policy Anal. 24 (4), 305–331.

Carnoy, M., Loeb, S., 2005. Revisiting external accountability effects on student outcomes: A cross-state analysis of NAEP reading and math results in the 1990s and early 2000s. Paper prepared for the Learning from Longitudinal Data in Education Conference. The Urban Institute.

Carnoy, M., Loeb, S., Smith, T., 2001. Do higher scores in Texas make for better high school outcomes? Consortium for Policy Research in Education, CPRE Research Report no. RR-047.

Chakrabarti, R., 2005. Do public schools facing vouchers behave strategically?. Harvard University, Working paper.

Chiang, H., 2007. How accountability pressure on failing schools affects student achievement. Harvard University, Working paper.

Clotfelter, C., Ladd, H., 1996. Recognizing and rewarding success in public schools. In: Ladd, H. (Ed.), Holding Schools Accountable: Performance-Based Reform in Education. Brookings Institution Press, pp. 23–64.

Clotfelter, C., Ladd, H., Vigdor, J., Diaz, R., 2004. Do school accountability systems make it more difficult for low performing schools to attract and retain high quality teachers? J. Policy Anal. Manag. 23 (2), 251–271.

Cronin, J., Kingsbury, G.G., McCall, M.S., Bowe, B., 2005. The impact of the No Child Left Behind Act on student achievement and growth, 2005 edition. Northwest Evaluation Association, Northwest Evaluation Association Technical Report.

Cullen, J., Reback, R., 2006. Tinkering towards accolades: School gaming under a performance accountability system. In: Gronberg, T., Jansen, D. (Eds.), Advances in Applied Microeconomics. 14, Emerald Group Publishing Limited, pp. 1–34, Improving School Accountability: Check-ups or Choice.

Dee, T., Jacob, B., 2009. The impact of No Child Left Behind on student achievement. National Bureau of Economic Research, NBER Working Paper No. 15531.

Deere, D., Strayer, W., 2001. Putting schools to the test: School accountability, incentives and behavior. Texas A&M University, Working paper.

Downes, T., Figlio, D., 1998. School finance reforms, tax limits, and student performance: Do reforms level-up or dumb down?. Department of Economics Tufts University, Discussion Papers Series 9805.

Education Week, 2001. Quality counts annual report 2001. Education Week.

Elmore, R., Abelmann, C.H., Fuhrman, S.H., 1996. The new accountability in state education reform: From process to performance. In: Ladd, H.F. (Ed.), Holding Schools Accountable: Performance-Based Reform in Education. Brookings Institution Press, pp. 65–98.

Feng, L., Figlio, D., Sass, T., 2009. School accountability and teacher mobility. Working paper. www.econ.wisc.edu/~scholz/Seminar/Figlio.pdf.

Ferrer, G., 2006. Estado de Situación de los Sistemas Nacionales de Evaluación de Logros de Aprendizaje en América Latina. Partnership for Educational Revitalization in the Americas.

Figlio, D., 2003. Fiscal implications of school accountability initiatives. Tax Pol. Ec. 17, 1–36.
Figlio, D., 2004. Measuring school performance: Promise and pitfalls. In: Stiefel, L., Schwartz, A.E., Rubenstein, R., Zabel, J. (Eds.), Measuring School Performance and Efficiency: Implications for Practice and Research. Eye on Education, pp. 119–136.
Figlio, D., 2006. Testing, crime and punishment. J. Public Econ. 90 (4–5), 837–851.
Figlio, D., Getzler, L., 2007. Accountability, ability and disability: Gaming the system? In: Gronberg, T., Jansen, D. (Eds.), Advances in Applied Microeconomics. 14, Emerald Group Publishing Limited, pp. 35–49, Improving School Accountability: Check-ups or Choice.
Figlio, D., Kenny, L., 2007. Individual teacher incentives and student performance. J. Public Econ. 91 (5–6), 901–914.
Figlio, D., Kenny, L., 2009. Public sector performance measurement and stakeholder support. J. Public Econ. 93 (9–10), 1069–1077.
Figlio, D., Ladd, H., 2007. School accountability and student achievement. In: Ladd, H., Fiske, E. (Eds.), Handbook of Research on Education Finance and Policy. Routledge.
Figlio, D., Lucas, M., 2004. What's in a grade? School report cards and the housing market. Am. Econ. Rev. 94 (3), 591–604.
Figlio, D., Rouse, C.E., 2006. Do accountability and voucher threats improve low-performing schools? J. Public Econ. 90 (1–2), 239–255.
Figlio, D., Winicki, J., 2005. Food for thought: The effects of school accountability plans on school nutrition. J. Public Econ. 89 (2–3), 381–394.
Fredericksen, N., 1994. The Influence of Minimum Competency Tests on Teaching and Learning. Educational Testing Services.
Frey, B., 2000. Motivation and human behaviour. In: Taylor-Gooby, P. (Ed.), Risk, Trust and Welfare. Macmillan, pp. 31–50.
Fuchs, T., Woessmann, L., 2007. What accounts for international differences in student performance? A re-examination using PISA data. In: Dustmann, C., Fitzenberger, B., Machin, S. (Eds.), The Economics and Training of Education. Physica-Verlag HD, pp. 209–240.
Goldhaber, D., Gross, B., Player, D., 2007. Are public schools really losing their "best"?: Assessing the career transitions of teachers and their implication for the quality of the teacher workforce. The Urban Institute Center for Analysis of Longitudinal Data in Education Research, Working Paper 12.
Hamilton, L., Berends, M., Stechter, B., 2005. Teachers' Responses to Standards-Based Accountability. RAND.
Haney, W., 2000. The myth of the Texas miracle in education. Educ. Policy Anal. Arch. 8 (41).
Hanushek, E.A., Kain, J., O'Brien, D., Rivkin, S.G., 2005. The market for teacher quality. National Bureau of Economic Research, Technical report.
Hanushek, E.A., Raymond, M., 2003. Lessons about the design of state accountability systems. In: Peterson, P.E., West, M.R. (Eds.), No Child Left Behind?: The Politics and Practice of School Accountability. Brookings Institution, pp. 127–151.
Hanushek, E.A., Raymond, M., 2005. Does school accountability lead to improved school performance? J. Policy Anal. Manag. 24 (2), 297–329.
Hanushek, E.A., Rivkin, S.G., 2010. Using value-added measures of teacher quality. National Center for Analysis of Longitudinal Data in Education Research, CALDER Brief 9.
Heneman III, H.G., 1998. Assessment of the motivational reactions of teachers to a school-based performance award program. J. Pers. Eval. Educ. 12 (1), 43–59.
Hoffman, J.V., Assaf, L.C., Paris, S.G., 2001. High-stakes testing in reading: Today in Texas, tomorrow? Read. Teach. 54 (5), 482–492.
Jacob, B., 2001. Getting tough? The impact of high school graduation exams. Educ. Eval. Policy Anal. 23 (2), 99–121.
Jacob, B.A., 2005. Accountability, incentives and behavior: The impact of high-stakes testing in the Chicago public schools. J. Public Econ. 89 (5–6), 761–796.
Jacob, B.A., Levitt, S.D., 2003. Rotten apples: An investigation of the prevalence and predictors of teacher cheating. Q. J. Econ. 118 (3), 843–878.

Jin, G.Z., Leslie, P., 2003. The effect of information on product quality: Evidence from restaurants hygiene grade cards. Q. J. Econ. 118 (2), 409–451.

Johnson, S.M., Birkeland, S.E., 2002. Pursuing a "sense of success": New teachers explain their career decisions. Am. Educ. Res. J. 40 (3), 581–617.

Jones, G., Jones, B., Hardin, B., Chapman, L., Yarbrough, T., Davis, M., 1999. The impact of high-stakes testing on teachers and students in North Carolina. Phi Delta Kappan 81, 199–203.

Kane, T., Staiger, D., 2002. Improving school accountability systems. National Bureau of Economic Research, NBER Working Paper, 8156.

Klein, S., Hamilton, L., McCaffrey, D., Stecher, B., 2000. What do test scores in Texas tell us? Educ. Policy Anal. Arch. 9 (49).

Koretz, D.M., Barron, S., 1998. The validity of gains on the Kentucky Instructional Results Information System (KIRIS). RAND Corporation, Working paper.

Koretz, D.M., Hamilton, L.S., 2003. Teachers' responses to high-stakes testing and the validity of gains: A pilot study. Center for Research on Evaluation, Standards, and Student Testing, CSE Technical Report 610.

Krieg, J., 2008. Are students left behind? The distributional impacts of the No Child Left Behind Act. Educ. Fin. Policy 3 (2), 250–281.

Ladd, H., 1999. The Dallas school accountability and incentive program: An evaluation of its impacts on student outcomes. Econ. Educ. Rev. 18, 1–16.

Ladd, H., 2001. School-based educational accountability systems: The promise and the pitfalls. Natl. Tax J. 54 (2), 385–400.

Ladd, H., Walsh, R., 2002. Implementing value-added measures of school effectiveness: Getting the incentives right. Econ. Educ. Rev. 21 (1), 1–17.

Ladd, H., Zelli, F., 2002. School-based accountability in North Carolina: The responses of school principals. Educ. Admin. Q. 38 (4), 494–529.

Lavy, V., 2007. Using performance-based pay to improve the quality of teachers. Future Child 17 (1), 87–109.

Lee, J., 2006. in: Is test-driven external accountability effective? A meta-analysis of the evidence from cross-state causal-comparative and correlational studies, Paper presented at the annual meeting of the American Education Research Association, April.

Linn, R.L., 2000. Assessments and accountability. Educ. Researcher 29 (2), 4–16.

Loeb, S., Cuhna, J., 2007. Have assessment-based accountability reforms influenced the career decisions of teachers and principals?. The Urban Institute, The Urban Institute Working Paper.

Loeb, S., Strunk, K., 2007. Accountability and local control: Response to incentives with and without authority over resource allocation and generation. Educ. Fin. Policy 2 (1), 10–39.

Luna, C., Turner, C.L., 2001. The impact of the MCAS: Teachers talk about high-stakes testing. Engl. J. 91 (1), 79–87.

Mathios, A.D., 2000. The impact of mandatory disclosure laws on product choices: An analysis of the salad dressing market. J. Law Econ. 43 (2), 651–677.

Mizala, A., Romaguera, P., Urquiola, M., 2007. Socioeconomic status or noise? Tradeoffs in the generation of school quality information. J. Dev. Econ. 84 (1), 61–75.

Neal, D., Schanzenbach, D., 2010. Left behind by design: Proficiency counts and test-based accountability. Rev. Econ. Stat. 92 (2), 263–283.

O'Day, J.A., Smith, M.S., 1993. Systemic reform and educational opportunity. In: Fuhrman, S. (Ed.), Designing Coherent Education Policy: Improving the System. Jossey Bass, pp. 250–312.

Peterson, P., Hess, F., 2006. Keeping an eye on state standards. Educ. Next 6 (3), 28–29.

Reback, R., 2008. Teaching to the rating: School accountability and the distribution of student achievement. J. Public Econ. 99 (5–6), 1394–1415.

Richards, C., Sheu, T., 1992. The South Carolina School Incentive Reward Program: A policy analysis. Econ. Educ. Rev. 11 (1), 71–86.

Rockoff, J., Turner, L., 2008. Short run impacts of accountability on school quality. National Bureau of Economic Research, NBER Working Paper No. 14564.

Romberg, T., Zarinia, E., Williams, S., 1989. The Influence of Mandated Testing on Mathematics Instruction: Grade 8 Teachers' Perceptions. National Center for Research in Mathematical Science Education, University of Wisconsin-Madison.

Rosenshine, B., 2003. High stakes testing: Another analysis. Educ. Policy Anal. Arch. 11 (24).

Rothstein, R., Jacobson, R., Wilder, T., 2008. Grading Education: Getting Accountability Right. Teachers College Press.

Rouse, C., Hannaway, J., Goldhaber, D., Figlio, D., 2007. Feeling the Florida heat? How low-performing schools respond to voucher and accountability pressure. Princeton University and University of Florida, Working paper.

Shepard, L.A., Dougherty, K.C., 1991. Effects of high-stakes testing on instruction, Paper presented at the annual meeting of the American Educational Research Association, April.

Sims, D., 2009. Going down with the ship? The effect of school accountability on the distribution of teacher experience in California. The Urban Institute, Working paper.

Smith, S.S., Mickelson, R.A., 2000. All that glitters is not gold: School reform in Charlotte-Mecklenburg. Educ. Eval. Policy Anal. 22 (2).

Stecher, B., Barron, S., Chun, T., Ross, K., 2000. The Effects of the Washington State Education Reform on Schools and Classrooms. Center for Research on Evaluation, Standards and Student Testing.

Stecher, B.M., Barron, S.I., Kaganoff, T., Goodwin, J., 1998. The effects of standards-based assessment on classroom practices: Results of the 1996–97 RAND survey of Kentucky teachers of mathematics and writing. Center for Research on Evaluation, Standards and Student Testing, CSE Technical Report 482.

Stiefel, L.A., Schwartz, E., Rubinstein, R., Zabel, J., 2005. Measuring School Performance and Efficiency: Implications for Practice and Research. Eye on Education.

Stullich, S., Eisner, L., McCrary, J., Roney, C., 2006. National Assessment of Title I: Interim Report. U.S. Department of Education.

Vegas, E., Petrow, J., 2008. Raising Student Learning in Latin America: The Challenge for the 21st Century. World Bank.

West, A., Pennell, H., 2000. Publishing school examination results in England: Incentives and consequences. Educ. Stud. 26 (4), 423–436.

Wiggins, A., Tymms, P., 2002. Dysfunctional effects of league tables: A comparison between English and Scottish primary schools. Public Money Manage 22, 43–48.

Wilson, M.B., Bertenthal, M.W., 2006. Systems for State Science Assessment. National Academies Press.

Woessmann, L., 2003. Central exit exams and student achievement: International evidence. In: Peterson, P., West, M. (Eds.), No Child Left Behind? The Politics and Practice of School Accountability. Brookings Institution Press, pp. 292–324.

Woessmann, L., 2005. The effect of heterogeneity of central exams: Evidence from TIMSS, TIMSS-Repeat and PISA. Educ. Econ. 13 (2), 143–169.

Woessmann, L., 2007. International evidence on school competition, autonomy, and accountability: A review. Peabody J. Educ. 82 (2–3), 473–497.

Wong, M., Cook, T.D., Steiner, P.M., 2009. No Child Left Behind: An interim evaluation of its effects on learning using two interrupted time series each with its own non-equivalent comparison series. Northwestern University Institute for Policy Research, Northwestern University, Working Paper Series WP-09-11.

Yin, L., 2009. Are school accountability systems contributing to adolescent obesity? University of Florida, Working paper.

Zimmer, R., Bettinger, E., 2008. Beyond the rhetoric: Surveying the evidence of vouchers and tax credits. In: Ladd, H.F., Fiske, E.B. (Eds.), Handbook of Research in Education Finance and Policy. Taylor and Francis, Inc., pp. 447–466.

CHAPTER 9

The GED☆

James J. Heckman,* John Eric Humphries,** and Nicholas S. Mader**
*University of Chicago, American Bar Foundation, University College Dublin, and Yale University
**University of Chicago

Contents

1. Introduction	424
2. Institutional Background and Functions of the GED	426
2.1 The GED test	429
3. The Effects of GED Certification	432
3.1 The direct benefit of GED certification	432
3.1.1 Average labor market outcomes	*432*
3.1.2 Heterogeneous labor market returns	*439*
3.1.3 Cognitive and noncognitive ability	*446*
3.2 Educational attainment	452
4. Changes and Growth in the GED Test Taking Population	458
4.1 Government education and training programs	458
4.2 Changes in the costs and benefits to education	461
4.3 Growth in high school–age test takers	467
4.4 Summing up the sources of growth of GEDs	470
5. Adverse Consequences of the GED	471
5.1 The GED induces would-be high school graduates to drop out	473
5.2 The GED inflates high school graduation statistics	475
5.3 The GED obscures the actual returns to education	477
6. Conclusion	478
References	480

☆ This research was supported by NIH R01-HD054702, the American Bar Foundation, The California Endowment, The Commonwealth Foundation, The Nemours Foundation, the Buffett Early Childhood Fund, the Spencer Foundation, an anonymous funder, and the J.B. and M.K. Pritzker Foundation. We are grateful for the helpful comments of the Handbook authors present at the CESIfo Munich conference. We also received helpful research assistance from Pana Alves and Joel Han. We would like to thank Lois M. Quinn, who provided valuable comments. The views expressed in this paper are those of the authors and not necessarily those of the funders or other parties listed here. A more complete description of the GED program is presented in our two books, Heckman, Humphries, and Mader (2010a,b).

Abstract

The General Educational Development (GED) credential is issued on the basis of an eight-hour subject-based test. The test claims to establish equivalence between dropouts and traditional high school graduates, opening the door to college and positions in the labor market. In 2008 alone, almost 500,000 dropouts passed the test, amounting to 12% of all high school credentials issued in that year. This chapter reviews the academic literature on the GED, which finds minimal value of the certificate in terms of labor market outcomes and that only a few individuals successfully use it as a path to obtain post-secondary credentials. Although the GED establishes cognitive equivalence on one measure of scholastic aptitude, recipients still face limited opportunity due to deficits in noncognitive skills such as persistence, motivation, and reliability. The literature finds that the GED testing program distorts social statistics on high school completion rates, minority graduation gaps, and sources of wage growth. Recent work demonstrates that, through its availability and low cost, the GED also induces some students to drop out of school. The GED program is unique to the United States and Canada, but provides policy insight relevant to any nation's educational context.

JEL classification: I21, J24, J31

Keywords

Returns to Education
GED
Dropouts
Graduation Rate
Noncognitive Skills

1. INTRODUCTION

The General Educational Development (GED) program has become a major factor in American education.[1] Dropouts from high school can take a seven hour battery of tests to obtain a GED credential. GEDs are widely held to be equivalent to individuals who receive a traditional high school diploma by taking courses and acquiring credit hours. Indeed, capturing this sentiment, many erroneously term the GED certificate as a "General Equivalency Degree." The GED program is quantitatively significant. Figure 9.1 shows that currently 12% of all high school credentials issued are GEDs,[2] and that there has been substantial growth over time in the number of GED certificates issued.

---

[1] The GED program is unique to the United States and Canada, but analysis of this program provides general insights into the limitations of using achievement exams to certify preparedness for schools and the workplace.

[2] Henceforth, "GED" refers either to the certificate itself or to an individual who has received a GED certificate, depending on the context. "GEDs" refer to individuals who choose to certify by the GED, "GED program" is used to refer to the entire program, and "GED test" refers to the test itself.

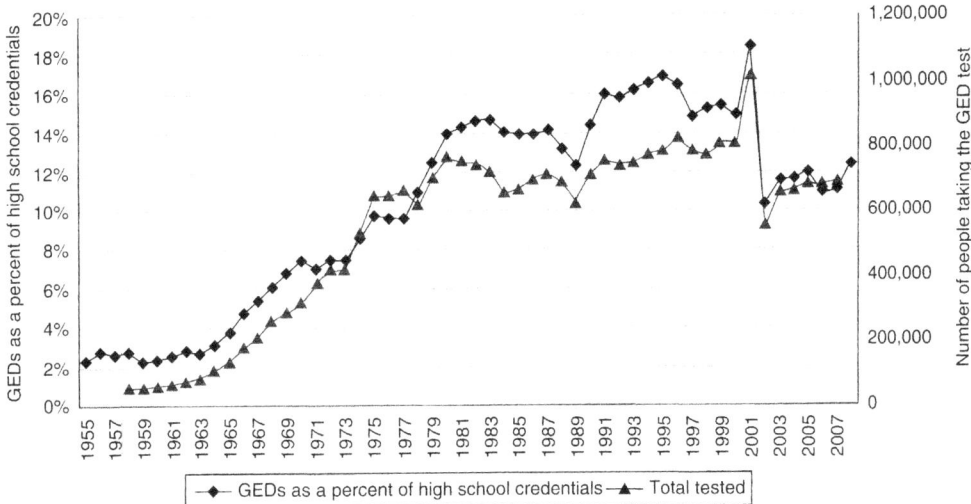

Figure 9.1 Growth in the GED—percent of high school credentials and number of takers. *Sources:* National Center for Education Statistics (Various years), and GED Testing Service (1958-2008). Notes: The spike and fall in 2001–2002 is from a change in test series combined with an increase in passing standards. The "percent of high school credentials" statistic is calculated by dividing the number of GEDs issued by the sum of diplomas and GEDs issued that year.

This chapter reviews a body of literature, starting with Cameron and Heckman (1993), that shows that GEDs are *not* equivalent to ordinary high school graduates. GEDs have higher achievement test scores than dropouts in part because they complete more years of high school. Controlling for their greater scholastic ability, GEDs are equivalent to uncredentialed dropouts in terms of their labor market outcomes and their general performance in society. On average, obtaining a GED does not increase the wages of dropouts. While GEDs go to college at higher rates than dropouts, few finish more than one semester. The same traits that lead them to drop out of school also lead them to leave from jobs early, to divorce more frequently, and to fail in the military.[3]

Given the preponderance of evidence against beneficial effects of GED certification for the average GED recipient, it is surprising that the GED program has grown so dramatically in the past 50 years. We examine explanations for its growth. A primary cause is the growth of government programs that promote the GED as a quick fix for addressing the high school dropout problem. Adult Education programs and programs designed to promote convict rehabilitation are major contributors, the latter being especially important for African-American males. We present evidence that high schools are increasingly promoting the use of the GED.

---

[3] See Heckman and Rubinstein (2001) and Laurence (forthcoming).

None of this would matter if the GED were harmless, like wearing a broken watch and knowing that it is broken. But the GED is not harmless. Treating it as equivalent to a high school degree distorts social statistics and gives false signals that America is making progress when it is not. A substantial part of the measured convergence of black and white high school attainment is fueled by prison-issued GEDs. Counting GEDs as dropouts, the African-American male high school graduation rate in 2000 is at the same level as it was in 1960. Improperly counting GEDs as high school graduates also overestimates the returns to college. We document how American social statistics are distorted by assuming that GEDs are equivalent to ordinary high school graduates. We also show how the GED *creates* problems. It induces students to drop out of school and lose the benefits of a high school degree.

There are larger lessons from a study of the GED program. GEDs are as smart as ordinary high school graduates, as measured by a scholastic achievement test. Yet, as a group, GEDs fail to perform at the level of high school graduates. We show that non-cognitive deficits—such as lack of persistence, low self-esteem, low self-efficacy, and high propensity for risky behavior—explain the lack of success for many GEDs. Deficits of what are sometimes called "soft" skills are often not taken into account in public policy discussions involving economic opportunity. A study of the GED shows the influence of personality traits on success in life and the need for public policies that address both cognitive and soft skill deficits.

This paper is organized as follows: Section 2 provides a short introduction to the GED, its structure, and a brief history. Section 3 looks at differences among dropouts, GEDs, and high school graduates, and discusses the evidence on labor market performance and educational attainment of GEDs. Section 4 presents evidence on the sources of growth of the GED program, and the changes over time in the demographic groups it serves. Section 5 reviews the adverse consequences of the GED. Section 6 concludes.

2. INSTITUTIONAL BACKGROUND AND FUNCTIONS OF THE GED

There are substantial consequences of being a high school dropout. Wage premia for education have increased over the last three decades. Using Census PUMs data, Goldin and Katz (2008) report that the wage differential between high school graduates and dropouts grew from 16.7% in 1970, to 21% in 1990, to 25.5% in 2000. Figure 9.2, reproduced from Autor, Katz, and Kearney (2008), shows that real wages by educational level have diverged across time for both males and females. At the same time that real wages for those with college are steadily increasing, real wages for male dropouts are currently below their 1963 levels, and real wages for female dropouts are effectively unchanged since 1970.

Figure 9.3 shows that across cohorts, college attendance and college completion have both increased.[4] The rate of college attendance conditional on finishing high

---

[4] Figure 9.3 does not count GEDs as high school graduates.

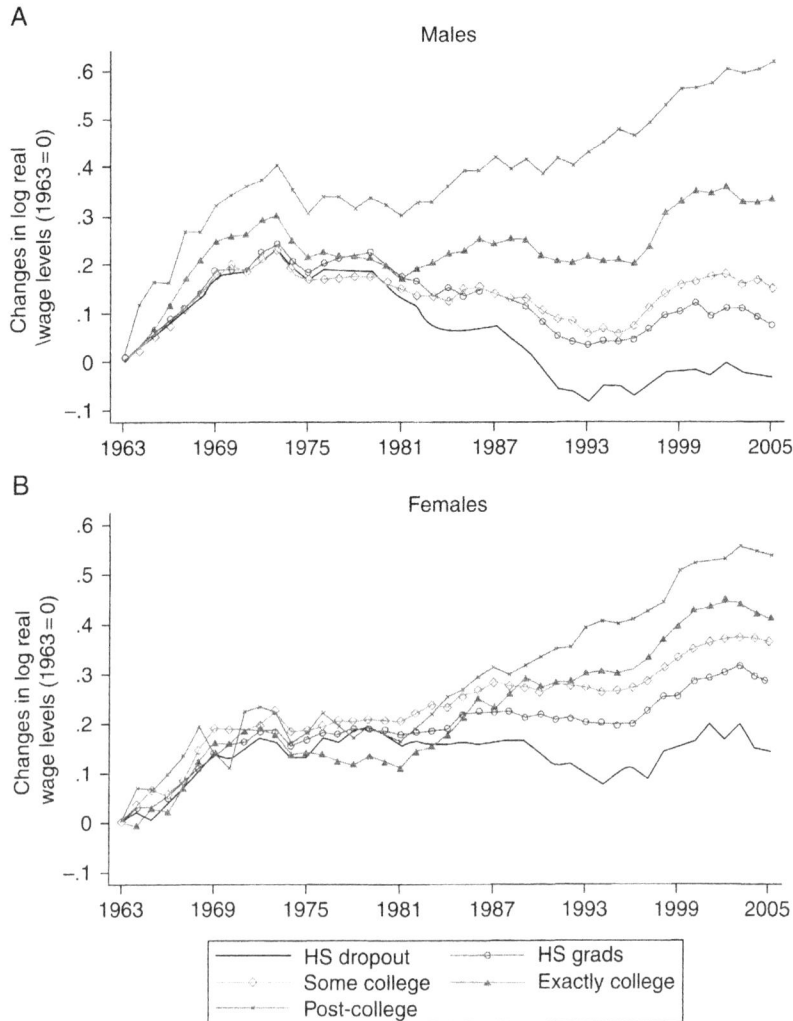

Figure 9.2 Log wage levels by education. *Source:* Reproduced from Autor et al. (2008, Figure 5).

school, and the rate of college graduation conditional on attendance have both trended upward. The outlier is the high school graduation rate, which has trended *downward* starting with the 1950 birth cohort. The growth in people seeking alternative certification through the GED is a major contributor to this trend. Figure 9.4 shows that dropout rates since 1970 have decreased if GEDs are counted as high school graduates, but have increased if they are counted as dropouts.

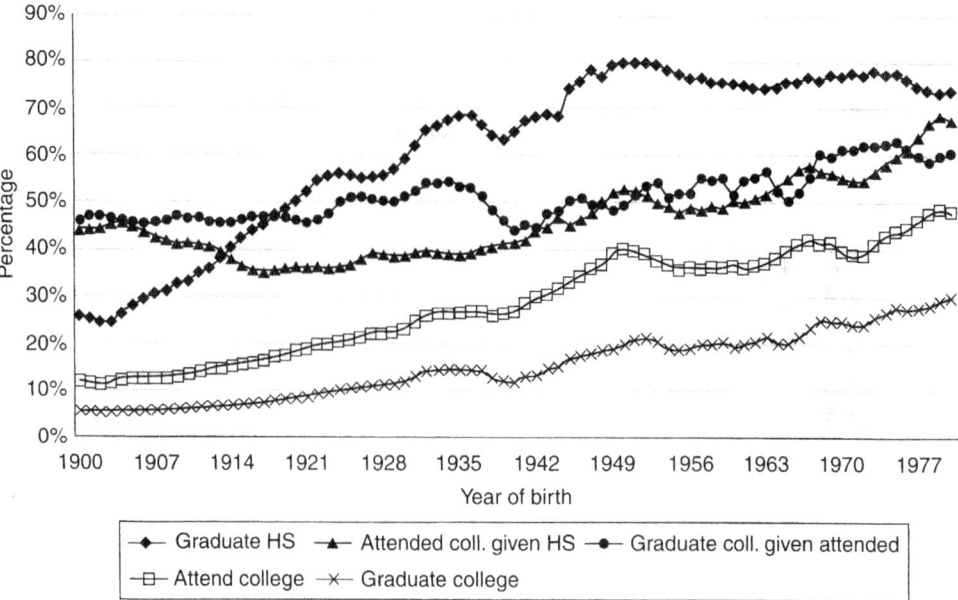

Figure 9.3 Trends in educational attainment. *Source:* Reproduced from Heckman and LaFontaine (2010, Figure XIII). Notes: 3-year moving averages based on Current Population Survey (CPS) October, Census, CPS March, and National Center for Education Statistics (NCES) data. HS graduates are those who obtained a regular public HS diploma (excluding GEDs) from the NCES. "Graduate HS" is the fraction of 8th grade enrollments for a given cohort who later report a regular HS diploma. "Attend Given HS" is the fraction of recent HS graduates who report being enrolled the fall of the year following graduation. "Attend College" is college enrollments of recent HS graduates as a fraction of 18-year-old cohort size. College graduates are those who report a bachelor's degree or higher by age 25. "Graduate Given Attend" is those who obtained a bachelor's degree as a fraction of the college enrollment total for that cohort. Associate's degrees are not included. "Graduate College" is the number of college graduates as a fraction of the 18-year-old cohort size. Population estimates are from the Census P-20 reports. HS diplomas issued by sex are estimated from CPS October data after 1982.

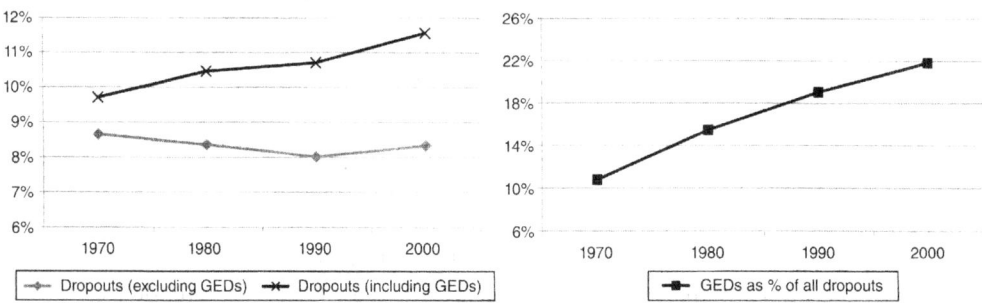

Figure 9.4 The effect of including/excluding GEDs in the calculation of the dropout rate. *Sources:* GED Testing Service (1958-2008), and U.S. Decennial Census 1970-2000. In the left-hand panel, all percentages are status dropout rates for 20-to-24-year-olds, except for 1970 which reflects status dropout rates for 20-to-23-year-olds. In the right-hand panel, the data series shows GEDs as a percentage of all credentialed and uncredentialed dropouts.

2.1 The GED test

The GED was introduced by the American Council on Education (ACE) in 1942 as a credential for returning World War II veterans who entered the armed services before completing high school.[5] The test was originally used as a tool for placing returning veterans in college and high school. It was quickly expanded as a method for earning high school diplomas or equivalency credentials.

States began to offer the test to civilians in the late 1940s and, by 1959, civilian GED test takers outnumbered veteran GED recipients (GED Testing Service (1959-2008), Quinn (2002)). Relative to its very targeted beginning, the GED program has expanded to serve dropouts across a wide population. The GED currently targets a large and diverse population, including many who are unqualified to join the military (Laurence (forthcoming)).[6]

The GED test: The GED exam has been a battery of five tests since its introduction. Its content has been updated three times with the introduction of new "series" designed to keep the test relevant to job skills and educational requirements (GED Testing Service (2009)). The current version of the GED test takes just over seven hours to complete and focuses on interpretation and analysis of information rather than on factual recall. The reading section has changed from being a general reading comprehension test to a test of reading "real life" work materials or newspaper articles. The math content demands more analysis and synthesis than factual recall. Examples of an easy and hard math problem are shown in Figure 9.5. The GED test introduced a short essay or writing sample starting

Mathematics

Easy sample question	If $8x + 16 = 32$, what is x? A) 8 B) 2 C) 4 D) 3 E) 7
Difficult sample question	Alex has a job working for Adam's apple orchard. Two hundred new apple trees just arrived, which Mr. Adams would like Alex to plant. Alex can plant an average of 15 trees per workday. At this rate, approximately how many workdays will it take Alex to plant the 200 trees? A) Between 7 and 9 B) Between 9 and 11 C) Between 11 and 13 D) Between 13 and 15 E) Between 15 and 17

Figure 9.5 GED sample questions. *Source:* Reproduced from Bobrow (2002). Notes: The source is a preparation guide for the most recent 2002 series of the GED test.

---

[5] See Quinn (2002) for a detailed exposition of the GED's history.
[6] Section 3 demonstrates that the value of the GED depends on characteristics of the test taker, and Section 4 demonstrates that changes in the demographic groups served by the GED have led to differences in composition away from the motivated, disciplined group of individuals to whom it was initially targeted.

in 1988, and the use of a calculator for part of the math subsection was introduced on the 2002 test series (GED Testing Service, 1958-2008).

It was initially decided that the pass score should be set so that 80% of graduation-bound high school seniors could pass (Boesel et al. (1998), Quinn (2002)). An analysis of the 1943 norming study suggests that the 80% pass rate overstates the actual difficulty of the original test (Quinn (2002)). Quinn (2002) also highlights that the original test included a high probability of passing due to chance. After three increases in the difficulty of the test, only 60% of current graduation-bound high school seniors are now estimated to be able to pass the entire test on their first try (GED Testing Service (1958-2008)).

Key changes to the GED test are displayed in Table 9.1, which also documents the expansion of the test. In 1947, New York was the first state to offer the test to civilian dropouts (Quinn (2002)). In 1974, California was the last state to offer a recognized GED certificate for passing the GED test. The table covers the three changes in test series as well as the three changes in test difficulty. For more details on the GED's history, content, standards, norming, and scoring procedures see Section A of the Web Appendix (*http://jenni.uchicago.edu/GEDHandbookChapter/*).

Table 9.1 Key Changes to the GED

Year	Changes to the GED Testing Program
1942	GED test introduced for veterans. 80% of graduation-bound high school seniors said to be able to pass all five batteries.
1947	New York offers GED test to civilian high school dropouts.
1959	More civilians taking the GED test than veterans.
1974	California becomes last state to introduce GED test for dropouts.
1978	Second series of the GED test introduced. Test time of 6 hours.
1981	Time limit extended to 6.75 hours. National minimum age for testing abolished.
1982	Passing standards made more difficult, 75% of graduation-bound high school seniors said to be able to pass the entire test.
1988	Third series of GED test introduced. First series to include a writing sample. Test time extended to 7.5 hours for taking the test.
1992	National minimum age for GED test-taking of 16 implemented.
1997	Passing standards made more difficult, 67% of graduation-bound high school seniors said to be able to pass the entire test.
2002	Fourth series of the GED test introduced. Calculator allowed for first time on parts of the math test. Passing standards made more difficult, 60% of graduation-bound high school seniors said to be able to pass the entire test. Test time of approximately 7 hours.

Sources: GED Testing Service (2009), Quinn (2002), and GED Testing Service (1958-2008).

GED preparation and means of benefit: The data on preparation times suggest that study for the GED is likely to lead to little or no human capital formation. In 1980, the median test taker had studied for 20 hours and, in 1989, had invested 30 hours of preparation (Quinn (2002), GED Testing Service (1959-2008)).[7] However, a sizable number of individuals study more than 100 hours, growing from 11.8% to 24.2% of takers in that same period. This indicates that certain populations may benefit somewhat from their preparation for the GED. To put this statistic into perspective, an average high school student spends approximately 1080 hours in class a year (Carroll (1990)). More recently, Zhang et al. (2009) find that, in 2006, the median study time for those who reported studying for the GED was 25 hours.

At the same time, the availability of the GED may induce a decrease in the effort spent on schooling. The academic literature often compares outcomes for GEDs to those for dropouts. However, for many individuals, the relevant counterfactual comparison is between the GED and high school graduation. As passing the GED requires substantially less effort than completing high school, its availability induces many students who would otherwise complete school to leave (Heckman et al. (2008), Humphries (2010)). This evidence is corroborated by a 2002 survey by the National Center for Education Statistics (2006) which found that 40.5% of surveyed high school dropouts listed "would be easier to get the GED" as among their reasons for leaving school. Behind "Missed too many school days," this was the second most frequently cited reason for leaving.

With the possible exception of individuals in the right-hand tail of the preparation time distribution, it seems unlikely that GED test takers are producing valuable human capital that will directly increase their wages. However, as a widely-recognized credential that tests for certain types of ability, it may serve as a signal to employers, the military, and post-secondary institutions that the individual is more capable than the average uncredentialed dropout.[8] A key caveat to the signaling argument is that the signaling value of a GED will reflect all associations due to sorting, such as through disproportionate receipt by the incarcerated or unmotivated takers who are able to complete high school but choose not to. The quality of the signal has changed over time due to shifts in the attributes of the GED-certified population.

GED acceptance: The extent to which employers and colleges treat the GED as equivalent to a high school diploma is uncertain. A poll reported by the Society for Human Resource Management (2002) finds that 96% of U.S. employers and training programs respond affirmatively to the question "Does your company accept applications with a GED credential for jobs requiring a high school degree?" (GED Testing Service (2009)). A positive response suggests that a GED is an acceptable prerequisite for consideration, but does not indicate what relative weight employers give to the GED.

The GED's wide acceptance as a valid prerequisite for admission to post-secondary institutions suggests that the GED might facilitate human capital development. A poll

---

[7] This amount applies only to test takers not qualifying as exceptions to the minimum age requirement.

[8] Spence (1973) is the classic reference on signaling.

by the The College Board (2007) finds that 98% of colleges respond positively to the prompt that "High school diploma is required and GED is accepted." Again, it is unclear if GEDs get equal consideration for admission relative to high school graduates.

3. THE EFFECTS OF GED CERTIFICATION

Section 3.1 reviews the literature on the value of the GED credential in labor markets. Section 3.2 focuses on the question of whether, and for whom, the GED leads to enrollment and completion of post-secondary education.

3.1 The direct benefit of GED certification

This section demonstrates that pre-existing differences in traits causally unrelated to the effect of the GED are responsible for the different labor market outcomes experienced by dropouts and GEDs. The early literature on the topic found that GED certification has little or no effect on labor market outcomes for the average test taker. Subsequent work has attempted to identify different populations and margins for which it might hold more value.

3.1.1 Average labor market outcomes

Raw comparisons of earnings, wages, and hours worked based on the National Longitudinal Study of Youth 1979 (NLSY79) data are displayed in Figure 9.6.[9] This figure shows the gap in wage income, hourly wages, and hours worked for terminal GEDs and terminal high school graduates over uncredentialed dropouts. There is a clear ordering among dropouts, GEDs, and traditional high school graduates in each measure. These differences persist across the life cycle, with the wage and hours premia for higher credentials increasing from their late 20s to their late 30s.

Background Differences Among Dropouts, GEDs, and High School Graduates: The differences in labor market outcomes among these three groups can be largely explained by pre-existing characteristics that generate economic returns, creating a non-causal association among education levels and wages. Tables 9.2 and 9.3 show comparisons of early life characteristics by final level of education for white males in the NLSY79 and in the National Longitudinal Survey of Youth 1997 (NLSY97) data sets.[10,11]

These tables show a clear ordering across final levels of education—notably highest grade completed, magazine subscriptions and home environment indices, family income,

---

[9] The NLSY79 is a survey starting in 1979 following a nationally representative cohort of individuals age 14 to 21 with follow-up interviews at least every two years on a wide range of social, educational, and economic variables. For more details on the NLSY79, see Section B.1 of the Web Appendix (http://jenni.uchicago.edu/GEDHandbookChapter/).

[10] The NLSY97 is a survey starting in 1997 following a nationally representative cohort of individuals age 12 to 16 with follow-up interviews every year on a wide range of social, educational, and economic variables. For more details on the NLSY97, see Section B.2 of the Web Appendix (http://jenni.uchicago.edu/GEDHandbookChapter/).

[11] These statistics are reported for other races and gender groups in Section C.1 of the Web Appendix (http://jenni.uchicago.edu/GEDHandbookChapter/). A similar pattern characterizes the other groups.

Table 9.2 Comparison of Key Characteristics by Educational level—White Males—NLSY79

	Dropout	GED No College	High School No College	Some College	Associate's Degree	Bachelor's Degree or More
Highest Grade Comp. 2006	9.44 (1.34)	10.70 (1.24)	11.90 (0.82)	13.50 (0.75)	14.10 (0.91)	17.00 (1.51)
South Age 14	0.39 (0.49)	0.36 (0.48)	0.23 (0.42)	0.26 (0.44)	0.26 (0.44)	0.25 (0.43)
Urban Age 14	1.38 (0.62)	1.31 (0.59)	1.37 (0.62)	1.26 (0.55)	1.31 (0.55)	1.21 (0.50)
Mother Worked Age 14	0.49 (0.50)	0.52 (0.50)	0.49 (0.50)	0.50 (0.50)	0.50 (0.50)	0.52 (0.50)
Father Worked Age 14	0.89 (0.32)	0.93 (0.26)	0.95 (0.21)	0.97 (0.18)	0.97 (0.16)	0.98 (0.14)
Magazines Age 14	0.42 (0.49)	0.61 (0.49)	0.68 (0.47)	0.75 (0.43)	0.79 (0.41)	0.88 (0.33)
Newspaper Age 14	0.71 (0.46)	0.85 (0.36)	0.89 (0.31)	0.91 (0.29)	0.91 (0.28)	0.94 (0.24)
Library Card Age 14	0.55 (0.50)	0.72 (0.45)	0.70 (0.46)	0.83 (0.38)	0.80 (0.40)	0.87 (0.34)
Mother's Highest Grade Comp.	10.30 (2.45)	10.70 (2.31)	11.50 (2.11)	12.20 (2.20)	12.10 (1.92)	13.30 (2.39)
Father's Highest Grade Comp.	9.57 (3.41)	10.50 (2.92)	11.50 (2.76)	12.80 (3.15)	12.60 (2.94)	14.30 (3.27)
Net Family Income 1979	15,001 (12,215)	19,162 (14,879)	23,060 (14,454)	23,072 (16,196)	25,781 (14,605)	28,598 (18,515)
Family Poverty Status 1979	0.24 (0.43)	0.15 (0.35)	0.06 (0.24)	0.08 (0.28)	0.06 (0.24)	0.07 (0.25)
Family Size	4.25 (1.90)	4.05 (1.89)	4.19 (1.81)	3.88 (1.84)	4.27 (1.75)	4.15 (1.76)

Source: National Longitudinal Survey of Youth 1979 (NLSY79). Notes: All results are from 1979 using nationally representative weights. Notes: Family size includes both parents and children. Net family income in 1979 dollars. Standard errors in parenthesis.

Table 9.3 Comparison of Key Characteristics by Educational level—White Males—NLSY97

	Dropout	GED No College	High School No College	Some College	Associate's Degree	Bachelor's Degree or More
Highest Grade Comp. Age 22	9.60 (1.21)	9.94 (1.00)	12.00 (0.00)	13.00 (0.00)	14.60 (0.49)	16.00 (0.21)
South Age 12	0.30 (0.46)	0.36 (0.48)	0.27 (0.44)	0.27 (0.45)	0.24 (0.43)	0.24 (0.42)
Urban Age 12	0.77 (0.42)	0.79 (0.41)	0.72 (0.45)	0.86 (0.35)	0.85 (0.36)	0.88 (0.32)
Inner City Age 12	0.21 (0.41)	0.19 (0.39)	0.17 (0.38)	0.19 (0.39)	0.20 (0.40)	0.14 (0.35)
Household Size Age 12	4.31 (1.41)	4.41 (1.45)	4.43 (1.32)	4.32 (1.20)	4.39 (1.21)	4.37 (1.07)
Broken Household Age 12	0.60 (0.49)	0.60 (0.49)	0.35 (0.48)	0.32 (0.47)	0.26 (0.44)	0.16 (0.36)
Mother's Highest Grade Comp.	11.70 (2.02)	13.10 (7.24)	12.70 (2.13)	13.60 (2.40)	14.30 (2.43)	14.60 (2.55)
Father's Highest Grade Comp.	11.50 (2.38)	12.70 (7.82)	12.70 (4.22)	13.50 (2.59)	14.60 (2.88)	15.30 (2.82)
Family Routine Index 1997	−0.19 (0.96)	−0.20 (0.84)	−0.09 (0.95)	0.07 (0.86)	0.13 (0.84)	0.06 (0.79)
Home Risk Index 1997	0.49 (1.08)	0.30 (1.11)	−0.05 (0.95)	−0.29 (0.87)	−0.59 (0.66)	−0.68 (0.54)
Physical Environment Index 1997	0.35 (0.97)	0.10 (0.91)	−0.11 (0.82)	−0.27 (0.78)	−0.47 (0.75)	−0.70 (0.45)
Enriching Environment Index 1997	−0.38 (0.93)	−0.20 (0.93)	−0.03 (0.88)	0.31 (0.88)	0.49 (0.87)	0.69 (0.83)
Deliquency Index 1997	0.91 (1.38)	0.86 (1.31)	0.34 (1.14)	0.31 (1.16)	−0.09 (0.83)	−0.21 (0.67)

Source: National Longitudinal Survey of Youth 1997 (NLSY97). Notes: All results are from 1997 using nationally representative weights. All index scores are standardized mean zero, standard deviation one. See Section B.2.2 of the Web Appendix (http://jenni.uchicago.edu/GEDHandbookChapter/) for detail on the construction of the family routine, home risk, physical environment, enriching environment, and delinquency indices. Standard errors in parenthesis.

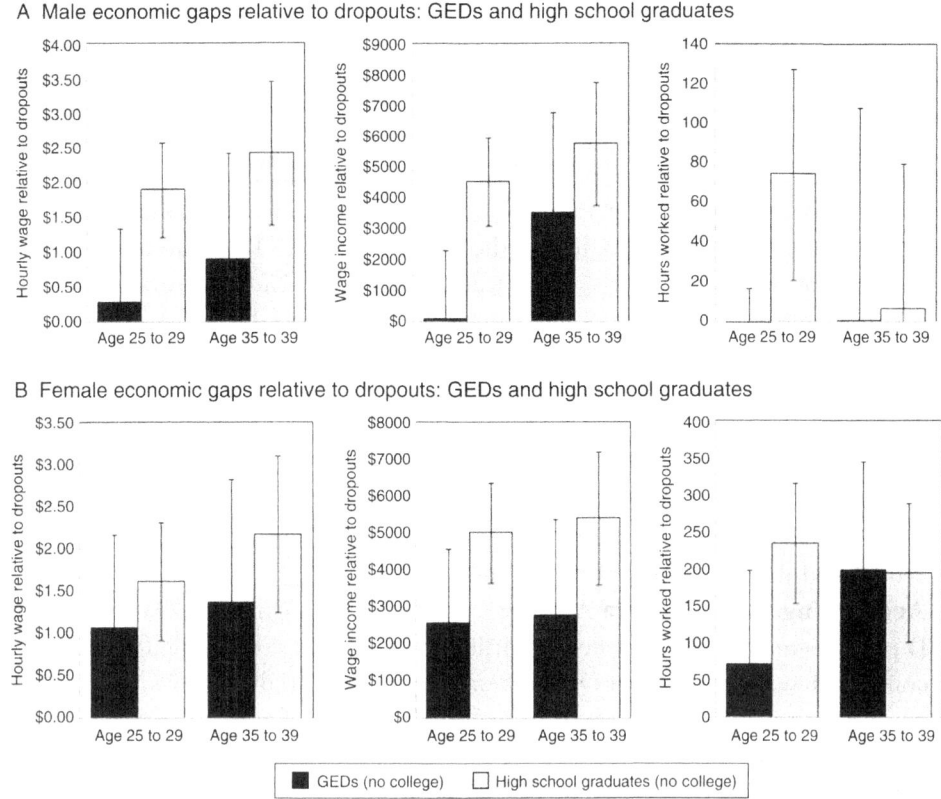

Figure 9.6 Economic gaps relative to dropouts: GEDs and high school graduates for males (A) and females (B). *Source:* National Longitudinal Survey of Youth 1979 (NLSY79). Notes: Regressions control for age, mother's highest grade completed, and dummies for urban residence at age 14, Southern residence at age 14, and race. The regressions use the cross-sectional subsample and minority oversamples of the NLSY79 data. The estimation sample is restricted to individuals who never attend college and who have not yet been incarcerated. Regressions for hourly wage and hours worked are restricted to those reporting more than $1/hour and less than $100/hour, and individuals working less than 4,000 hours in a given year. Wage income regressions are restricted to individuals reporting wage incomes between $1,000/year and $100,000/year. All monetary values are in 2005 dollars. Standard errors are clustered by individual. 95% confidence bands are displayed for each bar chart.

and poverty rates. Terminal GEDs (i.e., those who do not continue to college) generally fall between dropouts and terminal high school graduates. There are some exceptions. In the NLSY97, the parents of GED recipients are more educated than parents of high school graduates, and GEDs are as likely or more likely to come from a broken household than are dropouts.[12] The differences in these measures demonstrate the potential importance of controlling for pre-existing heterogeneity among educational groups.

---

[12] In Section C.1 of the Web Appendix (http://jenni.uchicago.edu/GEDHandbookChapter/) we show that minority GEDs have higher delinquency rates and higher home risk indices than dropouts.

Dropouts, terminal GEDs, and terminal high school graduates also differ in their performance on academic tests, which are predictive of earnings. The Armed Forces Qualification Test (AFQT) was administered in the NLSY79 and in the NLSY97, and is a commonly used measure of academic, or cognitive, ability.[13,14] When the AFQT was administered, the surveyed individuals were of different ages and had acquired different levels of schooling. These differences affect their measured performance. In order to make comparisons of academic ability, we adjust individual scores to account for the level of schooling at the time of the test. This adjustment controls for final educational attainment using a structural model as laid out in Hansen, Heckman, and Mullen (2004) and implemented in Heckman, Urzua, and Veramendi (2010). This allows comparisons of latent cognitive ability between dropouts, GED recipients, and high school graduates prior to schooling decisions.

The comparisons in Figure 9.7 show that, before entry into high school, individuals who eventually GED certify have higher cognitive ability than dropouts, and are very similar to terminal high school graduates. The cognitive ability distribution for GEDs is nearly identical to that of high school graduates and is strongly right shifted from uncredentialed dropouts for both males and females.

Accounting for Cognitive Ability: Cameron and Heckman (1993) find that the GED provides on average no benefit to male test takers after controlling for either years of completed schooling or AFQT scores. While their study follows the NLSY79 sample through age 28, subsequent analysis replicates this finding through later ages. Heckman and LaFontaine (2006) use later waves of the NLSY79 and find that the GED has no benefit on average log hourly wages after controlling for AFQT. They find that high school graduation is still associated with a positive wage premium. Once Heckman and LaFontaine correct for selection and control for AFQT scores, male GEDs earn on average 1% less per hour than dropouts while terminal high school graduates make 3.6% more per hour on average than dropouts. Similarly they find that female GEDs earn 1.7% more per hour than dropouts while terminal high school graduates earn 10.6% more per hour. They also show that the GED has little or no benefit after controlling for reported test scores using the National Adult Literacy Survey (NALS) data.

Figure 9.8 shows that, relative to the differences shown in Figure 9.6, the economic benefits associated with the GED are greatly reduced and become statistically insignificant

---

[13] The Armed Forces Qualification Test is an achievement test measuring numerical operations, arithmetic reasoning, paragraph completion, and word knowledge. The AFQT was administered to individuals in the NLSY79 in 1979 when they were aged 14 to 22, and to individuals in the NLSY97 in 1999 when they were age 14 to 18. The AFQT tests administered to each sample represented the same content, but differed in format and scoring procedure. See Section B.1.1 of the Web Appendix (*http://jenni.uchicago.edu/GEDHandbookChapter/*) for more details.

[14] Borghans, Golsteyn, Heckman, and Humphries (2010) show that the AFQT is predicted by both cognitive and noncognitive traits.

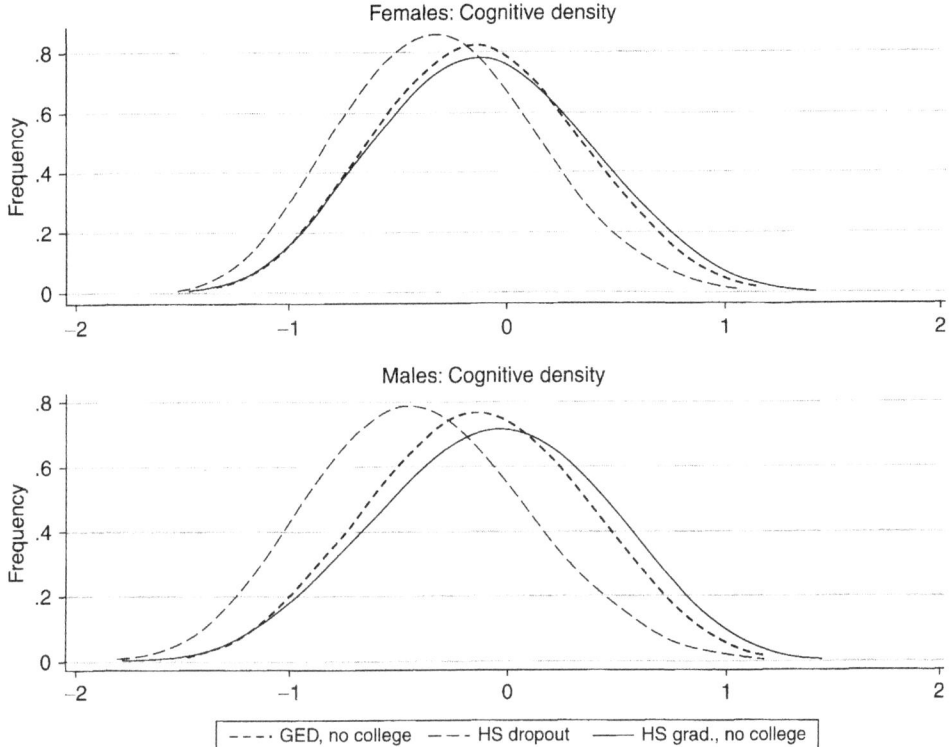

Figure 9.7 Cognitive ability by educational status (no college sample, all ethnic groups). *Source:* Reproduced from Heckman, Urzua, and Veramendi (2010). National Longitudinal Study of Youth 1979. Notes: The distributions above represent cognitive ability factors estimated using a subset of the Armed Services Vocational Aptitude Battery and educational attainment as laid out in Hansen, Heckman, and Mullen (2004). Sample restricted to the cross-sectional subsample for both males and females. Distributions show only those with no post-secondary educational attainment. The cognitive ability factors are separately normalized to be mean zero standard deviation one.

once pre-existing cognitive ability is controlled for.[15] For terminal high school graduates, however, economic benefits persist after controlling for pre-existing cognitive ability.

---

[15] To obtain the baseline standardized mean test score adjusted to the seventh grade level, we remove the estimated mean impact of schooling attained over the seventh grade level using the procedure of Hansen et al. (2004) as implemented in Carneiro et al. (2005). Let S_t be the random variable denoting schooling attained at year t (the date of the survey) and let s_t be its realized value. Let S_F be the random variable denoting the final level of schooling attained and s_F its realized value. Let $T(s_t, s_F)$ be the test score at time t for a person whose schooling at the time of the test is $S_t = s_t$ and whose final schooling level is $S_F = s_F$. The assumption of the procedure is that the unobservables generating $T(s_t, s_F)$ are mean independent of S_t given $S_F = s_F$. For each $S_F = s_F$, we can identify the causal effect of a year of schooling on the test score for each level of completed final schooling. Then we can adjust the mean test score to baseline levels $S_t = s_b$ by subtracting the term $E(T(s_t, s_F)|S_t = s_t, S_F = s_F) - E(T(s_b, s_F)|S_t = s_b, S_F = s_F)$. Both terms are identified, assuming in addition that at the time of the test for each level of $S_F = s_F$, there are some persons at schooling level $S_t = s_b$. Post schooling mean test scores are obtained in a similar fashion, but now adjusting to years of final schooling. See Section D of the Web Appendix for a detailed discussion of this procedure. See Hansen et al. (2004) for a more general procedure.

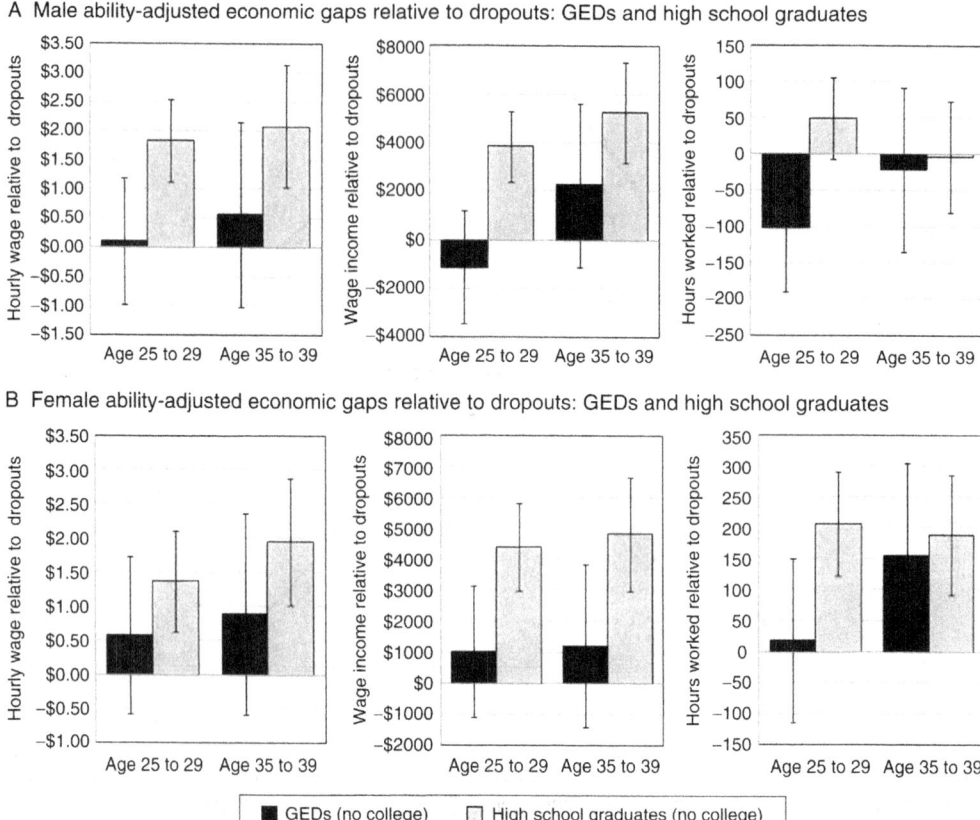

Figure 9.8 Ability-adjusted economic gaps relative to dropouts: GEDs and high school graduates for males (A) and females (B). *Source:* National Longitudinal Survey of Youth 1979 (NLSY79). Notes: Regressions control for baseline AFQT scores, age, mother's highest grade completed, and dummies for urban residence at age 14, Southern residence at age 14, and race. Baseline test scores are estimated using the procedure of Hansen et al. 2004 as implemented in Carneiro et al. (2005). The regressions use the cross-sectional subsample and minority oversamples of the NLSY79 data. The estimation sample is restricted to individuals who never attend college and who have not yet been incarcerated. Regressions for hourly wage and hours worked are restricted to those reporting more than $1/hour and less than $100/hour, and individuals working less than 4,000 hours in a given year. Wage income regressions are restricted to individuals reporting wage incomes between $1,000/year and $100,000/year. All monetary values are in 2005 dollars. Standard errors are clustered by individual. 95% confidence bands are displayed for each bar chart.

This suggests a causal effect of high school graduation. That high school still has value after controlling for pre-existing cognitive ability suggests high school graduates possess a valued trait not captured by an achievement test. Section 3.1.3 extends this discussion to encompass both cognitive and noncognitive ability. The next section follows the development of the literature in trying to identify specific populations that benefit from the GED.

3.1.2 Heterogeneous labor market returns

Recent work on the GED has sought to identify groups of test takers for which individual traits or circumstances contribute to a stronger signal or increased human capital development. This section focuses on several different potential margins of benefit, discusses hypotheses, and reviews the related literature.

Wage growth for GEDs with experience: It is argued that, similar to the pattern of returns to college, the benefits to a GED would increase with time in the labor market. Clark and Jaeger (2006) present evidence from the Current Population Survey (CPS) that is apparently consistent with the hypothesis that the wage premium to GED certification for males is increasing with age. Given the cross-sectional nature of the CPS data, this finding may be attributed to either experience effects or cohort effects. Using the NLSY79 sample, Heckman and LaFontaine (2006) show that this higher premium to older cohorts is explained by their greater ability. When not controlling for ability, the NLSY79 sample shows a wage premium for GED recipients that is comparable to that found in samples of individuals from the CPS data for the same birth cohorts. Once one controls for AFQT scores for the NLSY79 sample, there is no statistically significant effect of GED certification on wages.

Using longitudinal data on earnings in the NLSY79, Murnane et al. (1995) argue that the value of the GED increases with experience as recipients use the degree's signal for promotion, better job placement in the future, and on-the-job training. Consistent with Cameron and Heckman (1993), they find no treatment effect of the GED on mean wage levels at age 28, but they report a statistically significant 2.4% wage increase for every year of experience after receiving a GED. Murnane, Willett, and Boudett (1999) control for cognitive ability or individual fixed effects in different models specifications. They find that the complementarity of GED and years of experience is statistically significant only for individuals with low ability.

Murnane, Willett, and Boudett pool person-year observations in their regressions. They infer increasing returns to the GED from variables interacting GED receipt with years of experience. In contrast to this approach, Heckman and LaFontaine (2006) estimate separate regressions for earnings at different ages, allowing separate estimates of returns to ability and experience by age. They find that there is no statistically significant effect to GED certification at any age for both males and females.

Males vs. females: Males and females might derive different value from the GED through having different motivations for dropping out of school. Using data from the NLSY79 Market Experience survey, Rumberger (1983) presents differences in self-reported reasons for dropping out for males and females.[16] Males were 65% more likely than females to report school-related issues, indicating dislike of school, being expelled, and poor performance as their primary reason for leaving school. Among other explanations, males were more likely to leave school due to economic reasons while a third of all women left due to

---

[16] This table is reproduced in Section C.2 of the Web Appendix (*http://jenni.uchicago.edu/GEDHandbookChapter/*).

pregnancy or marriage. If there are gender differences in later-life motivations to work and seek higher education, there could be differential value of the GED for men and women.

Cao, Stromsdorfer, and Weeks (1996) test for the GED's direct effect on economic outcomes for women using data from the NLSY79 and from Washington state. Given their focus on women who may have custody of children and be eligible for public transfer programs, they attempt to eliminate selection bias related to both the decision to participate in the labor force and to not enroll in welfare. They find no statistically significant differences between the labor supplies of women of different education levels. The positive association of GED certification with hourly wage is eliminated by controlling for the number of years of schooling completed at the time people drop out.

Table 9.4 presents a comparison of qualitative findings for males and females from selected papers in the literature and information on which data sets and cohorts are studied. In addition, both Murnane et al. (2000) and Tyler et al. (2003) use the High School and Beyond (HSB) data set and find, respectively, positive effects of GED certification on the earnings of low ability males and on the hours worked by low ability females.[17] Because neither study can identify the sources of selection of each gender into dropout status—or selection into educational status and work in general—it is difficult to interpret these findings.

Using evidence from the NLSY79, CPS, and NALS, Heckman and LaFontaine (2006) establish that both male and female GEDs have higher wages than dropouts and that, for both genders, the explanation is sorting by ability and not a causal effect of the GED. They consistently find a small but statistically insignificant benefit for females of 1–2% on hourly wage which is not present or slightly negative for males. This finding is consistent with the hypothesis that females are more likely to drop out of high school for reasons unrelated to intrinsic labor market motivation, for example, due to pregnancy. Similarly, they find much larger benefits from high school graduation for females than for males.

Native vs. foreign born: While much has been written about the education and labor market performance of immigrants,[18] little attention has been paid to the value they receive from earning a GED. Clark and Jaeger (2006) argue that the GED might provide a signal of ability that is more familiar to employers than educational credentials earned outside the country, or may signal language ability and cultural assimilation. Clark and Jaeger use earnings data in the CPS and find that only foreign-born GEDs with no domestic credentials have a statistically significantly higher wage than native-born dropouts.

Heckman and LaFontaine (2006) examine the Clark and Jaeger (2006) analysis and find that their results are produced by data artifacts and limitations. One source of bias in the Clark and Jaeger (2006) analysis is that the CPS imputes values of missing wages for GEDs by sampling earnings of high school graduates, a process that contaminates comparisons of the outcome differences between those two groups and dropouts. A second source

---

[17] See Section B.5 of the Web Appendix (*http://jenni.uchicago.edu/GEDHandbookChapter/*) for more details on the High School and Beyond data set.
[18] See the edited volume Borjas (2000) and Betts and Lofstrom (2000) in particular.

Table 9.4 Literature Summary—Labor Market Effects—Males vs. Females

Study	Data	Population	Method/Identification	GED Effect	Findings
Cameron and Heckman (1993)	NLSY79 (1979–1987)	White males	Control for cognitive ability, correction for self-selection into working status	1/0 GED[1]	Income: no effect Wage: no effect
Murnane, Willett, and Boudett (1995)	NLSY79 (1979–1991)	Males	1/0 if ever got GED	(1/0 GED) × work experience	Income: no effect Wage: (+, **)
Cao, Stromsdorfer, and Weeks (1996)	NLSY79 (1979–1991), Washington State Family Income Study	Females	Correction for self-selection into working status	1/0 GED	Hours worked: no effect Wage: no effect
Heckman and LaFontaine (2006)	NLSY79 (1979–2001)	Males and females	Control for cognitive ability, correction for self-selection into working status	1/0 GED	Wage: no effect

Notes: [1] "1/0" refers to a binary indicator of the associated variable. For example, under GED Effect "1/0 GED" refers to 1 = receives GED, 0 = does not, indicating a simple binary treatment effect.
The study samples are statistically representative of the U.S. unless otherwise indicated in the "Population" field. The "Findings" field codes no statistically significant effect as "No effect," and otherwise shows (<indicator of a positive or negative finding>, <level of significance>) where * = $p < .10$, ** = $p < .05$, and *** = $p < .01$. See the Web Appendix (http://jenni.uchicago.edu/GEDHandbookChapter/) for tables with more detail on each paper's outcomes examined, lists of regressors, and point estimates for each regression specification.

of bias is the reliance on cross-sectional variation of wages. By making longitudinal comparisons with the CPS data, Heckman and LaFontaine (2006) find that receipt of a GED has no effect on earnings and explain Clark and Jaeger's findings as due to sorting along characteristics unmeasured in the CPS. Heckman and LaFontaine also analyze the NALS which also identifies the foreign born. They demonstrate no earnings premium to GED receipt for any group once selection and cognitive ability are controlled for. Table 9.5 shows a comparison of qualitative findings for native- and foreign-born individuals from selected papers in the literature and information on which data sets and cohorts are studied.

Table 9.5 Literature Summary— Labor Market Effects–Native vs. Foreign Born

Study	Data	Population	Method/ Identification	GED Effect	Findings
Clark and Jaeger (2006)	CPS	Foreign born, males and females	OLS	(1/0 GED[1]) × (foreign born)	Wage: (+, ***)
Heckman and LaFontaine (2006)	CPS, excluding wage imputation	Males and females	Individual fixed effects	1/0 GED	Wage: no effect
	NALS (1992)	Foreign born, males and females	Control for cognitive ability, correction for self-selection into working status	(1/0 GED) × (foreign born)	Wage: no effect

Notes: [1] "1/0" refers to a binary indicator of the associated variable. For example, under GED Effect "1/0 GED" refers to 1 = receives GED, 0 = does not, indicating a simple binary treatment effect.
The study samples are statistically representative of the U.S. unless otherwise indicated in the "Population" field. The "Findings" field codes no statistically signficant effect as "No effect," and otherwise shows (<indicator of a positive or negative finding>, <level of significance>) where $^* = p < .10$, $^{**} = p < .05$, and $^{***} = p < .01$.
See the Web Appendix (*http://jenni.uchicago.edu/GEDHandbookChapter/*) for tables with more detail on each paper's outcomes examined, lists of regressors, and point estimates for each regression specification.

Signaling: Tyler et al. (2000) use a difference-in-differences approach to examine the returns to the GED for individuals at the cusp of passing the test. Using variation in test score thresholds across states, they contend that focusing on individuals who would pass the GED under one regime but not under the other will identify the signaling effect of the GED for people at the margin. Using data from the GED Testing Service and Social Security Administration, they separate individuals into groups by performance on the GED exam and state of residence. Variation in the passing standards enforced by different states arguably creates a natural experiment where individuals with the same score do or do not pass the GED based on their state of residence. To understand their paper we use the notation in Table 9.6. Let "−" over a variable denote its mean.

Table 9.6 Outcomes by Treatment Classifications of Individuals in Tyler et al. (2000)

	Low GED Score ("LS")	High GED Score ("HS")
State of Residence has Low Passing Standard ("LP")	$Y_{LS,LP}$ (GED)	$Y_{HS,LP}$ (GED)
State of Residence has High Passing Standard ("HP")	$Y_{LS,HP}$ (no GED)	$Y_{HS,HP}$ (GED)

Their difference-in-differences estimator (DID) used by Tyler et al. (2000) is:

$$DID = \left(\overline{Y}_{LS,LP} - \overline{Y}_{LS,HP}\right) - \left(\overline{Y}_{HS,LP} - \overline{Y}_{HS,HP}\right). \quad (9.1)$$

In the notation of Table 9.6, $\overline{Y}_{A,B}$ represents the mean wage of individuals with score A in a state with passing standard B, where A is either low score (LS) or high score (HS), and B is either low passing standard (LP) or high passing standard (HP). Because their analysis only includes individuals measured in the neighborhood of GED passing standards, none of the individuals studied are high scoring in an absolute sense.

The first term in Equation (9.1) takes the difference in average earnings between individuals who have the same ability but different credential status. The second term is used to adjust for the possibility that wages in the two states in the first difference are unequal. The second difference is an estimate of the baseline wage difference across those states for individuals with the GED credential at the same low ability margin (in absolute terms).[19]

Tyler et al. (2000) report a 10–19% earnings benefit to GED certification at the margin for whites.[20] They argue that these estimates are consistent with earlier studies whose findings of no effect of certification only apply to the average test taker. They claim that for the particular margin they investigate–that of low-skilled takers–there are high signaling benefits to certification that are absent for the general population of test takers.

To defend the assumption of exogeneity of state passing standards with respect to individual earnings, they perform robustness checks accounting for selective migration, differential access to post-secondary training, differences in state labor markets, selective taking of the GED, and selective effort in studying across states. Rubinstein (2003)

---

[19] Tyler et al. (2000) implement this estimation in a linear regression to pool all states together and control for mean gender differences in earnings. See their paper for details.

[20] They suggest that their lack of a significant finding for nonwhites may be due to an institutional effect where both disproportionate representation of minorities in prison and the growth of GED programs for the incarcerated lead to negative associations with the test, thus decreasing its signaling value. See Section 4 below for evidence of these demographic trends in prison-based GED receipt. The separate estimation of the GED effect by race is rare in the literature, which typically includes regression controls for race but does not treat it as a separate conditioning variable. See Section E.1 of the Web Appendix (*http://jenni.uchicago.edu/GEDHandbookChapter/*) for a full account of study samples, treatment of race, and separate estimates by race.

discusses their paper, claiming that the endogeneity of studying effort would lead to upwardly-biased estimates. His model predicts that, at the margin, low ability individuals will exert more effort than high ability individuals when passing thresholds are higher. If these efforts have little or no effect on long-term productivity,[21] both $\overline{Y}_{LS,HP}$ and $\overline{Y}_{HS,HP}$ will include individuals whose true productivity is overstated, but abilities in $\overline{Y}_{LS,HP}$ will be overstated to a greater degree relative to $\overline{Y}_{LS,LP}$ than for $\overline{Y}_{HS,HP}$ relative to $\overline{Y}_{HS,LP}$. Greater downward bias in $\overline{Y}_{LS,HP}$ than in $\overline{Y}_{HS,HP}$ leads to upward bias in the DID estimate. He presents no direct empirical evidence on this bias. It is also possible that the higher passing standard discourages low ability persons from taking the test so that his conclusion is reversed.

Jepsen et al. (2010) show evidence of endogeneity of test taking effort in a single state with one passing standard. GED policy in Missouri permits individuals to pass the GED if their maximum scores on individual tests across retakes of the GED exam meet the passing standard.[22] Figure 9.9 shows the distribution of scores from the first administration of the test in its first panel, and the distribution of maximum scores across all administrations of the GED exam that each individual opted to take in its second panel, where a clear discontinuity arises at the passing standard of 2,250. This behavior introduces several possible sources of bias in the comparisons between GED certifiers and dropouts. Selective retaking will lead to low ability individuals being improperly counted in higher score groups. If changes in scores across retakes are due to unproductive cramming (as conjectured by Rubinstein (2003)) coupled with luck, this misclassification will lead to over-representation of low ability persons among GEDs producing a downward bias in comparisons of successful GED test takers with those who fail. On the other hand, if the choice to retake the test is associated with a trait of persistence that is productive in the workplace, these persons who become GEDs have high noncognitive skills that will moderate the downward bias due to their low ability. Jepsen et al. (2010) use Missouri administrative data on first test scores and final GED outcomes to implement a Fuzzy Regression Discontinuity (FRD) estimation of the effects of the GED.[23] They find no effects of GED receipt on earnings or employment for individuals at the margin of passing on their first attempt, but find a statistically significant increase in post-secondary schooling attendance of 10%.

Dropouts with low initial endowments: Tyler et al. (2000) focus on a low ability margin, and argue that low ability GEDs command higher wages relative to dropouts of comparable ability than high ability GEDs command relative to their

---

[21] Rubinstein assumes that these studying efforts represent "cramming," and do not represent durable investments in human capital.

[22] Thus top scores on the various subtests across retakes of the test are aggregated.

[23] See Imbens and Lemieux (2008) for discussion of the FRD method. See Hahn, Todd, and Van der Klaauw (2001) for the original paper.

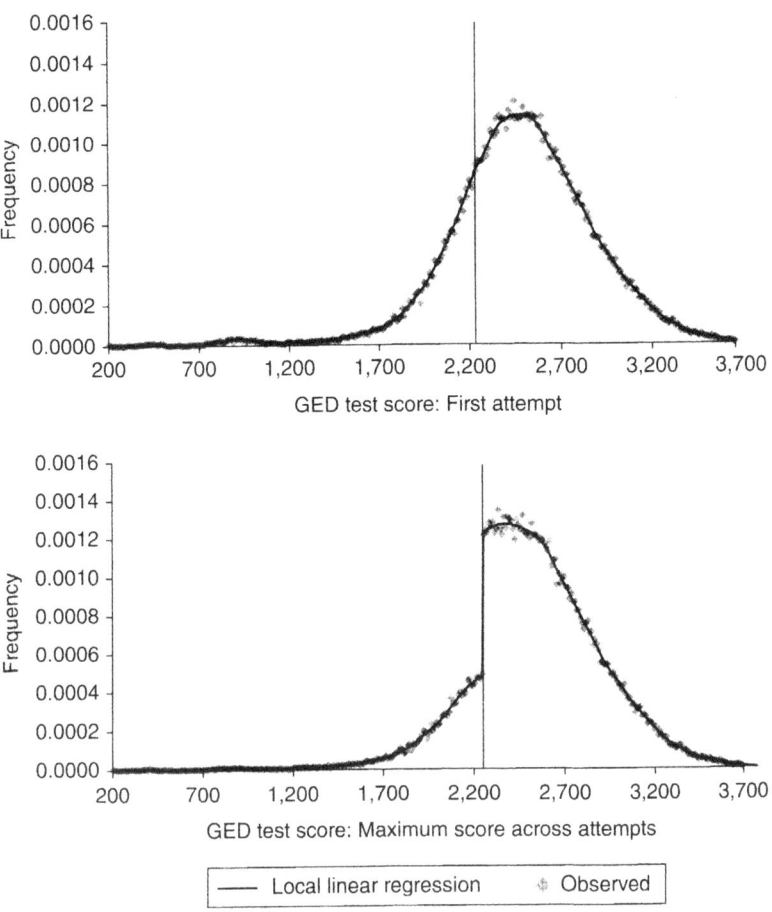

Figure 9.9 Distribution of first test scores and final test scores after retakes, Missouri. *Source:* Reproduced from Jepsen et al. (2010) using Missouri administrative records from 1995-2006. Notes: The first figure is the distribution of individual GED scores on the first test. The second figure represents the distribution of GED test score outcomes reflecting the maximum scores across all attempts of the GED that each individual elected to take. Passing the GED in Missouri requires a minimum score requirement on each subtest and a total score of 2,250.

non-GED counterparts. Murnane et al. (1999), Murnane et al. (2000), and Tyler et al. (2003) suggest a human capital explanation for large effects at a low ability margin where, in order to meet a uniform passing bar, GED recipients with the lowest academic ability when leaving school must have made the largest human capital investments in order to pass. That is, individuals with low initial ability may disproportionately comprise the sizable right tail in the distribution of preparation hours discussed in Section 2.1, and may thus generate a nontrivial amount of human capital. While no data sets combine information on GED preparation times, schooling at the time of dropping out, cognitive ability, and wages, the findings of these three papers are consistent with the hypothesis that low ability GEDs study more. As previously noted, the low ability GEDs who try repeatedly to pass and do so may have higher noncognitive traits than their low ability non-GED counterparts and this might explain their findings. The samples and qualitative findings of each paper are summarized in Table 9.7.

All of these papers find positive returns to the GED associated with low levels of academic ability. Murnane et al. (1999) control for individual heterogeneity using a long panel of earnings data from the NLSY79 sample to control for individual fixed effects. The wage returns are limited, with Murnane et al. (1999)'s analysis suggesting a statistically significant 6% hourly wage premium five years after GED certification. It would be instructive to compare the noncognitive skills of the low ability GEDs with those of dropouts who do not certify. To the best of our knowledge, this has not been done.

Murnane et al. (2000) use the High School and Beyond (HSB) data to examine growth in scores on subject tests that are administered with the initial wave when participants are in 10th grade, and tests that are administered in the next wave that is sampled two years later. Controlling for completion of 10th and 11th grade and baseline test scores, GEDs make larger test score gains than do dropouts. They note that while this finding may be due to differential returns to education or other unobserved heterogeneity, this pattern is consistent with the hypothesis that studying for the GED examination did increase the math skills of dropouts.

3.1.3 Cognitive and noncognitive ability

Just as cognitive ability is commonly a confounding factor in explaining the labor market returns to education, Heckman and Rubinstein (2001) demonstrate that dropping out is associated with negative social traits such as criminal behavior, divorce, risky social behaviors, and job turnover that are not controlled for in statistical studies. As a test of cognitive ability, the GED does not directly measure these negative social traits or induce sorting along the lines of positive traits. Heckman and Rubinstein introduce the idea that this association of the GED with negative social traits makes it a "mixed signal."

While Section 3.1.1 demonstrates that GEDs lie between dropouts and high school graduates in academic outcomes and home background, Figures 9.10 and 9.11 show that GEDs are similar to, or worse than, dropouts in terms of social outcomes.[24] This suggests that underlying behavioral characteristics can explain in part why GED recipients do not receive the benefit that high school graduates do from their credentials.

Heckman, Stixrud, and Urza (2006) test for the influence of cognitive and noncognitive skills on choices of schooling and the wage returns to schooling. They use

---

[24] These figures display different social outcomes due to the fact that the same measures are not surveyed in the NLSY79 and NLSY97.

Table 9.7 Literature Summary—Labor Market Effects by Ability

Study	Data	Population	Method/Identification	GED Effect	Findings
Murnane, Willett, and Boudett (1999)	NLSY79 (1979–1991)	Males, includes low-income sample	Individual fixed effects	post-GED work experience × (1/0 low cognitive ability)[1]	Income: no effect; Wage: $(+, ^{***})$ if low cognitive ability
Murnane, Willett, and Tyler (2000)	HSB (1980–1991)	Males	Control for cog quartile, OLS	(1/0 GED) × (1/0 low cognitive ability)	Income: $(+, ^{**})$
Tyler, Murnane, and Willett (2003)	HSB (1980–1991)	Females	Control for highest grade completed, OLS and Logit	(1/0 GED) × (1/0 low cognitive ability)	Income: no effect; Probability of working: $(+, ^{**})$; Work experience: $(+, ^{***})$
Heckman, Urzua, and Veramendi (2010)	NLSY79 (1979–2006)	White males	Dynamic discrete choice framework, latent factor analysis	(1/0 GED) × (cognitive ability, noncognitive ability)	Wage: $(+)^{2}$ if high cognitive and noncognitive ability

Notes: [1] "1/0" refers to a binary indicator of the associated variable. For example, under GED Effect "1/0 GED" refers to 1 = receives GED, 0 = does not, indicating a simple binary treatment effect.
[2] Heckman, Urzua, and Veramendi (2010) is a working paper that uses simulations to identify heterogeneous treatment effects. The most recent draft has distributions of treatments but has not yet bootstrapped the relevant standard errors.
The study samples are statistically representative of the U.S. unless otherwise indicated in the "Population" field. The "Findings" field codes no statistically significant effect as "No Effect," and otherwise shows (<indicator of a positive or negative finding>, <level of significance>) where $^{*} = p < .10$, $^{**} = p < .05$, and $^{***} = p < .01$. See the Web Appendix (http://jenni.uchicago.edu/GEDHandbookChapter/) for tables with more detail on each paper's outcomes examined, lists of regressors, and point estimates for each regression specification.

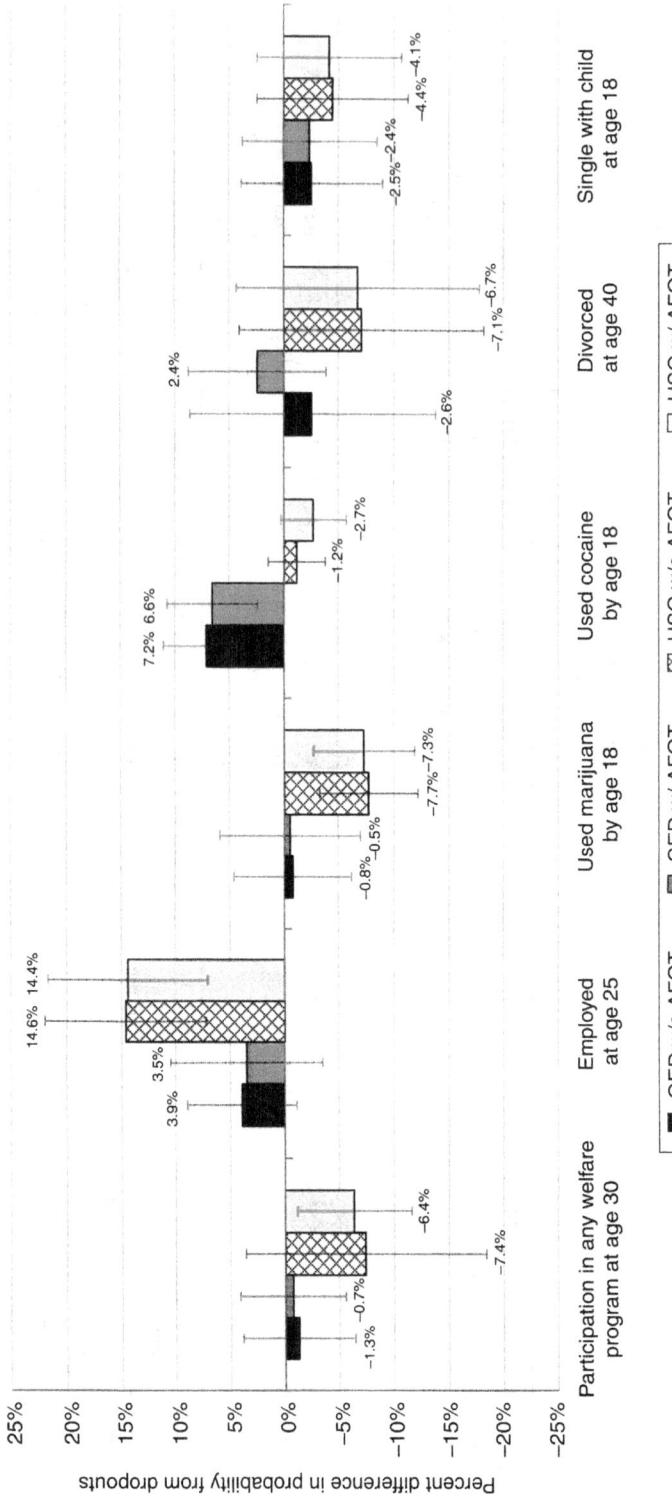

Figure 9.10 Gaps in the probability of various social outcomes compared to high school dropouts with and without controlling for scholastic ability (NLSY79). All demographic groups pooled unless otherwise noted. *Source*: National Longitudinal Survey of Youth 1979 (NLSY79). Notes: This analysis is restricted to the cross-sectional sample of NLSY79 reporting no completed years of college, having never been incarcerated, and having valid AFQT scores. "Single with Child at Age 18" includes only females. All regressions control for race, gender, Southern residence at age 14, and urban status at age 14. Regressions with controls for ability use "pre-8th grade" estimates of AFQT scores. Marginal effects reported 95% confidence intervals are displayed.

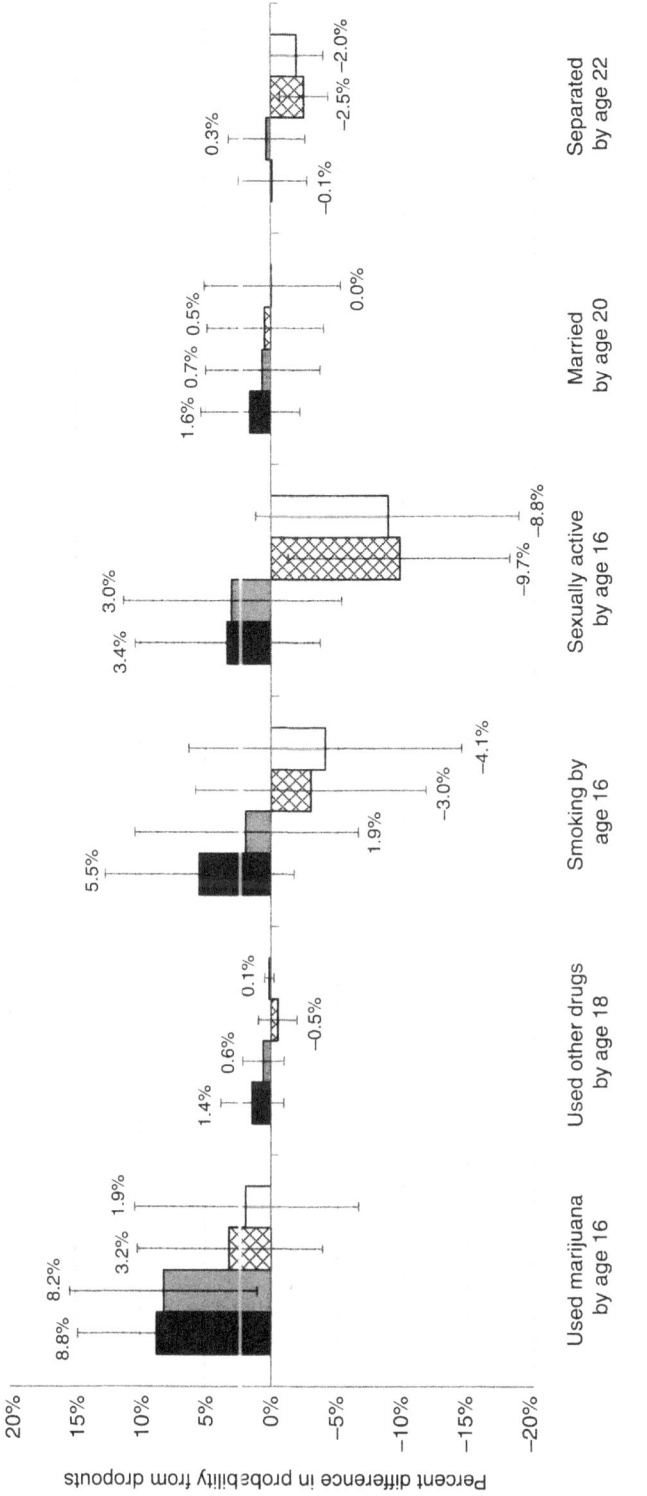

Figure 9.11 Gaps in the probability of various social outcomes compared to high school dropouts with and without controlling for scholastic ability (NLSY97). All demographic groups pooled unless otherwise noted. *Source:* National Longitudinal Survey of Youth 1997. *Notes:* This analysis is restricted to the cross-sectional sample of NLSY97 reporting no completed years of college at age 22, and having valid AFQT scores. "Separated by age 22" indicates that the individual is divorced or separated from one's spouse by age 22. All regressions include highest grade completed at 22, urban and rural status at age 12, and race and gender dummies. Regressions with controls for ability use "pre-8th grade" estimates of AFQT scores. Marginal effects reported. 95% confidence intervals are displayed.

the Rosenberg Self-Esteem Scale and Rotter Locus of Control,[25] both administered early in the NLSY79 panel to measure noncognitive skill.[26] Heckman, Urzua, and Veramendi (2010) similarly account for both cognitive and noncognitive ability, but anchor noncognitive ability in crime and risky behavior choices early in life. Figures 9.12 plots the noncognitive ability distributions from Heckman, Urzua, and Veramendi (2010) for males and females. Terminal GEDs and uncredentialed dropouts have nearly identical distributions of noncognitive ability while high school graduates are substantially right shifted.

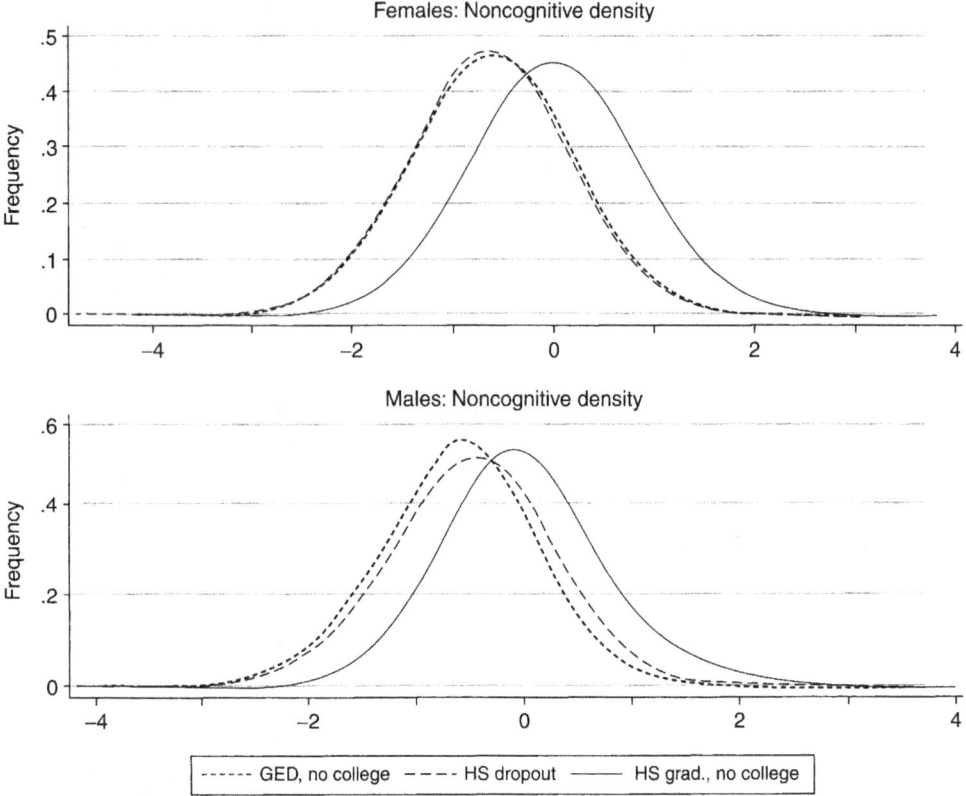

Figure 9.12 Noncognitive ability by educational status (no college sample, all ethnic groups). *Source:* Reproduced from Heckman, Urzua, and Veramendi (2010). National Longitudinal Study of Youth 1979. Notes: The distributions above represent noncognitive ability factors estimated using measures of early violent crime, minor crime, marijuana use, regular smoking, drinking, early sexual intercourse, and educational attainment as laid out in Hansen, Heckman, and Mullen (2004). Sample restricted to the cross-sectional subsample for both males and females. Distributions show only those with no post-secondary educational attainment. The noncognitive ability factors are separately normalized to be mean zero standard deviation one.

[25] The Rosenberg Self-Esteem Scale is a series of 10 yes or no questions to evaluate self-esteem. The Rotter Locus of Control is a set of four paired statements used to measure self-efficacy. The taker must indicate which she believes to be more true, then indicates if they believe this to be "somewhat true" or "very true."

[26] See Section B of the Web Appendix (*http://jenni.uchicago.edu/GEDHandbookChapter/*) for detailed descriptions of each measure.

Table 9.8, reproduced from Heckman, Stixrud, and Urzua (2006), shows that both cognitive and noncognitive[27] skills are valued in the labor market for individuals of all educational levels. The table reports the coefficients for the cognitive and noncognitive measures (which are standardized to mean zero, standard deviation 1) on log hourly wages by educational attainment. While the value of cognitive and noncognitive ability varies by education status and sex, noncognitive skills are of equal or greater importance at many educational levels as measured in effects on outcomes of unit changes in standard deviations.

Table 9.8 Coefficients from Log Wage Regression on Cognitive and Noncognitive Measures

	Males		Females	
Schooling Level	Cognitive	Noncognitive	Cognitive	Noncognitive
High school dropout	.113 (.076)	.424 (.092)	.322 (.125)	.208 (.103)
GED	.175 (.107)	.357 (.117)	.020 (.137)	.242 (.153)
High school graduate	.259 (.041)	.360 (.059)	.341 (.049)	.564 (.056)
Some college, no degree	.069 (.086)	.401 (.110)	.093 (.084)	.569 (.116)
2-year-college degree	.039 (.138)	.368 (.209)	.206 (.096)	.279 (.145)
4-year-college degree	.296 (.075)	−.060 (.175)	.290 (.066)	.379 (.103)

Source: Reproduced from Heckman, Stixrud, and Urzua (2006, Table 4). National Longitudinal Survey of Youth 1979 (NLSY79). Notes: Sample from NLSY79 males and females at age 30. Individuals are pooled across race/ethnic groups. The analysis uses the cross-sectional subsample of NLSY79, restricted to those not currently enrolled in college. The cognitive measure represents the standardized average over the raw ASVAB scores (arithmetic reasoning, word knowledge, paragraph comprehension, math knowledge, and coding speed). The noncognitive measure is computed as a (standardized) average of the Rosenberg Self-Esteem Scale and Rotter Internal-External Locus of Control Scale. The model also includes a set of cohort dummies, local labor market conditions (unemployment rate), region of residence, and dummies for race/ethnicity dummies. Standard errors are in parentheses.

Heckman, Stixrud, and Urzua (2006) and Heckman, Urzua, and Veramendi (2010) study the effect of education and noncognitive skills on earnings and other outcomes. Both papers use factor models to generate estimates of cognitive and noncognitive ability from multiple measures of those traits, and both consider choices of education levels and earnings outcomes as functions of those skills. Both papers use a generalized Roy model to control for selection into schooling and to estimate labor market returns to educational attainment that vary by levels of cognitive and noncognitive skill. While both papers measure cognitive ability from AFQT scores, Heckman et al. (2006) measure noncognitive factors using Rosenberg and Rotter scales in conjunction with educational choices. Heckman et al. (2010) construct noncognitive factors from measures of teenage behavior, specifically participation in minor and major illegal activity, smoking, drinking, drug use, involvement in after-school clubs, and sexual intercourse by the age of 15.

---

[27] Cognitive skill is measured by the Armed Services Vocational Aptitude Battery (ASVAB) which is used to construct the AFQT. Noncognitive skill is measured by the Rosenberg and Rotter scales.

Figure 9.13 shows the estimated distributions of noncognitive ability for dropouts and different types of GED recipients from Heckman and Urzua (2010). Consistent with differences displayed in Figures 9.10 and 9.11, it shows that all GEDs, except those with some college, are *below* uncredentialed dropouts in noncognitive ability. Figure 9.14, reproduced from Heckman et al. (2010), shows how the effect of GED certification on wages varies by levels of individual skill type. It shows that the marginal benefit of increasing a decile of noncognitive ability for GEDs, especially in the bottom two deciles, is greater than the marginal benefit of increasing a decile of cognitive ability. This analysis confirms the findings of Heckman et al. (2006) that there are positive returns to both noncognitive and cognitive ability in low skill labor markets.

A key observation is that GEDs are typically far down in the distribution of noncognitive ability. As discussed in the next section, noncognitive ability is also a key characteristic for predicting which individuals will successfully use the GED to obtain post-secondary training.

3.2 Educational attainment

Patterns of post-secondary enrollment and persistence: As noted above, the GED is widely accepted as a prerequisite for admission to post-secondary education. Thus it serves as an intermediate step to obtaining more valuable credentials. In 2008, 60% of GED test takers self-reported further education as a reason for taking

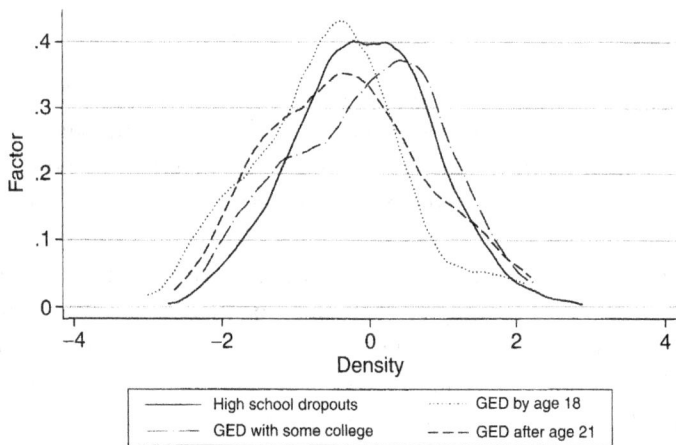

Figure 9.13 Distribution of noncognitive factor for GEDs and dropouts (white males). *Source:* Reproduced from Heckman and Urzua (2010). Notes: "GED after age 21" are those that GED certify at age 22 or later. "GED by age 18" are those that GED certify before the age of 19.

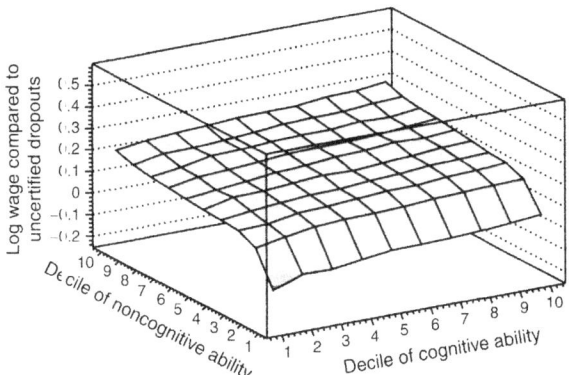
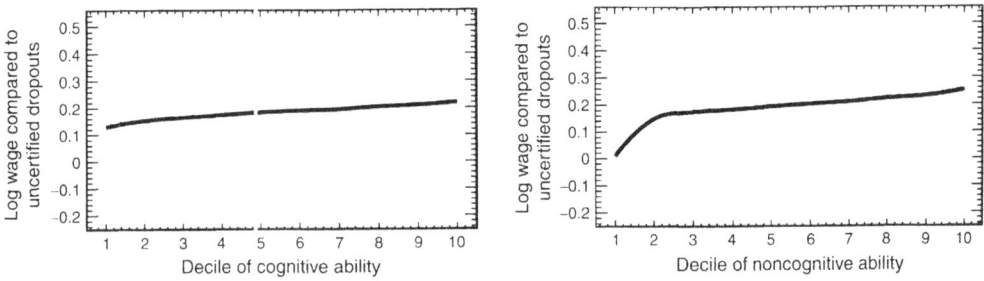

Figure 9.14 Log wage effects of GED recipient as a function of cognitive and noncognitive skills (white males). *Source:* Reproduced from Heckman et al. (2010). Notes: The top panel represents the log wage effect of GED receipt by joint distribution of cognitive and noncognitive ability. The lower panels show the log wage effect of GED receipt by marginal distributions of cognitive and noncognitive ability.

the test. Of this 60%, 20% planned on enrolling in four-year college, 28% in two-year college, and 22% in a technical or trade program (GED Testing Service (1958–2008)). Figure 9.15 presents time trends in the motivation to use the GED for post-secondary education, showing an awareness of the increasing returns to college. As the college–high school wage gap has grown, so has the percentage of GED recipients planning further education.

Few GEDs follow through with these plans. A recent study by the GED Testing Service (Patterson et al. (2009)) followed 1,000 randomly selected individuals who passed the GED test after the increase in test difficulty in 2002. It found that only 31% ever enrolled in a post-secondary institution of any kind, and that 77% of those who ever enrolled did so for only a single semester.

Figure 9.16 shows rates of enrollment and completion of various types of post-secondary education, comparing GEDs with high school graduates among the NLSY79

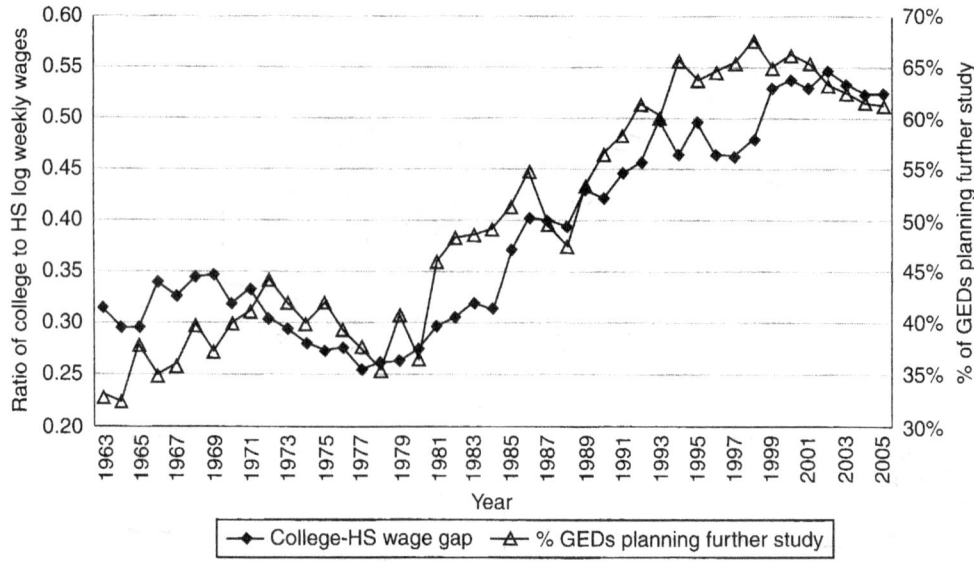

Figure 9.15 Returns to college and GED test takers seeking further education. *Source:* GED Testing Service (1958-2008) and Current Population Survey Data.

with NLSY97 cohorts at age 22.[28,29] As documented in the Patterson et al. (2009) report, many GEDs enrolled in college by age 22 but very few went on to ever earn degrees or complete a meaningful amount of post-secondary education. In contrast to the trend of self-reported plans in Figure 9.15, fewer GED recipients had enrolled by age 22 in NLSY97 than in NLSY79.[30] Figure 9.17 demonstrates that by 2006, when the NLSY79 sample is in their 40s, very few GEDs managed to earn four-year credentials although more earn associates degrees. As we discuss below, this trend may also be due to changes in the composition of GED test takers which is increasingly younger and more likely to attempt the GED through institutional requirements.

Causal analysis of outcomes pertaining to post-secondary education through the GED: GED recipients receive tangible improvements in their labor market outcomes when they complete post-secondary education. A summary of the

---

[28] We compare NLSY79 and NLSY97 at age 22 as it is the oldest age reached by the entire NLSY97 sample. The low rates of earned bachelor's/four year college degrees is explained by the fact that many students in this young sample are still working towards their degrees, given their relatively young age and the number of individuals reporting current enrollment in four year college in the NLSY97 survey.

[29] Murnane et al. (1997) contains a table that displays participation rates by extent of participation in post-secondary activities including on-the-job training, off-the-job training, college and military. These figures are divided by level of final educational attainment and by gender. Their table is reproduced in Section C.3 of the Web Appendix (http://jenni.uchicago.edu/GEDHandbookChapter/).

[30] Sampling variation may explain this trend across NLSY79 and NLSY97 samples given that relatively few GEDs attempt post-secondary training. Another possible factor, discussed below, is that the composition of GED test takers has changed for the worse.

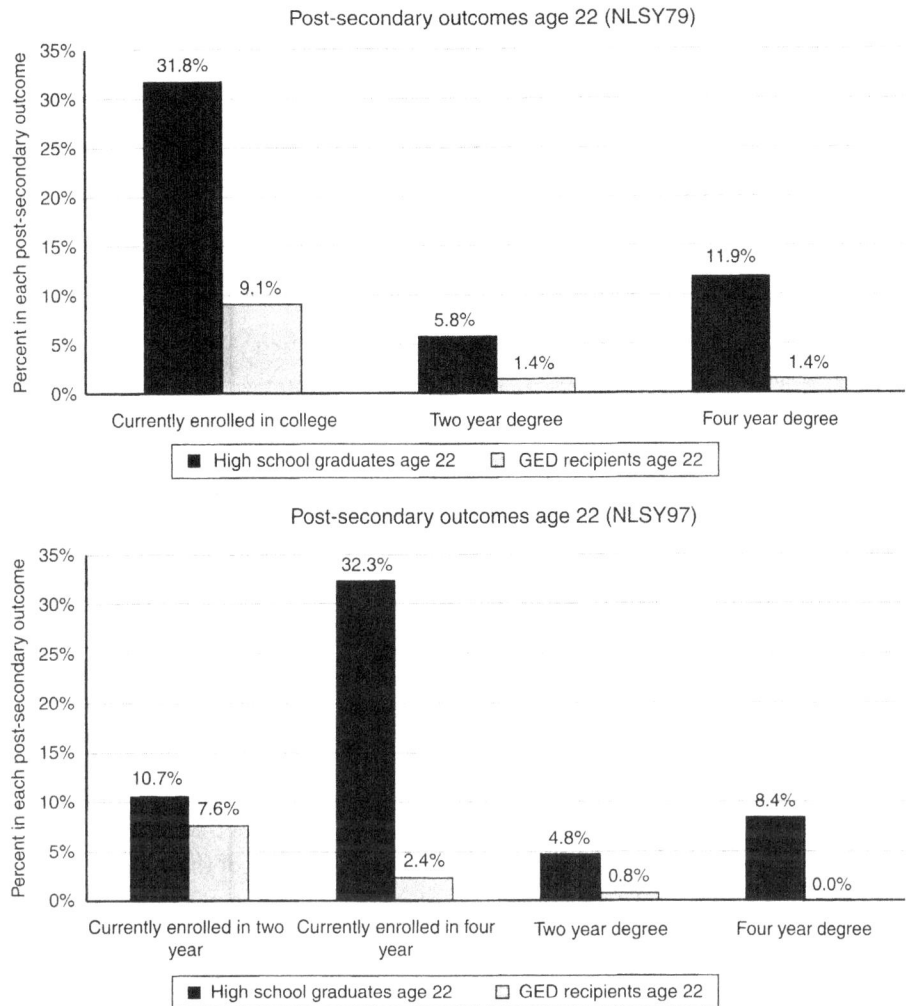

Figure 9.16 Post-secondary educational attainment at age 22 by high school certification type (all demographic groups). *Source:* National Longitudinal Survey of Youth 1979 (NSLY79) and the National Longitudinal Survey of Youth 1997 (NLSY97). Notes: Calculations are based on the cross-sectional subsample of each survey which are drawn to be representative of the full population. "Currently Enrolled in" variables are those who reported no two or four year degrees but reported being enrolled in college at age 22. "Four Year Degree" and "Two Year Degree" represent individuals who have earned such a degree by age 22.

qualitative findings and approaches of selected papers in this literature is presented in Table 9.9.

Cameron and Heckman (1993) calculate the option value or expected benefit of GED receipt through a wide array of types of post-secondary training—on- and off-the-job

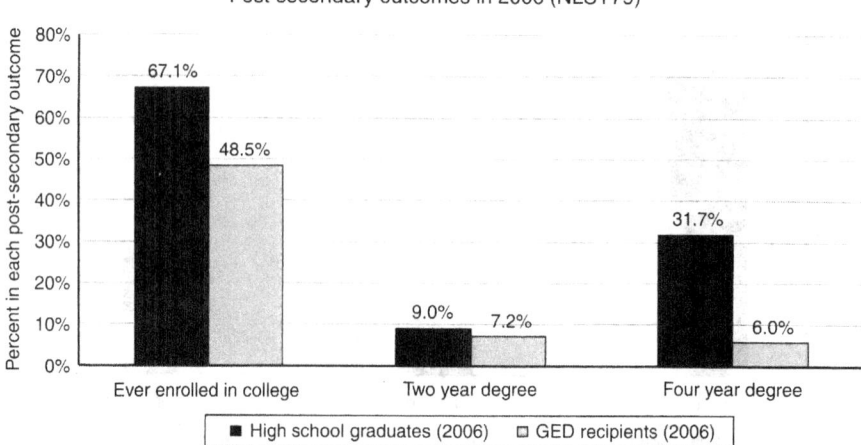

Figure 9.17 Post-secondary educational attainment in 2006 for the NLSY79 sample by high school certifcation type (all demographic groups). *Source:* National Longitudinal Survey of Youth 1979 (NSLY79). Notes: Calculations are based on the cross-sectional subsample of the NLSY79. "Ever Enrolled in College" is defined for the case that individuals ever report enrolling in college and is not conditional on completing any college.

training, military service, and two and four year college—as the benefit to each type of training times the expected amount of training obtained.[31] They find that the wage benefit associated with further education is much larger than the direct effect of GED receipt. Murnane et al. (1999) find strongly significant hourly wage and income premiums conditional on receiving these types of training, but note that few GEDs receive them. Murnane et al. (1997) use the same NLSY79 data as both of these studies and confirm that, net of controls, GEDs pursue more of these types of post-secondary education than dropouts, but that the predicted rates of completion are very low.

Heckman, Stixrud, and Urzua (2006), Heckman, Urzua, and Veramendi (2010), and Heckman and Urzua (2010) study the probability of selecting higher levels of educational attainment as a function of cognitive and noncognitive skills.[32] They find that both cognitive and noncognitive skills predict which individuals will drop out and use the GED for higher levels of education. Each approach studies the net present value (NPV) of income for individuals of a given skill set and choice of education level. Heckman and Urzua (2010) use a dynamic discrete choice framework where individuals make a sequence of

---

[31] Grubb (2002) surveys work that compares the wage and earnings returns to study in two year and four year colleges in terms of both completed degrees and individual credits earned at each type of institution. Whereas the value of a completed four year (bachelor's) degree is decisively higher than that for a complete two year (associate's) degree, there is no consensus on which type of college is associated with higher returns to earned credits that are not associated with degree completion.

[32] Like Heckman et al. (2006), Heckman and Urzua (2010) use the Rosenberg and Rotter scores to measure noncognitive ability.

Table 9.9 Literature Summary—Outcomes Pertaining to Post-Secondary Education through the GED

Study	Data	Population	Method/Identification	GED Effect	Findings
Cameron and Heckman (1993)	NLSY79 (1979–1987)	White males	Correction for self-selection into working status	1/0 GED × college[1]	Wage: no effect
Murnane, Willett, and Boudett (1997)	NLSY79 (1979–1991)	Males and females	Probit	1/0 GED, (1/0 GED) × post-GED work experience	Probability of acquiring training: (+,★★★) if Female
					Probability of acquiring training: no effect if Male
					Probability of attending college: (+,★★★) if Female and Male
Heckman and Urzua (2010)	NLSY79 (1979–2006)	White males	Dynamic decision framework, latent factor analysis	(1/0 GED) × (cognitive ability, noncognitive ability)	Educational option value: increasing in cognitive, noncognitive skills

Notes: [1] "1/0" refers to a binary indicator of the associated variable. For example, under GED Effect "1/0 GED" refers to 1 = receives GED, 0 = does not, indicating a simple binary treatment effect.
The study samples are statistically representative of the U.S unless otherwise indicated in the "Population" field. The "Findings" field codes no statistically significant effect as "No Effect," and otherwise shows (<indicator of a positive or negative finding>, <level of significance>) where ★ = $p < .10$, ★★ = $p < .05$, and ★★★ = $p < .01$.
See the Web Appendix (http://jenni.uchicago.edu/GEDHandbookChapter/) for tables with more detail on each paper's outcomes examined, lists of regressors, and point estimates for each regression specification.

decisions based on their expected income returns and psychological costs and payoffs (i.e. nonpecuniary factors that influence individual decisions beyond just income returns). Heckman and Urzua (2010) estimate "option values," which are the benefits conferred by completing one stage of education in terms of access to the returns of later stages of education. The option value associated with an educational choice at a given level of education is defined as the NPV of future educational decisions that choice opens up, net of the NPV of staying at the same level of education. For an individual with a given set of cognitive and noncognitive skills, the option value of the GED equals the returns that individual would receive from post-secondary education multiplied by the probability that they would choose and successfully complete that education.

Figure 9.18 shows for white males the respective probabilities of being a terminal dropout and of obtaining a GED based on population deciles of cognitive and noncognitive ability. "1" represents the lowest decile and "10" represents the highest. The first panel (A) shows that the probability of being a terminal dropout is primarily associated with low cognitive ability. The second panel (B) shows that, relative to the probability of dropping out, the probability of obtaining a GED is higher for higher levels of cognitive ability, and is higher for *lower* levels of noncognitive ability.

Figure 9.19 shows the estimated option values of the GED as a function of cognitive and noncognitive ability. The option value increases sharply in both cognitive and noncognitive ability. The axes of this graph represent population deciles. Very few dropouts are in the upper deciles of cognitive or noncognitive ability. As is evident from Figure 9.18(B), few individuals have the skills that produce a high option value for GED certification.

4. CHANGES AND GROWTH IN THE GED TEST TAKING POPULATION

Given the low returns to GED certification for the majority of GED test takers, the question remains why GED certification has reached such a large scale and continues to grow. As shown in Figure 9.1, the GED program grew from 50,000 takers in 1960 to over one million in 2001. A recent increase in the test's difficulty paired with the introduction of a new test series led to a decrease in takers in 2002, but growth resumed afterward with 700,000 people taking the test in 2008. In this section we review several explanations for the growth of the GED testing program over time. We show the significant role of government programs which both directly and indirectly subsidize the cost of GED certification. Much of the recent growth has occurred in populations such as younger teenagers and the incarcerated, populations that the literature shows have low expected benefit to GED certification.

4.1 Government education and training programs

Many government educational and job training programs have adopted the GED as a second chance program. These include government programs such as Job Corps, state

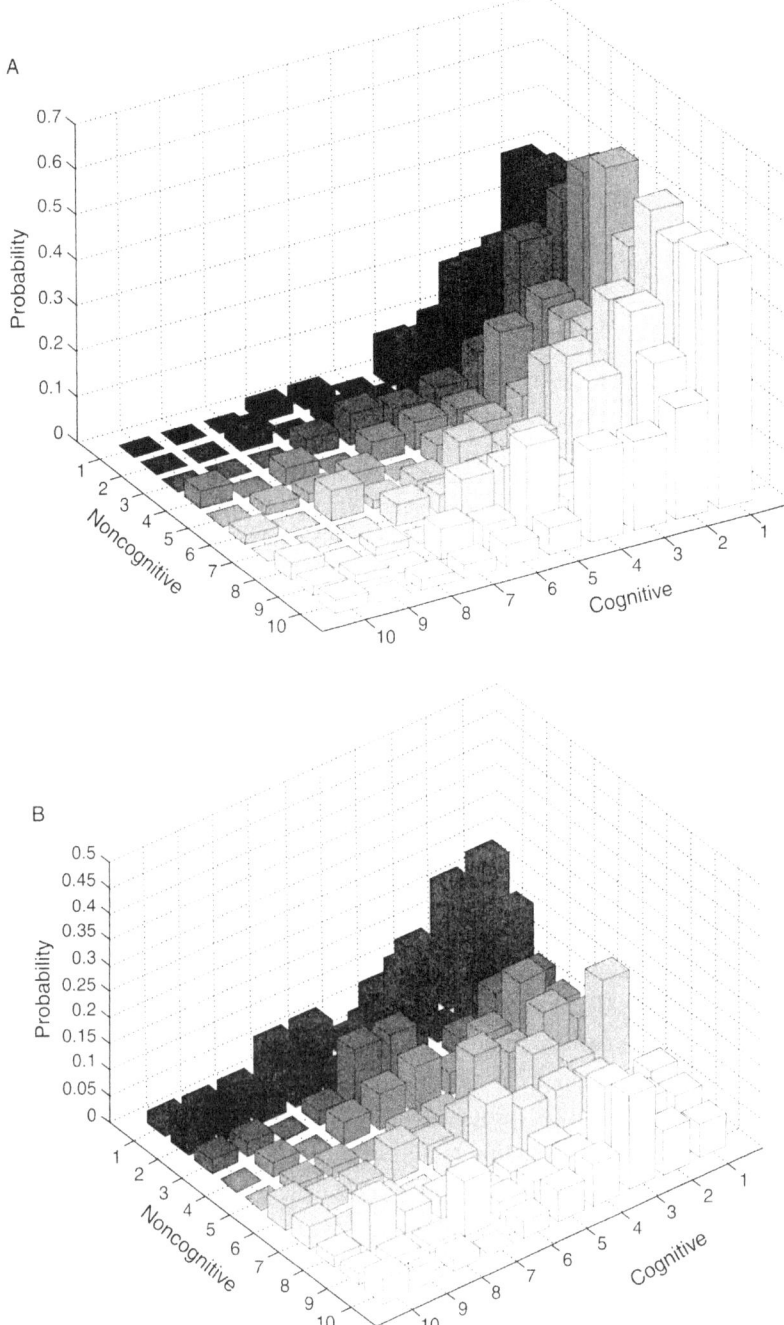

Figure 9.18 Distribution of probability of dropping out (A) and GED receipt (B) by cognitive and noncognitive ability (white males). *Source:* Reproduced from Heckman and Urzua (2010). Notes: x and y axes represent deciles of cognitive and noncognitive factors as defined in this section. "1" represents the lowest decile and "10" represents the highest decile.

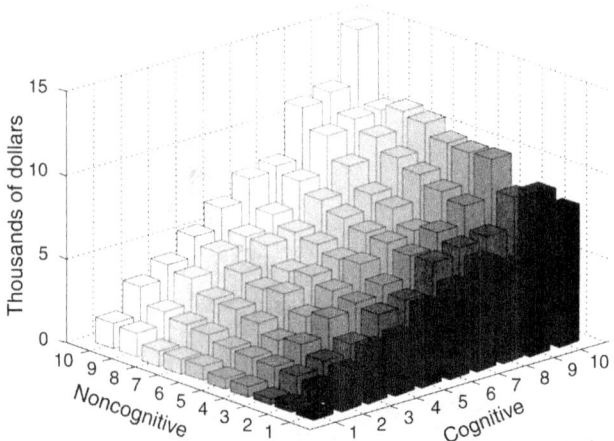

Figure 9.19 Distribution of GED option values by cognitive and noncognitive ability deciles for white males. *Source:* Reproduced from Heckman and Urzua (2010). Notes: Option value of GED certification for 17-year-old high school dropouts. x and y axes represent deciles of cognitive and noncognitive factors as defined in this section. "1" represents the lowest decile and "10" represents the highest decile.

anti-poverty programs,[33] and Adult Education programs. The GED test is used as a standardized, external measure of success for programs providing education. Figure 9.20 shows that 50% of individuals in the NLSY97 report obtaining the GED through either Adult Education programs or another job training program, demonstrating the role these government programs play in promoting the GED.

Adult Education is the largest government program promoting and subsidizing GED preparation and certification. The Adult Basic Education Act was signed into law in 1964. It was intended to provide funding for educating people aged 18 and older who lacked basic skills such as reading and basic arithmetic (National Advisory Council on Adult Education (1980)). The program expanded in 1970 to include Adult Secondary Education (ASE), which focused on high school-level learning (Rose (1991)).[34] The GED was quickly adopted by ASE programs as both a goal and a metric of program success. Adult Education programs are not homogeneous. They range from stand-alone GED classes to programs bundling job and vocational training with GED preparation.

---

[33] One example, documented in Quinn (2002), is of welfare reform initiatives in Ohio which paid mothers for sending their teenagers to attend GED classes.

[34] With the introduction of ASE, the age requirement was decreased to 16. Adult education was extended to incarcerated populations in 1981, though total expenditures on incarcerated education programs was capped at 20% of total Adult Education funding.

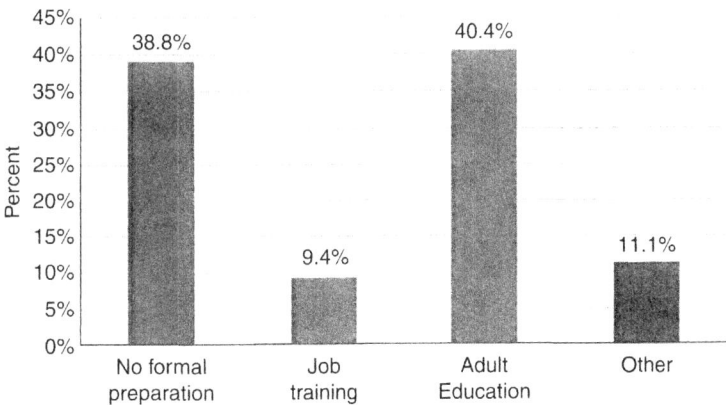

Figure 9.20 Route to GED certification taken by NLSY97 GED recipients. *Source:* National Longitudinal Survey of Youth 1997 (NLSY97). Notes: Statistics include all individuals who earn a GED by 2007.

Adult Education is a significant producer of GED certificates. In 1975, 26% of GED credentials were issued through Adult Education, increasing to 40% by 1980 and 50% in 1990 (U.S. Department of Education (Various years)). In 1995, six times as many people achieved a GED rather than a traditional high school diploma through Adult Education (National Advisory Council on Adult Education (Various years)). McLaughlin et al. (2009) examine the preparation methods for 90,000 GED test takers, and find that 46% of the sample took the GED through an Adult Education program.[35] Figure 9.21 shows Adult Education funding (both state and federal, in year 2000 dollars) graphed against the number of GED test takers. Expansion of Adult Basic Education promoted the growth of the GED. Figure 9.22 shows the proportions of individuals taking different routes of preparation for the GED test.

4.2 Changes in the costs and benefits to education

The costs and benefits of being a dropout, of GED certification, and of college completion have changed over time. These shifts play key roles in determining who selects into GED certification. As discussed in Section 2, the wage premium associated with getting any level of education above that of dropping out has been stable or increasing for both males and females in the last 25 years.

At the same time, both the financial and effort costs to education have changed. The difficulty of high school completion has increased in terms of class hours needed

---

[35] These 90,000 were chosen from a larger sample, removing individuals facing institutional influences on testing such as those in states requiring a practice test or being in prison.

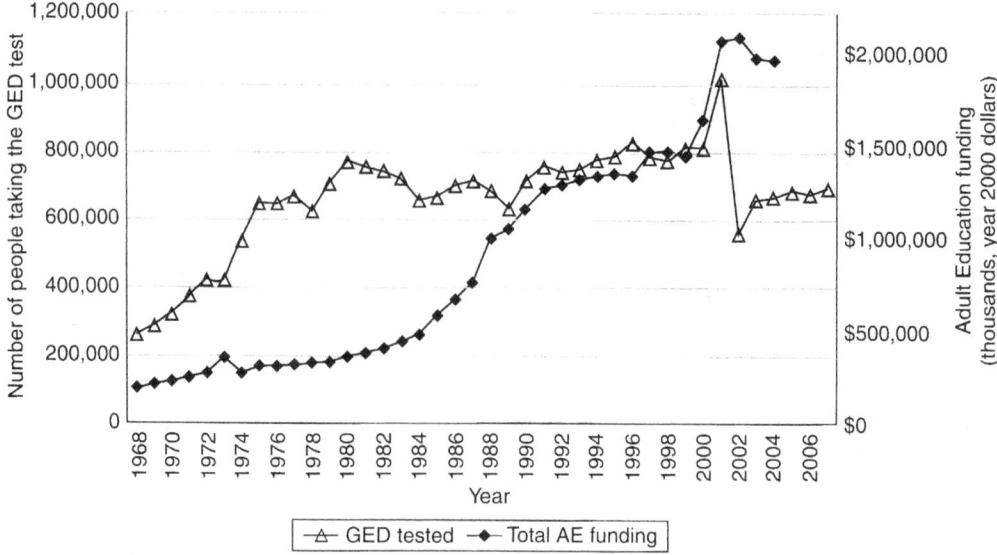

Figure 9.21 Adult Education funding and GED test taking. *Source:* GED Testing Service (1958–2008), U.S. Department of Education (Various years), and National Advisory Council on Adult Education (Various years).

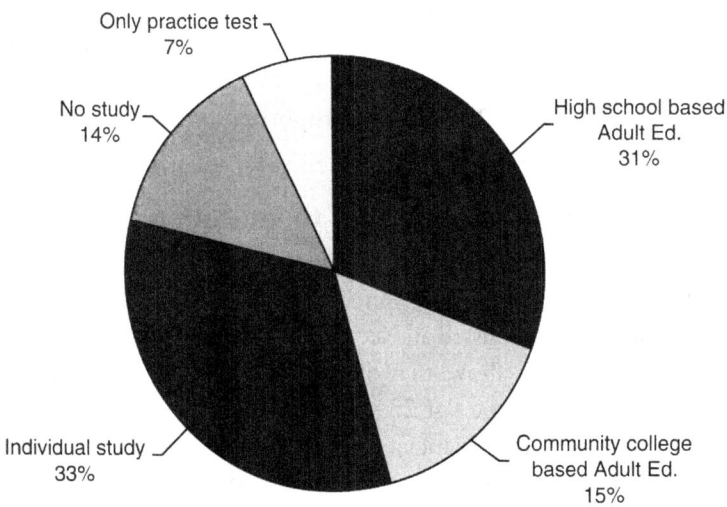

Figure 9.22 GED test takers by study type. *Source:* Constructed from McLaughlin et al. (2009). Notes: Results are from 90,000 test takers fitting into these categories without other restrictions on test taking such as being required to take a pretest in one's state of residence or being incarcerated.

to graduate (measured in Carnegie Units[36]) and through implementation of "exit exams" that must be passed in order to graduate. The late 1980s saw growth in the number of Carnegie Units required for graduation increasing from an average of 13.5 in 1985 to 17.4 in 1990. Only one state required an exit exam to earn a high school diploma in 1980, increasing to 22 states by 2008. Warren et al. (2006) show that completion rates decrease, and 16-to-19-year-old GED testing rates increase when high school exit exams are introduced. The increasing difficulty of high school may induce more students to drop out or to GED certify thinking that they can then go straight to college.

The monetary costs of college have also grown in the last three decades. From 1985 to 2005 the real cost of public and private four year colleges grew, respectively, by 95% and 83% (National Center for Education Statistics (Various years)). On the other hand, federal assistance may have lowered the cost for some individuals.[37] The establishment of Pell grants in 1972 decreased the costs of post-secondary education for individuals with high school–level credentials, including the GED. Figure 9.23 displays Pell grant

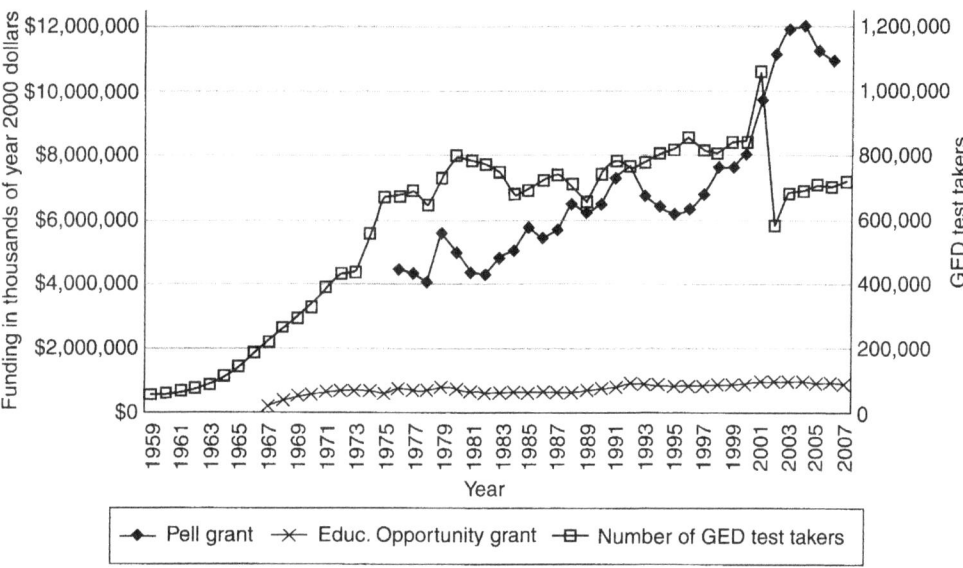

Figure 9.23 Federal aid for post-secondary education and GED test takers. *Source:* "2000 Status Report on the Pell Grant Program," Federal Campus-Based Programs Data Book (1998, 1999, 2000, 2001), U.S. Census Bureau, and GED Testing Service (1958–2008).

---

[36] Carnegie Units are standard measures of class hours. One Carnegie Unit is equivalent to one year-long high school class.
[37] See Section C of the Web Appendix (*http://jenni.uchicago.edu/GEDHandbookChapter/*) for the full trends of Carnegie Units, high school exit exams, and tuition costs of college.

funding and GED test taking rates across time. The spike in the average age of GED test takers in 1974, shown in Figure 9.26, is due to a number of older dropouts seeking the GED to become eligible for Pell grants when they first became available. This demonstrates the responsiveness of GED test taking to incentives to participate in complementary programs.

Monetary costs of GED certification have always been nominal. Testing fees for taking the GED range from $0 to $100, and enrollment in programs such as Adult Education often leads to reduced-fee or free testing (GED Testing Service (1958–2008)). On the other hand, the difficulty of passing the GED test has increased over time. National minimum difficulty has increased three times, but many states have consistently required higher passing standards. Figure 9.24 displays the population-weighted average GED difficulty, measured by the percentage of graduation-bound high school seniors estimated to be able to pass the GED in a single try. The effect of an increase in the difficulty of the test is seen in the dramatic decline in 2001 shown in Figure 9.23.

Incarceration and prison education The number of incarcerated individuals in the United States has grown rapidly since the mid-1970s. Figure 9.25 plots the total incarceration rate from 1926 to 2005, adding racial breakdowns starting in 1981. Growth occurs across all race groups, with a disproportionate amount coming from blacks. Faced with a growing population of the incarcerated, prison educational

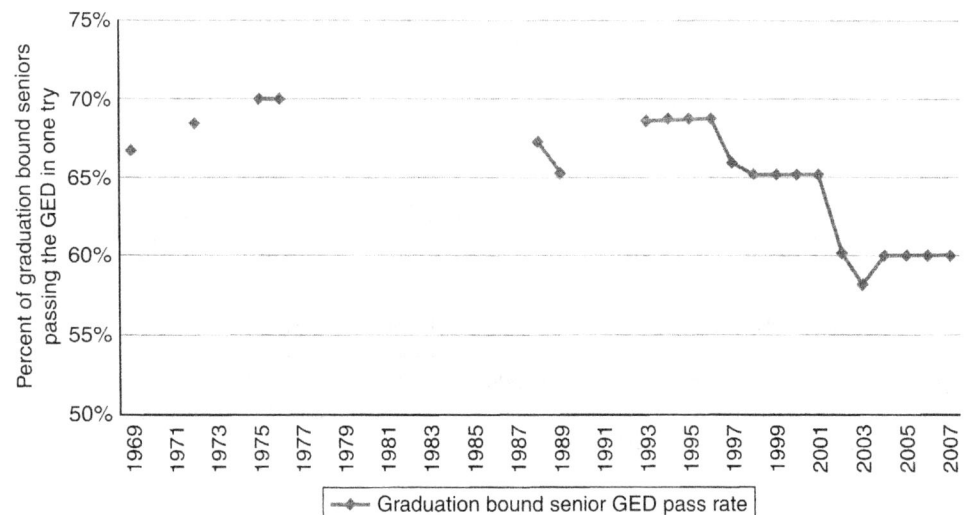

Figure 9.24 Estimated percent of graduation bound high school seniors able to pass the GED In first try. *Source:* GED Testing Service (2009), GED Testing Service (1958–2008), and GED Testing Service (Various years). Notes: Numbers are population weighted averages of State Requirements. Only years with 40 or more states reporting the passing requirement are displayed. Gaps are due to missing data.

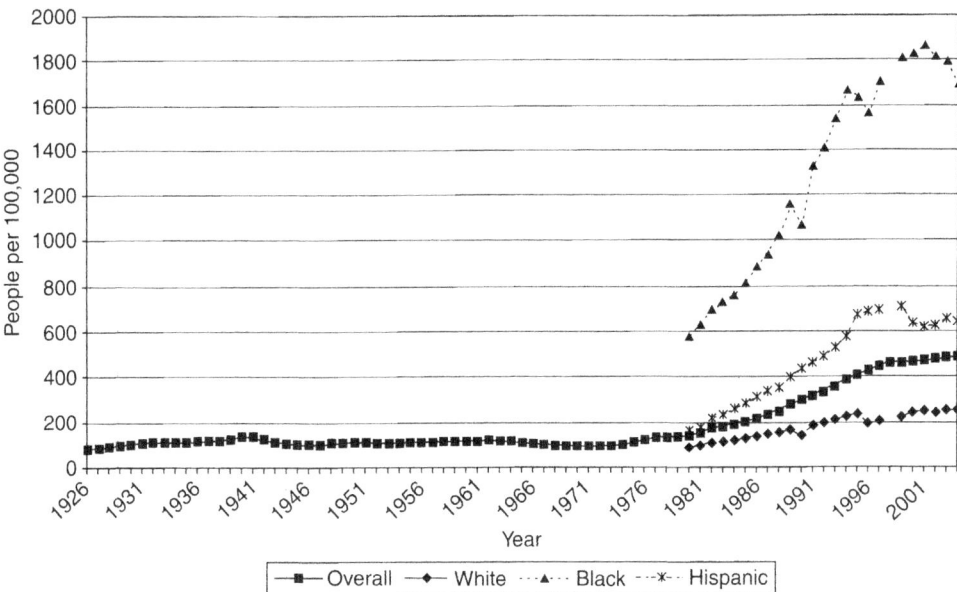

Figure 9.25 Growth in incarcerated populations by race. *Source*: Reproduced from Heckman and LaFontaine (2010). Bureau of Justice Statistics and the U.S. Census Bureau. Notes: Based on the U.S. Census Bureau estimated resident population, as of December 31 of each given year. Includes all persons under jurisdiction of federal and state authorities rather than those in the custody of such authorities. Represents inmates sentenced to minimum term of more than a year.

programs have been promoted on the basis of the belief that education will decrease recidivism. The GED has quickly become a key ingredient in prison education programs (United States Sentencing Commission (2009)). In federal prisons, inmates without a secondary degree are required to complete 240 hours of class work, or to GED certify (United States Sentencing Commission (2009)). Incarcerated individuals can qualify for monetary compensation for earning a GED as well as earning credits toward early release (Ekstrand (2001), U.S. Department of Justice (2008)). Furthermore, in 1995, the incarcerated made up 9% of all Adult Education participants (National Advisory Council on Adult Education (Various years)). A Bureau of Justice Statistics (BJS) special report states that in 1997, 26% of all prison inmates earned a GED in prison (Harlow, 2003).[38] Table 9.10 shows how the percent of GEDs produced in prison has grown consistently from 1994 to 2005. Overall, the GED has become a near-mandatory component of the prison education system. The growth of prison GEDs weakens its overall signaling value by its association with criminality.

---

[38] The BJS brief does not explain their methodology and there may be survey bias (people in prison longer are more likely to get GED and surveyed) or other statistical concerns.

Table 9.10 Percentage of GEDs Obtained in Prison Across Time

Year	Coverage	State Prisons	Federal Prisons	Total
1994	57.1%	6.7%	1.4%	8.1%
1995	71.9%	8.6%	1.2%	9.8%
1996	72.5%	9.2%	1.2%	10.4%
1997	73.1%	9.4%	1.4%	10.8%
1998	76.2%	9.6%	1.4%	11.0%
1999	75.4%	9.8%	1.5%	11.3%
2000	79.5%	9.8%	1.6%	11.4%
2001	55.9%	7.9%	1.6%	9.5%
2002	58.0%	11.3%	1.7%	13.0%
2003	58.4%	10.2%	1.6%	11.8%
2004	67.3%	11.0%	1.8%	12.8%
2005	60.5%	11.8%	1.8%	13.6%

Reproduced from Heckman and LaFontaine (2010). Sources: Various state Departments of Corrections and GED offices. Data for federal prisoners from GED Testing Service "Who took the GED?" (1958–2008).
Notes: State coverage represents the total number of GED credentials issued in those states with information available as a percentage of total GED credentials in the U.S. Total percentage of GED credentials issued in state prisons represent credentials issued in correctional institutions of those states that have prison information for a given year as a percentage of total GED credentials issued in those states. The percentage of GED credentials issued in federal prisons is calculated on total credentials issued in the U.S. (including federal prisons). Credentials issued in insular areas, freely associated states, Canada, overseas locations, and military bases are excluded.

Tyler and Kling (2007) study the post-release earnings of individuals who studied for the GED in prison. They use longitudinal data from the Florida Department of Corrections and other Florida state agencies to compare pre- and post-incarceration earnings for those who study for and receive GEDs. They find that GED preparation and receipt are associated with an increase in earnings for the first three years after release, but fade thereafter. The positive initial impact might be explained by non-random institutional sorting of individuals and by self-selection. To net out self-selection, the authors also compare earnings of those obtaining a GED with those that take GED preparation classes but do not earn a credential. They find no effect. Because both of these populations undertook some amount of study, this finding rules out a signaling effect of the GED.

There is a substantial literature that studies the impact of prison-based educational systems with a focus on recidivism, but this work faces significant challenges in addressing the endogeneity of educational attainment and the lack of baseline data on prior to imprisonment. Gaes (2009) surveys this literature and highlights the effect of GED receipt, as well as vocational training and Adult Basic Education training, on post-release wages and recidivism. Results from studies that he identifies as "methodologically sound" are generally mixed with effects that are either very modest or statistically insignificant.

4.3 Growth in high school–age test takers

In 1955, as more states began offering the GED to civilians, the American Council of Education implemented a minimum age of 20 for taking the GED test to prevent teen-aged students from seeking the GED as a replacement for high school (Quinn (2002)). In 1970, the national age requirement was lowered to 18. Following a period between 1981 and 1992 where there was no national age requirement, the national minimum has been set at 16. Many states set age requirements above the national minimum. Figure 9.26 shows the population-weighted average national age requirement for taking the GED and the average age of GED test takers over time. The sharp fall in both age requirement and average age in the early 1970s represents the expansion of the population eligible to take the GED.

Originally, states granted exceptions to age requirements in specific cases, such as teenage pregnancy. The number of exceptions to age restrictions has greatly increased over time, leading to growth in the number of 16-to-17-year-olds attempting the GED. The two relevant age restrictions for taking the GED are the statutory age requirement and, indirectly, the minimum age that students can drop out of high

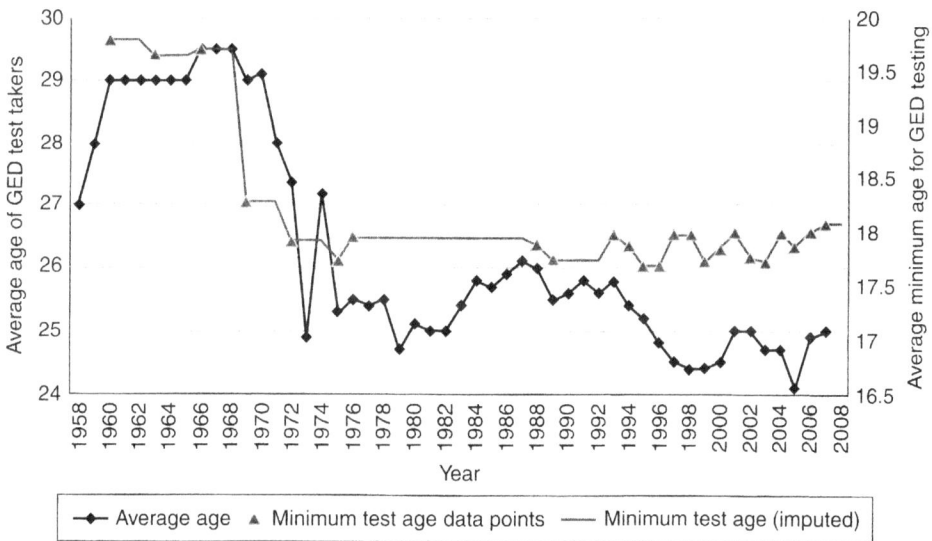

Figure 9.26 Minimum age requirement and average GED testing age. *Source:* GED Testing Service (1958–2008). Notes: The population-weighted average minimum age is calculated by weighting the states' age requirements by the state's total population. The national age requirement is assigned to states with requirements below the national age requirement.

school. Figure 9.27 plots the percentage of GED test takers qualifying as age exceptions to the minimum testing age, and the percentage of GED test takers qualifying as both an exception to the minimum testing age and the minimum age for compulsory high school attendance. Both series are increasing with GED age exceptions growing from 6% in 1980 to nearly 14% in 2007, and dual exceptions growing from 1% in 1990 to over 6% in 2007 (Humphries (2010)).

Trends in the age composition of GED takers reflect these changes in eligibility and institutional allowances. Figure 9.28 shows the number of test takers by age. The first panel shows that growth since the early 1980s is almost completely attributable to growth in 16-to-19-year-old takers. Test taking rates were distinguished between 16-to-17-year-old and 18-to-19-year-old takers in 1980. The second panel shows that 16-to-17-year-olds are responsible for virtually all growth in GED test taking within the 16-to-19 age group. Because these individuals are still of high school age, their growth as a group raises the question of whether the GED is serving as a true second chance opportunity or as a substitute for a more valuable high school degree. Of particular concern is the possibility that teenagers with the lowest levels of noncognitive skills are the most likely to opt out of high school in order to receive the GED and least likely to benefit from doing so.

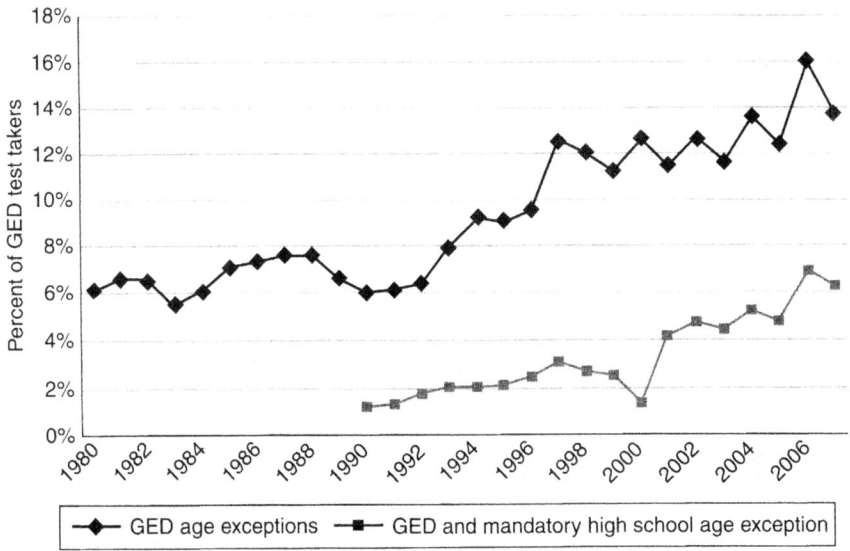

Figure 9.27 GED test takers qualifying as exceptions to age requirements. *Sources:* Reproduced from Humphries (2010). GED Testing Service (1958–2008), National Center for Educational Statistics Data. Notes: "GED Age Exceptions" are individuals taking the GED at ages below the minimum GED testing age. "GED & Mandatory High School Age Exceptions" are individuals from "GED Age Exceptions" who are also below the compulsory schooling age in their state, making them double exceptions.

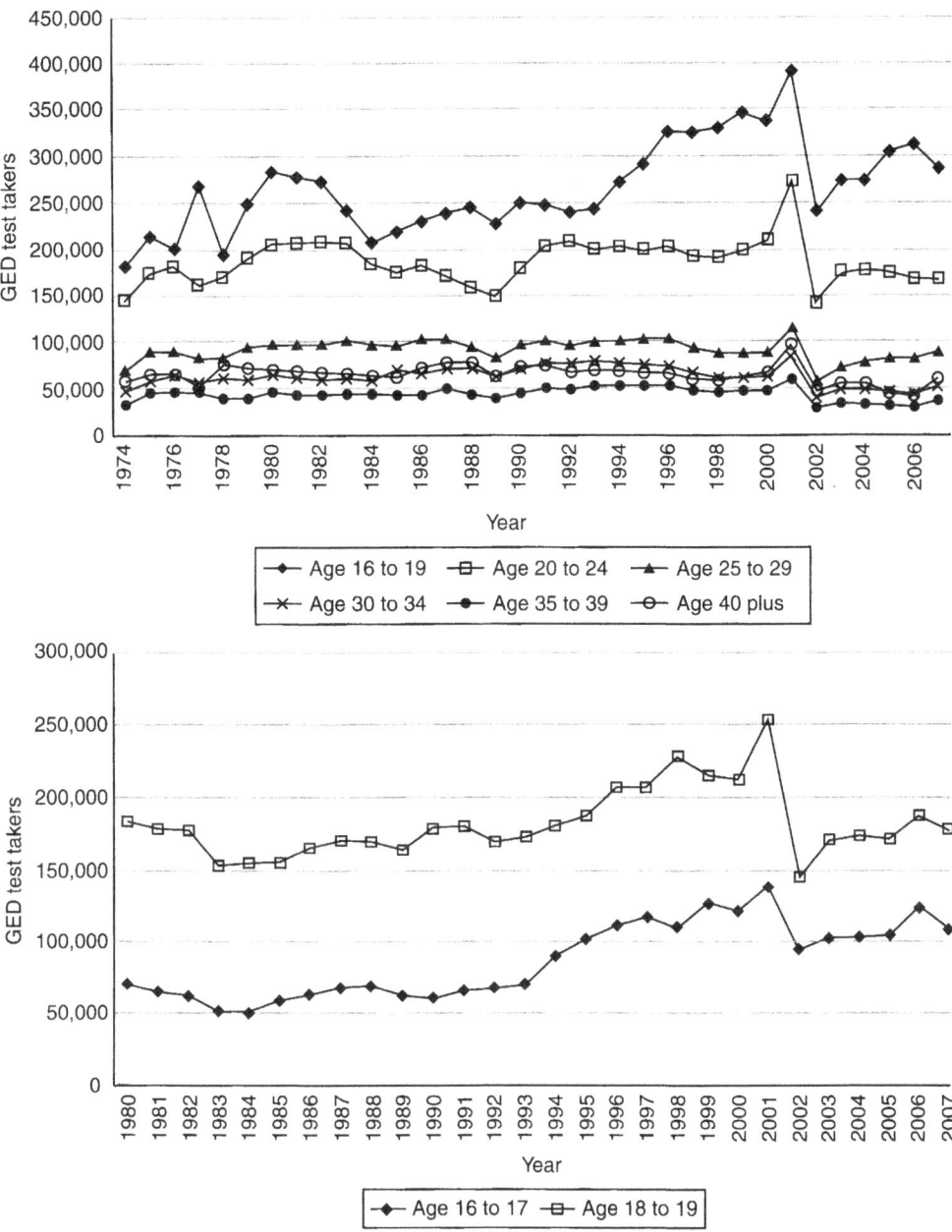

Figure 9.28 Test-taking populations by age. *Source:* GED Testing Service (1958–2008). Notes: 1974 is the year that test taking rates by age were first reported. Starting in 1980 the 16-to-19 age category is divided into 16-to-17 and 18-to-19-year-olds.

The decision-making process of teens may lead them to make choices that restrict their educational paths and earnings in a way that they later regret.[39] Given questionable teen decision-making, several institutional practices may increase the rate of ill-advised dropping out. Many state-issued GED certificates have names such as "Kansas State High School Diploma" or "Maryland High School Diploma" which mislead students into false expectations of equivalence with traditional high school (GED Testing Service (1958–2008)).

The GED Option Programs represent another institutional path to GED certification for high school students. In some states, the American Council on Education has approved programs which directly target at-risk students in high school and guide them toward GED certification. While states set their own determination of "at-risk," this commonly means students at risk of not graduating with their class.[40] Each state has its own set of requirements on what structure the GED Option Program takes and who is eligible. This introduces a range in the rigor of preparation across the 11 participating states. States vary in the hours of preparation required per week, requirements of complementary career-based training, practice-test policies, and in the study hours elicited from participants.[41] These programs have not been evaluated for their effect on labor market outcomes, but represent an institutional shift toward younger populations.

4.4 Summing up the sources of growth of GEDs

Since its introduction, the GED has grown rapidly. This rapid growth occurs despite the GED's low economic return. The growth of the GED can be credited to the adoption of the GED by government and non-profit entities, as well as the expansion of the GED into new populations. Figure 9.29 shows the number of total credentials issued each year, as well as the number of credentials contributed by Adult Education, prison populations, 16-to-17-year-old GED test takers, and 18-to-19-year-old GED test takers. These four categories each account for a large percentage of the credentials issued. Unfortunately, the promotion of the GED has pushed it further from

---

[39] The literature in psychology formally recognizes this as time-inconsistent preferences, where teens may discount future outcomes at a higher rate than they would at full maturity. Recent work in neuroscience gives concrete support to the common notion that teens in late adolescence—the period when the decision to drop out is made—make decisions that are inconsistent with their adult preferences. See Steinberg (2007) and Steinberg (2008).

[40] See the GED Option Statistical Report (GED Testing Service (2008)) for more detail on these programs.

[41] Virginia, for example, has a demanding Option Program requiring 15 hours of academic preparation per week, work- or career-based training for 10 hours a week, and scores of 450 on each subsection of the official practice test (higher than the 410 minimum/450 average state passing requirement for the GED) before GED certification is allowed. On the other hand, Oregon allows the requirements to be set to a much higher degree by the institution, allowing much more flexibility including self-study and technology-assisted study as a means of GED preparation. Similarly, the hours of studying and days enrolled in the option program also vary greatly. For example, Oregon's GED Option participants reported studying for a median of 20 hours with few explicit requirements. Louisiana, on the other hand, reported a mean of 150 hours and require 15 hours of academic preparation per week and 10 hours a week of job training.

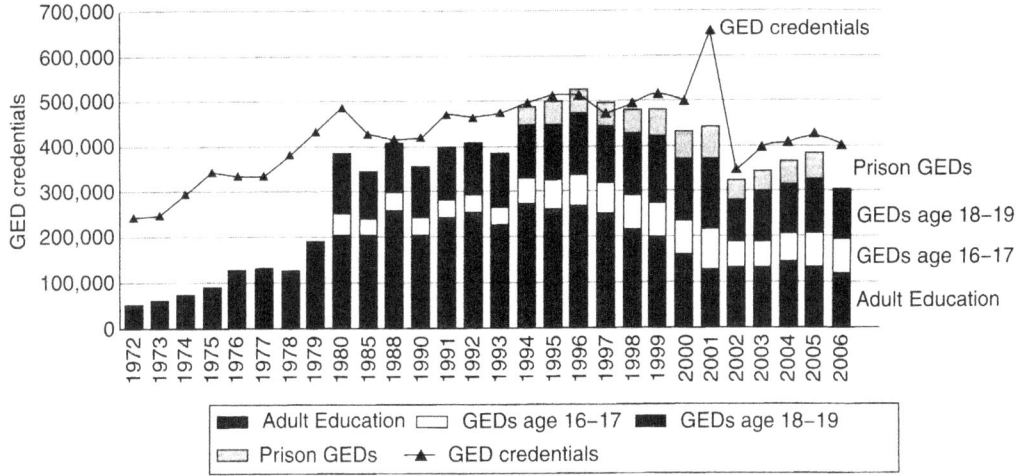

Figure 9.29 Decomposing growth in GED credentials. *Sources:* GED Testing Service (1958–2008), National Advisory Council on Adult Education (Various years), National Center for Education Statistics (Various years), U.S. Department of Education (Various years), and Heckman and LaFontaine (2010). Notes: The categories of GED credentials are not mutually exclusive; an individual may be counted in multiple categories. Years missing specific categories are due to missing data. Specific years have been excluded from the graph due to highly incomplete data. Prior to 1990, the age categories are imputed from the percent of GED test *takers* in the specific age category times the number of *credentials*. Adult Education statistics did not separate between GEDs and high school diplomas after 1996. From 1997 to 2006 the numbers are imputed by multiplying the total number of GEDs and high school diplomas issued by the average ratio of GEDs to GEDs plus high school diplomas from 1991 to 1996.

subpopulations that might potentially benefit from it. The test has expanded to younger populations which provides adverse incentives to high school–age individuals discussed in more detail below. Figures 9.30 and 9.31 provide a timeline of key events in the growth of the GED.

5. ADVERSE CONSEQUENCES OF THE GED

The GED's low returns may be unfortunate, but one might argue that its low costs and low returns balance and may not do much harm. In this section we show that its availability and scale does cause harm. One concern is that the availability of the GED as an easier-to-obtain secondary credential induces many individuals to drop out of high school. The alternative to GED receipt for these individuals is high school completion and not dropping out. An additional harm arises from counting GEDs in graduation statistics. This practice hides declines in traditional high school graduation rates and thus has disguised educational problems. Finally, the practice of improperly counting the GED as a high school diploma generates biased estimates of the returns to education.

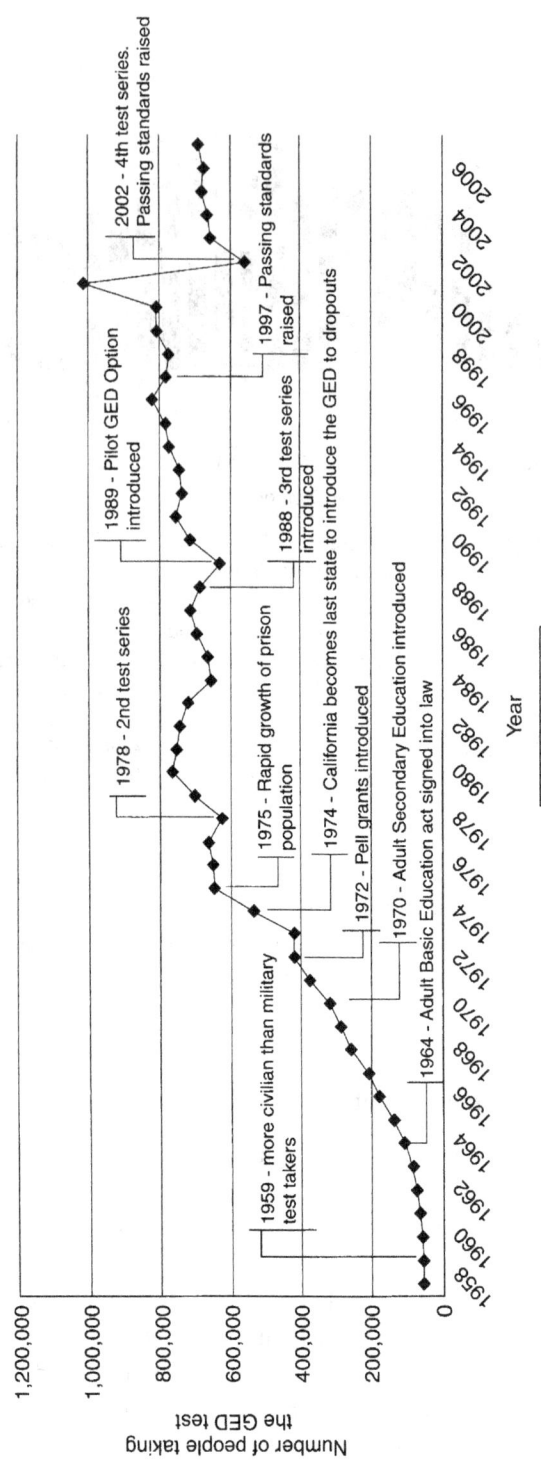

Figure 9.30 Key dates and the number of GED test takers. *Sources*: GED Testing Service (1958–2008), Quinn (2002), Rose (1991), GED Testing Service (2008), Heckman and LaFontaine (2010), and Boesel et al. (1998).

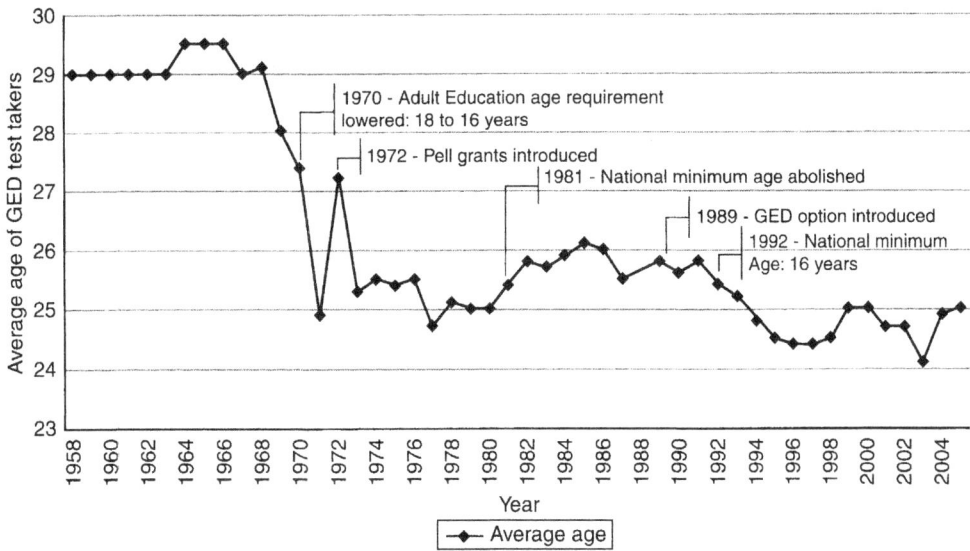

Figure 9.31 The average age of GED test takers and key changes in age policies. *Sources:* GED Testing Service (1958–2008), Quinn (2002), Rose (1991), GED Testing Service (2008), Heckman and LaFontaine (2010), and Boesel et al. (1998).

5.1 The GED induces would-be high school graduates to drop out

The availability of the test induces some students to drop out and seek a GED rather than persist in high school. Several papers in the literature demonstrate that changes in the relative costs of the GED certification and high school completion induce substitutions of one degree for the other at different margins. Lillard and DeCicca (2001) demonstrate that the number of students who drop out of high school (including GEDs) increases when the number of credits needed to graduate increases. They estimate that a standard deviation increase in the course graduation requirements in the U.S. would cause 26,000 to 65,000 individuals to drop out of high school. Chaplin (1999) provides descriptive evidence that high school–aged students are dropping out to take the GED and that requiring parental consent helps curb this practice. Humphries (2010) demonstrates that 16-to-17-year-old GED test taking rates respond to high school credit requirements, minimum high school dropout age, and the difficulty of the GED test. He estimates that a minimum dropout age of 18 policy would decrease state-wide GED test taking by 0.22% of the entire population of 16-to-17-year-olds. He also finds that an increase in the difficulty of the GED so that 10% fewer graduation-bound high school seniors could pass the test would decrease state-wide

GED test taking by 0.14% of the entire 16-to-17-year-old population.[42] Warren et al. (2006) demonstrate that 16-to-19-year-old GED test-taking rates respond to the presence of high school exit exams and other state high school policies. They report that a high school exit exam leads to a state-wide increase in GED test taking of 0.12% of the entire 16-to-19-year-old population.

Heckman et al. (2008) analyze two large natural experiments to study the effect of introducing the GED on inducing dropouts. The national minimum difficulty for passing the GED increased in 1997 which forced only a subset of states to increase their passing standards to be compliant. The increase raised the difficulty of the test so that only 60% rather than 66% of graduation-bound high school seniors would be able to pass the test on a single try. The study also looks at the effect of California's introduction of a GED credential in 1974. Difference-in-differences estimates show that these two policy changes resulted in a 1.3% decrease in dropout rates for states where the passing standard increased, and 3.1% fall in high school graduation rates when the GED became available.[43]

Humphries (2010) examines the effect of introducing GED Option Programs at the school district level using data from Oregon.[44] Using school district-level panel data from Oregon with fixed year and district effects, Humphries finds that introduction of these programs at the district level or in traditional high schools led to a fall of approximately 5% in four-year high school completion rates. Interestingly, in districts where the Option Program was only introduced in alternative institutions such as community colleges or charter schools, the effect was a decrease of only 1.8%.[45]

Heckman et al. (2008) and Humphries (2010) demonstrate that the GED induces some would-be high school graduates into dropping out, but we do not know which individuals drop out or how successful they would have been if they had stayed in high school. The dynamic model of Heckman and Urzua (2010) can be used to simulate counterfactuals. Table 9.11 contrasts the actual patterns of educational attainment of white males in the NLSY79 sample with predicted values if the GED were abolished. Not all GEDs persist as dropouts. Of the 3.7% of the sample that obtains a terminal GED or some college through the GED, only 2.3% remain as dropouts in the counterfactual state, whereas the rest either finish high school or complete higher levels of post-secondary education. While this line of structural research is still being refined, it has the promise of generating the likely effects on educational attainment arising from enforced age limits or increased test difficulty. The magnitudes in Table 9.11 are

---

[42] Median 16-to-17-year-old state population was 112,000 in year 2000.
[43] See Section E of the Web Appendix (*http://jenni.uchicago.edu/GEDHandbookChapter/*) for more in-depth description of these results.
[44] A full list of states implementing GED Option Programs can be found in GED Testing Service (2008).
[45] For further results see Section E of the Web Appendix (*http://jenni.uchicago.edu/GEDHandbookChapter/*).

Table 9.11 Simulated Response of Educational Attainment to Elimination of the GED

Schooling Level	Simulated with GED (1)	No GED (2)	Change in Rate (2)-(1)	% Change ((2)/(1)−1)%
Four Year College	25.5%	26.0%	0.5%	2.1%
Some Four Year College	7.0%	7.1%	0.1%	1.3%
Two Year College	7.2%	7.8%	0.6%	8.0%
Some Two Year College	10.2%	10.7%	0.6%	5.5%
Some College GED	2.5%	-		
High School Graduates	31.9%	34.0%	2.1%	6.5%
GEDs	3.7%	-		
High School Dropouts	12.0%	14.3%	2.4%	19.6%

Source: Reproduced from Heckman and Urzua (2010).
Note: The numbers in columns (1) and (2) are computed as fractions of the overall population.

broadly consistent with the estimates reported from natural experiments in Heckman et al. (2008).

5.2 The GED inflates high school graduation statistics

The high school graduation rate is a barometer of the health of American society and the skill level of its future workforce. Historically, the U.S. graduation rate continued to climb as schooling became increasingly important. This trend, however, counts GEDs as high school graduates. When GEDs are counted separately, the traditional high school graduation rate was falling until 2000.

Two commonly-used measures of the high school graduation rate are reported by the National Center of Education Statistics (NCES). The first is the "high school status completion rate" which counts the number of 18-to-24-year-olds possessing a high school credential and divides it by the population aged 18 to 24. The second is the "17-year-old graduation ratio," which is the number of diplomas issued in any given state divided by their 17-year-old population in a given year. The former includes the GED as a high school credential; the latter does not.

Figure 9.32 shows the time path of both measures, including the completion rate by race. The overall completion rate and 17-year-old graduation ratio were relatively similar in 1968 but diverged afterward. High school graduation was falling from the 1970s through about year 2000. The U.S. graduation rate has only recently returned to where it was 40 years ago.

The differences between status completion rates and the graduation ratio has previously been noted. Most of the gap comes from "alternative certifications" which are

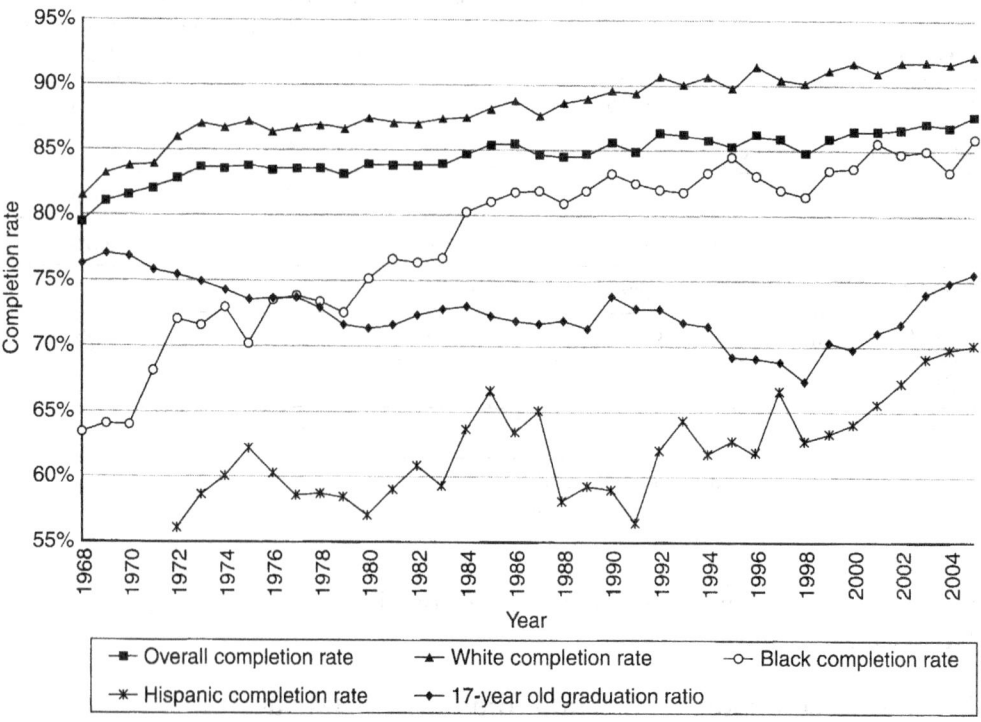

Figure 9.32 Trends in commonly-reported measures of high school graduation rates. *Source:* Reproduced from Heckman and LaFontaine (2010). Notes: Reproduced in part from the National Center for Educational Statistics (NCES) publication "Dropout Rates in the United States: 2005" (Laird et al. (2007)). Rates prior to 1972 are based on author's calculations using Current Population Survey (CPS) data. The status completion rate is the percentage of 18-to-24-year-olds not enrolled in secondary school who have a high school credential. High school credentials include regular diplomas and alternative credentials such as GED certificates. Hispanic ethnicity is not available before 1972. The 17-year-old graduation ratio is from the Digest of Education Statistics. HS graduates for the graduation ratio include both public and private school diplomas and exclude GED recipients and other certificates. October 17-year-old population estimates are obtained from Census Bureau P-20 reports from 1968–1971.

predominantly GEDs (Finn (1987)). Once the nonequivalence of GEDs to high school graduates is demonstrated, the growing gap in the status completion rate and graduation ratio becomes a great concern. Rather than an 88% graduation rate in the recent decade, estimates were reported as low as 66% as several researchers made efforts to construct correct high school graduation rates not counting GEDs as high school graduates (Greene (2001), Swanson (2004), Miao and Haney (2004), Warren (2005)). These corrected estimates varied depending on the data set and methodology used, leading to further confusion over which number was the "real" graduation rate.

Heckman and LaFontaine (2010) systematically examine each data set used in this debate and consider sources of bias in each data set in order to construct measures that are consistent across data sets.[46] They find that using year 2000 Census data, removing GEDs lowers overall graduation rates by 7.4%. Because of differential rates of alternative credentialing, graduation rates fall by different amounts for different groups: 8.1% for males, 6.6% for females, 10.3% for black males, and 8.7% for black females.

While the completion rates by race shown in Figure 9.32 show a decreasing white-black and white-Hispanic high school certification rate over time, those trends are fully explained by increasing rates of alternative certification. Figure 9.33 shows GED credentials as a percent of high school credentials issued broken down by race in 2005. GEDs account for 20% of black high school credentials, but only 11% of white credentials.[47] Over the last 40 years the minority education gap has been constant.

5.3 The GED obscures the actual returns to education

The misclassification of GEDs also affects estimates of the returns to education. While the dropout-to-high school and high school-to-college wage gaps have indeed been increasing, the GED misclassification is responsible for a sizable amount of this gap. Using the traditional CPS method of treating GED recipients and high school

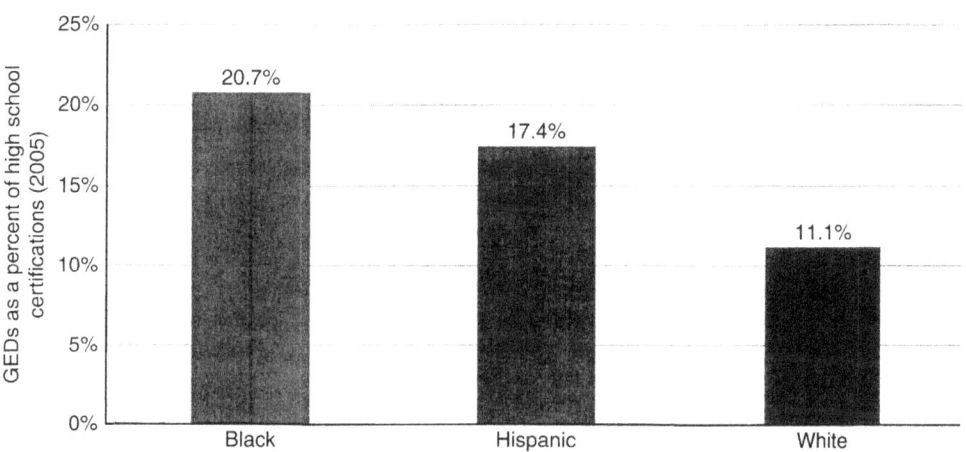

Figure 9.33 GEDs as a percent of HS credentials by race, 2005. *Source:* GED Testing Service (1958–2008).

---

[46] For bias extending beyond the GED across the Census, the Current Population Survey (CPS), and Common Core Data (CCD) see Heckman and LaFontaine (2010).

[47] See Section E of the Web Appendix (http://jenni.uchicago.edu/GEDHandbookChapter/) for tables demonstrating the differential effect on graduation rates for different races and genders of removing prisoners, immigrants, and military servicemen from calculations of the graduation rate.

graduates as equivalent, Cameron and Heckman (1993) estimate a 21% return to four year college completion. When classifying GEDs and high school graduates separately, the high school-to-college gap falls to 19.6%.

Heckman and LaFontaine (2006) show that the imputation method used by the CPS generates biased wages across educational levels. The CPS imputes missing wages by matching on socio-economic data using other observations in the same educational categories: 1) high school dropouts; 2) high school graduates with up to, but not including, a bachelor's degree; and 3) bachelor's degree or above. This procedure allocates missing GED wages with data drawn from high school graduates (including individuals with some college), and fills in missing high school graduate wages with data drawn from GEDs. Heckman and LaFontaine find that estimated returns to GED certification were overstated by 35% when CPS allocated wages are included for native-born males, and 25% for native-born females. Similarly, they find that excluding allocated earners lowers the returns to high school graduation for the full sample of males by 5% and the returns to college by 12%. The fact that the CPS increasingly reports missing values, coupled with the misallocation error of GED and high school wages, has led to increasingly biased estimates of the returns to education over time.

Table 9.12 displays evidence from three birth cohorts within the NLSY79 sample to compare how high school-to-college and dropout-to-high school wage differentials vary depending on how GED recipients are classified. Because the number of GED recipients grows from 9% of high school credentials to 20% across these birth cohorts, the bias the GED generates in returns to educational categories also increases over time. For the 1957–1958 birth cohort, GED misclassification accounts for 6.1% of the college-high school wage gap in log annual earnings. By the 1962–1964 birth cohort, GED misclassification grew to 9.5% of the college-high school wage gap in log annual earnings and 5.6% of the dropout-college wage gap.

6. CONCLUSION

This chapter reviews the scholarly literature on the General Educational Development certificate. The consensus in the literature is that the GED testing program does little good for the substantial majority of its takers in generating economic opportunity directly and in opening the door to post-secondary education. This finding is especially troubling given the size and rate of growth of the GED. Growth in the GED appears to be largely fueled by various government policies. Until recently, misclassification of the GED as a high school equivalent credential has hidden decreases in the high school graduation rate and has disguised the failure of minority graduation convergence. The study of the GED sheds considerable light on the value of noncognitive skills and the danger of relying solely on tests of scholastic aptitude to monitor the success of American educational policy.

Table 9.12 The Role of the GED in Explaining Rising educational Wage Gaps

A. Prevalence of GED as a	1957–1958 Birth Cohort	1959–1961 Birth Cohort	1962–1964 Birth
% of GED+HS Category	9.16%	13.82%	20.34%
% of GED+Dropout Category	38.29%	46.08%	60.14%
B. College-HS Wage Gap*			
Log Annual Earnings	.338	.411	.469
Log Weekly Wage	.297	.358	.418
Log Hourly Wage	.270	.311	.376
C. Bias in College-HS Gap from Counting GEDs as HS Graduates**			
Log Annual Earnings	.021	.030	.045
Log Weekly Wage	.010	.016	.025
Log Hourly Wage	.007	.010	.022
D. % of Current College-HS Gap Explained by GED			
Log Annual Earnings	6.1%	7.4%	9.5%
Log Weekly Wage	3.3%	4.5%	6.0%
Log Hourly Wage	2.6%	3.3%	5.9%
E. College-Dropout Wage Gap			
Log Annual Earnings	.635	.724	.747
Log Weekly Wage	.512	.593	.610
Log Hourly Wage	.474	.521	.555
F. Bias in College-Dropout Gap from Counting GEDs as HS Graduates†			
Log Annual Earnings	.029	.039	.056
Log Weekly Wage	.041	.051	.054
Log Hourly Wage	.044	.056	.049
G. % of Current College-Dropout Gap Explained by GED			
Log Annual Earnings	2.9%	3.9%	5.6%
Log Weekly Wage	4.1%	5.1%	5.4%
Log Hourly Wage	4.4%	5.6%	4.9%

Continued

Table 9.12 The Role of the GED in Explaining Rising educational Wage Gaps—continued

A. Prevalence of GED as a	1957–1958 Birth Cohort	1959–1961 Birth Cohort	1962–1964 Birth
Percentage of Overall Change Explained by GED Misclassification from 1957 to 1964			
	Annual Earnings	Weekly Wage	Hourly Wage
Growth in College-HS Gap	18.4%	12.8%	14.4%
Growth in College-Dropout Gap	23.7%	13.6%	5.5%

*Based on Model 1: Counting GEDs as HS graduates.
**Computed as the difference in the college-HS log wage gap in Model 1 vs. Model 2.
†Computed as the difference in the college-dropout wage premium in Model 1 vs. Model 3.
Source: Reproduced from Heckman and LaFontaine (2010) who use NLSY79 data on males and females aged 25–29.
Notes: The college category includes those with a four year degree or higher. Those with some college and no two or four year degree are included in the GED and HS categories, respectively, depending on their credential. Two year degree holders are estimated separately. All education dummies are mutually exclusive. Estimated wage gaps are based on the following 3 OLS specifications; Model 1: GEDs are included as HS graduates; Model 2: GEDs treated separately; and Model 3: GEDs treated as dropouts. Persons enrolled in school at each age are deleted as are those who are not working or self-employed. Those making less than $2 or more than $100 per hour are deleted as are those making less than $100 or more than $4,000 weekly. In addition, those making less than $2,000 or more than $200,000 are dropped. Region dummies are included in all regressions but are not shown. Percentages of GEDs are calculated using sampling weights. Weekly wage estimates are weighted by weeks worked last year. Hourly wage estimates are weighted by hours worked last year. Huber-White robust standard errors clustered by individual are reported.

REFERENCES

Autor, D.H., Katz, L.F., Kearney, M.S., 2008. Trends in U.S. wage inequality: Revising the revisionists. Rev. Econ. Stat. 90 (2), 300–323.

Betts, J.R., Lofstrom, M., 2000. The educational attainment of immigrants: Trends and implications. In: Borjas, G.J. (Ed.), Issues in the Economics of Immigration. University of Chicago Press, pp. 51–116.

Bobrow, J., 2002. GED (General Educational Development), first ed. Cliffs Notes, Indianapolis, IN.

Boesel, D., Alsalam, N., Smith, T.M., 1998. Educational and labor market performance of GED recipients. U.S. Dept. of Education, Office of Educational Research and Improvement, National Library of Education, Washington, DC.

Borghans, L., Golsteyn, B.H.H., Heckman, J.J., Humphries, J.E., 2010. IQ, achievement, and personality. University of Maastricht and University of Chicago. Unpublished manuscript (revised from the 2009 version).

Borjas, G.J. (Ed.), 2000. Issues in the economics of immigration. University of Chicago Press, Chicago, IL.

Cameron, S.V., Heckman, J.J., 1993. The nonequivalence of high school equivalents. J. Labor Econ. 11 (1, Part 1), 1–47.

Cao, J., Stromsdorfer, E.W., Weeks, G., 1996. The human capital effect of general education development certificates on low income women. J. Hum. Resour. 31 (1), 206–228.

Carneiro, P., Heckman, J.J., Masterov, D.V., 2005. Labor market discrimination and racial differences in pre-market factors. J. Law and Econ. 48 (1), 1–39.

Carroll, J.M., 1990. The Copernican plan: Restructuring the American high school. Phi Delta Kappan 71 (5), 358–365.

Chaplin, D., 1999. GEDs for teenagers: Are there unintended consequences?. The Urban Institute. Technical report.

Clark, M.A., Jaeger, D.A., 2006. Natives, the foreign-born, and high school equivalents: New evidence on the returns to the GED. J. Popul. Econ. 19 (4), 769–793. doi:10.1007/s00148-005-0037-8.

Ekstrand, L.E., 2001. Reintegration of offenders into communities. United States General Accounting Office, Washington, DC. Technical report GAO-01-966T. Testimony Before the Subcommittee on the District of Columbia, Committee on Government Reform, House of Representatives.

Finn Jr., C.E., 1987. The high school dropout puzzle. Public Interest 87 (2), 3–22.

Gaes, G.G., 2009. The impact of prison education programs on post-release outcomes. John Jay College of Criminal Justice, New York City. Presented at the Reentry Roundtable on Education, March 31 and April 1, 2008.

GED Testing Service, 2008. The GED Option Program statistical report. GED Testing Service, Washington, DC.

GED Testing Service, 2009. Technical Manual: 2002 Series GED Tests. GED Testing Service, Washington, DC.

GED Testing Service, Examiner's manual tests of General Educational Development. GED Testing Service, Washington, DC, various years.

GED Testing Service, Who Took the GED?: GED statistical report. American Council on Higher Education, Washington, DC, 1958–2008.

Goldin, C., Katz, L.F., 2008. The race between education and technology. Belknap Press of Harvard University Press, Cambridge, MA.

Greene, J.P., 2001. High school graduation rates in the United States. Center for Civic Innovation at the Manhattan Institute with Black Alliance for Educational Options. Civic report 31.

Grubb, W.N., 2002. Learning and earning in the middle, part I: National studies of pre-baccalaureate education. Econ. Educ. Rev. 21 (4), 299–321.

Hahn, J., Todd, P.E., Van der Klaauw, W., 2001. Identification and estimation of treatment effects with a regression-discontinuity design. Econometrica 69 (1), 201–209.

Hansen, K.T., Heckman, J.J., Mullen, K.J., 2004. The effect of schooling and ability on achievement test scores. J. Econom. 121 (1–2), 39–98.

Harlow, C.W., 2003. Education and correctional populations. Bureau of Justice Statistics, Washington, DC. Bureau of Justice Statistics special report NCJ 195670.

Heckman, J.J., Humphries, J.E., Mader, N., 2010a. Hard evidence on soft skills: The GED and the problem of soft skills in America. Under preparation, University of Chicago Press, Chicago, IL.

Heckman, J.J., Humphries, J.E., Mader, N., 2010b. Studies of the GED Testing Program. Under preparation, University of Chicago Press, Chicago, IL.

Heckman, J.J., LaFontaine, P.A., 2006. Bias corrected estimates of GED returns. J. Labor Econ. 24 (3), 661–700.

Heckman, J.J., LaFontaine, P.A., 2010. The American high school graduation rate: Trends and levels. Rev. Econ. Stat. 92 (2), 244–262

Heckman, J.J., Rubinstein, Y., 2001. The importance of noncognitive skills: Lessons from the GED testing program. Am. Econ. Rev. 91 (2), 145–149.

Heckman, J.J., Urzua, S., 2010. The option value and rate of return to educational choices. Northwestern University. Unpublished Manuscript.

Heckman, J.J., Stixrud, J., Urzua, S., 2006. The effects of cognitive and noncognitive abilities on labor market outcomes and social behavior. J. Labor Econ. 24 (3), 411–482.

Heckman, J.J., LaFontaine, P.A., Rodríguez, P.L., 2008. Taking the easy way out: How the GED testing program induces students to drop out. Under review, J. Lab. Econ.

Heckman, J.J., Urzua, S., Veramendi, G., 2010. The effects of schooling on labor market and health outcomes. Northwestern University. Unpublished Manuscript.

Humphries, J.E., 2010. Young GEDs: The growth and change in GED test takers. University of Chicago. Unpublished Manuscript.

Imbens, G., Lemieux, T., 2008. Regression discontinuity designs: A guide to practice. J. Econom. 142 (2), 615–635.

Jepsen, C., Mueser, P., Troske, K., 2010. Labor market returns to the GED using regression discontinuity analysis. Presented at the EALE-SOLE 2010 Third World Conference. June 17-19, 2010 at University College London.

Laird, J., Keinzl, G., DeBell, M., Chapman, C., 2007. Dropout rates in the United States: 2005. National Center for Education Statistics. Compendium report NCES 2007-059.

Laurence, J.H., forthcoming. The military performance of dropouts and GED holders. In: Heckman, J.J., Humphries, J.E., Mader, N.S. (Eds.), Studies of the GED Testing Program. University of Chicago Press, Chicago, IL.

Lillard, D.R., DeCicca, P., 2001. Higher standards, more dropouts? Evidence within and across time. Econ. Educ. Rev. 20 (5), 459–473.

McLaughlin, J.W., Skaggs, G., Patterson, M.B., 2009. Preparation for and performance on the GED test. American Council on Education: GED Testing Service, Washington, DC. Research studies 2009-2.

Miao, J., Haney, W., 2004. High school graduation rates: Alternative methods and implications. Education Policy Analysis Archives 12, 1–68.

Murnane, R.J., Willett, J.B., Boudett, K.P., 1995. Do high school dropouts benefit from obtaining a GED? Educ. Eval. Policy Anal. 17 (2), 133–147.

Murnane, R.J., Willett, J.B., Boudett, K.P., 1997. Does acquisition of a GED lead to more training, postsecondary education, and military service for school dropouts? Industrial Relations Review 51, 100–116.

Murnane, R.J., Willett, J.B., Boudett, K.P., 1999. Do male dropouts benefit from obtaining a GED, postsecondary education, and training? Eval. Rev. 22 (5), 475–502.

Murnane, R.J., Willett, J.B., Tyler, J.H., 2000. Who benefits from obtaining a GED? Evidence from High School and Beyond. Rev. Econ. Stat. 82 (1), 23–37.

National Advisory Council on Adult Education, 1980. A history of the Adult Education Act. National Advisory Council on Adult Education, Washington, DC.

National Advisory Council on Adult Education, Annual report to the President of the United States. National Advisory Council on Adult Education, Washington, DC, Various years.

National Center for Education Statistics, 2006. Education Longitudinal Study of 2002 (ELS:2004/04), first follow-up, student survey. National Center for Education Statistics, Washington, DC.

National Center for Education Statistics, Digest of Education Statistics. National Center for Education Statistics, Washington, DC, various.

National Center for Education Statistics, Digest of Educational Statistics. National Center for Education Statistics, Washington, DC, Various years.

Patterson, M.B., Song, W., Zhang, J., 2009. GED candidates and their postsecondary educational outcomes: A pilot study. GED Testing Service, Washington, DC. Research Studies 2009-5.

Quinn, L.M., 2002. An institutional history of the GED. WI: University of Wisconsin-Milwaukee Employment and Training Institute.

Rose, A.D., 1991. Ends or Means: An overview of the history of the Adult Education Act. Ohio State University, Columbus, OH. Information series 346, ERIC Clearinghouse on Adult, Career, and Vocational Education, Center on Education and Training for Employment.

Rubinstein, Y., 2003. The use of inter-states variation in GED passing standards for estimating the effect of a GED degree on labor market outcomes of high school dropouts - a critique. Brown University, Department of Economics. Unpublished manuscript.

Rumberger, R.W., 1983. Dropping out of high school: The influence of race, sex, and family background. Am. Educ. Res. J. 20 (2), 199–220.

Society for Human Resource Management, 2002. Does your company accept applicants with a GED credential for jobs requiring a high school degree? Online Poll, Retrieved January 25, 2008 from www.shrm.org/poll/results.asp?question=67.

Spence, A.M., 1973. Job market signaling. Q. J. Econ. 87 (3), 355–374.

Steinberg, L., 2007. Risk taking in adolescence - New perspectives from brain and behavioral science. Curr. Dir. Psychol. Sci. 16 (2), 55–59.

Steinberg, L., 2008. A social neuroscience perspective on adolescent risk-taking. Dev. Rev. 28 (1), 78–106.

Swanson, C.B., 2004. Who graduates? Who doesn't? A statistical portrait of public high school graduation, class of 2001. The Urban Institute Education Policy Center. Technical report, www.urban.org/url.cfm?ID=410934, Last accessed April 26, 2010.

The College Board, 2007. Annual Survey of Colleges. The College Board, New York, NY.

Tyler, J.H., Kling, J.R., 2007. Prison-based education and re-entry into the mainstream labor market. In: Bushway, S., Stoll, M., Weiman, D. (Eds.), Barriers to reentry? The labor market for released prisoners in post-industrial America. Russell Sage Foundation Press, New York, NY.

Tyler, J.H., Murnane, R.J., Willett, J.B., 2000. Estimating the labor market signaling value of the GED. Q. J. Econ. 115 (2), 431–468.

Tyler, J.H., Murnane, R.J., Willett, J.B., 2003. Who benefits from a GED? Evidence for females from High School and Beyond. Econ. Educ. Rev. 22 (3), 237–247.

United States Sentencing Commission, Western District of Texas, 2009. Regional hearing on the state of federal sentencing. Testimony of Harley G. Lappin, March 18.

U.S. Census Bureau. (1968-1971). "School enrollment in the United States." Report No. P20–234. U.S. Census Bureau, Population Division, Education and Social Stratification Branch. Available at http://www.census.gov/population/www/socdemo/school/past-schen.html.

U.S. Department of Education, Division of Adult Education and Literacy. Various years. Unpublished data. Office of Vocational and Adult Education, Washington, DC.

U.S. Department of Justice, 2008. Inmate work and performance pay. U.S. Department of Justice, Federal Bureau of Prisons, Washington, DC. Technical report.

Warren, J.R., 2005. State-level high school completion rates: Concepts, measures, and trends. Education Policy Analysis Archives 13, 1–34.

Warren, J.R., Jenkins, K.N., Kulick, R.B., 2006. High school exit examinations and state-level completion and GED rates: 1975 through 2002. Educ. Eval. Policy Anal. 28 (2), 131–152.

Zhang, J., Han, M.Y., Patterson, M.B., 2009. Young GED examinees and their performance on the GED tests. GED Testing Service. Research Studies 2009-1.

CHAPTER 10

Housing Valuations of School Performance

Sandra E. Black* and Stephen Machin**

*University of Texas at Austin, IZA, CESifo, and NBER
**University College London, London School of Economics, and CESifo

Contents

1. Introduction	486
2. Using Housing Expenditures to Value School Quality	486
2.1 Theoretical background	487
3. Data Issues Relating to House Prices and School Quality	489
3.1 Housing Valuations	490
3.2 Measuring School Quality	490
3.3 Matching of House Prices to Schools	492
4. Empirical Methodologies and Review of Evidence	493
4.1 Complications for Empirical Implementation: Sorting and Local Amenities	493
4.2 Empirical Approaches and Evidence	494
4.2.1 Regression Based Estimates	494
4.2.2 Parametric and Nonparametric Modeling of Unobservable Factors	495
4.2.3 Instrumental Variables Approaches	509
4.2.4 Discontinuity Methods Using Administrative Boundaries	509
4.2.5 Differences, Difference-in-Differences, Repeat Sales, and Quasi-Experimental Methods	511
4.2.6 Combined Methods and Alternative Approaches	514
4.3 Availability of Private Schooling	515
5. Conclusions	515
Acknowledgements	516
References	516

Abstract

In this Chapter, we critically review the sizable literature that values school quality and performance through housing valuations. While highly variable in terms of research quality, the literature consistently finds housing valuations to be significantly higher in places where measured school quality is higher. Thus parents are prepared to pay substantial amounts of money to get their children educated in better performing schools. This conclusion emerges from studies across many countries, using a variety of identification strategies, and at different levels of the education system.

JEL classification: C21; I20, H75; R21

Keywords

Housing Prices
School Quality
Hedonic Regressions

1. INTRODUCTION

For many years, economists have sought to understand how much, and along what dimensions, parents value better schools. This question has been approached in a number of ways, but the dominant research strategy uses housing market data to calculate how much more parents are willing to pay to live in an area that has a higher performing school. Given that residence often determines school attendance, the research attempts to compare prices of two houses that differ along only one dimension: one is associated with a better performing school than the other. The empirical challenge is, of course, that houses and areas are not otherwise identical and so one needs to carry out careful statistical analysis to accurately pin down the relationship between house prices and school quality.

In this chapter we discuss this line of research by critically appraising the now sizable literature on school quality and house prices. There are at least two main aims of this literature: first, to uncover how much parents are prepared to pay for the opportunity for their children to attend a better performing school and, second, to consider how school quality drives microgeographic patterns of house prices. In our review, we begin by describing the standard hedonic valuation method that is now widely used in empirical research in this area, with a particular focus on how it facilitates estimation of housing premia for local amenities like better schools. We then discuss common data issues and related methodological difficulties that arise when estimating these premia. Finally, we consider the evidence, again focusing upon how methodological improvements and refinements have altered the way in which credible estimates have been obtained. We discuss this in the context of the large body of U.S. and U.K. research, along with the smaller amount of evidence from elsewhere in the world, and we classify work according to the different methodological approaches that are adopted. We conclude by offering a critical assessment of what we learn from this literature and highlight aspects where more research is required.

2. USING HOUSING EXPENDITURES TO VALUE SCHOOL QUALITY

A long tradition of research in several branches of economics has used data on housing expenditures as a means of eliciting the prices of, or willingness to pay for, local amenities (see Sheppard (1999)). Usually this is motivated through the hedonic analysis of housing markets, whose theoretical underpinnings are described by Rosen (1974), and from which one can derive empirically implementable models that relate house prices to local amenities of interest. The approach, in various guises, has been widely used to study the demand for housing attributes and to value amenities like school quality, crime, and environmental factors.

Studies that derive empirical specifications using hedonics range from regression-based property value models relating micro house prices to local amenities in a reduced form setting, to the more technically complicated estimation of the structural demand and supply parameters of the Rosen model. We describe these different forms of modeling in this section, and make general comments on their success (or otherwise) in pinning down the empirical connection between housing values and school quality.

2.1 Theoretical background

To identify the house price premium associated with better school quality we need to consider the nature of empirical models that estimate how property characteristics and neighborhood attributes affect housing prices in local markets. The most common approach either begins with, or in some way bases itself upon, the Rosen (1974) analysis of the demand and supply of composite goods. The Rosen model describes a market equilibrium in which consumer choice over a composite good—like housing—results in choosing an optimum bundle of commodities, such as house characteristics (e.g., house size) and local amenities (e.g., school quality).

In equilibrium the Rosen model, for given consumer preferences and income, sets the marginal benefit of improving any part of that bundle (e.g., finding a bigger house, or living in a location with a better quality school) equal to the utility costs of the additional expenditure involved. This provides a justification for using expenditure on a house to monetize the benefits of its observable attributes. Thus if it is possible to estimate how much housing expenditures change with marginal changes in one attribute (holding the others fixed), then this can be interpreted as the marginal willingness to pay for that attribute, or its *implicit price*. The locus that traces out the relationship between housing expenditures and the quantities of its composite attributes has become known as the *hedonic* price function.

A second key insight from the Rosen model is that buyers (like sellers) in this kind of market are heterogeneous in their preferences and income. This heterogeneity means that the price of any particular housing attribute is not unique even in a single housing market. For instance, the "price" associated with an improvement in school quality may be low in areas of the market where school quality is generally bad, because buyers and sellers place little value on school quality (e.g., if buyers do not have children). Conversely, the price of school quality in higher quality areas may be very high, because buyers in this area of the market are willing to pay heavily for marginal improvements in their children's academic achievements. In other words, the hedonic price function can be highly nonlinear, with implicit prices that vary over the distribution of housing and neighborhood characteristics. The slope and shape of this relationship is anchored by the relative number (or density) of consumers (buyers) and suppliers (sellers, property developers) in different parts of the market (Epple (1987)).

Other factors influencing the supply of attributes will also interact with characteristics in the hedonic price function, especially alternative sources of supply for the commodities embodied in housing location. For example, in our area of interest, it seems natural that the price of high quality private education should cap willingness to pay for state school quality via the housing market. Similarly, if there is a lot of choice and competition among good local schools, then housing prices might be unresponsive to inter-school differences in quality within the choice set. These are issues we will return to when we look at empirical evidence on the value of schooling.

If the hedonic price function is correctly estimated (i.e., obtaining the equilibrium relationship between housing expenditures and the component attributes of housing and its location), it is possible to calculate the *implicit prices* of each of these attributes. The implicit price can be calculated as the estimated derivative of housing expenditures with respect to attributes. It is important to ask what these estimated implicit prices measure. If they are derived from a properly specified regression model, they can provide estimates of the *marginal* willingness to pay for changes in the corresponding housing attribute. However, for welfare analysis of nonmarginal policy changes, one would want to estimate the underlying consumer demand functions (or the parameters of consumer utility functions), at least for a representative consumer, and possibly for different types of consumers in the market.

Estimation of demand functions using estimated implicit prices is, however, often complex and difficult. Effectively, the problem is similar to the standard identification problem of supply and demand equations in econometrics. That is, we can observe variation in quantities of attributes (embodied in housing) and variation in the corresponding implicit prices, but this variation reveals only the equilibrium relationship between price and quantity and not the underlying demand or supply equations. Additionally, in the hedonic framework, there are multiple demand and supply equations in a single market at a given point in time, representing heterogeneous preferences of consumers and heterogeneous cost structures of suppliers.

Rosen's (1974) paper proposed a two-stage approach to estimate these demand functions (or inverse demand functions), and there have been many subsequent attempts to implement it. In the first step hedonic equation, the implicit prices are estimated from a regression of housing expenditures on housing and neighborhood attributes. In the second stage demand equation, the implicit price estimates are regressed on the observed attributes plus individual income and, on occasion, other buyer characteristics. However, since the implicit prices are simply calculated in the first stage as nonlinear combinations of the observed attributes, this approach relies for identification on ad hoc assumptions about functional form for the hedonic price function and demand function.[1]

---

[1] For instance, in a very simplistic setting for amenity x with a quadratic hedonic price function $m = \alpha_1 x + (\alpha_2/2)x^2$, the implicit price of x is $p = \alpha_1 + \alpha_2 x$, and regression of p on x recovers the coefficient α_2.

Alternatively, identification of the second stage demand functions requires some source of variation in prices and quantities that is driven by supply shifts alone, and not by demand shifts, as in "multiple markets" and instrumental variables approaches (Tauchen and Witte (2001)). Recent work by Ekeland, Heckman, and Nesheim (2002, 2004) has returned to the idea of using nonlinearities in the hedonic price function to allow estimation of the demand functions. Their papers show that the hedonic price function is inherently nonlinear, so the original idea of recovering the implicit prices from the hedonic price function and running a regression of prices on a linear demand function is not as arbitrary as it may first seem.

However, before we even consider estimates of the demand functions, estimates of the implicit prices are required. This in itself is a major challenge due to basic omitted variables and simultaneity (endogeneity) problems that plague all nonexperimental empirical research. In practice, the recent focus of most applied empirical work on micro housing models—particularly when considering local public goods, and neighborhood and community attributes, such as the quality of schooling—has shifted away from estimating demand function parameters. Instead, the focus tends to be more on the hedonic equation and estimation of the equilibrium implicit prices—that is, the equilibrium change in housing expenditure in response to changes in characteristics—using the tools used in other areas of empirical economics, particularly the research design approach that has become prevalent in labor economics (see Card (2006)).

This therefore forms the background for the empirical work considered in this chapter. It should be acknowledged that the work valuing school quality through the housing market varies significantly in terms of the closeness of its connection to the Rosen model. This is reflected in the different methodological approaches using a range of reduced form and more structural estimations that exist in the literature. We aim to discuss the large body of evidence on estimating implicit prices that has been brought to bear on the question of how much parents will pay for access to higher quality schooling. In doing so, there are a number of data and modeling issues that commonly feature in empirical work in this area. We will carefully discuss these before reviewing and appraising the literature.

3. DATA ISSUES RELATING TO HOUSE PRICES AND SCHOOL QUALITY

There are a number of practical data issues and difficulties that commonly occur when estimating a willingness to pay from hedonic price equations. In the context of inferring the implicit price of school quality from house price equations, these include: use of housing valuations data; measurement of school quality; the mapping of housing and school level data; the institutions associated with school admissions; and the definition of well-specified catchment areas.

3.1 Housing Valuations

The idea of using land values to value "place" has a very long history (e.g., the foundation works of Von Thunen (1826) or Hurd (1903), and the classic urban economics exposition of Alonso (1964)). The intuition that the value of a piece of land reveals something about the demand for the location of that land is straightforward. Less obvious is what we can learn when each place provides a large bundle of commodities of different types—related to the environment, schooling, labor market, accessibility, and so on—and we are interested in the value consumers place on each of these commodities separately. To further complicate matters, pure land values are rarely observed. Instead, the underlying value of place needs to be disentangled from the overall expenditure on whatever structure has been built on it.

This generates the need for statistical models that control for other confounding factors. In very general terms, this hedonic price function can be specified as relating the price (p in logs) of a house sale, with characteristics $x(c)$ in a geographical location c, as:

$$p = s(c)\beta + x(c)\gamma + g(c) + \varepsilon \quad (10.1)$$

In Equation (10.1) $s(c)$ represents the school *quality* that home buyers expect to be able to access by residence at c, measured on the basis of school characteristics at periods prior to the house sale. One can think of these attributes in a general sense as measures of school composition, resources, and effectiveness. The term ε represents unobserved housing attributes and errors that are assumed to be independent of x and c. The function $g(c)$ represents unobserved influences on market prices that are correlated across neighboring spatial locations, such that the price varies with geographical location, for example due to unobserved neighborhood characteristics and amenities (other than schooling). Location c can be specified in various ways, most flexibly in terms of a vector of geographical or Cartesian coordinates. As discussed below, for valuing school quality, the matching of houses to schools is critical for this.

There are a number of pertinent observations about this empirical model. First and foremost, we want the estimated coefficient on school quality, β, to reflect the causal impact of school quality on house prices. As we have already stated, the aim of our survey is to critically appraise the ability of research to identify this parameter. While we will discuss empirical strategies for estimating this parameter in future sections, substantial measurement issues exist and we consider these next.

3.2 Measuring School Quality

Up to this point, we have been somewhat vague in our description of measures of "school quality," $s(c)$. However, there is an extensive literature on determining what it is about schools that is important. One technique has been to examine which characteristics of a school are capitalized in housing prices.

If one looks at the standard education production function (see Hanushek (2006) or Todd and Wolpin (2003) for more extensive discussions), student performance is generally denoted as a function of a variety of inputs, including family characteristics, student ability, and school quality. In order to isolate the role of school quality, the production function can be estimated in first differences; as a result, the change in student performance is a function of the change in the school inputs, assuming other characteristics are unchanging over time and will therefore be differenced out. The value of a school can be thought of in a similar way; parents should pay for the additional learning that the school contributes. As a result, researchers have examined the role of value added in the hedonic housing price regressions.

Hayes and Taylor (1996) run a horserace to try to determine what it is about schools that parents value. Using data from the Dallas school district, they find that parents do not value changes in school expenditures but do in fact value changes in school test scores.[2] Dills (2004), using data on total housing values within Texas school districts, examines the effect of changes in house value associated with gains in test scores following the introduction of high stakes testing. She finds no effect of increasing passage rates of Texas Assessment of Academic Skills (TAAS) scores on housing values, suggesting either that parents do not respond to changes in school quality or the TAAS exam is a poor proxy for school quality. To test these competing hypotheses, she turns to other measures of student performance and examines the relationship between changes in SAT and ACT "passage rates" (defined as the percentage of graduates scoring above either 1000 on the SAT or 24 on the ACT) and changes in housing values. She finds that housing values do in fact respond, suggesting that value added, when perceived as true value added matters.

This finding has not been robust in the literature, however. Downes and Zabel (2002) use data from Chicago and conclude that parents value average test scores and not measures of value added. While they note that, theoretically, value added is what should matter, their evidence suggests the level is what does seem to matter to parents.

Brasington (1999) and Brasington and Haurin (2006a) both test the value-added model. In Brasington (1999), the author estimates 444 hedonic housing estimations and compares 37 different measures of school quality and concludes that, while expenditures per pupil and student test scores do have a significant effect on housing prices, the measure of value added does not. In Brasington and Haurin (2006a), the authors expand upon the earlier work by Brasington by using different measures of value added (relative to the urban area of each school district, not the state as in the previous paper) and use more test score data that enable them to follow a cohort of students over time. Again, they find little support for the value added model.

Much the same conclusion is reached in Gibbons, Machin, and Silva's (2009) work on English primary schools. They consider both the level of test scores at the end of the

---

[2] Note that their data consist of 288 houses.

primary school sequence and value added through the primary school years and conclude that parents value the level of test scores (which, incidentally, is the headline figure published in the English media). Considering other aspects of school quality does not affect this conclusion.[3] In related but separate work, Gibbons and Silva (2009) extend the range of possible valuation criteria to include measures of parent satisfaction with the school and (self-reported) child happiness. They find no relation between house prices and these subjective assessments, concluding that it is more concrete measures like test scores that parents value in choosing schools for their children to attend.

3.3 Matching of House Prices to Schools

A practical modeling concern for work in this area is that house prices and schools are not usually measured at the same level of (dis)aggregation. One then needs a means of matching house locations and school locations. The task is greatly simplified if there is a rigidly defined system of catchment areas or attendance zones, as is common in the U.S., since there then is a one-to-one mapping between residential location and school attended.

However, catchment area definitions—or indeed the very existence of catchment areas—differ considerably depending on the institutional setting. Figure 10.1 shows the

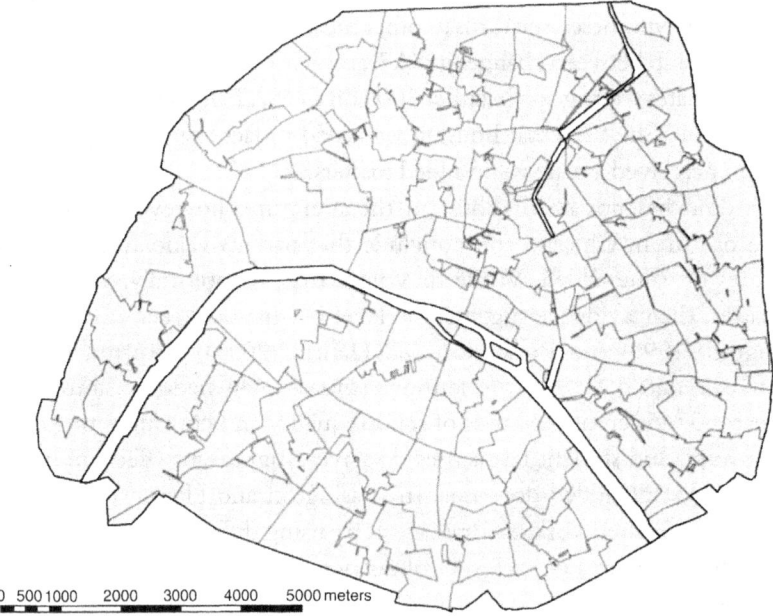

Figure 10.1 An example of catchment areas, Paris school year 2003–4.

---

[3] Expenditure per pupil, pupil–teacher ratio, number of full-time equivalent pupils and local housing taxes. Pupil characteristics include percentage of pupils eligible for free school meals, percentage of pupils from ethnic minorities, and percentage of pupils with special educational needs.

rigid catchment zones in Paris in Fack and Grenet's (2010) study. In other places, such as England (as in the work of Gibbons and Machin (2003, 2006)), proximity based attendance rules generate a much more fuzzy (often implicit) attendance zone which also depends on the demand for particular schools. In yet other places (like in Bogart and Cromwell's, (2000) study in Cleveland or Ries and Somerville's (2004) study of Vancouver) catchment zones may vary over time and, on occasion, be redrawn entirely.

The differing nature of catchment areas adds an important set of modeling concerns that matter for identification of the school quality premium, β. Consider a situation where formal, rigid attendance boundaries do not exist (e.g., in the case of the England where proximity of residence to a school is the key factor determining school admission). We can, given appropriate data, easily ascertain which schools are located close to specific properties in a data set. But which schools are relevant? Given that many pupils do not attend their nearest school (Briggs et al. (2006), Gibbons, Machin, and Silva (2008)), there is ambiguity in how to measure the characteristics of the school (or potential set of schools) associated with any particular house.

Without clearly defined catchment areas, considerable efforts need to be made to ensure that the link between residential location and accessible schools set up in the empirical analysis is a reasonable representation of the situation on the ground.

4. EMPIRICAL METHODOLOGIES AND REVIEW OF EVIDENCE

Our main focus is on the extent to which empirical investigations yield plausible estimates of the implicit prices of school quality attributes in housing models. In addition to the data and measurement issues mentioned previously, there are significant empirical challenges. Most notably, the full range of relevant housing characteristics and neighborhood attributes are never observed by empirical researchers, so estimates are plagued by standard omitted variables and endogeneity problems. We next explain the methods that have been used in the recent literature to try to circumvent these problems.

4.1 Complications for Empirical Implementation: Sorting and Local Amenities

There are numerous scenarios under which estimation of the implicit price of local public goods, community related amenities and other spatial goods via property value models presents the researcher with significant challenges; here we will discuss the two principal concerns. The first deals with the endogenous nature of the amenity. Theoretical work (such as that by Nechyba (2003a, 2003b), Epple and Romano (1998, 2003), or Bayer and McMillan (2005)) describes how voting on public school funding (and hence school quality) can be affected by the characteristics of the people in the neighborhood.[4] This introduces an endogeneity, or reverse causation, problem; the types of people who move

---

[4] The seminal work is by Tiebout (1956) and describes the sorting of individuals by preferences for public goods.

to a neighborhood then influence the characteristics of the neighborhood and schools. An easy example is school spending; if higher house prices lead to higher property tax revenues, a high willingness to pay for school quality could lead to an increase in school spending (and hence quality) itself. Unfortunately, researchers are severely limited in their ability to model this endogeneity; as a result, much of the research takes a partial-equilibrium perspective, assuming that marginal house buyers are not going to have a significant effect on neighborhoods and school quality.[5]

The second concern is that, because of the strong correlation between neighborhood characteristics and school quality, estimates of the value of school quality will be biased upward by omitted neighborhood or house quality characteristics. To the extent that the variables observed by the econometrician are an incomplete set of the characteristics observed by the homeowner (e.g., if, as is likely in practice, there are other unobserved local amenities correlated with house prices and/or school quality), this is very likely to be a problem. The following sections focus on how researchers have attempted to deal with the correlation between neighborhood characteristics (observed and unobserved) and schools we observe in the data.

4.2 Empirical Approaches and Evidence

We now move on to discuss the findings that emerge from the various different methodologies that have been used in the literature. We consider six of these, and classify papers by these groups[6]: regression based estimates; the use of parametric and nonparametric modeling of unobservable factors; instrumental variable approaches; discontinuity methods using administrative boundaries; differences, difference-in-differences, repeat sales, and quasi-experimental methods; and papers that combine a number of these approaches. We consider each of these in turn:

4.2.1 Regression Based Estimates

The most basic way of dealing with the empirical challenges presented by hedonic housing price regressions, and the approach adopted in many of the earlier studies, is to use multiple regression techniques to control for as many observable house price determinants as possible; the assumption is then that whatever price variation is left is essentially random noise and hence uncorrelated with school quality. The earliest work on school quality valuation applied this approach by estimating a simple hedonic regression with the price as the dependent variable and house and school characteristics as the independent variables. In Kain and Quigley (1970), the authors regress house

---

[5] Indeed, this issue becomes highly relevant in some contexts, for example in the U.S. and other countries where local property taxes generate a direct link between housing values and school quality working through the level of public expenditure on schooling.
[6] Some papers fall naturally into particular classifications, whereas others sometimes overlap. In the latter case, we classify according to what we view to be the dominant methodology adopted.

price or rental cost on structure characteristics (such as number bedrooms, bathrooms, etc.), neighborhood characteristics (such as median schooling of adults in census tract, racial composition of the neighborhood, etc.), and school characteristics (public school achievement). They find only marginally significant effects of school quality (and crime) on house prices; however, they note that this may be due to the strong correlation between school characteristics and neighborhood attributes.

Although Kain and Quigley do not find a robust effect of school quality on housing prices, since that time the literature has documented a significant relationship between the two. For example, Oates (1969), Sonstelie and Portney (1980), and Bradbury, Case, and Mayer (2001) all find a positive relationship between school spending and house prices, while Jud and Watts (1981), Fullerton and Rosen (1977), and Walden (1990) all document a positive relationship between student test scores and housing prices. The first panel of Table 10.1 gives details on the key findings from these and other similar regression based studies. Most studies uncover a sizable, statistically significant premium linked to school quality. However, more recent research has been quite critical of the strategies used in these "condition on observables" regressions as they are heavily plagued by omitted variable bias and, hence, unreliable.

Given the wide range of housing characteristics, the basic multivariate regression approach often yields unwieldy "kitchen-sink" regressions whose specification is governed largely by data availability. The decision as to which neighborhood characteristics to include in such specifications remains largely ad hoc; hence estimates are hard to interpret. Indeed, this traditional method is not an attractive way forward if we want credible amenity prices for policy purposes. More recent research in this field has adopted a number of empirical strategies to try to more rigorously address the problem of omitted variable bias. These strategies are based on isolating sources of variation in supply of school quality that are uncorrelated with other determinants of housing prices.

4.2.2 Parametric and Nonparametric Modeling of Unobservable Factors

An alternative, complementary approach to the traditional regression-based methods of including a number of controls for observable housing and neighborhood characteristics is to model part of the "unobserved" spatial variation in prices (the $g(c)$ function of Equation (10.1)) directly using information on the geographical location of house sales. For example, if there is an east-west downward trend in prices, and no observable demographic or physical characteristics explain this trend, then one could include the geographical coordinates of the house sales, just as one might include a time trend in a temporal model. More generally, house price models can include polynomials or elaborate parametric functions of x and y coordinates, or use *nonparametric* statistical methods to allow very flexible price surfaces in the x-y plane. The drawback in this method is that the researcher must make some judgment about when to stop in eliminating "nuisance" spatial variation, since the most flexible of specifications would eliminate the localized variation in prices and amenities that the researcher wishes to investigate.

Table 10.1 Summary of research findings, organized by methodological approach

Study	Setting	Data	Impact of school quality	Comments
4.2.1. Regression based estimates				
Oates (1969)	U.S. – New Jersey	Residential communities within 53 municipalities Census (1960). Expenditure per pupil.	Increase in spending per pupil from $350 to $450 per annum increases house prices by $1200 (1969 prices).	
Kain and Quigley (1970)	U.S. – St Louis	Survey of 1500 households (1969). Average eighth grade math score.	1 SD in school quality increase rent by $2.63–$5.05 per month	Very detailed information on housing quality. Basic hedonic modeling.
Grether and Mieszkowski (1974)	U.S. – New Haven	830 sales of single family homes (1962–1969). Reading percentiles for elementary schools from New Haven.	Moving from school district in 50th pctile to 90th pctile increase house value by 9% ($2000). PTR from 25 to 30 lowers price by 4.5% ($1000).	
Fullerton and Rosen (1977)	U.S. – New Jersey	Residential communities within 53 municipalities Census (1960/1970). Expenditure per pupil. Average reading/math scores 4th grade.	Increased reading and math score raises prices by 0.5 and 0.27 respectively. (No scale given.) Being in top decile relative to bottom increases price by $4300 (1970 prices).	Expenditure per pupil has no effect on house prices.
Brueckner (1979)	U.S. – New Jersey	53 municipalities Census (1960), Twenty-Third Annual Report of the Division of Local Government, State of New Jersey.	No effect of educational expenditure on house valuations.	

Sonstelie and Portney (1980)	U.S. – San Mateo County, California	Gross rent in single family dwellings (1969–1970). Elementary expenditure per pupil, average reading improvement from 1st to 3rd grade by school district.	Annual gross rent of a median house is increased by $52 for each additional month of average reading improvement. $1 increase in pupil expenditure increases gross rent of an 8-room house by $1.50.	The effect of expenditure per pupil increases with the number of bedrooms.
Jud and Watts (1981)	U.S. – Charlotte, North Carolina	Sales records from single family residential property (1977). School level average of 3rd grade performance on state reading test.	Increasing in performance by one grade level raises housing values by 5.2%.	
Atkinson and Crocker (1987)	U.S. – Chicago	1283 insurance valuations of detached single family residences (1967–67). Elementary school reading and maths scores, district means.	No effect.	
Walden (1990)	U.S. – Wake County, North Carolina	598 house sales in Wake County, North Carolina (1987). Use elementary and middle school California Achievement Test scores and SAT scores.	Elementary and SAT scores not significantly related. 1% point increase in middle schools scores increases house price by 0.2%. Reading had a larger effect than math.	Districts with magnet schools offer more school choice to parents and have less capitalization.

Continued

Table 10.1 Summary of research findings, organized by methodological approach—cont'd

Study	Setting	Data	Impact of school quality	Comments
Brasington and Haurin (1996)	U.S. – Ohio, 6 largest metropolitan regions	45,236 real-estate transactions (1991) % of fourth-grade students in each district who pass the reading proficiency test (1996).	2 SD increases in school quality differences increases house prices by 18%.	Capitalization of school quality differences occurs on a per lot basis rather than per square foot of land.
Case and Mayer (1996)	U.S. – Eastern Massachusetts	135,000 pairs of retail transactions (1981–1994). Spending per pupil.	High quality school districts appreciate in value slower than low quality districts.	
Hayes and Taylor (1996)	U.S. – Dallas, Northern and Southern	288 single family homes sold in July 1987. Nonschool data from 1990 Census of Housing and Population. Sixth-grade mathematics achievement.	1% increase in math scores increases house prices by 0.26% in northern Dallas.	No effect of pupil expenditure on house prices.
Brasington (1999)	U.S. – Ohio, 6 largest metropolitan regions	27,440 real-estate transactions (1991) % of fourth-grade students in each district who pass the reading proficiency test (1996).	No conclusive results, 3 significant positive, 2 significant negative. 1% increase in pass rate, increases log prices by 1%.	Investigates other school quality measures, including spending, PTR, teacher pay, and value added.
Cheshire and Sheppard (1998)	U.K. – Reading and Darlington	840 real-estate transactions (1984). Catchment area dummies.	Residences in a the catchment area of a "premium school" cost an extra 8% in Reading and 12% in Darlington.	

Clark and Herrin (2000)	U.S. – Fresno County, California	6837 residences from property tax data (1990–1994). SATs, dropout rate, PTR.	1 SD increase in taking the SAT raises 3.1%. An extra teacher per 100 students district-wide, increases housing prices by 16% (gross).	
Barrow (2002)	U.S. – District of Columbia	12,805 residences. High school mean SAT scores.	White households with children in the top income quintile are willing to pay $3300 for schools that generate a 100 SAT point advantage. No effect on black households.	Accounting for unobserved neighborhood factors by controlling for children present in household.
Brasington (2003)	U.S. – Ohio, 6 largest metropolitan regions	9509 houses real-estate transactions in 34 urban areas (1991) % of fourth-grade students in each district who pass 9th grade proficiency test on first attempt (1990).	1% increase in pass rate increases house prices by 0.01%.	The supply elasticity, 0.14, suggests nearly perfectly inelastic. Area residents require a large increase in price to induce them to supply an additional unit of public school quality.
Chiodo, Hernandez-Murillo, and Owyang (2003)	U.S. – Tucson, Arizona	9462 residential sales (1998–2003). School district dummies.	30–47% house price premium for houses in high value districts.	
Dills (2004)	U.S. – Texas	Total taxable value of single family residential property within school districts (1994–1999). Passage rates of Texas Assessment of Academic Skills (TAAS) and SAT/ACT.	TAAS pass rates have no effect on house values. 1 SD increase in pass rates on the ACT/SAT increases total house value by $2.8 million dollars (1.5% of the average total change over this period).	Parents only care about the passage rate of certain tests.

Continued

Table 10.1 Summary of research findings, organized by methodological approach—cont'd

Study	Setting	Data	Impact of school quality	Comments
Brasington and Haurin (2006a)	U.S. – Ohio, 7 urban areas	77,578 real-estate transactions over 310 school districts (2000). % of 4th and 9th grade students in each district 4 proficiency tests on first attempt.	1 SD increase in school quality increases house prices by 7.1%, using average tests scores. No relation to value added test scores.	OLS combined with spatial autoregressive model.
Brasington and Haurin (2006b)	U.S. – Ohio	40,116 real-estate transactions urban areas (1991) % of 4th grade students in each district who pass all 9th grade proficiency tests on first attempt (1990).	Price elasticity of demand for school quality −0.56 to −0.53. Income elasticity of demand 0.5.	
Chin and Foong (2006)	Singapore	13,790 real-estate transactions (1999–2003). Average primary and secondary school performance.	Access and prestige of primary schools appeared to be a more important consideration when making a home purchase than that of secondary schools.	
Crone (2006)	U.S. – Montgomery County, Pennsylvania	3150 home sales remaining in the 21 school districts Sales prices and previous sales price from property tax receipts (1998–1999). District and school level maths and reading tests for 5th and 11th grades.	1 SD increase in school quality increase house prices by 1.7%–2.4%.	District levels scores more significant than school level scores. *Intra-district* differences scores are not a significant determinant of house prices when controlling for district-wide averages.

Gravel, Michelangeli, and Trannoy (2006)	France – Val d'Oise	8200 housing units, over 33 cities in Val d'Oise (1985–1993). Number of pupils repeating a grade and pupil teacher ratio.	1 SD in school quality increase prices by 1.26% (1417 euros). Reducing class size by 1 increases value by 854 euros.	

4.2.2. Parametric and nonparametric modeling of unobservable factors

Bogart and Cromwell (1997)	U.S. – Cleveland Ohio	All arms-length sales of one-family owner-occupied houses in the three statistical planning areas, 11,000 (1976–1994).	High value school district is worth about $36 per month extra in rent.	Oaxaca decomposition of differences in average house prices across school jurisdictions into a component based on differences in observables and unobservable residual components.
Cheshire and Sheppard (2004)	U.K. – Reading	490 real-estate transactions (1999–2000). Primary School, proportion reaching target grade in maths science and English. Secondary School proportion achieving 5+ GCSEs A–C.	Primary schools: 9.8% for one standard deviation. Secondary schools: 4.0% for one standard deviation (own linear interpolation from authors reported results).	Model spatial distance parameters.
Brasington and Hite (2008)	U.S. – Ohio, 7 urban areas	Survey of 1606 homebuyer characteristics, 127,050 housing sales from 58 counties in Ohio (2000).	Mean elasticity of house price with respect to school quality is 0.19.	Uses mixed models.

Continued

Table 10.1 Summary of research findings, organized by methodological approach—cont'd

Study	Setting	Data	Impact of school quality	Comments
Derrick, Sedgley, and Williams (2008)	U.S. – Howard County, Maryland	3164 homes sold (2002). School mean pass rate of 6 subjects grades 3rd, 5th and 8th, SAT scores.	House price elasticizes: 3rd grade insignificant; 8th grade 0.16–0.22; SAT scores 0.12–0.3.	Spatial autocorrelation.

4.2.3. Instrumental variables approaches

Study	Setting	Data	Impact of school quality	Comments
Bradbury, Case, and Mayer (2001)	U.S. – Massachusetts	Use repeat sales house price information of 135,000 properties (1990–1995). Per pupil expenditure and combined math and reading MEAP test score for 8th graders in 1990.	1 SD increase in school spending (8.6%) increases house prices by 2%. Test scores have small but significant effect. Nonschool spending have insignificant effects.	Instruments include 1980 property tax rate, % nonresidential property, per capita income.
Downes and Zabel (2002)	U.S. – Chicago	American Housing Survey (1987–1991). Average district/school 8th grade reading component. Ownership information.	1 SD in school quality increases prices by 14%.	Home owners pay more attention to test scores than per-pupil expenditures, or value added test scores.
Rosenthal (2003)	England	350,000 real-estate transactions (1995–1998). Inspections of 3000 secondary schools and proportion achieving 5+ GCSEs A–C.	1 SD in school quality increases house prices by 2%. Elasticity of purchase price to school quality of 5%.	Instrument: Random timing of OFSTED school inspections.

4.2.4. Discontinuity methods using administrative boundaries

Black (1999)	U.S. – Boston, Massachusetts	All 22,679 real-estate transactions (1993–1995). Elementary reading and math scores.	1 SD in school quality (5%) increases prices by 2.5%.	Cross-sectional study using attendance boundary discontinuities.
Weimer and Wolkoff (2001)	U.S. – Monroe County, New York	1193 real estate transactions (1997). Elementary schools, average ELA test score.	Elasticity of city housing values with respect to average test score ranges from 0.6 to 4.7.	Effect of: Student body composition, test scores, student-teacher ratios. Use catchment areas where they do not coincide with boundaries for other public goods, with fixed effects.
Leech and Campos (2003)	U.K. – Coventry	Advertised prices from one issue of local property guide (13/7/2000). Catchment area dummies.	20% premium for two popular schools, and 16% for a third.	Use of catchment area dummies, with increased prices in oversubscribed school areas.
Davidoff and Leigh (2008)	Australia – Australian Capital Territory	580 transactions, excluding apartments (2003–2005) Secondary school's median University Admissions Index (UAI).	1 SD in school quality (5% in test scores) increases house prices by 3.5%.	Compare homes on either side of boundaries (600 m).
Fiva and Kirkeboen (2008)	Norway – Oslo	79,322 real estate transactions (2003–2006). Lower Secondary School, adjusted grade point average (1 internal, 2 external).	1 SD in school quality increases prices by 1.5%.	Exploit publication of school quality indicators on house prices. Grade point average adjusted for parental characteristics.

Continued

Table 10.1 Summary of research findings, organized by methodological approach—cont'd

Study	Setting	Data	Impact of school quality	Comments
Fack and Grenet (2010)	France – Paris	Real estate transactions (1997–2003). Middle school maths, geography, history and French scores.	1 SD in school quality increases prices by 2%.	Compare sales across school boundaries. Offering an outside option to parents, attenuates the capitalization of public school quality in the price of real estate.

4.2.5. Differences, difference-in-differences, repeat sales and quasi-experimental methods

Study	Setting	Data	Impact of school quality	Comments
Bogart and Cromwell (2000)	U.S. – Shaker Heights, Cleveland, Ohio	All arms-length sales of one-family owner-occupied houses in the three statistical planning areas, 11,000 (1983–1994).	Loss of high value school reduces house price by 9.9% ($5738 – 2000 prices).	Redistricting of high quality neighborhood school.
Dee (2000)	U.S. – California	School district level data (10,000) from National Center for Education Statistics School District Data Book and housing values from 1990 Census.	Court reform positively effected house prices. The poorest school districts found increases of 8%.	Changing educational expenditure due to court judgment.
Brunner, Murdoch, and Thayer (2002)	U.S. – Los Angeles	94,223 transactions of owner occupied single family homes (1975, 1980, 1985, 1990). District level average of 6th grade math and verbal scores.	1 point increase in performance increases price of homes by $300. $1 increase in spending per pupil increases price of homes by $6.	

Kane, Staiger and Samms (2003)	U.S. – Mecklenburg County, North Carolina	86,865 sales for 67,066 single-family homes with stable elementary school assignments between 1993–2001.	1 SD (school level) increase in scores increases house prices by 4–5%. 1 SD (student level) increased average house prices by 18–25%.	No evidence of volatility in housing prices to match the annual volatility in test scores.
Clapp and Ross (2004)	U.S. – Connecticut	100,000 housing transactions (1995–2000). 8th grade district mathematics score.	Math scores have no effect on house prices.	Simultaneous equations model, using price levels, school performance, and the racial and ethnic composition.
Figlio and Lucas (2004)	U.S. – Florida	73,782 properties in 481 elementary school zones (1999–2001) Elementary school grades based on government evaluation.	10% premium for schools receiving an "A" grade in each year.	Repeat property sales within small neighborhoods in Florida.
Ries and Somerville (2004)	Canada – Vancover	87381 repeat sales from 1996 to 2003 matched to information on 18 secondary and 69 elementary schools.	Cross section hedonics show strong school quality impacts, but once price trends are controlled for the only significant effects occur for the top quartile residences.	Rezoning that causes redrawing of catchment areas in January 2001 which took effect for school attendance in September 2001.

Continued

Table 10.1 Summary of research findings, organized by methodological approach—cont'd

Study	Setting	Data	Impact of school quality	Comments
Reback (2005)	U.S. – Minnesota	272 district-level residential property values (1989–1990 and 1997–1998). Index based on 7 test score measures over four school years. Elementary, middle secondary schools.	1 SD in school quality increases prices by 3.8–7.7%	Identify the capitalization effects associated with the diminished importance of school district boundaries.
Cellini, Ferreira, and Rothstein (2008)	U.S. – California	Real-estate transactions (1988–2005) averaged at census block. 3rd grade reading and math CAT, Stanford9.	An increase of $1 in educational spending increase house prices by $1.50. The total effect of spending on test scores would produce a housing price increase just over 1%.	Regression discontinuity on vote on education spending.
Clapp, Nanda and Ross (2008)	U.S. – Connecticut	356,829 real-estate transactions (1994–2004), 8th grade maths scores and demographic characteristics.	1 SD in school quality increases prices by 1.3–1.4%.	Proportions Black and Hispanic more important when looking at long run changes.
Caetano (2009)	U.S. – New Jersey	Restricted access 2000 U.S. Decennial Census data on 1 in 7 households in 200 New Jersey educational districts. Information on house composition, rental price and sales price.	A 5% increase in test scores increase rental prices per child by 2.7% for high school pupils, 1.6% for middle school pupils and 1.4% elementary school pupils.	

Machin and Salvanes (2010)	Norway – Oslo	15,495 real estate transactions (1995–2002). Secondary school maths, Norwegian and English scores. Socio-economic characteristic of home buyers.	1 SD in school quality increases prices by 2–9% with catchment areas, and 2–6% without.	Exploit admissions reform, removing catchment areas.
4.2.6. Combined methods				
Des Rosiers, Lagan, and Theriault (2001)	Canada – Quebec Urban Community	4300 transacted single-detached, owner-occupied housing units (1990–1).	Sales price decrease by CAN$2685 per km.	Investigates the nonmonotonicity of both the price–distance and price–size relationships with respect to primary schools.
Gibbons and Machin (2003)	England	Average transaction price in 7444 postcodes, by property type (1996–1999). Proportion reaching target grade in primary school maths, science and English tests.	1 SD in school quality increases prices by 4–9% (3.3–6.9% for 10 percentage point increase).	Semiparametric modeling of unobservable factors, discontinuities at school district boundaries, and instrumental variables.
Gibbons and Machin (2006)	U.K. – Greater London	All real-estate transactions involving a mortgage (1997–2002). Proportion reaching target grade in primary school maths, science and English tests.	1 SD in school quality increases prices by 3.8%.	Multiple methods used (IV, cross-boundary) with focus places on testing models where house price premia differ with distance to school.

Continued

Table 10.1 Summary of research findings, organized by methodological approach—cont'd

Study	Setting	Data	Impact of school quality	Comments
Kane, Riegg and Staiger (2006)	U.S. – Mecklenburg County, North Carolina	89,793 properties (1994–2001) Maths and reading scores in elementary schools.	1 SD in school quality increases prices by 10%.	Use differences in housing prices along boundaries and changes following the change in school assignments.
Bayer, Ferreira, and McMillan (2007)	U.S. – San Francisco Bay Area (6 counties)	Prices back engineered from 244,000 households tax forms (1978). Mean test scores by school over 2 years.	5% increase in school performance leads to 1% increase in prices.	Structural two stage approach based upon residential sorting, discontinuities at school district boundaries, and instrumental variables.

There are a few papers in the literature that take this approach. They are summarized in the second panel of Table 10.1 and include work by Bogart and Cromwell (1997) and Cheshire and Sheppard (2004). Consistent with the earlier multivariate regression approach, these papers also report significant house price or rent premia connected to better school quality. Typically, however, their additional modeling of unobservables in the ways they attempt add only marginally to the regression based approaches in panel I of the table, and there are still likely to be biases associated with other unobservables that can be controlled for using these methods.

4.2.3 Instrumental Variables Approaches

One natural means to try and identify the causal effect of school quality on house prices would be to adopt an instrumental variables (IV) strategy, which would rely on finding variation in school quality that is otherwise unrelated to housing prices. While this approach has recently been relatively successful in some areas of the economics of education (for example, in estimating the earnings returns to education as discussed in Card (1999)), in the area of valuing school quality it has proven hard to find credible instruments for school quality (or indeed other neighborhood amenities), and studies rarely use this method alone. Indeed, in this light it is not surprising that the literature contains very few such studies; panel 3 of Table 10.2 notes the papers by Bradbury, Case, and Mayer (2001), Downes and Zabel (2002), and Rosenthal (2003). From the IV strategies adopted in this work, it seems hard to conclude anything other than the fact that this approach has not been especially successful in this area.[7]

4.2.4 Discontinuity Methods Using Administrative Boundaries

By the early 1990s, researchers began to consider markedly different approaches for isolating the role of school quality from the role of neighborhood characteristics. One confounding factor is the fact that the boundaries that determine school quality and those that determine the provision of other public goods are coterminous. In an effort to circumvent this problem, Bogart and Cromwell (1997) compare houses in different school districts but within the same political jurisdiction, so that nonschooling public services are the same in the houses being compared. From this, the authors argue they are able to derive the net-of-tax value of the distinct public services (schooling) in the two jurisdictions.

While clearly innovative, this paper suffers from a number of limitations. Most of the public school districts were coterminous with political jurisdictions, thereby providing little clean variation in school quality. Secondly, the coefficient on the school characteristics provides a net-of taxes marginal valuation; because both taxes and school quality varies, it is not clear that the coefficient provides the parameter the authors would ideally like to estimate.

---

[7] Some of the quasi-experimental approaches considered below in 4.2.5 are clearly related to the search for exogenous variation in school quality that can be used to identify the causal impact on housing valuations.

Following on this idea was work by Black (1999); she uses what was later termed a "regression discontinuity" approach to distinguish the role of school quality on housing prices separate from neighborhood attributes.[8] In her work, she is looking within school districts in the Boston metropolitan area at houses on the opposite sides of elementary school attendance district boundaries. By comparing houses within a very close proximity to each other but associated with different elementary schools, one can argue that the houses are in the same neighborhood, so any difference in house price can be attributed to differences in school quality.

As expected, if earlier estimates were plagued by omitted variable bias, when she estimates the hedonic regressions with boundary fixed effects (which takes out all fixed characteristics of houses in the same neighborhood but on opposite sides of attendance district boundaries), the estimates of the effect of school test scores on housing prices go down dramatically from the more traditional specification regressing house prices on test scores with standard controls for house and neighborhood characteristics. She finds that house prices go up by approximately 2.5% for a 5% change in test scores.

One of the key assumptions of this strategy is that, while school quality changes discontinuously at attendance district boundaries, other characteristics such as neighborhoods change only smoothly. In the limit, you could look at observations epsilon distance from either side of the boundary and the only difference would be the school quality. To verify that this is the case, Black examines the characteristics of houses on opposite sides of attendance district boundaries and finds them to be similar. In addition, she reduces her range of comparison, first including all houses within 1/3 of a mile of the boundary, then 1/5 of a mile, and finally houses within .15 of a mile of the attendance district boundary. The results are robust to these specifications.

However, if other characteristics such as neighborhoods or house quality change discontinuously at the boundaries as well, the identification strategy no longer gives the marginal valuation of school quality. While Black (1999) showed that there appeared to be no differences in observable characteristics on opposite sides of boundaries, work by Kane, Riegg, and Staiger (2006) (listed in Table 10.1 under vi. combined methods) using data from North Carolina has suggested that there may be differences in neighborhood and house characteristics on opposite sides of attendance district boundaries.

Exploiting discontinuities at catchment area or administrative boundaries has been a feature of other modern empirical work in the area. In very different settings like English primary schools (Gibbons and Machin (2003, 2006); Gibbons, Machin, and Silva (2009)), middle schools in Paris (Fack and Grenet (2010)), and Australian secondary schools (Davidoff and Leigh (2008)), estimates based on the boundary approach have uncovered significant house price premia and, strikingly, the magnitudes of the

---

[8] See Imbens and Lemieux (2008) for discussion of the regression discontinuity approach.

estimates are rather similar to the U.S. work. A one standard deviation increase in school test scores seems to generate house price increases on the order of around 3–4%.

It is worth noting that the capitalization literature in general relies on the assumption that housing supply elasticity is close to zero; in urban areas, this may not seem unreasonable. Brasington (2002) argues that the boundary fixed effects methodology is particularly susceptible to violations of this assumption because of higher housing supply elasticities at the boundaries of urban areas. As a result, he argues we would expect to see weaker capitalization effects at the boundaries relative to the center of an urban area. Using data from housing transactions in Ohio in 1991, he finds evidence that this is the case. While this is less likely to be a problem in a densely populated metropolitan area, it does highlight the importance of our assumptions about the elasticity of housing supply necessary for inference in these models.

4.2.5 Differences, Difference-in-Differences, Repeat Sales, and Quasi-Experimental Methods

All of the methods discussed so far have relied on cross-sectional variation for identification. Given additional information on changes in the level of local amenities over time, there is scope for examining how the prices of individual houses, or the prices of neighborhood clusters of houses, respond to these changes. For example, another strategy is to compare housing prices before and after changes in school quality, thereby attributing the change in house prices to the change in school quality. Yet another is to take a more quasi-experimental approach, for example looking at policy driven changes in the provision of school quality such as school openings or closures or the introduction, redrawing, or withdrawal of school catchment boundaries. In these approaches the $g(c)$ term in Equation (10.1) is differenced out by looking at changes (or sometimes, differences-in-differences when a comparison group is also differenced).

There is a substantial literature that focuses solely on identifying the value of school quality by relating changes in house prices to changes in school quality. Work by Clapp and Ross (2004) and Clapp, Nanda, and Ross (2008) relate changes in house prices (two-year and ten-year, respectively) with changes in school performance and racial composition of a neighborhood.[9] By looking at changes, they are able to difference out fixed differences in neighborhoods, housing quality, and so on. They find that changing the demographic composition of the school does affect housing prices but find mixed evidence on the role of test scores.

A limitation of this type of analysis, however, is that the changes in school quality may be coincident with unobserved changes in neighborhood and, as a result, estimates of the relationship between school quality and housing prices will still be biased.[10]

---

[9] They use a simultaneous equations methodology to allow for endogeneity of the minority composition of the school.
[10] This type of analysis is particularly susceptible to measurement error. See Kane and Staiger (2002a, 2002b) and Chay et al. (2005).

Another strategy is to use an arguably exogenous shock to school quality induced by change in education policy and see how this change is related to housing prices.

The literature has consistently shown that shocks to school quality induced by changes in education policy are capitalized in housing prices. A number of papers have looked at how changes in finance or expenditures affect housing values. Dee (2000) examines the effect of changing educational expenditures induced by school finance reforms on housing prices. Using data from California, Dee finds that new school resources were in fact capitalized in house prices, with the poorest school districts showing an increase of at least 8%.[11]

Cellini, Ferreira, and Rothstein (2008) examine the effect of school investment in structures induced by bond passage on housing prices. Because districts that invest in infrastructure may be different from other districts and because the decision to invest may be correlated with other changes in the district, the authors compare districts that passed measures by a small margin to those that did not pass by a small margin, arguing that crossing the threshold is essentially "random." When they make this comparison, they find that school performance increases six years after the bond issue but that housing prices increase substantially more, concluding that much of the value of school facilities comes from dimensions of school output that are not reflected in student test scores.

School district structure can also affect parental perception of available school quality and hence housing prices. Reback (2005) looks at how housing prices are affected by the introduction of a limited amount of school choice. Using the implementation of inter-district choice in Minnesota, he finds that residential properties appreciated in school districts where students were able to transfer out to preferred school districts, while housing values declined in districts that accepted transfer students.

So far, we have assumed that parents know the school quality and, from there, have tried to estimate their valuation. But is this really the case? Or can the provision of "information" create changes in the housing market? There is a separate literature on the role of information about schools on housing prices. In this case, there may be no actual change in school quality but a change in the perception of school quality.

Figlio and Lucas (2004) use repeated sales in Florida to examine how the housing market responds to information on school quality. The introduction of school report cards in 1999 led to changes in residential property values beyond the estimated effects of test scores and the other components of school grades. This is somewhat surprising given that most of the school grades are purely functions of test scores and other publicly available data, suggesting that there the publication of these school quality grades in fact provided new information to parents.

---

[11] He also notes that the resulting house price increases offset the positive effect of increasing education quality by making it more costly to live in these neighborhoods.

Work by Kane, Staiger, and Samms (2003) uses data from Mecklenburg County, North Carolina, to look at the effect of school quality information introduced by school report cards on housing prices. In 1997, 13 out of 61 public elementary schools were labeled as low performing based on proficiency in end-of-grade exams. Despite finding strong and significant effects of average school test scores over a number of years on housing prices (using the boundary fixed effect method used in Black (1999)), the authors find no evidence of year to year fluctuations in school test scores having an effect on house price volatility.[12] This is in contrast to the findings of Figlio and Lucas (2004); the authors suggest that the absence of a response reflect the fact that most of these schools had been poor performing for some time and there was therefore little new information in the report cards.

In the context of a loss of neighborhood schools and school redistricting in Cleveland, Bogart and Cromwell (2000) adopt a quasi-experimental approach based upon the redrawing of catchment area boundaries. They study the case of Shaker Heights, Ohio, where the number of elementary schools was reduced from nine to six, and they find a significant loss in housing values when the realignment occurred.

Similarly, Ries and Somerville (2004) treat a redrawing of school catchment zones in Vancouver in January 2001 as an experiment that exogenously induces changes in school quality that in turn can affect housing valuations. This was a substantial rezoning that had a potential impact on around one in five Vancouver residences. Moreover, their analysis uses time series data to try and pin down the effects of the redrawing on housing values. The authors find significant effects of school quality on housing prices only for the most expensive quartile of residences, a finding they interpret as suggesting that these residences are purchased by high-income households who have strong preferences for good schools.

Finally, Machin and Salvanes (2010) consider an admissions policy reform in Oslo that generated a switch from zone based to open enrollment in the 1997/8 academic year. They exploit this change to estimate the house price premium associated with better school performance before and after the reform, hypothesizing that the value of being located in a higher school quality catchment area would decline with the introduction of school choice. They adopt a difference-in-difference type analysis (coupled with boundary discontinuities) and show that, while pre-reform there was a significant 2–4% increase in prices for a one standard deviation increase in school average pupil marks, this fell significantly post-reform as school choice was opened up and children could cross the old boundaries to attend school.

---

[12] Interestingly, their estimated effect of school test scores on housing prices is larger than that of Black (1999). They find that a one school-level standard deviation change in test scores is associated with a change in housing prices of 5 percentage points, over double the 2.2 percentage point difference found by Black.

4.2.6 Combined Methods and Alternative Approaches

There are a small number of papers that combine a variety of the methods discussed above to try and pin down the causal impact of school quality on house prices. Kane, Riegg, and Staiger (2006) apply two different strategies to identify the relationship between school quality and housing prices; the first is the boundary discontinuity method and the second relates the change in housing prices associated with a change in school district boundaries resulting from court ordered desegregation. Using data from the Charlotte-Mecklenburg school system, the authors find that both methods result in a positive and statistically significant relationship between housing prices and school quality. Consistent with earlier work, these estimates are substantially smaller than naive OLS estimates.

Gibbons and Machin (2003, 2006) also use multiple methods in their valuation of English primary schools. They adopt several of the approaches we have considered to date, including semiparametric modeling of unobservable factors, discontinuities at school district boundaries, and instrumental variables using historically determined school characteristics as instruments. They interpret their results as bounding the school performance effect; estimates range from 3–6.7% higher house prices associated with a one standard deviation increase in school quality. The IV estimate of 6.7% is very much viewed as an upper bound, with smaller effects from the discontinuity approach.

A rather different approach using multiple methods, but underpinned by a more structural modeling technique, is adopted by Bayer, Ferreira, and McMillan (2007). They estimate a model of residential sorting that considers the value of schooling from a general equilibrium perspective.[13] They implement a two-stage structural approach that imposes a particular functional form on the residential choice and sorting process (coupled with an instrumentation strategy). In particular, the authors follow the approach of Berry et al. (1995) and first specify a functional form for the indirect utility function of a household with given set of characteristics and given housing choice. This depends linearly on the characteristics of the housing choice and of the surrounding neighborhood, plus interactions between these attributes and household characteristics. They then estimate a multinomial logit model of actual housing choices to retrieve the set of parameters that characterize the mean indirect utility function of all households in a given housing choice and the household specific components. Finally, in the last step of their procedure, the authors use the estimated parameters to control for the effect of heterogeneous preferences in a standard hedonic price regression. The authors argue that, although the empirical work using boundary fixed effects methods give very small effects of school quality on housing prices (including their own estimates), when they

---

[13] Bayer, McMillan, and Rueben (2002) estimate a model of residential sorting that is more general and not explicitly focused on school quality.

consider the combined effect of housing prices and residential sorting, they find much larger effects of school quality. This highlights the importance of considering neighborhood sorting as well. While this approach does allow for general equilibrium effects, it is worth noting that this method relies on strong and hard-to-test assumptions about the shape of the indirect utility function and on the Independence of Irrelevant Alternatives (IIA) hypothesis invoked to estimate multinomial logit models.

4.3 Availability of Private Schooling

One final issue we need to consider is the fact that the literature focuses primarily on state-provided education. However, in most countries, private schooling alternatives are available. While a lot of the theoretical work on school quality concerns itself with choices between public and private schooling (see, *inter alia*, Epple and Romano (1998), Nechyba (1999, 2004)), much less of the empirical work considers this in detail. Fack and Grenet (2010) is one exception where, in their analysis of Paris middle schools, they explicitly argue that the presence of private schools has a mitigating influence upon the house-price–school-quality association. Their evidence shows significant spatial heterogeneity linked to private school density in the area, in that the effect of school quality is more pronounced for residences in areas with a low density of private schools (and nonexistent for areas in the upper quartile of private school density).

5. CONCLUSIONS

Estimating the extent to which parents are prepared to pay more for access to schools they perceive to be of higher quality has been a major preoccupation in the economics of education in the last 30 to 40 years. As our review makes evident, almost all of this work shows a significant statistical association between housing valuations and school quality. Indeed, much of the work reveals that parents, in a wide range of international contexts often with very different institutional features, are prepared to pay sizable sums of money for access to better performing schools.

One striking characteristic of the large body of work in this area has been the clear improvements and refinements of methodology over time. Traditional multivariate regression techniques have been replaced by regression discontinuity approaches, instrumental variables, and difference-in-differences approaches. This recent work can, in certain settings and under certain assumptions, identify the causal impact of school quality on housing valuations. Moreover, there is something of a consensus in this literature that school quality matters and significantly raises capitalized housing values. In our view a not unreasonable benchmark summary of the magnitude of the average causal impact is that a one standard deviation increase in test scores raises house prices by around 3%.

However, many research challenges remain. As better data become available, researchers can focus more on what features of a school make a "good" school as perceived by parents; this will be a good complement to the decidedly inconclusive literature on the role of school inputs on student outcomes. In addition, with access to more detailed data on the characteristics of homebuyers that registry data could provide, future work can help us better understand the sorting process involved in household location decisions.

ACKNOWLEDGEMENTS

We are very grateful to Richard Murphy and Felix Weinhardt for their research assistance help in identifying relevant research papers from the literature.

REFERENCES

Alonso, W., 1964. Location and Land Use. Harvard University Press.
Atkinson, S., Crocker, T., 1987. A bayesian approach to assessing the robustness of hedonic property value studies. J. Appl. Econom. 2, 27–45.
Barrow, L., 2002. School choice through relocation: Evidence from the Washington, D.C. area. J. Public Econ. 86, 155–189.
Bayer, P., Ferreira, F., McMillan, R., 2007. A unified framework for measuring preferences for schools and neighborhoods. J. Polit. Econ. 115, 588–638.
Bayer, P., McMillan, R., 2005. Sorting and competition in local education markets. NBER Working Paper No. 11802.
Bayer, P., McMillan, R., Rueben, K., 2002. An equilibrium model of an urban housing market: A study of the causes and consequences of residential segregation. Yale University, Unpublished manuscript.
Berry, S., Levinsohn, J., Pakes, A., 1995. Automobile prices in market equilibrium. Econometrica 63, 841–890.
Black, S., 1999. Do better schools matter? Parental valuation of elementary education. Q. J. Econ. 114, 578–599.
Bogart, W., Cromwell, B., 1997. How much more is a good school district worth? Natl. Tax J. 50, 215–232.
Bogart, W., Cromwell, B., 2000. How much is a neighborhood school worth? J. Urban Econ. 47, 280–305.
Bradbury, K., Case, K., Mayer, C., 2001. Property tax limits, local fiscal behavior, and property values: Evidence from Massachusetts under Proposition 2 1/2. J. Public Econ. 80, 287–311.
Brasington, D., 1999. Which measures of school quality does the housing market measure? J. Real Estate Res. 18, 395–413.
Brasington, D., 2002. Edge versus center: Finding common ground in the capitalization debate. J. Urban Econ. 52, 524–541.
Brasington, D., 2003. The supply of public school quality. Econ. Edu. Review 22, 367–377.
Brasington, D., Haurin, D., 1996. School quality and real house prices: Inter- and intra-metropolitan effects. J. Housing Econ. 5, 351–368.
Brasington, D., Haurin, D., 2006a. Educational outcomes and house values: A test of the value added approach. J. Regional Sci. 46, 245–268.
Brasington, D., Haurin, D., 2006b. The demand for educational quality: Combining a median voter and hedonic house price model. Louisiana State University Working paper.
Brasington, D., Hite, D., 2008. A mixed index approach to identifying hedonic price models. Reg. Sci. Urban Econ. 38, 271–284.

Briggs, A., Burgess, S., McConnell, B., Slater, H., 2006. School choice in England: Background facts. CMPO Working Paper, 06/159.

Brueckner, J., 1979. Property values, local public expenditure and economic efficiency. J. Public Econ. 11, 223–245.

Brunner, E., Murdoch, J., Thayer, M., 2002. School finance reform and housing values. Public Finance and Management 2, 535–565.

Caetano, G., 2009. Identification and estimation of parental valuation of school quality in the U.S. Mimeo.

Card, D., 1999. The causal effect of education on earnings. In: Ashenfelter, O., Card, D. (Eds.), Handbook of Labor Economics. 3A, Elsevier.

Card, D., 2006. Research design and the practice of labor economics. 2006 Royal Economic Society Lecture.

Case, K., Mayer, C., 1996. Housing price dynamics within a metropolitan area. Reg. Sci. Urban Econ. 26, 387–407.

Cellini, S., Ferreira, F., Rothstein, J., 2008. The value of school facilities: Evidence from a dynamic regression discontinuity design. NBER Working Paper No. 14516.

Chay, K., McEwan, P., Urquiola, M., 2005. The central role of noise in evaluating interventions that use test scores to rank schools. Am. Econ. Rev. 95, 1237–1258.

Cheshire, P., Sheppard, S., 1998. Estimating the demand for housing, land and neighbourhood characteristics. Oxford B. Econ. Stats. 60, 357–382.

Cheshire, P., Sheppard, S., 2004. Capitalising the value of free schools: The impact of supply characteristics and uncertainty. Econ. J. 114, F397–F424.

Chin, H., Foong, K., 2006. Influence of school accessibility on housing values. J. Urban Plan. D.-ASCE 132, 120–129.

Chiodo, A., Hernandez-Murillo, R., Owyang, M., 2003. Nonlinear hedonics and the search for school district quality. Federal Reserve Bank of St. Louis Working Papers: 2003–039.

Clapp, J., Nanda, A., Ross, S., 2008. Which school attributes matter? The influence of school district performance and demographic composition of property values. J. Urban Econ. 63, 451–466.

Clapp, J., Ross, S., 2004. Schools and housing markets: An examination of school segregation and performance in Connecticut. Econ. J. 114, F425–F440.

Clark, D., Herrin, W., 2000. The impact of public school attributes on home sale prices in California. Growth Change 31, 385–408.

Crone, T., 2006. Capitalization of the quality of local public schools: What do home buyers value? Federal Reserve Bank of Philadelphia, Working Papers: 06–15.

Davidoff, I., Leigh, A., 2008. How much do public schools really cost? Estimating the relationship between house prices and school quality. Econ. Rec. 84, 193–206.

Dee, T., 2000. The capitalization of education finance reforms. J. Law Econ. 43, 185–214.

Derrick, F., Sedgley, N., Williams, N., 2008. The effect of educational test scores on house prices in a model with spatial dependence. J. Hous. Econ. 17, 191–200.

Des Rosiers, F., Lagan, A., Theriault, M., 2001. Size and proximity effects of primary schools on surrounding house values. J. Prop. Res. 18, 149–168.

Dills, A., 2004. Do parents value changes in test scores? High stakes testing in Texas. Contrib. to Econ. Anal. Policy 3, Article 10.

Downes, T., Zabel, J., 2002. The impact of school characteristics on house prices: Chicago 1987–1991. J. Urban Econ. 52, 1–25.

Ekeland, I., Heckman, J., Nesheim, L., 2002. Identifying hedonic models. Am. Econ. Rev. Papers and Proceedings 92, 304–309.

Ekeland, I., Heckman, J., Nesheim, L., 2004. Identification and estimation of hedonic models. J. Polit. Econ. 112, S60–S109.

Epple, D., 1987. Hedonic prices and implicit markets: Estimating demand and supply functions for differentiated products. J. Polit. Econ. 95, 59–80.

Epple, D., Romano, R., 1998. Competition between private and public schools, vouchers and peer group effects. Am. Econ. Rev. 88, 33–62.

Epple, D., Romano, R., 2003. Neighborhood schools, choice and the distribution of educational benefits. In: Hoxby, C. (Ed.), The Economics of School Choice. University of Chicago Press.

Fack, G., Grenet, J., 2010. Do better schools raise housing prices? Evidence from Paris school zoning. J. Pub. Econ. 94, 59–77.

Figlio, D., Lucas, M., 2004. What's in a grade? School report cards and the housing market. Am. Econ. Rev. 94, 591–604.

Fiva, J., Kirkeboen, L., 2008. Does the housing market react to new information on school quality? CESifo Working Paper No. 2299.

Fullerton, D., Rosen, H., 1977. A note on local tax rates, public benefit levels, and property values. J. Polit. Econ. 85, 433–440.

Gibbons, S., Machin, S., 2003. Valuing english primary schools. J. Urban Econ. 53, 197–219.

Gibbons, S., Machin, S., 2006. Paying for primary schools: Admissions constraints, school popularity or congestion. Econ. J. 116, C77–C92.

Gibbons, S., Machin, S., Silva, O., 2008. Competition, choice and pupil achievement. J. Eur. Econ. Assoc. 6, 912–947.

Gibbons, S., Machin, S., Silva, O., 2009. Valuing school quality using boundary discontinuities. Centre for Economic Performance, LSE Mimeo.

Gibbons, S., Silva, O., 2009. School quality, child wellbeing and parents' satisfaction. Centre for the Economics of Education, Discussion Paper 103.

Gravel, N., Michelangeli, A., Trannoy, A., 2006. Measuring the social value of local public goods: An empirical analysis within Paris metropolitan area. Appl. Econ. 38, 1945–1961.

Grether, D., Mieszkowski, P., 1974. Determinants of real estate values. J. Urban Econ. 1, 127–146.

Hanushek, E., 2006. School resources. In: Hanushek, E., Welch, F. (Eds.), Handbook of the Economics of Education. 2, North Holland.

Hayes, K., Taylor, L., 1996. Neighborhood school characteristics: What signals quality to homebuyers? Economic Review: Federal Reserve Bank of Dallas 4, 2–9.

Hurd, R., 1903. Principles of City Land Values. Record and Guide.

Imbens, G., Lemieux, T., 2008. Regression discontinuity designs: A guide to practice. J. Econom. 142, 615–635.

Jud, G., Watts, J., 1981. Real estate values, school quality, and the pattern of urban development in Charlotte, North Carolina. Econ. Educ. Rev. 1, 87–97.

Kain, J., Quigley, J., 1970. Measuring the value of housing quality. J. Am. Statistical Assoc. 63, 532–548.

Kane, T., Riegg, S., Staiger, D., 2006. School quality, neighborhood and housing prices. Am. Law Econ. Rev. 8 (2), 183–212.

Kane, T., Staiger, D., 2002a. Volatility in school test scores: Implications for test-based accountability systems. Brookings Pap. Educ. Policy 235–269.

Kane, T., Staiger, D., 2002b. The promise and pitfalls of using imprecise school accountabilty measures. J. Econ. Perspect. 16, 91–114.

Kane, T., Staiger, D., Samms, G., 2003. School accountability ratings and housing values. Brookings-Wharton Papers on Urban Affairs 4, 83–137.

Leech, D., Campos, E., 2003. Is comprehensive education really free? A case study of the effects of secondary school admissions policies on house prices in one local area. J. R. Stat. Soc. Series A (Statistics in society) 166, 135–154.

Machin, S., Salvanes, K., 2010. Valuing school choice and social interactions: Evidence from an admissions reform. IZA Discussion Paper 4719.

Nechyba, T., 1999. School finance-induced migration patterns: The impact of private school vouchers. J. Public Econ. Theory 1, 5–50.

Nechyba, T., 2003a. School finance, spatial income segregation and the nature of communities. J. Urban Econ. 54, 61–88.

Nechyba, T., 2003b. Introducing school choice into multidistrict public school systems. In: Hoxby, C. (Ed.), The Economics of School Choice. University of Chicago Press.

Nechyba, T., 2004. Income and peer quality sorting in public and private schools. In: Hanushek, E., Welch, F. (Eds.), Handbook of the Economics of Education. 2, North Holland.

Oates, W., 1969. The effect of property taxes and local public spending on property values: An empirical study of tax capitalization and the Tiebout hypothesis. J. Polit. Econ. 77, 957–971.

Reback, R., 2005. House prices and the provision of local public services: Capitalization under school choice programs. J. Urban Econ. 57, 275–301.

Ries, J., Somerville, T., 2004. School quality and residential property values: Evidence from Vancouver Rezoning. Department of Economics, University of British Columbia Working paper.

Rosen, S., 1974. Hedonic prices and implicit markets: Product differentiation in pure competition. J. Polit. Econ. 82, 34–55.

Rosenthal, L., 2003. The value of secondary school quality. Oxford B. Econ. Stat. 65, 329–355.

Sheppard, S., 1999. Hedonic analysis of housing markets. In: Cheshire, P. (Ed.), Handbook of Urban and Regional Economics. Elsevier Science.

Sonstelie, J., Portney, P., 1980. Gross rents and market values: Testing the implications of Tiebout's hypothesis. J. Urban Econ. 7, 102–118.

Tauchen, H., Witte, A., 2001. Estimating hedonic models: Implications of the theory. NBER Technical Paper 271.

Tiebout, C., 1956. A pure theory of local expenditures. J. Polit. Econ. 64, 416–424.

Todd, P., Wolpin, K., 2003. On the specification and estimation of the production function for cognitive achievement. Econ. J. 113, F3–F33.

Von Thunen, J., 1826. Der Isolierte Staat in Beiziehung auf Landwirtschaft und Nationalokonomie. Berlin.

Walden, M., 1990. Magnet schools and the differential impact of school quality on residential property values. J. Real Estate Res. 5, 221–230.

Weimer, D., Wolkoff, M., 2001. School performance and housing values using non-contiguous district and incorporation boundaries to identify school effects. Natl. Tax J. 45, 231–254.

CHAPTER 11

Apprenticeship

Stefan C. Wolter* and Paul Ryan**
*University of Bern and CESifo
**Cambridge University

Contents

1. Introduction	522
2. Firm Behavior in Providing and Financing Apprenticeship Training	524
2.1 The human capital theory framework of Becker	525
2.2 Extensions to the Becker model	527
2.2.1 Information asymmetries	528
2.2.2 Compressed wage structures	530
2.2.3 Industry- or occupation-specific monopsonies	532
2.2.4 Product market competition	533
2.2.5 The "make or buy" decision	534
2.2.6 Reputation—advantages on the product markets	535
2.3 Training subsidies	535
2.4 Production-oriented training motivation	536
2.5 Conclusions and future research	538
3. Empirical Observations on the Specificity of Human Capital, Net Cost of Apprenticeship Training and the Business Cycle	539
3.1 Firm-specific vs. general training	539
3.2 Net cost of training	541
3.3 Production-oriented training: cheap labor?	546
3.4 Apprenticeship training and the business cycle	548
3.5 Conclusions and future research	549
4. Outcomes for Apprentices	550
4.1 Measurement and identification issues	550
4.2 Some recent evidence	551
4.3 Conclusions and future research	553
5. Institutional Foundations of Apprenticeship	553
5.1 Institutions and outcomes	555
5.1.1 Statutory framework	558
5.1.2 Employer representation	560
5.1.3 Employee representation: social partnership	562
5.1.4 Educational representation	566
5.1.5 Apprentice organization	567
5.2 Conclusions and future research	568
6. Conclusions	569
References	570

Abstract

Apprenticeship varies greatly across countries, in terms of both quantity (numbers trained) and quality (skill content); and across sectors and occupations within countries, in terms of its provision and finance by employers. This chapter outlines recent advances in both areas. Some firms engage in apprenticeship training, others do not; some of those that do, invest in their apprentices, whereas others make a surplus on them. Despite the advances of the last two decades, there is as yet no "general theory" to explain the full range of financial attributes seen in practice within, let alone between, countries. Indeed recent theoretical efforts have focused excessively on specific circumstances in occupational labor markets, and neglected the potential sensitivity of their conclusions to changes in assumptions about labor markets, for both skilled workers and trainees. We also consider evaluations of the benefits of apprenticeship for individuals. Finally, the chapter considers the coordination mechanisms, principally employer bodies (associations, chambers) and employee representation and social partnership (trade unions, works councils, and joint regulatory bodies). Economic analysis indicates various ways in which such institutions may affect economic efficiency. Diversity of institutions across the countries with successful apprenticeship systems suggests, however, that there is no unique recipe for success.

JEL classification: I2, J3, J4, J5, J6, O5

Keywords

Apprenticeship
Training
Institutions

1. INTRODUCTION[1]

Apprenticeship normally combines part-time formal education with training and experience at the workplace. As such, it involves four parties—employers, trainees, educators, and government—as potential bearers of its costs and recipients of its benefits. The conditions under which they are willing to bear those costs and can receive those benefits constitutes a fruitful area of contemporary research, both theoretical and empirical.

The issue is particularly important for employers. Full-time vocational education involves the employer and the labor market only indirectly, as agent and arena respectively for the trading of human capital after its creation. Apprenticeship, by contrast, involves both directly, as part of the creation of human capital. Following Becker, a key question is: why would any employer provide and finance training for an asset, viz. employee skills, that it does not own and for any investment in which it cannot in competitive markets extract a return?

---

[1] We thank the editors, the participants at the Munich conference, Simon Field, Kathrin Hoeckel, Malgorzata Kuczera, Samuel Mühlemann, Harald Pfeifer and Eric Verdier for information, comments and suggestions.

The wider benefits of apprenticeship have also attracted scientific interest. Many observers, including economists, educators, managers, and policy makers alike, view apprenticeship as superior to full-time schooling as a source of efficient skill development. Its potential benefits include: (a) the cognitive and motivational effects of integrating theory and practice in skill learning; (b) a closer correspondence between the content of skills and the requirements of actual production systems; and (c) increased youth employment rates, and better school-to-work transitions in general (Streeck (1989); Grubb (1995); Ryan (2001); Field et al. (2009)).

The evidence does not uniformly favor apprenticeship: traditional and unregulated apprenticeship often shows limited learning content and a poor integration of theory—where present in the first place—with practice. Nor does apprenticeship invariably induce superior labor market outcomes for participants. Apprenticeship is more vulnerable to fluctuations in both economic activity and the youth population than is full-time schooling. Moreover, occupation-specific training such as apprenticeship may be better suited to incremental than to radical innovation, resulting in a slower adaptation of new technology and possibly a slower growth rate (Hall and Soskice (2001); Krueger and Kumar (2004a,b)). These drawbacks have not however prevented widespread policy interest in apprenticeship in advanced economies since the 1970s (OECD (1999)).

Scientific interest in apprenticeship is promoted also by the high dispersion of training activity across sectors, occupations, and countries. A standard indicator is the share of educational enrollments at upper secondary level that involve part-time training at workplaces. Across 17 advanced economies in 2006, this indicator had a coefficient of variation of 92%, as compared to 5% for the enrollment rate in all programs, and 64% for that in full-time vocational programs. In Germany and four of its smaller neighbors, apprentices account for between one-third and two-thirds of upper-secondary enrollments; in Belgium, South Korea, and Sweden, for very few or none (OECD (2008b, tables C1.1, 2.2)). Why do countries differ so much in so potentially important an aspect of skill formation?

We define apprenticeship as programs that comprise both work-based training and formal education, in most countries at upper-secondary level, and lead to a qualification in an intermediate skill, not just to semiskilled labor.[2] Apprenticeship is therefore distinct from three activities for which it is often an alternative: full-time vocational education, standalone on-the-job training, and labor market programs.[3] Even then, the term "apprenticeship" covers a heterogeneous reality. Definitions of apprenticeship vary from country to country and comparative data on it are limited.

---

[2] Although vocational education is present at lower-secondary level in many advanced economies, because young people at ages subject to compulsory schooling are excluded from mainstream employment, formal apprenticeship training usually starts when school-leavers attain full age. Apprenticeship training can also be part of tertiary education. We do not in principle differentiate the levels at which apprenticeship training can lead to educational credentials, because those differences are not relevant to most of the analysis.

[3] We use "apprenticeship" in principle as a functional rather than a conventional term. However, we do not cover other forms of vocational preparation that functionally fall under our definition but are not conventionally labeled as such—e.g., pupilages in the English legal profession.

The outline of the chapter is as follows. The next section tracks developments in the literature on employer-provided training, given that the firm's willingness to train apprentices is the *conditio sine qua non* for an apprenticeship system. We present the diverse analyses in the training literature—some competing, some complementary—of the firm's motivation for training. Most of these theoretical developments have been prompted by one-off empirical observations, and can therefore be expected to hold only if the relevant evidence is representative of a larger set of apprenticeship situations. That is why Section 3 considers recent empirical developments that refocus attention on specific issues and relativize some common views on the economics of apprenticeship. Section 4 summarizes recent empirical studies on the effects of training for apprentices themselves. As there is no comprehensive microeconomic theory that might explain differences in the scale of apprenticeship across countries, Section 5 discusses institutional factors, which provide the most promising analysis of those differences. The conclusions are presented in Section 6.

2. FIRM BEHAVIOR IN PROVIDING AND FINANCING APPRENTICESHIP TRAINING

This section analyses the firm's behavior in offering and financing apprenticeship training. Although the training literature, and human capital theory in particular, offers no specific theory of apprenticeship training, apprenticeship has often served not just as an illustration of its predictions but also as catalyst for new theoretical developments.[4] However, apprenticeship training, in contrast to standard "on-the-job-training," is in most cases heavily regulated by governments and social partners, and so particular aspects of it are not considered in the mainstream training literature, in which decisions are based solely on market-based interactions between atomistic employers and employees. This section has two goals: to trace developments in the training literature[5] over the last five decades, and to check the appropriateness of its assumptions and predictions in the context of apprenticeship.

Most of the training literature sees firms as having three options and choosing whichever promises the most profit. (1) They can either use nonskilled or skilled labor in production. If they choose skilled labor, they can either (2) train their own skilled labor, or (3) hire skilled labor on the external labor market, where skilled workers have been trained by other firms. For reasons of simplicity we assume in this section that skills can either be acquired efficiently only at the workplace or require on-the-job experience to develop full productivity, and that therefore once a firm has a demand

---

[4] Examples for this include: Lindley (1975), introducing the distinction between a production and an investment motive for firms to provide apprentices, using data on the net cost of training in England; Stevens (1994a), applying her investment model of firms' training to explain the collapse in the demand for apprentices in the English engineering industry in the 1980s; and Acemoglu and Pischke (1999a), using the observation of von Bardeleben et al. (1995), that the average German firm incurs considerable net cost during the training period of apprentices to motivate their extension of the classical Becker model (see also 2.2.).

[5] See also Leuven (2005) for a more extensive survey of the training literature.

for skilled labor its sole options are to offer training or to hire former apprentices that have been trained by other firms.[6]

2.1 The human capital theory framework of Becker

Human capital theory, formalized by Becker (1962) but contemporaneously developed by others, helps us understand the training activities of firms. It (re-)introduced the view that education and training represent investment in future productivity and not just consumption of resources. In this perspective, firm and workers alike depend on investments in human capital to increase competitiveness, profits, and pay. Although the benefits are obvious, these investments come at a cost. From the firm's point of view, investments in human capital differ from those in physical capital, in that the firm does not acquire a property right over its investments in skills, so it and its workers have to agree on the sharing of costs and benefits of those investments. Whereas investments in physical capital are strictly the company's own decision, investments in the skills of its workforce involve interaction with the employees to be trained. In the basic formulation, Becker, assuming that product and labor markets are perfectly competitive, introduced the distinction between firm-specific and general human capital to solve the question: who bears the costs of training?

General human capital is defined as all skills that are identically useful to many firms, including the training company. Firm-specific skills, in contrast, increase productivity only in the firm in which the skills were acquired. In a competitive market setting, workers always get a wage that equals their marginal productivity and thus, in the case of general human capital, workers earn the same wage wherever they work. Therefore the answer to the question "who bears the costs of general human capital investment?" is straightforward. As firms—in the absence of a contractual specification of an enforceable remedy for breach of contract—would lose all their investment were a worker to leave the training company, and because the worker is indifferent to the identity of the employer, there is no reason for any firm to finance the investment. Expenses are borne by the worker, either through an up-front payment or through a wage reduction during training. Although firms do not have an incentive to finance general human capital, workers are prepared to finance it up to the point where the marginal increase in their productivity (and wages) equals the marginal increase in their cost of training, and the amount of training provided by firms is then socially efficient, provided that no credit or liquidity constraints prevent the workers from financing the optimal amount of training.

If the training is firm-specific, the optimal financing scheme becomes more complicated, as neither the firm nor the worker has an incentive to pay its full cost. The reason is that both parties lose their entire investment in the event of a separation after

---

[6] However, the role of the state as a provider of education and training, which is of little importance for induction training and simple on-the-job training, is crucial for apprenticeship training, and that also motivates our discussion of institutions (below).

training. Becker conjectured that the firm and the worker would share costs and benefits in that case. Hashimoto (1981) formalized an optimal sharing rule, based on the minimization of inefficient post-training separations. With optimal cost-sharing, the investment in specific human capital is also socially efficient.[7]

In Becker's analysis, firms invest the efficient amount in training as long as trainees are willing and able to pay for the investment, whether directly out of their pockets or by accepting lower pay during training. At least historically it was the case that in many countries apprentices had to pay an apprentice premium (fee) that potentially covered the net cost of their training. Since this practice ended, apprentices pay has typically been substantially lower than the average pay of unskilled labor, which suggests that apprentices bear at least part of total training costs, in the form of lower pay.[8]

Two features of apprenticeship increase the analytical suitability of Becker's model to the financing and provision of apprenticeship training. First, and different from adult workers, apprentices are mostly young and living with their parents, and therefore less likely to be liquidity constrained or to reject low pay in order to finance training. Also, statutory minimum wages which might otherwise prevent wages from falling sufficiently for trainees to pay for training, typically do not apply to apprentices.[9]

Second, regulation of the length of apprenticeship contracts (Malcomson et al. (2003)) can further enhance efficiency.[10] Training very often involves an up-front investment for the training company, in the sense that the apprentice receives most of the training in the first phase of the apprenticeship and works productively only in the second phase. In such cases, the apprentice would have no incentive to accept low pay and stay with the training company for the second phase, if she could receive pay equal to her marginal product with another employer. Such situations are

---

[7] An important outcome of human capital theory is that in competitive markets there is no market failure in the provision of training and therefore also no cause for governments to intervene in the training market. Employers provide the efficient amount of general and specific skills.

[8] However, the observation that apprentice pay is lower than the wage of an unskilled worker does not necessarily establish that training costs are fully borne by the apprentice. Apprentices do not spend all their time at work (as a result of part-time schooling or formal training spells at the workplace) and the training company incurs expenses for trainers and materials. For the apprentice to bear all of the cost, the wage reduction would have to cover both the loss of production while the apprentice is away from work and the training expenses incurred by the company.

[9] In some countries the minimum wage applies to all categories of worker; others have a youth-specific subminimum wage, such as the SMIC (*Salaire minimum interprofessionelle de croissance*) rate in France for young workers and apprentices. In some theoretical models, minimum wages are the rationale for employer financed general training (e.g., Acemoglu and Pischke (2003)).

[10] This need not be the case, as some employers may want contract lengths that are inefficiently long in order to profit more from their apprentices. One has to note, however, that the length of the contract cannot be arbitrarily long to allow firms to recoup their training expenses. From the perspective of the apprentice, time spent in apprenticeship generates opportunity costs and therefore if a longer training period does not increase her productivity, apprenticeship training becomes a less attractive option compared to nontraining or a full-time schooling education (see e.g., Oosterbeek and Webbink 2007). An efficient contract length therefore must correspond to the time needed to learn the relevant occupational skills. Mühlemann et al. (2007b) show that the differentiation in the length of apprenticeship training programs in Switzerland is—on average—well-adapted to learning requirements.

common. The contract therefore commits the apprentice to stay to its completion, thereby permitting the training company to recoup its training expenses. Such contracts are less frequent and more difficult to enforce in the case of standard on-the-job training. Although it would also be quite difficult for employers to sue apprentices who quit their training before completion, the difference between on-the-job-training, which is typically uncertified, and a completed apprenticeship, which provides an educational credential, makes that unnecessary: the apprentice has an incentive to complete the contract in order to obtain the educational qualification. Even apprentices who do not set a high value on the qualification may be deterred from quitting by the reputational damage and, in some cases, increased difficulty of access to regulated occupations.

According to the Becker model, when all training in an apprenticeship is general, firms should bear no net costs for the training period as a whole. At the end of training, labor turnover should be high, and former apprentices should earn the same pay whether they stay or leave. If the training is firm-specific, in whole or part, companies should finance some of the net training cost during the apprenticeship and turnover after training should be lower. Assuming that all apprentices receive the same mix of firm-specific and general skills, stayers should earn more than movers, as the latter lose all the productivity derived from firm-specific human capital. Nontraining firms should not be able to make a profit from the investments made by the training firm or its apprentices (no poaching) as they have to pay a wage equal to the marginal productivity of the hired worker.

Although the Becker model offers an elegant analysis of the training decisions of firms, two sources of concern led to its extension. First, its predictions are potentially sensitive to its rather strict assumptions, viz. a perfectly competitive market system, with no distortions and with full information. This raised the question: how would the predictions change if these assumptions were relaxed? Becker's model might still constitute an important benchmark for alternative models, and the choice among alternative models might depend on the realism of their assumptions. Second, if empirical results contradict the predictions of the Becker model, a model that conforms better to those observations might be preferred.

2.2 Extensions to the Becker model

The basic human capital model has been extended in the last three decades in response to empirical findings that contradicted the prediction that firms never pay for general training. Indeed, Becker's model was seen to fail to explain the existence of apprenticeship systems such as the German one. The skills learned in German apprenticeships, because they conform to a national curriculum and are certified by external bodies, should be transferable to many companies and are therefore more general than firm-specific in content. If so, according to the Becker model, the turnover of apprentices after training should be high and, more important, firms should not pay for the training. However, the evidence showed that many firms incur substantial net costs over the training period as a whole and, although skills are in principle transferable, labor turnover after training, especially immediately after, is not particularly high.

2.2.1 Information asymmetries

Katz and Ziderman (1990) argued that there might be an information asymmetry concerning the amount and quality of training a worker receives.[11] If just the training firm knows how much and what type of general training a worker received, that would impose substantial information-based costs on external firms that seek to recruit its ex-trainees. The pay of the trained worker in the external market would therefore be lower than her true productivity. In such a situation the firm becomes willing to invest in general training as the informational advance over its competitors gives it bargaining power when negotiating the wage after training. All actions that help the training firm to disguise the true amount and the nature of general training it provides to its workers increase the rent that it can earn on its ex-trainees. Conversely, all measures that reveal its training reduce the informational asymmetry and thus its willingness to invest in general training. In particular, skill certification awards workers an effective property right over their general training and increases their potential mobility. But it also returns us to the Beckerian situation, in which apprentices must bear all the cost of their training. As apprenticeship training is in most countries externally certified, the model seems therefore not to explain why firms might pay for general training. Katz and Ziderman (1990, p. 1157) themselves noted that in their model the (West) German apprenticeship system appears anomalous, as the training is certified externally but firms bear the bulk of the training costs.

Acemoglu and Pischke (2000) introduced a framework in which external certification is not only compatible with firms' sharing or bearing the costs of general training but may even be a necessary condition that the predictions of the Katz and Ziderman model can be confirmed. The underlying intuition is that, whereas asymmetric information generates monopsony power for the firm over its skilled workers, and thus encourages it to invest in training, it also reduces the incentive for workers to invest in training themselves. If the effort that trainees put into their learning itself increases the effect of training on productivity, and that effort cannot be monitored by the training firm, then the firm faces a dilemma. It could, in principle, using its monopsony power, extract a rent on its training investment, but doing so reduces the incentive of trainees to exert effort and thereby reduces the value of the firm's investment. External certification can solve this dilemma as it ensures that workers receive more of the return to their general training and encourages workers to exert effort during training. It also has the advantage that it commits the training firm to provide a specific amount and quality of training, which otherwise would be legally difficult to enforce. In the model of Dustmann and Schönberg (2007),

---

[11] Chang and Wang (1996) provides formal model that borrows from Katz and Ziderman.

if firms are not able to commit to training provision because of the absence of an external regulatory framework, training activity is substantially lower, because apprentices are not willing to accept wage cuts to finance their share of the investment.

The idea that the monopsony power of training firms stems from an asymmetry in information over the content of general training is unlikely to explain fully firms' investments in general human capital in most apprenticeship systems.[12] The prospective exceptions are countries in which decisions about training and certification are company-based rather than institutionalized and external, as is largely the case in England, Italy, and Spain (Ryan (2000), Bassanini et al. (2007)) or certification requires only low attainments, leaving room for information asymmetry for the nonmandatory part of training.

When information about the ability and the productivity of skilled workers is not perfect, additional types of asymmetry can be exploited by training firms. The argument that adverse selection due to information asymmetries can generate rents on firms' investments is an application of Akerlof's (1970) "lemons" problem to labor markets. Models built on this idea assume that the ability of trainees cannot be (fully) observed in the moment of hiring. Therefore all unskilled recruits receive the same amount of training or no training at all. After training the company learns their true ability and makes a second-period wage offer that is contingent on ability and training. The training company can offer low-ability workers a wage equal to their productivity and high-ability workers the market wage. In the external market, firms observe the presence of training but not the ex-trainee's ability and so offer a wage that equals the expected ability of workers in the market. Assuming that some turnover is exogenous there will always be some high-ability workers in the market and wages will be strictly greater than the productivity of low-ability workers. Consequently, all low-ability workers have an incentive to leave the training firm and expected productivity in the market is strictly lower than the productivity of high-ability workers. Although the high-ability worker's productivity is higher than the market wage, she will not get a higher outside wage because the nontraining firms cannot observe individual ability in the market and so they always pay the market wage. Therefore by retaining high-ability workers after training, the training company can make a profit because the market wage is always less than the productivity of high-ability workers. If ability and training are complementary, so that high-ability workers profit more from training than low-ability workers, the information asymmetry automatically leads to a compressed wage structure, with reduced pay differences between untrained and trained workers (Acemoglu and Pischke 1998), which further encourages firms to investment in general training (see Section 2.2.2., below).

If firms do not know the ability of recruits, then another gain from training can be that training programs allow workers to signal their ability. These models (e.g., Autor (2001), Cappelli (2004)) also assume complementarity between training and ability. In

---

[12] Clark (2001) tests asymmetric information empirically, finding little evidence that German firms subsidize training to obtain (asymmetric) information about their trainees' attributes and choices.

this case, those workers who believe themselves to have high ability apply to training firms; workers who do not, apply to nontraining firms. Providing training helps the firm to access a pool of high-ability workers.[13] During the training period the firm learns the true ability of workers and, as above, it exploits its informational advantage about worker ability, because adverse selection depresses the market wage. The high-ability workers retained by training firms have a higher productivity than the average in the external "secondhand" worker pool, but because they cannot signal that to outside employers, the training firm pays them a wage below their true productivity.

2.2.2 Compressed wage structures

Acemoglu and Pischke (1998, 1999a,b) addressed the same anomaly—firms bearing a large share of the costs of training for skills that are predominantly general—as in the German apprenticeship system, explaining it also in terms of imperfect competition in labor markets. Frictions in the labor market lead to a compressed wage structure that makes it profitable for firms to invest in general training.[14] Wage compression denotes a situation in which pay increases with training less strongly than does productivity, creating a wedge between productivity and pay that is higher at greater levels of skill (Acemoglu and Pischke (1999a, p. F120).

Empirically, the ratio of pay at the highest decile to that at the lowest decile of the pay distribution differs substantially between countries. Assuming that the structure of productivity as a function of training is similar in all industrialized countries, this suggests that in some countries the wage structure is more compressed than in others; and Bassanini and Brunello (2008) show that firm-sponsored training is—as expected—more widespread in countries with pronounced wage compression than in other countries.

Wage compression may have several causes:

Information asymmetries. Asymmetric information between the training firm and its competitors in the labor market can cause wage compression through two channels. First, the training provider may know more about the amount of training it provides; second, it may know more about the ability of its trained workers. Either informational asymmetry leads to wage compression if ability and training are complements (Acemoglu and Pischke (1998)). This is plausible since more able workers are likely to benefit more from training and will therefore acquire more training.

Search costs and matching frictions. If workers must incur search costs in order to find a new employer and if frictions in matching make some employer-employee matches

---

[13] Similarly workers may view the training activities of firms as a signal of workplace quality, whether or not they themselves are interested in the particular training program. Backes-Gellner and Tuor (2010) find that German firms that provide apprenticeship have superior recruitment outcomes for skilled blue-collar workers, because such programs signal a high-quality workplace. In such cases the employer may recoup its net costs for apprenticeship training by enjoying lower recruitment costs.

[14] On the difference between absolute and relative wage compression see Booth and Zoega (2004).

more productive than others, the result is bilateral monopoly and a sharing of the match-specific surplus, with workers paid less than their marginal products. Although skilled workers usually have more bargaining power than unskilled workers, more skill also means higher search costs for workers; as it becomes increasingly difficult to find a good match, the bargaining power of skilled workers falls relative to that of unskilled ones, which also means wage compression.

Moreover, labor market regulations, in the form of firing costs, potentially augment search costs and matching frictions. If firing costs are negligible then in the case of a bad match firms can just lay off workers and bear the search cost for new recruits. Otherwise, firing costs add to the potential for mismatch. If firing costs are higher for skilled workers ("golden parachutes") than for low-skilled workers this in turn means greater wage compression.

Moral hazard. Acemoglu and Pischke (1998) argue that, if the company cannot monitor perfectly the work effort of employees, it may have to pay a higher (efficiency) wage to deal with moral hazard, that is, to incentivize effort. Such a wage floor would also compresses the wage structure. However, additional frictions (e.g., mobility costs) that create a surplus (i.e., a gap between marginal product and pay) must be present for the firm to offer training in the first place. The surplus may be invariant with respect to the level of skill. When a surplus exists, the introduction of the wage floor compresses pay structure and gives the firm an incentive to incur the cost of training up to the point where pay (which equals marginal product minus the surplus) exceeds the wage floor.[15]

Collective bargaining. A wage floor can also result from collective bargaining, for example, if trade unions seek to ensure for their members some minimum living standard. Dustmann and Schönberg (2009) test the effects on apprentice training in Germany using movements by firms between coverage and noncoverage by collective bargaining in order to control for selection biases potentially caused by unobserved employer attributes. As in Acemoglu and Pischke (1999a), the model predicts both more compressed pay structures and more apprenticeship training in firms with bargaining coverage. The evidence is consistent with the predictions: the number of noncovered firms that provide apprenticeship, although positive, is close to zero and significantly lower than the share of training firms among covered firms.[16]

A further effect of the equalizing effects of unions may be that low-ability members earn more than in the nonunion sector whereas high-ability workers earn less (Hirsch and Schumacher (1998)). Wage compression again gives unionized firms an incentive to invest in general human capital. However, additional frictions, such as information asymmetries, must also be present, because otherwise nontraining firms would poach trained workers and appropriate some of the rent on their skills (Stevens (1994b)).

---

[15] In the Becker model of general training, minimum wages reduce training when they prevent workers from paying for their training through lower pay.

[16] The recent literature on skilled labor markets has ignored a further source of imperfect competition that was historically important for manual skills and remains important in the liberal professions: seller organization and market power, as exercised notably by craft trade unions and professional associations.

Interaction between firm-specific and general skills. Training is never exclusively firm-specific or entirely general, but comprises instead some mix of general and firm-specific components.[17] In Becker's model, firms and workers share costs and benefits for firm-specific skills and firms pay nothing for general skills. Acemoglu and Pischke (1999b) argue that if firm-specific and general skills are independent, a component of specific skills simply generates economic rent for the firm but does not encourage them to invest in general skills, because that rent is independent of the amount of training in general skills.[18] If, however, firm-specific and general skills are complements, either because the production of one of those types of skill is less costly when accompanied by the other, or because skills of one category are more productive in the presence of the other category, the value of firm-specific skills increases as the amount of general skills increases, and with it the surplus from specific skills and the extent of wage compression.

2.2.3 Industry- or occupation-specific monopsonies

Other deviations from Becker's assumptions that may also explain firms' investments in general training do not involve wage compression. One is that firms possess monopsony power. Even if one would assume that all skills are technically general, their specificity to an industry or an occupation makes them *de facto* specific to firms (Bishop (1996)). Lazear (2003) formalized this idea in his skills weight model.[19] The fact that because of the specific combination (skills weight) of general skills turns them into *de facto* industry or occupation-specific skills, creates monopsony powers because it limits the number of firms that compete for a particular set of skills and thus increases the cost of changing jobs. Firms of course can further reduce the transferability of training in differentiating their skills requirement so as to generate market power (Stevens (1994b)). Occupation- or industry-specific skill requirements play an important role

---

[17] Even if the worker learns a mix of specific and general skills, it is not clear whether the two types are learned independently of each other or as complements, or even as substitutes. Feuer et al. (1987), Stevens (1994b), and Franz and Soskice (1995) argue that specific and general skills are likely to be complements. If they are complements in production, the firm can hedge its investment in the general component with its investment in the specific one.

[18] In Kessler and Lülfesmann (2006), however, the rent on specific skills depends on the level of general skills. In this case there are incentives for firms to invest in general human capital, without having specific and general skills necessarily as technical complements or substitutes in costs or output. In their bargaining model, specific and general skills are complementary from the point of view of firms because a higher share of general skills increases the firm's share of the rent on specific human capital. The authors also argue that the combination of specific and general skills might explain why bigger firms have on average higher investments (net costs) in apprenticeship training per trainee than do smaller firms: "... it is not immediate why informational asymmetries or search costs should systematically differ ... However, it seems quite plausible that firm-specific training is of considerable importance in large enterprises which are characterized by complex internal structures. ... a high relevance of specific training leads not only to low turnover rates, but goes hand in hand with a more pronounced provision of firm-sponsored general training." (ibid.: 919).

[19] Applying the skills weights approach to apprenticeship, Geel et al. (2010) calculate a skills weight for every occupation learned in apprenticeship in Germany, and find that, the more specific the skill portfolio in an occupation compared to other occupations, the higher are the net costs that firms bear for apprenticeship in that occupation.

in apprenticeship training and create conflicts of interests between employers and workers (Smits (2007)). Those conflicts are often addressed by the state, which typically holds the right to impose a training curriculum on the training firm. In doing so, the state has to balance the interests of the workers (more transferable skills increase the lower bound on wages and increase options for external mobility) and employers (industry- or occupation-specific skills increase their market power).

There is thus a policy tradeoff between the goals of a mobile and employable workforce and of firms' willingness to provide and finance training. The importance of the definition of the curriculum in apprenticeship training and the role it plays in keeping firms in a sector interested in providing training places can be seen in extended negotiations between governments and social partners not only about curriculum content, and thereby the mix of firm-specific and general skills, but also about the number of recognized training occupations. A higher number of occupations increases the occupational specificity of training but it increases the willingness of firms to incur training costs.[20]

Monopsony power may also be generated by the regional distribution of firms. Assuming again that skills are to some degree industry- or occupation-specific, then a high spread of the firms in a sector across regions promotes monopsony power, that is, reduces the probability that skilled workers will be poached by competitors. Conversely, economic density can increase training through the "agglomeration effect." If training produces positive spill-overs, for example, because training is a complement to innovation (Acemoglu (1997)), a greater concentration of firms in a particular region increases firms' willingness to provide and finance training. However, Harhoff and Kane (1997) and Mühlemann and Wolter (2007) show for Germany and Switzerland respectively that the higher the number of competitor firms in the same region, the lower the probability that they are active in apprenticeship training. Brunello and de Paola (2008) and Brunello and Gamberotto (2007) show similar results for general on-the-job training in the U.K. and Italy. It seems that a greater density of economic activity increases the threat of poaching more than it creates positive training spill-overs.

2.2.4 Product market competition

As well as labor market regulation and competition, competition in the product market may also influence firms' training decisions. Theoretically different outcomes may result from more product market competition. A model of Gersbach and Schmutzler (2006) concludes that if product market competition is high and product differentiation low, training incidence is lower because workers enjoy better outside options and therefore employers have less bargaining power. On the other hand, if competition is weak and the skills of trained workers are homogeneous, firms may invest in nonfirm-specific training if others do the same, to avoid competitive disadvantage or the need to

---

[20] The traditional training literature, which is more concerned about continuous education and workplace training of adults than specifically apprenticeship training, underestimates the importance of certification authority in countries with extensive apprenticeship training systems (e.g., Busemeyer (2009)).

pay higher wages in order to attract trained workers. However, other models lead to the opposite prediction: Bassanini and Brunello (2007) conclude that if the number of firms rises as a result of a reduction in product market regulations, the output gain from training rises, which encourages firms to invest more in training. They estimate the relationship between product market regulation and training incidence for on-the-job-training in 15 European countries and find that more product market competition significantly increases training incidence. Goerlitz and Stiebale (2008) with a similar approach find for Germany no relationship between product market competition and training incidence. Thus theory does not produce consistent predictions, nor is the empirical evidence conclusive concerning the effect of product market deregulation on training.

2.2.5 The "make or buy" decision

Differences in hiring and training costs may also affect the firm's supply of training. A firm can obtain skilled workers either by hiring from the external labor market or by training apprentices internally and retaining them after training: the "make or buy" decision. A profit-maximizing firm trains apprentices only if it is cheaper than recruiting already skilled workers. If there are no economies of scale in training or recruitment and all firms have the same cost structure, then either all firms train or no firm does. But if there are diminishing returns in training and rising costs of recruitment, firms may use both sources of skill; and if firms' cost structures differ, then some firms do more training, others more recruitment.[21]

So some firms may train apprentices because they have a low relative cost in training relative to recruitment. Cost-benefit surveys of apprenticeship in Germany (e.g., Beicht and Walden (2002)) and Switzerland (Mühlemann et al. (2007b)) find substantial differences in net training costs across companies that provide training, even in the same occupation and industry. Generalizing to all firms, Mühlemann et al. (2007a) show for Switzerland that differences in net training costs affect significantly the probability that a firm trains apprentices. Recruitment costs may be similarly variable across firms, encouraging some firms to train and others to recruit.

Concerning the tendency for firms to use both training and recruitment, Blatter et al. (2011) find evidence that the marginal cost of recruitment increases with its scale, and the higher the recruitment cost, the greater the volume of training. Among Swiss firms with positive net training costs, the estimated elasticity of training volume with respect to recruitment cost, computed at sample means, is that one standard deviation in hiring costs for skilled workers increases the number of apprentices by 2.7 standard deviations. Therefore firms invest in training partly to reduce their recruitment costs.

---

[21] A third potential source of skilled labor is the upgrade training of less skilled employees, which can offer firms a more cost-effective source of skilled labor than either apprenticeship or recruitment (Ryan et al. (2007)).

2.2.6 Reputation—advantages on the product markets

A further incentive for firms to bear part of the costs of apprentice training may arise from reputation effects (Sadowski (1980)). Training apprentices may signal not only a high-quality workplace in the eyes of future recruits in the labor market but also, in imperfectly competitive product markets, product quality, and social commitment in the eyes of consumers, thereby increasing the firm's sales and profits. If so, the firm's net costs for the training of apprentices does not entail any corresponding reduction in profits. The argument is popular with policy makers but, apart from some firms' declarations of their motives for training, there is no scientific evidence either way on its existence or importance.

2.3 Training subsidies

As Becker emphasized, if training involves both general skills and positive net costs for the firm, and labor markets are perfectly competitive, firms do not train. The most obvious ways to stimulate firms to offer training would then be to subsidize training costs, including tax deductibility of training expenses (Bishop (1996), Stevens (1999, 2001)).[22] In many countries with well-established apprenticeship systems, firms also benefit directly from more or less generous state support, as in Denmark (Albaek (2009)).[23]

A handful of evaluation studies show that, while subsidies tend to increase participation in training by firms or apprentices, substantial deadweight loss is typically involved. It is difficult for governments to target subsidies on firms that would not otherwise have done any training.[24] Moreover, the state rarely knows with any precision firms' net training costs, and therefore the extent to which individual firms should be subsidized, if at all. Finally, if subsidies are uniformly distributed across sectors, distortions are to be expected in the labor market: sectors with low training costs expand training, even if the skills involved are not the ones most needed in the present or the future. It is unlikely that governments possess the information necessary to circumvent this problem by targeting subsidies on particular sectors.

---

[22] Public subsidies to apprenticeship that do not involve direct support for firms normally focus on the public funding of part-time courses for apprentices in vocational schools and colleges (Ryan (2000, table 4)).

[23] Another way to subsidize apprenticeship is to direct public subsidies to the demand side, aiming at trainees who are credit and liquidity constrained, as is likely to be common when apprenticeship is aimed more at young adults than teenagers, as is the case to some extent in Denmark (e.g., Dohlmann Weatherall (2009)). The subsidy to trainees reduces apprentices' pay, so that ideally the surplus of apprentices' productivity over pay covers the firm's training costs.

[24] Mühlemann et al. (2007a) simulated the costs of an introduction of subsidies in Switzerland and reached the conclusion that the deadweight loss would be so big that the costs for an additional training post would exceed the costs of full-time schooling. Although Rasmussen and Westergaard-Nielsen (1999) calculated subsidy costs for an additional training post in apprenticeship training in Denmark that amounted only to one sixth of the costs of full-time schooling, they concluded that the efficiency of the measure could have been greatly improved, if it would have been limited to a few industries.

2.4 Production-oriented training motivation

The extensions to the classical Becker discussed above concern the training strategy that Lindley (1975) labeled investment-oriented: the firm provides training, and finances it at least in part, with a view to ensuring its future skill supply. Although it is not always clear whether the firm really invests in future skilled workforce or just needs to retain its former apprentices in order to pay back the firm's training expenses.[25] The theoretical focus on investment-oriented training may be motivated by the fact that investing in general training makes no sense if the firm has no intention to keep the apprentice after training. In any case, theory has not accommodated evidence that is potentially inconsistent with mainstream theories of both perfect competition (Becker) and imperfect competition in skilled labor markets (Acemoglu and Pischke (1998), Stevens (1994b)).

The anomalous evidence contains three strands. Firstly, while studies of the net cost of apprenticeship to the firm during the training contract (see Section 3.2.) always reveal great heterogeneity in firms' net costs, they also show that a substantial share of firms make a net profit—that is, incur negative net costs—*during* the training period itself.[26] Secondly, in some apprenticeship systems, notably the Swiss one, inter-firm mobility of apprentices during the early post-training years is so high as to call into question its compatibility with an investment-oriented training motivation for firms (e.g., Wolter and Schweri (2002)). In Germany, the distribution of post-training retention rates by employers who train apprentices is bimodal, with peaks at 0 and 100% (Mohrenweiser and Backes-Gellner (2010)). The lower mode points strongly to production-oriented training. Thirdly, the industrial disputes that apprentices have occasionally conducted in pursuit of higher pay (see Section 5) could not have succeeded had their employers trained them in general skills and borne part or all of the net cost, as they are taken to do in the theories discussed above.[27] These three types of evidence suggest that the provision of apprenticeship by some firms has more to do with their current production costs than with their future skills supplies.

In production-oriented training, the firm provides apprenticeships because it can substitute toward apprentices for work that would otherwise be done at higher pay by unskilled or skilled workers. Even when, because of external regulation or technology, firms train for transferable skills, they may find that the value of apprentices' output (net

---

[25] Autor (2001) shows that firms that hire out temporary workers share the costs for general skills without having an investment strategy; although the firm does not wish to keep the ex-trainees itself, the extra skill allows it to charge higher prices to other firms that seek temporary labor.

[26] E.g., Beicht et al. (2004), Mühlemann et al (2007b), and Mühlemann et al (2010). Similarly, Mohrenweiser and Zwick (2009) find that in Germany a higher ratio of apprentices to employees is associated with higher (current) labor productivity and profitability (at least in the nonmanufacturing sectors), which suggests that more apprenticeship improves the firm's current performance.

[27] Apprenticeship was widely criticized in West Germany before the 1969 Vocational Training Act as a vehicle for cheap production labor (Palmer (1981)). Similar issues arose in Britain under the Youth Training Scheme in the 1980s (Ryan (1995)).

of the firm's direct training costs) exceeds apprentices' pay, that is, the firm's net training costs are negative. In production-oriented training, the firm offers training not because it is more profitable than recruitment as a source of skilled labor, but because it is profitable to substitute apprentices for unskilled or skilled workers in production.

Cases in which net training costs to the firm are negative may be termed exploitation, in the Robinsonian sense: apprentices' pay is less than their (net) marginal product, which, in the absence of wage regulation, is evidence of monopsony power. Were competition for apprentices, on whom the firm earns a surplus, perfect, apprentice pay would be bid up until the firm's rent was driven to zero.[28]

While the conditions for production-oriented training have yet to be theorized, a promising direction can be suggested. Assuming a market without external regulation of training content and asymmetric information about the content of the firm's training program,—that is, the firm knows, but other employers do not know, the amount and content of the training it provides its apprentices—the firm can then increase profit, in the short term at least, by offering little training to each apprentice, at given apprentice pay. Only the firm's concern for (i) its future skill supplies and (ii) its reputation as a trainer, and thus its ability to attract trainees, potentially stand between the apprentice and low training content. Under asymmetric information the latter constraint may be weak (Katz and Ziderman (1990); Ryan (1994); Chang and Wang (1996); Malcomson et al. (2003); Stevens (2004); Smits (2007); Dustmann and Schönberg (2007)). But the threat of inadequate content (quality) provides a rationale for externally mandated training standards (see Section 5).

The firm profits more from production-oriented training when apprentice pay can be low without jeopardizing the supply of apprentice labor—as when young people have poor external alternatives, whether because of high unemployment for unskilled young workers or because of rationing of access to full-time schooling. Finally, the firm may enjoy literal monopsony power over its apprentices, as a result of fewness of employers and an absence of collective bargaining in the labor market for youth services (see Section 3).

In the limit, production-oriented training becomes production pure and simple. As long as apprentices' pay is less than their marginal product (relative to other sources of labor), the firm benefits from reducing the amount of training they receive in order to increase their output. As the amount of training given to apprentices tends to zero, they become production labor in all but name. Such "training" is analyzed with the standard theory of production with heterogeneous labor (Mohrenweiser and Zwick (2009)).

Apart from that extreme case, the firm's decisions concerning the number of trainees and the content of their training require analysis: to what extent do firms that pursue production-oriented training take on *more* trainees, as well as offering each one less training, and fire more of them after training, than do firms that invest in training?

---

[28] Under what Leuven (2005, p. 89) terms the "free entry at the start of period 1" assumption, which characterizes most mainstream models of training, the pay of apprentices is set by competitive market clearing.

Production-oriented training has connotations of cheap labor and trainee exploitation. However, it is not always to the detriment of the apprentice: when apprentices are substituted for *skilled* workers, production and learning tend to be complementary during training, to the potential advantage of the firm, the trainee, and the economy (see Section 3).

2.5 Conclusions and future research

There is as yet no comprehensive theory of the firm's behavior in relation to apprentice training. The dominant view at present is that, if the skills learned in apprenticeship are mainly general and trainee pay is not so low as to mean that apprentices bear all the costs of training, then the firms' provision of apprenticeship is—from a policy perspective—a matter of steering between the *Charybdis of regulated labor markets* and the *Scylla of a scarceness of apprenticeship posts*. Because then apparently only labor market frictions or government subsidies, which create other distortions, can incentivize firms to pay for apprenticeship training. A third policy option would be to emphasize firm-, industry- or occupation-specific skills in training, which could be expected to harm labor mobility and workers' employability. As all three options seem to be second-best solutions, this raises the fundamental question, for economist and policy maker alike, as to whether apprenticeship training entails a problematic choice between a viable firm-sponsored training system and frictionless, competitive markets with high labor mobility.[29]

Moreover, firms may undertake training for production-oriented reasons. In the absence of external skill standards, the result are undesirable outcomes for trainees. More evidence is therefore needed if we are to understand the firm's choice of training strategy and the influence thereon of the regulatory framework.

The development of a comprehensive theory of apprenticeship training might focus on several factors: a) labor market regulation (no external training standards vs. enforced external standards); b) the skill requirements of production, given technology and job design; c) substitutability in production between trainee and other labor (skilled and unskilled); d) asymmetric information about the content of training programs; e) alternatives open to trainees (full-time education and unskilled employment); and f) monopsony power of firms over trainees, not just over skilled workers.

---

[29] See, for example, Acemoglu and Pischke (1999b, pp. 548–9) who note that "naturally, in practice, increased frictions will have a number of allocative costs, such as lower employment ... [but] in any case, the implications of labor market frictions on training are worth bearing in mind when suggesting labor market reforms. For example, proposals for reducing union power and removing other regulations in the German labor market, which are on the current agenda, could have unforeseen consequences regarding the German apprenticeship system, where employers pay for the general training of their workers." Similarly Beckmann (2002, p. 385) argues that "the results of this empirical investigation emphasize, among other things, the role of unions and works councils as sources of wage compression encouraging firm-sponsored training. A continuing deregulation in terms of weakening the influence of unions or works councils would probably be at the expense of the firms' willingness to pay for general skill accumulation."

3. EMPIRICAL OBSERVATIONS ON THE SPECIFICITY OF HUMAN CAPITAL, NET COST OF APPRENTICESHIP TRAINING AND THE BUSINESS CYCLE

Two assumptions are central to the preceding extensions of Becker's analysis of the cost of work-based training: first, that the human capital provided by firms is general and second, that firms pay for it, in part at least. Were the skills involved firm-specific and firms shared the cost, or were the skills general but firms bore no cost, everything would align with the Becker model. Therefore when we observe cost-sharing by firms and trainees the possibility arises that the firm is simply bearing its share for the firm-specific component of the skills, and similarly if certain that the skills are transferable (general), that the firm has not actually made any net investment. This section reviews evidence on whether the human capital acquired by apprentices really is general, and whether training firms truly bear net cost when training apprentices.

Because economic factors are likely to influence the supply of apprentice places more strongly than that of full-time schooling, we consider also the effect of business cycles. The issue is important because if apprenticeship activity reacts strongly to the economic cycle, countries in which apprenticeship is a substantial part of upper-secondary schooling would have to identify policies that would offset the cycle, instead of relying only on markets to provide all school-leavers with training opportunities.

3.1 Firm-specific vs. general training

Although apprenticeship training in most countries is certified so as to ensure that apprentices acquire at least some transferable skills, there is always a certain degree of firm-specificity to the employer. Certification in most cases guarantees only that the minimum set of qualifications required to practice a particular occupation have been acquired. It therefore leaves room for an indefinite additional amount of firm-specific knowledge and skills. It is almost impossible to measure the specificity of skills directly,[30] but indirect evidence can be found in the pay loss suffered by apprentices when moving from the training company to another firm. The loss should increase with the amount of firm-specific skills: the outside firm will not pay for skills that it cannot use. If, however, the skills involved are wholly general, apprentices who move to another firm at the end of their training should earn as much as had they stayed put. So if stayers earn more than movers, the implication is that their skills are at least partly firm-specific.

However, estimating the firm-specificity of skills based on pay comparisons between movers and stayers faces two obstacles. First, even when assuming that the decision to quit is entirely exogenous, so that therefore movers and stayers do not on average differ in ability and productivity, the interpretation of the observed pay

---

[30] See however Gathmann and Schönberg (2010), Geel et al. (2010) and Spitz-Oener (2006).

differential is not necessarily conclusive. If movers and stayers earn the same pay, that could be because labor markets are competitive and the skills are general, or that labor markets are not competitive and, although the skills are partly firm-specific, monopsony power allows firms to hold down the pay of stayers.

Second, the assumption that the quit decision of former apprentices is exogenous is unlikely to be valid. Firms acquire information about their apprentices while training them and one of the advantages of training for the firm is the option to release the trainee after training at no cost. The firm will want to do that if the productivity of the apprentice falls short of expectation. Apprentices who select into moving should therefore earn less than those who select into staying even when their skills are purely general. Without controlling for the endogeneity of turnover after training, we cannot tell the extent to which the pay differential between movers and stayers reflects selection by unobserved individual attributes rather than firm-specificity in training.

The evidence available on the pay of stayers and movers is therefore less than conclusive. Euwals and Winkelmann (2004) find that stayers do not earn more than movers, which they take (assuming that all skills are transferable) as evidence that firms bear no net training costs, and that a negative selection into moving takes place.[31] Werwatz (2002) on the other hand, controlling for selection effects, finds that only a minority of movers faces wage losses, but that most move into skilled jobs with higher wages, suggesting positive self-selection into moving with skills that are mostly general.[32]

Acemoglu and Pischke (1998) analyze wage differentials between movers and stayers, focusing in particular on the quits induced among German ex-apprentices by compulsory military service. As "military quits" can be taken to be exogenous, the average ability of such movers should be lower than that of stayers, assuming that the best are retained by the training firm, but higher than that of other movers, most of whom the firm has chosen to lay off. In the evidence, both stayers and military quitters (in their subsequent employment) earn significantly more than other movers, while military quitters earn more than stayers. The authors conclude (as latter Euwals and Winkelmann (2004)) that, while military quitters are paid their marginal product by their new employers, training firms can extract a rent from stayers and thus recoup their investment in training. As these results are not readily reconciled with firm-specificity of skills, which should mean that military quits do not earn more than stayers, they suggest that the skills that apprentices learn are highly general.

---

[31] Winkelmann (1996) concluded from the smooth transitions made by apprentices and the high mobility (by five years after training) that most of the skills learned must be transferable. Euwals and Winkelmann (2002) interpreted their finding that the job duration of stayers was longer than that of movers, and that of stayers in big firms even longer than that of stayers in small companies, as evidence that the firms with the highest investment in (net cost of) training had a better chance of recouping their investment.

[32] Positive self-selection into moving is also inferred by Fitzenberger and Kunze (2005).

With a quite different approach, Dustmann and Schönberg (2007, p.6) using data from self-assessments of the utility of skills learned in an occupation for the present occupation and demonstrate the importance of occupation specific skills. From their data they conclude that only 5% of skills are firm-specific but some 35% of the learned skills are occupation-specific; this would leave 60% of the learned skills to be completely transferable. The degree of occupation-specificity is likely to depend largely on the type of employer-provided training and results therefore certainly differ from country to country (see e.g. Loewenstein and Spletzer, (1998) using self-assessment data from the National Longitudinal Survey of Youth (NLSY) in the United States).

3.2 Net cost of training

Repeated observations that German firms that train apprentices incur positive net costs have stimulated the theories of training that center on labor market frictions and informational failures (see Section 2). However, cost sharing by firms and workers for work-based training is not actually straightforward to observe. Even when explicit payments are made by firms, as typically for externally provided courses of continuous training, trainees may bear part of the cost in terms of pay less than marginal product. Empirical investigations usually do not find lower pay for trainees than for comparable employees who are not in training (Cappelli (2004)). But trainees may still share the cost: selection into training may be positive by ability, so that trainees would otherwise earn higher pay than nontrainees. More useful evidence would require exogenous assignment to training, which is likely to be rare.

Representative cost-benefit analyses of apprenticeship training exist for just a couple of countries.[33] The most often quoted ones follow the methodology developed in Germany by the Edding Commission in the 1970s to estimate the cost to firms of apprenticeship training. More recent estimates for Germany, while not free of restrictive assumptions and potential shortcomings, have provided a key stimulus to the contemporary training literature (see Section 2.3).[34] They have recently acquired a Swiss counterpart, which raises the question to what extent the results for the two countries are analogous. If they are not, it may be that the net cost estimates for Germany do not represent those of other apprenticeship systems.

These cost-benefit studies obtain from a random sample of establishments detailed information about their training costs and in particular the benefits, with the productive contribution of apprentices during training as a key ingredient. Briefly, the gross cost (C) of an apprentice (i) at a training site (j) and in an apprenticeship year (t) comprises primarily the apprentice's wages ($_a w$), the trainers' wages ($_b w$), and the materials

---

[33] Cost studies of work-based training in British apprenticeship are confined to one or a few case studies (e.g., Jones (1986)) or to nonrandom samples of firms offering apprenticeship (Hasluck et al. (2008)).

[34] Acemoglu and Pischke (1999a, pp. F114–116) describe in detail the German cost-benefit analyses of von Bardeleben et al. (1995).

expenses (X) involved in providing the training. The number of training years is n. For simplicity there is no discounting.

$$C_{ij} = \sum_{t=1}^{n} {}_a w_{ijt} + {}_b w_{ijt} + X_{ijt} \qquad (11.1)$$

Trainers' pay is present in the costing framework because the "dual system" does not simply involve the apprentice working part of the week and attending school the rest of the time: part of the training takes place at the worksite. It also indicates that the training differs also from simple learning by doing, in normally requiring specialist trainers, which involves additional costs.

The benefit derived by the firm from training (B) during the training period comprises the production generated by the apprentice when she or he is at work, that is, not being trained off the job or away in school. The benefit is calculated on the assumption that the productive work done by an apprentice would—in the absence of the apprentice—be performed by either skilled or unskilled workers at the wage levels usually paid them by the firm. Allowance is made for the possibility that not all of the work of apprentices is productive and that some apprentice time is spent on exercises.

The benefit is broken down into production activities that would otherwise be performed by unskilled workers (P_I) and skilled workers (P_{II}). It is assumed in the first case that the apprentice's performance has the same value as that of the average unskilled employee. In the second case the value of the apprentice's performance (relative productivity) is estimated by comparison to that of a fully skilled worker (γ). Type I production is multiplied by the wages paid to an unskilled worker ($_u w$), while for type II the wages paid to a skilled worker in the relevant occupation ($_p w$) are used.[35] As is to be expected, the proportion of type I productivity (α) varies according to the year of apprenticeship and in general declines as the apprenticeship progresses, while the share of skilled work, with higher apprentice productivity (γ), increases as the training proceeds. The precise pattern depends on the detailed organization of the firm's apprenticeship program, the training occupation, and the quality of the trainee.

$$B_{ij} = \sum_{t=1}^{n} \alpha_{ijt} *_u w_j + (1-\alpha)_{ijt} *_p w_j * \gamma_{ijt} \qquad (11.2)$$

The net cost of apprenticeship training (NC) to the firm is calculated by simply subtracting benefits (Equation 11.2) from costs (Equation 11.1). The costs borne by apprentices are not estimated.

---

[35] The possibility that the wages are less than marginal product for skilled employees need not influence the calculations, which are based on the opportunity cost principle. If the productive contribution of apprentices is multiplied by a salary of a skilled worker, which lies below productivity, the benefit is not underestimated, as in the case of no apprenticeship training, the firm would have to pay the same wage for a skilled worker—as long, that is, as the firm could otherwise obtain the additional services from skilled workers at the existing wage, which may be the case only in perfect competition.

The net cost of training an apprentice in the von Bardeleben et al. (1995) survey, quoted by Harhoff and Kane (1997) and Acemoglu and Pischke (1999a) as evidence of firms' financing of general training, ranged from 15,000 to 25,000 DM ($7,500 to $25,000 at 1991 exchange rates). The presence of substantial net costs was subsequently confirmed by similar surveys in 2000 and 2008 (Beicht and Walden (2002)). In 2000 an identical survey was carried out in Switzerland, a country whose apprenticeship system is in scale and content comparable to the German one (Wolter and Schweri (2002)). Data from the national surveys were subsequently merged, and net costs calculated on the same basis for each country (Dionisius et al. (2009)). Matching techniques were applied to calculate the net costs of training for similar firms in similar occupations. Table 11.1 shows the results for an average firm training an apprentice in a three-year program.

The results are quite different for the two countries. In Switzerland, firms on average obtain a net benefit (i.e., incur a negative net cost) when training apprentices, whereas German firms typically incur a substantial net cost. In both countries, net cost varies from firm to firm, as indicated by the standard deviations. Taking the two dimensions together, in Switzerland 60% of all training firms obtain positive net benefits, while in Germany, 93% of training firms incur net costs. A complementary difference between the countries shows up in labor turnover. In Germany more apprentices remain with their training company after completion than in Switzerland: 50% and 36% of apprentices stay put for at least a year afterwards, respectively.[36]

Three factors explain the large difference between Germany and Switzerland in the firms' net cost for apprentice training. First, the relative pay of apprentices (compared to skilled pay in the training occupation) is around twice as high in Germany as in Switzerland (Ryan et al. (2010)). Second, there are marked differences in the tasks

Table 11.1 Net Cost to the Firm of Training an Apprentice (3-Year Program) in Germany and Switzerland (2000, €; Standard Deviations in Parentheses)

	Gross Costs	Benefits[a]	Net Costs
Germany	46,608	24,024	22,584
	(15,050.35)	(11,922.24)	(16,694.65)
Switzerland	54,393	57,132	−2,739
	(21,413.4)	(17,589.25)	(24,292.89)

Note: euro/dollar exchange rate in 2000 approximately 0.9.
[a]Excluding any benefits that accrue after the completion of training.
Source: Dionisius et al. (2009, tables 2, 4).

---

[36] In Germany's western federal states, in which estimated firms' net training cost is higher than the national average, the one-year retention rate is also higher (64%) than the national rate.

allocated to apprentices when they work in production. German apprentices spend more time doing practice exercises, Swiss ones doing productive work, and particularly doing skilled tasks. Third, although Swiss apprentices spend similar time in part-time vocational education, they are nevertheless more often present at work, as they have less vacation time, take fewer sick days, and spend less time in external and internal courses. Table 11.2 shows the results of simulations in which these three parameters are changed in order to simulate Swiss training conditions for a German firm, and vice versa. First relative wages are changed to the other country average, then the same is done for days present at the workplace, and finally for task allocation (exercise vs. productive work). The three adjustments taken together more or less transform the training costs of the average German company into those of the average Swiss one, and vice versa.

In terms of net cost, an average German firm, training apprentices with relative wages, attendance days, and task allocations as in Switzerland, would face a net cost of less than €3000, whereas a Swiss company training under German conditions would have to bear a net cost of nearly €24,000. The biggest change in net cost is caused by changing task allocation, as the productive contribution of German apprentices is considerably lower than that of Swiss ones.[37]

The next question is whether the difference in net cost between the two countries can be attributed also to differences in training standards: for example, were lower training standards in Switzerland to allow Swiss firms to provide less training to their apprentices? Training standards in the two countries cannot be compared directly.[38] Nevertheless, given the similarity in the two countries' training system and industry structure, the relative productivity of an apprentice in her final year provides a proxy measure of training quality. The average productivity of a final year German apprentice relative to that of a fully trained worker amounts to 68%, as compared to 75% in

Table 11.2 Mean Net Cost of Training for German and Swiss Apprenticeship Training (3-Year Programs), with and without Treatment (€, 2000)

Country	No Treatment	Relative Wages Only	Relative Wages + Attendance	Relative Wages + Attendance + Task Allocation
Germany	22,584	19,206	16,578	2,802
Switzerland	−2,739	9,231	13,053	23,754

Source: Calculations based on Dionisius et al. (2009, tables 2, 4).

[37] The low amount of productive work of German apprentices had already been noted in the German-French-comparison of Fougère and Schwerdt (2002).

[38] Some governments interested in apprenticeship training intend to measure learning outcomes directly, as do the OECD's PISA studies of the competencies of early school-leavers (e.g., Winther and Achtenhagen (2009)).

Switzerland (Dionisius et al. (2009)). Differences in training standards do not therefore appear to explain lower costs for firms in Switzerland.

Two questions remain, however: why do German firms incur high net costs, if Swiss firms can do the training at lower cost, and why do so many Swiss firms have net benefits in the first place? Were the training market highly competitive, one would expect that profits on training would be driven to zero.

Concerning the first question, the net cost incurred during training and the profits German companies can make after training, relying on labor market frictions, may be opposite sides of the same coin.[39] If the social partners agree on labor market regulations and frictions that allow firms to earn economic rent on their skilled employees, thereby earning a return on their training investments, then free entry into the training market results in higher wages of apprentices—or, as can seen by the empirical observations, less use of apprentices in productive activities during the training period.[40]

A further factor may be the greater strength of employee representation in Germany than in Switzerland. Both high relative pay and low relative productivity may result from the greater strength of trade unions and works councils in Germany. Unions and councils might favor less use of apprentices for production because they see it as the substitution of apprentices for adult members, whether skilled or unskilled workers. The issue is taken up in Section 5, below.

There is as yet no conclusive explanation for why numerous Swiss firms obtain substantial net benefits during apprentice training, but there are several entry barriers to apprenticeship training that hinder free competition. The most promising answer is that apprentices are required to undertake practical work and training in the chosen occupation and if a company does not have many skilled workers in the respective occupation, the firm would simply not have much occupation-specific work to give its apprentices, which lowers the potential benefit of training. Therefore the size of the company and the nature of its activity limit the immediate profitability of training. Wolter et al. (2006), simulating the net cost of training for nontraining firms, show that those firms differ from training firms mainly in the benefits from training apprentices (Table 11.3). The main reason for nontraining is therefore a high net cost were the firm to provide training, which in turn reflects a lack of adequate work to give to potential apprentices—which would also imply that due to the differences in the net costs of training between firms, competition for apprentices is imperfect and training firms make a profit on average.

---

[39] Mohrenweiser and Zwick (2009) analyze whether firm profits are influenced by the share of apprentices and find no impact of the share of apprentices (relative to the share of nonskilled workers) on profits. We interpret this empirical finding as proof that German firms have the possibility to reap substantial benefits from their trainees after training due to labor market rigidities that are sufficient to offset positive net-costs in the training period.

[40] "Because of the free-entry condition firms bid up workers' wages until they make zero profits in the long-run. As firms make positive profits in the second period…, first period wages are higher than workers' expected productivity," (Dustmann and Schönberg (2009)).

Table 11.3 Gross cost, benefit, and net cost of training in Swiss firms, 2000, €

	Gross Cost	Benefit	Net Cost
Training Firms	58,295	61,276	−4,116
Nontraining Firms	72,427	31,524	28,263

Note. All values are predicted econometrically, so net costs for training firms differ somewhat from the survey-based estimates in Table 11.1.
Source: Wolter et al. (2006); converted from Swiss francs at 1€: 1.5CHF.

It is also possible that more Swiss than German firms enjoy monopsony power, not over trained workers but over youth labor, which allows them to keep apprentices wages low.[41] Mühlemann et al. (2011) find that the pay of Swiss apprentices is lower, relative to that of unskilled workers, in districts with a lower density of potentially competing firms.

3.3 Production-oriented training: cheap labor?

As outlined in Section 2.4., using apprentices as substitutes for other employees because their lower pay more than compensates for their lower productivity might be termed a "cheap labor" strategy. However, two things have to be kept in mind, when interpreting the low pay of apprentices. First, apprentices do not spend all their time at the workplace and are therefore not as productive as skilled workers at least. Second, firms incur direct training costs that have to be covered, if a surplus cannot be earned after training, during training by way of a lower apprentice wage. Therefore the relative pay of apprentices does not in itself reveal whether the firm's motivation to train is indeed the substitution of more expensive with less expensive labor. When, however, firms earn a substantial surplus on apprentices during the training contract itself, the question arises whether that indicates the exploitation of trainees. In the scientific sense that is the case: exploitation occurs by definition when an employee is paid less than her marginal product—defined for the apprentice as net of her direct training costs—whether apprentices do unskilled or skilled work. But which of the latter applies is important, both for the apprentice and for public policy. If the apprentice is underpaid for doing skilled work, concern is limited, as she is acquiring skills that she could probably not obtain through formal off-the-job training. So from the perspective of the apprentice and the public interest the "exploitation" is potentially acceptable, as it leads to greater skill and productivity in future. The same does not however apply when the tasks performed by the apprentice are unskilled. In order to judge production-oriented

---

[41] Although there are industry guidelines and recommendations, in all but one Canton, apprentices' wages can be set freely by the training company.

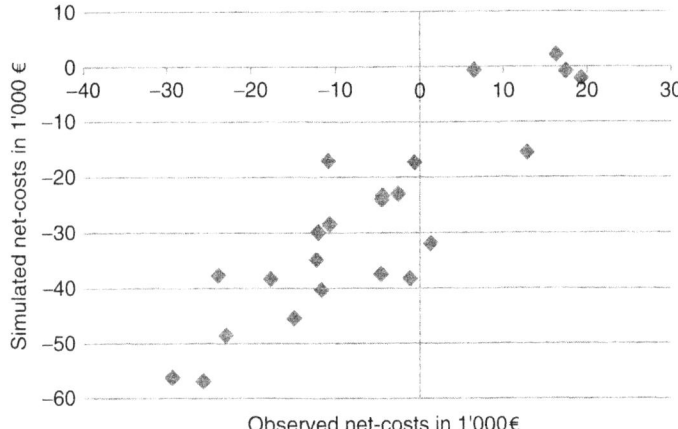

Figure 11.1 Observed and simulated net cost of apprentice training for the largest occupations, Switzerland (€) Note: $n = 2200$ firms; conversion to euros as in Table 11.3. *Data source: Mühlemann et al. (2007b)*.

training, one needs therefore to know whether the firm's net benefit during training is generated by using apprentices for unskilled or for skilled tasks.

Evidence can be taken from the same surveys of training costs. Figure 11.1 shows the observed average net cost in the 23 largest training occupations in Switzerland. Training produces on average a net cost in six and a net benefit in the other 17 occupations. The simulation reestimates net cost on the assumption that the cost parameters (training methods, apprentice pay, and apprentice productivity in skilled and unskilled tasks) remain the same, but the contribution of apprentices to production is confined to unskilled tasks. The effect is dramatic. Were employers to confine apprentices to unskilled work only, their net training cost would fall (or the benefit would increase) by around €22,000, and in no occupation would the typical employer make any worthwhile surplus during training. The simulated change in net cost is not significantly associated with actual net cost, meaning that the observed negative net-costs are not just the result of a heavier use of apprentices in these occupations for unskilled labor.[42] The implication is that, in Switzerland at least, production-oriented training involves a preponderance of skilled rather than unskilled work by apprentices.

These results raise the question: what deters training firms from exploiting apprentices more intensively, given the scope for firms to increase profits from all training occupations by giving apprentices more unskilled work to do? The potential reasons include externally mandated minimum training standards, to which in Switzerland as in Germany firms must adhere in order to be allowed to continue to train apprentices.

---

[42] The correlation between observed net cost and the difference between simulated and observed cost caused is 0.17.

Second, firms would choose not to do it if they intend subsequently to employ their apprentices as skilled workers and if doing skilled work and learning skills are complements—though when the firm intends to release most or all its apprentices after training, this factor is secondary or absent. Thirdly, were firms to use apprentices only to maximize current production, their reputation on the training market would suffer, and they might attract only low-ability apprentices with deficient output even in unskilled work. The limitations of the second and third constraints suggests that external training standards are central to the viability of high quality in the apprentice training market (see Section 5).

3.4 Apprenticeship training and the business cycle

Economic fluctuations have two potential effects on apprenticeship activity, depending on the firm's training strategy. First, the firm's demand for skilled labor falls during an economic downturn, which may in turn cut its demand for apprentices, when apprenticeship is integral to the firm's acquisition of skilled labor (Stevens (1994a), Brunello and Medio (2001), Brunello (2009)). If the firm trains apprentices because that is less expensive at the margin than recruiting skilled workers, an economic downturn not only reduces the demand for skilled workers but also cuts recruitment costs, as the external supply of skilled workers rises. Both effects reduce the demand for apprentices. However, as apprenticeship programs typically last between two and four years, the economic cycle may not affect the provision of training strongly, because firms may expect economic recovery before new apprentices have finished training.

Alternatively, if the firm trains for production-oriented motives, economic fluctuations may affect the benefit of using apprentices in production. In prosperous times, when order books are long, there may be abundant work, skilled as well as unskilled, to give to apprentices. With low apprentice pay, the firm has an incentive to expand training in the short-run in order to increase production. However, Merrilees (1983) noted that the firm may not adjust its demand for apprentices immediately. In an economic boom, the firm might prefer to switch its trainers from training apprentices to production in order to increase output. In recession, the demand for apprentices would not fall in proportion to incoming orders because apprentices are initially not very productive (because they first need to be trained in skilled work) and therefore periods of lower economic activity could be used for training instead of work.

In sum, theoretical considerations imply that, while business cycles have potentially important effects on the supply of apprentice training by firms, there are countervailing effects that may weaken those effects.

The evidence suggests that fewer apprenticeships are offered during economic downturns and when unemployment rates are high. Dietrich and Gerner (2007) find in establishment-level panel data for Germany during 1993–2003 that firms' training efforts respond to short-term business expectations: a one percentage point increase in the firm's expected business volume increases its supply of new apprenticeships by 0.35 percentage points. For the U.K., Hart (2005) finds that although fewer apprenticeships were offered during the Great Depression, firms seemed to lay off skilled workers more rapidly than they did apprentices. Merrilees (1983) found for 1963–1979 a negative relationship between new apprenticeship contracts and unemployment, and a positive one with output. For Norway, Askilden and Nilsen (2005) find that the supply of apprenticeships decreases with unemployment. Rasmussen and Westergaard-Nielsen (1999) find that firms' demand for apprentices is positively related to demand for skilled labor in Denmark.

For Switzerland, Schweri and Müller (2007) find a positive effect from the recent GDP growth rate on a firm's propensity to train. Mühlemann et al. (2009) find a significant, although also small, impact of unemployment rates and changes in the growth of cantonal income on the number of new apprenticeship contracts: across Swiss Cantons from 1988– 2004, a standard deviation increase in the unemployment rate (1.9 percentage points) reduces the number of new apprenticeship contracts by around 0.6%.

The business cycle can affect not only a firm's offer of apprenticeships, but also quitting by apprentices. Bilginsoy (2003) finds for the United States that apprentices are more likely to leave their training program if unemployment is low, since outside options increase if the labor market is tight.

The empirical evidence shows a significant but modest impact of business cycles on the provision of apprenticeships, provided that what is involved is indeed cyclical downswing rather than structural decline. Therefore the fear that apprenticeship training is a problematic component of upper-secondary educational opportunities, because the number of training positions may show booms and busts, is exaggerated.

3.5 Conclusions and future research

The evidence, based as it is predominantly on apprenticeship training systems in German-speaking countries, suggests that given that the skills learned in apprenticeship are predominantly general, frictions in the market for skilled labor contribute importantly to the willingness of firms to offer training. They make it possible for employers to invest in general skills without facing the prospect of being unable to make a return on it after the apprenticeship contract has ended. Indeed, the same frictions require employers to bear some of the cost of training, as apprentices respond to their inability to acquire all the returns by refusing to bear all of the costs.

At the same time, some firms train apprentices not so much for their future supply of skilled labor as for their immediate usefulness in production. A minority of firms in Germany, and a majority in Switzerland, reap net benefits rather than incur net costs over the training contract as a whole.

The conditions under which firms adopt one training strategy or the other are only partly understood. The contributory factors potentially include collective bargaining and the goals of trade unions and works councils, and, in the absence of either of those constraints, employers' power in the labor market, in relation to apprentices as well as skilled workers. External training standards are also important, in limiting the scope for firms to use apprentices in production for short-term profit. Moreover, the extent to which skilled work and formal training are complementary is potentially important.

The evidence invariably shows up extensive heterogeneity among employers. A leading research question is therefore why in situations involving the same economic and regulatory framework some firms find it profitable to invest in their apprentices whereas others train apprentices but make a surplus during training, while yet others do neither—and what consequences follow for young people these different choices by employers, a topic taken up partly in the next section.

4. OUTCOMES FOR APPRENTICES
4.1 Measurement and identification issues

Determining the effects of apprenticeship training on individuals is complicated by at least four problems.

First, one has to implement the counterfactual: that is, compare outcomes for apprenticeship to those under the alternative foregone when someone takes an apprenticeship. Taking apprentices to be engaged in part-time upper secondary education, the principal potential alternatives are (i) full-time upper secondary education, general or vocational, and (ii) labor market experience, including various mixtures of employment, unemployment, and labor market programs. The issue of what constitutes the alternative for young people is of course essentially an empirical one.

Second, the allocation of young people to upper-secondary programs is unlikely to be random. For example, more talented young people may take an apprenticeship rather than enter the labor market directly, while still more talented young people may remain in full-time schooling. If "talent' represents any and all unobserved individual attributes, then, in the absence of effective statistical controls for differences therein, estimates of the effect of apprenticeship that are based on comparisons to labor market experience and to full-time schooling will be biased: upward-biased and downward-biased, respectively. A meaningful analysis therefore requires controls, whether experimental (natural or social experimentation) or statistical (econometric), for unobserved individual heterogeneity.

Thirdly, apprenticeship might be superior to other forms of learning for particular skills and occupations, but inferior for others. Therefore some occupations may be learned through apprenticeship, others through full-time education or simple labor market experience. In such situations, comparisons of outcomes by mode of learning overlap with and are potentially biased by uncontrolled occupation-specific factors. This points empirical work toward situations in which apprenticeship and full-time education result in the same qualifications, as in many occupations, for example, in France and the Netherlands, but not in Germany and Switzerland.

Fourth, the outcomes chosen must be appropriate. Employment, unemployment, and pay are the obvious ones for economists. But apprenticeship may also induce youngsters to remain in post-compulsory education, both during and after their training programs. The benefits of any induced increase in educational attainment are captured only partly by labor market outcomes. However, where apprenticeship functions as an educational terminus, it may be educationally damaging, as if it reduces educational attainment by those who would otherwise have remained in full-time schooling (Ryan (2003)).

Finally, human capital theory is couched in terms of rates of return, which involves a comparison of discounted costs and benefits. In practice, however, given the paucity of data-sets with information on both costs and benefits, empirical studies of individual "returns" focus on gross returns (in pay and employment probability) from training, and do not estimate either costs or net returns for apprentices.

Given these difficulties, we now offer not a comprehensive survey of methods and findings in the empirical literature but rather a selection of recent papers that use innovative methods and data to analyze the effects of apprenticeship on individuals.

4.2 Some recent evidence

The papers discussed here estimate the economic effects of apprenticeship on participants using potentially informative evidence taken primarily from papers that use potentially exogenous variation arising from social or natural experiments, which have involved either changes in school laws or the failure of firms or econometric techniques to overcome selection problems.[43] Broader surveys of the literature prior to 2000 are provided by Ryan (1998, 2001).[44]

A potential advantage of apprenticeship in comparison with full-time schooling, particularly in the context of high youth unemployment, is the smoothing of the transition from school to work (Sofer (2004)). Bonnal et al (2002) show for France that students who come through apprenticeship subsequently experience less long term unemployment as young adults than do those who go through full-time vocational schooling. Plug and Groot (1998) show for the Netherlands a similar benefit, which does not involve lower pay than for former full-time vocational students.

---

[43] We include a paper concerning the effects of vocational education instead of apprenticeship training (Oosterbeek and Webbink 2007) because of its pertinence to apprenticeship.
[44] Ryan concluded that apprenticeship is associated unevenly with economic advantages, primarily as a source of more stable employment for young male adults, but with low returns for females, and more in comparison to labor market experience than to full-time upper secondary schooling.

Some papers take into account the internal heterogeneity of apprenticeship systems. Countries with large apprenticeship systems have many training occupations with differentiated entry requirements. Selection into particular training occupations clearly depends on educational performance in compulsory schooling, but does the subsequent transition to the labor market after training depend on occupation? Bertschy et al. (2009) find that once the transition to training occupation is taken out, and using PISA results to control for ability, apprentices with poor educational results are not further penalized once they complete apprenticeship training.[45] They also find significant advantages in the transition to the labor market for apprentices compared to full-time vocational students.

Concerning effects on pay, selection into different educational tracks is a potential source of bias, which few studies have tried to correct—that is, when they go beyond simply treating years of education as homogenous across tracks. Fersterer et al. (2008) analyze the individual return to apprenticeship training in Austria using instrumental variables estimation, specifically by concentrating on apprentices whose employer failed before they had completed training. Such apprentices have a significantly higher risk of never completing their apprenticeship. The time that those apprentices spent in apprenticeship before the bankruptcy provides an instrumental variable for years of apprenticeship. The results differ little however from those produced by ordinary least squares, which does not involve any controls for selection by ability in setting the length of training for apprentices as a whole. A year of apprenticeship training is estimated to generate an increase in pay of slightly more than 5%.

By contrast, Oosterbeek and Webbink (2007) use a natural experiment and a difference-in-difference approach. In 1975 all vocational programs in Dutch schools were required to last four years, whereas previously one half had lasted only three years. The general education component of the curriculum was increased at the same time. The authors study the long-term returns to an extra year of basic vocational education comparing the cohorts that studied before the reform to those that came after it.[46] The reform did not affect labor market outcomes for young people, which suggests that an extra year in vocational education and work experience had similar effects—possibly because the skills learned in vocational education can readily be learned on-the-job instead.

Finally, Malamud and Pop-Eleches (2010) assess the effects of vocational education, including apprenticeship, in Romania, with the alternative taken to be full-time

---

[45] Büchel (2002) cautioned against this view in an analysis of different cohorts covering the time from 1948–1992. He found the same labor market entry quality for trainees with different levels of attainment in compulsory schooling only in the older cohorts.

[46] The study parallels analyses of the return to schooling that use extensions of the compulsory school leaving age (Pischke and von Wachter (2008)).

general education.[47] The focus is the educational reform of 1973, which prevented students from entering vocational schools or apprenticeship after only eight years of compulsory schooling, required them to receive an additional two years of general education, and shortened the duration of vocational training. A regression discontinuity approach compares the long term labor market outcomes (1992, 2002) of cohorts affected by the 1973 reform and earlier ones that had not been affected by it. Although the reform provoked the intended sharp increase in general educational attainment, the pay and family income of the pre- and post-reform cohorts did not differ significantly. The results demonstrate that increased general education did not improve labor market outcomes relative to vocational education and that graduates of vocational programs have done just as well on the labor market, even in times of rapid technological change.

4.3 Conclusions and future research

The evidence on the economic effects of apprenticeship on individuals is still too limited to draw general conclusions. The well-documented benefits of apprenticeship for the transition from school to work—once selection into different training options is taken into account—are followed by economic returns in early adulthood that in some countries are similarly favorable but that in others involve smaller pay gains and more unstable employment. In some results apprenticeship compares favorably to full-time school-based vocational programs; in others, it even beats general ones. This heterogeneity in the empirical results arises less from differences in research methods and data than from differences in the scale and content of apprenticeship itself. Consequently, results for specific countries or programs can rarely be generalized to apprenticeship training *per se*. The further empirical research that is therefore needed should a) employ convincing methods, whether econometric or experimental, to control for selectivity across programs, and b) allow for the heterogeneity of apprenticeship and thereby isolate the attributes of the variants that work for young people themselves.

5. INSTITUTIONAL FOUNDATIONS OF APPRENTICESHIP

The introduction noted the high dispersion of apprenticeship activity across countries. How might such differences be explained?

The previous two sections have discussed microeconomic theories of work-based training, and presented evidence derived primarily from single-country micro-data. That evidence is consistent with theories of imperfect competition in occupational labor markets. Such theories are less suited however to an explanation of differences

---

[47] The authors cannot differentiate between people having obtained a degree from full-time vocational school or apprenticeship training. Therefore vocational schools and apprenticeship training are treated as one category and compared to general schooling.

in apprenticeship across countries. Most of the factors that they highlight, including skill specificity and informational asymmetries, are technological attributes, which are not expected to vary greatly from country to country. Others, including external wage compression, might be expected to vary more, but they in turn require explanation, rather than being treated as exogenous.

The great variability of national institutions is the starting point for institutional analyses of labor markets (Freeman 2008). The roles of such institutions as employers' associations, trade unions and works councils vary greatly, with potential influence on the training-related decisions of employers and individuals.

Microeconomic and institutional explanations are often treated as alternatives, and their merits contested across academic disciplines within the social sciences. We view them as complements when it comes to explaining cross-national training patterns. Neither is plausibly sufficient for an explanation. On the one side, the institutions that might promote apprenticeship can arguably perform that task only in the presence of labor market imperfections: under perfect competition, as Becker demonstrated, employers could not finance general training at all, and collective action aimed at getting them to do so would fail. On the other side, while imperfect competition makes it possible for employers to provide and finance training in transferable skills, it does not require them to do so, and the extent to which they do varies across countries in ways that can be linked, both logically and empirically, to institutions (Ryan (2001)). This section addresses that task.

Causal inference is particularly problematic in institutional research. Four types of empirical difficulty stand out. The first concerns measurement problems. Some institutional attributes are qualitative and unmeasurable; others are measurable, but only as ordinal variables, and characterized by measurement error, missing observations, and limited validity, as the terms and their meaning vary across countries. Moreover, even simple outcomes, such the rate of youth participation in apprenticeship, are potentially distorted by the interest of national governments in improving their country's standing in international league tables such as those compiled by the OECD. Secondly, some institutions are multidimensional, and their effects on apprenticeship may differ by subdimension. Thirdly, institutions may interact in determining outcomes, as suggested by the concept of "institutional complementarity" (Höpner (2005))—between, for example, industrial relations and corporate ownership—a factor that places additional strain on the evidence. Finally, the data are usually country-year observations, which means small sample sizes and identifying variation based more on differences between countries than on changes over time. Country-specific fixed effects can therefore distort the results. Firm conclusions are therefore elusive in institutionally-oriented research. For institutionalists, however, the importance of the issues trumps the limitations of the evidence.

The result is a literature dominated by qualitative evidence and binational comparisons. We prefer here to relate quantifiable outcomes to quantifiable institutional attributes across a heterogeneous set of countries, and thereby to suggest potentially fruitful directions for further research. We rely in particular on a database on national institutional attributes that was compiled primarily with pay setting in mind, but which potentially applies to training as well (Visser (2009)).

As to the meaning of "institutions," we follow contemporary practice in political economy and focus both on the organizations that sustain collective action, such as employers' associations, trade unions, and labor market authorities, and on their relationships with each other, including collective bargaining and joint regulation. These relationships affect individual agents' choices in market contexts—for example, the decision of employers to offer apprenticeships—which in turn renders sterile any dichotomy between markets and institutions.

5.1 Institutions and outcomes

Institutionalists typically identify several types of institution as foundations on which successful national apprenticeship systems stand. The set includes public regulation (legislation), employer organizations (employers' associations, chambers of trade and commerce), employee organizations (trade unions, works councils), and educational organizations (vocational colleges, educational professionals). To this list we add youth and trainee organization.

A prominent theme in institutionalist accounts is efficiency: such institutions may correct training-related market failures. Such perspectives dominate personnel economics, or the "new efficiency-oriented institutionalism", and the "varieties of capitalism" literature (Lazear (2000), Hall and Soskice (2001)). Other institutionalists prefer historical contingency and path dependence to functionalist determinism, with more scope for economically undesirable outcomes (Streeck (2005), Hall and Thelen (2009)). We avoid any dichotomy between these approaches: the potential efficiency-improving functions of the various institutions are analyzed, while potential dysfunctions and historical processes are kept in mind.

We attempt here only a preliminary empirical analysis of a potentially fruitful research field. Our analysis is confined to eight advanced economies (Table 11.4), for all of which reasonably comprehensive data on institutional attributes are readily available—which unfortunately rules out the Czech Republic, for example. We select them so as to span a wide range of both institutional attributes and intensity of operation.

Table 11.4 shows the most accessible indicator of apprenticeship's intensity of operation: the share of educational enrollments at upper secondary level that are part-time (i.e., combined school-based and workplace-based). In Switzerland and Germany, the share of apprentices is 58% and 44% respectively; in Sweden and South Korea, zero.

This indicator of apprenticeship activity is imperfect in various ways. First, it measures the quantity but not the quality of training. Second, its coverage of apprentices is

Table 11.4 Apprenticeship Activity and Institutional Attributes, Selected Countries, 2006

	Switzerland	Germany	Netherlands	France	Ireland	U.K.	Sweden	South Korea
1. Enrollment share of part-time vocational education (%)	57.8	44.2	18.3	11.6	2.4	[1.4][a]	0	0
2. Year of key apprenticeship legislation	1930 2003	1969	1966 1993	1971 1987	1987	[2009]	none	none
3. Employers' association membership density (%)	37	72	79	74	39	54	56	n.a.
4. Mandatory extension of collective agreements (index)	0	1	1	2	0	0	0	0
5. Union membership density (%)	19	21	22	8	35	29	75	10
6. Collective bargaining coverage (%)	48	63	82	95	n.a.	34	92	10[b]
7. Works Council powers (index)	0	3	3	2	1	1	2	0
8. Tripartite national council present (index)	0	0	1	1	1	0	0	0
9. Joint body, national socio-economic policy (index)	2	1	2	1	2	0	2	0
10. Joint bodies, sector employment policy: (index)	1	2	2	1	0	0	2	1
11. Powers over workplace training, external body (index)	1[c]	1	1	1	1	0	n.a.	n.a.
12. Representation of vocational teachers (index)	0	1	1	0	1	0	n.a.	n.a.

Variables

1. Enrollments in vocational upper secondary programs in which off-the-job education accounts for less than one-quarter of the curriculum as a percentage of the 15–19-year-old population
2. Year of key (enabling or codifying) statute for apprenticeship
3. Share of employees within the domain of the employer peak organization who are covered by it, 1995 or 1996
4. Mandatory extension of collective agreements to nonorganized firms. Coding: 2 extension applied regularly and to significant share of employees; 1, available, but not widely used; 0, not available
5. Union membership net of nonemployees as percentage of employees in employment
6. Employees covered by collective pay bargaining as percentage of those with the right to coverage
7. Rights of works councils: 3, codetermination of company economic policies; 2, major consultation rights over social policies, including training; 1, information rights; 0, no representation or no rights
8. Existence of tripartite national council concerned with socio-economic policy in private sector: 1, yes; 0, no
9. Formal involvement of organizations of employers and employees in determination of social and economic practices: 2, routine; 1, occasional; 0, rare or nonexistent
10. Sector-level organization of employers and unions, or joint bodies, for negotiation, dispute settlement, training and/or recruitment: 2, present throughout economy; 1, present in some sectors only; 0, absent
11. Powers over the operation of apprenticeship within the company for an external joint body, including sector-level or occupation-level committees, and German chambers: 1, any; 0, none
12. Mandatory representation of vocational teachers on joint apprenticeship committees, at national, sector or district level; 1, yes; 0, no

Notes. n.a.: not available or not applicable.

[a] Learner volumes, Level 3 Advanced Apprenticeship; <19 year olds 2006/07 (England only).
[b] Lower bound estimate, 2000.
[c] Public (cantonal) body is responsible for quality of training at workplace, but occupational associations (*Berfusverbände*) examine apprentices (Hoeckel et al. 2008, p. 14).

Sources (1) OECD (2008, table C1.1); Kuczera et al. (2009); Learning and Skills Council, Post 16 Education and Skills Tables, Statistical First Release June 2009; ONS, Principal Population Projection, 2006-based, England. (3) Traxler (2008, table II.4). (4–10) Visser (2009); Kuczera, Kis, and Wurzburg (2009); OECD (2004, table 3.3); OECD Statistics database. (2, 11, 12) Ryan (2000, table 3); Ni Cheallaigh (1995, Annex 5).

incomplete, and in ways that may lead it to understate the dispersion of activity across countries.[48]

Table 11.4 also lists 11 quantifiable institutional attributes that potentially influence the scale of apprenticeship. Five categories are covered: public law, and the representation of employers, employees, educators, and trainees themselves. The list of institutions is also less than comprehensive. Particular institutions may contain additional dimensions: for example, the influence of employers' associations potentially depends on their powers vis-à-vis their members as well as the share of the economy that they cover. A second difficulty is that training decisions may also be affected by institutions not included in Table 11.4—notably, corporate ownership and finance (Black, Gospel and Pendleton (2007)).

Moreover, no listing of individual attributes can capture complementarities between institutions. For example, the "varieties of capitalism" approach classes market economies as "liberal" or "coordinated" according to the importance of supra-market coordination by organized interest groups (Hall and Soskice (2001)). Each category is described in terms of a set of organizational attributes, including industrial relations, corporate ownership, and product market strategies, that complement each other within a wider whole. Apprenticeship is treated as a leading area of institutional complementarities, though the content of those complementarities remains controversial (Crouch et al. (2005)).

We now examine the extent to which the scale of apprenticeship is associated across countries with their institutional attributes.

5.1.1 Statutory framework

Some countries have passed laws that define apprenticeship and provide for its organization and administration (Table 11.4, row 2). The best-known example is Germany's Vocational Training Act of 1969, which extended the prior recognition and regulation of apprenticeship in small artisanal firms to larger employers in industry and the services. One of the act's central functions has been to stipulate how apprenticeship is to be organized, in that it defines the responsibilities, membership categories, and powers of the relevant multilevel bodies. The broader connotation of the 1969 Act is the devolution of public powers to bodies representing the interested parties, such

---

[48] The OECD's measure in principle excludes: firstly, apprentices older than 19 years, who constitute a majority of apprentices in Germany and the U.K.; secondly, apprentices in post-secondary education, whose numbers have risen rapidly in France; and thirdly, learners who are not enrolled in formal education, who are the majority of "apprentices" in the U.K. The excluded categories are large in some countries with larger systems, notably Germany and France, but not in Switzerland, where most apprentices start training after lower secondary education. On a more comprehensive measure, for the share of a population cohort that undertakes an apprenticeship at any age, Switzerland and Germany scores are much closer, at around two-thirds and three-fifths respectively (Wolter and Schweri (2002), Ryan and Unwin (2001)).

as employers' associations, conditional on their using those powers in the public interest rather than in sectional ones (Streeck et al. (1987), Deiβinger 1996).

A similar approach was adopted around the same time by Germany's smaller apprenticeship-oriented neighbors and by France in 1987. The Dutch and Irish statutes, for instance, integrated traditional apprenticeship into the formal education system. The French reform made apprenticeship a recognized path to existing vocational qualifications at all levels of attainment, including post-secondary ones (Combes (1988), Ryan (2000)). In Switzerland, vocational education was exempted by law in 1930 from the general devolution to canton level of the regulation of formal schooling and has since then constituted the exceptional federal responsibility in educational matters (Bauder and Osterwalder (2008)). By contrast, until recently British apprenticeship lacked a statutory basis, and in Sweden and South Korea, in the effective absence of apprenticeship, that remains the case.

The potential functions of enabling legislation start with the mobilization of decentralized and scarce information about training needs and methods in particular occupations, sectors, and employers. Members of the officially recognized regulatory bodies have information about a wider range of circumstances than can be obtained by public administration alone. Secondly, by providing for the public definition of both training occupations and minimum training standards in those occupations, and also for the regulation by external organizations of the actual content of training at the workplace, a counterweight is installed to the threat of low quality training within the firm—a matter of particular concern when production-oriented training firms are left entirely to their own devices (see Sections 2 and 3). More broadly, to define the educational standing and contribution of apprenticeship is to point it away from narrow job training and toward vocational education, and, in most countries, general education too.

The problems potentially caused by statutory regulation include the restriction of innovation in training agency and training methods. Thus Britain's (until recently) nonstatutory, subsidy-based system has encouraged a proliferation of training providers, including commercial specialists. The potential gains are greater cost reduction and faster innovation. As the same providers have increasingly displaced public colleges, the potential losses include training standards and the educational contribution of apprenticeship, along with a low commitment by employers to apprenticeship (Dustmann and Schönberg (2007), Lewis and Ryan (2009)).

Table 11.4 suggests that the scale of apprenticeship is associated with statutory regulation, and in particular that a statutory basis may be necessary for a substantial system. The countries with mid-sized or large apprenticeship systems all have such laws, whereas those without apprenticeship—not surprisingly—lack such laws. However, as the countries with a statutory basis for apprenticeship include Ireland, which has only a small system, legislative support appears to be less than sufficient for success.

5.1.2 Employer representation

The viability of apprenticeship is frequently taken to require collective action by employers. Two institutional types are potentially relevant: employers' associations, at the level of the sector and the economy; and chambers of trade or commerce, organized across sectors at district or regional level.

The potential contributions of employer representation are widely recognized. Firstly, it may ensure that the content of apprenticeship—in contrast to vocational education based wholly in educational institutions—remains relevant to the skill requirements of production. Moreover, external employer representation may discourage firms from providing narrow, firm-specific training, and prompt them instead to contribute to a pool of transferable skills from which all companies benefit. Similarly, when it is employer representatives, whether from the sector or district, rather than public officials, who assess the quality of an employer's training program, the legitimacy of the assessment in the eyes of that particular employer is potentially greater.

Secondly, according to employer representatives, trust is fostered when they play an important part in the design and administration of the apprenticeship system. Individual firms are encouraged to share types of information about their skill requirements and training options that they would not otherwise willingly share with outsiders, particularly public officials. The result is a better design and functioning of the training system (Culpepper (2003)).

Thirdly, there is the threat of noncooperative outcomes in the prisoners' dilemma "game" of "train or recruit" that employers who use costly transferable skills must play: that is, under uncoordinated decisions, employers do not provide enough training, and use recruitment excessively instead. In that context, employer collectives may coordinate strategy choices around the jointly beneficial cooperative outcome, in which more firms do more training than they would if left entirely to their own devices. (This potential benefit is relevant only to employers with an investment-oriented training strategy.) Attaining the superior outcome may however require that the employers' association possess formal powers that allow it to punish any defecting employers. Those powers may be based either on compulsory membership or on extension rules, which require nonmembers to observe the terms established by the association. The contribution of employer collectives to building "dialogic capacity" and exerting peer pressure on individual employers may however be sufficient (op. cit.).

Finally, chambers of commerce, which are organized by district and across sectors, may be able to use attachment to the local community to mobilize employers to provide more training, in terms of quality as well as quantity, than they would if left purely to their own devices.

The potential dysfunctions of devolved administration by employer representatives start with the threat of rent extraction: instead of pursuing the general good, those representatives may feather their own nests. The threat is particularly acute for employers' associations, with their sector-specific basis. Firms that compete in the same product market may find it easier to coordinate their product market strategies when they can meet legitimately to coordinate their training decisions.

A second consideration is conflict between the interests of large and small firms. To the extent that large companies favor investment-oriented training and small ones production-oriented training, and small firms dominate employers' associations, the result is higher volume and lower quality in the apprenticeship system, along with fewer opportunities for educational progression after apprenticeship (Culpepper (2007)).

Third, powers exercised by chambers of commerce over training at the workplace may mean under-informed decisions, to the extent that employers in other sectors fail to understand or share the concerns of the company providing training.

What quantitative evidence is there on the association between employer organization and apprenticeship? The answer is: unfortunately little. The indicator that is available for the largest number of countries is the coverage of the national peak employers' association. It varies considerably across countries, and it is particularly high in three of the four largest apprenticeship systems, those of Germany, France, and the Netherlands (Table 11.4, row 3).

Such an association would align with the failure of the government's attempt to develop a German-type apprenticeship in South Korea in the 1990s, which resulted partly from the absence of employer organizations capable of generating and coordinating suitable responses—a lacuna that continues to handicap public training policy (Jeong (1995); Kuczera et al. (2009)).

The apparent association between employers' associations and the scale of apprenticeship cannot however be close. In Switzerland, the country with the largest apprenticeship system, the coverage of the peak employers' association is relatively low. Sweden has no apprenticeship training but highly developed institutions of employer coordination.

The evidence is not however compelling. The coverage of the peak association may not capture well the role of employers' associations, particularly as it is at sector-occupation level rather than national level that the coordination of training decisions is potentially most important. The countries with the largest apprenticeship systems, Switzerland again excepted, devolve to sector-level employers' associations powers over the organization and administration of apprenticeship, whereas three with smaller systems (Britain, Sweden, and South Korea) do not. Second, other bodies may be able to perform the task of coordinating employers' training decisions. In Switzerland the job is done by occupational associations (*Berufsverbände*), whose presence is mandated for all apprenticeable occupations, and which are dominated in part or whole by employer representatives (Hoeckel et al. (2009, p. 16)). Finally, employers' associations often face a divergence of interests between large and small member firms. The greater the membership share of small firms—as in Austria relative to Switzerland—the more the association becomes likely to favor production-oriented training in general, and narrowly defined training standards in particular (Culpepper 2007).

A positive association with the scale of apprenticeship is less clear for chambers of commerce. Comparative data on these bodies are particularly scarce.[49] In Germany chambers hold the power to approve an employer's training programs and to assess apprentices at the end of training. This is however a specifically German approach. In the Netherlands and Ireland, much or all of that set of tasks falls to sector-based or occupation-based bodies, who in Switzerland and England share the relevant tasks with public inspectorates (Ryan (2000); Hoeckel et al. (2009, p. 21)).

Further evidence on the role of employer organization comes from *within-country* differences in employer organization and training activity. A striking example is the electrical contracting component of British construction, in which an employers' association managed for many decades to coordinate its members' provision of apprenticeship training. At the same time, lacking direct statutory support, the employers' association could not sustain training on a scale commensurate with its members' needs, let alone those of the wider industry (Gospel and Druker (1998)).

That weakness points to statutory support, in the shape of extension rules that require nonparticipating employers to adopt decisions made by their sector's employers' association, that may contribute to the effectiveness of employer organizations. The evidence in Table 11.4 (row 4) is broadly consistent with that proposition. Three of the four countries with the largest apprenticeship systems operate extension rules in at least some parts of the economy; in the four with the smallest systems, they do not operate them anywhere. Switzerland again proves the exception.

Finally, an important role for employer organization is suggested also by the government attempts in France and the new federal states (*Länder*) in Germany in the 1990s to increase employers' provision of apprenticeship. The few regions and states in which those efforts succeeded were those in which intra-sector cooperation by employers was most successfully fostered, in particular by the devolution of public powers to their representatives, whereas in those in which public officials imposed their own decisions, failure was normal (Culpepper (2003)).

5.1.3 Employee representation: social partnership

Social partnership denotes the involvement of representatives of employees, as well as those of employers, on joint bodies that are given responsibility for some combination of strategic advice and administration in relation to the apprenticeship system. These

---

[49] For example, Traxler et al. (2001), studies the organization and effects of employers' associations, both sector and economy-wide, but does not touch on the organization and role of chambers.

joint bodies may operate on a simply bipartite basis, as in Denmark, or on a tripartite one, including government representatives, as in Switzerland.

The bodies that represent employees in relation to apprenticeship issues are trade unions and works councils. In Germany, trade union officials have parity of representation with employers on the joint bodies that steer and operate the apprenticeship system, ranging from the board of the Federal Vocational Training Institute (BIBB), down to the committees that the district-level chambers—which in other functions are purely employer-based bodies—set up to validate individual employers as trainers and to assess apprentices' skills. At company and workplace levels, works councils have the right to codetermine both how training regulations are implemented at the workplace and the content of employment decisions concerning training staff. They have established a plant-level training committee in most large establishments (Streeck et al. (1987); Münch (1991); Müller-Jentsch (1995, p. 71)).

In some accounts, employee representation, as part of joint regulation by employer and employee representatives, is a key requirement for the success of an apprenticeship system (Raggatt (1988), Streeck (1989)); in other accounts, it is a secondary or optional extra (Hall and Soskice (2001)).

The potential contributions of employee representation to the success of apprenticeship depend on the goals of trade unions and works councils. Theoretical generalization on that matter is difficult. A simple starting point is the assumption that employee representatives press for more and better training. To the extent that they do so, their involvement in training-related decisions increases support for those goals, compared to cases of "employer coordination only." This is potentially important both at central level (the definition of training standards for particular occupations), which typically involves national union officials, and at workplace level (training content that exceeds minimum standards, a higher volume of training), which potentially involves works councils and workplace union representatives. Support for quality is potentially most important when the employer adopts a production-oriented training strategy; support for quantity, is when an investment-oriented strategy is involved. The former situation arises mostly in small firms, where employee representation is least extensive, and therefore least able to improve training. In the investment-oriented case, support for high training standards is less necessary, but a works council with codetermination powers may press to make the firm's apprenticeship program larger and its content less firm-specific than they would otherwise be, which may reduce market failure.

Secondly, employee representation may improve information and reduce distrust, and thereby also potentially improve apprenticeship. To the extent that works councils reduce the cost and asymmetry of information on skills-related issues between managers and employees, and increase trust between the two parties, the efficiency of apprenticeship training can improve (Rogers and Streeck (1995)). In particular, works councils, workplace training committees, and union training representatives are well-placed to monitor the quality of training, and thereby to reassure employees and trade unions that their interests are not unduly threatened by the substitution of apprentices for adult employees (see Section 2; Ryan (1994)).

Indirect channels may also be present. Firstly, to the extent that unions and councils press for more skill-intensive methods of production, both the employer's demand for skill and the supply of apprenticeships may be higher. Secondly, when an employer possesses monopsony power over trainees, as is sometimes the case for production-oriented training, collective bargaining can raise apprentices' pay and weaken the incentive to the employer to offer high quantity and low quality training. This constraint is potentially important when effective external training standards are absent. Finally, to the extent that trade unions succeed in strengthening employment protection law, employers seeking to screen candidates for future employment are encouraged to offer apprenticeship rather than recruit already skilled workers, both because an apprenticeship contract makes it easier to lay off individuals (i.e., when it expires, at the end of the training contract) than does an employment contract, and because it is more expensive to recruit skilled workers when layoffs are restricted by law.

Employee representation and social partnership may however have dysfunctional effects. First, trade unions may make pay a higher priority than training. When that leads to higher apprentice pay, training costs are higher and the employer's supply of training places lower—a pathology that was prominent in post-war Britain. Unions may pursue such goals for various reasons: to increase employment for adult members, to increase their bargaining power, to respond to youth discontent, or to increase recruitment (Ryan (1987); Marsden and Ryan (1991); Ryan (2010)).

Second, trade unions may seek to curb the supply of apprenticeships in order to generate scarcity in occupational labor markets, and thereby to raise pay for their skilled members. The strategy is encountered most frequently among occupationally based employee organizations (craft unions and professional associations). The resulting volume of training is inefficiently low.

Finally, trade unions may be reluctant to engage in political-economic exchange in the first place. Where trade unionism has a strong political or ideological component, and militancy is preferred to negotiation, the prospects for the joint regulation of work-based training may be impaired from the supply side. The difficulties of apprenticeship in South Korea may have resulted from such attributes in the labor movement, not just the weakness of employer coordination (Jeong (1995)).

Turning to works councils, although usually they operate under a "peace obligation" (i.e., prohibition of industrial action) and are formally excluded from pay bargaining, they may be diverted from improving training into rent acquisition ("plant egotism"), by negotiating establishment-specific advantages in pay and working conditions (Thelen (1991)).

Second, works councils may use their powers over training at the workplace to "protect" trainees by reducing their involvement in production during training, which raises costs to the employer and, under investment-oriented training, potentially cuts both the effectiveness of training and the supply of places.[50] Similarly, works councils have been seen in Germany to push the employer to retain after training more apprentices than it would otherwise do, thereby reducing the contribution of apprenticeship to the screening of future employees and more generally to the matching of workers and jobs in occupational labor markets Ryan et al. (2010).

Finally, social partnership at national level may reduce innovation in training content and methods. Training schedules have to be revised in response to technical change in products and processes; the need for agreement means more discussion and slower decision-making, particularly under the consensus requirements for decision-making. The issue remains open, however, as the cost of slower decisions may be outweighed by the benefit of better decisions.

The cross-country evidence suggests some association between indices of employee representation and apprenticeship activity (Table 11.4, rows 5–11). The countries with small or nonexistent apprenticeship systems tend to score low in terms of both the background attributes of social partnership (trade union membership and collective bargaining coverage) and the foreground ones (powers of works councils at the workplace, and of joint committees at sector and national levels).

A comparison between South Korea and Ireland illustrates the relationship. Korea's weak and highly conflictual industrial relations system helped frustrate its government's German-inspired attempt to introduce apprenticeship in the 1990s (Jeong (1995)). By contrast, the growth of social partnership in Ireland since the mid-1980s, while originally oriented to macroeconomic management, soon embraced the reform of a traditional "time served" apprenticeship system. The success of that reform, relative to its British counterpart, is consistent with the importance of social partnership in Ireland and its near absence in Britain. An Irish-British comparison is particularly informative for involving institutional changes over time, not just institutional differences at a point in time (Ryan (2000); Field and O'Dubhchair (2001)).

Nevertheless, social partnership appears not to meet the more stringent requirements for status as necessary or sufficient for the success of apprenticeship. On the sufficiency side, Sweden scores highly on all indicators except national policy-making but has no apprenticeship. That is perhaps not surprising: as Sweden had previously opted to replace apprenticeship system by full-time vocational education, it may be a case of

---

[50] Any council-induced reduction of apprentice learning might conflict with the case for apprenticeship as a means of learning. If skills are better learned not only by being learned at the workplace but also by performing actual production tasks, apprentices who are less involved in productive work in order for a works council to curb substitution for skilled workers learn less. A cross-sectional study finds the greater the share of their time at the workplace that apprentices spend in productive work, the more cross-curricular skills they learn (Bieri-Buschor et al. (2002)).

institutional suitability combined with lack of political interest in developing apprenticeship (Crouch et al. (1999, p. 117 seq.)). One test would be whether, should the Swedish government try to recreate apprenticeship, the country's well-developed institutions of social partnership will generate success.

On the necessity side, extensive employee representation and social partnership may not be essential for large-scale apprenticeship. Switzerland lacks mandatory works councils, most Swiss employees neither belong to unions nor are covered by collective bargaining, yet the country has a large apprenticeship system. Swiss law does however give the "organizations of the world of work" (employers' associations, trade unions, and occupational associations) responsibility for the design and operation of apprenticeship (BBT (2009)). That shows up in Table 11.4 in the role of joint bodies in the formulation of social and economic policy at both national and sector levels. The Swiss case therefore both calls into question the necessity of employee representation for the success of apprenticeship and suggests that, insofar as social partnership does matter, the important attribute is training-related joint representation, not high levels of employee organization *per se*.

One potentially necessary condition must be noted. In almost all of the countries with apprenticeship systems, including Switzerland, joint bodies external to the firm possess powers over the content of training at workplaces. Those powers involve variously the specification of minimum training standards, the validation of the employer's eligibility to train apprentices, or the assessment of apprentices' learning.[51] To that extent, some external regulation of workplace training appears to be a necessary ingredient of apprenticeship training. Doubt again centres on Switzerland, where the relevant powers of occupational associations are limited to the assessment of apprentice skills, and many associations are employer-dominated and, as such, do not involve strong social partnership.

5.1.4 Educational representation

Social partnership may also involve educational institutions and educators in the design and administration of apprenticeship. In Germany, representatives of vocational teachers enjoy parity of representation with employers and employees on the vocational training committees of the federal states (*Länder*), which are responsible for the vocational education (*Berufsschule*) component of apprenticeship (Streeck et al. (1987, p. 17)). The examination committees that the chambers set up for the assessment and certification of apprentice learning must contain a vocational teacher (Münch (1991)).

The potential contributions of such representation rights are all quality-related: the bolstering of the more educational components of apprentices' learning and its

---

[51] The exception is the U.K., where the powers of the external body (Sector Skills Council) are limited to restricting eligibility for public training subsidies to firms that adhere to a training "framework," and where those external bodies are "employer led," i.e., need not involve employee representatives.

external, disinterested assessment, and of the monitoring of training content at the workplace. These contributions are potentially valuable across the board, but particularly so when employers adopt a production-oriented training strategy and have an incentive to cut corners in organizing training.

The potential dysfunctions of educational representation include the reorientation of apprenticeship toward narrowly academic goals and methods, to the detriment of apprentice motivation and learning—which undermines the case for apprenticeship as opposed to full-time vocational schooling. Vocational educators may also resist pedagogical innovations that reduce training cost without compromising quality, not just those that cut quality as well as cost. Fear of such dysfunctions may account in Germany for the lack of direct representation of vocational teachers on the Central Board and the sectoral training committees of the Federal Vocational Training Institute, responsible respectively for the overall design of the system and the specification of training regulations at occupation level (Streeck et al. (1987)).

Cross-national data on the role of vocational educators in apprenticeship systems are scanty. In the European countries with moderate or extensive apprenticeship systems, such representation is typically mandatory, whether on the national steering body, on the sector-level or district-level committees that regulate work-based training, or on both (Table 11.4, row 12). That does not however apply in either France or Britain. Its absence in Britain reflects political hostility to both social partnership and any systematic educational orientation in apprenticeship (Lewis and Ryan (2009)).

5.1.5 Apprentice organization

The final category of actor is apprentices themselves. Their role has been widely neglected. Institutionalists have paid little attention to the individual trainee. Indeed, the governance of apprenticeship usually accords no place to apprentices, beyond the indirect representation of their interests by trade unions. Nevertheless, under particular circumstances, dissatisfied apprentices have organized independently, acted collectively, and thereby affected how their training programs function.

The effects of trainee organization involve occurrence, goals, and methods. Dissatisfaction becomes more widespread, and collective action more likely, when employers adopt a production-oriented training strategy and trainee pay is low by the standards of the time and place. Even then, collective action is likely only when three conditions are met: first, external training standards are either absent or poorly enforced, so that little learned; second, the alternatives open to discontented apprentices are few and poor, for example, as a result of job scarcity or monopsony power; third, apprentices expect to face excess supply in occupational labor markets after qualifying. Career prospects are then too poor to compensate young people for low pay relative to productivity during training. Apprentices may then act collectively, and press employers either for better training or for higher pay during training.

Apprentice activism is neither commonplace nor easy to measure. In the absence of systematic cross-country data, evidence can be taken from particular times and places. Three examples stand out. The first is the strike movements conducted by apprentices in British metalworking between 1912 and 1964, mostly in pursuit of higher pay. Those actions episodically increased the relative pay of apprentices and the cost to employers of training them, and arguably contributed to the decline of apprenticeship (Ryan (2004, 2010)). The second example concerns the unofficial strikes conducted by German apprentices between 1968 and 1972, in which the primary demand was better training not higher pay, but which appear to have had little effect on either (Blanke (1972)). Thirdly, there are the strikes conducted in recent decades by teaching assistants—viewed as apprentices' functional equivalents in higher education—in some large public U.S. universities, including Wisconsin and Berkeley, in pursuit of higher pay and reduced workloads (Cohen (2000), Julius and Gumport (2003)).

Apprentice activism that leads to more training per apprentice potentially increases efficiency, insofar as market-based training involves under-provision. When it raises apprentice pay, the effect on efficiency depends on whether low pay during training reflects monopsony power or simply a paucity of alternatives to apprenticeship (see Section 4.2.3). If the former, efficiency potentially increases, but if the latter, it falls—although a case for the change may still exist in equity.

5.2 Conclusions and future research

The evidence suggests, first, that countries with larger apprenticeship systems tend to have more elaborate institutions for the coordination of training related decisions, both market-based and nonmarket-based, than do those with smaller ones or no system at all. The principal dimensions along which institutional elaboration is observed are: statutory underpinning, employer organization, and social partnership.

Second, a functionalist analysis of those institutions indicates various ways in which they can reduce market failure and increase efficiency. Two loci are particularly important: in the presence of investment-oriented training, by increasing the quantity of training provided (number of apprentices); in the presence of production-oriented training, by improving training standards, and thus the amount of training per apprentice.

The evidence considered here is consistent with the view that such institutional attributes influence the success of apprenticeship across countries. Three reservations must however be registered. First, the evidence is too limited to "prove" the hypothesis overall, let alone determine the interactions between institutions in the setting of outcomes. Second, some potential institutional effects, including those of corporate ownership and finance, have not been covered here. Third, it appears unlikely that, even confining attention to the institutional attributes that have been considered, any combination is either necessary or sufficient for the success of apprenticeship. Concerning necessity, the successful countries include Switzerland, whose "liberal corporatism" involves weaker roles for employee representation and social partnership than do the neighboring countries with comparably large apprenticeship systems (Fluder and Hotz-Hart (1998)). Concerning sufficiency, high levels of coordination in Sweden have only recently led to attempts to create an apprenticeship system in place of the one abandoned decades ago.

The evidence has a bearing on the efforts of governments to develop apprenticeship in many countries, including France, Ireland, the U.K., and South Korea, which had previously either no apprenticeship system or only a traditional or moribund one. The evidence suggests that neither of the polar positions that are sometimes taken in discussions of such policies—"no need for serious institutional development" and "no prospect for policy borrowing, given institutional stasis"—is valid. Countries that lack institutions for employer coordination and social partnership do indeed face serious difficulties, whether in expanding high-quality work-based training without institutional support, or in developing suitable institutional support in the first place—as notably in South Korea. But the institutional obstacles are less than absolute. Ireland and France have both expanded apprenticeship and increased its quality with less powerful—albeit nontrivial—support from employer coordination and social partnership.

Promising directions for future research include improved measurement of institutional attributes, leading to the inclusion of more countries and more detailed institutional attributes, at sectoral and regional as well as national levels. It may then become possible to identify more clearly the roles of and complementarities between institutions in the operation of apprenticeship, and to analyze institutional change more effectively (Thelen (2009)).

6. CONCLUSIONS

Apprenticeship varies greatly across countries, in terms of both quantity (numbers trained) and quality (skill content); and across sectors and occupations within countries, in terms of its provision and finance by employers. Therefore it is not easy to explain the heterogeneity of apprenticeship. Despite the theoretical advances of the last two decades, as yet no general theory explains the full range of financial attributes observed, even ignoring cross-national heterogeneity. Indeed recent theoretical efforts have focused to a greater extent than is widely recognized on specific circumstances in occupational labor markets, and the potential sensitivity of the conclusions to changes in assumptions about trainee labor markets is not widely recognized. The economics of information and imperfect (monopsonistic) competition potentially explains why many employers invest substantial amounts in transferable ("general") skills, despite the poaching externality. But empirical observations show not only a large degree of heterogeneity in the training costs that firms share but also that many firms reap net benefits even during the training of apprentices.

This can be partly explained by the phenomenon of production-oriented training, in which employers earn a surplus during training, release many trainees at the end of the training contract, and, in the absence of external training standards, use apprentices as cheap labor. However, production-oriented training is less well-understood than investment-oriented training and more research is needed to understand why in some cases production-oriented training leads to a qualitative collapse of the training market and why in others it operates alongside a high-skill, high volume training market.

Microeconomic models of market choices by firms and young people require institutional elaboration in order to effectively address cross-national differences in apprenticeship, partly because informational failure and skill specificity are not expected to vary greatly, and partly because institutional attributes do vary considerably, across countries. Successful apprenticeship systems involve nonmarket coordination mechanisms, comprising principally employer bodies (associations, chambers) and also social partnership, drawing upon employee representatives (trade unions, works councils) and educators. Economic analysis indicates various ways in which such institutions may reduce market failure and increase efficiency. Countries with successful apprenticeship systems do however differ among themselves in terms of institutional content, particularly the importance of social partnership. The relevant institutions may also produce economically dysfunctional effects. Path dependence in institutional development may hamper the scope for suitable institutional development. This means research is needed into institutional development and the interplay of institutions, to fully understand under what circumstances and in what combinations institutions improve outcomes for young people, employers, and the economy as a whole.

Many questions await conclusive answers, including: does apprenticeship increase educational participation and attainment, as it should do if it improves motivation and cognition in vocational education, and if it provides improved job prospects to young people? This is suggested by the positive cross-country association between overall educational participation and the enrollment share of apprentices. The association is not strong, as many nonapprenticeship countries have high enrollments (Sweden, Belgium), but the lowest enrollment rates are in countries with little or no apprenticeship (U.S.) or little or no educational content in apprenticeship (U.K.). The association is in any case at most suggestive, given potential distortion by national fixed effects.

REFERENCES

Acemoglu, D., 1997. Training and innovation in an imperfect labour market. Rev. Econ. Stud. 62, 445–464.

Acemoglu, D., Pischke, J.S., 1998. Why do firms train? Theory and evidence. Q. J. Econ. 79–119.

Acemoglu, D., Pischke, J.S., 1999a. Beyond Becker: Training in imperfect labour markets. Econ. J. 108, F112–F142.

Acemoglu, D., Pischke, J.S., 1999b. The structure of wages and investment in general training. J. Pol. Econ. 107 (3), 539–572.

Acemoglu, D., Pischke, J.S., 2000. Certification of training and training outcomes. Eur. Econ. Rev. 44 (4–6), 917–927.

Acemoglu, D., Pischke, J.S., 2003. Minimum wages and on-the-job training. In: Polachek, S.W. (Ed.), Worker well-being and public policy. Vol. 222. 159–202. Res. Labour E.

Akerlof, G.A., 1970. The market for "lemons": Quality uncertainty and the market mechanism. Q. J. Econ. 84 (3), 488–500.

Albaek, K., 2009. The Danish apprenticeship system, 1931–2002: The role of subsidies and institutions. App. Econ. Q. 55 (1), 39–60.

Askilden, J.E., Nilsen, O.A., 2005. Apprentices and young workers: A study of the Norwegian youth labour market. Scot. J. Polit. Econ. 52 (1), 1–17.

Autor, D., 2001. Why do temporary help firms provide free general skills training? Q. J. Econ. 116 (4), 1409–1448.

Backes-Gellner, U., Tuor, S., 2010. Avoiding labor shortages through employer signaling—on the importance of good work atmosphere and labor relations. Ind. Labor Relat. Rev. forthcoming.

Bassanini, A., Brunello, G., 2007. Barriers to entry, deregulation and workplace training. IZA Working Paper, No. 2746.

Bassanini, A., Brunello, G., 2008. Is training more frequent when the wage premium is smaller? Evidence from the European Community Household Panel. Labour Econ. 15 (2), 272–290.

Bassanini, A., Booth, A., Brunello, G., de Paola, M., Leuven, E., 2007. Workplace training in Europe. In: Brunello, G., Garibaldi, P., Wasmer, E. (Eds.), Education and Training in Europe. Oxford University Press (Chapters 8–13).

Bauder, T., Osterwalder, F., 2008. 75 Jahre eidgenössisches Berufsbildungsgesetz. Politische, pädagogische, ökonomische Perspektiven. HEP Verlag.

BBT, 2009. Vocational education and training in Switzerland. In: National Report to the OECD's Learning for Jobs Review. Bundesamt für Berufsbildung und Technologie.

Becker, G., 1962. Investment in human capital: a theoretical analysis. J. Polit. Econ. 70 (5), 9–49.

Beckmann, M., 2002. Wage compression and firm-sponsored training in Germany: Empirical evidence for the Acemoglu-Pischke model from a zero-inflated count data model. App. Econ. Q. 48 (3–4), 368–389.

Beicht, U., Walden, G., 2002. Wirtschaftlichere Durchführung der Berufsbildung—Untersuchungsergebnisse zu den Ausbildungskosten der Betriebe. Berufsbildung in Wissenschaft und Praxis, Heft 6.

Beicht, U., Walden, G., Herget, H., 2004. Kosten und Nutzen der betrieblichen Berufsausbildung in Deutschland. BIBB.

Bertschy, K., Cattaneo, M.A., Wolter, S.C., 2009. PISA and the transition into the labour market. Labour: Rev. Lab. Econ. & Ind. Relations 23, 111–137.

Bieri-Buschor, C., Forrer, E., Maag-Merki, K., 2002. The willingness of young Swiss to participate in continuing education and training: Initial findings from a survey of young adults. Education + Training 44 (4–5), 224–232.

Bilginsoy, C., 2003. The hazards of training: Attrition and retention in construction industry apprenticeship programs. Ind. Labor Relat. Rev. 57 (1), 54–67.

Bishop, J.H., 1996. What we know about employer-provided training: A review of literature. Cornell University, Center for Advanced Human Resources Studies, Working Paper 96–09.

Black, B., Gospel, H., Pendleton, A., 2007. Finance, corporate governance and the employment relationship. Ind. Relat. 46 (3), 643–650.

Blanke, T., 1972. Funktionswandel des Streiks im Spätkapitalismus: am Beispiel des Lehrlingsstreikrechts. Fischer.

Blatter, M., Mühlemann, S., Schenker, S., Wolter, S.C., 2011. Hiring costs for skilled workers and the supply of firm-provided training. IZA Discussion Paper. forthcoming.

Bonnal, L., Mendes, S., Sofer, C., 2002. School-to-work transition: Apprenticeship versus vocational school in France. Int. J. Manpower 23 (5), 426–442.

Booth, A., Zoega, G., 2004. Is wage compression a necessary condition for firm-financed general training? Oxf. Econ. Pap. 56, 88–97.

Brunello, G., 2009. The effect of economic downturns on apprenticeships and initial workplace training: A review of the evidence. Empirical Research in Vocational Education and Training 1 (2), 145–171.

Brunello, G., de Paola, M., 2008. Training and the density of economic activity: Evidence from Italy. Labour Econ. 15 (1), 118–140.

Brunello, G., Gambarotto, F., 2007. Agglomeration effects on employer-provided training: Evidence from the UK. Reg. Sci. Urban Econ. 37 (1), 1–22.

Brunello, G., Medio, A., 2001. An explanation of international differences in education and work place training. Eur. Econ. Rev. 45 (2), 307–322.

Büchel, F., 2002. Successful apprenticeship-to-work transitions: On the long-term change in significance of the German school-leaving certificate. Int. J. Manpower 23 (5), 394–410.

Busemeyer, M.R., 2009. Asset specificity, institutional complementarities and the variety of skill regimes in coordinated market economies. Socio-Economic Rev. 7 (3), 375–406.

Cappelli, P., 2004. Why do employers pay for college? J. Econom. 121, 213–241.

Chang, C., Wang, Y., 1996. Human capital investment under asymmetric information: The Pigovian conjecture revisited. J. Labor Econ. 14 (3), 505–519.

Clark, D., 2001. Why do German firms subsidize apprenticeship training? Tests of the asymmetric information and mobility cost explanations. Vierteljahreshefte zur Wirtschaftsforschung 70 (1), 102–106.

Cohen, W., 2000. The economics of doctoral education in literature. Publications of the Modern Language Association of America 115, 1165–1187.

Combes, M., 1988. La loi de 1987 sur l'apprentissage. Formation Emploi. 22, 83–97.

Crouch, C., Finegold, D., Sako, M., 1999. Are Skills the Answer? The Political Economy of Skill Creation in Advanced Industrial Economies. Oxford University Press.

Crouch, C., Streeck, W., Boyer, R., Amable, B., Hall, P., Jackson, G., et al., 2005. Dialogue on "institutional complementarity and political economy. Socio-Economic Review 3 (3), 359–382.

Culpepper, P., 2003. Creating Cooperation: How States Develop Human Capital in Europe. Cornell University Press.

Culpepper, P., 2007. Small states and skill specificity. Comp. Polit. Stud. 40 (6), 611–637.

Deißinger, T., 1996. Germany's Vocational Training Act: Its function as an instrument of quality control within a tradition-based vocational training system. Oxford Rev. Educ. 22, 317–336.

Dietrich, H., Gerner, H.D., 2007. The determinants of apprenticeship training with particular reference to business expectations. J. Labour Market Res. (ZAF) 40 (2–3), 221–233.

Dionisius, R., Mühlemann, S., Pfeifer, H., Walden, G., Wenzelmann, F., Wolter, S.C., et al., 2009. Costs and benefits of apprenticeship training. A comparison of Germany and Switzerland. Appl. Econ. Q. 55 (1), 5–38.

Dohlmann Weatherall, C., 2009. Do subsidized adult apprenticeships increase the vocational attendance rate? Appl. Econ. Q. 55 (1), 61–82.

Dustmann, C., Schönberg, U., 2007. Apprenticeship training and commitment to training provision. Universities of Zurich and Bern: Leading House Working Paper Series No. 32.

Dustmann, C., Schönberg, U., 2009. Training and union wages. Rev. Econ. Stat. 91 (2), 363–376.

Euwals, R., Winkelmann, R., 2002. Mobility after apprenticeship training – evidence from register data. Appl. Econ. Q. 48 (3–4), 256–278.

Euwals, R., Winkelmann, R., 2004. Training intensity and first labour market outcomes of apprenticeship graduates. Int. J. Manpower 25, 447–462.

Fersterer, J., Pischke, J.S., Winter-Ebmer, R., 2008. Returns to apprenticeship training in Austria: Evidence from failed firms. Scand. J. Econ. 110 (4), 733–753.

Feuer, M., Glick, H., Desai, A., 1987. Is firm-sponsored education viable? J. Econ. Behav. Organ. 8 (1), 121–136.

Field, J., O'Dubhchair, M., 2001. Recreating apprenticeship: Lessons from the Irish standards-based model. J. Vocational Educ. Training 53 (2), 247–261.

Field, S., Hoeckel, K., Kis, V., Kuczera, M., 2009. Learning for jobs. In: OECD Policy Review of Vocational Education and Training: Initial Report. OECD.

Fitzenberger, B., Kunze, A., 2005. Vocational training and gender: Wages and occupational mobility among young workers. Oxford Rev. Econ. Pol. 21, 392–415.

Fluder, R., Hotz-Hart, B., 1998. Switzerland: Still smooth as clockwork? In: Ferner, A., Hyman, R. (Eds.), Changing Industrial Relations in Europe. Blackwell, pp. 262–282.

Fougère, D., Schwerdt, W., 2002. Are apprentices productive? Appl. Econ. Q. 48 (3–4), 317–346.

Franz, W., Soskice, D., 1995. The German apprenticeship system. In: Butler, F., Franz, W., Schettkat, R., Soskice, D. (Eds.), Institutional Frameworks and Labor Market Performance. Routledge, London, pp. 208–234.

Freeman, R.B., 2008. Labour market institutions around the world. In: Blyton, P., Bacon, N., Fiorito, J., Heery, E. (Eds.), The SAGE Handbook of Industrial Relations. SAGE Publications, pp. 640–658.

Gathmann, C., Schönberg, U., 2010. How general is human capital? A task-based approach. J. Labor Econ. 28 (1), 1–50.

Geel, R., Backes-Gellner, U., Mure, J., 2010. Specificity of Occupational Training and Occupational Mobility: An Empirical Study Based on Lazear's Skill-Weights Approach. Education Economics, forthcoming.

Gersbach, H., Schmutzler, A., 2006. A product-market theory of industry-specific training. University of Zurich, Socioeconomic Institute Discussion Paper No. 0610.

Goerlitz, K., Stiebale, J., 2008. Does product market competition decrease employers' training investments? Evidence from German establishment panel data. Ruhr Economic Paper No. 41.

Gospel, H., Druker, J., 1998. The survival of national bargaining in the electrical contracting industry: A deviant case? Br. J. Ind. Relat. 36 (2), 249–267.

Grubb, W.N., 1995. Education through Occupations. Teachers' College Press.

Hall, P., Soskice, D., 2001. An introduction to varieties of capitalism. In: Hall, P., Soskice, D. (Eds.), Varieties of Capitalism: The Institutional Foundations of Comparative Advantage. Oxford University Press (Chapter 1).

Hall, P., Thelen, K., 2009. Institutional change and varieties of capitalism. Socio-Economic Review 7 (1), 7–34.

Harhoff, D., Kane, T.J., 1997. Is the German apprenticeship system a panacea for the U.S. labour market? J. Popul. Econ. 10, 171–196.

Hart, R.A., 2005. General human capital and employment adjustments in the Great Depression: Apprentices and journeyman in UK engineering. Oxf. Econ. Pap. 57 (1), 169–189.

Hashimoto, M., 1981. Firm-specific human capital as a shared investment. Am. Econ. Rev. 71 (3), 475–482.

Hasluck, C., Hogarth, T., Adam, D., 2008. The Net Benefit to Employer Investment in Apprenticeship Training. Institute of Employment Research, University of Warwick.

Hirsch, B.T., Schumacher, E.J., 1998. Unions, wages, and skills. J. Hum. Resour. 33 (1), 201–219.

Hoeckel, K., Field, S., Grubb, W.N., 2008. Learning for Jobs. OECD Reviews of Vocational Education and Training: Switzerland. OECD.

Höpner, M., 2005. What connects industrial relations and corporate governance? Explaining institutional complementarity. Socio-Economic Review 3 (2), 331–358.

Jeong, J., 1995. The failure of recent state vocational training policies in Korea from a comparative perspective. Br. J. Ind. Relat. 33 (2), 237–252.

Jones, I.S., 1986. Apprentice training costs in British manufacturing establishments: Some new evidence. Br. J. Ind. Relat. 24 (3), 333–362.

Julius, D.J., Gumport, P.J., 2003. Graduate student unionization: Catalysts and consequences. Rev. High. Educ. 26 (2), 187–216.

Katz, E., Ziderman, A., 1990. Investments in general training: The role of information and labour mobility. Econ. J. 100 (403), 1147–1158.

Kessler, A.S., Lülfesmann, C., 2006. The theory of human capital revisited: On the interaction of general and specific investments. Econ. J. 116, 903–923.

Krueger, D., Kumar, K.B., 2004a. Skill-specific rather than general education: A reason for U.S.–Europe growth differences? J. Econ. Growth 9 (2), 167–207.

Krueger, D., Kumar, K.B., 2004b. US–Europe differences in technology-driven growth: Quantifying the role of education. J. Monetary Econ. 51 (1), 161–190.

Kuczera, K., Kis, V., Wurzburg, G., 2009. Learning for jobs. In: OECD Reviews of Vocational Education and Training: Korea. OECD.

Lazear, E., 2000. The future of personnel economics. Econ. J. 110 (November), F611–F639.

Lazear, E., 2003. Firm-specific human capital: A skill-weights approach. NBER Working Paper No. W9679.

Leuven, E., 2005. The economics of private sector training: A survey of the literature. J. Econ. Surv. 19 (1), 91–111.

Lewis, P., Ryan, P., 2009. Does external inspection under-rate apprenticeship training by employers? Evidence from England. Empirical Research in Vocational Education and Training 1 (1), 39–63.

Lindley, R.M., 1975. The demand for apprentice recruits by the engineering industry, 1951-71. Scot. J. Pol. Econ. 22, 1–24.

Loewenstein, M.A., Spletzer, J.R., 1998. General and specific training, evidence and implications. J. Hum. Resour. 710–733.

Malamud, O., Pop-Eleches, C., 2010. General education versus vocational education: Evidence from an economy in transition. Rev. Econ. Stat. 92 (1), 43–60.

Malcomson, J.M., McGaw, J.W., McCormick, B., 2003. General training by firms, apprentice contracts, and public policy. Euro. Econ. Rev. 47, 197–227.

Marsden, D., Ryan, P., 1991. Initial training, labour market structure and public policy: Intermediate skills in British and German industry. In: Ryan, P. (Ed.), International Comparisons of VET for Intermediate Skills. Falmer Press, pp. 251–285.

Merrilees, W.J., 1983. Alternative models of apprentice recruitment: With special reference to the British engineering industry. Appl. Econ. 15 (1), 1–21.

Mohrenweiser, J., Zwick, T., 2009. Why do firms train apprentices? The net cost puzzle reconsidered. Labour Econ 16 (5), 631–637.

Mohrenweiser, J., Backes-Gellner, U., 2010. Apprenticeship training - what for: investment or substitution?, Int. J. Manpower, forthcoming.

Mühlemann, S., Wolter, S.C., 2007. Regional effects on employer provided training: Evidence from apprenticeship training in Switzerland. Journal for Labour Market Research (ZAF) 2–3, 135–147.

Mühlemann, S., Schweri, J., Winkelmann, R., Wolter, S.C., 2007a. An empirical analysis of the decision to train apprentices. Labour: Rev. Lab. Econ. & Ind. Relations 21 (3), 419–441.

Mühlemann, S., Wolter, S.C., Fuhrer, M., Wüest, A., 2007b. Lehrlingsausbildung - ökonomisch betrachtet. Rüegger Verlag.

Mühlemann, S., Wolter, S.C., Wüest, A., 2009. Apprenticeship training and the business cycle. Empirical Research in Vocational Education and Training 1 (2), 173–186.

Mühlemann, S., Pfeifer, H., Walden, G., Wenzelmann, F., Wolter, S.C., 2010. The financing of apprenticeship training in the light of labor market regulations. Labour Econ.17 (5), 799–809.

Mühlemann, S., Ryan, P., Wolter, S.C., 2011. Monopsony power, compressed pay structures and training. IZA Discussion Paper.

Müller-Jentsch, W., 1995. Germany: From collective voice to co-management. In: Rogers, J., Streeck, W. (Eds.), Works Councils. Consultation, Representation and Cooperation in Industrial Relations. University of Chicago Press, pp. 53–78.

Münch, J., 1991. Vocational Training in the Federal Republic of Germany. CEDEFOP.

Ni Cheallaigh, M., 1995. Apprenticeship in the EU Member States. CEDEFOP.

OECD, 1999. Preparing Youth for the 21st Century: The Transition From Education to the Labour Market. OECD.

OECD, 2004. OECD Employment Outlook 2004. OECD.

OECD, 2008a. Education at a Glance: OECD Indicators. OECD.

OECD, 2008b. Systematic Innovation in the Swiss VET System. Centre for Educational Research and Innovation. OECD.

Oosterbeek, H., Webbink, D., 2007. Wage effects of an extra year of basic vocational education. Econ. Educ. Rev. 26 (4), 408–419.

Palmer, M.E., 1981. Education and Work in the Federal Republic of Germany. Anglo-German Foundation.

Pischke, J.S., von Wachter, T., 2008. Zero returns to compulsory schooling in Germany. Rev. Econ. Stat. 90 (3), 592–598.
Plug, E., Groot, W.J.N., 1998. Apprenticeship versus vocational education: Exemplified by the Dutch situation. TSER/STT Working Paper 10–98.
Raggatt, P., 1988. Quality control in the dual system of West Germany. Oxford Rev. Educ. 14 (2), 163–186.
Rasmussen, A.R., Westergaard-Nielsen, N., 1999. The impact of subsidies on the number of new apprentices. Res. Labor E. 18, 359–375.
Rogers, J., Streeck, W., 1995. The study of works councils: Concepts and problems. In: Rogers, J., Streeck, W. (Eds.), Works Councils. Consultation, Representation and Cooperation in Industrial Relations. University of Chicago Press, pp. 3–26.
Ryan, P., 1987. Trade unionism and the pay of young workers. In: Junankar, P. (Ed.), From School to Unemployment? The Labour Market for Young People. Macmillan, pp. 119–142.
Ryan, P., 1994. Training quality and trainee exploitation. In: Layard, R., Mayhew, K., Owen, G. (Eds.), Britain's Training Deficit. Avebury, pp. 92–124.
Ryan, P., 1995. Trade union policies towards the Youth Training Scheme: Patterns and causes. Br. J. Ind. Relat. 33 (1), 1–33.
Ryan, P., 1998. Is apprenticeship better? A review of the economic evidence. Journal of Vocational Education and Training 50 (2), 289–325.
Ryan, P., 2000. The institutional requirements of apprenticeship: Evidence from smaller EU-countries. International Journal of Training and Development 4, 42–65.
Ryan, P., 2001. The school-to-work transition: A cross-national perspective. J. Econ. Lit. 39 (1), 34–92.
Ryan, P., 2003. Evaluating vocationalism. Euro. J. Educ. 38 (2), 147–162.
Ryan, P., 2004. Apprentice strikes in the twentieth century UK engineering and shipbuilding industries. Historical Studies in Industrial Relations (Autumn) 18, 1–63.
Ryan, P., 2010. Apprentice strikes, pay structure and training in twentieth century UK metalworking industry. In: Brown, C., Eichengreen, B., Reich, M. (Eds.), The Great Unraveling: New Labour Market Institutions and Public Policy Response. Oxford University Press.
Ryan, P., Unwin, L., 2001. Apprenticeship in the British "training market" Natl. Inst. Econ. Rev. 178, 99–114.
Ryan, P., Gospel, H., Lewis, P., 2007. Large employers and apprenticeship training in Britain. Br. J. Ind. Relat. 45 (1), 127–153.
Ryan, P., Wagner, K., Teuber, S., Backes-Gellner, U., 2010. Financial attributes of apprenticeship training in England, Germany and Switzerland. Report to Hans-Böckler-Stiftung, Dusseldorf.
Sadowski, D., 1980. Berufliche Bildung und betriebliches Bildungsbudget. Poeschel.
Schweri, J., Müller, B., 2007. Why has the share of training firms declined in Switzerland? Journal for Labour Market Research (ZAF) 2–3, 149–167.
Smits, W., 2007. Industry-specific or generic skills? Conflicting interests of firms and workers. Labour Econ. 14, 653–663.
Sofer, C., 2004. Human Capital over the Life Cycle: A European Perspective. Edward Elgar Publishing.
Spitz-Oener, A., 2006. Technical change, job tasks, and rising educational demands: Looking outside the wage structure. J. Labor Econ. 24 (2), 235–268.
Stevens, M., 1994a. An investment model for the supply of training by employers. Econ. J. 104, 556–570.
Stevens, M., 1994b. A theoretical model of on-the-job training. Oxford Econ. Pap. 46 (4), 537–562.
Stevens, M., 1999. Human capital theory and UK vocational training policy. Oxford Rev. Econ. Pol. 15, 16–32.
Stevens, M., 2001. Should firms be required to pay for vocational training? Econ. J. 111, 485–505.
Stevens, M., 2004. Wage-Tenure contracts in a frictional labour market: Firms' strategies for recruitment and retention. Rev. Econ. Stud. 71 (2), 535–551.
Streeck, W., 1989. Skills and the limits of neo-liberalism: The enterprise of the future as a place of learning. Work Employ. Soc. 3 (1), 89–104.
Streeck, W., 2005. Rejoinder: On terminology, functionalism, (historical) institutionalism and liberalization. Socio-Economic Review 3 (3), 577–588.

Streeck, W., Hilbert, J., van Kevelaer, K.H., Maier, F., Weber, H., 1987. The Role of the Social Partners in Vocational Training and Further Training in the Federal Republic of Germany. CEDEFOP.

Thelen, K., 1991. Union of Parts: Labour Politics in Postwar Germany. Cornell University Press.

Thelen, K., 2009. Institutional change in advanced political economies. Br. J. Ind. Relat. 47 (3), 471–498.

Traxler, F., 2008. Employer organisations. In: Blyton, P., Bacon, N., Fiorito, J., Heery, E. (Eds.), The SAGE Handbook of Industrial Relations. SAGE Publications, pp. 225–241.

Traxler, F., Blaschke, S., Kittel, B., 2001. National Labour Relations in Internationalised Markets. Oxford University Press.

Visser, J., 2009. ICTWSS: Database on institutional characteristics of trade unions, wage setting, state intervention and social pacts in 34 countries between 1960 and 2007, Version 2. AIAS, University of Amsterdam. www.uva-aias.net/208.

Von Bardeleben, R., Beicht, U., Fehér, K., 1995. Betriebliche Kosten und Nutzen der Ausbildung: Repräsentative Resultate aus Industrie, Handel und Handwerk. Bertelsmann.

Werwatz, A., 2002. Occupational mobility after apprenticeship—How effective is the German apprenticeship system? Appl. Econ. Q. 48 (3–4), 279–303.

Winkelmann, R., 1996. Employment prospects and skill acquisition of apprenticeship-trained workers in Germany. Ind. Labour Relat. Rev. 49, 658–672.

Winther, E., Achtenhagen, F., 2009. Measurement of vocational competencies—A contribution to an international large-scale assessment on vocational education and training. Empirical Research in Vocational Education and Training 1 (1), 85–102.

Wolter, S.C., Schweri, J., 2002. The cost and benefit of apprenticeship training: The Swiss case. Appl. Econ. Q. 48 (3–4), 347–367.

Wolter, S.C., Mühlemann, S., Schweri, J., 2006. Why some firms train apprentices and many others not. Ger. Econ. Rev. 7 (3), 249–264.

INDEX

Note: Page numbers followed by f, t and n indicate figures, tables and notes, respectively.

A

Aaronson, Daniel, 67, 68t
Abdulkadiroglu, A., 309
Accountability, 5–6, 48, 139. *See also* Educational achievement; No Child Left Behind
  achievement distribution and, 80–82
  benefits of, 387
  in California, 415–416
  consequences of, 388–389
  cross-state studies, 407, 408–409t
  defining, 384
  differential effects of, 410–411
  district, 394, 404, 405–406t
  domains, 389–391
  draconian elements of, 389
  early adoption of, 411–412
  education quality and, 77–82
  educational achievement and, 145–146
  effectiveness of, 389
  English Language Learners and, 394
  evidence, 402–412
  exclusions, 394–395
  failure/inability to respond to incentives and, 401–402
  Florida and, 414–415
  future research in, 416–417
  growth model, 400
  heterogeneity in programs of, 81
  high/low stakes, 398–399
  housing markets and, 389
  for individual teachers, 387
  information content in, 386–387
  introduction to, 384–386
  late adoption of, 411–412
  limitations to, 387
  measurement error, 395
  mobility and, 394
  narrowing curriculum in response to, 389–390
  nature of, 388–397
  in North Carolina, 415
  not improving performance, 397–402
  principal-agent problem, 386
  psychostimulants and, 399
  racial achievement gap and, 410–411
  ratings, 384
  rationale for, 386–388
  reforms and, 413
  resulting in generalized learning, 397–398
  sanctions, 388, 389
  scope, 389–391
  shock, 415
  short-term, 401
  size, 412
  special needs and, 395
  state specific, 404, 405–406t
  strategic behaviors and, 399–400
  strength of, 414
  subgroup identification, 395–396
  teacher effectiveness and, 413
  teacher turnover and, 412–416
  test scores and, 391
  theory of action behind, 411
  time period for, 396–397
  universal inclusion, 394
  voluntary contributions and, 388
ACE. *See* American Council on Education
Acemoglu, D., 22–23, 528, 530–531, 538n29, 540
Achievement gap
  accountability on racial, 410–411
  black-white test score, 267
  gender, 158
  test scores, 267
  tracking and, 156
"Acting white," 266–267
Adda, Jerome, 44
Adoption
  age at, 230
  intergenerational transmission and, 222
  nonrandom selection of, 232
  parental education and, 230
  studies, 226–227t

Index

Adult Basic Education Act, 460
Adult Education program, 460, 464, 465
    funding, 462f
Adult Literacy and Life Skills Survey (ALLS), 102, 104t, 161n43
Adult Secondary Education (ASE), 460
Afonso, A., 125t
AFQT. *See* Armed Forces Qualification Test
Africa
    international tests and, 102
    Sub-Saharan, 186
    tracking in, 372–374, 377
AFT. *See* American Federation of Teachers
Age
    at adoption, 230
    dropouts and, 473
    education level and, 9, 34
    GED and, 464, 467–470, 469f, 473f
    GED and exceptions to, 468f
    GED and minimum, 467f
    retirement, 10
    at starting school, absolute, 123n22
    tracking, 239, 240, 363–368
Agglomeration effect, 533
Air Force Academy, 270, 271
Akerlof, G.A., 529
Alcohol drinking
    binge, 252, 254
    peer effects, 252, 254, 268, 270
ALLS. *See* Adult Literacy and Life Skills Survey
Altinok, N., 129t, 176t
Altonji, J.G., 27, 60
American Council on Education (ACE), 429, 467
American Federation of Teachers (AFT), 292, 305
    membership of, 305n31
American Time Use Survey (ATUS), 286n12
Ammermueller, A., 120t, 122t, 125t, 126, 129t, 143t, 262t, 366, 367
Amrein-Beardley, A., 408t, 409t
Angrist, J., 22–23, 38, 58t, 64–65, 261t, 263, 334
Angrist, J.D., 22
Antonovics, K.L., 225t, 229
Appleton, S., 177t
Apprentice
    activism, 568
    organization, 567–568
Apprenticeship training

    advantages to, 551
    benefits of, 523
    business cycle and, 548–549
    contract lengths, 526n10
    contract regulation, 526
    cost-benefit surveys of, 534
    criticism of, 536n27
    defining, 522
    demand collapse, 524n4
    developing comprehensive theory of, 538
    drawbacks to, 523
    educational representation, 566–567
    efficiency, 526
    employee representation in, 562–566
    employer representation in, 560–562
    entry requirements, 552
    features of, 526
    as functional term v. conventional term, 523n3
    industry-specific monopsonies and, 532–533
    influences on scale of, 558
    information asymmetries and, 528–530, 554
    investment-oriented, 536
    laws defining, 558
    "make or buy" decision and, 534
    minimum wage and, 526
    motive for, 524n4
    movers v. stayers, 540
    occupation-specific monopsonies and, 532–533
    on-the-job training v., 524
    optimal sharing rule, 526
    parties, 522
    product market competition and, 533–534
    release option, 540
    reputation and, 535
    restriction of innovation in, 559
    skills weight model and, 532n19
    social partnership, 562–566
    spillovers, 533
    statutory framework, 558–559
    subsidies, 535
    successful, 570
    technological attributes of, 554
    trust and, 560
    wage compression and, 530–532
    within-country differences in, 562
    work-based, 539
Apprenticeship training, firm behavior in, 524–538
    future research in, 538

Apprenticeship training, institutional foundations, 553–569, 556–557t
  causal inference and, 554
  future research, 568–569
  measurement problems, 554
  outcomes and, 555–568
Apprenticeship training, net cost of, 541–546
  Germany v. Switzerland, 543–546, 543t, 544t, 546t
Apprenticeship training, production-oriented, 536–538
  as cheap labor, 536n27, 546–548, 570
  as exploitation, 537
Apprenticeship training outcomes, 550–553
  evidence, 551–553
  future research, 553
  identification issues, 550–551
  institutions and, 555–568
  measurement issues, 550–551
Argys, L.M., 268, 349–350, 353
Armed Forces Qualification Test (AFQT), 436, 436n13
ASE. See Adult Secondary Education
Ashenfelter, O., 207t
"Asian values," 112
Askilden, J.E., 549
Assortative mating, 221, 222
  controlling for, 224
ATE. See Average treatment effect
Atherton, P., 177t
Atkinson, S., 497t
ATT. See Average treatment on the treated
Attanasio, O., 46
ATUS. See American Time Use Survey
Autonomy, 139
  educational achievement and, 146–148
Autor, D., 536n25
Average treatment effect (ATE), 13, 28, 39–40
Average treatment on the treated (ATT), 13, 39–40

B

Ballou, Dale, 68t, 69, 308
Barro, R.J., 124t, 175t
Barrow, Lisa, 67, 68t, 499t
Bassanini, A., 534
Bauer, P., 368–369
Baumol effect, 130n25

Bayer, Patrick, 74t, 75–76, 508t, 514
Becker, Gary, 202, 213–214, 525–527
Beckmann, M., 538n29
Bedard, K., 120t, 123, 123n22, 170t
Behrman, J.R., 224, 225t, 229
Berliner, D., 408t, 409t
Bertschy, K., 552
Betts, J.R., 262t, 264, 266, 349, 353–356, 370
BIBB. See Federal Vocational Training Institute
Bilginsoy, C., 549
Bingley, P., 225t, 229
Birth-order effects, 208, 209, 234–236
  biological differences and, 235
  confluence model of, 235
  divorce and, 235
  IQ and, 235
  intergenerational transmission and, 234–236
  negative, 236
  testing for, 235–236
Birthweight
  differences in monozygotic twins, 223
  maternity leave and, 238
Bishop, J.H., 140t, 141t, 145
Björklund, A., 207t, 218, 219, 226t, 230
Black, S.E., 74t, 75, 227t, 231, 503t, 510
Blatter, M., 534
Blau, F.D., 170t
Bleaney, M., 177t
Blundell, R.W., 37, 42–44, 59n52
Bobonis, G.J., 268
Bogart, W., 501t, 504t, 509, 513
Boisjoly, J., 270
Bokhari, F., 399
Books-at-home, 117
  educational achievement and, 117
  as measure of socio-economic status, 157
Boozer, M.A., 261t, 263
Boston's Metco busing program, 263
Bosworth, B.P., 175t
Boudett, K.P., 441t, 447t, 457t
Boyd, D., 328t
Bradbury, K., 502t
Bramoullé, Y., 257–258
Brasington, D., 491, 498t, 499t, 500t, 501t, 511
Bratti, M., 129t
Braun, H., 409t
Breastfeeding, 238
Brewer, D.J., 329t, 349–350, 353

Brueckner, J., 496t
Brunello, G., 143t, 361–363, 534
Brunner, E., 504t
Budget constraints. *See* Credit constraints
Burke, M.A., 264
Bush, George H.W., 385

C

Cacciola, S.E., 261t, 263
Caetano, G., 506t
California, 415–416
Cameron, S.V., 441t, 457t
Campos, E., 503t
Cao, J., 441t
Capitalism, varieties of, 555, 558
Card, D., 21, 58t, 61
Carman, K., 262t
Carnegie Units, 463
Carneiro, P., 228t, 231, 233–234
Carnoy, M., 407, 408t
Carrell, S.E., 267, 270
Cartwright, G.P., 374
Cascio, E., 140t
Case, A., 268
Case, K., 498t, 502t
Catchment area
 definitions, 492–493
 differing nature of, 493
 example of, 492f
 exploiting discontinuities at, 510–511
 redrawing, 513
Catholic Church, 151–152
CBEEE. *See* Curriculum-based external exit exam
Cellini, S., 506t, 512
Cesarini, D., 218–219
Cheating, 270
Checchi, D., 129t, 143t, 361–363
Chernozhukov, V., 18
Chesher, A., 27
Cheshire, P., 498t, 501t
Chevalier, A., 227t, 231
Chiang, H., 406t
Child development, 203–204
Child labor, educational achievement and, 123
Child-rearing endowments, 221
 mother's education and, 222
Children of twins (COT), 222n9
Chin, H., 500t

Chiodo, A., 499t
Choice, 6, 48
 education quality and, 77–82
 school quality/housing value and, 512
Christensen, K., 225t, 229
Church going, 268
Ciccone, A., 176t
Civic education, 98n8, 191
Clapp, J., 505t, 506t
Clark, D., 140t, 499t
Clark, M.A., 442t
Class size, 5, 48, 250n4
 academic preparation and, 56
 allocation of, 133
 application of regression discontinuity, 65
 attenuation bias, 60
 benefits of reduced, 56
 bias in conventional estimates of, 134
 disruption level and, 55, 56
 educational achievement and, 133
 empirical analyses of, 57–66, 58t
 end-of-year achievement and, 62
 enrollment cut off dates and, 133
 estimating effects of, 55
 Iceland, 137
 improvement in quality of instruction time due to smaller, 57
 initial achievement and, 57
 learning and, relationship between, 55
 licensure and, 66n56
 maximum, 136
 model, 55–57
 natural fluctuations in, 133
 peer effects and, 263
 probability of finding correctly signed, 131
 quasi-experimental strategies and, 133
 rules, 136
 rules, exploiting, 136–137
 Singapore and, 134, 135f
 students in grade of school and average, 136
 teacher education and, 137
 teacher experience and, 66n56
 teacher quality and, 137, 159
 tracking and, 343n2
 wages and, 59–60
 within-school variation in, 134
Classroom disruption
 class size and, 55, 56

domestic violence and, 267
peer effects and, 267
Clotfelter, C.T., 328t, 415
Coleman, James, 202, 250
Coleman report, 202, 250
Collective bargaining
  teachers, 283, 297, 305–309
  wage compression and, 531
College, 7
  analyzing differences between, 95n5
  bounds to return to, 43t
  completion probability, 16
  decision rule, 11
  distance to, 231
  earnings function for, 9
  expected utility from, 10
  flow utility for, 9
  peer effects in, 252
  utility shock, 10
  value of attending, 10
  wage returns to, 13
Collins, S.M., 175t
Commitment, 191
Communications ability, 161n40
Comparative advantage, 11
  education level and, 15, 32
Competition, 5, 139
  education quality and, 77–82
  among schools and housing prices, 488
Computer-based instruction, 285n11
Congestion effects, 39
Conley, D., 207t
Consumer protection, licensure and, 318
Cook, T.D., 402, 403t
Cooley, J., 265–266
Coradi Vellacott, M., 120t
Corten, R., 140t
COT. *See* Children of twins
Coulombe, S., 175t
Cramming, 444n21
Credit constraints
  educational underinvestment and, 214
  long-term, 234
  quality v. quantity and, 234
  reasons for, 215
  short-term, 234
Criminal behavior
  dropouts and, 446

peer effects and, 253, 268
Crocker, T., 497t
Cromwell, B., 501t, 504t, 509, 513
Crone, T., 500t
Cronin, J., 403t
Cross-country comparisons
  advantages of, 93–94
  causation and, 182–184
  concerns with, 94–95
  economic motivation for, 96–98
  on educational achievement, 124–125t
  on equity of educational achievement and institutions, 143–144t
  on institutions and level of educational achievement, 141–142t
  scope of, 95–96
  on student background, 124–125t
Cullen, J.B., 72, 78t
Cunha, F., 51, 54
Curriculum-based external exit exam (CBEEE), 139
Currie, J., 234

D

Davidoff, I., 503t
Dearden, L., 46n31, 58t, 59, 72, 226t, 230
DeCicca, P., 473
Decker, P.T., 328t, 330
Dee, T., 403t, 504t
Demand functions
  identification of second stage, 489
  inverse, 488
  two-stage approach to, 488
Denny, K., 162t
Derrick, F., 502t
Des Rosiers, F., 507t
DeSimone, J.S., 270
Devereux, P.J., 227t, 231
Devroye, D., 170t
Dhuey, E., 120t, 123, 123n22
Diaz, R., 415
Dietrich, H., 548–549
Dills, A., 491, 499t
Distance learning, 285n11
Divorce
  birth order effects and, 235
  dropouts and, 446
Djebbari, H., 257–258

Dolton, P., 125t, 129t
Domestic violence
    classroom disruption and, 267
    test scores and, 267
Downes, T., 491
Dronkers, J., 140t
Dropouts, 22
    age and, 473
    consequences of, 426
    criminal behavior and, 446
    divorce and, 446
    economic gaps relative to, 435f
    economic gaps relative to, ability-adjusted, 438f
    GED inducing, 473–475
    with low initial endowments, 444–446
    negative social traits and, 446
    noncognitive skills and, 452f
    peer effects and, 268
    probability of, 459f
    reasons for, 431
    social outcome probabilities of, 448f, 449f
Dropouts, rate of
    GED and calculating, 428f
    increasing with credit increases, 473
Drug use, 253, 268, 270
Duflo, E., 266, 372–374
Duncan, G., 254, 270
Dupas, P., 266, 372–374
Dustmann, Christian, 44, 528–529, 531, 541
Dynamic multisector model of education choice, 32–34

E

Early learning, 233–234
Earnings
    beyond working life, 12
    after completing education, 16
    education level and, 34
    experience and growth in, 9
    family background and, 156
    function, 9
    for individual over time, 16
    skills translating into, 160
    test scores and, 168f, 168n52
Eccles, J., 270
ECIEL. *See* Programa de Estudios Conjuntos para la Integración Económica Latinoamericana
Eckstein, Z., 44

Economic growth
    cognitive skills and, 171–190, 175–177t, 179f
    human capital and, 97
    intelligence quotient and, 189t
    school attainment and, 180f
    trends in test scores and trends in, 184, 185f
Edding Commission, 541
Education. *See also* Parental education
    earnings after completing, 16
    future optimal decision to continue, 11–12
    month of birth and differences in, 22
    net payoff to, 33
    prelabor market investments in, 20
    selection mechanism into different, 11
    shocks to, 15
    total outcomes of, 97
Education, return to, 2–3
    bounds and, 34–37
    bounds and, worst-case, 41
    discrete choice model, 14
    education policy and, 46–48
    estimation of, 14–19, 82
    estimation of, simulation, 17–19
    family background and, 167f
    GED and, 454f
    GED obscuring, 477–478
    heterogeneous, 9, 25–30
    ignoring nonworkers and underestimating, 41
    labor force participation and, 40–46
    Mincer wage equations and, 19–31
    participation bias, 40–41
    reforms and, 22
    wage equations and, 6–40
Education, wage return to, 19–31
    distribution of, 25–26
    dynamic discrete education choice model, 32–34
    learning abilities and, 25
    nonparametric models of, 23–24
Education choice
    binary, 38–40
    informal assumptions, 31
    modeling, 8–13
    as once-and-for-all, 33
    reduced form model for, 26, 31
    sequential nature of, 32
    structural model of, 29, 31
    true model generating, 26
    wages and, 30–31

wages and, cross equation restrictions between, 14
Education cost, 11, 131n27, 231
 changes to, 461–467
 function, 30
 GED and, 461–467
 opportunity, 6
 random shocks to, 9
Education costs
 discrete, 24
 money, 21
 time, 21
Education for All, 187
Education level, 6, 7. *See also* School attainment
 age and, 9
 comparative advantage and, 15, 32
 earnings function for, 9
 expected utility from, 10
 to maximize wages minus costs, 30
 mean earnings for age and, 34
 optimal choice of, 30
 retirement age and, 10
 uncertainty and, 32
 wage equations for, 7–8
Education Maintenance allowance, 46n31
Education policy, 236–241
 general equilibrium effects and, 48
 intergenerational transmission and, 236
 returns to education and, 46–48
Education production functions, 393, 491
 concerns, 111
 example of international, 114–115t
 family background and, 114t
 identification of, 111
 inputs in, 111
 international evidence on, 111–116
 student characteristics, 114t
Education quality, 48. *See also* School quality
 accountability and, 77–82
 choice and, 77–82
 competition and, 77–82
 reforms changing, 22
Educational achievement. *See also* Accountability
 accountability and, 145–146
 autonomy and, 146–148
 books-in-home and, 117
 child labor and, 123
 class size and, 133

cross-country studies on, 124–125t
cross-country studies on institutions and equity of, 143–144t
cultural bias and, 145
dispersion of, 155
earnings and, 160
evidence across countries, 126–132
evidence within different countries, 132–138
expenditure per student and, 127f
family background and, 119, 123, 155, 204–211
institutions and, 138–158
institutions and, cross-country studies on level of, 141–142t
institutions and, within country studies on, 140t
licensure and, 317, 335
No Child Left Behind and, 402, 403t
preprimary education and, 157–158
pressure for, 215
private schools and, 148–153
school attainment and, separating, 165n48
school inputs and, within country studies on, 128–129t
school inputs of, 126–138
school resources and, 132
school structure and, 183n70
signaling, 139
in Singapore, 134, 135f
spillovers, 146n35
student background and, 119, 123
teacher compensation and, 289–290
teacher quality and, 316
tracking and, 153–157
within-country studies on student background and, 120–122t
Educational achievement, international
 challenges to estimation of, 112
 cultural values and, 112
 determinants of, 111–160
 economic consequences of, 160–190
 family background and, 115, 116–126
 student background and, 116–126
Educational productive functions, 91
 at country level, 113
 at individual level, 113
 institutions and, 115t
 microeconomic estimations of, 134
 school inputs and, 114–115t
 at school level, 113

Efficient contracts, 285
Ehrenberg, R., 285n9
Eisenberg, D., 268
Elder, Todd, 60
Emmerson, C., 46n31
Employment protection laws, 166
Endowments, 213, 221. *See also* Child-rearing endowments
    dropouts with low initial, 444–446
English Language Learners, 394
Entorf, H., 121t
Entrepreneurial intentions, 191
Environment
    intergenerational transmission and prenatal, 233
    Intergenerational transmission and socio-economic, 233
    IQ and, 188n74
Evans, W.N., 268
Evertson, C.M., 326
Expenditure per student, 130, 131, 283
    change in, 130f
    comparisons, 130–131
    educational achievement and, 127f
    exchange rate and, 131
    increase in, 130
    mathematics and, 126
    in preprimary education, 157–158
    test scores and, 130–131
Exploitation
    accepting, 546–547
    defining, 546
    deterrence, 547
    production-oriented apprenticeship training as, 537, 546–548

F

Fack, G., 504t, 515
Factor price equalizations, 47n33
Fairlie, R.W., 370
Falch, T., 142t
Family
    location, 50
    size, 234–236
Family background, 216–220
    cognitive skills and, 164
    cultural, 213
    earnings and, 156
    educational achievement and, 116–126, 119, 123, 155, 204–211
    effects in different countries, 118f
    international education production function and, 114t
    measurements, 116
    return to education and, 167f
    test scores and, 155, 205
    tracking and, 366, 367, 370
Father's education, 229
    adoptive, 230
Federal Vocational Training Institute (BIBB), 563
Feng, L., 414–415
Ferrall, C., 170t
Ferreira, Fernando, 74t, 75–76, 506t, 508t, 512, 514
Ferri, J., 58t, 59, 72
Fertig, M., 124t
Figlio, D.N., 267, 355, 388, 399, 406t, 410, 414–415, 505t, 512
Filippin, A., 129t
FIMS. *See* First International Mathematics Study
Finan, F., 268
Finland, 360–361
Firing costs, 530–531
FIRS. *See* First International Reading Study
First International Mathematics Study (FIMS), 97, 100t
First International Reading Study (FIRS), 100t
First International Science Study (FISS), 100t, 178
Fischer, J.A.V., 142t
FISS. *See* First International Science Study
Fiva, J., 503t
Florens, J.P., 28–30, 30–31
Florida, 414–415
Flynn, James, 188n74
Flynn effect, 188n74
Foong, K., 500t
Foreign languages, 98n8, 191, 233
Fortin, B., 257–258
Foshay, Arthur W., 90
Frayne, C., 46n31
Fredericksen, N., 408t
Freeman, R.B., 170t
Fryer, R.G., 144t
Fuchs, T., 125t, 141t
Fullerton, D., 496t
Functionalist determinism, 555

G

Gaes, G.G., 466–467
Galindo-Rueda, F., 359–360, 368
Gamoran, A., 352
Gang membership, 268
Gauss Newton iterative process, 14, 18
Gaviria, A., 268
GED. *See* General Educational Development
Geel, R., 532n19
Gender. *See also* Women
   equal culture, 158
   GED and, 439–440, 441t
   peer groups and, 257, 260
General Educational Development (GED)
   acceptance of, 431–432
   adverse consequences of, 471–478
   age and, 464, 467–470, 469f, 473f
   age exceptions to, 468f
   availability of, 431
   average labor market outcomes and, 432–436
   calculating dropout rate and, 428f
   certification effects, 432–458
   changes in, 458–471
   cognitive skills and, 436–438, 446, 450–452, 453f
   costs of, 464
   current version of, 429
   decomposing growth in credentials of, 471
   direct benefit of, 432–452
   education cost and, 461–467
   expected benefit of, 455–456
   functions of, 426–432
   gender and, 439–440, 441t
   government education and, 458–461
   growth in, 425, 425f, 458–471
   heterogeneous labor market returns to, 439
   immigration and, 440, 442, 442t
   inducing dropouts, 473–475
   inflating graduation statistics, 475–477
   institutional background of, 426–432
   introduction to, 424–426, 429
   key changes to, 430
   key dates and number of participants, 472f
   means of benefit, 431
   minimum age and, 467f
   mixed signals of, 446
   native v. foreign born and, 440, 442
   noncognitive skills and, 446, 450–452, 452f, 453f
   Option Programs, 470, 474
   option value of, 455–456, 458, 460
   parental consent for, 473
   passing, 430, 464, 464f
   preparation, 431
   prison education and, 465–467
   problems with, 426
   reasons for, 452–453
   retaking, 445f
   return to, 446
   return to, overstating, 478
   return to education, obscuring, 477–478
   return to education and, 454f
   route to, 461f
   sample questions, 429f
   school attainment and, 452–453, 457t
   as second chance program, 458–461
   signaling and, 442–444
   simulated response to elimination of, 475t
   by study type, 462f
   terminal, 435
   timeline, 430t
   training programs and, 458–461
   treatment classifications, 443t
   value increasing, 439
   wage benefit and, 456
   wage gaps and, 479–480t
   wage growth with experience and, 439
   women and, 440
General equilibrium effect, 39, 47
   education policies and, 48
   feedback effects from, 48
   heterogeneous agents and, 47
Genetics, IQ and, 188n74
Germany, net cost of training in Switzerland v., 543–546, 543t, 544t, 546t
Gerner, H.D., 548–549
Gersbach, H., 533–534
Gibbons, S., 74t, 76–77, 266, 491–492, 507t, 514
Glauber, R., 207t
Glazerman, S., 328t
Gmelin, J., 128t
Goals 200: Educate America Act, 385
Goerlitz, K., 534
Goldberger, A.S., 225t, 229
Golden parachutes, 531

Goldhaber, D.D., 328t, 329t
Gordon, N., 140t
Gosling, A., 37, 42–44
Graham, B.S., 258–259
Gravel, N., 501t
Grenet, J., 504t, 515
Grether, D., 496t
Grossman, P., 328t
Grubb, W.N., 456n31
Guiso, L., 143t
Gundlach, E., 128t, 175t
Gunnarsson, V., 125t
Guryan, J., 334

H

Hægeland, T., 225t, 227t, 229
Hagwon schools, 298
Hahn, J., 64–65, 66
Hannaway, J., 329t
Hanushek, E.A., 58t, 61–64, 68t, 71–72, 78t, 80–82, 110n13, 124t, 128t, 143t, 162t, 173–174, 174n61, 175t, 176t, 177t, 178, 262t, 264, 267, 333–334, 364–366, 367, 368, 409t, 410–411
Harmon, C., 21, 162t
Harris, J.R., 250n3
Hart, R.A., 549
Hashimoto, M., 526
Haurin, D., 491, 498t, 500t
Hawley, W.D., 326
Hayes, K., 498t
Head Start, 234, 236–237
Health
  cognitive skills and, 181n66
  maternity leave and, 237
Heckman, J.J., 26, 28, 29, 30–31, 32–33, 34, 39, 48, 51, 54, 233–234, 441t, 442t, 447t, 450, 451–452, 456, 457t, 458, 474, 477, 478
Heckman selectivity corrections, 355
Hedonic price functions, 489
Heijke, H., 120t, 129t
Hernandez-Murillo, R., 499t
Herrin, W., 499t
Hess, F., 400
Heyneman, S.P., 128t
Hierarchical lineal modeling (HLM), 57
High school, 7
  benefits from, 15
  completion probability, 15
  decision rule, 11
  earnings function for, 9
  expected utility from, 10
  flow utility for, 9
  status completion rate, 475
  trends in graduation, 476f
  utility shock, 9–10
  value of attending, 10
High School and Beyond Survey, 333–334
HISD. See Houston Independent School District
Hite, D., 501t
HLM. See Hierarchical lineal modeling
Hoekstra, M.L., 267
Hoffer, T.B., 352, 355
Holmlund, H., 225t, 227t, 228t, 229
Hong, H., 18
Housing
  accountability and, 389
  choice, 4, 49–50
  demand, 487
  relocation of, 49
Housing location
  equilibrium, 49
  matched to school locations, 492
Housing values, 490
  bond passage on, 512
  expenditure changes and, 512
  finance changes and, 512
  matching to schools, 492–493
  test scores and, 491
Housing values, school quality and, 5, 48, 73–77, 486–489
  alternative approaches to, 514–515
  choice and, 512
  combined methods, 507–508t, 514–515
  competition and, 488
  data issues, 489–493
  differences methods, 504–507t, 511–513
  differences-in-differences methods, 504–507t, 511–513
  discontinuity methods using administrative boundaries, 503–504t, 509–511
  eliminating "nuisance" spatial variation, 495
  empirical methodologies, 493–515
  evidence of, 493–515
  instrumental variables approach, 502t, 509
  kitchen sink regressions, 495

local amenities and, 493–494
nonparametric modeling of unobservable factors, 495, 501–502t, 509
parametric modeling of unobservable factors, 495, 501–502t, 509
private schools and, 515
quasi-experimental methods, 504–507t, 511–513
regression based estimates, 494–495, 496–501t
repeat sales and, 504–507t, 511–513
research summary, 496–508t
sorting and, 493–494
theoretical background, 487–489
trends, 511
two-stage structural approach to, 514
Houston Independent School District (HISD), 327, 330
Hoxby, C.M., 251, 253, 254–255, 257, 260, 261t, 262t, 265, 272, 283, 307
Human capital
acquiring, 2
assumptions, 97
cognitive skills and, 92, 96, 164
cost of, 525
defining, 525
economic growth and, 97
empirical observations on specificity of, 539–541
endogenous accumulation of, 44
future shocks to, 7
international differences in, 178
investments in, 525
lags in, 8
measuring, 97, 164
parental, 213, 214
physical capital v., 525
pricing of, 6–8
production function, 20
production function for child's, 213–214
school enrollment ratios as proxy for, 171
substituting levels of, 8
in terms of school attainment, 92
types of, 6–8, 7
Human capital theory, 525–527
extensions to, 527–535
failure of, 527
Human resource policy, 309
Humphries, J.E., 474
Hurricane Katrina evacuees, 264

I

IAEP-I. *See* International Assessment of Educational Progress I
IAEP-II. *See* International Assessment of Educational Progress II
IALS. *See* International Adult Literacy Survey
Iceland, 137
Ichimura, H., 37, 42–44
IEA. *See* International Association for the Evaluation of Educational Achievement
Illposed inverse problem, 25
Imbens, G., 27–28, 29, 38
Imberman, S., 264
Immigration, 117
employment rate and, 166
GED and, 440, 442, 442t
tracking and, 370
wages and, 188
Incarceration, 464–467
GED and, 465–467
growth by race, 465f
India, 187
Indirect inference approach, 14
Infant mortality
cognitive skills and, 181n66
maternity leave and, 238
Information technology, 98n8, 191
Institutional complementarity, 554
"Institutionalism, new efficiency-oriented," 555
Institutions
apprenticeship training and, 553–569, 556–557t
cognitive skills and, 183n69
educational achievement and, 138–158
educational achievement and, within country studies on, 140t
equity of educational achievement and, cross-country studies on, 143–144t
level of educational achievement and, cross-country studies on, 141–142t
meaning of, 555
variability of, 554
Instruction time, measures of, 131
Instructional material, shortage of, 131
Intelligence quotient (IQ)
birth order and, 235
critical period for improving, 233
differences among nations, 187
environment and, 188n74

Intelligence quotient (IQ) (*cont.*)
   fixed-factor view, 187
   genetics and, 188n74
   labor force quality and, 188
   macroeconomic growth and, 189t
   models, 187–190
Intergenerational transmission, 116, 202n1.
      See also Parental education
   adoption and, 222
   birth-order effects and, 234–236
   causal effect of, 220–233
   child quantity v. quality and, 234
   cultural, 215
   early learning and, 233–234
   education policy and, 236
   equation, 216
   estimates of, 210t
   family size and, 234–236
   generic reduced form model of, 221
   main mechanisms for, 211, 213
   money input, 232–236
   prenatal environment and, 233
   public policies and, 215
   in school attainment, 209
   socio-economic environment and, 233
   theory of, 211–216
   time input, 232–236
   tracking and, 360–361
International Adult Literacy Survey (IALS), 102, 103t, 105, 158, 161, 166f, 181
International Assessment of Educational Progress I (IAEP-I), 102, 103t
International Assessment of Educational Progress II (IAEP-II), 102, 103t
International Association for the Evaluation of Educational Achievement (IEA), 98, 100–101t
   expansion of, 99
International educational achievement. *See* Educational achievement, international
International tests, 98–111, 100–101t, 103–104t
   Africa and, 102
   beginning of, 98
   criticism of, 105, 110
   cultural bias in, 110
   expanding through regional tests from developing countries, 184–186
   focusing on reading, 178n63
   Latin America and, 102
   in nontraditional subjects, 191
   participation in, 102f, 191–192
   participation overview of, 98–105
   performance by country on, 106–109t
   robustness checking, 113
   sample selection, 105, 110
   sampling quality, 110
   scaling of, 172
   school background questionnaires, 146
   timing of, 182
   validity of, 105, 110–111
Inverse Mills terms, 355
Iowa Test of Basic Skills, 263
IQ. *See* Intelligence quotient
Isacsson, G., 207t

J

Jacob, B.A., 72, 78t, 403t, 405t, 408t
Jaeger, D.A., 442t
Jamison, D.T., 176t
Jamison, E.A., 176t
Jäntti, M., 218
Jencks, C., 203n2
Jenkins, S.P., 119, 121t
Jensen, V.M., 225t, 229
Jepsen, C., 66n56, 444
Job Corps, 458–459
Jones, G., 189t
Joplin plan, 352
Jud, G., 497t
Juku schools, 298, 345
Jürges, H., 124t

K

Kahn, L.M., 162t, 170t
Kain, J.F., 58t, 68t, 71–72, 262t, 264, 267, 494–495, 496t
Kakuma, R., 238
Kämpf, S., 189t
Kane, T.J., 68t, 69–71, 329t, 505t, 508t, 513, 514
Kaplan, 298n22
Katz, E., 528
Katz, L., 268
Keane, Michael P., 44
Kennan, J., 49–50
Kenny, L., 388
Kerr, S., 360–361

Kershaw, J.A., 292
Kessler, A.S., 532n18
Kimko, D.D., 124t, 174n61, 175t
Kingdon, G., 129t, 308
Kirkebøen, L., 225t, 227t, 229, 503t
Klein, S., 405t
Kling, J.R., 465
Knowledge acquisition, 4
  cumulative nature of, 50
Kooreman, P., 268
Kramarz, F., 263
Kramer, M.S., 238
Krantz-Kent, R., 286n12
Krauth, B., 268
Kremer, M., 266, 269, 270, 372–374
Krueger, A.B., 22, 58t, 61, 66
Kugler, A., 264
Kumon, 298n22

L

Labor force participation. *See* Participation
Labor force quality, 174
  IQ and, 188
Labor supply, licensure restricting, 319–321, 331–334
Laboratorio Latinoamericano de Evaluación de la Calidad de la Educación (LLECE), 185–186
Ladd, H.F., 328t, 405t, 415
LaFontaine, P.A., 441t, 442t, 477, 478
Lagan, A., 507t
Land values, 490
Lang, K., 261t, 263
Lankford, H., 328t
LATE. *See* Local average treatment effect
Latin America
  cognitive skills and, 185–186
  international tests and, 102
  school attainment in, 185
Lavy, V., 58t, 64–65, 261t, 263, 266
Laws
  changes in compulsory schooling, 231
  defining apprenticeship training, 558
  school resources and, 50
Lazear, E., 56, 532
Learning
  class size and, relationship between, 55
  dynamics, 50–55
  wage returns to education and, 25

Lee, D.W., 48, 124t, 175t
Lee, T.H., 175t
Leech, D., 503t
Lefgren, L., 262t, 266
Legislation changes, 21
Leigh, A., 283, 283n4, 503t
Leisure, 45
Lemons problem, 529
Leuven, E., 123n22, 162t
Levitt, S.D., 72, 78t, 144t
Levy, D., 270
Licensure
  alternatives to, 316, 324
  background, 316–317
  class size and, 66n56
  consumer protection and, 318
  costs of, 321
  costs of, reducing, 333
  criticisms of, 316
  definitions of, 327
  educational achievement and, 317, 335
  educational achievement and, studies linking, 328–329t
  educational major and, 322t
  empirical evidence on impact of, 325–335
  examination prior to entering teacher education program and, 322t
  examination prior to receipt of, 322–323t
  hiring decisions and, 334–335
  hiring decisions and, changes in, 336
  major hurdles associated with, 333
  policy effectiveness, 326n13
  pressure for, 326n13
  restricting labor supply, 319–321, 331–334
  student backgrounds and, 327
  supporters of, 317
  Teach for America and, comparison between, 330
  teacher quality and, 317, 319f, 320f, 326–331
  theoretical arguments for/against, 318–321
  undergraduate studies and, 322t
  in U.S./abroad, 321–325
  variations requirements for in, 322–323t
  work force and, 331–334
Licensure requirements, 331–334
  establishment of, 318
  state, 321
Lillard, D.R., 473

Limit set, 33, 34, 36
Lindahl, L., 212t
Lindahl, M., 123n22, 219, 225t, 226t, 227t, 228t, 229, 230
Lindley, R.M., 524n4, 536
Literacy, 158
　document, 161
　prose, 161, 161n42, 168
　quantitative, 161
LLECE. *See* Laboratorio Latinoamericano de Evaluación de la Calidad de la Educación
LLR. *See* Local linear nonparametric regression
Local average treatment effect (LATE), 38–39, 64
　interpreting, 39
Local linear nonparametric regression (LLR), 65
Lochner, L., 48
Loeb, S., 328t, 407, 408t
Lovenheim, M., 307
Loxley, W., 128t
Lucas, M., 505t, 512
Luedemann, E., 142t, 144t
Lülfesmann, C., 532n18
Luo, X., 176t
Luque, J.A., 128t

M

Machin, S., 74t, 76–77, 226t, 230, 263, 491–492, 507t, 513, 514
Magnac, T., 32
Maimonides Law, 64–65
Malamud, O., 241, 552–553
Malmstrom, F.V., 270
Manning, A., 360, 368
Manski, C., 41, 43, 256
Marascuilo, L.A., 375
Marcenaro-Gutierrez, O.D., 125t
Mare, R.D., 352
Markman, J.M., 262t, 264
Markov Chain Monte Carlo methods, 18–19
Marmaros, D., 271
Marshall, Alfred, 92n1
Marshall, J.H., 124t
Matching frictions, 530–531
Maternity leave, 237–239
　birthweight and, 238
　health and, 237
　infant mortality and, 238
　long-term outcomes of, 238
　mandatory job-protected, 237
　short-term outcomes of, 237
Mathematics
　achievement in Singapore, 134, 135f
　expenditure per student and, 126
Matzkin, R., 27
Maurin, E., 228t, 231
Mayer, C., 498t, 502t
Mayer, D.P., 328t
Mazumder, B., 207t
McEwan, P.J., 124t
McIntosh, D.K., 374
McKean, R.N., 292
McMillan, Robert, 74t, 75–76, 508t, 514
McNally, S., 228t, 231
McSweeny, M., 375
Meghir, C., 21–22, 28, 30–31, 37, 42–44, 46, 46n31, 58t, 59, 72, 228t, 231, 357–359
Merit pay. *See* Teacher performance pay
Merrilees, W.J., 548, 549
Method of moments approach, simulated, 14, 18
Meyer, J., 176t
Michaelowa, K., 128t
Michelangeli, A., 501t
Mickelson, R.A., 405t
Micklewright, J., 119, 121t
Mieszkowski, P., 496t
Miguel, E., 269
Mihaly, K., 268
Military Academy, 270
Miller, P., 206t
Mincer, J., 160n39
Mincer earnings model, 160, 163
Mincer wage equations, 3
　basic, 19–20
　return to education and, 19–31
　theoretical foundations of, 19
　underlying choice model of, 19
Minimum wage, 168, 171n54. *See also* Salaire minimum interprofessionalle de croissance
　apprenticeships and, 526
Minoiu,. N., 121t
Mohrenweiser, J., 545n39
Monotone instrumental variables, 43
Monte, F., 143t
Moral hazard, 531
Morale, 191
Mother's education, 229

adoptive, 230
child-rearing endowments and, 222
natural experiments and, 223
Moving to Opportunity (MTO), 269
MTO. *See* Moving to Opportunity
Mühlemann, S., 535n24, 549
Müller, B., 549
Murdoch, J., 504t
Murname, R.J., 441t, 446, 447t, 456, 457t

N

NAEP. *See* National Assessment of Educational Progress
NALS. *See* National Adult Literacy Survey
Nanda, A., 506t
NASDTEC. *See* National Association of Directors of Teacher Education and Certification
A Nation at Risk, 290
National Adult Literacy Survey (NALS), 436
National Assessment of Educational Progress (NAEP), 102, 173, 397–398
National Association of Directors of Teacher Education and Certification (NASDTEC), 321
National Board for Professional Teaching Standards Certification Program, 69
National Center for Education Statistics (NCES), 289, 475
National Center on Teacher Quality, 306n32
National Commission on Excellence in Education, 290
National Education Association (NEA), 292, 305
membership of, 305n31
National Education Longitudinal Study (NELS), 268
National Educational Longitudinal Survey, 333
National Labor Relations Act (NLRA), 305
National Longitudinal Study of Youth 1979 (NLSY79), 432, 432n9, 448f
National Longitudinal Study of Youth 1997 (NLSY97), 432, 432n10, 433t, 434t, 449f
Nature v. nurture, 123, 214, 216–220, 242
criticism of, 217n5
Navarro, S., 32, 34
NCES. *See* National Center for Education Statistics
NCLB. *See* No Child Left Behind
NEA. *See* National Education Association
Neal, D., 78t, 79, 402, 403t

Nechyba, T.S., 262t, 264–265
Neighbor demographics, 75–76, 205, 210
sibling correlations and, 212t
Neighborhood effect, school quality and, 493–494, 509
NELS. *See* National Education Longitudinal Study
Nested fixed point (NFP), 14
possible infeasibility of, 14–15
Newey, W., 23–24, 27–28, 29
NFP. *See* Nested fixed point
Nilsen, O.A., 549
NLRA. *See* National Labor Relations Act
NLSY79. *See* National Longitudinal Study of Youth 1979
NLSY97. *See* National Longitudinal Study of Youth 1997
No Child Left Behind (NCLB), 66–67, 216, 326n13, 385, 394, 395, 400. *See also* Accountability
educational achievement and, 402, 403t
isolating, 402
reauthorization of, 391–392
Nonworkers
accounting for, 41–44
endogeneity and, 44–46
missing wages for, 40
proportion of, 40
underestimating returns to education and, 41
worst-case bounds and, 42
North Carolina, 415

O

Oakes, J., 356
Oates, W.E., 268, 496t
Obama, Barack, 384
OECD. *See* Organisation for Economic Co-operation and Development
Oosterbeek, H., 123n22, 162t, 552
Ophem, H., 162t
Opportunity, equality of, 202
enhancing, 240
measures of, 116
normative approach to, 203n2
private schools and, 152n37
reforms enhancing, 203
student background and, 116
tracking and, 155
tracking and, early, 156

Orazem, P.F., 125t
Oreopoulos, P., 227t, 231
Organisation for Economic Co-operation and Development (OECD), 98, 100–101t, 324
  expansion of, 99
Ouazad, A., 263
Overlapping generations model, 47, 213–214
Owyang, M., 499t

P

Pace, R.R., 333–334, 355
Page, M.E., 227t, 231
Pallas, A.M., 57, 58t, 59
Palme, M., 21–22, 357–359
Papaioannou, E., 176t
Parental education, 209. *See also* Father's education; Intergenerational transmission; Mother's education
  adoption and, 230
  causal effect of, 220–233, 225–228t
  comparison across methods of, 232–233
  misrepresentation of, 223
Parental work
  long-term outcomes of, 238
  short-term outcomes of, 237
Parents
  biological, 219
  consent for GED, 473
  human capital, 213
  power couple, 229
  skills, 213, 215
  twins as, 222–223
Parents, adoptive, 219
  education of, 230
Parey, M., 228t, 231
Participation (labor market). *See also* Nonworkers
  returns to education and, 40–46
PASEC. *See* Programme d'Analyse des Systèmes Educatifs des Pays de la CONFENEM
Paserman, D., 266
Patience, 215
Peer effects, 39
  Air Force Academy and, 270, 271
  alcohol drinking, 268, 270
  aspirations and, 266
  attitudes and, 270
  bad apple model of, 255, 255t
  binge drinking, 252, 254
  boutique model of, 255t, 256, 265
  cheating, 270
  church going, 268
  class size and, 263
  classroom disruption and, 267
  in college, 252
  common approaches to identifying, 257
  contextual, 256
  correlated, 256
  criminal behavior, 253, 268
  defining, 250
  dropping out and, 268
  drug use, 253, 268, 270
  empirical results on, 260–267
  endogenous, 256
  exogenous, 256
  focus model of, 255t
  gang membership, 268
  Hurricane Katrina evacuees and, 264
  identification of, 256–260
  identification using excess variance, 258–260
  invidious comparison model of, 255t, 256
  limited to externalities, 250
  Military Academy and, 270
  models of, 253–256
  movers and, 263
  nonlinear, 265–266
  nonlinear, testing for, 254
  nontest outcomes of, 268–269
  older peers and, 268
  overview, 250–253
  "percent female" and, 260, 263, 272
  in post-secondary education, 269–271
  in primary/secondary education, 260–267, 272
  rainbow model of, 255t, 256
  reflection problem, 256
  roommates and, 269
  sexual activity, 270
  shining light model of, 255t, 256
  single crossing model of, 255t
  size of, 250, 272
  smoking, 268
  social multiplier, 259–260
  teen pregnancy and, 253, 268
  test scores and, 251, 261–262t, 264
Peer effects, linear-in-means model of, 251–252, 255t, 265, 272
  expanding, 254

problems with, 253
social welfare point of view on, 253
test scores and, 261–262t
Peer group
 career selection and, 271
 gender mix in, 257, 260
 policies to generate random variation in, 257
 racial mix in, 260, 266–267
 shocks to, 257
 tracking changing, 343, 344
Pekkarinen, T., 360–361
Pell grants, 463–464
Pepper, J., 43
Perry Preschool program, 236–237
Personnel costs, 131
Peterson, P.E., 121t, 400
PIAAC. See Programme for the International Assessment of Adult Competencies
PIRLS. See Program in International Reading Literacy Study
PISA. See Programme for International Student Assessment
Pischke, J.S., 122t, 126, 262t, 360, 368, 528, 530–531, 538n29, 540
Plug, E., 219, 225t, 226t, 227t, 228t, 229, 230
Podgursky, M., 308
Pong, S., 57, 58t, 59
Pop-Eleches, C., 241, 552–553
Portney, P., 497t
Postbirth factors. See Nature v. nurture
Poverty, 131n27
Powell, J., 23–24, 28
Prebirth factors. See Nature v. nurture
Prenatal environment, 233
Preprimary education, 139
 advantage of, 157
 educational achievement and, 157–158
 expenditure per student for, 157
 structural quality of, 157
Preschool reforms, 237–239
Primer Estudio Internacional Comparativo (LLECE), 103t
Princeton Review, 298n22
Principal quality, 251
Prison education, 464–467
 GED and, 465–467
Prisoners' dilemma, 560
Private schools, 94, 139
 decision to attend, 77–79
 defining, 148
 education achievement and, 148–153
 equality of opportunity and, 152n37
 external inspection of, 149
 funding dimensions of, 150
 international education achievement and, 112
 operation of, 150
 performance comparisons, 149
 school quality/housing prices and, 515
 teacher compensation in public school v., 288–289
 teacher wage-setting units in, 297, 297f
Productivity collapse, 131
Program in International Reading Literacy Study (PIRLS), 91, 100t, 101t, 154f
Programa de Estudios Conjuntos para la Integración Económica Latinoamericana (ECIEL), 103t
Programme d'Analyse des Systèmes Educatifs des Pays de la CONFENEM (PASEC), 103t
Programme for International Student Assessment (PISA), 91, 100t, 101t, 105, 145, 154f, 173n60
 design of, 98
 news coverage of, 91
 participation in, 191–192
Programme for the International Assessment of Adult Competencies (PIAAC), 102n11, 161n43
PROGRESA conditional cash program, 46
Psychostimulants, 399

Q

Quantile structural function, 28
Quigley, J., 494–495, 496t

R

Raaum, O., 206t, 212t, 225t, 227t, 229
"Race to the Top," 302, 384
Ram, R., 189t
Ramirez, F., 176t
Raphael, S., 268
Rasmussen, A.R., 535n24, 549
Raymond, M.E., 78t, 80–82, 409t, 410–411
RD. See Regression discontinuity
Reading. See also Literacy
 international tests focusing on, 178n63

Reagan, Ronald, 290
Reback, R., 333, 506t, 512
Recidivism, 466–467
Redmond, S., 162t
Reed, H., 226t, 230
Rees, D.I., 268, 349–350, 353
Reforms, 21–22, 236–241
   accountability and, 413
   education quality and, 22
   enhancing equality of opportunity, 203
   general equilibrium effects and, 23
   preschool, 237–239
   returns to education and, 22
   tracking and, 357–363
   tracking and comprehensive, 239–241
Regression discontinuity (RD), 64–65
   approach to school quality, 510
   class size application of, 65
Regularization, 25
Religious affiliation, 78–79, 289
Retirement
   cost side of teacher, 299–300
   education level and age of, 10
   employer contribution to, 299–300f
   incentives in teacher pension plans, 298n24
Richards, C., 405t
Riegg, S., 508t, 514
Ries, J., 505t, 513
Riphahn, R.T., 368–369
Risk
   aversion, 9, 215
   preferences, 213
Rivkin, S.G., 58t, 61–64, 66n56, 68t, 71–72, 262t, 264, 267
Robert, P., 140t
Robin, Jean-Marc, 44
Robin, S., 140t
Rockoff, J.E., 67, 68t, 69, 329t, 406t
Rosen, H., 496t
Rosen, S., 487, 488
Rosenberg Self-Esteem Scale, 450, 450n25, 451
Rosenshine, B., 409t
Rosenzweig, M.R., 224, 225t, 229, 235
Ross, S., 505t, 506t
Rothstein, J., 67, 506t, 512
Rotter Locus of Control, 450, 450n25, 451
Rouse, C., 207t, 406t, 410
Roy model of decision making, 2–3

Rubenstein, Y., 444
Rudman, D., 175t
Rust type problem, 15
Ryan, C., 283n4

S

Sacerdote, B., 219, 226t, 230, 264, 269, 270–271
SACMEQ I. *See* Southern and Eastern Africa Consortium for Monitoring Educational Quality
SACMEQ II. *See* Southern and Eastern Africa Consortium for Monitoring Educational Quality II
Salaire minimum interprofessionalle de croissance (SMIC), 526n9
Salary schedules, 280, 290–296
   costs of, 296
   equalizing pay, 295–296
   example, 291t
   problems with, 293–296
   suppressing differentials by schools within districts, 295
   suppressing pay differentials by field, 293–295
   women's struggle for pay equity and, 292
Salvanes, K.G., 225t, 227t, 229, 231, 507t, 513
Samms, G., 505t, 513
Sánchez, M.A., 125t
Sander, William, 67, 68t, 69
Santiago, A., 46
Sapienza, P., 143t
SASS. *See* School and Staffing Survey
Sass, T.R., 264, 414–415
Schanzenbach, D., 402, 403t
Schettkat, R., 170t
Schlosser, A., 261t, 263, 266
Schmutzler, A., 533–534
Schneeweis, N., 144t
Schneider, H., 399
Schneider, K., 124t
Schneider, W.J., 189t
Schnepf, S.V., 119, 121t
Schofer, E., 176t
Schönberg, U., 528–529, 531, 541
School. *See also specific types*
   background questionnaires, 146
   distance from, 21
   efficiency, 393
   estimating input effects of, 48–82

mobility rates, 52
political/judicial processes determining finances of, 50
price deflators for, 130n25
relative maturity at entry to, 123n22
social segregation between, 119
structure and educational achievement, 183n70
utility maximizing choices of, 50
School and Staffing Survey (SASS), 289, 334, 414
School attainment. *See also* Education level
by certification type, 455f
cognitive skills and, 174n61, 178, 179f, 437f, 451t
comparison of key characteristics by, 433t, 434t
economic growth and, 180f
educational achievement and, separating, 165n48
GED and, 452–458, 457t
intergenerational correlations in, 209
in Latin America, 185
model, 217
noncognitive skills and, 450f, 451t
school enrollment and, 453–454
sibling correlations and, 205
skill differences and, 163
trends in, 428f
wage and, 426, 427f
School attendance zone boundaries.
See also Catchment area
housing comparisons across, 73
test scores and, 75
School enrollment
absolute age at starting, 123n22
cut off dates for, 123
cut off dates for, class size and, 133
lottery, 79–80
open, 79–80
ratios as proxies for human capital, 171
school attainment and, 453–454
School quality. *See also* Education quality
awareness of, 215
capitalization models, 73
cognitive skills and, 164
as constant, 163
growth measures, 391–393
measurement errors, 393
measuring, 490–492
neighborhood effects and, 493–494, 509
parental perceptions of, 486
price associated with improvement in, 487
regression discontinuity approach to, 510
school attainment and, 97
school resources and, 163
status measures, 391–393
willingness to pay for, 76
School quality, housing market and, 5, 48, 73–77, 486–489
alternative approaches to, 514–515
choice and, 512
combined methods, 507–508t, 514–515
competition and, 488
data issues, 489–493
differences methods, 504–507t, 511–513
differences-in-differences methods, 504–507t, 511–513
discontinuity methods using administrative boundaries, 503–504t, 509–511
eliminating "nuisance" spatial variation, 495
empirical methodologies, 493–515
evidence of, 493–515
instrumental variables approach, 502t, 509
kitchen sink regressions, 495
local amenities and, 493–494
nonparametric modeling of unobservable factors, 495, 501–502t, 509
parametric modeling of unobservable factors, 495, 501–502t, 509
private schools and, 515
quasi-experimental methods, 504–507t, 511–513
regression based estimates, 494–495, 496–501t
repeat sales and, 504–507t, 511–513
research summary, 496–508t
sorting and, 493–494
theoretical background, 487–489
trends, 511
two-stage structural approach to, 514
School resources
educational achievement and, 132
laws and, 50
school quality and, 163
tracking and, 349–350
Schuetz, Gabriela, 117, 120t, 142t–144t, 369, 370
Schwab, R.M., 268
Schwerdt, G., 138
Schweri, J., 549
Search costs, 530–531

Second International Mathematics Study (SIMS), 98n9, 100t
Second International Reading Study (SIRS), 100t
Second International Science Study (SISS), 100t
Sedgley, N., 502t
Segundo Estudio Regional Comparativo Explicativo (SERCE), 104t
SERCE. *See* Segundo Estudio Regional Comparativo Explicativo
17-year-old graduation ratio, 475
Sexual activity, 270
Sheepskin effects, 29
Sheppard, S., 498t, 501t
Sheu, T., 405t
Shkolnick, J.L., 266, 349, 353–356
Shocks
 accountability, 415
 college utility, 10
 education, 15
 to education cost, 9
 future human capital, 7
 high school utility, 9–10
 to peer groups, 257
 sequential revealment of, 10
 timing of, 10
Sibling correlations, 208, 210, 215, 217, 241
 comparisons of, 209t
 neighborhood correlations and, 212t
 school attainment and, 205, 206–207t
Siblings. *See also* Birth-order effects; Twins
 closely spaced, 208
 differential treatment of, 205
 interactions between, 208
 time resources differing across, 235
 types, 218
 widely spaced, 208
Sieben, I., 206t
Silva, O., 74t, 76–77, 266, 491–492
SIMS. *See* Second International Mathematics Study
Sims, D., 415–416
Singapore
 class size effects in, 134, 135f
 math achievement in, 134, 135f
SIRS. *See* Second International Reading Study
SISS. *See* Second International Science Study
Skills, 522. *See also* Cross-country comparisons
 basic, 187–190
 distribution of, 168

economic outcomes of labor-force, 160
elasticity of substitution between, 8
firm-specific, 525
firm-specific v. general, 532, 539–541
identically useful, 525
labor market effects by, 447t
manual, 531n16
parenting, 213, 215
preferences, 215
school attainment and differences in, 163
soft, 426
source of, 97
supply/demand for, 163
transferable, 539
translating into earnings, 160
Skills, cognitive
 advantages of measuring, 96
 critical periods for investment in, 233
 development of, 51
 distribution of economic outcomes and, 168–171
 distribution of economic outcomes and, studies on, 170t
 economic growth and, 171–190, 175–177t, 179f
 economic growth and, evidence on role of, 174–181
 family background and, 164
 GED and, 436–438, 446, 450–452, 453f
 health and, 181n66
 human capital and, 92, 96, 164
 individual labor-market outcomes and, 160–167
 individual labor-market outcomes and, studies on, 162t
 infant mortality and, 181n66
 inherited, 213
 institutional measures and, 183n69
 Latin America and, 185–186
 macroeconomic growth and, 171–190
 macroeconomic growth and, studies on, 175–177t
 measuring, 161
 measuring, aggregate, 172–174
 nonschool influences on, 164
 policy standpoint on, 182
 returns to, 166f
 school attainment and, 174n61, 178, 179f, 437f, 451t
 school quality and, 164

Skills, noncognitive, 161n40
    development of, 51
    dropouts and, 452f
    earnings and, 451–452
    GED and, 446, 450–452, 452f, 453f
    school attainment and, 450f, 451t
Skills weight model, 532
    apprenticeship training and, 532n19
Slavin, R.E., 351–352, 356, 372, 374–375
Slective migration, 61
SMIC. *See* Salaire minimum interprofessionalle de croissance
Smith, R., 285n9
Smith, S.S., 405t
Smoking, 268
Social norms, acceptance of, 161n40
Social segregation, 119
Solon, G., 212t, 218
Somerville, T., 505t, 513
Sonstelie, J., 497t
Southern and Eastern Africa Consortium for Monitoring Educational Quality (SACMEQ I), 103t
Southern and Eastern Africa Consortium for Monitoring Educational Quality II (SACMEQ II), 104t
Special needs, 395
Sprietsma, M., 122t, 141t
St. Aubyn, M., 125t
Staiger, D.O., 68t, 69–71, 329t, 505t, 508t, 513, 514
Statutory schooling
    earnings function for, 9
    expected utility from, 10
Steiner, P.M., 402, 403t
Stevens, A.H., 227t, 231
Stevens, M., 524n4
Stiebale, J., 534
Stixrud, J., 450, 451–452, 456, 458
Stromsdorfer, E.W., 441t
Student, expenditure per, 130, 131, 283
    change in, 130f
    comparisons, 130–131
    educational achievement and, 127f
    exchange rate and, 131
    increase in, 130
    mathematics and, 126
    in preprimary education, 157
    test scores and, 130–131
Student background
    cross-country studies on, 124–125t
    educational achievement and, 116–126, 119, 123
    equality of opportunity and, 116
    in international education production function, 114t
    licensure and, 327
    measurements, 116
    within-country studies on educational achievement and, 120–122t
Students
    fixed effects model, 52
    heterogeneity influence on teachers, 69
    monitoring of, 145
    purposeful allocation of, 60
    teacher value-added and sorting, 69–71
    teachers matched with, 50
Student-teacher ratio, 60, 62, 130, 130n26, 283, 284f, 350
    measurement error in, 60
    teacher quality and, 60, 62
    uncertainty in, 60
Subsidies
    deadweight loss, 535, 535n24
    school, 46–48
    training, 535
Sweden, 357–359
Switzerland, 543–546, 543t, 544t, 546t
Sylvan Learning Centers, 298n22

T

TAAS. *See* Texas Assessment of Academic Skills
Taber, C., 48, 60
Tach, L., 203n2
Tanaka, S., 238
Tardiness, 191
Taylor, C., 329t
Taylor, L.L., 61–64, 287, 498t
Teach for America (TFA), 322n6, 326, 327, 327n14
    effectiveness of, 327
    traditional licensure and, comparison between, 330
Teacher benefits, 280, 287, 288t
    defined, 300
    occupational choice model of, 283

Teacher compensation, 280
  deferred, 298–301
  educational achievement and, 289–290
  historical development of, 291–292
  market-based, 280n1, 301–305
  nonteacher compensation v., 286–289
  performance-based, 303t
  private school v. public school, 288–289
  structure, 290–301
  studies of relative, 281–283
  teacher experience and, 291–292
  for women, 282–283
Teacher education
  class size and, 137
  measures of, 132
Teacher effectiveness
  accountability and, 413
  rewarding, 295–296
Teacher employment, nonteacher employment v., 284f
Teacher experience
  class size and, 66n56
  teacher compensation and, 291–292
  teacher quality and, 293
Teacher Follow-Up Survey (TFS), 414
Teacher Incentive Fund (TIF), 302, 309
Teacher mobility, 289
  pension and, 301
Teacher pension, 298–301
  early retirement incentives in, 298n24
  mobility costs of, 301
Teacher performance pay, 51, 296, 302–303, 303t, 387
  nature of teaching thesis of, 308
  political cost thesis of, 308
Teacher quality, 5, 48, 251, 280
  class size and, 137, 159
  compensatory intervention and, 73
  concern over measurement methods of, 67
  crowding thesis, 281, 282
  decline in, 282
  educational achievement and, 316
  elimination of labor market barriers for women and, 281
  as endogenous intervention of parents/schools, 72
  false positives, 320f
  licensure and, 317, 320f, 326–331

  money and, 72
  observing, 320
  problem in examining long-term trends in, 281–282
  quantity v., 283–285
  selected research on variance in, 68t
  student heterogeneity influence on, 69
  student-teacher ratio and, 60, 62
  teacher experience and, 293
  teacher fixed effects and, 69–71
  time and, 72
  within-school variance of, 72
Teacher retirement pay, 280
  cost side of, 299–300
  employer contribution to, 299–300f
Teacher salary, 280. See also Salary schedules
  structure, 280
Teacher turnover
  accountability and, 412–416
  cost of, 413
Teacher unions
  charter schools and, 308–309
  cross-state variation in, 307
  dues, 285n10
  educational achievement and, 306
  productivity and, 306
  teacher compensation and, 306
Teacher value-added
  estimation of, 66–73
  student sorting and, 69–71
  test scores and, 72
  true teacher effect and, 67, 72
  validity of nonexperimental estimates of, 69–71
  variation within/between groups, 332f
Teacher wage-setting units, 296–298
  in charter schools, 297, 297f
  in private schools, 297, 297f
  in public schools, 296, 297f
Teachers. See also Licensure; Student-teacher ratio
  accountability for individual, 387
  bonuses for teaching in shortage fields, 303
  children of, 286
  collective bargaining, 283, 297, 305–309
  concentration, 287
  filling vacancies for, 293, 294t
  full-time equivalent, 296–297
  incentives, 146

incentives to teach in low-performing schools, 302
matched with students, 50
monitoring, 145, 149
motivation effect, 295–296
out of field, 293
professional development bonus, 302
recruitment bonuses, 304–305, 305t
shortages, 285, 324
students heterogeneity influence on teachers, 69
tenure, 296–298
tracking and, 373
underpaid, 281
work at home, 286n12
work weeks, 286
Teacher-student gender interaction, 138
"Teaching to the test," 390, 397
Teal, F., 308
Teamwork, 161n40
Teen pregnancy, 253, 268
Telhaj, S., 266
Tennessee STAR experiment, 66, 257, 257n6, 258–259
Test preparation market, 298n22
Test scores. *See also* International tests
  accountability and, 391
  artificially improving, 399
  black-white achievement gap in, 267
  domestic violence and, 267
  earnings and, 168f, 168n52
  expenditure per student and, 130–131
  experimental evaluations of, 410
  family background and, 155, 205
  housing values and, 491
  measures of, 97
  peer effects and, 251, 261–262t, 264
  pressure, 413–414
  scale of, 54, 72
  school attendance zone boundaries and, 75
  teacher value-added and, 72
  tracking and, 354f, 363, 372
  trends in economic growth rates and trends in, 184, 185f
  willingness to pay for higher, 76
Texas Assessment of Academic Skills (TAAS), 260, 398, 491
Texas Schools Project, 264
TFA. *See* Teach for America

TFS. *See* Teacher Follow-Up Survey
Thayer, M., 504t
Theriault, M., 507t
Thesmar, D., 32
Third International Mathematics and Science Study, 100t
Thomas, D., 234
Thornton, R., 269
Threshold crossing model, 39
TIF. *See* Teacher Incentive Fund
Time preferences, 213
TIMSS. *See* Trends in International Mathematics and Science Study
Todd, P., 64–65, 66, 72
Toma, E.F., 120t, 123, 126, 140t
Tomes, N., 213–214
Tracking, 139, 265–266, 342
  ability grouping and, 353, 355
  achievement gap and, 156
  across-school, 351–356
  across-school variations in, 346–347
  in Africa, 372–374, 377
  age, 239, 240, 363–368
  American style, 350
  average effects of, 348–349
  basic considerations of, 344–346
  benchmark data generation process of, 348–349
  between-school, 378
  categorization data for, 343
  changing peer groups, 343, 344
  class size and, 343n2, 349
  controversy, 153
  definitions of, 342
  early work on, 351–352
  educational achievement and, 153–157
  efficiency and, 351, 368, 372
  empirical approaches to, 343–349
  empirical approaches to estimating effects of, 351–375
  endogeneity of, 347–348, 370–371
  equality of opportunity and, 155
  European style, 343, 350
  experiments with random assignments, 371–375
  external validity, 377
  family background, 366, 367, 370
  in Finland, 360–361
  future research agenda for, 375–380
  geographical variation approaches to, 357–371

Tracking (cont.)
  helping mechanisms of, 373
  immigration and, 370
  incentive effects of, 360
  inequality and, 354, 367–368, 373, 376, 377–378
  informal, 347
  intergenerational transmission and, 360–361
  late, 378
  long-term, 361–363
  measurement error, 346–347
  nationally representative samples, 352–356
  observations for researching, 355–356
  opponents of, 343
  political beliefs and, 370–371
  political debate over, 343–344
  positive effects from, 266
  postponement of, 155, 240
  proponents of, 343
  reasons for, 347
  reforms and, 357–363
  reforms and, comprehensive, 239–241
  school resources and, 349–350
  selectivity bias controls, 352
  socio-economic status and, 156f, 343
  in Sweden, 357–359
  teachers and, 373
  teaching style and, 344
  test scores and, 354f, 363, 372
  theoretical foundations of, 344–349
  tutoring and, 345
  in United Kingdom, 359–360
  within-school, 342, 344, 351–356, 378
Tracking, early, 154, 363
  equality of opportunity and, 156
Training. See also Apprenticeship training
  GED and, 458–461
  subsidies, 535
  vocational, 38, 523n3
Trannoy, A., 501t
Treatment effect. See also Average treatment effect; Average treatment on the treated; Local average treatment effect
  parameters, 39–40
Tremblay, J.F., 175t
Trends in International Mathematics and Science Study (TIMSS), 91, 100t, 101t, 105
  design of, 98, 133

participation in, 191–192
Tuition costs, 30
Turner, L., 406t
Tutoring, 345
Twins, 164. See also Siblings
  children of, 222n9
  dizygotic, 208
  income differences, 164n47
  as parents, 222–223
  as parents studies, 225t
Twins, monozygotic, 208, 217
  birthweight differences in, 223
Tyler, J.H., 443–444, 447t, 465

U
Uncertainty
  education levels and, 32
  student-teacher ratio, 60
Unions, 168, 171n54
  teacher, 285n10, 306, 307
  threat effect, 306
United Kingdom, tracking in, 359–360
Ursprung, Heinrich, 117, 120t, 143t, 369, 370
Urzua, S., 32–33, 447t, 450, 451–452, 456, 457t, 458
Uusitalo, R., 360–361

V
Van de Klaauw, W., 64–65, 66
Van der steeg, M., 369
Van Elk, R., 369
Vandenberghe, V., 140t
Vella, F., 28
Veramendi, G., 447t, 450, 451–452, 456, 458
Vigdor, J.L., 262t, 264–265, 328t, 415
Vignoles, A., 359–360, 368
Vocabulary, 233
Vocational training, 38, 523n3
Vocational Training Act, 536n27, 558
Vytlacil, E.J., 26, 28, 30–31, 32–33, 39

W
Wage compression
  apprenticeship training and, 530–532
  collective bargaining and, 531
  firing costs and, 530–531
  firm specific v. general skills and, 532
  information asymmetries and, 530

matching frictions and, 530–531
moral hazard and, 531
search costs and, 530–531
Wage equations
education choice and, 8–13
education level and, 7–8
estimations of, 2–3
Mincer, 3–4, 19–31
quarter of birth and, 22
returns to education and, 6–40
role of ability in, 20n16
selectivity corrected, 41
Wages. *See also* Minimum wage
benefit of GED, 456
class size and, 59–60
education and, 2–3
education choice and, cross equation restrictions between, 14
education level to maximize, 30
estimating life cycle profiles of, 8
GED and gaps in, 479–480t
growth with experience and GED, 439
immigration and, 188
IQ and, 188
return to college, 13
return to education, 19–31
school attainment and, 426, 427f
Walden, M., 497t
Waldinger, F., 143t, 366–367
Walker, I., 21
Walker, J.R., 49–50
Warren, J.R., 474
Watts, J., 497t
Wealth constraints. *See* Credit constraints
Webbink, D., 123n22, 369, 552
Weede, E., 189t
Weeks, G., 441t
Weimer, D., 503t
Weingarth, G., 251, 253, 254–255, 262t, 265, 272
Weinhardt, F., 266
West, J.E., 270
West, M.R., 128t, 142t, 144t
Westergaard-Nielsen, N., 535n24, 549

Whitmore, D., 261t, 263
Willet, J.B., 441t, 447t, 457t
Williams, N., 502t
Windmeijer, F., 59n52
Woessmann, L., 110n13, 113, 117, 120t, 121t, 124t, 125t, 126, 128t, 129t, 141t, 142t, 143t, 144t, 173–174, 175t, 176t, 177t, 178, 205, 240, 364–366, 367, 368, 369, 370, 411
Wolkoff, M., 503t
Wolpin, K.I., 44, 72, 235
Wolter, S.C., 120t, 545
Women. *See also* Gender
cultural attitudes towards, 158
GED and, 440
peer effects and percent of, 260, 263, 272
political empowerment of, 158
struggle for pay equity and, 292
teacher compensation for, 282–283
teacher quality and elimination of labor market barriers for, 281–282
Wong, M., 402, 403t
Wright, Paul, 68t
Wright, R.E., 124t
Wuppermann, A., 138
Wyckoff, J.H., 328t

X
Xu, Z., 329t

Y
Youth Training Scheme, 536n27

Z
Zabel, J., 491
Zajonc, R.B., 235
Zau, A., 262t, 264
Zhang, L., 162t, 262t
Ziderman, A., 528
Zimmer, R.W., 120t, 123, 126
Zingales, L., 143t
Zlotnik, M., 326
Zwick, T., 545n39

Edwards Brothers Malloy
Ann Arbor MI. USA
July 22, 2014